Handbook of Special Education

Research and Practice

Volume 1

Other titles of related interest

WANG et al.	Handbook of Special Education, Volume 2: Mildly Handicapped Conditions
WANG et al.	Handbook of Special Education, Volume 3: Low Incidence Conditions
WANG et al.	Handbook of Special Education, Volume 4: Emerging Programs
WANG et al.	Special Education: Research and Practice: Synthesis of Findings
DUNKIN	The International Encyclopedia of Teaching and Teacher Education
PSACHAROPOULOS	Economics of Education: Research and Studies
POSTLETHWAITE	The Encyclopedia of Comparative Education and National Systems of Education
KEEVES	Educational Research, Methodology and Measurement: An International Handbook
TITMUS	Lifelong Education for Adults: An International Handbook
ERAUT	International Encyclopedia of Educational Technology
WALBERG	The International Encyclopedia of Educational Evaluation
THOMAS	Encyclopedia of Human Development and Education
LEWY	The International Encyclopedia of Curriculum
REYNOLDS	Knowledge Base for the Beginning Teacher

Handbook of Special Education
Research and Practice

Volume 1

Learner Characteristics and Adaptive Education

Edited by

MARGARET C. WANG
Temple University, Philadelphia, USA

MAYNARD C. REYNOLDS
University of Minnesota, Minneapolis, USA

HERBERT J. WALBERG
University of Illinois at Chicago, USA

PERGAMON PRESS

OXFORD · NEW YORK · SEOUL · TOKYO

U.K. Pergamon Press plc, Headington Hill Hall, Oxford OX3 0BW, England

U.S.A. Pergamon Press Inc., Maxwell House, Fairview Park, Elmsford, New York 10523, U.S.A.

KOREA Pergamon Press Korea, KPO Box 315, Seoul 110-603, Korea

JAPAN Pergamon Press, 8th Floor, Matsuoka Central Building, 1-7-1 Nishi-Shinjuku, Shinjuku-ku, Tokyo 160, Japan

---

First edition 1987
Reprinted 1989, 1991

Library of Congress Cataloging in Publication Data

Handbook of special education
Contents: v. 1. Learner characteristics and adaptive education
1. Special education literature—United States
I. Wang, Margaret C. II. Reynolds, Maynard Clinton
III. Walberg, Herbert J., 1937-
LC3965.H263 1987 371.9 87-18965

British Library Cataloguing in Publication Data

Handbook of special education: research and practice
Vol. 1: Learner characteristics and adaptive education
1. Exceptional children—Education—United States
I. Wang, Margaret C. II. Reynolds, Maynard C. III. Walberg, Herbert J.
371.9'0973 LC3981
ISBN 0-08-033383-4

Information included in this publication is the result of a project funded at least in part through Federal funds from the U.S. Department of Education under contract number 300–84–0194. The contents of this publication do not necessarily reflect the views or policies of the U.S. Department of Education; nor does the mention of trade names, commercial products or oganizations imply endorsement by the U.S. Government.

Printed in Great Britain by BPCC Wheatons Ltd, Exeter

Contents

Preface

In the United States, as in many other parts of the world, we are engaging in a new wave of education reform efforts, particularly the improvement of schools' capabilities to serve students who have greater-than-usual needs for educational support but were often either left out of earlier reform movements or kept on the sidelines. The term "students with special needs" is used here to refer to students with physical, behavioral, or cognitive disabilities; students from economically, culturally, or language disadvantaged backgrounds; and students with chronic low achievement or those who otherwise can be considered academically at risk.

Significant progress has been made, especially in the past decade, in providing equal access to free and appropriate schooling for students. At this point in our history, nearly all school-age children in the United States and other industrialized countries attend school. This effort to achieve universal and effective education is based on a recognition of the rights of children to basic education that enables them to thrive in a complex society, as well as a realization that technological and economic growth is facilitated by increasing the numbers of students, even those with poor academic prognoses, who are, in fact, successful in school learning. Thus, recent and current efforts to improve schooling serve both private and social interests.

This three-volume publication, the *Handbook of Special Education: Research and Practice*, represents a commitment to examine the research base, broadly defined to represent current knowledge or the "state of the art," that can be used in formulating plans to improve the chances of schooling success for all students, especially students with special needs. Each of the 45 chapters comprising the *Handbook* summarizes the well-confirmed knowledge in a particular area, giving attention first to the research literature, broadly defined, and then to the tested experience and practices of leading professionals. The authors include in their reviews estimates of the state of practice in their respective topic areas and then proceed to recommend improvements for effectively linking practice with the state of the art. Thus, the research syntheses provide state-of-the-art standards against which the state of practice can be judged.

Several perspectives provided the specific context for this *Handbook*. First, the reviews of research and practice mark the impact of a decade of intensive research and program development in the United States aimed at improving the chances of educational success for students with special needs. Since 1975, the year of the enactment of the Education for All Handicapped Children Act (PL 94-142), schools have made major advances in providing for handicapped students and others with special needs. Consequently, there is reason to celebrate the 10th anniversary of what has proven to be an extremely powerful and influential piece of legislation. During the same period, there have been important advances in educational research, thus adding to the impetus for careful review of both research and practice at this time.

The second perspective derives from the movement to provide more inclusive arrangements for disabled persons and for others who often find themselves at the margins of schools and other institutions. These efforts are variously described as deinstitutionalization, normalization, and mainstreaming. Even persons with severe impairments are less often segregated in special enclaves and more often mainstreamed into ordinary community situations. As a result, it is critical that the findings from research on persons with special needs be made available to broader groups than ever before, and that future research be conducted in new settings and on the specific processes of change involved in implementing new policies. In a sense, research needs to be "mainstreamed." Accordingly, the reviews reported here join the work of special education researchers with that of the broader community of researchers in general education and human behavior.

The need to coordinate services across a wide range of caretakers and agencies provided a third perspective for the research syntheses. Specifically, special education must be coordinated with services such as health and welfare, family services, correction, rehabilitation, and employment assistance. Many of the "new morbidities," such as child abuse, drug addiction, and the erosion of "natural" support systems as a consequence of broken family structures and incomplete mother–child attachments, have grave effects on school children. Often, children who are referred to special education programs come from unsupportive families and disordered communities. Schools must respond by linking up with other community agencies in order to construct high-quality, broadly coordinated programs for students and families with special needs. At the same time, it is necessary to recognize and delimit the special functions of the schools. In this context, the research reviews reported in this *Handbook* were designed to be instructionally relevant, while also acknowledging the larger networks of service to which educational processes can be linked.

The dependence of special education on public policy and legal imperatives is yet another perspective that guided the research syntheses. Several reports, court decisions, and policies have enlarged this perspective in recent years. Examples include Nicholas Hobbs's 1975 work entitled, *The Futures of Children* (San Francisco, CA: Jossey–Bass); and the 1982 report by the National Academy of Sciences Panel on Selection and Placement of Students in Programs for the Mentally Retarded, entitled *Placing Children in Special Education: A Strategy for Equity* (K. A. Heller, W. H. Holtzman, and S. Messick, Editors, Washington, DC: National Academy Press). These and other reports by leading scholars cast doubt on some of the traditional practices of special education.

The courts, moreover, have had far-reaching effects on educational policy. For instance, the 1972 decision of *Larry P. v. Riles* (Civil action N.L.–71–2270, 343 F. Supp. 1306, N.D. Cal., 1972) held that the use of intelligence tests as a prime determiner of the classification and placement of children as educable mentally retarded is unconstitutional. Similar court decisions have been the basis for many program changes. Clearly, the field of special education is held accountable to the procedural standards and practices outlined by binding court decisions. Thus, the research reviews reported in this work were sensitive to studies of policy and policy related developments.

Finally, the research syntheses took account of the rising public concern over the general quality of schools, as expressed in the widely heralded 1983 report by the National Commission on Excellence in Education entitled, *A Nation at Risk: The Imperative for Educational Reform* (Washington, DC: U.S. Department of Education), as well as at least a dozen other recent and significant national reports. They reflect growing public demand for better instruction and for a greater focus on all forms of school accountability, including a commitment to provide the greater-than-usual educational interventions required by students who are difficult to teach. Because recent developments in special education (e.g., more individualized planning, closer partnerships with parents, better measurements of instructional outcomes) are congruent with the increasing general demands made of schools, it should be possible, as we see it, for special educators to complete the necessary reforms. To this end, the authors of the chapters in these volumes sought to define the knowledge base and extend its application in the field of special education in the broadest and most helpful way. Just as students with special needs are no longer isolated in the schools, research in special education should no longer be treated in isolation.

As we have noted, 1986 is a year in which schools in the United States entered into a second decade under the mandates of changed national policy concerning special education and related services for students with special needs. However, the authors of the research syntheses were also mindful of the international scope of the research literature and of the similarity in trends and problems surrounding special education throughout the world.

This publication was initiated, in part, as a culminating activity of a project entitled, "Research Integration of Selected Issues in the Education of Handicapped Children," which was funded by the Office of Special Education and Rehabilitative Services of the United States Department of Education. The 45 chapters are organized in three volumes under nine major topic areas or sections. The chapters in Volume 1 focus on the topic areas, Learning Characteristics of Handicapped Students and the Provision of Effective Education, Effectiveness of Differential Programming in Serving Handicapped Students, and Noncategorical Programming for Mildly Handicapped Students. Volume 2 consists of writings in the areas of Mild Mental Retardation, Behavioral Disorders, and Learning Disabilities. Volume 3 includes chapters in the topic areas, Education of Deaf Children and Youth, Education of Visually Handicapped Children and Youth, and Handicapped Infants.

An eight-member advisory board played a major role at important stages in the substantive development and preparation of the research syntheses. They participated in the initial selection of areas of research in special education and related fields, in the identification of authors who would conduct the research syntheses, and in the reviewing of manuscripts. The members of the advisory board were Joseph Fischgrund from the Lexington School for the Deaf in New York; James Gallagher from the University of North Carolina; Reginald Jones from the University of California, Berkeley; Stephen Lilly from Washington State University; Daniel Reschly from Iowa State University; Judy Schrag from the Washington State Department of Education; Phillip Strain from the University of Pittsburgh; and Martha Ziegler from the Federation for Children with Special Needs based in Boston, Massachusetts.

A group of scholars, each of them nationally and internationally known and active in research, provided substantive leadership to the authors in the nine topic areas. These scholars assisted the editors of this *Handbook* in overseeing the quality and breadth of the content coverage. They also wrote Introductions that provide overviews of the topics addressed in the nine areas. The names of these individuals and the topic areas in which they worked are Verna Hart from the University of Pittsburgh—Handicapped Infants; Kenneth Kavale from the University of Iowa—Effectiveness of Differential Programming in Serving Handicapped Students; Barbara Keogh from the University of California, Los Angeles—Learning Disabilities; Daniel Reschly from Iowa State University—Mild Mental Retardation; Maynard Reynolds from the University of Minnesota—Noncategorical Programming for Mildly Handicapped Students; Geraldine Scholl from the University of Michigan—Education of Visually Handicapped Children and Youth; E. Ross Stuckless from the National Technical Institute for the Deaf—Education of Deaf Children and Youth; Margaret Wang from Temple University—Learning Characteristics of Handicapped Students and the Provision of Effective Education; and Frank Wood from the University of Minnesota—Behavioral Disorders.

The chapters were reviewed during various draft stages by persons representing a broad range of expertise in research, personnel preparation, curriculum development, and educational practice. The contributions of these reviewers helped to enhance the comprehensiveness and relevance of the individual research syntheses.

The comprehensiveness of the research syntheses was further enhanced by making available to all authors the findings from computerized literature searches. These covered the two major indices of the Educational Resources Information Centre (ERIC)—the Resources in Education Index and the Current Index to Journals in Education. In addition, the authors made use of technical reports and other documentation on more than 100 research projects in special education that were conducted in the United States in recent years.

As a final note, we wish to acknowledge the contributions of several others who played important roles in facilitating the development and production of this *Handbook*. Funding from the Office of Special Education and Rehabilitative Services provided the necessary support to commission the writing of most of the chapters. Judy Fein and Nancy Safer from that agency's staff were the source of continuing advice and encouragement. Special acknowledgments go to Mary Kay Freilino for her efficient orchestration of the myriad administrative details involved in the manuscript reviewing process and her efforts in overseeing the substantive and technical details of conducting computerized literature searches for authors; to K. Charlie Lakin whose substantive input during the reviewing of many of the manuscripts was consistently insightful; to Rita Catalano for her editorial and administrative leadership throughout the preparation of this work; to Jackie Rubenstein for her technical editing expertise and her diligence in monitoring the details of a Herculean editing assignment; and to Regina Rattigan for her contribution as a member of the technical editing team. Finally, we are grateful to Barbara Barrett from Pergamon Press for her constant support and guidance throughout the editing and production process.

Margaret C. Wang
Maynard C. Reynolds
Herbert J. Walberg
Editors

SECTION 1

Learning Characteristics of Handicapped Students and the Provision of Effective Education

Introduction

MARGARET C. WANG

Temple University Center for Research in Human Development and Education

The commitment to provide greater-than-usual educational and related services that enable students with special needs to experience schooling success has been a guiding force in the design and implementation of "special" educational alternatives. In fact, the provision of educational experiences that are adaptive to the widely varying learning characteristics and needs of individual students is essentially what makes these alternative educational approaches "special." Theoretical and technical advances in research on learning and effective schooling, particularly those which have occurred during the past decade, have greatly influenced the nature and type of information on individual differences that has been considered in instructional planning and the educational placement of students with special needs. The authors of the five chapters in this section focused their reviews on changing conceptions and technical advances in the characterization and description of instructionally relevant individual difference variables and their implications for furthering understanding of the process of learning and for improving educational practices.

Several prevailing themes or trends can be traced in the recent research literature on learning characteristics and the provision of effective schooling for students with special needs. Viewed collectively, they represent a movement toward strengthening the correspondence between the learning needs of individual students and standards for the design and delivery of special education and related services. A widely noted finding is the adverse effects of prevailing practices whereby student differences are characterized as part of classification and labeling systems that marshal funding and other resource supports for special education and related services but are viewed as having little relation to instructional needs. There is increasing recognition of the need for a data base for deriving descriptions of learner characteristics that reflect the cognitive and social competence (entering knowledge and skills) required for students' achievement of intended learning outcomes. Such descriptions are considered essential for the design of effective interventions and for instructional planning.

The shift toward instructionally relevant descriptions of the learning characteristics and needs of individual students has been accompanied by growing dissatisfaction with descriptions of learner differences that are based solely on traditional measures of learning ability, aptitude, and other social and personality attributes. Designed with an outcomes orientation for normative and predictive purposes, such measures do not take into account the cognitive-affective and social processes that are intrinsic to learning and performance. There has come to be increasing attention to the dynamic nature of the instructional-learning process and the role of this interactive process in mediating distinct types of learning and, thereby, improving performance. The heightened emphasis on the learning process has led to examination of learning characteristics as partly the evolutionary product of individual students' interactions with fluid and complex learning environments that include factors such as teacher behaviors and attitudes, program design features, and peer relationships.

These developments in the conceptualization and description of individual differences contrast sharply with the more traditional view of learning characteristics as static qualities and with the classification and labeling of groups of students based on rather grossly defined diagnostic categories. There is a growing realization that learning characteristics become increasingly alterable as we become more knowledgeable about the learning process, and that different competencies and attributes are required to succeed in different types of learning and in different learning situations. By building upon these changing views of learning characteristics and the learning process, it is possible to enhance the potential for individual students with a wide range of unique characteristics to achieve success in their performance of a variety of learning tasks.

Another notable theme in the literature is the changing conception of the role of the learner in the learning process. Recent research on the nature of learning and instruction has many implications for reexamination of the role of the learner. It suggests, for example, that essentially all learning involves both internal and external adaptation. External adaptation occurs in the ideas and content that are to be learned and in the modes and forms in which the content is presented to the learner. Internal adaptation takes place in the learner's mind as new content is assimilated and internal mental structures are modified to accommodate the new content. Thus, students are seen as active processors, interpreters, and synthesizers of information in the learning process. They are expected to take responsibility for managing, monitoring, and evaluating their own learning, while also playing an instrumental role in adapting the learning environment to accommodate the demands of the learning process. Students' ability to carry out this role is highly influenced by their prior knowledge and skills as well as their self-perceptions of their cognitive and social competence. Therefore, the characteristics required to support an active learner role have come to be considered among the broad array of instructionally relevant learning characteristics.

Finally, the trend toward examining learning characteristics from an ecological perspective should be noted. This perspective recognizes the importance of establishing the external validity of characteristics and interpretations of individual differences in learning characteristics. It calls attention to family influences on individual students' unique learning characteristics, including the impact of differences in socioeconomic, linguistic, and ethno-cultural backgrounds, as well as the effects of particular handicapping conditions.

These themes that seem to be predominant in the literature provided the guiding framework for the reviews discussed in the chapters in this section. Several common questions are salient in the reviews. These questions, which are listed below, also point to future directions for continuing research and development aimed at incorporating information on the learning characteristics of students with special needs in the provision of effective instruction.

— Do differences in learning characteristics make a difference in learning and performance? Under what conditions do they make a difference?
— Can learning characteristics be modified through training, especially for students with special learning needs?
— In the context of the broad spectrum of schooling tasks that are required of all students, including students with special needs, are certain learning characteristics more critical than others for successful mastery of certain types of tasks?
— Recognizing that there is always a gap between what we know and what we can do (or actually do), to what extent and how is our knowledge of learning and performance, and of the conditions that foster learning in individual students, reflected in current practice in special education? What is the relevance of this knowledge base for designing and managing instruction and learning for students with special needs?
— What are some of the common and unique design features of special education programs that incorporate information on student learning characteristics and the nature of learning tasks in the process of instructional programming? Are particular management and organization patterns associated with effective implementation of these programs?
— Given the impact of current policies and funding guidelines on the definition of special education and the implementation of special education programs, and given the state of the art of research on learning characteristics and the implications for instruction and effective schooling, what, if any, policy and implementation reforms are necessary?

The authors of the individual chapters approached these questions from a variety of perspectives. In their chapter, entitled "Ethnocultural and Social-Psychological Effects on Learning Characteristics of Handicapped Children," Ellen Brantlinger and Samuel Guskin present findings from their review to support the contention that students from various cultural, social, and linguistic backgrounds differ markedly in terms of school performance and the likelihood of being classified as handicapped. The authors examine a number of theories about the reasons for differential school achievement among various groups of students, and they review research that relates schooling to socioeconomic class, race, and ethnic status. Brantlinger and Guskin include discussions of discriminatory referral, assessment, classification, and placement; the impact of the school environment on various learners; the role of the home environment in influencing learning characteristics; the social consequences of being labeled as handicapped; and educational interventions for a number of specific groups of more severely handicapped students.

Daniel Reschly's chapter is entitled "Learning Characteristics of Mildly Handicapped Students: Implications for Classification, Placement, and Programming." He discusses research on the basic learning characteristics of mildly handicapped children and youth in relation to the current exceptional child classification system, the range of students' individual differences, the need for alternative or adaptive educational programming, and the revision of public policy. He considers a wide range of similarities and differences in the learning problems of mildly handicapped and economically disadvantaged students, and he argues for the need for systematic, broad-based, and well-integrated programs that focus on basic literacy skills, academic content, social skills, and career/vocation. Reschly includes in the recommendations for future directions the development of flexible and finely graduated special programming, including new combinations of general and special education practices and programs.

Margaret Wang and Stephen Peverly summarize relevant research and practice on "The Role of the Learner: An Individual Difference Variable in School Learning and Functioning." They present their discussion in the context of a model for the study of the self-instructive process in classroom learning situations. A major premise of this model's design is that variations in students' ability to be self-instructive are an individual difference variable that has significant implications for systematic instructional planning and for student learning outcomes. In addition to explicating the theoretical and empirical basis for the conception of the active mediating function that students play in their own learning, Wang and Peverly propose a program of research that consists of the development of a descriptive data base on the role of the learner in classroom learning situations as well as the conducting of instructional design experimentations aimed at creating learning environments and facilitating teaching practices that foster the development and use of self-instructive skills in learning.

In the next chapter of this section, entitled "Advances in Improving the Cognitive Performance of Handicapped Students," the focus changes from explicating the nature and implications of instructionally relevant learner characteristics to consideration of a specific instructional approach to accommodating diverse student learning characteristics and needs. Annemarie Palincsar and Ann

Brown review the research and practice of cognitive strategy instruction as an approach to improving the academic achievement of students with mild learning problems. They characterize cognitive instruction as instruction that increases students' awareness of task demands, teaches the use of appropriate strategies to facilitate task completion, and prepares students to monitor the application of these strategies. Their review includes findings from evaluation research on the impact of cognitive strategy instruction on student learning in reading, written language, mathematics, and problem solving, as well as implications for classroom implementation.

In the final chapter of this section, Herbert Walberg and Margaret Wang discuss "Effective Educational Practices and Provisions for Individual Differences." They review findings from four major syntheses of research. Their summary of results from these quantitative studies includes findings on the influence of student aptitude, instruction, and environment on learning, as well as the characteristic features and related processes and student outcomes of various instructional models that make effective educational provisions for student differences.

Ethnocultural and Social-Psychological Effects on Learning Characteristics of Handicapped Children

ELLEN ANDERSON BRANTLINGER AND SAMUEL L. GUSKIN

Indiana University

Abstract—Students from various cultural, social, and linguistic backgrounds differ markedly in the extent to which their performance in school meets the standards set by schools and in their likelihood of being classified as handicapped. This chapter examines a number of theories about the reasons for differential school achievement among various groups and reviews research related to schooling and socioeconomic class, race, and ethnic status. Included are discussions of discriminatory referral, assessment, classification, and placement; the impact of the school environment on various learners; the role of home environments in influencing learning characteristics; the social consequences of being labeled as handicapped; and educational interventions for a number of specific groups of more severely handicapped children. The chapter concludes with recommendations for practice and future research.

There appears to be almost universal recognition among academics, professionals, and the public at large that students from various social class, ethnic, and racial backgrounds differ markedly in the extent to which their performance in school meets the standards set by schools. It is also well recognized today that students from these varying backgrounds differ in the extent to which they are likely to be classified as handicapped and in need of special education services. Perhaps only somewhat less widely accepted, at least among special educators, is the assumption that students who are classified as handicapped are viewed negatively by their peers, their families, and their teachers. However, once one moves beyond these presumed relationships to their perceived causes, the consensus falls apart. Interpretations range from genetic causes, to deprived environments, to societal discrimination and teacher prejudice.

It is important to examine the processes that might mediate the influence of a number of ethnocultural and social-psychological variables. Some processes may mask others or may simply be correlates of important variables. Thus, low socioeconomic status (SES), which is one of the most consistently found correlates of poor academic achievement and mild mental retardation, is a composite index of a number of variables (parental education, occupation, income), which themselves may only indirectly influence a child. There is no shortage of assumed explanations of the processes underlying these relationships. A list of some of these assumptions is presented below.

1. There is a relationship among ethnic and/or social-class status, school achievement, and handicap classification.
2. There is a bias in the referral rates, assessment strategies, and types of placements of minority and/or low-income learners.
3. School environments have an impact on the learning characteristics of minority students.
    a. There are inequities in the distribution of material and human resources between high-income and low-income schools.
    b. Differential (i.e., inferior) learning environments tend to be developed within heterogeneous (i.e., class- and race-desegregated) schools.
    c. The social class and racial compositions of schools have an impact on learning characteristics.
    d. Minority individuals are not passive, static recipients of educational services but come to school with their own agendas, their own feelings about school, and their own unique reactions to what happens in school.
4. Home environments influence learner characteristics.
    a. Early childhood environments have an impact on learners' readiness for and response to the educational setting.
    b. Cognitive styles vary according to socialization patterns.
    c. Self-concepts, aspirations, and motivation are influenced by parental values and student identification patterns and are further shaped by school climate variables.
5. Being classified as handicapped has an impact on the future school and life careers of individuals.
6. Specific handicapped minorities have difficulty in gaining access to and benefiting from appropriate educational interventions.

Literature related to these six assumptions are discussed in subsequent sections of this chapter. The chapter closes with a summary of findings and recommendations for future work.

Relationship Among Ethnic and/or Social Class Status, School Achievement, and Handicap Classification

Special educators have traditionally been concerned about distinguishing handicapped individuals from the general population; however, recent investigations have focused on similarities between the groups (Deshler, Schumaker, Alley, Warner, and Clark, 1982; Mercer, 1973b; Ysseldyke, Algozzine, Shinn, and McGue, 1982). In 1984, Moran combined handicapped learners and nonclassified learners in order to describe a larger body of students with school problems and arrived at a figure of 36% for pupils experiencing school difficulties. Others have argued that evaluation procedures used for classification as handicapped do not clearly differentiate between handicapped and nonhandicapped persons. Ysseldyke, Algozzine, and Epps (1983) found, in a study of 243 third-, fifth-, and twelfth-grade students, that 85% of nonlabeled low-achieving students could be classified as learning disabled. They maintained that no defendable system exists for classifying learning disabled students and that learning disability is becoming simply a category of low achievement (Algozzine & Ysseldyke, 1983). Thus, this chapter examines the larger group of lower achieving children as well as those children classified as handicapped.

It has long been documented that low-income and minority students' IQ and achievement scores are lower than those of high-income and majority children. Ramey and Campbell (1979) claimed that social class has a pronounced effect on scores on developmental tests. Children in upper social classes have shown progressive gains in their rates of development beginning in infancy, while children of lower SES have shown progressive declines relative to norms. In a study of approximately 26,000 black and white 4-year-olds, Broman, Nichols, and Kennedy (1975) found that SES was the best single predictor of IQ. Kushlick and Blunder (1974) described the relationship between social class and retardation as so strong that, in higher socioeconomic groups, only children with pathological conditions had IQs of less than 80. They claimed this phenomenon has been demonstrated cross-culturally by a series of epidemiological studies. Mare (1981) projected an increasing dependence of educational attainment on social origins.

Racial and ethnic status are correlated similarly with achievement and cognitive measures. Yet Levine, Kukuk, and Meyer (1979) wrote that the correlation of race and achievement does not mean that racial composition is independently related to achievement apart from SES. Results of their analysis indicate that racial composition generally added nothing at all to the prediction. Thus, when SES is controlled, racial differences in test results tend to disappear.

Even when IQ is held constant, achievement scores fluctuate according to race and social class. In 1976, Gordon reported on a study involving 1,102 Chicago area fifth and sixth graders who were aggregated into seven cohorts of approximately equal IQ scores. She found that, among children with average IQ scores (95–104.9), white children scored higher on achievement tests than black children of the same sex and SES and that middle-class children had a similar advantage over working-class children of the same sex and race. Gordon concluded that overachievement and underachievement among children with similar IQ scores were consistently related to race and class.

Proportionately more black and other minority children are placed in special classes (Anderson & Anderson, 1983; Argulewicz, 1983; Educational Testing Service, 1980; Ford, Mongon, & Whelan, 1982; Pink, 1982; Polloway & Smith, 1983; Ysseldyke, Algozzine, & Richey, 1982), and linguistically different children are even more disproportionately represented (Aguirre, 1979; Argulewicz, 1983; Bernal, 1983; Ochoa, Pacheco, & Omark, 1983). Bernal (1983) maintained that many "normal," limited-English-proficient children are placed in special classes in systems that have resisted bilingual programming. In 1984, Gerber expressed concern about the erroneous classification and inequitable treatment of those children labeled as handicapped in the educational system.

Finn's (1982) examination of the 1978 Office of Civil Rights Surveys of the assignment of minority children to special education programs provides evidence that (a) minorities are overrepresented in programs for educable mentally retarded students; (b) on a national basis, overrepresentation is greatest and most consistent for black students, though there is considerable regional variation in the magnitude of this effect; (c) Hispanic students, although not overrepresented in national statistics, are overrepresented in educable mental retardation programs in small, predominantly Hispanic districts and underrepresented in educable mental retardation programs in large, predominantly black school districts; (d) in areas where a high percentage of Hispanic students are in bilingual education programs, Hispanic students are less likely to be overrepresented in educable mental retardation programs; (e) Hispanic students tend to be overrepresented in learning disability programs in the same districts in which they are overenrolled in educable mental retardation programs; (f) students from Asian or Pacific Island backgrounds are generally underrepresented both in educable mental retardation and in learning disability programs; (g) Alaskan natives are substantially overrepresented in educable mental retardation classes, though this is not the case for American Indians in other states; and (h) disproportions of minorities in educable mental retardation classes are lower in districts of higher SES that also have the smallest proportions of students in educable mental retardation programs.

The Referral, Assessment, and Placement of Minority and/or Low-Income Children

A frequent explanation for the higher special education placement rates for certain groups is that assessment procedures are biased. *Biased assessment* refers to a constant error in the decisions, predictions, and inferences about members of particular groups (Cleary, Humphreys, Kendrick, and Wesman, 1975), which discriminates against children whose sociocultural backgrounds differ from that of the cultural majority for whom the assessment was designed (Chinn, 1979; Hobbs, 1978). Assessment is used at various levels of the instructional process: screening, classification/placement, instructional planning, individual pupil evaluations, and program evaluation (Duffey, Salvia, Tucker, and Ysseldyke, 1981). Bias at any level influences the type of education that minority and/or poor children receive. In a California decision, *Larry P. v. Riles* (1979), the constitutionality of using IQ tests for the placement of black children and the appropriateness of labeling and placement were challenged (Cremins, 1981). The 1974 meeting of the National Association for the Advancement of Colored People (NAACP) and the 1978 Delegate Assembly International Convention of the Council for Exceptional Children (CEC) called for a moratorium on the use of IQ testing for special education placement.

Others have denied that standardized testing procedures are biased (e.g., Jensen, 1980). Gordon and Rudert (1979) claimed there is evidence that IQ predicts important criterion variables equally well across social classes and racial samples. They accused test critics of endorsing, for the purpose of public argument, a definition of test bias that opportunistically relies on considerations of face validity.

The Education for All Handicapped Children Act of 1975 (PL 94-142) specifies that the procedures and materials for the assessment and classification of special needs individuals be selected and administered so as not to be racially, culturally, or sexually discriminatory. They are, for instance, to be provided and administered in a pupil's native language. Nevertheless, fair assessment practices appear to be very difficult to implement. Although precautions such as the involvement of multidisciplinary evaluation teams in assessment and program decision making are required by PL 94-142 to assure adequate and appropriate testing, Junkala (1977) found that the only pupil variables that related significantly with any magnitude to placement decisions were IQ scores.

Salvia and Ysseldyke (1978) claimed that acculturation is the most important characteristic being evaluated in a child's performance on a test. Tests have been developed for the purpose of preventing cultural bias; however, culture-fair tests have not demonstrated good predictive validity, perhaps because they are poor predictors of success in monocultural school systems. Biased tests are better predictors of negative school outcomes for minority learners, whose styles do not match those of their schools (Almanza & Mosely, 1980).

It has been estimated that the language factor accounts for over 50% of the total test variance on IQ and achievement test measures for fourth graders and 60–90% of the variance for seventh graders (Oller, 1981). Translations of existing tests are often not acceptable because translation can modify item difficulty and destroy the applicability of existing norms so that predictive validity is not good (Duffey et al., 1981). Literal translation may not render concepts understandable; thus, the tests remain invalid for certain cultural groups (Omark & Watson, 1983). Non-English-proficient children may never have received reading or writing instruction in their home language, so a test requiring literacy skills would not be an appropriate measure. Language translations may not be translated into local dialects; for example, children from Mexico, Cuba, and Puerto Rico speak different versions of the Spanish language.

Alternative culture-specific tests that are based on concepts specifically familiar to inner-city black children have been developed (e.g., Black Intelligence Test of Cultural Homogeneity, Williams, 1972). These, too, have demonstrated low predictive validity (Duffey et al., 1981). In fact, one might suspect a negative correlation between a high score on a cultural minority test and success in a cultural majority school. However, the tests have been useful in illustrating the point of cultural specificity to members of the dominant culture.

Alternative or supplementary tests and assessment strategies have been recommended by a number of professionals working in the field. Mercer (1972), a prominent proponent of this approach, was among the first to assert that IQ tests were simply testing the middle-class and/or Anglo-American characteristics of students. She suggested that it would be more appropriate to examine students' adjustment to their own life surroundings to determine if special education programming might be justifiable. Truly retarded individuals would demonstrate low competence across all social roles (Reschly, 1981). As a result, Mercer and Lewis (1977) developed the System of Multicultural Pluralistic Assessment (SOMPA), which includes an adaptive behavior measure. Grossman (1973) defined adaptive behavior as "the effectiveness or degree with which the individual meets the standards of personal independence and social responsibility expected of his age and cultural group" (p. 11). Besides SOMPA, a number of other adaptive behavior scales have been developed or revised in response to the American Association of Mental Deficiency's recommendation that intellectual assessment be accompanied by social competence ratings (Grossman, 1973). Bailey and Harbin (1980), however, reviewed issues in adaptive behavior assessment and concluded that there is little consensus among professionals as to what comprises the adaptive behavior construct. Items in different scales are not equivalent. They questioned the validity of using parent interviews or teacher reports (techniques utilized in adaptive behavior scales) in the collection of information.

Another strategy suggested by Mercer (1973b) for reducing cultural bias in assessment for special education placement is to adjust IQ scores for cultural background correlates. This approach utilizes separate ethnic group norms and a regression formula that takes into account variables such as family size and educational background. The adjusted IQ score is called the Estimated Learning Potential (ELP), while the unadjusted IQ score is termed the School Functioning Level (SFL). Thus, although the average, poor, black child might have an IQ or SFL of less than 85, he or she should obtain an ELP of 100. When the SOMPA is used to assess whether a child is mentally retarded, the child must score two standard deviations below the norm on the SFL, the ELP, and the Adaptive Behavior Inventory for Children (Mercer, 1979). As a study by Talley (1979) illustrates, applying SOMPA to reduce ethnic discrimination may have dramatic effects on placement patterns. The most noticeable change may be in the reduced number of children found eligible for mental retardation classification if SOMPA criteria are strictly used. In short, strict application of SOMPA criteria not only reduces bias but it also almost eliminates the educable mental retardation category. Talley (1979) found, however, that, although the SOMPA battery was employed, the criteria for actual placement were more traditional (IQ scores only).

Conditions for testing have been found to have an impact on test results. Labov (1973) convincingly describes the asymmetry of a testing situation in which the examiner and examinee are not of the same race or social class. Establishing rapport and being warm, responsive, and receptive, but firm, may favorably influence test performance (Oakland & Matuszek, 1977).

Many recommendations have been made that evaluation should focus on specific skills required in academic settings (Bailey & Harbin, 1980; Hilliard, 1976; Siegel & Leahy, 1974). Padilla and Garza (1975) stated that existing tests should be used for diagnosis, the purpose for which they were originally invented, rather than for the normative ranking of students, since abuses arise from the use of these instruments for selection.

Assessment is not the only area that is affected by cultural differences. Assigning grades, making referrals, classifying deviance, and recommending services all involve subjective decision making, which can be influenced by preconceptions and attitudes (Duffey et al., 1981). Ethnic and social class background have been reported to affect teacher expectancy and behavior toward students (Jackson & Cosca, 1974; Rosenthal & Jacobson, 1968). In responding to a fictitious case study involving Anglo- and Mexican-American identification of the same subject, special education teachers were found to feel that special education placement was more appropriate for Mexican-American children (Zucker & Prieto, 1977), and, in a later study, regular class teachers made similar judgments (Prieto & Zucker, 1981). These investigators hypothesize that an association linking ethnicity, lower SES, and academic difficulty resulted in the ethnically biased results. The same phenomenon was replicated in a study involving behavior problems and placement in classes for emotionally disturbed students (Prieto & Zucker, 1981). This negative expectancy for ethnic minorities may be part of the reason that the referral step has been found to be a major factor contributing to disproportionate ethnic representation in special education (Argulewicz & Sanchez, 1983; Richmond & Waits, 1978). In fact, Argulewicz and Sanchez (1983) stated that psychoeducational evaluation by a team moderated the original excessive ethnic minority referrals. However, in her study, Mercer (1973a) found that most of the bias in placement decisions resulted from the psychological evaluation (i.e., IQ testing) and very little from the teacher referral.

Impact of School Environments on Minority Learners

One explanation given for social class and ethnic differences in achievement is that school conditions are not equal for poor and rich children. Bowles and Gintis (1976) asserted that class inequities in education are intentional and result from deliberate efforts on the part of a power elite to maintain advantage. This position holds that schools reflect the social structure of the larger society (Tyack, 1974), serving as gatekeepers to entrance into power positions (Sizemore, 1978; Walberg & Rasher, 1979) and sorting out students to fit into a hierarchical socioeconomic class structure (Taylor, 1976). From this perspective, middle-class interests, rather than a subordinate minority culture, are responsible for the persistence of inequalities in educational opportunities and outcomes (Roberts, 1980). The recent basic skills and minimum competency emphases appear to focus on instrumentalities, for example, toughening the admission or exit standards, necessary to maintain middle-class advantage in the labor market (Shapiro, 1983).

Neo-Marxist Sally Tomlinson (1982) observed that special education in England is permeated by an ideology of benevolent humanitarianism, which provides the moral framework for professionals and the rationale for exclusion. The powerful categorize the weaker group and treat them unequally. Parents accept professional judgment as legitimate authority and assume they are doing what is best for their children. According to Moran (1984), parents and other advocates have been led to accept the "outgroup" status of their children and to agree that segregated instruction is in the students' best interests. Drummond (1982) maintained that to suggest that a handicap, such as mental illness, resides solely within the individual is the power elite's lie.

There are those who believe that American schools, unlike other social and economic institutions, have traditionally been reformist and egalitarian in structure, allowing for social mobility. Such a meritocratic school system is perceived as necessary in preventing a free enterprise economy from becoming a rigid caste-based society and in educating a responsible, assertive, and cooperative electorate in a democracy. Thus, the allocation of rewards is to be based on achievement rather than inheritance or influence. Yet, historically, the actual working of a meritocracy has been disputed (Cohen & Lazerson, 1977). There is unequal influence among citizens in school matters as in other political affairs (Reitman, 1981). In response to the question of why schools are not effective in educating poor students, Edmonds (1982) wrote:

We happen to live in a society that values some of its people more than it values others. Educators, like all social servants, serve those they think they must and when they need not, they do not. Unfortunately, most of the children who do not get these services, in general and in education in particular, happen to be members of politically impotent groups—children who are either poor, of color, or both. (p. 272)

Inequities Between High-Income and Low-Income Schools

Sexton (1961), in her classic book, *Education and Income*, described numerous disparities between schools with rich and poor children in the Detroit area. Jencks (1972), in his book, *Inequality*, estimated that the most extensively educated fifth of the population received about 75% more than its share of the nation's educational resources, while the least educated fifth received about half of its share. Some people receive protracted schooling and schooling that costs more annually. Jencks claimed that the eventual resource disparity between the most and least favored students is at least 4 to 1 and perhaps more. A more recent related survey found that 80% of the country's 2,000 largest and richest public high schools now have at least one microcomputer as compared to only 40% of the 2,000 poorest schools (Faflick, 1982).

Interdistrict disparities in funding have been widely documented. In Texas, it was found that the poorest district could spend only $400 per child, whereas the richest could spend $7,300. In a California Supreme Court case, *Serrano v. Priest* (1971), the plaintiff argued successfully that the tradition of using property taxes to finance schools prevented children in low-income districts from obtaining an educational equivalent to that offered to children in high-income districts. The *Lau v. Nichols* (1974) decision and the remedies it called for set a legal precedent for schools to provide increased funding and unique programming so that certain groups of children would receive an equal education.

Besides funding, another important area in the allocation of resources is the distribution of teacher competencies among schools. Research indicates that teachers generally prefer to teach in middle-class schools (Jencks, 1972). Both within districts, where principals of high-income schools have more teachers to select from, and between districts, where higher income districts are also able to pay higher salaries, low-income schools are likely to attract the teachers who have been rejected by other schools. Once teachers are in low-income schools, conditions may further diminish their competencies. Scheffler (1980) reported that teachers in low-income schools were "overwhelmed" and "demoralized" and that relationships between teachers and pupils and among staff members had a high degree of conflict.

In a qualitative study of five schools (two working-class, one middle-class, one affluent professional, and one executive elite), Anyon (1980) used classroom observation, interviews with students and staff, and assessment of curriculum and materials to document differences in the school environments. Anyon concluded that a "hidden curriculum" and class bias had a profound effect on the achievement of children and that everyday activities in schools and classrooms reproduced the unequal structure of economic and political relations in the larger society. Surprisingly, few of these differences among schools have been found to have sizable effects on achievement (Coleman, Campbell, Hobson, McPartland, Mood, Weinfeld, & York, 1966; Jencks, 1972). One explanation may be that there are important differences among groups in the environments they experience within schools.

Differential Learning Environments Within Schools

Even when poor or minority children attend integrated schools, their education is often inferior because of differential learning environments within schools resulting from tracking procedures, discriminatory counseling, and inequitable relationships with staff (Weinstein, 1983). Jones, Erickson, and Crowell (1972) concluded that race had been systematically used to relegate black students to the general and basic tracks. In analyzing track assignment when controlling achievement level, they found that SES still played a major factor in the placement of seventh-grade students. Eighty percent of the upper class students, as compared to 47% of the lower class, who qualified for placement in the top track were so placed, and only 2% of the upper class pupils, as contrasted with 85% of the lower class, who qualified for placement were actually placed in the low tracks. Between the seventh and ninth grades, the downward track-mobility rate for black students was 39% but only 23% for white students. Eder (1981) and Rowan and Miracle (1983) observed differential treatment of various ability groups, and Weinstein and Middlestadt (1979) found that students discerned the relative standing and differential treatment of the groups.

Differential teacher treatment has been reported by numerous investigators (Becker, 1952; Chaikin, Sigler, & Derlega, 1974; Dotts, 1978; Harvey, 1980; Oakes, 1982; Rist, 1970; Rosenthal & Jacobson, 1968). Goodlad (1983) found that teachers expressed a preference for teaching upper tracks. Investigators have observed differential (i.e., inferior) curricula (Meier, 1982; Pink, 1982; Sieber, 1982; Young, 1976) and discriminatory disciplinary policies (Balch & Kelly, 1974; Leacock, 1969) for poor and minority children.

Tracking, also called streaming or homogeneous ability grouping, has been shown to result in de facto segregation of social classes and minority groups. In desegregated schools, tracking can be a form of resegregation (Amato, 1980; Beck, Jencks, Keddie, & Young, 1976; Jencks, 1972). Some schools may actually have selected tracking for that purpose—or are at least not careful and objective in determining track placements—and are therefore guilty of de jure segregation. Children who are intended to be integrated are instead isolated into homogeneous racial and/or social class groups. A study by McPartland (1967), done in New England and Mid-Atlantic schools, indicates that, for black students, the academic advantage of being in desegregated schools depended upon their being in the same classes with middle-class students. An individual student's academic gains are directly affected by only those students with whom he or she shares classroom experiences and interpersonal relations. Peer influence is reported to be a small but consistent correlate of educational outcomes (Ide, Parkerson, Haertel, & Walberg, 1981).

Litigation has resulted in decisions against ability grouping. In the *Hobson v. Hanson* (1967) case, the judgment was rendered that Washington, D.C. schools must stop tracking, based on the evidence that both achievement and intelligence tests used to form groups were discriminatory. In a 1976 California case, *Spangler v. Pasadena Board of Education*, racial imbalance in tracks was attributed to conscious policies and practices on the part of the school district to maintain disproportionate racial distributions, and schools were ordered to abolish the track system.

Similar to the finding regarding special education referrals, Findley and Bryan (1971) concluded, in a study of ability-grouping practices and effects, that teachers' recommendations produced even greater social class disproportions in tracks than standardized tests. Findley and Bryan felt this was a result of teachers' social class stereotypes. Rist's (1970) study revealed that, within 8 days after the beginning of school, a black teacher of an all-black kindergarten class had put her students into ability groups that corresponded to the socioeconomic distinctions of her pupils.

Empirical studies of the effects of ability grouping provide mixed evidence. Generally, the findings are that achievement is better with random grouping of children of middle- and low-achievement levels (Kelly, A.V., 1978). Some, but not all, studies show that tracking resulted in better achievement for children in higher tracks with homogeneous ability grouping (Borg, 1966). But, these results must be interpreted with care. One must question whether the occasionally superior results in the tracked conditions for high-ability students were due to the effects of ability grouping per se or were the result of preferential treatment received by students in those groups. Perhaps random grouping would have resulted in equally high achievement with the same advantaged conditions. A United Nations Educational, Scientific, and Cultural Organization (UNESCO) study of grouping (Yates, 1966) found that the most competent and popular teachers were assigned to higher tracks, that the most interesting and challenging assignments were given in higher tracks, that teachers spent more time preparing to teach higher tracks and more time grading papers, and that children in advanced tracks received better labs and books and experienced smaller teacher–pupil ratios. Rist (1970) also observed that children in different groups received qualitatively different treatment from teachers in the areas of praise, attention, distance from the teacher, and classroom responsibilities. Such differential treatment could be expected to increase the disparity between pupils over time. Several researchers have concluded negative effects of tracking for children, claiming that tracking deprives the less advanced groups of self-respect, stimulation by higher achieving peers, access to the world of college-bound peers, and helpful teacher strategies and expectations (Cave & Davies, 1977; Eder, 1981; Esposito, 1973; Kelly, A.V., 1978; Pink, 1982).

Research on children's perceptions of tracking indicates that children are very aware of the status of their group. Bayer (1981) found that, in the first grade, there was already an established social hierarchy within class reading-group assignments. Members of the top group had more social prestige, and students lost status as they moved down the hierarchy. She questioned whether this form of social stratification promoted maximum language growth on the part of the largest number of students. Bayer (1981) concluded that a hidden curriculum pervades reading activities. Students learned to value the completion of isolated reading tasks as a means of maintaining or acquiring status rather than learning to value reading as a tool for communication. Balch and Kelly (1974) reported that students at the high school level were aware of the status of their tracks, and these investigators claimed that negative teacher reaction and differential treatment were the result of the students being in certain tracks. Ability grouping clearly conveys to students their academic status in the classroom. Boersma, Chapman, and MacGuire (1979) found a high correlation between confidence in academic ability and satisfaction with school.

Despite the potentially negative effects of ability grouping, it has been found that teachers approve of tracking by ability and prefer to teach homogeneous groups (Winn & Wilson, 1983). Special education has been described as a special case of tracking because it separates children into ability levels for instruction (Madden & Slavin, 1983). Special educators must take a particularly critical look at the situation. It is clear that, in school environments where nonhandicapped, low-achieving peers are not integrated with more successful learners, it is unlikely that handicapped students, whose skills are more disparate compared to mainstream students, can be successfully integrated. Although many mildly handicapped students might succeed in lower tracks, in which the curriculum is less advanced than in heterogeneous classrooms, it is questionable whether integration within a low track can be considered as mainstreaming for either the handicapped or lower track students.

Class and Race Desegregation

In their major study, *Equality of Educational Opportunity*, Coleman et al. (1966) found that the most significant variable affecting the achievement of minority youth was attending school with white peers. In racial terms, the concept of equal educational opportunity translated into integrated schooling, which is enforced through the Civil Rights Act and amendments. Regarding social class, Coleman (1976) stated the following:

> If integration had been limited to racial integration, if there had not been an attempt to carry out widespread class integration, then the fear of racial incidents would have been much less, and the experience with integration would have been much more positive. (p. 11)

The implication here is that class integration is more troublesome to implement than racial or ethnic integration within the same socioeconomic class.

The social class composition of schools has been found to have an impact on the achievement of low-income students. In California, Wilson (1967) found that the social class composition of the primary schools in this study had the largest independent effect upon the sixth-grade reading level of his subjects. Wilson concluded that school desegregation strategies needed to be conducted along class as well as racial lines. A study by Levine and Havighurst (1977a, 1977b) of approximately 600 schools in Chicago, Illinois; Cincinnati, Ohio; Cleveland, Ohio; Kansas City, Missouri; and St. Louis, Missouri also showed a significant relationship between reading scores and the SES characteristics of elementary schools. Low-income students are more likely than middle-class students to be influenced by peer-group effects (Alexander & Campbell, 1964; Gronlund, 1979; Jencks, 1972; Ornstein, 1978); that is, the achievement scores of middle-class children do not decline when these students attend class-integrated schools, but those of working-class children improve.

There are a number of hypotheses about the reasons for the enhanced achievement of poor and minority students in integrated schools, and a great deal of empirical evidence supports these hypotheses. According to Kirp (1969), the apparent benefit of a student body with a high proportion of white students comes not from the racial composition per se but from the better educational background and higher educational aspirations that are, on the average, found among white students. Alexander and Campbell (1964) found that the educational plans of students tend to be similar to those of the students who they name as best friends. Perhaps in integrated schools, achievement orientation patterns are observed and imitated by low-income children. Picou and Carter (1976) surmised that influence on aspirations can be delineated into "definer" and "model" effects and that proximity affects the strength of either. When people of different cultures meet, aspects of the cultures are likely to be interchanged. In well-integrated schools, low-income children have the opportunity to learn middle-class values and styles, including language styles, and these are beneficial for getting ahead in school and in society in general. Furthermore, these styles enable them to perform better on standardized tests. Unfortunately, many studies of desegregation have found that segregated interactional patterns among students and faculty continue in desegregated settings (Crain, Mahard, & Narot, 1982; Schofield, 1978, 1982).

One explanation for the finding that more low-income children aspire to go to college and actually begin and complete college if they have attended desegregated schools (Armor, 1972) is perhaps that contact with middle-class children gives working-class children more realistic perceptions of their own intellectual abilities than they would have in isolation. They may find that the differences are not as great as they appear from a distance. They hear about college from their peers and teachers, and they consider the possibility of college for themselves.

Sieber (1982) found that a group of influential middle-class parents managed to manipulate preferential treatment for their children in an integrated inner-city school in a neighborhood where they had recently moved. Olson (1983) described how middle-class parents in Canada were able to divert funds for a general bilingual language-immersion program designed to promote national unity into specialized and prestigious bilingual schooling for their children. Parents in suburban schools have a sense of entitlement in demanding results from schools (Lightfoot, 1981). This vigilance of middle-class parents, whose power to influence the educational situation is similar to that of school authorities, appears to be important in maintaining quality schools and may be among the strongest arguments for having class-desegregated schools.

In the end, perhaps the most likely theory for the improved performance of low-income children in middle-class schools is that they are exposed to better learning conditions, better instruction, and more committed teachers. They spend more time attending to learning tasks and have more advanced, diverse, enriched, and stimulating curricula. In other words, they are able to take advantage of the better learning environments traditionally available to middle-class children (Anyon, 1981a; Lightfoot, 1983).

Havighurst's (1966) study of dropouts concluded that a boy from a low-income family who attended elementary school with a majority of middle-class pupils was more likely to stay in school than one who attended predominantly low-income schools. Felice and Richardson (1977) found minority students less likely to drop out when they were bussed to higher SES schools. Wilson (1967) found that a low-income boy attending school with predominantly middle-class pupils was more likely to get good grades than if he attended a school with a predominance of low-income pupils. A recent study by Brantlinger (1985a) found that, although low-income parents felt that their children would have various problems in social class integrated schools, the majority preferred to have their offspring in class-heterogeneous schools.

Minority Persons' Reactions to Schooling

The reactions of low-income people to the inequitable educational system are reputed to be alienation (Newman, 1981; White, 1980), perceptions of powerlessness, a sense of low control, feelings of meaninglessness, cultural estrangement (Seeman, 1975), feelings of futility (DeLone, 1979), and resignation to mediocrity (Havighurst, 1966). Low-income people are said to suffer passively or to express their suffering in ways that irritate the larger society (Leighton, 1979). Bott (1957) suggested that the "us–them" imagery of the working class tends to reduce the class members' desire to join the "other side" (i.e., the middle class and the middle-class school establishment) and results in rejection of what are perceived to be the values and goals of the group. In contrast to the perception of a dropout as a "loser," Fine and Rosenberg (1983) maintained that many dropouts are capable of academic achievement but leave school because of institutional inadequacies and discrimination. According to Kelly, D.H. (1978), alienated low-income students dislike school and authority figures and are rewarded for misconduct through their peer structures. These attitudes may not be limited to education or to the school years. Barbagli and Dei (1977) believed that the general attitude toward authority that pupils acquire in their relationships with teachers is transformed into a political orientation: Apparently, alienated and hostile pupils become alienated and hostile citizens.

There are few actual studies of low-income parents' perceptions of education. Lightfoot (1981) found that much of the discontent that parents felt about school inadequacies was focused on school staff and that the parents' perceptions of personnel as uncaring led to distance and the need to blame. Beckman (1976) and Vernberg and Medway (1981) also found that parents tended to hold teachers responsible for students' school problems, though teachers did not attribute children's difficulties to themselves. In England, Johnson and Ransom (1980) found that low-income parents were not apathetic about their children or about how their children did in school. They wanted their children to have a good education but did not express their concerns vociferously to local school authorities. Others (Cloward & Jones, 1963; Roberts, 1980) have written that low-income parents have positive attitudes toward education and high aspirations for their offspring (Seginer, 1983).

It is quite possible that these findings are not as contradictory as they appear. Ideally, education may be viewed as an avenue for advancement and success, yet, in reality, parents may find that their children do not have the same opportunities as the children of wealthier citizens. Brantlinger (1985a) found that the majority of low-income parents interviewed in her study perceived class discrimination in school settings and described their local low-income schools as inferior to other schools in the district. Seginer (1983) suggested that black parents may reject school achievement criteria because they are disillusioned with white society and its institutions. Felice (1981) proposed an "exchange model," which states that as long as the minority student perceives the educational relationship to be efficacious in terms of either immediate or future benefits, he or she will remain in school.

Impact of the Home Environment on Learning Characteristics

Because many ethnic groups have a similar status in society and are affected by the same environmental pressures, they may ultimately share certain characteristics. Chan and Rueda (1979) reported that 13.6% of Americans live in poverty but that 34.6% of black Americans, 23.5% of Hispanics, and 39.7% of American Indians live in poverty. Although this index was based on per capita income, poverty can also be defined as a physical and sociopsychological environment in which individuals have severely limited amounts of money, power, and social status (Farran, Haskins, & Gallagher, 1980). As Henderson (1981) pointed out, social class is not in itself an explanatory variable for a lack of school success but is related to the behaviors, attitudes, values, and living conditions of families of various socioeconomic levels.

Early Childhood Environments

Research on the importance of the quality of an infant's environment dates back to Skodak and Skeels (1949). Their findings provided the incentive for the preschool intervention studies that flourished in the early 1960s (Lazar & Darlington, 1982) and resulted in national interest in and federal funding of the Head Start program (Scott-Jones, 1984). Many of the studies concentrated on school-based interventions, but some also included a home intervention component. The Milwaukee Project (Garber & Heber, 1982) involved very early and intensive school-based intervention, which continued until a child was 6 years old, and it utilized parent training as well. Early evaluation indicated dramatic gains on cognitive measures for the experimental group, who had a mean IQ at age 6 of 124, whereas the mean IQ for the control group was 94. A follow-up evaluation 4 years later resulted in a substantially lower mean score (104), but this score remained higher than that of the control group. This finding is similar to the major conclusion of a reanalysis of 12 group-setting, preschool interventions, in that children showed considerable gains on cognitive measures in the first year of the program, but, 1 or 2 years after termination, they showed a progressive decline, so that third- and fourth-year follow-up analyses revealed no remaining effects (Bronfenbrenner, 1974).

In spite of this washout of IQ gains, a follow-up study of the Perry Preschool Project (Weikart, 1970) 9 years later found that experimental subjects did differ in terms of academic achievement (which was 1.2 grade levels above that of the control group); teacher ratings; and grade placement (Schweinhart & Weikart, 1981). Schweinhart and Weikart (1981) attributed these gains to motivational differences and adaptive functioning, both of which originated during the preschool period. Lazar and Darlington (1982), in a collaborative follow-up study, assessed the long-term effects of several preschool interventions and found lasting effects in four areas: school competence (i.e., students were less likely to be retained or to be in special education classes); achievement, attitudes, and values (i.e., students were proud of their school performance); impact on family (e.g., maternal attitudes toward school performance); and vocational aspirations. Yet, the IQs of both the experimental and control groups were one standard deviation below the national average. Clarke (1984) asserted that a short-term preschool intervention should not be expected to provide an effective long-term barrier to the ongoing environmental problems suffered by poor children and that long-term rearing environments have cumulative effects on children.

In the early 1960s, many prominent writers in the area of mental retardation attributed the "cognitive deficiencies" of lower income children to environmental causes such as "cultural deprivation." Many investigations were conducted in an attempt to find causes in children's impoverished surroundings (usually in the mother and/or in the home), or to intervene to prevent or reverse deficiencies (Bereiter & Engelmann, 1966; Deutsch, 1965; Gray & Klaus, 1965; Hess & Shipman, 1969; John & Goldstein, 1964). Bernstein (1961), for example, reported that low-income children were inferior to middle-class children in several dimensions of language. Besides language patterns, the home studies focused on such factors as concept formation, the amount or focus of stimulation received, educational materials in the home, and maternal teaching styles.

These 1960s studies were followed by criticism not only from the genetic perspective (Jensen, 1969) but also from sociolinguists (Baratz, 1969; Labov, 1973; Stewart, 1967), who carefully analyzed black English and argued that urban black children received a good deal of verbal stimulation, participated in a highly verbal culture, and were exposed to more well-formed, grammatically consistent sentences than middle-class children. Thus, the early home studies focusing on the inadequacies of the parents or in the home situations of poor children were followed by critical works, such as *The Myth of Cultural Deprivation* (Keddie, 1973), which claimed that researchers of the cultural-deprivation school were ethnocentric, naive about the customs and behavior patterns of low-income and minority families, and careless in their research methodologies. The writers of these works maintained that the language and culture of lower SES groups were different from, but not inferior to, those of the white majority and that researchers ought to focus on school and societal inadequacies instead of "blaming the victim" of societal problems (Ryan, 1971).

Another perspective in home characteristic analyses comes from conflict theory, an example of which is the theoretical work of Bowles and Gintis (1976) on class reproduction. They applied Gramsci's (1949) concept of hegemony to the American educational scene. Gramsci defined hegemony as the success of the ruling class in persuading subordinate classes to accept its own moral, political, and cultural values, the very values that contribute to their continuing subservient role in society.

In order to examine why social class status is intergenerationally transmitted, Kohn (1969, 1977) studied the child-rearing values of parents and, in general, found that middle-class parents were more likely to emphasize self-direction (e.g., self-control, responsibility, curiosity) while low-income parents stressed conformity to external authority (e.g., cleanliness, good manners, obedience). Kohn reasoned that child-rearing practices, as well as school practices, correspond to the job duties of different classes and, thus, ultimately prepare children for their roles in a class-stratified society. Kohn's perspective might be challenged by the assertion of Howell and McBroom (1982) that conventional measures of SES and specific contemporary measures of a father's job conditions account for 3% or less of variation in molar parent–child relations. Morgan, Alwin, and Griffin (1979) maintained that achievement and, therefore, achievement expectations, may involve conformity as much as initiative, ingenuity, and creativity. They also reported an absence of an effect of parental values on grades. Rollins and Thomas (1979) found that parental support produced greater conformity, while coercive attempts to control reduced conformity and were associated with antisocial behavior in offspring.

Unlike Kohn, who ultimately posited major blame for class inequities in the dominant classes, Fotheringham and Creal (1980) maintained that efforts to improve the academic achievement of the "lower end" of the population are unlikely to produce much success if they operate through modification of the existing school system or attempt to eliminate material poverty. After interviewing sixty-two mothers of high-, average-, and low-achieving third graders, they concluded that there was a need to transmit learning styles and attitudes. Thus, it appears that the conflict over and criticism of home studies has not eliminated the broad acceptance of home inadequacy theories. It is generally assumed that middle-class mothers raise their children differently and that there is a hidden curriculum in the middle-class home that results in greater school success for its members (Chan & Rueda, 1979).

Perhaps the more recent studies of home environments have been more cautiously designed and the results more objectively interpreted. At least efforts are being made to specifically define home variables, as reflected in the number of home environment rating scales recently developed (Adams, Campbell, & Ramey, 1984; Caldwell & Bradley, 1979; Elardo, Bradley & Caldwell, 1977; Laosa, 1980; Meyers, Mink, & Nihira, 1977; Mink, Meyers, & Nihira, 1984; Moos & Moos, 1976). Although researchers are still examining the reliability and validity of these scales, that is, their ability to predict high-risk behaviors, most have found some correlation between home environment and eventual school achievement. The home-environment rating scales include such indicators as the physical environment of the home, the emotional and verbal responsiveness of parents, parents' aspirations, educational opportunities, and family cohesiveness and harmony in the home. These indicators are being tied to environmental forces that might have an impact on achievement or behavior in school. Marjoribanks (1974) defined eight environmental forces affecting achievement: press for achievement; press for activeness; press for intellectuality; press for independence; press for English; press for ethnolanguage (i.e., use of home language); father dominance; and mother dominance. Marjoribanks (1979) distinguished "contextual effects," or the influences of the sociopsychological learning environment that a family creates for its children, from "individual effects" on children's performance, which might include a child's interpretations of his or her social status position. Nicassio (1983) observed dyads of school-age children and their parents completing an instructional task. Analyses indicate differential speech acts, performance rates, and task outcomes across achievement levels, suggesting a relationship among achievement, SES, language, and task performance.

Wright (1983) contended that particular forms of language functioning, resulting from certain patterns of socialization, contribute positively to successful performance in formal educational settings. Yet, Wright also maintained that, even if there were no stable relationship between language socialization and academic achievement, negative attitudes about particular groups would result in differential learning opportunities. Smitherman (1983) classified "standard English" as a class concept, and Maehr and Stallings (1975) maintained that language behaviors may exert most of their effect by shaping teachers' expectations rather than by producing interference in the verbal dialogue accompanying teaching. Anderson and Anderson (1983) claimed that American Indian English dialects are distinctive for different tribes and carry important identity roles. They recommended that dialects be accepted even though various "errors" in English tend to stem from dialect interference. Gere and Smith (1979) listed steps in the process of changing teachers' attitudes toward language. Although it appears that language performance and school achievement are correlated, there is considerable disagreement on the factors that account for that relationship.

Cognitive Styles

In 1965, Lesser, Fifer, and Clark reported different patterns of ability among school-age children in different ethnic groups (i.e., Chinese, Jewish, Negro, Puerto Rican) in New York City. Although the level of the scores varied, the patterns were maintained across socioeconomic strata and interethnic integration patterns (i.e., ethnic minorities in Anglo-oriented schools produced patterns similar to those of their ethnic peers in ethnic enclaves). The results of this study have been interpreted by some as reflecting innate capabilities and by others as supporting a differential socialization hypothesis. Proponents of theories of discontinuous relationships between school expectations and learners' styles have suggested that the diversity found in task and academic competence is precipitated by differences in culturally induced psychological, cognitive, and behavioral strategies rather than by differences in ability (Shade, 1982). Home and school environments have their own specific demand characteristics, and success in school depends on the degree of overlap of the demand characteristics of the school environment and the attributes of the individual (Laosa, 1979). *Cognitive style* has been defined as modes of perceiving, remembering, and thinking found to be related to students' interests, behavior, and performance (Kogan, 1971). On the one hand, Hess (1981) maintained that parental beliefs, expectations, and aspirations are cognitive mediators of parents' interactions with their children. On the other hand, Laosa (1982) claimed that mothers who have had more schooling tend to imitate the academic style of the classroom: they teach their children as they themselves have been taught by teachers.

A number of researchers have described those differences in the cognitive styles of particular ethnic groups that they attribute to socialization differences in the home. Shade (1982) reviewed the literature on Afro-American cognitive style and concluded that the Afro-American outlook on the world, interpersonal interaction patterns, and ideal role models differed from those of other American ethnic groups and, notably, from those of the white Anglo-Saxon Protestant (WASP) ethnic group, which controls many of the important institutions in society. Unfortunately, many of the studies Shade reviewed are situationally specific; that is, the findings of a particular study may be true for the specific group studied but may not be generalizable to supposedly similar groups in other locations or of other socioeconomic levels.

Ethnographic studies, such as those done by Cazden, Carrasco, Maldonado-Guzman, and Erickson (1980) of Mexican-American school children in Chicago, Illinois and by Philips (1982) of American Indians in the Northeastern United States, are important not necessarily because their specific results are valid for an entire ethnic group, but because they illustrate subtle diversities among individuals that often go unnoticed. It is important to heed Henderson's (1981) remarks that within-group differences in ethnic groups are greater than between-group differences. Hence, there is sure to be substantial variation within any particular group. Yet, carefully conducted ethnographic or naturalistic research is valuable in sensitizing educators to a variety of differences (e.g., communication styles, unique agendas for schooling, cognitive styles) that might affect interaction and achievement in the classroom. Remembering that categorizing behaviors and groups often results in stereotyping them, we proceed cautiously to review some of the evidence that has been documented about differences in style.

Hilliard (1976) stated that Afro-Americans process information in the environment uniquely. He claimed that they tend to view things in entirety rather than in isolated parts; that they prefer intuitive to deductive or inductive reasoning; and that they approximate concepts of space, number, and time rather than aim for exactness or complete accuracy. Hilliard contended that black children prefer people stimuli to object stimuli and rely on nonverbal as well as verbal communication. Cureton (1978) claimed that black students have a learning style preference for action-oriented teaching (i.e., intense groups and interpersonal lessons) that differs significantly from traditional, individually oriented teaching. Cureton maintained that a group-conscious, cooperative, sociocentric, and affective orientation underlies Afro-American culture.

Although there are numerous American Indian tribes with independent tribal traditions, a number of writers believe that there are some common characteristics across the different tribes. Fuchs and Havighurst (1972) focused on the American Indian life-style and concluded that the Indian family background is a handicap in school achievement because the majority of families are poverty stricken and provide a non-English environment. In addition, their Indian culture is often discontinuous with the demands of schooling. The general Indian reservation culture is different from the urban industrialized culture of the surrounding society; the former is characterized by family solidarity and cooperation among kinfolk rather than by competition among members of a given age group, belief in the value of a tribal tradition, belief in tribal religion, and a tribal language. These characteristics are believed to sometimes conflict with the competitive, individualistic achievement demands of school.

Zintz (1970) contrasted the characteristics of American Indian children and Anglo-American teachers. He observed that an Indian child is taught to live in harmony with nature, to believe in mythology for causal explanations, and to follow the ways of old people, whereas an Anglo-American teacher believes in mastery over nature, in scientific explanations of events, and in climbing the ladder of success, even if success requires overlooking tradition. According to Zintz, an Anglo-American teacher is concerned about using time efficiently and about working to get ahead in the future, whereas an Indian child has a present-time orientation and sees time as infinite.

Anderson and Anderson (1983) described various cultural behaviors that they feel lead to lower teacher evaluations of Indian children, stating that Indians value cooperation over competition, avoid public recognition, tend to produce a lower level of language in Anglo-dominated classrooms, value individual autonomy, refuse to defend themselves against accusations made by Anglo authority figures, respond to authority by looking down or away, and value an orientation toward the present rather than the future. Anderson and Anderson claimed that Indian children show a definite preference for visual learning experiences and demonstrate advanced fine-motor coordination. They suggested that the preference for visual demonstrations rather than verbal instructions might be a result of limited-English proficiency. They claimed that Indian children show low motivation for school attendance, and they suggested that this may be because education does not increase the Indian children's chances of getting jobs.

Guinn (1977) reported a number of values held by Chicanos that differ from those of Anglos, such as an emphasis on being rather than doing, a limited stress on material objects, a present-time orientation, an emphasis on group cooperation, a belief in the importance of family relations, an attitude of fatalism, and a belief in tradition. However, in a study of the interpersonal tactics of Anglo-American and Mexican-American mildly mentally retarded and nonretarded students, Rueda and Smith (1983) found no ethnic differences. Since nonretarded children were found to utilize cooperation and temporary withdrawal more often than retarded children, these investigators suggested that experiences associated with retardation may have a more pervasive influence on social development than ethnic group membership.

Analyses of maternal teaching patterns reveal that Chicano mothers use modeling, visual cues, and directive and negative physical control as teaching strategies more frequently than non-Hispanic white mothers, who use inquiry and praise more frequently (Laosa, 1980). However, the Anglos in this study were from higher socioeconomic strata and had more schooling. Laosa (1982) asserted that schooling exerts a powerful, pervasive, and enduring influence on the cultural patterns of family interaction, perhaps more than any other experience. He found that more highly schooled Chicano mothers taught using a more conversational style (inquiry) rather than by motoric demonstration (modeling) and that they especially included verbal reinforcement. Laosa (1980) also cited evidence that a parent's choice of teaching strategies influenced his or her child's development of characteristic learning strategies or cognitive styles. He hypothesized that the intellectual disadvantage observed among many ethnic minority children can be explained by the fact that ethnic minority parents, on the average, attained fewer years of schooling than nonminority parents. If the education level is held constant, ethnic differences disappear.

Self-Concept, Aspirations, and Motivation

Purkey (1970) noted a persistent and significant relationship between self-concept and academic achievement. Recent studies have found this to be true of white students, but Adam (1978) argued that the connections are not as straightforward as they first appeared. Although it might be assumed that inferiorized students (i.e., students subjected to the prejudice of others) would have low self-esteem, recent research shows that this is not the case for black students (Pugh, 1976; Simmons, 1978; Stephen & Rosenfield, 1978). Apparently, the effect of academic achievement upon self esteem varies, depending upon the patterns of students' associations with other students, social comparison processes, and the values that determine status in different situations. Faunce (1984) found that high status was correlated with academic success yet maintained that a student's "self-investment" in academic achievement is a selective process through which activities become differentially imbued with significance for the maintenance of self-esteem. Students choose to associate with others who evaluate them as they wish to be evaluated, and their response to negative evaluation is the withdrawal of self-investment as a way of coping with threats to concept of self.

St. John (1972) found that inner-city mothers, especially black mothers, have estimations of their children's potential and aspirations that are high or optimistic. She found that maternal expectations and aspirations were better predictors of children's attitudes than family SES. Entwisle and Hayduk (1978) reported a "painful discrepancy" between low-income black parents' expectations and the first school reports received by the children of these parents. Parents' aspirations for their children are reputed to have an impact on school success, yet, after a thorough review of related literature, Seginer (1983) concluded parents' expectations appear to be both a cause and an effect of academic achievement. In general, school feedback has a corrective effect on parents' perceptions of their children, but one way parents deal with the situation is to deny the validity of school feedback (Entwisle & Hayduk, 1978). In most cases, estimates of ability correlate with actual classroom performance at about the second grade (Rosenholtz & Simpson, 1984).

Ideal aspirations for educational attainment and occupational status are fairly similar for all social classes (Laosa, 1980), but expectations (real aspirations) decrease as the amount of parental schooling decreases. According to Rodman and Voydanoff (1978), all parents desire their offspring to achieve high status, but different social classes put "floors" in different places. These investigators' interviews with parents reveal that lower social status was correlated with a wider range of aspirations; low-income parents were more content with their offspring having lower status jobs. Gottfredson (1981) also found that classes differed in where along the prestige continuum they would draw the line, even though there was evidence that all social groups shared the same image of occupations. In most cases, youngsters take the group of which they are a member as their reference group: a low-SES child is likely to orient himself or herself to lower SES norms and to adopt these standards of success, and a middle-class child will orient himself or herself to the more demanding standards of the middle class. Brantlinger (1985c) found that parental aspirations were affected by school reports of performance and that educational attainment was perceived by low-income parents as not necessarily enhancing chances for life success. In other words, interviewed parents had low expectations of the power of schools to change the life circumstances of their children. Thus, definitions of success vary across individuals, tasks, and situations (Frieze & Snyder, 1980), and perceptions of the relationship of schooling to success also vary.

The attainment of aspirations is correlated with parents' stratification positions (Sewell, Haller, & Ohlendorf, 1969). Olneck and Bills (1980) found that social-class background had an effect on persistence in school. Students whose fathers had more schooling acquired more schooling. When a student's parent has gone to college, it may be taken for granted that the student will attend college, and when students report that it is taken for granted that they will attend college, they usually do (Conklin & Daily, 1981). Achieving one's aspirations may depend on the development of a rational plan of action for status outcomes. Hoelter (1982) found that white persons had more rational plans of action for status attainment than black persons in either segregated or desegregated settings, although segregated black persons had the least rational plans for college attendance of all groups. By definition, high-income parents are better able to pay for college than low-income parents; thus, taking college attendance for granted and having a rational plan for attendance (i.e., parents will pay) are naturally more likely among children of high-income families.

For low-income students, "significant others" are usually not college educated and, thus, cannot model status attainment as middle-class parents can. Impoverished adults may be so estranged from societal success models that they do not know the preferred traits that underlie mobility (Laosa, 1979). Low-income parents are reported to express ambitions for their children in terms of dissatisfaction with their own lot, offering themselves as models to be avoided (Newson, Newson, & Barnes, 1977).

One factor that affects aspirations is the perceived accessibility of occupations (Gottfredson, 1981). For a variety of class-related reasons, low-income students have fewer educational and occupational options. Rather than seeing differential attainment as due to variations in learned motives and skills, as in a socialization model, Kerckhoff (1976) offered an allocation model in which attainment is viewed as due to application of the structural limitations and the selection criteria of society.

Covington and Beery (1976) contended that achievement behavior is motivated by the desire to maintain a high self-image of ability or self-efficacy. Students will try hard to maintain a positive sense of self and status in the classroom. Yet, unlike ability, effort is volitional and amenable to change (Weiner, 1979). Therefore, attributing failure to factors, such as inefficient effort, bad luck, or task difficulty, allows individuals to avoid admitting that they lack ability and the resulting shame and distress of such an admission (Covington & Omelich, 1979).

Success attained with less perceived effort promotes self-efficacy more than that achieved with greater effort (Bandura, 1982). Katz, Cole, and Baron (1976) found that low achieving students were more self-critical than high-achieving students when working at an easy task, even though the two groups performed similarly. They maintained that harsh self-criticism represents an internalization of predominately negative reactions on the part of parents and teachers to a child's striving for competence.

Rosenholtz and Simpson (1984) maintained that, in our society, intelligence is defined as an inevitable, stable, general, and diffuse quality of individuals that is reliably measured. Thus, Roth and Kubal (1975) stated that negative feedback leads students to believe that they have failed problems that measure important human abilities and that this persistent perception of failure results in learned helplessness. (Learned helplessness is a concept used to describe children who attribute academic difficulty to low ability [Diener & Dweck, 1978].) As a result, these children are unlikely to attempt school tasks they perceive as difficult. This phenomenon is usually seen in older children because younger children are less likely to be influenced by failure or to make attributions to lack of ability (Ruble & Rhodes, 1981). Thomas (1979) pointed out that the learned helplessness pattern was characteristic of children classified as learning disabled.

Henderson and Hennig (1979) asserted that, within the norm-referenced world of the classroom, children may be likely to discern their progress in relation to their peers because of the salience of implicit and explicit comparison processes. Classrooms, in fact, constitute one of the few social settings in which children are routinely subjected to public comparisons of performance (Henderson & Hennig, 1979). Wang and Lindvall (1984) maintained that students' sense of personal control greatly affects their classroom behavior and learning processes, which in turn affect student achievement. They suggested that students' sense of personal control can be modified through instructional interventions. Ames, Ames, and Felker (1977) maintained that failure is less likely to result in self-deprecation in classrooms in which a cooperative goal structure is employed than in those characterized by norm-referenced competition.

Social Consequences of Being Known as Handicapped

In the previous sections, we discussed the social factors that may cause a child to be defined as handicapped. In this section, we examine selected findings from investigations of the social consequences of being seen as handicapped. Most of the research on this issue has been summarized elsewhere under the topics of attitudes toward handicapped persons (Guskin & Jones, 1982; Jones, 1984); or classification of handicapped persons (Hobbs, 1975); and under the more widely investigated of the specific topics, attitudes toward mentally retarded children (Gottlieb, 1975; Gottlieb, Corman, & Curci, 1984) and labeling mentally retarded persons (Guskin, 1978; MacMillan, Jones, & Aloia, 1974).

The literature in this field can be readily categorized into the following topics, which mirror the sequence proposed by labeling theory: (a) stereotypes of handicapped individuals; (b) effects of the handicap label on others' perceptions of a handicapped individual; (c) effects of the label, stereotype, and expectations on the behavior of others and on a handicapped individual's behavior; (d) reactions of others to the behavior of persons labeled as handicapped; and (e) effects of instructional settings on reactions.

Stereotypes of Handicapped Individuals

Stereotypes of handicapped individuals are beliefs held in common by members of the public about handicapped persons. Investigators of these stereotypes try to identify beliefs about the characteristics of handicapped groups. Although this has not been an area of recent interest, stereotypes of mentally retarded persons have been examined in studies by Gottwald (1970); Guskin (1963a, 1963b); and Willey and McCandless (1973). These studies have suggested, among other things, that retardation is associated with helplessness rather than aggressiveness. The existence of stereotypes of handicapped groups is assumed, though not directly studied, in most investigations of labeling and expectancy effects. That is, it is assumed that those who react to persons labeled as mentally retarded or learning disabled have images of a typical member of the group and that these preconceptions are aroused when they come in contact with a person so labeled.

Labeling Effects

Labeling studies have examined how knowledge of an individual's membership in a handicap group influences the way the individual is perceived. It is assumed that the handicap label will lead others to view a labeled individual as more like the stereotype of the group than he or she would otherwise be perceived. In these studies, information about a person's handicap is either given or not given to the perceiver along with a verbal description, photo, audiotape, film, or videotape of the individual to be judged. Findings suggest that the impact of the label depends on other available information. Thus, mental retardation labels have been ignored when a child's academic competence has been apparent (Gottlieb, 1974; Yoshida & Meyers, 1975), while in another case, the mental retardation label enhanced the negative reaction to an aggressively behaving child (Gottlieb, 1975). Although most studies of responses to the learning disabled label (as reviewed by Reid, 1984, for example) have found that it leads to negative judgments by teachers, a recent study by Sutherland, Algozzine, Ysseldyke, and Freeman (1983) found no effects of the learning disability label in a study in which the observed behavior of the child and positive reputed attributes did influence judgments by children.

Expectancy Effects

Studies of expectancy effects are defined here as those that examine the consequences of labels, such as a handicap label, for others' interactive behavior with a labeled person as well as for a labeled individual's own behavior. It is assumed that a handicap label arouses expectations of relatively incompetent performance, which lead others to modify the demands they place on labeled children to learn; a modification that in turn reduces a labeled individual's achievement. There are very few studies examining the interactive-behavior consequences of handicap labels. Many studies, of course, have examined a related phenomenon, the effect of believing that someone is a good or poor student upon teaching and learning. A consensus appears to have developed on this body of literature that suggests that artificially induced labels tend to be ineffective except in laboratory-like situations, whereas a teacher's natural labeling of a child as a good or poor student is more consistently related to the teacher's classroom behavior with this student (Dusek, 1975).

Reactions to the Behavior of Handicapped Individuals

Several studies have examined students' acceptance or rejection of educable mentally retarded or learning disabled children in regular classes. This work was recently reviewed by MacMillan and Morrison (1980), who concluded: "Despite wide variations in sociometric techniques and criteria for sociometric choice, the literature on mildly handicapped learners in regular grades reveals a consistent picture: These children are less well accepted and more frequently rejected than are nonhandicapped peers" (p. 102). These findings seem to occur whether or not the mildly handicapped children have ever been formally classified. That is, they appear to indicate a generally positive correlation between intelligence (or achievement) and sociometric status.

Effects of Settings on Reactions

One argument in favor of mainstreaming handicapped persons is that negative attitudes toward handicapped children are based on a lack of knowledge and experience and that increasing day-to-day contacts will lead to more realistic views, closer relationships, and, thus, more favorable attitudes. Gottlieb et al. (1984) reviewed several studies on the effects of mainstreaming on peer acceptance and reported consistently negative findings, that is, less favorable reactions to integrated than to segregated educable mentally retarded students. The sociometric findings reported above should suggest that, under ordinary circumstances (i.e., without special structuring), peers will not react favorably to mildly handicapped children. That favorable circumstances for contact can be designed has been demonstrated by the positive findings of Ballard, Corman, Gottlieb, and Kaufman (1978); Johnson and Johnson (1984); and Voeltz (1980). Other efforts to improve attitudes toward handicapped persons have been recently reviewed by Donaldson (1980) and Towner (1984).

Conclusion About Social Reactions to Handicapped Individuals

Guskin and Jones (1982) suggested the need to qualify widely held assumptions about social reactions to handicapped persons. They concluded:

> Attitudes toward handicapped persons are, in general, less favorable than toward nonhandicapped individuals. However, the magnitude of negative reactions varies with the severity and type of handicap. Attitudes have varied considerably from culture to culture and time period to time period but there does not appear to be a progression associated with either time or "civilization." Reactions to the handicapped do seem to be related to reactions toward other lower status and dependent individuals such as children, minorities, and the poor. Although reactions to handicap and associated labels may be negative and formal treatment programs may have unfortunate consequences, reactions to individual handicapped persons appear to be more influenced by the behavior and competence of the person than by knowledge of the handicap. Contact, as in integration of handicapped persons, may not lead to their acceptance by the public, by teachers, or by peers. Nevertheless, attitudes toward handicapped persons can be improved if exposure to the handicapped is carefully structured to reduce stereotypes and interpersonal tension and to foster equal status or otherwise satisfying contacts. (p. 192)

Educational Interventions for Culturally, Linguistically, and/or Situationally Unique Handicapped Children

Most of the issues related to social class, race, ethnic heritage, and education are relevant to the mildly handicapped population; however, there are a number of important concerns about minority children who are either more severely handicapped, who have sensory or physical deficits that interfere with language development, or whose situations interfere with effective programming. In addition, there are a number of children who present problems in programming because they are handicapped and have other special education needs as well. This section of the chapter focuses on programming for such children, including rural children, American Indian children, children of migrant workers, and limited-English-proficient children.

Rural Children

People living in certain rural areas, such as Appalachia, are often referred to as an ethnic group. However, the term *Appalachians* is linked with the Appalachian Mountains and is thus specific, whereas the term *rural* more generally refers to those in isolated situations who share similar conditions regardless of their specific locale. Usually, handicapped children in rural areas lack access to appropriate programs because of the sparseness of the population and their distance from population concentrations. They may be one of a kind and, therefore, be unable to be grouped with similar peers for effective programming. This problem is not limited to a few Appalachian-type individuals: Helge (1983) estimated that 11,000 school districts (i.e., 67% of all school districts) were considered rural and experienced problems of access and availability. Helge (1981) conducted a survey of nineteen state education agencies (SEAs) with rural populations and found that 94% claimed that recruiting adequately trained, competent staff was a problem. Eighty-eight percent reported that rural districts were resistant to change, and 72% said attitudinal problems such as suspicion of external (federal and state) interference contributed to difficulties in implementing PL 94-142. Fifty-five percent of those surveyed said economic conditions, which resulted in a low tax base, affected the rural districts' ability to deliver full services. Cultural differences, such as varying belief in the value of education, was perceived by 66% to be a problem. Language barriers, presenting problems in appropriate assessment and intervention for non-English-speaking pupils, were named by 44% of the SEAs.

Helge (1983) hypothesized that rural parents tended to perceive teachers as experts and therefore assumed a passive role in their offsprings' education. She noted that local education agencies (LEAs) did not favor expenditures for handicapped students, who they felt would not ultimately become productive. This position is supported by the research of Tunick, Platt, and Bowen (1980), who found that rural Colorado farmers and farm workers had negative attitudes toward handicapped people.

After a period when mass production ideologies seemed to have been generalized to mass education ideologies and when the consolidation and closing of rural schools were the mode, there now appears to be a trend of focusing on the advantages of rural schools (Alexander, 1978; Skenes & Carlyle, 1979). Suggested advantages are that small groups are easier to manage and that greater participation among members results in a more personable atmosphere. Rural schools can give students a sense of belonging with the possibility of close relationships among school personnel, families, pupils, and community leaders, including school board members.

One advantage of rural schools for mildly handicapped individuals might be that the school structure may be somewhat open, with cross-age grouping, peer-tutoring, and individualized instruction being commonplace for all students, not just for those experiencing learning problems. Flexibility in grouping and curriculum is possible (Alexander, 1978), and this may be to the advantage of mildly handicapped individuals, who can be readily mainstreamed because of strategies rural teachers generally use to teach heterogeneous groups. Thus, mainstreaming (or nonidentification) may happen quite naturally. Clearly, if education is provided in a rural setting, teachers in these settings will be more acquainted with local customs and more likely to understand the unique characteristics of rural children (Snider, 1979), whereas their behaviors in another locale might appear deviant or disturbed.

Students with more severe handicaps, those whose conditions require quite specialized programming (e.g., students who are visually impaired, hearing impaired, physically handicapped, autistic, or moderately/severely/profoundly handicapped or multiply handicapped), are likely to suffer in rural situations because of the lack of access to appropriate interventions and adequately trained personnel. Their geographical isolation might render it impossible for them to receive services locally.

American Indian Children

American Indians living on reservations experience conditions similar to those of other rural residents in that many of their problems spring from their isolated geographical location. Havighurst (1981) reported that, as of 1978, 38% of Indians were being educated in public schools with 50–90% Indian enrolment contiguous to reservations, 18% were in public schools with 10–50% Indian enrolment in rural communities or small cities, 17% were in boarding or day schools operated by the Bureau of Indian Affairs (BIA), 11% were in public schools on reservations, 11% were in public schools with less than 10% Indian enrolment that were located mainly in large cities, 3% were in mission or other private schools, and 1% were in Indian-controlled schools with BIA contracts. It is apparent that many American Indian children are being educated in fairly segregated settings, out of the mainstream of American society. In sparsely populated areas, students must board away from home or leave reservations, moves that families often resist.

Chiago (1981) summarized the 1969 Senate Committee report on the status of Indians, stating that approximately 16,000 Indian children were not in school, that dropout rates were twice the national average, and that the level of individuals' formal education was half that received by the average person. Indian unemployment was ten times the national average, and the average Indian income was $1,500. Though Havighurst (1981) claimed that American Indian children are at least as intelligent as American European children, American Indian children consistently underachieve, or their achievement scores are below what would be predicted from their intelligence scores. What is more, Chiago (1981) found that Indian children, more than any other group, believed themselves to be below average in intelligence and, in the twelfth grade, had the poorest self-concept of all minority groups tested.

Anderson and Anderson (1983) reported that acceptance of handicapped persons varies among Indian tribes, but, in many cases, the family assumes responsibility, which leads to overprotection and isolation. Many of the handicapped persons are reluctant to obtain treatment; thus, many unrepaired cleft lips or minor untreated orthopedic conditions exist. The prevalence of conductive hearing loss, congenital hip deformity, and other handicaps is greater than in the general population, presumably due to poor nutrition and poor prenatal and postnatal care.

Reports of new programs, such as the St. Stephen's School at Wind River, Wyoming (Reilly, 1980) and the Rough Rock School on a Navajo Reservation, an Indian-run, BIA-contract school (Havighurst, 1981), can perhaps serve as models, as they develop curricula and strategies for successful education of Indian children. Foerster and Little Soldier (1974) recommended open education, that is, student-centered education that promotes sharing and cooperation; increased student communication and interaction; and flexible use of time and space as well suited to the characteristics of Indian children. Although there appears to be little direct information about special education programming in the literature, provision for it is included in the Indian Education Act of 1973 (Ryan, 1982). Strategies suggested for general classroom practice (Foerster & Little Soldier, 1974; Havighurst, 1981; Reilly, 1980) resemble techniques often used in special education classrooms.

Children of Migrant Workers

A third minority population, migrant children, shares many problems with the other two groups. Poor economic conditions, deplorable living conditions, inadequate health care, and a life expectancy of 49 years—the national average is 73 years—characterize migrant families (Barresi, 1982). Achievement patterns are similar, but children of migrant workers underperform all other groups. Educational attainment averages the fourth or fifth grade, only 12% of those who start school graduate from high school, and 20% never enroll in school (Barresi, 1982). The majority of migrant school children are non-English speaking: 74.7% are Hispanic, and 20.2% are black (Inter-American Research Association, 1978). Therefore, they share the problems common to other non-English-speaking groups in the public schools and the discrimination problems of other minority racial or ethnic groups.

The unique aspect of migrant children is that they are a mobile population, and their nomadic life-style adversely affects their access to appropriate educational services and the continuity of these services once determined (Hunter, 1982). Pyecha and Ward (1982) conducted a telephone survey to determine the extent to which a sample of 153 handicapped migrant children were identified and had Individualized Educational Programs (IEPs) prepared by schools where they were enrolled from January 1978 through June 1979. Findings indicate that (a) various schools were inconsistent in their identification of pupils and in the preparation of IEPs, (b) IEPs were developed less frequently for the most mobile than for the least mobile migrant students, (c) only a small percentage of students had IEPs developed at more than one school, and (d) IEPs and IEP-related information were rarely transmitted between schools. Barresi (1982) outlined a number of reasons for problems in identification: (a) when a student is enrolled in a district only 3 months a year, there is no incentive to expand diagnostic resources; (b) teachers do not have time to become familiar with migrant children's needs since the children often move before the special education referral and placement process is completed; and (c) cultural and language differences cause difficulties in accurate diagnoses.

In addition to identification problems, Barresi described a number of barriers impeding service delivery: (a) interstate differences in special education eligibility requirements; (b) residency requirements (e.g., Florida charges nonresidents tuition); (c) waiting periods and limited program options; (d) scheduling problems and model program inadequacies; (e) lack of communication and cooperation between agencies serving migrant students; and (f) interstate differences in minimum competency testing and graduation requirements. As possible solutions, Barresi recommended programming options such as trial placements; extending class size with an aide while migrant students are present (to avoid opening new classes that will be underenrolled when students leave); flexible scheduling (weekend, evening, and summer instruction to accommodate work schedules); or providing tutors to work around the work hours of migrants. Frith (1982) suggested that a broader use of paraprofessionals, especially those with some connection to the migrant community, might be beneficial in various components of educational programming.

The Education Commission of the States Interstate Migrant Education Project, initiated in June 1976, evolved in response to a need for coordinated planning and implementation of migrant programs among states (Perry, 1982). The Migrant Student Record Transfer System (MSRTS), a computerized student-data network headquartered in Little Rock, Arkansas, was created to improve educational continuity for migrant students by providing centralized storage of migrant student records. The MSRTS provides the official count of migrant children for computations of state allocations of federal funds. Presently, it provides information on more than a half million children from 5 to 17 years of age (Barresi, 1982). Pyecha and Ward (1982) suggested more active strategies for assuring that copies of assessment reports and/or IEPs follow these children as they move from one school to another. They recommended that a "mini-IEP," or a standard form that would be transmitted through the MSRTS, should be developed to become part of that service to provide consistency in programming for migrant handicapped children. Sauer (1982) stated that, in spite of the belief that New York State has a successful program for migrants, handicapped individuals are not adequately served because regulations intended to protect their rights interfere with efficient service delivery. Sauer also observed that the MSRTS is presently not capable of dealing with special education information and that it would be more useful if it were expanded to do so.

Limited-English-Proficient Children

Limited-English-proficient or non-English-speaking children are often referred to as bilingual children, which is a misnomer precisely because their major problem is their lack of dominant-language (English) proficiency. Bilingual more accurately refers to the programs offered to limited-English-proficient children, yet even this may be a fallacious title because the major purpose of many bilingual programs is to encourage the use of English and perhaps to extinguish the use of the mother language.

As of 1976, more than 2.5 million limited-English-proficient children had been identified. Spanish-speaking children comprised the largest group (1,789,500), including primarily Mexican-Americans, mainland Puerto Ricans, and Cubans (Omark & Erickson, 1983). These Spanish-speaking children are part of a larger group of Hispanics (3 million) who are presently being educated in American schools. The educational statistics for Hispanics are similar to those for the other minority groups mentioned in this chapter: Hispanic students 14–19 years old were twice as likely as white students not to complete high school, and among the 8- to 13-year-old group, underachievement was double the rate for Anglo students (Santiago & Feinberg, 1981). Santiago and Feinberg (1981) reported that one-third of Hispanic students attended schools with 90–100% minority enrolment and another one-third attended schools with a 50–89% minority enrolment. This statistic is crucial to remember when the language settings of limited-English-proficient students are considered.

There are major issues related to assessment of and intervention with limited-English-proficient children. One issue, concerning appropriate assessment, has been dealt with in a previous section of this chapter. A second issue involves the most efficacious programming for children whose major language use is other than English. This issue is relevant for both handicapped and nonhandicapped school enrolments. A third issue involves the language of instruction for limited-English-proficient pupils who exhibit language acquisition problems in their home language.

There has been considerable debate about bilingual education through the years (Otheguy, 1982). The Civil Rights Act of 1964 addressed the rights of ethnic minorities, and the Bilingual Education Act of 1968 designated language minority students as a special needs population in terms of education and provided federal funds for program development at the LEA level but did not establish specific instructional strategies (Omark & Erickson, 1983). The Supreme Court decision reached in *Lau v. Nichols* (1974) firmly established the principle that "equality of educational opportunity" is not the same as "equal education," and, although it did not specifically mandate bilingual instruction, it was an important factor in further legitimizing bilingual education alternatives (Omark & Erickson, 1983).

Although bilingual education has been validated by some studies (Troike, 1978), other studies have not documented the impact of bilingual programs on academic achievement (Epstein, 1977), and the timing and focus of this second group of studies have been criticized (Tymitz, 1983). There is even some disagreement within the Hispanic community on the efficacy of bilingual intervention (Rodriquez, 1981), and funding continuation is insecure. The remedies of the *Lau v. Nichols* (1974) decision have not been enforced (Foster, 1982), and school districts have been allowed to determine for themselves the kind of programming they need, an option that often results in no programming.

Bilingual education is a complex issue, and a variety of factors must be considered before programming decisions are made. Different levels of programming have different goals, and these goals profoundly affect the nature of instruction. For example, a full biliterate/bilingual program has the objective of developing full proficiency in both languages and offers equivalent amounts of instruction in both languages in all subjects. By contrast, a partial biliterate/bilingual program develops literacy skills in both languages, but mother-tongue instruction is restricted to certain subjects, which are related mainly to cultural heritage fields, while English is used in all technical spheres and is the main instructional language (Gaarder, 1977). The goal of this approach is native-language maintenance and culture-identity development but not equal usage of the two languages. Monoliterate bilingualism promotes conversational development in both languages but not literacy skills in the non-English language. Transitional bilingualism has the goal of easing non-English speakers off the mother tongue and onto English gradually and supportively. The native language is used in the early years to the extent necessary to allow students to adjust to school and to master subject matter. There is, however, no attempt at either written or oral development or maintenance of the home language. The goal of transitional bilingual programming is to improve achievement and to facilitate the shift to the dominant language. Generally, the bilingual approach used by schools has been transitional in that there is no attempt to improve non-English proficiency. In fact, transitional bilingual education programs that limit individual students' participation to one year, are the only ones eligible for federal funds (Foster, 1982). Baca and Cervantes (1984) challenged this approach, emphasizing that children with weak language skills should work on their native language problems before being introduced to a second language.

Eligibility for bilingual instruction is another factor for consideration. The Hispanic school population is about 3 million (Santiago & Feinberg, 1981), yet only 1.8 million are considered limited in English proficiency (Omark & Erickson, 1983). Thus, in the implementation of a bilingual program for handicapped or nonhandicapped students, facility in English is a factor. Cummins (1977, 1983) contended that there is a linguistic threshold that must be attained in order to avoid cognitive deficits among limited-English-proficient children. He cautioned that surface-structure deviance should not imply cognitive deficits—nor should adequate surface structure in English necessarily imply English proficiency (1981). He suggested that it takes 5 years of English use to approach grade norms in aspects of English proficiency.

Proficiency depends on variables such as the number of generations of residency (Cummins, 1981; Laosa, 1981), contact with English speakers, and motivation to learn English, which may in turn depend on feelings about the dominant culture and the desire to assimilate. Like intelligence testing, tests of language proficiency have validity and reliability problems. Langdon (1983), who has worked both with mainland Puerto Ricans and with Mexican Americans, made a number of suggestions about formal and informal instruments available to assess the first- and second-language skills of bilingual or limited-English-proficient students. Wilson and Fox (1982) recently described microcomputer courseware developed to provide interactive, receptive language testing and training for bilingual, language-handicapped individuals.

Situational variables need to be considered in the development of bilingual programming. Bilingual programming in a school with a predominantly limited-English-proficient enrolment is substantially different from programming in a school with a small minority of pupils or with pupils whose mother language is a less common one than Spanish. When a school district separates limited-English-proficient students for instruction in an area with many minority students, it may risk segregation and discrimination charges.

Media and materials are often not relevant to the needs of Spanish-speaking students, and those that exist are often prohibitively expensive (Bland, Sabatino, Sedlak, & Sternberg, 1979). The availability of materials and instructional approaches becomes a major obstacle in the case of more obscure languages.

Finding personnel who are fully trained to implement bilingual education is an often-recognized problem in special or general education (Baca & Bransford, 1982; Benavides, 1980; Plata & Santos, 1981). Recruiting minority individuals for teacher-training programs is one approach, and another is offering language and multicultural training to nonminority teachers, an approach described by Benavides (1984) as designed to increase the supply of bilingual special education teachers in the Chicago, Illinois area. Teacher competencies for bilingual handicapped programs have been described by Ortiz (1981) and by Rueda, Rodriguez, and Prieto (1981). Plata and Jones (1982) have described a bilingual, interdisciplinary, vocational education program for handicapped children involving three instructional approaches (i.e., vocational, bilingual, and special education).

Handicapped learners and limited-English-proficient children are each very heterogeneous groups with tremendous variations both in characteristics and in needs. The multiple eligibility of some children for bilingual and special education programs can cause scheduling or placement problems. Thus, assessment and intervention issues are very complex and necessitate multifaceted considerations in programming.

Most mildly handicapped limited-English-proficient individuals, if provided with appropriate instruction, can benefit from education in English—and they will probably need English proficiency to achieve in the dominant culture. However, this may not be the case for more severely handicapped children. Many such children have major deficits in acquiring their mother language, and instruction in another language may well be counterproductive in that it could hinder development in the first language or interfere with training in more relevant and useful survival skills. For more severely retarded pupils who have physical handicaps or hearing impairments, or who are autistic, a number of related variables may need to be considered before the language of instruction is determined. Factors such as the predominant language of the child's community, the child's prospective place in the community, and his or her language facility and language contacts, all need to be considered in order to make legitimate program decisions.

Summary and Recommendations

In the major sections of this chapter, we have examined the factors that might explain the effect of minority status on schooling and handicap classification; the social consequences of being known as handicapped; and educational interventions for culturally, linguistically, and/or situationally unique handicapped children.

In addressing this large body of literature, space limitations have made it impossible to provide detailed critiques of individual studies. However, it is important that the reader be aware that much of the research in this area has serious conceptual and methodological weaknesses as well as limitations in the extent to which findings can be applied to practice.

Conceptually, we find that most studies are either atheoretical in their examination of empirical relationships among large sets of variables or overly broad in their use of frameworks such as labeling theory, normalization, and neo-Marxism, which are heavily value-laden and thus filled with unverified and often unverifiable assumptions.

Methodologically, most research in this area is vulnerable because it is primarily correlational, regardless of the methods and sophistication of the data analysis employed. Attemps to unravel causal relationships between sociocultural variables and learner achievement or handicap status are necessarily limited by the potential influence of unmeasured or imperfectly measured variables. This is true even when the direction of influence initially appears obvious. Thus, for instance, while it is apparent that a young child's school achievement is not the cause of his or her parents' SES, SES is obviously influenced by the parents' own school achievement, and numerous other genetic and environmental variables can be involved in the relationship between parents' and children's school achievement.

Experimental intervention (e.g., preschool) studies have not been without their own problems. Even in those few cases in which random assignment to conditions, blind and reliable measurement procedures, carefully implemented treatment procedures, and long-term follow-up have been employed, it is difficult to remove the influence of extraneous variables. Thus, if a preschool program's mode of instruction makes a child more able to answer questions, such as those on an IQ or reading-readiness test, the child is unlikely to be placed in special education programs, even if he or she does poorly in school. The problems are, of course, even greater when the effects of large-scale, policy-based interventions such as desegregation and mainstreaming are examined (Jones, Gottlieb, Guskin, & Yoshida, 1978). On the one hand, initial findings may be influenced by a variety of factors that may not exist once programs are institutionalized. On the other hand, more controlled laboratory studies, such as labeling experiments, gain their internal validity at the price of external validity. That, is, they fail to be representative of the natural events to which researchers may wish to generalize them.

The implications of these criticisms are that we should be careful about the generalizations that abound in this area and that research is more valuable for challenging common assumptions, raising questions, and suggesting possibilities than for convincingly demonstrating truths or validating practical solutions. It is with these limitations in mind that we provide the conclusions and recommendations that follow. Although it is not easy to summarize all of our findings, we can draw together much of the material by reexamining the assumptions presented in the previous sections of this chapter.

1. *There is a relationship among ethnic and social-class status and school achievement and handicapped classification.* A review of research indicates that this assumption is to some extent true, although results vary depending on the location and the characteristics of the sample studied. Further investigations of the factors precipitating this phenomenon are needed, particularly, careful studies of those variables in school climates that might account for differences in the achievement of high- and low-income learners. Studies of school and classroom climate, teacher behavior, and teacher–pupil interaction in the tradition of Anyon (1981a, 1981b), Eder (1981), Leacock (1969), Lightfoot (1973), McDermott and Gospodinoff (1979), Mehan (1979), and Rist (1970) could continue to provide meaningful information for educators. Meanwhile, national, state, and local education associations should attempt to rectify discrimination by fair funding patterns and/or by checks on school practices such as tracking, teacher assignments, and discipline procedures.

2. *There is a bias in referral rates, assessment strategies, and types of placements of minority and/or low-income children.* This assumption appears to be true. Multicultural pre-service and in-service training, which sensitizes personnel to minority learner needs and makes them aware of personal prejudices, can be expanded and improved. Additional nondiscriminatory assessment tools and methods need to be developed and expanded. The most fair and objective assessment strategies currently available must be implemented scrupulously by assessment teams. Furthermore, schools must be certain that they place children in the least restrictive appropriate environment and provide the resources to make that placement possible.

3. *School environments have an impact on the learning characteristics of minority students.* Although the Coleman et al. (1966) report diverted attention away from school environment variables with the exception of student composition, recent studies have pinpointed other influential variables.

a. *There are inequities in the distribution of materials and human resources between high-income and low-income schools.* Investigations indicate that school inequities are real. Resources, both material and human, need to be more equitably distributed. Advocates for low-income minorities need to pressure school administrators at all levels to work to improve funding patterns. Similarly, checks on within-district enrolment patterns would undoubtedly reveal de jure and de facto ethnic and social class segregation, perhaps even illegal racial segregation. National, state, and local education associations should take a meaningful stand against such discriminatory practices.

b. *Differential (i.e., inferior) learning environments tend to be developed within heterogeneous (i.e., class- and race-desegregated) schools.* The investigations of tracking, discriminatory counseling, and disciplinary practices show such development to be the case. There is a vast literature on the negative impact of tracking and ability grouping on less advanced children that clearly needs dissemination among practitioners. Perhaps similar due-process procedures need to be delineated and followed for track and group placement as are currently necessary for special education placement. Multicultural education might help teachers and school administrators understand and appreciate all the children in their care.

c. *The social class and racial compositions of schools have an impact on learning characteristics.* Although racial desegregation is mandated, further attention should be directed at developing effective implementation strategies. Comprehensive studies of desegregation have concluded with numerous suggestions for practice (e.g., Crain, Mahard, & Narot, 1982; St. John, 1971; Schofield, 1982). Unlike racial desegregation, social-class desegregation is not compulsory, yet, the rationale for social-class desegregation is practically identical to that for race. Additional research needs to be focused on the impact of social-class desegregation on low-achieving students.

d. *Minority individuals are not passive, static recipients of educational services but come to school with their own agendas, their own feelings about school, and their own unique reactions to what happens in school.* There is considerable evidence available on the impact of the school setting on characteristics of a learner, particularly on those of a low-achieving learner. Minority and low-income individuals have been found to have perceptions of and opinions about the nature of schooling and about their roles in relation to school personnel. Unlike wealthier persons, low-income people usually have little power to implement their ideas about school reform. Consumer (i.e., parent and child) opinion must be actively sought both by researchers and by educational implementors.

4. *Home environments influence learning characteristics.* Studies indicate that this assumption is true.

a. *Early childhood environments have an impact on learners' readiness for and response to the educational setting.* Although early home studies were often ethnocentric and faulty in methodology, current researchers are attempting to develop more objective measures for discerning the variables that influence early childhood development. Investigations comparing preschool and day-care services for rich and poor families would probably reveal discrepancies that might be more alterable than those produced by family factors. Studies of the efficacy of parenting courses at the secondary level, which are frequently combined with school-based day-care internships, might prove meaningful.

b. *Cognitive styles vary according to socialization patterns.* Most people have a hunch that this assumption is true, although concrete evidence on the topic is not readily available. Information on socialization processes, as well as on cognitive differences, is often based on the theories and conjecture of insiders (i.e., members of the group being studied). It is difficult for an outsider to be an unobtrusive observer in the home. There is considerable information from laboratory research in which the interaction patterns of parent–child dyads were observed through one-way mirrors. Such reports are valuable but do not tell the whole story. Determining the obtuse processes involved in both socialization and cognition and the interrelationship of these processes is a complex undertaking. Even if results appear to be valid, home intervention is difficult, and postponing treatment to modify cognitive style until school entrance may reduce the chances of treatment success. Additionally, advocating the modification of either home socialization or unique cognitive style may be considered an ethnocentric pursuit.

c. *Self-concept, aspirations, and motivation are influenced by parental values and student identification patterns and are further shaped by school climate variables.* Again, past and present investigations are of mixed value because of inadequate conceptualizations of the topic and inadequate research design. Laboratory research has provided considerable information on psychological characteristics; however, applied research is needed to validate lab results. Self-report inventories are frequently utilized for measuring these constructs. Unfortunately, they operate under the constraints of set categories and forced choices. Naturalistic designs are likely to be more effective in exploring the parameters of the topic and in obtaining more realistic information from respondents.

5. *Being classified as handicapped has an impact on the future school and life careers of individuals.* The influence that the handicap label has on a student depends heavily upon that student's own behavior and achievement as well as on the educational setting in which the student is placed. Most studies find that handicapped and low-achieving students are poorly accepted in regular classes. One problem with such efficacy studies is that they focus on the regular classroom as it is and not as it ideally could be. Creative strategies for improving the chances of successful learning and adjustment for low-achieving and handicapped students in regular classrooms have finally begun to appear in the literature (e.g., Block, 1984; Johnson, Maruyama, Johnson, Nelson, & Skon, 1981; Oden, 1976; Reynolds & Wang, 1983; Slavin, 1984). Specially designed programming and instructional organization for the class as a whole can facilitate the maintenance of diverse students in regular classes. At a time when the referral of low-achieving and behaviorally difficult children is apparently a valued option for regular classroom teachers, incentives need to be found and support provided to encourage teachers to maintain diverse learners in the mainstream setting and to accommodate their needs.- Studies of noncategorical service delivery models hold promise for the future.

6. *Specific handicapped minorities have difficulty in gaining access to and benefiting from appropriate educational interventions.* A number of handicapped, limited-English-proficient children who are seasonally mobile or who live in isolated areas are presently not receiving adequate services. The MSRTS attempts to improve educational services for the children of migrant laborers, although it needs to be expanded to fit the needs of handicapped children. Similar projects, preferably with national dissemination of results, need to be developed in response to other widespread concerns. Local model programs, materials, computer-assisted instruction, and policies need to be developed and communicated between service providers with similar special needs populations.

Conclusion

Making school a viable institution suited to the needs and interests of a variety of youngsters is imperative. Methods must be found to provide incentives for failing students to succeed and for alienated students to become involved so that schools can become truly efficacious in terms of immediate and future benefits for all students. The state of the art and the state of practice in this area are succinctly described by Edgerton (1981) as follows:

> Because we know that subcultural differences can be important we may be lulled into the belief that we have adequately taken them into account, but our knowledge of subcultural factors is so inadequate that we cannot have provided for differences. (p. 320)

Besides school reform, efforts to provide multicultural, nonsexist, and handicap-sensitive pre-service and in-service training to regular elementary and secondary teachers must be continued and improved. Perhaps more important, administrators must have comprehensive training in dealing fairly with, and encouraging the success of, all children. It has been consistently found that school leadership is very important in this area. Efforts to recruit minority personnel or other personnel with particular characteristics suitable to the teaching of minority children, or to purge ineffective or inadequate staff, are essential. On a broader level, it is important that citizens concerned with equal rights and opportunity issues be vigilant observers of local, state, and federal laws and policies that might have an impact on the schooling of poor, minority, and handicapped groups. It must be remembered that school concerns are closely related to and, in fact, inseparable from, other political, economic, and social issues.

Author Information

Ellen Anderson Brantlinger is Assistant Professor of Special Education and Samuel L. Guskin is Professor of Special Education both at Indiana University.

References

Adam, B. D. (1978). Inferiorization and self-esteem. *Social Psychology*, **41**, 47–53.

Adams, J. L., Campbell, F. A., & Ramey, C. T. (1984). Infants' home environments: A study of screening efficacy. *American Journal of Mental Deficiency*, **89**, 133–139.

Aguirre, A. (1979). Chicanos, intelligence testing and the quality of life. *Educational Research Quarterly*, **4**(1), 3–12.

Alexander, C. N., & Campbell, E. Q. (1964). Peer influences on adolescent educational aspirations and attainments. *American Sociological Review*, **29**, 568–575.

Alexander, R. (1978). Is the country school the newest thing in education? *Instructor*, **88**, 106–111.

Algozzine, B., & Ysseldyke, J. (1983). Learning disabilities as a subset of school failure: The over-sophistication of a concept. *Exceptional Children*, **50**, 242–246.

Almanza, H. P., & Mosely, W. J. (1980). Curriculum adaptations and modifications for culturally diverse handicapped children. *Exceptional Children*, **46**, 608–614.

Amato, J. (1980). Social class discrimination in the schooling process: Myth and reality. *Urban Review*, **12**(3), 121–130.

Ames, C., Ames, R., & Felker, D. W. (1977). Effects of competitive reward structure and valence of outcome on children's achievement attributions. *Journal of Educational Psychology*, **69**, 1–8.

Anderson, G. R., & Anderson, S. K. (1983). The exceptional Native American. In D. R. Omark & J. G. Erickson (Eds.), *The bilingual exceptional child* (pp. 163–180). San Diego, CA: College-Hill Press.

Anyon, J. (1980). Social class and the hidden curriculum of work. *Journal of Education*, **162**(4), 67–92.

Anyon, J. (1981a). Elementary schooling and distinctions of social class. *Interchange*, **12**(2), 118–132.

Anyon, J. (1981b). Schools as agencies of social legitimation. *International Journal of Political Education*, **4**, 195–218.

Argulewicz, E. N. (1983). Effects of ethnic membership, socioeconomic status, and home language on LD, EMR, and EH placements. *Learning Disabilities Quarterly*, **6**, 195–200.

Argulewicz, E. N., & Sanchez, D. T. (1983). The special education evaluation process as a moderator of false positives. *Exceptional Children*, **49**, 452–454.

Armor, D. J. (1972). The evidence on busing. *The Public Interest*, **28**, 90–126.

Baca, L. M., & Bransford, J. (1982). *An appropriate education for handicapped children of limited English proficiency.* Reston, VA: Council for Exceptional Children.

Baca, L. M., & Cervantes, H. T. (Eds.). (1984). *The bilingual special education interface.* St. Louis, MO: Times Mirror/Mosby.

Bailey, D. B., & Harbin, G. L. (1980). Nondiscriminatory evaluation. *Exceptional Children*, **46**, 590–596.

Balch, R. W., & Kelly, D. H. (1974). Reactions to deviance in a junior high school: Student views of the labeling process. *Instructional Psychology*, **1**, 25–38.

Ballard, M., Corman, L., Gottlieb, J., & Kaufman, M. J. (1978). Improving the social status of mainstreamed retarded children. *Journal of Educational Psychology*, **69**, 605–611.

Bandura, A. (1982). Self-efficacy mechanism in human agency. *American Psychologist*, **37**, 122–147.

Baratz, J. C. (1969). Linguistic and cognitive assessment of Negro children: Assumptions and research needs. *Asha*, **11**, 87–91.

Barbagli, M., & Dei, M. (1977). Socialization into apathy and political subordination. In J. Karabel & A. H. Halsey (Eds.), *Power and ideology in education* (pp. 423–431). New York: Oxford University Press.

Barresi, J. G. (1982). Educating handicapped migrants: Issues and options. *Exceptional Children*, **48**, 473–488.

Bayer, A. (1981). Social status hierarchy: Reading groups. *Viewpoints in Teaching and Learning*, **57**(3), 49–57.

Beck, J., Jencks, C., Keddie, N., & Young, M. F. D. (1976). *Toward a sociology of education.* New Brunswick, NJ: Transaction Books.

Becker, H. S. (1952). Social class variations in teacher-pupil relationships. *Journal of Educational Sociology*, **25**, 451–465.

Beckman, L. J. (1976). Causal attributions of teachers and parents regarding children's performance. *Psychology in the Schools*, **13**, 212–218.

Benavides, A. (1984). Planning effective special education for exceptional language minorities. *Teaching Exceptional Children*, **17**, 127–133.

Bereiter, C., & Engelmann, S. (1966). *Teaching disadvantaged children in the pre-school.* Englewood Cliffs, NJ: Prentice-Hall.

Bernal, E. M. (1983). Trends in bilingual special education. *Learning Disability Quarterly*, **6**, 424–431.

Bernal, E. M. (1983). Trends in bilingual special education. *Learning Disability Quarterly*, **6**, 424–431.

Bernstein, B. (1961). Social structure, language and learning. *Educational Research*, **3**, 163–176.

Bland, E., Sabatino, D. A., Sedlak, R., & Sternberg, L. (1979). Availability, usability and desirability of instructional materials and media for minority handicapped students. *Journal of Special Education*, **13**, 157–167.

Block, J. H. (1984). Making school learning activities more play-like: Flow and mastery learning. *Elementary School Journal*, **85**, 64–75.

Boersma, F. J., Chapman, J. W., & MacGuire, T. O. (1979). The student perception of ability scale: An instrument for measuring academic self-concept in elementary school children. *Educational and Psychological Measurement*, **39**, 135–141.

Borg, W. R. (1966). *Ability grouping in the public schools.* Madison, WI: Denbar Educational Research Services.

Bott, E. (1957). *Family and social network.* London, England: Tavistock.

Bowles, S., & Gintis, H. (1976). *Schooling in capitalist America.* New York: Basic Books.

Brantlinger, E. A. (1985a). Low-income parents' opinions about the social class composition of schools. *American Journal of Education*, **93**, 319–408.

Brantlinger, E. A. (1985b). Low-income parents' perceptions of favoritism in the schools. *Urban Education*, **20**, 82–102.

Brantlinger, E. A. (1985c). What low-income parents want from schools: A different view of aspirations. *Interchange*, **16**(4), 14–28.

Broman, S. H., Nichols, P. L., & Kennedy, W. A. (1975). *Preschool IQ: Prenatal and early developmental correlates.* Hillsdale, NJ: Erlbaum.

Bronfenbrenner, U. (1974). *A report on longitudinal evaluation of preschool programs. Vol. 2. Is early intervention effective?* Washington, DC: Department of Health, Education, and Welfare.

Caldwell, B. M., & Bradley, R. (1979). *Home observation for measurement of the environment.* Little Rock, AR: University of Arkansas.

Cave, R. G., & Davies, B. (1977). *Mixed ability teaching in the elementary school.* London, England: Ward Lock Educational.

Cazden, C. B., Carrasco, R., Maldonado-Guzman, A. A., & Erickson, F. (1980). The contribution of ethnographic research to bicultural-bilingual education. In J. E. Alatis (Ed.), *Current issues in bilingual education* (pp. 64–80). Washington, DC: Georgetown University Press.

Chaikin, A. L., Sigler, E., & Derlega, V. J. (1974). Nonverbal mediators of teacher expectancy effects. *Journal of Personality and Social Psychology*, **30**, 144–149.

Chan, K., & Rueda, R. (1979). Poverty and culture in education: Separate but equal. *Exceptional Children*, **45**, 422–428.

Chiago, R. (1981). Making education work for the American Indian. *Theory Into Practice*, **20**, 20–25.

Chinn, P. C. (1979). The exceptional minority child: Issues and some answers. *Exceptional Children*, **45**, 532–536.

Clarke, A. M. (1984). Early experience and cognitive development. In E. W. Gordon (Ed.), *Review of research in education* (pp. 125–157). Washington, DC: American Educational Research Association.

Cleary, T., Humphreys, L., Kendrick, S., & Wesman, A. (1975). Educational uses of tests with disadvantaged students. *American Psychologist*, **30**, 15–41.

Cloward, R. A., & Jones, J. A. (1963). Social class, educational attitudes and participation. In A. H. Passow (Ed.), *Education in depressed areas* (pp. 198–216). New York: Bureau of Publications, Teachers College.

Cohen, D., & Lazerson, M. (1977). Education and the corporate order: Merit and equality. In J. Karabel & A. H. Halsey (Eds.), *Power and ideology in education* (pp. 393–585). New York: Oxford University Press.

Coleman, J. S., Campbell, E. Q., Hobson, C. J., McPartland, J., Mood, A. M., Weinfeld, F. D., & York, R. L. (1966). *Equality of educational opportunity* (Report of the Office of Education to the Congress and the President). Washington, DC: U.S. Government Printing Office.

Coleman, J. S. (1976). Liberty and equality in school desegregation. *Social Policy*, **6**(14), 9–13.

Conklin, M. E., & Daily, A. R. (1981). Does consistency of parental educational encouragement matter for secondary school students? *Sociology of Education*, **54**, 254–262.

Covington, M. V., & Beery, R. G. (1976). *Self-worth and school learning.* New York: Holt, Rinehart & Winston.

Covington, M. V., & Omelich, C. L. (1979). Effort: The double-edged sword in school achievement. *Journal of Educational Psychology*, **71**, 160–182.

Crain, R. L., Mahard, R. E., & Narot, R. E. (1982). *Making desegregation work: How schools create social climates.* Cambridge, MA: Ballinger.

Cremins, J. J. (1981). Larry P. and the EMR child. *Education and Training of the Mentally Retarded*, **16**, 158–161.

Cummins, J. (1977). Cognitive factors associated with the attainment of intermediate levels of bilingual skills. *The Modern Language Journal*, **61**, 3–12.

Cummins, J. (1981). Four misconceptions about language proficiency in bilingual education. *National Association for Bilingual Education Journal*, **5**, 31–45.

Cummins, J. (1983). Bilingualism and special education: Program and pedagogical issues. *Learning Disability Quarterly*, **6**, 373–386.

Cureton, G. O. (1978). Using a black learning style. *The Reading Teacher*, **31**, 751–756.

DeLone, R. H. (1979). *Small futures: Children, inequality, and the limits of liberal reform.* New York: Harcourt, Brace, Jovanovich.

Deshler, D. D., Schumaker, J. B., Alley, G. R., Warner, M. M., & Clark, F. L. (1982). Learning disabilities in adolescent and young adult populations: Research implications. *Focus on Exceptional Children*, **15**(1), 221–227.

Deutsch, M. (1965). The role of social class in language development and cognition. *American Journal of Orthopsychiatry*, **35**, 78–88.

Diener, C. I., & Dweck, C. S. (1978). An analysis of learned helplessness: Continuous changes in performance, strategy, and achievement cognitions following failure. *Journal of Personality and Social Psychology*, **36**, 451–462.

Donaldson, J. (1980). Changing attitudes toward handicapped children: A review and analysis of research. *Exceptional Children*, **46**, 504–514.

Dotts, W. (1978). Black and white teacher attitude toward disadvantage and poverty. *Education*, **99**, 48–54.

Drummond, H. (1982). Power, madness and poverty. *Behavioral Disorders*, **7**, 101–109.

Duffey, J. B., Salvia, J., Tucker, J., & Ysseldyke, J. (1981). Nonbiased assessment: A need for operationalism. *Exceptional Children*, **47**, 427–434.

Dusek, J. B. (1975). Do teachers bias children's learning? *Review of Educational Research*, **45**, 1–684.

Eder, D. (1981). Ability grouping as a self-fulfilling prophecy: A micro-analysis of teacher-student interaction. *Sociology of Education*, **57**, 151–162.

Edgerton, R. B. (1981). Another look at culture and mental retardation. In M. J. Begab, H. C. Haywood, & H. L. Garber (Eds.), *Psychosocial influences in retarded performance* (Vol. I, pp. 309–323). Baltimore, MD: University Park Press.

Edmonds, R. (1982). The last obstacle to equity in education: Social class. *Theory Into Practice*, **20**, 269–272.

Educational Testing Service (1980). New vistas in special education. *Focus* **8**(2), 1–20.

Elardo, R., Bradley, R., & Caldwell, B. M. (1977). A longitudinal study of the relation of infants' home environments to language development at age three. *Child Development*, **48**, 595–603.

Entwisle, D. R., & Hayduk, L. A. (1978). *Too great expectations: The academic outlook of young children.* Baltimore, MD: Johns Hopkins University Press.

Epstein, N. (1977). *Language, ethnicity, and the schools.* Washington, DC: George Washington Institute for Educational Leadership.

Esposito, D. (1973). Homogeneous and heterogeneous ability grouping: Principal findings and implications for evaluating and designing more effective educational environments. *Review of Educational Research*, **43**, 163–179.

Faflick, P. (1982, November 15). Peering into the poverty gap: Will the rich get smarter while the poor play video games? *Time*, 69.

Farran, D. C., Haskins, R., & Gallagher, J. J. (1980). Poverty and mental retardation: A search for explanations. In J. J. Gallagher (Ed.), *Ecology of exceptional children* (Vol. 1, pp. 47–65). San Francisco, CA: Jossey-Bass.

Faunce, W. A. (1984). School achievement, social status, and self-esteem. *Social Psychology Quarterly*, **47**, 3–14.

Felice, L. G. (1981). Black student dropout behavior: Disengagement from school, rejection and racial discrimination. *Journal of Negro Education*, **50**, 415–424.

Felice, L. G., & Richardson, R. L. (1977, November/December). Effects of desegregation on minority student dropout rates. *Integrated Education*, **15**, 47–50.

Findley, W., & Bryan, M. (1971). *Ability grouping: Status, impact and alternatives*. Athens, GA: University of Georgia Press.

Fine, M., & Rosenberg, P. (1983). Dropping out of high school: The ideology of school and work. *Journal of Education*, **165**, 257–272.

Finn, J. B. (1982). Patterns in special education placement as revealed by the OCR surveys. In K. A. Heller, W. H. Holtzman, & S. Messick (Eds.), *Placing children in special education: A strategy for equity* (pp. 322–381). Washington, DC: National Academy Press.

Foerster, L. M., & Little Soldier, D. (1974). Open education and Native American values. *Educational Leadership*, **32**, 41–45.

Ford, J., Mongon, D., & Whelan, M. (1982). *Special education and social control: Invisible disaster*. London, England: Routledge & Kegan Paul.

Foster, S. G. (1982, May 5). Bell confirms shift from "Lau Rules": Bilingual-education decisions left to schools. *Education Week*, 9.

Fotheringham, J. B., & Creal, D. (1980). Family socioeconomic and educational-emotional characteristics as predictors of school achievement. *Journal of Educational Research*, **73**, 311–317.

Frieze, I., & Snyder, H. (1980). Children's beliefs about the causes of success and failure in school settings. *Journal of Educational Psychology*, **72**, 186–196.

Frith, G. H. (1982). Educating migrant students: The paraprofessional component. *Exceptional Children*, **48**, 506–509.

Fuchs, E., & Havighurst, R. J. (1972). *To live on this earth*. New York: Doubleday.

Gaarder, A. B. (1977). *Bilingual schooling and the survival of Spanish in the United States*. Rowley, MA: Newbury House.

Garber, H., & Heber, R. (1982). Modification of predicted cognitive development in high-risk children through early intervention. In D. K. Detterman & R. Sternberg (Eds.), *How and how much can intelligence be increased?* (pp. 180–194). Norwood, NJ: Ablex.

Gerber, M. M. (1984). The Department of Education's Sixth Annual Report to Congress on PL 94–142: Is Congress getting the full story? *Exceptional Children*, **51**, 209–224.

Gere, A. R., & Smith, E. (1979). *Attitudes, language, and change*. Urbana, IL: National Council of Teachers of English.

Goodlad, J. I. (1983). *A place called school*. New York: McGraw-Hill.

Gordon, M. T. (1976). A different view of the IQ-achievement gap. *Sociology of Education*, **49**, 4-11.

Gordon, R. A., & Rudert, E. E. (1979). Bad news concerning IQ tests. *Sociology of Education*, **52**, 174–190.

Gottfredson, L. S. (1981). Circumscription and compromise: A developmental theory of occupational aspirations [Monograph]. *Journal of Counseling Psychology*, **28**, 545–579.

Gottlieb, J. (1974). Attitudes toward retarded children: Effects of labeling and academic performance. *American Journal of Mental Deficiency*, **79**, 268–273.

Gottlieb, J. (1975). Attitudes toward retarded children: Effects of labeling and behavioral aggressiveness. *Journal of Educational Psychology*, **67**, 581–585.

Gottlieb, J., Corman, L., & Curci, R. (1984). Attitudes toward mentally retarded children. In R. L. Jones (Ed.), *Attitudes and attitude change in special education: Theory and practice* (pp. 143–156). Reston, VA: Council for Exceptional Children.

Gottwald, H. (1970). Public awareness about mental retardation. *Research Monograph*. Reston, VA: Council for Exceptional Children.

Gramsci, A. (1949). *Quaderni del carcere. Vol. 2. Gli intellettuali e l'organizzazione della cultura*. Turin, Italy: Einaudi.

Gray, S. W., & Klaus, R. A. (1965). Experimental preschool programs for culturally deprived children. *Child Development*, **36**, 887–898.

Gronlund, N. E. (1979). *Sociometry in the classroom*. New York: Harper & Row.

Grossman, H. J. (Ed.). (1973). *Manual on terminology and classification in mental retardation* (1973 revision). Washington, DC: American Association of Mental Deficiency.

Guinn, R. (1977, January). Value clarification in the bicultural classroom. *Journal of Teacher Education*, **28**, 46–47.

Guskin, S. L. (1963a). Measuring the strength of the stereotype of the mental defective. *American Journal of Mental Deficiency*, **67**, 569–575.

Guskin, S. L. (1963b). Social psychologies of mental deficiency. In N. R. Ellis (Ed.), *Handbook of mental deficiency* (pp. 325–353). New York: McGraw-Hill.

Guskin, S. L. (1978). Theoretical and empirical strategies for the study of the labeling of mentally retarded persons. In N. R. Ellis (Ed.), *International review of research in mental retardation* (Vol. 9, pp. 127–158). New York: Academic Press.

Guskin, S. L., & Jones, R. L. (1982). Attitudes toward the handicapped. In H. F. Mitzel (Ed.), *Encyclopedia of educational research* (5th ed.) pp. 189–193). New York: Free Press.

Harvey, M. R. (1980). Public school treatment of low-income children. *Urban Education*, **15**, 279–323.

Havighurst, R. J. (1966). *Education in metropolitan areas*. Boston, MA: Allyn & Bacon.

Havighurst, R. J. (1981). Indian education: Accomplishments of the last decade. *Phi Delta Kappan*, **62**, 329–331.

Helge, D. I. (1981). Problems in implementing comprehensive special education programming in rural areas. *Exceptional Children*, **47**, 514–520.

Helge, D. I. (1983). Increasing preservice curriculum accountability to rural handicapped populations. *Teacher Education and Special Education*, **6**, 137–142.

Henderson, R. W. (1981). Home environment and intellectual performance. In R. W. Henderson (Ed.), *Parent-child interaction* (pp. 3–29). New York: Academic Press.

Henderson, R. W., & Hennig, H. (1979). Relationships among cooperation-competition and locus of control in social and academic situations among children in traditional and open classrooms. *Contemporary Educational Psychology*, **4**, 121–131.

Hess, R. D. (1981). Approaches to the measurement and interpretation of parent-child interaction. In R. W. Henderson (Ed.), *Parent-child interaction* (pp. 207–230). New York: Academic Press.

Hess, R. D., & Shipman, V. (1969). Early experience and socialization of cognitive modes in children. *Child Development*, **36**, 869–886.

Hilliard, A. G. (1976). *Alternatives to IQ testing: An approach to the identification of gifted minority children.* Sacremento, CA: State Department of Education.

Hobbs, N. (1975). *Issues in the classification of children.* San Francisco, CA: Jossey-Bass.

Hobbs, N. (1978). Classification options. *Exceptional Children*, **44**, 494–497.

Hobson v. Hanson, 269F. Supp. 401 (D.C. 1967).

Hoelter, J. W. (1982). Segregation and rationality in black status aspiration processes. *Sociology of Education*, **55**, 31–39.

Howell, F. M., & McBroom, L. W. (1982). Social relations at home and at school: An analysis of the correspondence principle. *Sociology of Education*, **55**, 40–52.

Hunter, B. (1982). Policy issues in special education for migrant students. *Exceptional Children*, **48**, 469–472.

Ide, J. K., Parkerson, J., Haertel, G. D., & Walberg, H. J. (1981). Peer group influence on educational outcomes: A qualitative synthesis. *Journal of Educational Psychology*, **73**, 472–484.

InterAmerican Research Associates. (1978). *An evaluation of access to and availability of human services for migrant and seasonal farm workers in Region X* (Contract No. HEW 101–76–0010). Washington, DC: Department of Health, Education, and Welfare.

Jackson, G., & Cosca, L. (1974). The inequality of educational opportunity in the southwest: An observational study of ethnically mixed classrooms. *American Educational Research Journal*, **11**, 219–229.

Jencks, C. (1972). *Inequality: A reassessment of the effect of family and schooling in America.* New York: Harper & Row.

Jensen, A. R. (1969). How much can we boost IQ and scholastic achievement? *Harvard Educational Review*, **39**, 1–123.

Jensen, A. R. (1980). *Bias in mental testing.* New York: Free Press.

John, V. P., & Goldstein, L. S. (1964). The social context of language acquisition. *Merrill-Palmer Quarterly*, **10**, 265–275.

Johnson, R. T., & Johnson, D. W. (1984). Building friendships between handicapped and nonhandicapped students: Effects of cooperative and individualistic instruction. *American Educational Research Journal*, **18**, 415–423.

Johnson, D. W., Maruyama, G., Johnson, R., Nelson, D., & Skon, L. (1981). Effects of cooperative, competitive and individualistic goal structures on achievement: A meta-analysis. *Psychological Bulletin*, **89**, 47–62.

Johnson, D., & Ransom, E. (1980). Parents' perceptions of secondary schools. In M. Craft, J. Raynor, & L. Cohen (Eds.), *Linking home and school: A new review* (3rd ed.) (pp. 177–189). London, England: Harper & Row.

Jones, J. D., Erickson, E. L., & Crowell, R. (1972). Increasing the gap between whites and blacks: Tracking as a contributory source. *Education and Urban Society*, **4**, 339–349.

Jones, R., Gottlieb, J., Guskin, S., & Yoshida, R. (1978). Evaluating mainstreaming programs: Models, caveats, considerations, and guidelines. *Exceptional Children*, **44**, 588–601.

Jones, R. L. (1984). *Attitudes and attitude change in special education: Theory and practice.* Reston, VA: Council for Exceptional Children.

Junkala, J. J. (1977). Teachers' assessments and team decisions *Exceptional Children*, **44**, 31–32.

Katz, I., Cole, O. J., & Baron, R. M. (1976). Self-evaluation, social reinforcement, and academic achievement of black and white school children. *Child Development*, **47**, 368–374.

Keddie, N. (Ed.). (1973). *The myth of cultural deprivation.* Harmondsworth, Middlesex, England: Penguin Education.

Kelly, A.V. (1978). *Mixed-ability grouping: Theory and practice.* London, England: Harper & Row.

Kelly, D. H. (1978). *How the school manufactures misfits.* Pasadena, CA: Newcal Publications.

Kerckhoff, A. C. (1976). The status attainment process: Socialization or allocation? *Social Forces*, **55**, 368–381.

Kirp, D. L. (1969). The poor, the schools, and equal protection. In J. S. Coleman (Ed.), *Equal educational opportunity* (pp. 139–172). Cambridge, MA: Harvard University Press.

Kogan, N. (1971). Educational implications of cognitive styles. In G. S. Lesser (Ed.), *Psychology and educational practice* (pp. 242–292). Glenview, IL: Scott-Foresman.

Kohn, M. L. (1969). *Class and conformity: A study of values.* Homewood, IL: Dorsey Press.

Kohn, M. L. (1977). *Class and conformity; a study of values, with a reassessment, 1977* (2nd ed.). Chicago, IL: University of Chicago Press.

Kushlick, A., & Blunder, R. (1974). The epidemiology of mental subnormality. In A. M. Clarke & A. B. D. Clarke (Eds.), *Mental deficiency: The changing outlook* (3rd ed.) (pp. 47–65). New York: Free Press.

Labov, W. (1973). The logic of nonstandard English. In N. Keddie (Ed.), *The myth of cultural deprivation* (pp. 21–66). Harmondsworth, Middlesex, England: Penguin Education.

Langdon, H. W. (1983). Assessment and intervention strategies for the bilingual language-disorder student. *Exceptional Children*, **50**, 37–47.

Laosa, L. M. (1979). Social competence in childhood: Toward a developmental, socioculturally relativistic paradigm. In M. W. Kent & J. E. Rolf (Eds.), *Primary prevention of psychopathology* (Vol. 3, pp. 253–279). Hanover, NH: University Press of New England.

Laosa, L. M. (1980). Material teaching strategies and cognitive styles in Chicano families. *Journal of Educational Psychology*, **72**, 45–54.

Laosa, L. M. (1981). Maternal behavior: Sociocultural diversity in modes of family interaction. In R. W. Henderson (Ed.), *Parent–child interaction: Theory, research, and prospects* (pp. 125–167). New York: Academic Press.

Laosa, L. M. (1982). School, occupation, culture, and family: The impact of parental schooling on the parent–child relationship. *Journal of Educational Psychology*, **74**, 791–827.

Larry P. v. Riles. United States District Court for the Northern District of California, 1979 495 F. Supp. 926.

Lau v. Nichols, 414 U.S. 563 (1974).

Lazar, I., & Darlington, R. B. (1982). Lasting effects of early education. *Monographs of the Society for Research in Child Development*, **47**, (2–3, Serial No. 195).

Leacock, E. B. (1969). *Teaching and learning in city schools.* New York: Basic Books.

Leighton, D. C. (1979). Community integration and mental health: Documenting social change through longitudinal research. In R. F. Munoz, L. R. Snowden, J. G. Kelly, and Associates (Eds.), *Sociological and psychological research in community settings* (pp. 275–304). San Francisco, CA: Jossey-Bass.

Lesser, G. S., Fifer, G., & Clark, D. H. (1965). Mental abilities of children from different social-class and cultural groups. *Monographs of the Society for Research in Child Development*, **30**, (4, Serial No. 102).

Levine, D. U., & Havighurst, R. J. (1977a). *Concentrations of poverty and reading achievement in five big cities.* Kansas City, MO: Center for the Study of Metropolitan Problems in Education.

Levine, D. U., & Havighurst, R. J. (1977b). *The future of big-city schools; desegregation policies and magnet alternatives.* Berkeley, CA: McCutchan.

Levine, D. U., Kukuk, C., & Meyer, J. K. (1979). Poverty in big cities. In H. J. Walberg (Ed.), *Educational environments and effects* (pp. 331–352). Berkeley, CA: McCutchan.

Lightfoot, S. L. (1973). Politics and reasoning through the eyes of teachers and children. *Harvard Educational Review*, **43**, 197–244.

Lightfoot, S. L. (1981). Toward conflict and resolution: Relationships between families and schools. *Theory Into Practice*, **20**, 97–104.

Lightfoot, S. L. (1983). *The good high school: Portraits of character and culture.* New York: Basic Books.

MacMillan, D. L., Jones, R. L., & Aloia, G. F. (1974). The mentally retarded label: A theoretical analysis and review of research. *American Journal of Mental Deficiency*, **79**, 241–261.

MacMillan, D. L., & Morrison, G. M. (1980). Correlates of social status among mildly handicapped learners in self-contained special classes. *Journal of Educational Psychology*, **72**, 437–444.

Madden, N., & Slavin, R. E. (1983). Mainstreaming students with mild handicaps: Academic and social outcomes. *Review of Educational Research*, **53**, 519–569.

Maehr, M. L., & Stallings, W. M. (Eds.). (1975). *Culture, child and school: Sociocultural influences of learning.* Monterey, CA: Brooks/Cole.

Mare, R. D. (1981). Change and stability in educational stratification. *American Sociological Review*, **46**, 72–87.

Marjoribanks, K. (1974). Environment, social class and mental abilities. In K. Marjoribanks (Ed.), *Environments for learning* (pp. 127–136). Great Britain: National Foundation for Educational Research.

Marjoribanks, K. (1979). Family environments. In H. J. Walberg (Ed.), *Educational environments and effects, evaluation, policy and productivity* (pp. 15–37). Berkeley, CA: McCutchan.

McDermott, R. P., & Gospodinoff, K. (1979). Social contexts for ethnic borders and school failure. In A. Wolfgang (Ed.), *Nonverbal behavior.* Toronto, Canada: Ontario Institute for the Study of Education.

McPartland, J. (1967). *The relative influence of school desegregation and classroom desegregation on the academic achievement of ninth grade Negro students.* Baltimore, MD: Johns Hopkins University Press.

Mehan, H. (1979). *Learning lessons: Social organization in the classroom.* Cambridge, MA: Harvard University Press.

Meier, D. (1982, May 26). Planning to keep them in their place. *In These Times*, 11.

Mercer, J. (1972, September). IQ: The lethal label. *Psychology Today*, 44–47, 95–97.

Mercer, J. R. (1973a). The myth of 3% prevalence. In G. Tarjan, R. K. Eyman, & C. E. Meyers (Eds.), *Sociobehavioral studies in mental retardation* (pp. 1–16). Monographs of the American Association of Mental Deficiency.

Mercer, J. R. (1973b). *Labeling the mentally retarded.* Berkeley, CA: University of California Press.

Mercer, J., & Lewis, J. (1977). *System of Multicultural Pluralistic Assessment.* New York: The Psychological Corporation.

Mercer, J. R. (1979). *System of Multicultural Pluralistic Assessment: Technical Manual.* New York: The Psychological Corporation.

Meyers, C. E., Mink, I. T., & Nihira, K. (1977). *Home quality rating scale.* Pomona, CA: University of California at Los Angeles/Neuropsychiatric Institute, Pacific State Research Group.

Mink, I. T., Meyers, C. E., & Nihira, K. (1984). Taxonomy of family life styles: 2 Homes with slow-learning children. *American Journal of Mental Deficiency*, **89**, 111–123.

Moos, R. H., & Moos, B. S. (1976). A typology of family social environments. *Family Process*, **15**, 357–371.

Moran, M. R. (1984). Excellence at the cost of instructional equity? The potential impact of recommended reforms on low-achieving students. *Focus on Exceptional Children*, **16**(7), 1–12.

Morgan, W. R., Alwin, D. F., & Griffin, L. J. (1979). Social origins, parental values and the transmission of inequality. *American Journal of Sociology*, **85**, 156–166.

Newman, F. M. (1981). Reducing student alienation in high schools: Implications of theory. *Harvard Educational Review*, **51**, 546–564.

Newson, J., Newson, E., & Barnes, P. (1977). *Perspectives on school at seven years old.* London, England: George Allen & Unwin.

Nicassio, F. J. (1983). Parent–child communication during a home instruction task. *Journal of Educational Research*, **76**, 335–342.

Oakes, J. (1982). Classroom social relationships: Exploring the Bowles and Gintis hypothesis. *Sociology of Education*, **55**, 197–212.

Oakland, T., & Matuszek, P. (1977). Using tests in non-discriminatory assessment. In T. Oakland (Ed.), *Psychological and educational assessment of minority children* (pp. 52–69). New York: Brunner/Mazel.

Ochoa, A. M., Pacheco, R., & Omark, D. R. (1983). Addressing the learning disability needs of limited-English proficient students: Beyond language and race issues. *Learning Disability Quarterly*, **6**, 416–423.

Oden, C. W. (1976). Desegregation and mainstreaming: A case of deja vu. In R. L. Jones (Ed.), *Mainstreaming and the minority child* (pp. 53–64). Reston, VA: Council for Exceptional Children.

Oller, J. W. (1981). Language as intelligence? *Language in Learning*, **31**, 465–492.

Olneck, M. R., & Bills, D. B. (1980). What makes Sammy run? An empirical assessment of the Bowles–Gintis correspondence principle. *American Journal of Education*, **89**, 27–61.

Olsen, C. P. (1983). Inequality remade: The theory of correspondence and the context of French immersion in Northern Ontario. *Journal of Education*, **165**, 75–98.

Omark, D. R., & Erickson, J. G. (1983). *The bilingual exceptional child.* San Diego, CA: College-Hill Press.

Omark, D. R., & Watson, D. L. (1983). Psychological testing and bilingual education: The need for reconceptualization. In D. R. Omark & J. G. Erickson (Eds.), *The bilingual exceptional child* (pp. 24–54). San Diego, CA: College-Hill Press.

Ornstein, A. C. (1978). *Education and social inquiry.* Itasca, IL: Peacock.

Ortiz, R. D. (1981, January/April). Developing Indian academic professionals. *Integrated Education*, **19**(1), 38–41.

Otheguy, R. (1982). Thinking about bilingual education: A critical appraisal. *Harvard Educational Review*, **52**, 301–314.

Padilla, A. M., & Garza, B. M. (1975). IQ tests: A case of cultural myopia. *The National Elementary Principal*, **54**(4), 53–58.

Perry, J. (1982). The ECS interstate migrant education project. *Exceptional Children*, **48**, 496–500.

Philips, S. U. (1982). *The invisible culture: Communication in classroom and community on the Work Springs Indian Reservation*. New York: Longman.

Picou, J. S., & Carter, T. M. (1976). Significant-other influence and aspirations. *Sociology of Education*, **49**, 12–22.

Pink, W. T. (1982). School effects, academic performance, and school crime. *Urban Education*, **17**, 51–72.

Plata, M., & Jones, P. (1982). Bilingual vocational education for handicapped students. *Exceptional Children*, **48**, 538–540.

Plata, M., & Santos, S. L. (1981). Bilingual special education: A challenge for the future. *Teaching Exceptional Children*, **14**, 97–100.

Polloway, E. A., & Smith, J. D. (1983). Changes in mild mental retardation: Population, programs, and perspectives. *Exceptional Children*, **50**, 149–159.

Prieto, A. G., & Zucker, S. H. (1981). Teacher perception of race as a factor in the placement of behavior disordered children. *Behavioral Disorders*, **7**, 34–38.

Pugh, M. D. (1976). Statistical assumptions and social reality: A critical analysis of achievement models. *Sociology of Education*, **49**, 34–40.

Purkey, W. W. (1970). *Self-concept and school achievement*. Englewood Cliffs, NJ: Prentice-Hall.

Pyecha, J. N., & Ward, L. A. (1982). A study of the implementation of PL 94–142 for handicapped migrant children. *Exceptional Children*, **48**, 490–495.

Ramey, C. T., & Campbell, F. A. (1979). Compensatory education for disadvantaged children. *School Review*, **87**, 1711–1789.

Reid, B. W. (1984). Attitudes toward the learning disabled in school and home. In R. L. Jones (Ed.), *Attitudes and attitude change in special education: Theory and practice* (pp. 157–170). Reston, VA: Council for Exceptional Children.

Reilly, R. (1980). Wind River changes its course: The St. Stephens experience. *Phi Delta Kappan*, **62**, 200–202.

Reitman, S. W. (1981). *Education, society, and change*. Boston, MA: Allyn & Bacon.

Reschly, D. J. (1981). Psychological testing in educational classification and placement. *American Psychologist*, **36**, 1094–1102.

Reynolds, M. C., & Wang, M. C. (1983). Restructuring "special" school programs. *Policy Studies Review*, **2**(1), 198–212.

Richmond, B. O., & Waits, C. (1978). Special education: Who needs it? *Exceptional Children*, **44**, 279–280.

Rist, R. C. (1970). Student social class and teacher expectations: The self-fulfilling prophecy in ghetto education. *Harvard Educational Review*, **40**, 411–449.

Roberts, K. (1980). Schools, parents, and social class. In M. Craft, J. Raynor, & L. Cohen (Eds.), *Linking home and school: A new review* (3rd ed.) (pp. 41–55). London, England: Harper & Row.

Rodman, H., & Voydanoff, P. (1978). Social class and parents' range of aspirations for their children. *Social Problems*, **25**, 333–344.

Rodriguez, R. (1981). *Hunger of memory: The education of Richard Rodriguez*. Boston, MA: David R. Godine.

Rollins, B. C., & Thomas, D. L. (1979). Parental support, power and control techniques in the socialization of children. In W. R. Burr, R. Hill, F. I. Nye, & I. L. Reiss (Eds.), *Contemporary theories about the family: Research-based theories* (Vol. 1, pp. 317–364). New York: Free Press.

Rosenholtz, S. J., & Simpson, C. (1984). The formation of ability conceptions: Developmental trend of social construction? *Review of Educational Research*, **54**, 31–63.

Rosenthal, R., & Jacobson, L. (1968). *Pygmalion in the classroom: Teacher expectation and pupils' intellectual development*. New York: Holt, Rinehart & Winston.

Roth, S., & Kubal, L. (1975). The effects of noncontingent reinforcement on tasks of differing importance: Facilitation and learned helplessness effects. *Journal of Personality and Social Psychology*, **32**, 680–691.

Rowan, B., & Miracle, A. W. (1983). Systems of ability grouping and the stratification of achievement in elementary schools. *Sociology of Education*, **56**, 133–144.

Ruble, D. N., & Rhodes, W. S. (1981). The development of children's perceptions and attributions about their social world. In J. H. Harvey, W. Ickes, & R. F. Kidd (Eds.), *New directions in attribution research* (Vol. 3). Hillsdale, NJ: Erlbaum.

Rueda, R. S., Rodriquez, R. F., & Prieto, A. G. (1981). Teachers' perceptions of competencies for instructing bilingual/multicultural exceptional children. *Exceptional Children*, **47**, 268–270.

Rueda, R. S., & Smith, D. C. (1983). Interpersonal tactics and communicative strategies of Anglo-American and Mexican-American mildly mentally retarded and nonretarded students. *Applied Research in Mental Retardation*, **4**, 153–161.

Ryan, W. (1971). *Blaming the victim*. New York: Random House.

Ryan, F. A. (1982). The Federal role in American Indian Education. *Harvard Educational Review*, **52**, 423–433.

St. John, N. (1971). Thirty-six teachers: Their characteristics and outcomes for black and white pupils. *American Educational Research Journal*, **8**, 635–648.

St. John, N. (1972). Mothers and children: Congruence and optimism of school-related attitudes. *Journal of Marriage and the Family*, **34**, 422–430.

Salvia, J., & Ysseldyke, J. E. (1978). *Assessment in special and remedial education*. Boston, MA: Houghton-Mifflin.

Santiago, R. L., & Feinberg, R. C. (1981). The status of education for Hispanics. *Educational Leadership*, **38**, 292–297.

Sauer, R. A. (1982). Issues in the education of migrants and other mobile handicapped students. *Exceptional Children*, **48**, 503–505.

Scheffler, W. (1980). Therapy for a school. *American Education*, **16**(7), 25–28.

Schofield, J. W. (1978). School desegregation and intergroup relations. In D. Bar-Tal & L. Saxe (Eds.), *Social psychology of education: Theory and research* (pp. 329–363). Washington, DC: Hemisphere.

Schofield, J. W. (1982). *Black and white in school: Trust, tension, or tolerance?* New York: Praeger.

Schweinhart, L. J., & Weikart, D. P. (1981). Perry preschool effects nine years later: What do they mean? In M. J. Begab, H. C. Haywood, & H. L. Garber (Eds.), *Psychosocial influences in retarded performance* (Vol. 2, pp. 113–126). Baltimore, MD: University Park Press.

Scott-Jones, D. (1984). Family influences on cognitive development and school achievement. In E. W. Gordon (Ed.), *Review of research in education* (Vol. 2, pp. 259–304). Washington, DC: American Educational Research Association.

Seeman, M. (1975). Alienation studies. In A. Inbeles, J. Coleman, & N. Smelser (Eds.), *Annual review of sociology* (Vol. 1, pp. 91–123). Palo Alto, CA: Annual Reviews.

Seginer, R. (1983). Parents' educational expectations and children's academic achievements: A literature review. *Merrill-Palmer Quarterly*, **29**, 1–23.

Serrano v. Priest, 5 Cal. 3d 584, 487 P. 2d 1241, 96 Cal. 601 (1971).

Sewell, W. H., Haller, A. O., & Ohlendorf, G. W. (1969). The educational and early occupational attainment process. *American Sociological Review*, **34**, 82–92.

Sexton, P. (1961). *Education and income: Inequalities of opportunity in our public schools*. New York: Viking.

Shade, B. J. (1982). Afro-American cognitive style: A variable in school success? *Review of Educational Research*, **52**, 219–244.

Shapiro, H. S. (1983). Class, ideology, and the basic skills movement: A study in the sociology of educational reform. *Interchange*, **14**(2), 14–24.

Sieber, R. T. (1982). The politics of middle-class success in an inner-city public school. *Journal of Education*, **164**, 30–47.

Siegel, A. L., & Leahy, W. R. (1974). *Nonverbal and culture-fair performance prediction procedures: III. Cross validation.* Wayne, PA: Applied Psychological Services.

Simmons, R. G. (1978). Blacks and high self-esteem: A puzzle. *Social Psychology Quarterly*, **41**, 54–57.

Sizemore, B. (1978). Education: Integration, welfare, and achievement. In F. Aquila (Ed.), *School desegregation: A model at work* (pp. 13–23). Bloomington: School of Education.

Skenes, R. E., & Carlyle, C. (1979). CAL community school; Small, rural and good! *Phi Delta Kappan*, **60**, 589–593.

Skodak, M., & Skeels, H. M. (1949). A final follow-up study of 100 adopted children. *Journal of Genetic Psychology*, **75**, 82–125.

Slavin, R. E. (1984). Team assisted individualization: Cooperative learning and individualized instruction in the mainstreamed classroom. *Remedial and Special Education*, **5**(6), 33–42.

Smitherman, G. (1983). Language and liberation. *Journal of Negro Education*, **52**, 15–23.

Snider, S. J. (1979). Cultural characteristics and their relationship to disruptive behavior among Appalachian students. *Clearing House*, **53**, 177–180.

Spangler v. Pasadena City Board of Education, 44 USLW 5114 (1976).

Stephan, W. G., & Rosenfield, D. (1978). Effects of desegregation on race relations and self-esteem. *Journal of Educational Psychology*, **70**, 670–679.

Stewart, W. (1967). Sociolinguistic factors in the history of American Negro dialect. *Florida Foreign Language Reporter*, **5**(2), 6–12.

Sutherland, J. H., Algozzine, B., Ysseldyke, J. E., & Freeman, S. (1983). Changing peer perceptions: Effects of labels and assigned attributes. *Journal of Learning Disabilities*, **16**, 217–220.

Talley, R. (1979). *Consequences of implementing the System of Multicultural Pluralistic Assessment (SOMPA)*. Unpublished doctoral dissertation, Indiana University.

Taylor, C. P. (1976). *Transforming schools: A social perspective.* New York: St. Martin's Press.

Thomas, A. (1979). Learned helplessness and expectancy factors: Implications for research in learning disabilities. *Review of Educational Research*, **49**, 200–221.

Tomlinson, S. (1982). *A sociology of special education*. London, England: Routledge & Kegan Paul.

Towner, A. G. (1984). Modifying attitudes toward the handicapped: A review of the literature and methodology. In R. L. Jones (Ed.), *Mainstreaming the minority child* (pp. 223–257). Reston, VA: Council for Exceptional Children.

Troike, C. (1978). *Research evidence for the effectiveness of bilingual education.* Arlington, VA: Center for Applied Linguistics.

Tunick, R. H., Platt, J. S., & Bowen, J. (1980). Rural community attitudes toward the handicapped: Implications for mainstreaming. *Exceptional Children*, **46**, 549–550.

Tyack, J. B. (1974). *The one best system*. Cambridge, MA: Harvard University Press.

Tymitz, B. L. (1983). Bilingual special education: A challenge to evaluation processes. In D. K. Omark & J. G. Erickson (Eds.), *The bilingual exceptional child* (pp. 359–378). San Diego, CA: College-Hill Press.

Vernberg, E. M., & Medway, F. J. (1981). Teacher and parent causal perceptions of school problems. *American Educational Research Journal*, **18**, 29–37.

Voeltz, L. M. (1980). Children's attitudes toward the handicapped. *American Journal of Mental Deficiency*, **84**, 455–464.

Walberg, H. J., & Rasher, S. P. (1979). Achievement in fifty states. In H. J. Walberg (Ed.), *Educational environments and effects* (pp. 353–369). Berkeley, CA: McCutchan.

Wang, M. C., & Lindvall, C. M. (1984). Individual differences and school learning environments. In E. W. Gordon (Ed.), *Review of research in education* (Vol. 11, pp. 161–226). Washington, DC: American Educational Research Association.

Weiner, B. (1979). A theory of motivation for some classroom experiences. *Journal of Educational Psychology*, **71**, 3–25.

Weinstein, R. S. (1983). Student perceptions of schooling. *Elementary School Journal*, **83**, 286–312.

Weinstein, R. S., & Middlestadt, S. E. (1979). Student perceptions of teacher interactions with male high and low achievers. *Journal of Educational Psychology*, **71**, 421–431.

White, R. (1980). *Absent with cause: Lessons of truancy*. London, England: Routledge & Kegan Paul.

Willey, N. R., & McCandless, B. R. (1973). Social stereotypes for normal, educable mentally retarded, and orthopedically handicapped children. *Journal of Special Education*, **7**, 283–288.

Williams, R. L. (1972). *The black intelligence test of cultural homogeneity*. Bethesda, MD: National Institute of Mental Health. (ERIC Document Reproduction Services No. ED 070 799).

Wilson, A. B. (1967). Educational consequences of segregation in a California community. In U.S. Commission on Civil Rights, *Racial isolation in the public schools* (pp. 180–181). Washington, DC: U.S. Government Printing Office.

Wilson, M. S., & Fox, B. J. (1982). Computer-administered bilingual language assessment and intervention. *Exceptional Children*, **49**, 145–149.

Winn, W., & Wilson, A. P. (1983). The affect and effect of ability grouping. *Contemporary Education*, **54**, 119–125.

Wright, R. L. (1983). Functional language, socialization, and academic achievement. *Journal of Negro Education*, **52**, 24–34.

Yates, A. (Ed.). (1966). *Grouping in education: A report sponsored by the UNESCO Institute for Education.* Hamburg, NY: Wiley.

Yoshida, R., & Meyers, C. E. (1975). Effects of labeling as educable mentally retarded on teachers' expectancies for change in a student's performance. *Journal of Educational Psychology*, **67**, 521–527.

Young, M. (1976). On the politics of educational knowledge. In J. Beck, C. Jencks, N. Keddie, & M. Young (Eds.), *Toward a sociology of education* (pp. 134–158). New Brunswick, NJ: Transactional Books.

Ysseldyke, J. E., Algozzine, B., & Epps, S. (1983). A logical and empirical analysis of current practice in classifying students as handicapped. *Exceptional Children*, **50**, 160–166.

Ysseldyke, J. E., Algozzine, B., & Richey, L. (1982). Judgment under uncertainty: How many children are handicapped? *Exceptional Children*, **48**, 531–534.

Ysseldyke, J. E., Algozzine, B., Shinn, M. R., & McGue, M. (1982). Similarities and differences between low achievers and students classified learning disabled. *Journal of Special Education*, **16**, 73–85.

Zintz, M. (1970). American Indians. In D. Horn (Ed.), *Reading for the disadvantaged* (pp. 41–48). New York: Harcourt, Brace & World.

Zucker, S. H., & Prieto, A. G. (1977). Ethnicity and teacher bias in educational decision. *Instructional Psychology*, **4**, 2–5.

Learning Characteristics of Mildly Handicapped Students: Implications for Classification, Placement, and Programming

DANIEL J. RESCHLY

Iowa State University

Abstract—Research on the basic learning characteristics of mildly handicapped children and youth are discussed in relation to the current exceptional child classification system, the range of students' individual differences, the needs for alternative or adaptive educational programming, and the revision of public policy. Similarities and differences among learning problems of mildly handicapped and economically disadvantaged students are discussed. Systematic, broadly based, and well-integrated programs are needed to address the following needs: basic literacy skills, academic content, social skills, and career/vocation. Dilemmas in determining program objectives and strategies in view of the myriad needs are identified. Development, more flexible and finely graduated special programming, perhaps through new combinations of regular and special education, are recommended.

A fundamental assumption in the research and theory concerning education of exceptional children and youth is that the educational needs of handicapped students are sufficiently different from those of nonhandicapped students to require special programming in order to ensure appropriate education. Although it has been recognized for many years that the needs of handicapped students may vary substantially, the absolutely bedrock assumption has been the need for significantly different educational services due to the handicapping conditions. The focus of this chapter is on special education needs and (a) the basic learning characteristics of handicapped students that underlie those needs; (b) the exceptional child classification system used to determine which children are eligible to receive special education; (c) the placement options used with students classified as handicapped; and (d) the implications of learning characteristics, the classification system, and placement options for instruction.

The four topics addressed in this chapter are related, with no clear-cut boundaries differentiating one from another. In fact, the implicit rationale for the current special education system suggests that learning characteristics, classification, placement, and instruction are (or, at least, should be) closely related. Unfortunately, these relationships are far from clear cut, consistent, reliable, or valid.

Ideally, the relationships among educational needs, learning characteristics, instructional procedures, the classification system, and placement options would be critically examined through an exhaustive consideration of empirical studies on each of the variables and the myriad empirical relationships among them. However, empirical bases for each of the variables are far from complete. The data base for the relationships among the variables is even more uncertain. Despite these gaps in knowledge, the data *are* sufficient to conclude confidently that all is not well with current practices. Data-based alternatives to these practices need to be considered, implemented, monitored, evaluated, revised as needed, and then disseminated widely. All of this seems straightforward, if not simple. The problems, though, are enormously complex, due only in part to the incomplete data base for policy decisions. There are intense disagreements *within* and *between* major constituencies in what might be regarded as the special education establishment. One very important constituency is practitioners in direct service roles such as special education teachers, consultants, and related services personnel. Another constituency is advocacy groups, often formed by parents who are intensely interested and deeply committed to the availability of special education services for their handicapped sons or daughters. Still another constituency is the research community, by and large university faculty, who usually have background and experience in one or more of the handicapping conditions. A final constituency is the public policy decision makers, including administrative staff at the state and federal levels, legislators, and so on. The disagreements within and between these constituencies cause an exponential expansion of the already complex problems of determining policies and effecting changes in current practices. It is, therefore, important to consider not just the data base but also the sociopolitical realities that support current practices, especially the heavy hand of custom and tradition, which, sometimes, appears to be the only identifiable basis for a current practice. However, in a dynamic situation, which education for handicapped students certainly is, something more than custom and tradition ultimately is needed to preserve current practices.

Scope of the Review

The literature review in this chapter addresses several topics, each of which might be the subject of a chapter-length review. The treatment is intended to examine general trends and research results in each of the areas, with primary attention devoted to the *relationships* among the variables. The major topics examined are the educational needs of handicapped children, the exceptional child classification system, learning research with handicapped students, placement options, and instructional procedures. The treatment of each of the topics is not exhaustive, but references to further information in this and other volumes are provided.

Limitations and Definitions

The major problem with the literature and the data base represented in the literature is the partial, incomplete nature of results. There are numerous studies on relevant topics that use appropriate samples. However, there are almost always serious questions concerning the generalizability of results to other samples of similar subjects as well as concerns about extrapolating from one age group to another or from one mildly handicapping condition to another. At the outset, it is worth cautioning that any major reform involving the overall system of services to handicapped students would, by necessity, involve considerable extrapolation from the present data base. The last section of this chapter reviews the data base for changes and discusses the kind of extrapolation that would be involved in various reforms. It is also important to note that the political interests of various constituent groups exert a major limitation on what can be studied or attempted, particularly on a broad scale. But broad-scale research is just what is needed. Research that attempts to apply data-based procedures across different age groups and different handicapping conditions, and in diverse geographic and sociopolitical settings, is what is needed most to rectify the large gaps in current knowledge.

The discussion in this chapter is restricted to mildly handicapped students. The handicap areas of primary concern are learning disability, serious emotional disturbance or behavioral disorders, and mild or educable mental retardation. Most of the controversies concerning whether or not particular students ought to be classified, and whether their educational needs are sufficiently different to justify classification as handicapped and the provision of special education services, are restricted to mildly handicapped students. These students are neither obviously different from others nor easily recognized by nonprofessionals, characteristics that make classification and assessment related to classification very complex.

Paradoxes

There are a number of paradoxes apparent in the recent literature on the education of handicapped children. These paradoxes arise, at least in part, because of the limited data base that is available to guide policy decisions, but also, in part, because of the competing interests of different constituencies. Paradoxes involving contradictory themes strongly supported by different constituencies set the stage for the present examination of literature. It is important to note that at least one (and sometimes more than one) of the major constituencies is firmly committed to each side of the paradox. Resolution of these contradictory themes, a topic discussed in the last section of this chapter, represents a major challenge to the research community in special education.

Paradox 1

On one hand, several very capable and prominent scholars have concluded that mildly handicapped students, particularly learning disabled students, are just about any students someone wishes to diagnose as such. By contrast, other equally capable and prominent scholars conclude that vast differences separate students currently classified as learning disabled from classroom averages.

Paradox 2

Regular educators, plagued by declining resources and increased pressures for educational excellence, are increasingly concerned about the nature, degree, and kind of mainstreaming for mildly handicapped students. Most regular educators suggest less mainstreaming because of insufficient time to meet the needs of mildly handicapped learners. By contrast, the current trend among many scholars and some practitioners in special education is toward far greater, perhaps total, mainstreaming for mildly handicapped students. Both groups express concern about the achievement of mildly handicapped students, and both contend that their solutions, contradictory as they may be, will lead to greater benefits for mildly handicapped students.

Paradox 3

Careful assessment for use in designing instruction is nearly universally endorsed, but commonly used assessment procedures with mildly handicapped students are sharply disputed. Some scholars claim that traditional measures are irrelevant, unreliable, and invalid. By contrast, other scholars claim that the newer direct measures are excessively narrow, limited, and superficial.

Paradox 4

Precise distinctions between the mildly handicapping conditions of learning disability, mild or educable mental retardation, and emotional disturbance are regarded as absolutely essential by some constituencies and, just as absolutely, irrelevant by other constituencies. All would agree that making such distinctions is a complex, time-consuming activity.

PARADOX 5

Matching instructional method to a handicapped student's strengths is regarded as crucial by some, irrelevant by others, and downright fraudulent by still others, all of whom claim the support of empirical results.

In view of the paradoxes just cited, healthy skepticism, almost always a prudent attitude in evaluating evidence, seems especially appropriate. Some of the contradictions represent people looking at different aspects of the same reality, while others represent genuine conflicts based on various combinations of research evidence and practical experience. It is, perhaps, important to note that these disputes do have a significant impact on educational services for children and youth and that the strongly held opinions belong to sincere individuals who are deeply committed to what they perceive as best for handicapped children and youth. It is equally important to note that these contradictory themes cannot all be explained away as different opinions or contrasting perceptions of the same reality. The effort that follows represents an attempt to separate evidence from custom and fact from opinion—all of which must be considered when these topics are evaluated.

Exceptional Child Classification

The current exceptional child classification system evolved gradually, haphazardly, and inconsistently over the past century. Most of the current disability classifications were recognized earlier, sometimes in a surprisingly modern form (Ysseldyke & Algozzine, 1984). However, there is no official classification system; there are no universal definitions or uniform classification criteria; and, most important, there is no unifying hierarchy, or overall structure. In fact, the current system is probably best understood as the product of diverse forces, countervailing trends, historical accident, and compromise among competing constituencies.

One very disquieting note from a thorough review of the literature is that no one, absolutely no one, is a strong advocate of the current classification system. Everyone has concerns about the current system, usually expressed as discomfort with labeling, or doubts about the degree of homogeneity within each of the disabilities, or questions about the usefulness of the disability classifications for instructional purposes. Thus, everyone has reservations about the current system, which leads to the obvious question, Why isn't a more rational system established and implemented? Although answers to this question are admittedly speculative, one answer may be that, although everyone is against the current system, the opposition occurs in varying degrees and for varying reasons. And this is perhaps the most crucial feature of the current situation: the varying (and contradictory) reasons for opposition. The consensus that the current system should be changed would, in all likelihood, dissolve into total anarchy if serious consideration were devoted to alternatives. Thus, although there is a consensus at a very general level concerning dissatisfaction with the present classification system, there is no consensus concerning the kind of classification system that should replace what exists now.

Federal Definitions

Perhaps the closest facsimile to a uniform classification system are the definitions in the "Regulations Implementing Education for All Handicapped Children Act" (1977). These definitions constitute relatively brief conceptualizations of eleven handicapping conditions that state and local education agencies are required to serve in order to receive federal monies. The eleven conditions are as follows: deaf, deaf–blind, hard-of-hearing, mentally retarded, multihandicapped, orthopedically impaired, other health impaired, seriously emotionally disturbed, specific learning disability, speech impaired, and visually handicapped.

All of the definitions of handicapping conditions in PL 94-142 are relatively brief and provide no specific classifaction criteria. For example, the definition of mental retardation is as follows: "mentally retarded means significantly subaverage general intellectual functioning existing concurrently with deficits in adaptive behavior and manifested during the developmental period, which adversely affects a child's educational performance" ("Regulations Implementing Education for All Handicapped Children Act," 1977, p. 42478).

There is nothing in the mental retardation definition, nor is there any additional information in the federal rules and regulations, concerning what is meant by *significantly subaverage general intellectual functioning* or what kind and degree of deficits are required in adaptive behavior. These matters, intelligence and adaptive behavior, are fundamental to the definition of mental retardation. However, a great deal is left undefined, which, not surprisingly, results in widely varying state and local practices regarding mental retardation classification (Bickel, 1982; Patrick & Reschly, 1982). The one exception in the federal rules and regulations is the area of learning disability, the subject of a subsequent set of rules and regulations published later in 1977 in "Procedures for Evaluation of Specific Learning Disabilities" (1977). These additional rules and regulations were formulated by the Bureau of Education for the Handicapped at the insistence of Congress, which was, as it turns out, quite properly concerned about the possible excessive use of the classification of learning disability with students who have achievement difficulties but who are not handicapped. However, these subsequent rules and regulations are not very precise in determining classification criteria. These regulations require that a severe discrepancy be established between ability and achievement in one or more of seven areas, but nothing is specified concerning assessment of ability or the achievement areas, nor is the nature or degree of discrepancy indicated. It is not surprising that considerable variation also exists in how learning disabilities are determined (Mercer, Hughes, & Mercer, 1985).

Although definitions are provided, relatively little direction is provided by federal legislation. This lack of direction allows considerable variation within states and local districts, a subject discussed in a later section concerning the influence of social system factors on prevalence.

Dimensions of Behavior

The present system uses seven general dimensions of behavior or individual characteristics as the basis for classifying students as handicapped. These dimensions, which are used in various combinations to define each of the handicapping conditions specified by federal law, are discussed briefly below.

INTELLIGENCE

A major dimension of exceptionality is intelligence. Intelligence is a critical factor in the conceptual definitions used in the classification criteria for all types or levels of mental retardation and for learning disability. Volumes have been written about intelligence, including its measurement and use with various populations. Intellectual assessment is highly controversial for a number of reasons, not the least of which is a concern about overrepresentation of minority students in special classes for mildly retarded students (Heller, Holtzman, & Messick, 1982; Reschly, 1981b; Sattler, 1982). A question addressed later in this chapter is whether intelligence should be a part of the classification system, based on the contribution of intelligence to accurate classification, instructional programming, and placement decisions.

ACHIEVEMENT

A second dimension used very frequently in the classification of students as handicapped is achievement. Achievement is central to all areas since a typical requirement in most states is that a student must meet eligibility requirements *and* be in need of special education services in order to receive an appropriate education. Therefore, achievement is assessed with virtually all handicapped or potentially handicapped students. Achievement is perhaps most central to the learning disability diagnostic construct, which defines a learning disability in general terms as a severe discrepancy between ability and achievement in one or more areas. Assessment of achievement is considerably less controversial than intellectual assessment, but numerous problems and controversies do exist (Bennett & Shepard, 1982; Coles, 1978; Deno, Mirkin, & Chiang, 1982; Reynolds, 1984; Salvia & Ysseldyke, 1985).

SOCIAL BEHAVIOR AND EMOTIONAL ADJUSTMENT

A third dimension of exceptionality is social behavior and emotional adjustment, especially important factors in the classification of students as seriously emotionally disturbed. For the most part, the major concern in most settings is with social behavior that can be characterized as aggressive, disruptive, and intrusive. The vast majority of students classified as emotionally disturbed or behaviorally disordered are so classified due to conduct disorders involving aggressive, acting-out kinds of behaviors. The relative nature of these kinds of behaviors is generally quite obvious. Whether or not a behavior is regarded as aggressive and disordered depends very much upon the context, the role of the participant, the expectations for that role, and the persons making judgments.

The assessment of social behavior and emotional adjustment factors is generally regarded as important to all handicapping conditions. All students classified as handicapped should at least be screened for difficulties in these areas. It is also the case that many students classified in other disability areas have difficulties in social behavior or emotional adjustment. These problems are often inseparable from overall intellectual abilities, achievement, and classroom performance. The study of these factors in conjunction with learning disability has been prominent in the literature in recent years (see the chapter by Gresham in Volume 2 of this work).

COMMUNICATION/LANGUAGE

Communication skills and language development are central to several handicapping conditions, particularly speech impairment. All students who receive preplacement or reevaluations should at least be screened for possible communication disorders, which are encountered more frequently in persons with various mildly handicapping conditions than in the normal population. Communication/language disorders vary markedly, from relatively straightforward misarticulation difficulties, which may be resolved by short-term therapy or even no remedication at all, to severe stuttering, to total communication/language impairment requiring intensive interventions over many years.

SENSORY STATUS

Sensory status, particularly auditory and visual acuity, is the basis for the handicapping conditions of deaf, hard-of-hearing, deaf–blind, and visually handicapped, and it should be at least screened with all students in the regular population. Impairments in sensory status as secondary conditions also occur with many primary handicapping conditions, such as orthopedically impaired and other health impaired, and with severe levels of mental retardation.

MOTOR SKILLS

Motor impairments are a sixth dimension used in classifying students as exceptional. Many students with motor impairments have other disabilities, although, for some, the motor impairment may be the primary and only handicapping condition. Motor impairment is another area that should be screened with all students suspected of being handicapped. Most motor impairments are, however, obvious even to a casual observer, so that the question of whether or not a motor impairment exists is not at all difficult to resolve.

Health Status

Overall health status is a final dimension that may be used in classifying students as handicapped. A wide variety of disorders, many of which are life threatening, are grouped within this dimension. Some of the students classified as orthopedically impaired or other health impaired have very serious disorders that require careful monitoring and the availability of emergency intervention.

Although many dimensions exist that constitute the basis for classifying students as exceptional, the most frequently used dimensions are intelligence, achievement, social and emotional status, and communication or language. These are the principal dimensions used with the students of primary concern in this chapter, those who are educable mentally retarded, learning disabled, and seriously emotionally disturbed. These dimensions are used primarily with social system model handicaps (discussed in the next section), which, within the exceptional child population, are also characterized as high-prevalence exceptionalities.

Models of Exceptionality

The current exceptional child classification system involves a mixture of models (Hobbs, 1975a, 1975b). Two models are prominent: the medical model and the social system model. Much of the confusion in recent years concerning the meaning of exceptionality and the basis for determining handicaps results from confusion of these two models.

Medical Model

The term *medical model* is perhaps unfortunate in that it suggests that the assumptions and approaches to problems described in the medical model are typical of how professionals in medicine solve problems. Kauffman and Hallahan (1974) pointed out large differences between the concept of the medical model as it is used in the behavioral sciences and the approach to solving problems actually used in medicine. Therefore, the term medical model should be seen as a heuristic device, and should not be taken literally as indicative of practices in medicine. The characteristics of the medical model as an approach to the development of assessment devices and as an approach to conceptualizing child deviance were described by Mercer and Ysseldyke (1977) and Mercer (1979). The most important characteristic of the medical model for the purposes of this analysis is that abnormal patterns of behavior or development are attributed to underlying biological pathology. The etiology, or the cause, direct or indirect, of deviant behavior is seen as stemming from biological anomalies. Another important characteristic of the medical model is that it is cross cultural; that is, the same underlying biological abnormalities cause approximately the same deficits in behavior regardless of the social status or cultural group of the individual involved. Further, the medical model is seen as a deficit model, and an underlying biological anomaly is viewed as an inherent part of an individual.

The medical model is probably useful in the description and classification of some, but not all, of the exceptional conditions defined by federal law. The conditions of deaf, deaf–blind, hard-of-hearing, multihandicapped, orthopedically impaired, other health impaired, visually handicapped, and certain levels of mental retardation are probably best regarded as medical model handicaps in that there are underlying biological anomalies and identifiable physiological differences associated with and, frequently, known to be the direct cause of observed deficits in behavior. Moreover, these underlying deficits cause approximately the same kinds of anomalies in patterns of development or behavior regardless of cultural context or social status. For example, Down's Syndrome, usually associated with moderate to severe levels of mental retardation, has the same underlying chromosomal aberration and causes approximately the same limitation in development regardless of social status or cultural group.

Although a number of controversies exist regarding medical model handicaps, these controversies generally do not involve questions of whether or not special education is needed and whether or not the students involved should be classified as handicapped. Moreover, there is universal agreement on the importance of early diagnosis of and early intervention with these kinds of handicaps. Finally, there is no substantial overrepresentation of economically disadvantaged or minority students with medical model handicaps, a problem encountered frequently with social system model handicaps.

Social System Model

In contrast to the medical model, the social system model uses a strongly ecological perspective (Mercer, 1979). Deviant behavior or abnormal patterns of development are not seen as inherent characteristics of the individual but rather as reflections of a discrepancy between what an individual has learned in a cultural context and the expectations for normal behavior associated with a specific social role and social setting. Judgments about behavior or the classification of certain patterns of behavior as exceptional involve applications of social norms within a particular social setting to observed patterns of behavior. The norms or expectations for behavior are determined by the larger society. Judgments of deviance are based on an interaction between the learned patterns of behavior on the part of an individual, the social setting in which a specific behavior is judged, the social role in which the individual is engaged, and the expectations associated with the social role and the social context. This social system model suggests that social and cultural factors are extremely important in the determination of what an individual learns to be appropriate behavior and in the determination of expectations for behavior in a specific role and setting.

Many of the handicapping conditions listed in the federal definitions—specifically those of most of the students classified as mentally retarded, seriously emotionally disturbed, specific learning disabled, or speech impaired—should be regarded as social system model handicaps. All of these handicaps are best understood as persistent patterns of behavior that do not conform to social norms. These classifications account for the vast majority of the students classified as handicapped, perhaps even as many as 80% to 90% (Algozzine & Korinek, 1985). To illustrate the distinction between medical model handicaps and social system model handicaps, it might be useful to consider the following questions: Would someone be classified as learning disabled due to a severe reading disorder in an illiterate or preliterate society? Would someone with severe neuromotor damage, resulting in paraplegia, be regarded as handicapped in a preliterate or illiterate society? It is highly likely that the classifications of learning disability or mild mental retardation would not exist if we did not have compulsory school attendance laws and nearly universal public education for children between the ages of approximately 5 and 17. Social system model handicaps, the central focus of this chapter, are best understood as a function of the demands and expectations placed upon students in a highly techological society, particularly the demands and expectations for the development of abstract thinking and literacy skills.

Although some rarely encountered instances of mild mental retardation, learning disability, and emotional disturbance do have identificable underlying biological anomalies, the overwhelming majority do not. For the overwhelming majority of students classified as handicapped, there is no biological explanation, no underlying physical disorder, to account for the handicapping condition.

Failure to understand the social system nature of most handicapping conditions leads to a great deal of confusion and miscommunication. In many instances, the question raised is, Is the student *really* handicapped? An answer to this query depends on what is meant by handicapped. If the inquiry is based on the underlying assumption that handicapped persons have obvious physical disorders due to underlying biological anomalies, then the vast majority of students classified as handicapped are not really handicapped. On the other hand, if the underlying assumption is that a handicap involves significant discrepancies between actual and expected patterns of behavior as well as significant difficulties in coping with the demands placed on all children, then the overwhelming majority of students now classified as handicapped are indeed correctly classified. It is crucial to note that the distinctions between social system model and medical model kinds of handicaps, as well as the bases for social system model handicapping conditions, essentially are derived from a consensus concerning what is expected of children and the kinds of significant discrepancies from expectations that constitute disabling conditions.

The mental retardation classification is especially confusing because both social system and medical model concepts are prominent, depending on level or degree of severity (Grossman, 1983). Mildly mentally retarded students are best understood from a social system model perspective, while those with moderate, severe, and profound levels of mental retardation are best understood as having medical model kinds of handicaps. Unfortunately, the characteristics of the more severe levels of mental retardation (biological anomalies, comprehensive handicaps, and permanence) are incorrectly attributed to mildly retarded students. This confusion, which is inherent in the current system, accounts for at least part of the greater stigma associated with mild mental retardation than with other mildly handicapping categories. The need for reforms in this part of the classification system is especially acute (Polloway & Smith, 1983, Volume 2 of this work; Reschly, 1982, 1984).

Prevalence and Severity

Further distinctions between the medical and social system model handicaps can be found in the prevalence and severity of these handicaps. These distinctions are discussed below.

Prevalence. The prevalence of medical and social system model handicaps varies considerably. All of the medical model handicaps are of relatively low prevalence, meaning that very few school-age students exhibit these handicapping conditions. Students with medical model handicaps constitute less than 20% of the population of students currently classified as handicapped, or less than 2.5% of the total school-age population. By contrast, students with social system model handicaps constitute 80% or more of the current population of students classified as handicapped (Algozzine & Korinek, 1985), or from about 7% to as much as 9.5% of the total school-age population.

The information on prevalence provides an illustration of the social system nature of mildly handicapping conditions. The Office of Special Education Programs of the United States Department of Education is required to gather data on the prevalence of the eleven handicapping conditions defined by federal law. These prevalence data are to be reported to Congress annually. The sixth and seventh annual reports to Congress on the implementation of PL 94-142 (U.S. Department of Education, 1984, 1985) provide ample data concerning rather large variations in the prevalence of mildly handicapping conditions across the states. Variations among states in the prevalence of learning disabilities range from a low of 3% to a high of 7%. In other words, depending on the state, the proportion of the school-age population classified as learning disabled may be as low as 3% or as high as 7%. Similar variations occur in the area of mental retardation, in which the lowest rate is about 0.5% and the highest rate is nearly 4%. There are about 8 times as many mentally retarded persons in the highest prevalence state as in the lowest prevalence state. However, the overall prevalence of all types of handicapping conditions among school-age children varies only from 9% to 11.5%. The overall prevalence of all types of handicapping conditions and the prevalence of medical model handicaps are relatively similar across the different states. The enormous variations exist within the social system model mild handicap areas of learning disability, educable mental retardation, and emotional disturbance. These enormous variations are related, at least in part, to the nearly decade-long trend of expanding numbers of students classified as learning disabled and diminishing numbers of students classified as mentally retarded (Gerber, 1984; Polloway & Smith, 1983, Volume 2 of this work).

One of the reasons for the widely differing prevalences of learning disability, educable mental retardation, and emotional disturbance is state rules and regulations concerning definitions and classification criteria. Recent studies of definitions and classification criteria in mental retardation (Patrick & Reschly, 1982) and learning disability (Mercer et al., 1985) reveal rather large differences among the states. In the area of mental retardation, widely varying classification criteria exist, with IQ scores as high as 85 to as low as 70 required in order to classify a student as mildly retarded. The states also vary considerably in the relative importance attached to adaptive behavior, in conceptions of adaptive behavior, and in decision rules concerning adaptive behavior. Similar variations were reported by Mercer et al. (1985) for learning disability. These variations of state criteria make it entirely possible for a student to be classified as mildly retarded in one state, only to move across state boundaries and be reclassified as learning disabled. It is also entirely possible for a student to be classified as handicapped in one state, but not to be so classified in another sate. These variations in classification criteria are further illustrations of the social system model nature of mildly handicapping conditions.

A further source of variation in the prevalence of handicapping conditions, particularly within a state or a district, is the variety of systemic factors described quite persuasively by Bickel (1982), Keogh (1983), MacMillan and Borthwick (1980), and MacMillan, Meyers, and Morrison (1980). Further systemic influences include variations in teachers' tolerance for individual differences, variations in how referrals are screened and in the availability of options within regular education to provide remedial services, and variations in the extent to which special programs are available for students who are considered for classification. All of these factors interact in very complicated ways to influence whether or not a specific youngster is classified as handicapped and placed in a special education program.

Before leaving this subject, it is, perhaps, worthwhile to note the enormous decline in the numbers of students classified as mentally retarded over the past decade (Haywood, 1979; Polloway & Smith, 1983; Reschly, 1981a). The recent reports to Congress cited above indicate that the number of students classified as mentally retarded in the United States declined by 300,000 from 1976 to 1983. At the same time, the number of students classified as learning disabled increased by one million. Some of the decline in mental retardation can undoubtedly be attributed to more stringent classification criteria, greater concern for assessment of adaptive behavior, and caution in classifying minority students as mildly retarded (Tucker, 1980). It is also true that relatively slight variations in classification criteria, such as increasing or decreasing the IQ cut-off score by 5 points, can produce rather large differences in the numbers of students eligible for classification as mentally retarded (Reschly, 1981a; Reschly & Jipson, 1976). However, these factors probably do not explain the large decline in mental retardation classification, which, almost undoubtedly, affected the numbers of students classified as mildly retarded rather than those classified as having other levels of mental retardation (Polloway & Smith, 1983). (For further discussion of issues in the area of mild mental retardation, see the section on this topic in Volume 2 of this work.)

Thus, the huge variations in prevalence among states, among districts within states, and among attendance centers within districts provide overwhelming evidence of social system influences on who is classified as handicapped. The vast majority of handicapping conditions are relative, best understood from a social system perspective. Efforts to reform the current system must take into account the very complex characteristics of this social system.

Severity. Social system and medical model handicaps also vary considerably in regard to severity. Almost all social system handicaps are best regarded as mildly impairing in that discrepancies in behavior are fairly subtle, relatively modest in degree, and, usually, situation specific. In nearly all instances, social system model handicaps are not recognized prior to school attendance. Within school, mild handicaps exist only with regard to certain roles. Finally, persons with such conditions are typically not recognized, at least officially, as handicapped during their adult years. By contrast, medical model handicaps can range widely in severity, such as from mild losses of visual acuity that are easily correctable to severe losses of visual acuity that are not correctable. However, sensory losses are typically officially regarded as handicapping only when there is significant interference with normal activities. Thus, students classified as having medical model handicaps usually are regarded as having moderate or severe degrees of impairment. This is due, at least in part, to the fact that very mild or subtle anomalies of a medical model nature can be corrected or compensated for or do not in and of themselves significantly interfere with classroom performance. In discussions of handicapping conditions, considerable clarity would be achieved if we would think in terms of two quite different kinds of exceptional or handicapping conditions: one kind related to underlying biological anomalies, usually causing rather serious disabilities and typically occurring very rarely; and the other kind much more subtle in nature, usually recognized formally only in the public school setting and occurring with a relatively higher prevalence, perhaps approaching 10% of the total school-age population.

Validity and Reliability of Classification Systems

The most important characteristics of a good classification system are validity and reliability. As part of an earlier effort to produce reforms in exceptional child classification, not unlike some of the current efforts reflected in these volumes, Cromwell, Blashfield, and Strauss (1975) suggested criteria to be used in judging the usefulness of classification systems. Cromwell et al. identified two kinds of information that can be used as a basis for classifying individuals: individuals can be classified according to historical information having to do with previous events, developmental history, and the like and/or on the basis of currently assessable characteristics. Some diagnostic constructs involve a combination of both kinds of information. The reliability of a classification system is determined by the degree to which independent judges examining the same information concerning historical characteristics and/or currently assessable characteristics arrive at the same classification.

Cromwell et al. (1975) suggested that reliability, although important, is far less important than validity. Validity is the degree to which a classification is related to specific treatments or interventions *and* to knowledge about the effectiveness of these treatments or interventions. A valid classification system, therefore, involves diagnoses that are clearly related to different treatments or interventions which, in turn, are known to be effective in improving competencies and expanding opportunities. Diagnoses not related to treatment and outcome were regarded by Cromwell et al. as relatively useless, at least for the individual. Cromwell et al. also noted that many classifications were related to popular and sometimes faddish treatments or interventions about which little or nothing was known regarding effectiveness. Circumstances today in the exceptional child classification system are, unfortunately, much the same.

Validity and reliability are absolutely essential characteristics of a useful classification system. Classification as handicapped involves certain risks for an individual, particularly possible labeling effects and the creation of stigma. Classification is in the best interest of an individual, however, despite the risks, if treatments or interventions are provided that are sufficiently powerful to overcome the risks (Gallagher, 1972). In any analysis of current classifications, particularly concerning high-prevalence, mild handicaps, which represent failures to meet social system expectations, the risks–benefits ratio is of paramount importance. Questions that must be addressed include the degree to which current classifications are related to beneficial treatments (see Heller et al., 1982; Reschly, 1979, 1984; Reynolds & Wang, 1983). A second consideration has to do with the degree of stigma associated with the current classification system. The obvious objective is to develop a classification system that is as free of stigma as possible and, at the same time, as valid as possible with respect to effective treatments or interventions. On the basis of these criteria, the current classification system leaves much to be desired. Classification system reform needs to be guided by concerns about reliability and validity, efforts to incorporate relevant learning phenomena, valid interventions, effective placement options, and minimization of stigma. These variables are considered in the following sections of this chapter.

Learning Research With Mildly Handicapped Students

Increasingly sophisticated research investigating basic learning phenomena with mildly handicapped students, particularly those who are learning disabled and mildly mentally retarded, has appeared in recent years. This research corrects a somewhat persistent older view that measured intellingence has little or no relationship to the acquisition, processing, and retrieval of information. This older view, popular among at least some psychologists through the 1960s (e.g., Gagne, 1967), suggested that the amount or quantity of learning separated less intelligent children from average cohorts. This view seemed quite preposterous to many teachers and others who worked closely with mildly handicapped students.

Recent research has suggested significant qualitative and quantitative differences between mildly handicapped and average children and youth on a variety of information processing variables, including efficiency of learning, availability of prior knowledge, strategies for processing information and metacognitive operations used by the learner to direct the learning process. In addition to these intellectual or cognitive differences, recent research has also established significant differences in motivation, attention, social skills, and locus of control. These findings, although relatively recent and, in some cases, tentative, have significant implications for instructional procedures and classification system reforms.

Information Processing

Campione, Brown, and Ferrara (1982) showed that the view that intelligence is largely unrelated to learning is true under a very special set of circumstances. Their finding of no differences between mildly retarded and normal persons was restricted to learning tasks involving simple, automatic, nonmeaningful, and concrete associations as in simple, paired-associate learning using nonsense syllables. However, research on learning processes using problems that involve complex, abstract, and meaningful content reveals substantial differences between mildly retarded and normal subjects.

Outstanding work in the area of basic learning phenomena with mildly retarded students has been conducted by Brown and her associates for about the past 10 years (see Campione et al., 1982; Palincsar & Brown, this volume). They have suggested that four basic variables in the learning process differ significantly as a function of intelligence or ability. These basic variables are (a) the speed or efficiency in elementary information processing operations; (b) the knowlege base from previous learning; (c) the use of strategies in acquisition, memory, and problem solving; and (d) metacognitive operations. Campione et al. (1982) then reviewed research on each of these variables. Citing massive amounts of empirical research, they concluded that mildly retarded students differed significantly from average students in the basic variables of speed or efficiency, knowledge base, strategies, and metacognition.

Deficits in the use of strategies have received considerable attention and comment (see also Robinson & Robinson, 1976) for at least a decade. The basic research in this area suggests that mildly retarded persons can be taught to use strategies but that there is relatively little transfer to new situations or generalization to slightly different tasks in the same situation. Perhaps a basic, fundamental characteristic of mildly retarded persons is their failure to transfer knowledge appropriately to new situations, a characteristic that Campione et al. (1982) suggested is due to poorer abilities to learn incidentally or to profit from incomplete instruction.

The deficits that have been reported concerning metacognitive processes are not surprising in view of the apparent difficulties with spontaneous development and the use of strategies. Metacognitive processes appear to require the availability of different strategies, which can then be examined and applied as appropriate.

Findings similar to those of Brown and her colleagues have been reported by Brooks and McCauley (1984) based on a continuing program of research directed toward identifying basic cognitive process differences between mentally retarded and average ability persons. Again, processing efficiency for semantic or meaningful content was found to differ for mildly retarded and normal persons. These investigators suggested that the deficit was probably due to attention processes, a conclusion also suggested by Borkowski, Peck, and Damberg (1983). The Borkowski et al. review focused on fundamental deficits in attention and short-term processing and complements the treatment of the literature by Campione et al. (1982), which focused more on the use of strategies and metacognitive functions.

Attention difficulties are also among the learning process problems identified with learning disabled students (Hallahan & Sapono, 1984). In addition to the studies cited in the reviews by Borkowski et al. and Campione et al., findings that are typical of recent information processing research can be examined in studies of semantic processing speed reported by Davies (1981) and in studies of abstract and concrete learning reported by Dean and Kundert (1981).

Research on basic information processing variables with children classified as learning disabled appears to be less well developed and more recent than comparable research with mildly retarded children. (It should be noted here that information processing research is not the same as the correlated process literature in the area of learning disabilities. Information processing research is generally based on cognitive psychology and very precise experimental methods.) The literature on learning disabled students has yielded results similar to those reported for mildly retarded students. The Teachers College Institute for Research on Learning Disabilities (Conner, 1983) conducted intensive studies of the information processing abilities of learning disabled children. Conner's conclusion was, "these studies all show pervasive performance deficits of learning disabled children on deliberate memory tasks" (p. 27). Conner also reported successful results with improving the use of strategies through direct instruction procedures. However, cautions were expressed concerning the transfer and generalizability of the improved strategies, a problem noted above with mildly retarded students. Basic research reporting deficits in strategy use and metacognitive processes for learning disabled students have been reported by Bauer (1979), Short and Ryan (1984), and Swanson (1982). These studies establish the existence of basic information processing deficits among learning disabled students and suggest the beginnings of intervention programs that may ameliorate these deficits.

Motivation and Attributions

In addition to basic deficits in information processing, mildly handicapped students typically display affective characteristics that may interfere with efficient, successful, classroom learning. These motivational differences have long been ascribed to mildly retarded students (MacMillan, 1982; Robinson & Robinson, 1976; Zigler, 1962). There appears to be considerable agreement, supported by reasonably strong, but not definitive, evidence, that mildly retarded persons are more subject to failure-set phenomena (involving reduced motivation and less efficient learning even on simple tasks subsequent to experiencing failures); that they have greater tendencies to attribute success or failure to the behaviors of other persons or to context variables rather than to individual competence or effort; and that they exhibit greater dependence on external reinforcement. As suggested above, much of the evidence for these generalizations is now dated, perhaps, in part, due to a decline in research in mildly retarded persons (Haywood, 1979; Polloway & Epstein, 1985; Polloway & Smith, 1983). Nevertheless, motivational factors—including attributions for success or failure, since these are believed to be related to effort—are important considerations in designing instruction for mildly retarded students.

Recent research on learning disabled students suggests motivational and attributional deficits similar to those reported earlier for mildly retarded students. In Volume 2 of this work, Gresham summarizes the literature in this area concerning learning disabled students. Two other kinds of research in this area are especially noteworthy. Bryan, Pearl, Donahue, Bryan, and Pflaum (1983) reported extensive research on the social skills and social competencies of learning disabled students, some of which have significant implications for motivation related to learning. Adelman and Taylor (1983, 1984) also reported motivational differences with learning disabled students, including external locus of control of reinforcement and tendencies toward attributing success to external factors. These investigators also reported procedures for enhancing motivation through greater involvement of students in decision-making processes, contractual agreements, and specific positive feedback concerning performance. Work by Deshler, Schumaker, and Lenz (1984) with learning disabled adolescents also emphasized the existence of motivational differences that must be considered in the development of interventions.

Although the literature in this area is relatively sparse, the results to date are quite impressive concerning the importance of motivational factors. Again, considerable similarity, at least with respect to general kinds of problems, has been reported for mildly retarded and learning disabled students. However, these and other results contrasting groups of mildly handicapped students with average or normal students must be interpreted cautiously, a topic discussed in the next section.

Caution in Interpreting Group Differences

Before going further with the discussion of learning research with mildly handicapped students, it is essential to recognize the hazards of applying the results from studies of contrasted groups to practical issues in classification and instruction. The modern history of the psychology of exceptional individuals and special education is replete with instances in which efforts were made to directly apply the results from studies of contrasted groups. There is every reason to believe that these kinds of difficulties may confound efforts to directly apply the research on information processing and affective characteristics.

Some of the major difficulties associated with applying the results from contrasting groups to practical decisions have to do with the differences between laboratory, or experimental, situations, and classroom, or real-world, applications. Some areas of difference are the degree of control over variables and the opportunity to carefully select kinds of participants. These differences are generally recognized but infrequently accounted for in real-world applications.

A less obvious but, perhaps, more important confounding factor has to do with the size of differences among groups, or the effect size of the independent variable. What is often not reported or studied sufficiently is the degree of difference among constrasted groups and the degree of overlap in distributions. Some studies that contrast students performing at the average level with students performing at a lower level (e.g., mildly mentally retarded students) occasionally yield results suggesting large differences and virtually no overlap of distributions. However, if students in all ranges (i.e., mildly mentally retarded to average students, including those sometimes characterized as low average and slow learning) are studied, the differences between mildly retarded and other learners are less apparent. Failure to take into account the overlap of distributions and the size of differences probably explains, at least in part, the difficulties recently emphasized regarding similarities between students classified as learning disabled and low achieving in regular classrooms, as well as the rather unhappy history of attempting to identify and intervene with learning disabled students using correlated process measures. Much of this literature can best be understood through a consideration of aptitude-by-treatment research.

Aptitude-by-Treatment Interaction

Much of modern special education, particularly the area of learning disability, has been significantly influenced by the concept of and assumptions about aptitude-by-treatment interactions. Aptitude-by-treatment interaction means that learners varying on some characteristic respond differentially, depending on the nature of the treatment. (Treatment usually means instruction in special education.) In the psychological literature, aptitude, as a construct, is used quite broadly. This broad use is especially apparent in the theory and research on aptitude-by-treatment interaction (Cronbach & Snow, 1977; Snow, 1980). Here, aptitude means virtually any psychological characteristic, including neurological organization (Reynolds, 1984), that predicts differences among people in later learning or training situations. Included in this very broad conception of aptitude are general abilities, such as intelligence, specific cognitive skills and prior achievement; cognitive or information processing characteristics; and personality/affective characteristics, such as locus of control over reinforcement, achievement motivation, and so on.

During the late 1960s and much of the 1970s, the assumption of aptitude-by-treatment interaction was fundamental to special education, particularly in the area of learning disability. Terminology used in special education typically included *learning process by instructional method* or *modality-by-teaching approach*. The assumption clearly was identical to what Snow and others defined as aptitude-by-treatment interaction, since it was assumed that matching teaching method to modality strength would enhance learning. The aptitudes prominent at that time were a variety of psycholinguistic skills and perceptual processes, such as auditory discrimination, visual perception, auditory reception, and so on. The prevailing point of view was that learning disabled children should be identified by deficits in psychological processes, which should then be the basis of remedial efforts. The remedial efforts were to be carried out by teaching the deficit skills and/or by compensation through teaching subject-matter content, such as reading, through intact processes or processing strengths.

In a series of articles that appeared beginning in the mid-1970s, these assumptions were severely criticized, and the correlated process approach to identification and remediation of learning disabilities declined dramatically. The major problems with the correlated process approach were that (a) most of these special aptitude or process measures had poor psychometric characteristics, including low reliability and doubtful validity; (b) there was little evidence that the processes could be successfully taught and even less evidence that improvements in these processes led to better performance in relevant academic subjects (Hammill & Larsen, 1974, 1978; Newcomer, Larsen & Hammill, 1975; however, another perspective on this literature is provided by Lund, Foster, & McCall-Perez, 1978; Minskoff, 1975); and (c) there was virtually no evidence in support of aptitude-by-treatment interactions including the use of these process measures and currently available teaching methods (for a recent review, see Ysseldyke & Mirkin, 1982). For these reasons, as well as the development of other criteria for classifying children as learning disabled, there has been a steady decline in the use of process measures in public school settings, at least until recently.

Many of the negative findings in the aptitude-by-treatment research with mildly handicapped students may be attributable, at least in part, to methodological considerations, a point stressed by Minskoff (1975) in her response to Hammill and Larsen's (1974) criticism. In recent years, there has been increasing sophistication regarding measurement and design considerations with aptitude-by-treatment research (Snow, 1978; Van der Linden, 1981; Ysseldyke & Salvia, 1980). This increasing methodological sophistication may account, at least in part, for the growing number of successful aptitude-by-treatment studies of aptitude measures including ability, affect, and motivation with a variety of nonhandicapped groups (Alesandrini, 1981; Bernard & Davis, 1982; Delaney, 1978; Holtan, 1982; James & Knief, 1978; Kulik & Kulik, 1982; McGivern & Levin, 1983; Peterson, 1979, 1981; Veldman & Sanford, 1984; Winn, 1980). It is essential to note, though, that the successful studies just cited involved nonhandicapped learners, some of whom were college students. These successful studies suggest increasing methodological sophistication and an expanding knowledge base of what kinds of aptitudes interact with what kinds of treatments. However, it is premature to apply these findings to mildly handicapped students.

Despite these cautions, it is appropriate to identify some recent, successful, and promising aptitude-by-treatment interaction studies with handicapped students. Gettinger (1983) reported an interaction of learner ability and amount of time required for learning with fourth-grade students. This study, though preliminary, may yield useful information concerning the amount of time required for mastery of essential academic content, a very significant question in designing instruction for handicapped students. In another promising study, Pascarella, Pflaum, Bryan, and Pearl (1984) were able to show the interaction of the affective characteristic of locus of control with kind of teacher response and feedback. Learning disabled students with high internal locus of control learned best when they were responsible for determining the correctness of their responses. By contrast, learning disabled students with high external locus of control learned best when teachers determined the correctness of their responses. It is essential to note the preliminary nature of these studies and the rather unsuccessful history of aptitude-by-treatment interaction research with exceptional children. However, these studies do provide support for Snow's (1984) plea for continued use of aptitude constructs, including global intelligence, and for further research on aptitude-by-treatment interaction with exceptional students.

The relative paucity of positive aptitude-by-treatment interaction findings seriously undermines the assumption that matching unique methodologies to unique learner characteristics is the fundamental basis for special education. The present state of knowledge simply does not provide an empirical basis for this matching process. Until positive aptitude-by-treatment interactions are established for exceptional children, and the aptitudes and treatments used by researchers are within the realm of use in practical situations, the notion of a science and practice of special education based on matching students to different teaching methodologies will be impossible. The absence of the aptitude-by-treatment interaction basis for special education is part of the reason for the kinds of reforms that are discussed later in this chapter.

Summary

The results of the review of the literature on learning characteristics and mildly handicapped students are mixed. In recent years, significant advances have occurred regarding understanding of basic learning phenomena and the identification of differences between mildly handicapped and normal cohorts in basic learning phenomena. The technology required to assess these differences, and the research and technology required to relate them to instruction, are not sufficiently well developed to provide a basis for exceptional child classification, placement, and instruction. Further developments in this knowledge base and its associated technology are anticipated in the years ahead. However, for the present, and in the foreseeable future, these results must be regarded as preliminary, though fascinating.

Individual Differences as the Basis for the Exceptional Child Classification System

As discussed earlier, individual differences, or variations among learners, are the basis for the current exceptional child classification system. It is assumed that individual differences in characteristics related to instruction are sufficiently large that learners at the lowest levels of distributions are appropriately regarded as handicapped and that special education services are required in order to provide them with an appropriate education. It is critical to note that both of these criteria of individual differences must be met prior to classification and placement of a student in a special education program. That is, the student's performance must be sufficiently different from average levels of performance to meet eligibility requirements, and the student must also require special education services. Meeting only one of these criteria is not sufficient for classification and placement.

In this section, the *magnitude* of individual differences on variables related to the mildly handicapped/exceptional child classification system is considered. The primary focus is on the variables noted earlier as most important to the social system model of handicapping conditions: intelligence, achievement, and social/emotional characteristics. Several perspectives guide the consideration of individual differences. Mildly handicapped students are compared with average or normal students, with low-achieving students, and with students classified as economically disadvantaged. In addition, students classified as mildly handicapped, particularly those classified as mildly mentally retarded and learning disabled, are compared. These comparisons are then discussed in terms of instructional needs, a discussion that sets the stage for a consideration of appropriate educational interventions with mildly handicapped students.

Comparisons With Classroom Averages

In recent years, comparisons of the performance of mildly handicapped students with average levels of performance have devoted decreasing attention to the magnitude of differences on a host of variables. Much of the recent literature has focused on the absence of differences between mildly handicapped and low-achieving students, a topic covered in the next section. Despite all of the systemic influences and variations in state classification criteria, there is overwhelming evidence establishing the enormous differences between students classified as mildly handicapped and students with average levels of performance on measured intelligence, achievement, and social/emotional behaviors (Bryan & Bryan, 1978; Bryan et al., 1983; Conner, 1983; Gresham & Reschly, 1986; Meyers, MacMillan, & Yoshida, 1978; Reschly, Gresham, & Graham-Clay, 1984; Richmond & Walts, 1978; Schumaker, Deshler, Alley, & Warner, 1983; Scott, 1979; Yoshida, MacMillan, & Meyers, 1976). The size of the differences in average performance usually range from 1.5 to as much as 2.5 to 3 standard deviations. Differences of this magnitude suggest relatively little overlap of distributions and large differences in levels of academic skills. A major challenge in educational programming in mainstream placements is providing for these differences, especially in advanced grades.

It is not surprising that such differences exist between the performance levels of mildly handicapped and average-achieving students. Differences of this magnitude are required in the areas of intelligence, achievement, and social/emotional behaviors in order to meet eligibility requirements. Although there are well-documented instances of relatively poor assessment practices, particularly with regard to determination of the discrepancy between intelligence and achievement required by many states in their classification criteria for learning disabilities (Reynolds, 1984; Shepard, 1983; Shepard & Smith, 1981), even these studies show substantial differences between levels of academic achievement for learning disabled and average-achieving students.

These differences do not connote nearly identical performance levels for mildly handicapped students in different districts, nor do they mean that achievement for mildly handicapped students varies from state to state. The essential pattern of substantial differences has always been the case in studies comparing the performance of mildly handicapped and average-achieving students.

Another intriguing result from studies comparing mildly handicapped to average levels of performance is the low level of social skills usually displayed by mildly handicapped students, even when social competence or social skills are not included in classification criteria. There is now substantial evidence indicating that mildly mentally retarded and learning disabled students perform at a level 1.5–2 or more standard deviations below classroom averages on measures of social skills, even though social skills are not part of the criteria used in classifying students as learning disabled or educable mentally retarded (Bryan et al., 1983; Gresham, 1982; Reschly et al., 1984). These differences in social skills may account for the reasons that some children are referred and then classified as learning disabled while other students with approximately the same performance deficits in ability and achievement are not referred.

Thus, enormous differences are reported when the performance levels of mildly handicapped students are compared to average levels of performance in ability, achievement, and social/emotional behaviors. These differences have significant implications for instructional design.

Comparisons With Low-Achieving Students

In contrast to the unequivocal findings of substantial differences discussed above, comparisons of mildly handicapped to low-achieving students result in far more equivocal findings. These equivocal findings are especially prominent with students who are classified as learning disabled, who, apparently, are not substantially different from other low-achieving students in the same regular education classrooms. This particular set of findings has been emphasized in numerous publications by a group of investigators in Minnesota, Ysseldyke and his colleagues (Algozzine & Ysseldyke, 1983; Ysseldyke, Algozzine, & Epps, 1983; Ysseldyke, Algozzine, Shinn, & McGue, 1982; Ysseldyke, Thurlow, Graden, Wesson, Algozzine, &

Deno, 1983). These findings of essentially no differences between students classified as learning disabled and those defined, according to standardized test results, as low achieving have been interpreted as indicating that almost anyone could be classified as learning disabled or that learning disabled students are merely those whom someone decides, perhaps arbitrarily and capriciously, to classify as such. These findings certainly do call into question the concept of learning disability as a handicap separate from low achievement, a problem exacerbated by confusion on definitions and by problems with assessment procedures. However, it is important to note that the notion that a "learning disabled person can be anybody" is restricted to the relatively small population of low-achieving students and to those currently classified as learning disabled.

Other findings, such as those of Schumaker et al. (1983), indicate that differences between low-achieving and learning disabled adolescents exist on academic and cognitive variables. It should also be noted that the findings of the Minnesota group were severely criticized by McKinney (1983), who pointed out the potential for misinterpretation and misuse of the findings of no differences between learning disabled and low-achieving students. McKinney criticized this work because, although the Minnesota studies failed to differentiate learning disabled and low-achieving groups on psychometric measures, the results meant only that the Minnesota studies did not find differences, not that such differences did not exist. McKinney also criticized the suggestion by the Minnesota group that special education services for learning disabled children are ineffective—perhaps even harmful, unnecessary, and unwarranted. He noted that these findings are quite inconsistent with the findings of other learning disability research institutes. Ysseldyke, Algozzine, and Thurlow (1983) responded to McKinney by reasserting their position concerning the uselessness of the concept of learning disability and their suggestion that the classification stage be skipped because the classification of learning disability has little or no instructional validity. In this article, Ysseldyke, Algozzine, and Thurlow suggested that interventions be developed for low-achieving students without consideration of special education classification, a topic addressed in a later section of this chapter.

Comparable studies involving precise contrasts between mildly retarded and low-achieving students have not appeared in the literature to date. However, other studies provide findings that may have some bearing on these concerns. These studies suggest that relatively small differences would exist between most slow-learning or low-achieving persons and those who are mildly mentally retarded. Both groups have significant educational needs that are related, in large part, to inefficient learning and low achievement (Gresham & Reschly, 1986; Meyers et al., 1978; Richmond & Waits, 1978; Scott, 1979).

One further consideration in comparisons of mildly handicapped to low-achieving students is, again, the nature of social system model deficits. Deficits from the social system model perspective exist on a continuum, usually with normal or near-normal overall distributions. This means that there are fine gradations from average levels of performance to the lowest possible levels of performance. It should, therefore, not be surprising that considerable overlap exists between low-achieving and learning disabled students, both of whom are defined, by and large, by deficits in achievement. Perhaps the problem is not with the concept of learning disability as such, or, for that matter, with the concept of low achievement, but, rather, with the unequivocal, dichotomous, either/or decisions required by our current system of exceptional child classification. For this system to reflect the results reported in this section, there would need to be fine gradations in classification and placement decision making, with many more instructional options.

Overlap With Economically Disadvantaged Students

Before examining opinion and evidence concerning the similarities and differences between mildly handicapped and low-achieving economically disadvantaged students, it is important to dispel several stereotypes. Henderson (1980, 1981) discussed the inaccuracies of applying information about the mean differences among sociocultural groups to individual students. In many instances, there are mean differences that meet the criterion of statistical significance but that are not typical of the group in question. Henderson pointed out stereotypes of the black matriarchal family and of male dominance among the Hispanic population as examples of stereotypes that are based on group differences but that are neither typical nor found even among the majority of persons in the sociocultural group. Reschly (1986) provides a thorough treatment of the issues related to economic and cultural factors in childhood exceptionality. There are many controversies in this area, including quite legitimate concerns about appropriate assessment and classification of minority children and youth (Burke, 1975; Franks, 1971; Hilliard, 1980; Neer, Foster, Jones, & Reynolds, 1973; Tucker, 1980). Concerns about overrepresentation of minority students, particularly overrepresentation in segregated special classes for mildly retarded students, have prompted litigation in several states (Reschly, 1981b, 1986, in press).

Several review articles have noted similarities between economically disadvantaged students, who often are minority students as well, and mildly handicapped students (Chan & Rueda, 1979; Chinn, 1979; Kavale, 1980; Mackie, 1968). Kavale (1980) noted considerable similarity in behavioral characteristics, including low achievement, inefficient learning, difficulties in correlated processes, such as visual and auditory perception, and social/behavioral difficulties.

The question of the similarity between mildly handicapped students and low-achieving, economically disadvantaged students has implications far beyond better understanding of student characteristics and cultural influences. As is noted in a later section of this chapter, there are, currently, two major systems for delivering remedial or compensatory education services to children and youth. If the characteristics and instructional needs of mildly handicapped and low-achieving, economically disadvantaged students are sufficiently similar, greater compatibility among—and, perhaps, even a merger of—these two systems might be appropriate. If, on the other hand, the characteristics and needs of these groups are substantially different, then a merger of the systems would not be appropriate. Unfortunately, we do not have carefully conducted studies comparing low-achieving, economically disadvantaged students, many of whom are currently served in a compensatory education program called Chapter 1, and mildly handicapped students. There is some anecdotal evidence, as well as some preliminary findings, suggesting that, when both programs are available, students placed in programs for mildly handicapped students have more severe deficits (*Marshall et al. v. Georgia,* 1984; Reschly & Kicklighter, 1985). Even if there are differences in *degree* of deficit, but the general needs of these groups are similar, it might still be sensible to combine the systems and then attempt to match the intensity of the intervention to the degree of need.

Finally, the controversies concerning the overrepresentation of economically disadvantaged minority students in special education need to be underscored. The litigation on this issue has had a substantial influence on the Protection in Evaluation Procedures Provisions included in PL 94-142 (Bersoff, 1982; "Regulations Implementing Education for All Handicapped Children Act," 1977; Reschly, 1983, in press). Moreover, plaintiffs representing minority students have, in at least two instances, asked federal district courts to correct overrepresentation in programs for mildly retarded students and underrepresentation in programs for learning disabled students so that approximately the same proportions of white and black students would be found in learning disability and educable mental retardation programs. This request was granted in the case of *Mattie T. v. Holladay* (1979) but denied in *Marshall et al. v. Georgia* (1984). Plaintiffs' efforts to reduce placement rates in educable mental retardation programs and to increase placement rates in learning disability programs probably reflect the lesser degree of stigma associated with learning disability (Collins & Camblin, 1983). These contentions by plaintiffs also bring up the issue of the similarity between learning disability and educable mental retardation, a topic covered in the next section.

Learning Disability, Educable Mental Retardation, and Emotional Disturbance: Similarities and Differences

One of the most controversial issues in the education of exceptional children is whether the primary categories for the mildly handicapped categories of learning disability, educable or mild mental retardation, and emotional disturbance should be combined into a generic category that might simply be called mildly handicapped, or whether different categories and separate programming should continue. This can be a highly emotional issue, particularly among parents and teachers of learning disabled students, who generally are staunchly opposed to any merger of the learning disability classification or programs with classifications and associated programs of other mildly handicapping conditions. As noted in the previous section, advocates for minority groups have suggested either a merger of the categories or an elimination of the barriers that exist to greater numbers of minority students in learning disability programs (and, of course, fewer minority students in special classes for mildly retarded students). The major debate seems to be over the categories of learning disability and educable mental retardation and, to a lesser extent, the category of emotional disturbance. There are two important differences associated with the learning disability and educable mental retardation categories that further complicate study of this issue. First, there is considerably greater stigma associated with the educable mental retardation label than with the learning disability label. Apparently, if one has to experience failure in a public school setting, it is far better to have that failure attributed to learning disability than to educable mental retardation. The second difference between the two labels concerns their associated, typical placement options, with self-contained, largely segregated special class placement far more common with mildly retarded than with learning disabled students. The difference, then, between the learning disability and educable mental retardation categories is more than what name is attached to very low educational performance. The names themselves have considerable implications for the degree of stigma associated with classification and placement as well as for the kind of placement that might be assigned.

Although conducting studies comparing mildly retarded and learning disabled students would appear to be relatively easy (since there are considerable numbers of both kinds of students in most large school districts), there have been very few empirical studies published. Most of the literature in this area consists largely of the opinions of persons closely associated with learning disability services and of many professional special educators, who, generally, voice strong opposition to merging categories (e.g., Chandler & Jones, 1984; Gaar & Plue, 1983; Lieberman, 1980; Phipps, 1982). Very strong opposition to this sort of merger is also expressed by parents and others associated with learning disability advocacy groups. Much of this opposition does not appear in academic or professional journals but in state and national newsletters. This opposition should not be underestimated because these parents and advocates are often politically highly motivated and sophisticated. The likelihood of broad-scale reforms that might lead to a merger of categorical programs will depend upon either changing the minds of these persons or on developing a sufficiently large amount of political support to overcome their opposition.

Persons conducting research in special education, particularly those not directly tied to learning disabilities, frequently suggest that there is greater similarity than difference among the categories of learning disability, educable mental retardation, and emotional disturbance (Boucher & Deno, 1979; Hallahan & Kauffman, 1977; Neisworth & Greer, 1975). These scholars typically emphasize the similarities in kinds of educational needs as well as the fact that a common approach, now frequently termed direct instruction, works well with all three groups (see also Heller et al., 1982).

The relatively infrequent empirical studies of the similarities and differences among the three categories have yielded mixed results. Nearly everyone who has studied the issue has concluded that mildly retarded students typically obtain IQ scores below the IQ averages for learning disabled students, but the IQ differences are not as large as might be anticipated since samples of learning disabled students typically obtain IQ scores that are approximately halfway between the top score that can be used in the state for classification as mildly retarded and statewide averages. In other words, learning disabled students also typically obtain IQ scores below average, but not as far below average as the educable mentally retarded students (Becker, 1978; Gajar, 1979). Other studies have suggested that educable mentally retarded students score lower on conceptual tasks and are more field dependent than learning disabled students (Becker, 1978) and that non-task-oriented behavior, or being off task, varies for educable mentally retarded and learning disabled students (Sherry, 1981). Furthermore, Carri (1985) reported that teachers of learning disabled, educable mentally retarded, and behaviorally disordered students reported different continuing education needs, which may suggest that different skills are required for teaching these students. However, no data were reported on actual teaching behaviors, nor were there comparisons among teachers of students in different categories. Finally, McKinney and Forman (1982) reported different perceptions among teachers concerning the three categories. However, these different perceptions may be based more on stereotypes of the students involved rather than on actual differences in the students' behavior.

There is considerable opinion—but little empirical evidence—concerning the similarities and differences among mildly handicapped students. Reviews of the literature, particularly the literature on teaching methodology and instructional needs, suggest considerable similarity among mildly handicapped students, particularly between learning disabled and educable mentally retarded students. There clearly is, however, no evidence suggesting that the use of different remedial or compensatory education procedures depends on a student's classification. The same procedures apparently work with students with either classification. If the same procedures work for students with either classification, then the primary remaining question about whether or not the students ought to be grouped together has to do with the degree of difference, an essentially quantitative consideration, between the mildly handicapped groups. Further information on the degree of difference would certainly assist in settling this rather important issue.

The State of Practice

In this section, contemporary practices regarding classification, placement, and instructional interventions for mildly handicapped and low-achieving students are considered in relation to the current state of knowledge, with emphasis placed on discrepancies between what is known and what is currently implemented. However, prior to these considerations, some contemporary realities should be emphasized.

Contemporary Realities

Some of the recent literature concerning the education of handicapped students seems incredibly naive. It seems that some people believe that all that needs to be done is to apply better techniques of individualization, to stop labeling kids, and to inform regular education to do more for low-achieving students. These rather naive discussions usually fail to consider a number of realities of the contemporary educational scene. These realities are discussed briefly below.

Addressing Individual Differences

Individual differences. Individual differences in achievement are probably far greater than persons without intensive experience with both low- and high-achieving students are likely to understand. These differences are so large that very low achievers, by sixth- or seventh-grade level, may be unable to read textbooks written at a third-grade level or below. Interested persons without intensive experiences with very high-achieving and very low-achieving students are encouraged to examine samples of printed media carefully tied to grade-level standards. Many will be quite surprised at the magnitude of differences that exist. Furthermore, the absolute magnitude of individual differences probably increases as students progress through the grades, although relative positions within normative groups remain relatively stable. The fact is that individual differences are large and become increasingly problematic as students progress through the schooling experience.

Individualization and individual differences. Mastery learning and direct instruction procedures are sometimes suggested as sufficient means to cope with the magnitude of individual differences encountered in typical classrooms. The underlying assumption appears to be that very careful individualization will reduce the range of individual differences or, at least, enable low-achieving students to learn rapidly enough to prevent any further widening of discrepancies with average performance. This view is probably naive. When individualization of instruction is well implemented, the effects are likely to be experienced by all students, not just low-achieving students. The effects of greater individualization as well as those of more effective instruction will, in all likelihood, increase rather than diminish individual differences (Campione et al., 1982).

Multiple Dimensions

The literature reviewed in previous sections suggests rather strongly that students classified as mildly handicapped display a variety of problems. Problems exist not only in achievement and intelligence but also in a variety of information processing operations related to efficient acquisition, retention, and problem solving. In addition to these cognitive difficulties, mildly handicapped students also display problems in motivation, social skills, and self-efficacy. Effective programs for students now classified as mildly handicapped need to take into account these multiple problems rather than focus only on achievement (Deshler, Schumaker, & Lenz, 1984). Although improved achievement has a positive influence on these other problems, special programming for the broader social/affective deficits is still needed.

Sociopolitical Influences

School reform movement. The school reform movement, provoked in part by the report, *A Nation at Risk* (National Commission on Excellence in Education, 1983), may well be counterproductive with respect to greater tolerance for individual differences and the commitment of resources to remedial education programs. School reform has meant tougher academic standards, greater demands for achievement, and, very likely, less tolerance of persons who fail to meet tougher standards (Keith, 1982; Keith & Page, in press; Walberg, 1984).

Parent advocacy. A final contemporary reality is the influence of parent advocacy groups, particularly groups interested in learning disabilities. Efforts to reform current special education classification, programming, and instructional practices must take into account the influence of these groups. Efforts to change programs or to reduce resources now devoted to learning disabled students are especially likely to encounter strong opposition.

These contemporary realities are important considerations in evaluating the discrepancies between what is known and what might be implemented.

Interventions Needed by Mildly Handicapped and Low-Achieving Students

Recent reviews of eductional programming for mildly handicapped and low-achieving students have resulted in fairly good agreement on the characteristics of effective programs (Heller et al., 1982; Leinhardt, Bickel, & Pallay, 1982). These characteristics, as well as some of the programming dilemmas that must be addressed, are discussed in this section.

Direct Instruction

There is now nearly universal agreement that direct instruction is effective for low-achieving and mildly handicapped students. Direct instruction methods were described clearly about 20 years ago by Bereiter and Englemann (1966). The major features of direct instruction are clear specification of objectives, systematic presentation of content, high rate of learner response, frequent assessment and immediate feedback on performance, periodic review, and reinforcement for correct performance. The elements of this approach can be delivered in a variety of settings by means of a variety of techniques. Generally, however, small class size is a significant asset in carrying out direct instruction (Glass & Smith, 1978; Leinhardt et al., 1982).

Learning Efficiency

The second need of low-achieving students is for greater efficiency in processing information and in problem solving. Recognition of this need is based on recent studies in which information processing constructs were used to compare the learning performance of mildly handicapped and average-achieving students. Although problems with using results from contrasted groups are likely to apply here, there is evidence to suggest that the learning efficiency of low-achieving and/or mildly handicapped students can indeed be improved (Campione et al., 1982; Conner, 1983; Feuerstein, Haywood, Rand, & Hoffman, 1982; Hallahan & Sapona, 1984). The problem is the transfer and generalization of improved information processing skills. If broad generalization and transfer effects can be produced, it would make entirely good sense to emphasize information processing as a means to improve overall learning performance, which would then improve academic achievement. On the other hand, if broad transfer effects of information processing do not occur, there would likely be relatively little effect on achievement and intense conflict over whether to attempt to improve academic skills or broaden thinking skills.

Adult Adjustment

One of the most important kinds of evidence that should be considered in programming for mildly handicapped students comes from studies of transition from school to work and from longitudinal studies of the adult adjustment of students classified at school as mildly handicapped. Several such studies have been published (Baller, Charles, & Miller, 1967; Edgerton, 1967, 1984; Edgerton & Bercovici, 1976; Edgerton, Bollinger, & Herr, 1984). Similar studies have begun to appear recently concerning students classified as learning disabled (Deshler, Schumaker, Lenz, & Ellis, 1984; Horn, O'Donnell, & Vitulano, 1984; Vetter, 1983). These studies clearly indicate that mildly handicapped students continue to have problems in adjustment, caused, in part, by the same kinds of difficulties that led to their original referral, classification, and placement. The problems of mildly handicapped children do not simply disappear in adulthood, even though most mildly handicapped persons are not classified officially as handicapped during their adult years. Research clearly indicates continued problems with basic academic skills and abstract thinking operations, which create difficulties in social and vocational adjustment. These studies also suggest the importance of good social competencies and the availability of mechanisms that are useful in compensating for deficiencies in basic skills. These results as well as other information suggest certain dilemmas in programming for low-achieving or mildly handicapped students.

Programming Dilemmas

The dilemmas inherent in decisions about appropriate programming goals for mildly handicapped persons are apparent from a careful review of studies on longitudinal adjustment. The dilemmas were also described very well by Deshler, Schumaker, Lenz, and Ellis (1984) in the context of resolving the difficult problem of what to emphasize in the curriculum for adolescent learning disabled students. These investigators suggested that four different approaches to curriculum could be used: the tutorial, emphasis on basic skills remediation, compensatory instruction, or information processing strategies. A strong rationale for each of these emphases would not be hard to formulate, but determining which is most important for mildly handicapped, low-achieving students, particularly at higher grade levels, is extraordinarily difficult. The question becomes, Direct instruction on what? This problem is not easily resolved, since time and remedial resources are limited, and results of longitudinal studies suggest the importance of all of the possible emphases described above.

Classification, Placement, and Instruction

Efficacy of Special Education

The efficacy of special education has long been an intense concern (Carlberg & Kavale, 1980; Dunn, 1968; Johnson, 1962). This concern with effects of special programs has certainly not been restricted to special education (e.g., Glass, 1983; Glass, McGaw, & Smith, 1981; Jensen, 1969). Despite the general tenor of studies that indicate either modest or insignificant program effects, there clearly are some well-established findings concerning the effectiveness of programs. Perhaps the most important factor in improving efficacy in special education is the clear delineation of program objectives. If program objectives are clearly delineated, and direct instruction procedures are applied in smaller classes, there seems to be little question about whether such programming can be effective. The problem, though, lies in reaching a clear consensus on desirable program objectives and in delivering the necessary services for direct instruction to be effective. The lack of strong efficacy data supporting special education clearly indicates that some of these necessary requirements have not, to date, been met. There is, undoubtedly, much more that can be done to enhance direct instruction.

Prevalence and Incidence Concerns

Much of the current concern about contemporary practices has to do with the perception that excessive numbers of students are being classified as mildly handicapped. This appears to be a central concern in the work of the Minnesota group (see Ysseldyke et al. references) and of Gerber (1984). There is no unequivocal way to resolve this concern about excessive numbers. An analysis of this problem results in a near tautology, since mildly handicapped students are best understood by social system factors, which, in turn, are blamed by critics of excessive numbers as causing the problem. Before this topic is dismissed, though, as merely a matter of opinion, it is useful to cite estimates of the percentages of students regarded as handicapped from the pre-1975 era, prior to the time when mandatory special education established the funding basis for the systemic effects now observed. Kirk (1962), for example, suggested an overall prevalence of handicapped students for that era that is above current prevalence figures. Thus, the question of systemic effects and how many students ought to be classified as handicapped and served in special education really needs to be rephrased.

The relevant question should be, What is the most effective system for allocating scarce resources to enhance the academic skills and later adjustment of students who achieve at very low levels? One definite answer, it seems to me, is that the amount of time and energy now devoted to preplacement and reevaluations, which are dominated by determination of eligibility, represents an excessively costly and ineffective use of resources (Davis & Smith, 1984; Shepard, 1983). This excessive emphasis on determining eligibility, which in and of itself rarely has much to do with intervention, is one of the most obvious inefficiencies of the present system.

Assessment Problems

Much has already been said in the literature about the difficulties with the conception and assessment of learning disability. The only point needing further stress here is that reforms in the classification system and a variety of graduated interventions could render moot much of the debate over assessment and classification of students as learning disabled.

Recommendations

A number of reforms in the present system would go far toward alleviating some of the problems identified thus far as well as produce a closer match between what is known and what is done concerning the education of handicapped students. Four specific areas of reform are recommended here—the reform of the current classification system, the building of a closer relationship between regular and special education, the identification and use of finely graduated interventions, and a greater emphasis on prevention.

Reforms of the Classification System

Although formidable barriers exist to significant revisions in the present exceptional child classification system, reforms at various levels need to be undertaken. A modest reform in the current classification system, though an extremely important one in protecting students from excessive stigma (MacMillan, Jones, & Aloia, 1974), would be to separate the terminology now used to refer to the mild or educable level from that used to refer to the other levels of mental retardation. As noted earlier, the mild or educable level of mental retardation is substantially different on several important dimensions from the more severe levels of mental retardation. A revision in terminology for the mild level to, for example, *learning handicapped* or *educationally handicapped,* is long overdue. This change could be made with very little impact on the current classification system.

A somewhat more significant change would be to combine the mild handicap categories of learning disability, mild or educable mental retardation, and emotional disturbance. The new category might be called *mildly handicapped*, if it were absolutely necessary to continue to apply classifications to students. An even better method would be to label the interventions instead of the child, an idea advanced in an earlier effort to reform the classification system (Hobbs, 1975a, 1975b). One such intervention classification, *extraordinary educational service (EES),* was suggested by Leinhardt et al. (1982). We should not, however, delude ourselves about the long-term, salutary effects of changing names. Words or phrases that have entirely neutral meanings can acquire negative connotations quite rapidly. Some negative effects in the form of stigma will always accrue to any nomenclature that identifies students according to their learning problems. There are a variety of other ways that might be used to classify services rather than students. These, too, should be considered in classification system reform.

The kinds of reforms suggested here would contribute to the development of finely graduated interventions to be discussed later. By labeling services it may be possible to move away from the either/or, dichotomous kinds of decisions required today and toward decision-making options more consistent with the nature of mildly handicapping problems.

Closer Relationship Between Regular and Special Education

In order to implement the changes in the classification system suggested above as well as the finely graduated interventions described in the next section, massive changes will be required in the current relationship between regular and special education. The required changes are complicated by a host of factors, including legal precedents concerning the rights of handicapped students, current funding patterns, mandatory special education legislation, the interests of various constituencies, and, of course, the inertia associated with any well-entrenched system. However, basic research on learning phenomena and on the nature of individual differences in achievement and ability all suggest fine gradations over a rather large continuum from the average level through the level now associated with mildly handicapped students. As noted before, the cut-off points separating mildly handicapped students from those who are low-achieving are arbitrary. There are few, if any, meaningful differences between those students who barely meet eligibility requirements and those who just miss meeting eligibility requirements.

Another purpose of producing a closer regular and special education relationship is to improve the effectiveness of educational programs for all students (Hersh & Walker, 1983). Although the number of students who might be regarded as low achieving is entirely arbitrary, Leinhardt et al. (1982) suggested that about 20–25% of the student population might be regarded as achieving well below average and in need of remedial education services. A closer relationship between regular and special education would likely enhance the possibilities of providing appropriate services to greater numbers of students. The monies no longer required for expensive preplacement evaluations (see Davis & Smith, 1984; Shepard, 1983) might be reallocated to the development of other interventions.

One step toward a closer relationship between regular and special education would be a merger of Chapter 1 and special education services for mildly handicapped students, both of which provide remedial or compensatory education services to low-achieving students. Chapter 1 is now part of regular education, designed for economically disadvantaged students who also are low achieving (Carter, 1984; Leinhardt et al., 1982). Leinhardt et al. discussed the quite different assumptions and origins of Chapter 1 and special education programs for mildly handicapped students. However, they also noted the similarity in the needs displayed by students served in the programs as well as the commonality among the programs' effective instructional practices. However, the possible risks associated with merger of these programs also need to be considered. These risks include possible loss of resources and specialized training among special educators as well as loss of other features of Chapter 1, such as community action, which are important to producing stronger ties between schools and economically poor parents.

Further discussion of the risks associated with merger of programs was provided recently by Wang and Reynolds (1985). As these investigators noted, the "Catch-22" of special education reform is the loss of resources due to current funding patterns that require classification of students as handicapped in order for services to be provided. These services, in turn, are paid for from special education funds. Programs that declassify students, even when very effective, run the risk of eliminating scarce resources for the enlightened districts that implement such programs. This Catch-22 situation establishes the need for systemic changes (Reynolds & Wang, 1983) that would enable promising programs to be implemented over several years (Wang & Birch, 1984).

The systemic reforms suggested here, and discussed in far greater depth in other chapters of this work, are extraordinarily complicated. However, such reforms are needed in order to better reflect our knowledge of learning processes and individual differences. There are numerous barriers to such reforms, not the least of which is possible loss of resources.

Finely Graduated Interventions

Reform in the types of interventions used is needed to match the knowledge we have about individual differences and learning processes. If the classification and systemic reforms suggested above are made, the provision of graduated interventions, that is, a far greater set of remedial instruction or behavioral treatments than now exists, will be easier to establish. We now have several promising models for producing graduated interventions.

One model, reported by Wang and Birch (1984), involves use of an adaptive instruction approach to facilitate full-time mainstreaming. This program is apparently just as effective as the resource teaching program, by far the most popular of current special education placement options (Gerber, 1984). Implementation of this program in one large urban setting, however, was not continued because of the potential loss of special education monies. Further data are needed with respect to the program's effects over time, grade levels for which it is appropriate, and robustness in the range of interventions needed by mildly handicapped students in later grades. Nevertheless, it represents one type of graduated intervention—provision of special education services in regular classrooms—rather than the use of some sort of pull-out model.

A second example of a graduated intervention is the use of consultation services by related services personnel, such as psychologists, special education consultants, and social workers, as a means of developing interventions within regular classrooms. One of the strongest areas of development in special education today is prereferral intervention, which involves efforts to resolve learning or behavioral problems in regular education settings. Prereferral interventions may reduce the amount of testing by related services personnel, which, in turn, would allow more time for consultive and direct services to children. There are some reasonably well-established models for this kind of consultation service (Bergan, 1977; Bergan & Kratochwill, 1985; Graden, Casey, & Christianson, 1985). These consultive models involve the use of interviews with teachers, careful examination of educational records, and observations of students as the basis for the development of interventions that are usually carried out in regular classrooms by regular education personnel. Thus, the first response to referrals from teachers is not a preplacement evaluation involving a lot of testing designed to determine whether or not a student can be classified as handicapped. Rather, the first response is to develop interventions within regular education that may resolve the student's problem. Evaluation data related to consultive services are quite promising (Bergan, 1977; Graden, Casey, & Bonstrom, 1985). However, this is unlikely to be a panacea because there are, again, significant systemic barriers to the full implementation of these techniques (Graden, Casey, & Bonstrom, 1985; Piersel & Gutkin, 1983). Moreover, this approach may work well in the short term and with relatively younger students at lower grade levels, but it may be insufficient over the long term, especially with older students at higher grade levels. Further evaluation and research with the consultive approach is essential.

Another model worthy of mention is that provided by Hewett, Taylor, and Artuso (1968) a number of years ago in what was called the Santa Monica Project. This project involved fewer barriers between regular and special education, with nearly all students who had been placed in special education transferred back to regular education. The purpose of this program was to provide intensive experiences that would allow the students to return to regular education environments with additional skills designed to enhance their performance.

Many additional interventions could be developed for delivering special services to students. These options provide a better match to the nature of learning deficits and individual differences found with low-achieving and mildly handicapped students. Moreover, these options appear to have considerable promise for better utilization of existing resources.

Greater Emphasis on Prevention

A further consideration in reforming the present system is the placement of greater emphasis upon the prevention of low achievement and mildly handicapping conditions. Although the prevention literature is extremely complicated, with considerable doubt raised periodically about the effectiveness of compensatory programs such as Head Start and Follow Through (Jensen, 1969), there is evidence that mildly handicapping conditions, particularly among economically disadvantaged persons, can be prevented. The evidence in this area needs to be interpreted cautiously, particularly the results of the Milwaukee Project (Garber & Heber, 1981), which now are regarded as suspicious in some commentaries (Sommer & Sommer, 1983). However, a very well-conducted study (Ramey & Campbell, 1984) also reported promising, though not quite as astounding, results. The use of preventive educational treatments in the preschool years, or very early in the school careers of high-risk students (Feuerstein et al., 1982), is perhaps the most important reform, and, potentially, the most beneficial. Unfortunately, support for these kinds of programs has been difficult to establish and maintain, particularly in recent years with strong efforts on the part of governments at various levels to curtail spending on social programs.

Conclusions

Considerable controversies and numerous paradoxes exist today regarding classification, placement, and instructional programming for mildly handicapped students. Basic research in individual differences and learning processes suggests a number of deficiencies in present practices. Perhaps the greatest deficiency is the absence of finely graduated classification, placement, and instructional interventions. Finely graduated interventions, such as full-time mainstreaming with greater efforts toward individualization, consultation, and so on, appear to be promising alternatives to present practices, in which there are dichotomous decision making, considerable separation of special and regular education, and rather few instructional alternatives. Although there are numerous barriers to producing the changes that appear to be needed, including deficiencies in the knowledge base, the most compelling rationale for these changes is the possibility of more effective interventions for greater numbers of students at the same cost now expended on special and compensatory education programs. Concerted effort on the part of all of the major constituencies associated with special education is needed to expand the knowledge base needed for these changes, to change administrative structures and funding priorities, to develop and implement new skills, and to evaluate the effectiveness of innovative programs. The work involved with design, implementation, and evaluation of the regular-special education of the future will be challenging and exciting for everyone who makes a commitment to these changes.

Author Information

Daniel J. Reschly is Professor of Psychology at Iowa State University.

References

Adelman, H. S., & Taylor, L. (1983). *Learning disabilities in perspective.* Glenview, IL: Scott, Foresman.

Adelman, H. S., & Taylor, L. (1984). Enhancing motivation for overcoming learning and behavior problems. *Annual Review of Learning Disabilities,* **2**, 102–109.

Alesandrini, K. L. (1981). Pictorial-verbal and analytic-holistic learning strategies in science learning. *Journal of Educational Psychology,* **73**, 358-368.

Algozzine, B., & Korinek, L. (1985). Where is special education for students with high prevalence handicaps going? *Exceptional Children,* **51**, 388–394.

Algozzine, B., & Ysseldyke, J. (1983). Learning disabilities as a subset of school failure: The over-sophistication of a concept. *Exceptional Children,* **50**, 242–246.

Baller, W., Charles, D., & Miller, E. (1967). Mid-life attainment of the mentally retarded. *Genetic Psychology Monographs,* **75**(2), 235–329.

Bauer, R. H. (1979). Memory, acquisitions and category clustering in learning disabled children. *Journal of Experimental Child Psychology,* **27**, 365–383.

Becker, L. D. (1978). Learning characteristics of educationally handicapped and retarded children. *Exceptional Children,* **44**, 502–511.

Bennett, R. E., & Shepard, M. J. (1982). Basic measurement proficiency of learning disability specialists. *Learning Disability Quarterly,* **5**, 177–184.

Bereiter, C., & Englemann, S. (1966). *Teaching disadvantaged in the preschool.* New York: Prentice-Hall.

Bergan, J. (1977). *Behavioral consultation.* Columbus, OH: Merrill.

Bergan, J., & Kratochwill, T. (1985). *Behavioral consultation.* New York: Plenum.

Bernard, F., & Davis, J. K. (1982). Effect of field-independence match or mismatch on a communication task. *Journal of Educational Psychology,* **74**, 29–31.

Bersoff, D. N. (1982). The legal regulation of school psychology. In C. R. Reynolds & T. B. Gutkin (Eds.), *The handbook of school psychology* (pp. 1043–1074). New York: Wiley.

Bickel, W. E. (1982). Classifying mentally retarded students: A review of placement practices in special education. In K. A. Heller, W. H. Holtzman, & S. Messick (Eds.), *Placing children in special education: A strategy for equity* (pp. 182–229). Washington, DC: National Academy Press.

Borkowski, J. G., Peck, V. A., & Damberg, P. R. (1983). Attention, memory and cognition. In J. L. Matson & J. A. Mulick, *Handbook of mental retardation* (pp. 479–497). New York: Pergamon General Psychology Service.

Boucher, C. R., & Deno, S. L. (1979). Learning disabled and emotionally disturbed: Will the labels affect teacher planning? *Psychology in the Schools,* **16**, 395–402.

Brooks, P. H., & McCauley, C. (1984). Cognitive research in mental retardation. *American Journal of Mental Deficiency,* **88**, 479–486.

Bryan, T., & Bryan, J. (1978). Social interactions of learning disabled children. *Learning Disability Quarterly,* **1**, 33–38.

Bryan, T., Pearl, R., Donahue, M., Bryan, J., & Pflaum, S. (1983). The Chicago Institute for the Study of Learning Disabilities. *Exceptional Children Quarterly,* **4**, 1–22.

Burke, A. A. (1975). Placement of black and white children in educable mentally handicapped and learning disability classes. *Exceptional Children,* **41**, 438–439.

Campione, J. C., Brown, A. L., & Ferrara, R. A. (1982). Mental retardation and intelligence. In R. J. Sternberg (Ed.), *Handbook of human intelligence* (pp. 392–490). Cambridge, England: Cambridge University Press.

Carlberg, C., & Kavale, K. (1980). The efficacy of special versus regular class placement for exceptional children: A meta-analysis. *Journal of Special Education,* **14**, 295–309.

Carri, L. (1985). Inservice teachers' assessed needs in behavioral disorders, mental retardation, and learning disabilities: Are they similar? *Exceptional Children,* **51**, 411–416.

Carter, L. F. (1984). The sustaining effects study of compensatory and elementary education. *Educational Researcher,* **13**(1), 4–13.

Chan, K. S., & Rueda, R. (1979). Poverty and culture in education: Separate but equal. *Exceptional Children,* **45**, 422–428.

Chandler, H. N., & Jones, K. E. (1984). Learning disabled or emotionally disturbed: Does it make any difference? Part II. *Annual Review of Learning Disabilities,* **2**, 15–18.

Chinn, P. C. (1979). The exceptional minority child: Issues and some answers. *Exceptional Children,* **45**, 532–536.

Coles, G. S. (1978). The learning disabilities test battery: Empirical and social issues. *Howard Educational Review,* **48**, 313–340.

Collins, R., & Camblin, L. D. (1983). The politics and science of learning disability classification. *Contemporary Education,* **54**, 113–118.

Conner, F. P. (1983). Improving school instruction for learning disabled children: The Teachers College Institute. *Exceptional Child Quarterly,* **4**, 23–44.

Cromwell, R., Blashfield, R., & Strauss, J. (1975). Criteria for classification systems. In N. Hobbs (Ed.), *Issues in the classification of children* (pp. 4–25). San Francisco, CA: Jossey-Bass.

Cronbach, L. J., & Snow, R. E. (1977). *Aptitudes and instructional methods.* New York: Wiley (Halstead Press).

Davies, D. (1981). Intelligence related differences in semantic processing speed. *Journal of Experimental Child Psychology,* **31**, 387–402.

Davis, A., & Smith, M. L. (1984). The history and politics of an evaluation: The Colorado learning disabilities study. *Educational Evaluation and Policy Analysis,* **6**, 27–37.

Dean, R. S., & Kundert, D. K. (1981). Intelligence and teachers' ratings as predictors of abstract and concrete learning. *Journal of School Psychology,* **19**, 78–85.

Delaney, H. D. (1978). Interaction of individual differences with visual and verbal elaboration instructions. *Journal of Educational Psychology,* **70**, 306–318.

Deno, S. L., Mirkin, P. K., & Chiang, B. (1982). Identifying valid measures of reading. *Exceptional Children,* **49**, 36–45.

Deshler, D. D., Schumaker, J. B., & Lenz, B. K. (1984). Academic and cognitive interventions for LD adolescents. *Annual Review of Learning Disabilities,* **2**, 57–66.

Deshler, D. D., Schumaker, J. B., Lenz, B. K., & Ellis, E. (1984). Academic and cognitive intervention for LD adolescents: Part II. *Annual Review of Learning Disabilities,* **2**, 67–76.

Dunn, L. (1968). Special education for the mildly retarded: Is much of it justifiable? *Exceptional Children,* **35**, 5–22.

Edgerton, R. (1967). *The cloak of competence: Stigma in the lives of the mentally retarded.* Berkeley, CA: University of California Press.

Edgerton, R. B. (Ed.). (1984). *Lives in process: Mentally retarded adults in a large city.* Washington, DC: American Association on Mental Deficiency.

Edgerton, R., & Bercovici, S. (1976). The cloak of competence: Years later. *American Journal of Mental Deficiency,* **80**, 485–497.

Edgerton, R. B., Bollinger, M., & Herr, B. (1984). The cloak of competence: After two decades. *American Journal of Mental Deficiency,* **88**, 345–351.

Feuerstein, R., Haywood, H., Rand, Y., & Hoffman, M. (1982). *Examiner manuals for the learning potential assessment device.* Jerusalem, Israel: Hadassah-WIZO-Canada Research Institute.

Franks, D. J. (1971). Ethnic and social characteristics of children in EMR and LD classes. *Exceptional Children,* **37**, 537–538.

Gaar, B. L., & Plue, W. V. (1983). Separate vs. combined categories for mental retardation and specific learning disabilities. *Learning Disability Quarterly,* **6**, 77–79.

Gagne, R. E. (Ed.). (1967). *Learning and individual differences.* Columbus, OH: Merrill.

Gajar, A. (1979). Educable mentally retarded, learning disabled, and emotionally disturbed: Similarities and differences. *Exceptional Children,* **45**, 470–472.

Gallagher, J. (1972). The special education contract for mildly handicapped children. *Exceptional Children,* **38**, 527–535.

Garber, H. L., & Heber, R. (1981). The efficacy of early intervention with family rehabilitation. In M. J. Begab, H. C. Haywood, & H. L. Garber (Eds.), *Psychosocial influences in retarded performance. Vol. II. Strategies for improving competence* (pp. 71–87). Baltimore, MD: University Park Press.

Gerber, M. M. (1984). The Department of Education's Sixth Annual Report to Congress on PL 94–142: Is Congress getting the full story? *Exceptional Children,* **51**, 209–224.

Gettinger, M. (1983). Effects of learner ability and instructional modification on time needed for learning and retention. *Journal of Educational Research,* **76**, 362–369.

Glass, G. V. (1983). Effectiveness of special education. *Policy Studies Review,* **2**, 65–78.

Glass, G. V., McGaw, B., & Smith, M. L. (1981). *Meta-analysis in social research.* Beverly Hills, CA: Sage.

Glass, G. V., & Smith, M. L. (1978). *Meta-analysis of the research on the relationship of class size and achievement.* San Francisco, CA: Far West Laboratory for Educational Research and Development.

Graden, J. L., Casey, A., & Bonstrom, O. (1985). Implementing a prereferral intervention system: Part II. The data. *Exceptional Children,* **51**, 487–496.

Graden, J. L., Casey, A., & Christianson, S. L. (1985). Implementing a prereferral intervention system: Part I. The model. *Exceptional Children,* **51**, 377–384.

Gresham, F. (1982). Misguided mainstreaming: The case for social skills training with handicapped children. *Exceptional Children,* **48**, 422–433.

Gresham, F. M., & Reschly, D. J. (1986). Social skill deficits and low peer acceptance of mainstreamed learning disabled children. *Learning Disability Quarterly,* **9**, 23–32.

Grossman, H. J. (Ed.). (1983). *Classification in mental retardation.* Washington, DC: American Association on Mental Deficiency.

Hallahan, D., & Kauffman, J. (1977). Labels, categories, behaviors: ED, LD, and EMR reconsidered. *Journal of Special Education,* **11**, 139–149.

Hallahan, D. P., & Sapona, R. (1984). Self-monitoring of attention with learning disabled children: Past research and current issues. *Annual Review of Learning Disabilities,* **2**, 97–101.

Hammill, D., & Larsen, S. (1974). The effectiveness of psycholinguistic training. *Exceptional Children,* **41**, 5–14.

Hammill, D., & Larsen, S. (1978). The effectiveness of psycholinguistic training: A reaffirmation of position. *Exceptional Children,* **44**, 402–414.

Haywood, H. C. (1979). What happened to mild and moderate mental retardation? *American Journal of Mental Deficiency,* **83**, 429–431.

Heller, K., Holtzman, W., & Messick, S. (Eds.). (1982). *Placing children in special education: A strategy for equity.* Washington, DC: National Academy Press.

Henderson, R. (1980). Social and emotional needs of culturally diverse children. *Exceptional Children,* **46**, 598–605.

Henderson, R. W. (1981). Nonbiased assessment: Sociocultural consideration. In T. O. Oakland (Ed.), *Nonbiased assessment* (pp. 34–55). Minneapolis: University of Minnesota, National School Psychology Inservice Training Network.

Hersh, R. H., & Walker, H. M. (1983). Great expectations: Making schools effective for all children. *Policy Studies Review,* **2**, 147–188.

Hewett, F. M., Taylor, F. D., & Artuso, A. A. (1968). The Santa Monica Project. *Exceptional Children,* **34**, 387.

Hilliard, A. (1980). Cultural diversity and special education. *Exceptional Children,* **46**, 584–588.

Hobbs, N. (1975a). *The futures of children.* San Francisco, CA: Jossey-Bass.

Hobbs, N. (Ed.). (1975b). *Issues in the classification of children.* (Vols. 1–2). San Francisco, CA: Jossey-Bass.

Holtan, B. (1982). Aptitude × treatment interaction research in mathematics education. *School Science and Mathematics,* **82**, 593–602.

Horn, W. F., O'Donnell, J. P., & Vitulano, L. A. (1984). Long-term follow-up studies of learning disabled persons. *Annual Review of Learning Disabilities,* **2**, 77–90.

James, M. A., & Knief, L. A. (1978). Interaction of general, fluid, and crystallized ability and instruction in sixth-grade mathematics. *Journal of Educational Psychology,* **70**, 319–323.

Jensen, A. R. (1969). How much can we boost IQ and scholastic achievement? *Harvard Educational Review,* **39**, 1–123.

Johnson, G. O. (1962). The mentally handicapped: A paradox. *Exceptional Children,* **29**, 62–69.

Kauffman, J., & Hallahan, D. (1974). The medical model and the science of special education. *Exceptional Children,* **41**, 97–102.

Kavale, K. (1980). Learning disability and cultural-economic disadvantage: The case for a relationship. *Learning Disability Quarterly,* **3**, 97–112.

Keith, T. Z. (1982). Time spent on homework and high school grades: A large-sample path analysis. *Journal of Educational Psychology,* **74**, 248–253.

Keith, T. Z., & Page, E. B. (in press). Homework works at school: National evidence for policy changes. *School Psychology Review.*

Keogh, B. K. (1983). Classification, compliance, and confusion. *Journal of Learning Disabilities,* **16**, 25.

Kirk, S. A. (1962). *Educating exceptional children.* Boston: Houghton Mifflin.

Kulik, C. L., & Kulik, J. A. (1982). Effects of ability grouping on secondary school students: A meta-analysis of evaluation findings. *American Educational Research Journal,* **19**, 415–428.

Leinhardt, G., Bickel, W., & Pallay, A. (1982). Unlabeled but still entitled: Toward more effective remediation. *Teachers College Record,* **84**, 391–422.

Lieberman, L. M. (1980). The implications of non-categorical special education. *Journal of Learning Disabilities,* **13**, 65–68.

Lund, K., Foster, G., & McCall-Perez, F. (1978). The effectiveness of psycholinguistic training: A reevaluation. *Exceptional Children,* **44**, 310–321.

Mackie, R. P. (1968). The handicapped benefit under compensatory education programs. *Exceptional Children,* **34**, 603–606.

MacMillan, D. (1982). *Mental retardation in school society* (2nd ed.). Boston, MA: Little, Brown.

MacMillan, D., & Borthwick, S. (1980). The new educable mentally retarded population: Can they be mainstreamed? *Mental Retardation,* **18**, 155–158.

MacMillan, D., Jones, R., & Aloia, G. (1974). The mentally retarded label: A theoretical analysis and review of research. *American Journal of Mental Deficiency,* **79**, 241–261.

MacMillan, D., Meyers, C. E., & Morrison, G. (1980). System-identification of mildly mentally retarded children: Implications for interpreting and conducting research. *American Journal of Mental Deficiency,* **85**, 108–115.

Marshall et al. v. Georgia, CV482-233. (U.S. District Court for the Southern District of Georgia, 1984).

Mattie T. v. Holladay, C. A. No. 75-31-S. (U.S. District Court for the Northern District of Mississippi, 1979).

McGivern, J. E., & Levin, J. R. (1983). The keyword method and children's vocabulary learning: An interaction with vocabulary knowledge. *Contemporary Educational Psychology,* **8**, 46–54.

McKinney, J. D. (1983). Contributions of the institutes for research on learning disability. *Exceptional Education Quarterly,* **4**(1), 129–144.

McKinney, J. D., & Forman, S. G. (1982). Classroom behavior patterns of EMH, LD, and EH students. *Journal of School Psychology,* **20**, 271–279.

Mercer, C. D., Hughes, C., & Mercer, A. R. (1985). Learning disabilities definitions used by state education departments. *Learning Disability Quarterly,* **8**, 45–55.

Mercer, J. (1979). *System of multicultural pluralistic assessment technical manual.* New York: Psychological Corporation.

Mercer, J., & Ysseldyke, J. (1977). Designing diagnostic-intervention programs. In T. Oakland (Ed.), *Psychological and educational assessment of minority children* (pp. 70–90). New York: Brunner/Mazel.

Meyers, C., MacMillan, D., & Yoshida, R. (1978). Validity of psychologists' identification of EMR students in the perspective of the California decertification experience. *Journal of School Psychology,* **16**, 3–15.

Minskoff, E. (1975). Research on psycholinguistic training: Critique and guidelines. *Exceptional Children,* **42**, 136–144.

National Commission on Excellence in Education. (1983). *A nation at risk: The imperative for educational reform.* Washington, DC: Author.

Neer, W., Foster, D., Jones, J., & Reynolds, D. (1973). Socioeconomic bias in the diagnosis of mental retardation. *Exceptional Children,* **40**, 38–39.

Neisworth, J., & Greer, J. (1975). Functional similarities of learning disability and mild retardation. *Exceptional Children,* **42**, 17–21.

Newcomer, R., Larsen S., & Hammill, D. (1975). A response to Minskoff. *Exceptional Children,* **42**, 144–148.

Pascarella, E. T., Pflaum, S. W., Bryan, T. H., & Pearl, R. A. (1984). Interaction of internal attribution for effort and teacher response mode in recoding instruction: A replication note. *American Educational Research Journal,* **20**, 269–276.

Patrick, J., & Reschly, D. (1982). Relationship of state educational criteria and demographic variables to school-system prevalence of mental retardation. *American Journal of Mental Deficiency,* **86**, 351–360.

Peterson, P. L. (1979). Aptitude × treatment interaction effects of teacher structuring and student participation in college instruction. *Journal of Educational Psychology,* **71**, 521–533.

Peterson, P. L. (1981). Aptitude × treatment interaction effects on children's large group and small group approaches. *American Educational Research Journal,* **18**, 453–473.

Phipps, P. M. (1982). The merging categories: Appropriate education or administrative convenience. *Journal of Learning Disabilities,* **15**, 153–154.

Piersel, W. C., & Gutkin, T. B. (1983). Resistance to school-biased consultation: A behavioral analysis of the problem. *Psychology in the Schools,* **20**, 311–320.

Polloway, E. A., & Epstein, M. H. (1985). Current research issues in mild mental retardation: A survey of the field. *Education and Training of the Mentally Retarded,* **20**, 171–174.

Polloway, E. A., & Smith, J. D. (1983). Changes in mild mental retardation: Population, programs, and perspectives. *Exceptional Children,* **50**, 149–159.

Procedures for evaluation specific learning disabilities. (1977). *Federal Register,* **42**(250), pp. 65082–65085.

Ramey, C. T., & Campbell, F. A. (1984). Preventive education for high risk children: Cognitive consequences of the Carolina Abecedarian Project. *American Journal of Mental Deficiency,* **88**, 515–523.

Regulations Implementing Education for All Handicapped Children Act of 1975 (Public Law 94–142). (1977). *Federal Register*, **42**(163), pp. 42474–42518.

Reschly, D. (1979). Nonbiased assessment. In G. Phye & D. Reschly (Eds.), *School psychology: Perspectives and issues* (pp. 215–253). New York: Academic Press.

Reschly, D. (1981a). Evaluation of the effects of SOMPA measures on classification of students as mildly mentally retarded. *American Journal of Mental Deficiency*, **86**, 16–20.

Reschly, D. (1981b). Psychological testing in educational classification and placement. *American Psychologist*, **36**, 1094–1102.

Reschly, D. (1982). Assessing mild mental retardation: The influence of adaptive behavior, sociocultural status and prospects for nonbiased assessment. In C. Reynolds & T. Gutkin (Eds.), *The handbook of school psychology* (pp. 209–242). New York: Wiley Interscience.

Reschly, D. (1983). Legal issues in psychoeducational assessment. In G. Hynd (Ed.), *The school psychologist: Contemporary perspectives* (pp. 67–93). Syracuse, NY: Syracuse University Press.

Reschly, D. J. (1984). Beyond IQ test bias: The national academy panel's analysis of minority EMR overrepresentation. *Educational Researcher*, **13**(3). 15–19.

Reschly, D. (1986). Economic and cultural factors in childhood exceptionality. In R. Brown & C. Reynolds (Eds.), *Psychological perspectives on childhood exceptionality* (pp. 423–466). New York: Wiley.

Reschly, D. (in press). Assessing educational handicaps. In A. Hess & I. Weiner (Eds.), *Handbook of Forensic Psychology*. New York: Wiley.

Reschly, D. J., Gresham, F. M., & Graham-Clay, S. (1984). *Multi-factored nonbiased assessment: Convergent and discriminant validity of social and cognitive measures with black and white regular and special education students.* Final Project Report. Ames: Iowa State University, Department of Psychology. (ERIC Document Reproduction Service No. ED 252034)

Reschly, D. J., & Jipson, F. J. (1976). Ethnicity, geographic locale, age, sex, and urban–rural residence as variables in the prevalence of mild retardation. *American Journal of Mental Deficiency*, **81**, 154–161.

Reschly, D. J., & Kicklighter, R. J. (1985, August). *Comparison of black and white EMR students from Marshall v. Georgia.* Paper presented at the Annual Convention of the American Psychological Association, Los Angeles, CA. (ERIC Document Reproduction Service No. ED 271911)

Reynolds, C. R. (1981). Neuropsychological assessment and the habitation learning: Considerations in the search for aptitude × treatment interaction. *School Psychology Review*, **10**, 343–349.

Reynolds, C. R. (1984). Measurement issues in learning disabilities. *Journal of Special Education*, **18**, 445–471.

Reynolds, M. C., & Wang, M. C. (1983). Restructuring "special" school programs: A position paper. *Policy Studies Review*, **2**, 189–212.

Richmond, B. O., & Waits, C. (1978). Special education—Who needs it? *Exceptional Children*, **44**, 279–280.

Robinson, N., & Robinson, H. (1976). *The mentally retarded child* (2nd ed.). New York: McGraw-Hill.

Salvia, J., & Ysseldyke, J. (1985). *Assessment in special and remedial education* (3rd ed.). Boston, MA: Houghton Mifflin.

Sattler, J. M. (1982). *Assessment of children's intelligence and special abilities* (2nd ed.). Boston, MA: Allyn & Bacon.

Schumaker, J. B., Deshler, D. D., Alley, G. R., & Warner, M. M. (1983). Toward the development of an intervention model for learning disabled adolescents: The University of Kansas Institute. *Exceptional Evaluation Quarterly*, **4**, 45–74.

Scott. L. S. (1979, August). *Identification of declassified students: Characteristics and needs of the population.* Paper presented at the Annual Convention of the American Psychological Association, New York.

Shepard, L. A. (1983). The role of measurement in educational policy: Lessons from the identification of learning disabilities. *Educational Measurement: Issues and Practice*, **2**, 4–8.

Shepard, L., & Smith, M. L. (1981). *Evaluation of the identification of perceptual-communicative disorders in Colorado: Final Report.* Boulder: University of Colorado, College of Education. (ERIC Document Reproduction Service No. ED 216037)

Sherry, L. (1981). Non-task oriented behaviors of educable mentally retarded, emotionally handicapped, and learning disabled students. *Educational Research Quarterly*, **6**(1), 19–29.

Short, E. J., & Ryan, E. B. (1984). Metacognitive differences between skilled and less skilled readers: Remediating deficits through story grammar and attribution training. *Journal of Educational Psychology*, **76**, 225–235.

Snow, R. E. (1978). Theory and method for research on aptitude processes. *Intelligence*, **2**, 225–278.

Snow, R. E. (1980). Aptitude and achievement. In W. B. Schrader (Ed.), *Measuring achievement: Progress over a decade? New directions for testing and measurement* (pp. 99–131). San Francisco, CA: Jossey-Bass.

Snow, R. E. (1984). Placing children in special education: Some comments. *Educational Researcher*, **13**(1), 12–14.

Sommer, R., & Sommer, B. A. (1983). Mystery in Milwaukee: Early intervention, IQ, and psychology textbooks. *American Psychologist*, **38**, 982–985.

Swanson, L. (1982). Conceptual process as a function of age and enforced attention in learning disabled children: Evidence for deficient rule learning. *Contemporary Educational Psychology*, **7**, 152–160.

Tucker, J. (1980). Ethnic proportions in classes for the learning disabled: Issues in nonbiased assessment. *Journal of Special Education*, **14**, 93–105.

United States Department of Education. (1984). *Executive summary: Sixth annual report to Congress on the Implementation of Public Law 94–142: The Education for All Handicapped Children Act.* Washington, DC: Office of Special Education Programs.

United States Department of Education. (1985). *Executive summary: Seventh annual report to Congress on the Implementation of Public Law 94–142: The Education for All Handicapped Children Act.* Washington, DC: Office of Special Education Programs.

Van Der Linden, W. J. (1981). Using aptitude measures for the optimal assignment of subjects to treatments with and without mastery scores. *Psychometrica*, **46**, 257–274.

Veldman, D. J., & Sanford, J. P. (1984). The influence of class ability level on student achievement and classroom behavior. *American Educational Research Journal*, **21**, 29–44.

Vetter, A. A. (1983). *A comparison of the characteristics of learning disabled and non-learning disabled young adults.* Unpublished doctoral dissertation. University of Kansas, Lawrence.

Walberg, H. J. (1984). Improving the productivity of America's schools. *Educational Leadership*, **41**, 19–30.

Wang, M. C., & Birch, J. W. (1984). Comparison of a full-time mainstreaming program and a resource room approach. *Exceptional Children,* **51**, 33–40.

Wang, M. C., & Reynolds, M. C. (1985). Avoiding the "Catch 22" in special education reform. *Exceptional Children,* **51**, 497–502.

Winn, W. (1980). The effect of block-word diagrams on the structuring of science concepts as a function of general ability. *Journal of Research in Science Teaching,* **17**, 201–211.

Yoshida, R., MacMillan, D., & Meyers, C. (1976). The decertification of minority group EMR students in California: Student achievement and adjustment. In R. Jones (Ed.), *Mainstreaming and the minority child* (pp. 215–233). Reston, VA: Council for Exceptional Children.

Ysseldyke, J. E., & Algozzine, B. (1984). *Introduction to special education.* Boston, MA: Houghton Mifflin.

Ysseldyke, J., Algozzine, B., & Epps, S. (1983). A logical and empirical analysis of current practice in classifying students as handicapped. *Exceptional Children,* **50**, 160–166.

Ysseldyke, J., Algozzine, B., Shinn, M., & McGue, M. (1982). Similarities and differences between underachievers and students labeled as learning disabled. *Journal of Special Education,* **16**, 73–85.

Ysseldyke, J., Algozzine, B., & Thurlow, M. (1983). On interpreting institute research: A response to McKinney. *Exceptional Child Quarterly,* **4**, 145–147.

Ysseldyke, J. E., & Mirkin, P. K. (1982). The use of assessment information to plan instructional interventions: A review. In C. R. Reynolds & T. B. Gutkin (Eds.), *The handbook of school psychology* (pp. 395–409). New York: Wiley.

Ysseldyke, J. E., & Salvia, J. (1980). Methodological considerations in aptitude-treatment interaction research with intact groups. *Diagnostique,* **6**, 3–9.

Ysseldyke, J. E., Thurlow, M., Graden, J., Wesson, C., Algozzine, B., & Deno, S. (1983). Generalizations from five years of research on assessment and decision making: The University of Minnesota Institute. *Exceptional Education Quarterly,* **4**(1), 75–93.

Zigler, E. (1962). Rigidity in the feebleminded. In E. P. Trapp & P. Himelstein (Eds.), *Readings on the exceptional child* (pp. 141–162). New York: Appleton-Century Crofts.

The Role of The Learner: An Individual Difference Variable in School Learning and Functioning

MARGARET C. WANG

Temple University Center for Research in Human Development and Education

STEPHEN T. PEVERLY

Teachers College, Columbia University

Abstract—Recent theoretical advances and expanded empirical bases on the processes of learning and effective teaching suggest the educational value of developing competencies and attitudes that enable students to learn in an active and deliberate manner. These findings, however, have had little influence on the design and implementation of practices for improving learning efficiency and effectiveness. This chapter focuses on the rationale and design of a conceptual model for the study of the self-instructive process in classroom learning situations. One major premise of the model's design is that variations in students' ability to be self-instructive are an individual-difference variable that has significant implications for systemic instructional planning and for student learning outcomes. The chapter includes: a discussion of students' perceptions of personal control over and development of self-responsibility for their learning and a discussion of the findings from intervention research; an overview of the conceptual model; an explication of contemporary theories and the empirical basis for the conception of the active mediating function that students play in their own learning, and a discussion of the relationship between the self-instructive process in learning and the dynamic interactions between the personal characteristics of individual students and a given classroom learning environment; and a proposed program of research to develop a descriptive data base on the role of the learner in classroom learning situations and to conduct experiments in instructional design to create learning environments and encourage teaching practices that foster the development and use of self-instructive skills in learning.

A prominent and recurring theme in the history of school reform efforts has been the recognition that one fundamental task of effective schooling is to enable individual students to become active learners who assume responsibility for acquiring knowledge and skills and sustain a pattern of self-directed, lifelong learning. Recent theoretical advances and expanded empirical work on the nature of learning and instruction and the effects of innovative educational programming provide a rich research base for analyzing and characterizing the role of the learner in knowledge and skills acquisition. The twofold purpose of this chapter is to synthesize major findings from a review of this research base and to discuss their implications for examining the role that students are required to play as they learn and cope with the intellectual and social demands of schooling.

Specifically, this chapter reports the findings from a review of contemporary theories, research, and practices concerning the role of the learner in the learning process. It advances the conceptualization of the active role that learners play in their learning as an individual difference variable with significant implications for furthering understanding of the functioning of successful and less successful students in their learning process and for the design of effective instruction. The present review of research on the role of the learner focuses on two critical categories of learner competence: students' ability to be responsible for their own learning and behavior, and students' ability to be self-instructive in the learning process. The former refers to perceptions of self-responsibility as well as capabilities for assuming self-responsibility. The latter category of competence is concerned with the ability to effectively coordinate the relationship of one's own cognitive and affective characteristics with the structure and demands of learning tasks and the task environment.

It is important to note at the outset that, although an extensive and intensive attempt was made in identifying source material for the present review to locate studies focusing on the learning of students with special learning needs, the limited extant data base in special education made it necessary to draw primarily from the literature on research and practice related to learning and classroom instruction in the context of regular education. Nevertheless, it is anticipated that the findings from this review will have significant implications for broadening our knowledge and ability to improve the chances of schooling success for all students, including, and particularly, those students who are identified as academically at risk; those receiving services under compensatory programs such as Chapter 1; and/or those classified as mildly handicapped (i.e., students who are classified as learning disabled, educable mentally retarded, or socially and emotionally disturbed).

The present review is based on an integrative analysis of the results of the work of three groups of researchers: cognitive psychologists interested in the cognitive and metacognitive processes underlying knowledge and skills development, social psychologists whose work in social cognition and achievement motivation focuses on the learner's perception of self-control and self-competence, and researchers interested in the study of students' mediating function in classroom learning situations and in innovative practices that foster self-instruction and promote student self-responsibility.

The next two major sections consist of discussions of findings from a review of the extant research base related to the characterization and development of two categories of learner competence: self-responsibility for learning and behavior, and the self-instructive process for mediating learning. The concluding section of the chapter presents an agenda for research and innovative program development aimed at increasing students' competence as active, self-responsible, and self-instructive learners.

Self-Responsibility for Learning

The conception of successful learners as those who are capable of assuming responsibility for their learning and behavior is grounded in theory and research that posit a close relationship between school achievement and students' perceptions of their ability to exert personal control over their learning (Coleman, Campbell, Hobson, McPartland, Mood, Weinfeld, & York, 1966; Crandall, Katkovsky, & Crandall, 1965; Dweck & Elliot, 1983; McCombs, 1982a; Nicholls, 1979; Thomas, 1980; Uguroglu & Walberg, 1979). Research in this area has shown that students who believe they can influence their learning are more likely to succeed than those who believe that learning is controlled by powerful others (e.g., teachers) or that achievement is related to a stable intelligence unaffected by effort (Dweck & Elliot, 1983). Success in learning also strengthens students' perceptions of self-competence and personal control, whereas repeated failure weakens such perceptions. Furthermore, perceptions of self-competence and personal control tend, in turn, to instill a desire to learn new skills and meet new schooling challenges.

Theories and investigations of the "self" as a learner have generated a multiplicity of definitions. They include constructs such as self-efficacy, self-competence, locus of control, and self-responsibility. Two common elements of the widely varying definitions are a concern with students' perceptions of the source of control over their academic achievement and rewards—either internal control (e.g., personal competence, effort) or external control (e.g., luck, task difficulty)—and a concern with the subsequent implications for school learning. Investigators interested in the social-psychological determinants of learning have generally based their studies on the relationship between success in learning and perceptions of self on two interrelated hypotheses: that academic achievement fosters a positive perception of self; and that a positive perception of self is associated with achievement motivation, which, in turn, influences student behavior and learning.

Research aimed at examining perceptions of self as an antecedent of successful learning generally focuses either on investigations and theoretical formulations of causal relationships between perceptions of self and achievement or on intervention studies designed to foster the development of positive perceptions of self. Among the efforts with the former research focus are Bandura's (1977) conception of self-efficacy and learning; the work of Covington and his associates (Covington & Beery, 1976; Covington & Omelich, 1979) on the relationship between the development of perceptions of self-worth and school learning; the formulation of relationships between perceptions of locus of control and learning (Lefcourt, 1982; Rotter, 1966); Weiner's (1976, 1979) theory of motivation, based on attributions of causality for success and failure; the self-evaluation maintenance model developed by Tesser and Campbell (1982) for examining school performance in relation to students' self-definitions; and Wang's (1983) conceptual analysis of the development of students' perceptions of, and competence in, taking self-responsibility for learning. Instructional intervention research in this area generally includes investigations aimed at developing students' perceptions of control over their learning behaviors and processes (e.g., deCharms, 1976; Heckhausen & Krug, 1982; McCombs, 1982b; Wang & Stiles, 1976b); increasing the effectiveness of attribution training (e.g., Dweck, 1975; Schunk, 1982; Weiner, 1983); and developing perceptions of self-competence and efficacy (e.g., Bandura & Schunk, 1981; Schunk, 1984a).

Perceptions of Personal Control and School Learning

Researchers and practitioners alike have paid much attention to both the general concept of personal control and the specific nature of the relationship between perceptions of personal control and school performance. Two areas of research in particular—how students feel about themselves as learners, and how much control they feel over their life situations (e.g., events, behavior, consequences)—have been shown to be positively related to school learning processes and outcomes. Perceptions of personal control have been a topic of central concern, particularly in research aimed at examining correlates of academic success, whether these perceptions have to do with control over personal behavior or with the outcomes of an event. In other words, success or failure is viewed as less important than a student's perception of the causes of the success or failure. A basic premise of research in this area is that success enhances self-perceptions of competence only if a student perceives or accepts responsibility for success. Students' perceptions of their ability, and students' expectations of success or failure, have important and enduring effects on their school learning behavior. Performance improves when students accept responsibility for their success and understand that effort on their part can overcome failure.

Rotter's concept of locus of control (Rotter, 1966) has greatly influenced research in this area. According to Rotter, an individual identifies the force responsible for an experience as either internal or external. Individuals with an internal locus of control perceive themselves as determining events in their environment; those whose locus of control is external perceive forces outside themselves as determining such events. Although the specific definition of locus of control has varied from study to study, Rotter's formulation has been the basis of most definitions.

The theoretical and empirical bases for hypothesizing an interrelationship among internal locus of control, positive attitudes toward mastery, and competence behavior in both children and adults have been noted in the literature. Bandura (1981), for example, postulated that the ability to process information conveyed by an event, weigh all elements of the situation, and then organize and execute necessary actions is intrinsically related to perceptions of self-efficacy and self-competence. Furthermore, these perceptions are thought to influence students' choices of activities, work situations, and persons with whom to interact and work, as well as the amount of effort, vigor, and persistence expended on learning.

An internal locus of control has been noted to be positively related to outcomes such as classroom participation, academic performance, and scores on academic achievement tests (cf. Findley & Cooper, 1983). One major finding of the Findley and Cooper (1983) meta-analysis of nearly 100 research reports was the significant and positive relationship between locus of control and academic achievement. Evidence also suggests a relationship between students' sense of personal control and their tendencies to seek and use information in problem solving (Davis & Phares, 1967; Phares, 1968) and to persist in difficult intellectual tasks (Crandall, 1966; Gagné & Parshall, 1975; Gordon, Jones, & Short, 1977). Students with an internal locus of control have been found to demonstrate greater reflectivity and attentiveness, as well as better performance and higher rates of knowledge acquisition, than students with an external locus of control (Chance, 1968).

In their formulation of the relationship between perceptions of self-worth and school achievement, Covington and Beery (1976) stressed that feelings of personal efficacy and self-worth must be considered in any complete understanding of the dynamics of school achievement behavior. They contended that "the individual's sense of worth is threatened by the belief that his value as a person depends on his ability to achieve, and that if he is incapable of succeeding, he will not be worthy of love and approval" (p. 6). In a similar vein, Weiner's (1979) analysis of the motivation for classroom achievement from the perspective of attributional theory suggests that the source of information can have a causal effect on achievement. The underlying assumption is that the "search for understanding is the (or a) 'spring of action'" (p. 3). One postulate of attributional theory is that perceptions of the reasons for an event are important determinants of subsequent action and that modifications of perceptions of causality produce different actions (Weiner, 1983).

The results of a series of studies of the role of perceived causes (attribution) in the alteration of learned helplessness (Diener & Dweck, 1978, 1980; Dweck, 1975) support the hypothesis of a relationship between perceptions of causes (in this case, helplessness) and school achievement. These findings indicate that students oriented toward helplessness differed in several important ways from students oriented toward mastery. Students in the former group tended to perceive failure as indicative of low ability, whereas those in the latter group tended to attribute failure to modifiable factors such as effort. Moreover, there is evidence that persons can be trained to attribute success to effort and that such training can result in greater persistence in the face of failure (Andrews & Debus, 1978; Chapin & Dyck, 1976).

The interrelationship between students' perceptions of agency and achievement is also suggested in work based on the competence-motivation theories of White (1959) and others (e.g., Deci, 1975; Harter, 1974). According to these theorists, a child's intrinsic motivation to learn and his or her mastery of a task produce feelings of efficacy and competence that, in turn, reinforce further attempts at mastery. Harter, for one, has found that the pleasure of mastery is greatest when the subject accepts responsibility for success (Harter, 1974, 1982).

Overall, the relationship between students' perceptions of self and their performance in school seems evident from the empirical evidence of research that has addressed this matter from diverse theoretical perspectives. An underlying premise of work in this area is that the amount of personal control students perceive themselves as having is an individual difference variable in learning, and such a conceptualization has significant implications for furthering understanding of individual differences in processes of learning and academic achievement. Research suggests that persons who believe they can control their destinies are likely to use previously learned skills to acquire new skills (Baird & White, 1982; Lefcourt, 1982; Paris, Lipson, & Wixson, 1983), and perceptions of increasing personal control can lead to greater self-responsibility, achievement motivation, and learning (Bandura, 1982; Findley & Cooper, 1983; Schunk, 1984b; Stipek & Weisz, 1981; Thomas, 1980; Wang, 1983). Thus, although the locus of control construct may have different meanings or emphases in the work of researchers with various theoretical perspectives, its centrality to student learning seems clear.

Development of Self-Responsibility for Learning

The research on the relationship between students' sense of personal control and their assumption of responsibility for the social and academic outcomes of their schooling (e.g., Coleman et al., 1966; Crandall, Katkovsky, & Preston, 1962; Stallings & Kaskowitz, 1974) has been the impetus for parallel developments in instructional interventions aimed at fostering students' perceptions of personal control over their learning environment and behavior. Findings from intervention research in this area have shown that special instructional interventions can change an individual's perception of locus of control and that changes in an individual's perception of locus of control, in turn, influence learning.

Shore, Milgram, and Malasky (1971) reported, for example, that their educational enrichment program, compared to programs in regular classrooms, contributed to changes in children's feelings of control over their environment. Children from 5 to 7 years of age who participated in the enrichment program became significantly more internally oriented. deCharms (1972) found that personal causation training resulted in changes in behavior related to locus of control. Similarly, a study of inner-city adolescents by Nowicki and Barnes (1973) showed that a highly structured summer camp experience, which focused on the relationship between behavior and reinforcement, tended to strengthen internal control. The data from Reimanis' (1974) investigations, in which attempts were made to deliberately alter the locus of control of students in different age groups, also corroborate other findings in this area.

Evidence of the positive influence of educational environments that promote student autonomy and choice and encourage students to take responsibility for their learning and behavior is also noted in the findings from a series of intervention studies conducted by Wang and her associates (e.g., Wang, 1983; Wang & Birch, 1984a, 1984b; Wang, Peverly, & Randolph, 1984). The findings from these studies, which were conducted in preschool and elementary grades and in classes that included moderately and mildly handicapped mainstreamed students, consistently show that teaching and expecting students to assume responsibility for their learning and behavior generally produced significant increases in their task completion rates and their perceptions of personal control and self-competence.

Further demonstration of the performance effects of students' perceptions of self-responsibility comes from the work of Arlin and Whitley (1978), Matheny and Edwards (1974), and Wang and Walberg (in press). Data from the Arlin and Whitley study suggest that the number of opportunities students had to control their learning affected their perceptions of the amount of control they had over their learning outcomes. In their study of exemplary classrooms of eight different instructional models, Wang and Walberg found a significant relationship between achievement and students' sense of personal control in classrooms where certain program design features were implemented to promote autonomy and choice and where students were taught and expected to be responsible for their own learning and behavior.

The implications of intervention research for the development and consequences of students' self-responsibility for learning are evidenced by research findings. They support the hypothesis of a relationship among students' perceptions of personal control, development of self-responsibility, and school performance, and, furthermore, they suggest that an individual's sense of agency is malleable.

Perceptions of Personal Control and Handicapped Students' Learning

Findings on the relationship between perceptions of personal control and school success suggest the wisdom of including the development of students' sense of self-responsibility as an educational goal. This is particularly crucial for students who have histories of academic failure and poor perceptions of self-competence and personal control—characteristics that are most frequently cited in the literature or associated with students classified in the various categories of handicaps (cf. Keogh, 1982). Yet, the nature of the relationship between learning in school and students' perceptions of personal control, and the subsequent effects on the learning performance of students with varied handicapping conditions, have received very little attention in special education research. Moreover, the data base that does exist in this area is from investigations with study samples comprised mainly of students classified as learning disabled.

In a review article based on findings from seven studies of the perceptions of locus of control of learning disabled children, Dudley-Marling, Snider, and Tarver (1982) discussed the results of their investigation in terms of three dimensions: overall locus of control orientation, locus of control orientation in academic and nonacademic situations, and orientation toward failure and success. They noted that, like other groups who experience academic failure, learning disabled children were, overall, more likely to perceive an external locus of control than were children whose achievements were at or above the norm. In particular, learning disabled students were found to be more likely than the latter students to attribute their success to external factors and to accept responsibility for failure. The researchers found a positive relationship between groups who failed, including students who were classified as learning disabled or were otherwise handicapped, and external locus of control. Six of the seven studies reviewed by Dudley-Marling et al. found that an external locus of control was characteristic of learning disabled populations. These findings are corroborated by the results of several other studies (Boersma & Chapman, 1981; Keogh & Cahill, 1971; Pearl, Bryan, & Donahue, 1980).

Boersma and Chapman (1981), for example, investigated affective development in eighty-one learning disabled and eighty-one normal-achieving students in Grades 3 through 6 and found marked differences in three affective variables. Overall, the learning disabled group scored significantly lower on measures of self-perceptions of ability. The learning disabled subjects also had significantly lower expectations for future academic success than the subjects in the control group. Furthermore, the data from measures of students' perceptions of academic locus of control suggested that, although the learning disabled and the normal-achieving students accepted responsibility for academic failure to a similar extent, the learning disabled students were relatively unable to take credit for their successes. Adelman and Taylor (1983) also noted this tendency of learning disabled students to attribute success to external factors.

Pearl (1982) examined the attributions of third- and fourth-grade learning disabled students and found that the students did not always interpret success as a positive reflection of themselves, and they perceived that failure could not be overcome with effort. Furthermore, the learning disabled students considered luck to play a larger role in their successes than in their failures. The learning disabled third graders were less inclined than were the nonlearning disabled third graders to believe that their ability was responsible for success on puzzle tasks. The learning disabled fourth-grade students were likewise less inclined than were the non-learning disabled, fourth-grade students to consider their successes in reading to be the result of ability.

A study by Perna, Dunlap, and Dillard (1983) produced similar findings. They examined the relationships of the scores on internal locus of control, the gains in academic achievement, and the IQ scores of 63 mildly to moderately emotionally disturbed male students from 10 to 15 years of age. Perna et al. found that the students who felt a high degree of self-responsibility for success and failure also showed greater gains in academic achievement, regardless of age and IQ score.

Three major conclusions can be drawn from the findings of research on handicapped student populations that are related to development of these students' sense of self-responsibility and their school learning performance. First, handicapped students generally perceive an external locus of control; that is, handicapped students are more likely than nonhandicapped students to attribute academic and nonacademic success and failure to forces outside of themselves. Second, handicapped students are more likely to accept responsibility for failure than for success, although they generally do not recognize ability or effort as controllable determinants of either success or failure in school learning. Finally, as research on effective learners in the general population also suggests, handicapped students who assume high levels of responsibility for their learning tend to achieve more academically than those who do not. Nevertheless, it is important to note that, since the research base on handicapped students' perceptions of control and on the relationship between their perceptions of control and learning outcomes comes mainly from studies with learning disabled populations, the extent to which the conclusions drawn here can be generalized across students classified in other categories of handicaps remains an empirical question.

Instructional Intervention Approaches

There are two widely reported general approaches to fostering students' self-responsibility for learning. The first involves training students to accept responsibility for their learning success and failure; the other employs interventions designed to foster a sense of personal control by training students to manage their learning and behavior. The former is based on research on learned helplessness and attribution retraining; the latter on classroom research on improving achievement through direct instruction in taking self-responsibility for learning and behavior.

Attribution Retraining

A consistent finding from research related to the general topic area of locus of control is that students with low academic success (a characteristic of handicapped students) are more likely, compared with high-achieving students, to be externally oriented and to accept responsibility for failure but not for success. These findings suggest the potential of interventions designed to improve performance by fostering self-responsibility for learning outcomes. As Meyer's (1979) work indicates, certain groups of children —retarded children, for instance—might need to be taught more explicitly the relationship between self-responsibility and learning success and to be encouraged to take actions that lead to optimal performance. Research suggests, for example, that the negative attribution pattern exhibited by learning disabled students may be mediated by generalized learned helplessness, which may require intervention in addition to academic remediation. These students may have difficulty in maintaining self-esteem if they believe they are powerless to influence their environment, be it academic or nonacademic. This belief may also affect their willingness to employ learning strategies and to recognize the influence of these strategies on their social relationships (Sabatino, 1982).

There is a growing research base on the attributional approach to improving student achievement (e.g., Andrews & Debus, 1978; Chapin & Dyck, 1976; Diener & Dweck, 1980; Dweck, 1975; Schunk, 1981; Zoeller, 1979). Although research suggests the potential of systematic retraining in attribution for reducing the learned helplessness of academically at-risk students, there have been very few attempts to systematically implement established interventions in the schools. Two interventions have been cited most frequently in the literature. They are the attribution retraining program developed by Dweck (1975) and deCharms' (1976) teacher training program for fostering student motivation through the concept of "origin-pawn" behavior. These programs are described briefly here.

Dweck's (1975) program basically provides either attribution retraining or "success-only" treatment for learned-helpless students. The former type of training teaches students to assume responsibility for failure and to attribute failure in learning to a lack of effort. By contrast, the success-only treatment exposes students exclusively to successful experiences without attempting to change their perceptions of failure. The results of Dweck's research suggest that, on the one hand, attribution retraining helped students whose previous performance had deteriorated after academic failure to persist in their learning (i.e., to maintain or increase the number of problems completed). The performance of students who received the success-only treatment, on the other hand, continued to decrease markedly after experiences of failure.

deCharms' teacher training program is designed to promote origin (internally caused) rather than pawn (externally caused) behavior. It consists of two phases: training teachers to apply the origin concept in the classroom, and implementing an instructional program designed to foster achievement motivation, realistic goal setting, and origin behavior. deCharms' findings show that training students in the middle-childhood age range (from Grades 5 through 7) to set goals and to use realistic learning strategies had an impact beyond that which could be attributed to development. Personal causation training, along with school curriculum, was found to contribute to improved academic achievement.

Development of Student Self-Responsibility

Intervention programs designed to improve academic performance by developing students' sense of control and self-responsibility for learning are generally based on the assumptions that there is a close relationship between a sense of control and positive learning processes and outcomes and that instructional intervention can modify students' perceptions of personal control (e.g., Coleman et al., 1966; Crandall et al., 1965; Wang & Stiles, 1976b). Among the interventions that have successfully modified students' sense of personal control and resulted in improved achievement are direct instruction in self-management skills and the provision of opportunities for self-managed learning (e.g., Felixbrod & O'Leary, 1974; Ross & Zimiles, 1974). One such intervention program is the Self-Schedule System (Wang, 1976).

The Self-Schedule System is a classroom management system designed to foster students' sense of personal control in school learning situations. One assumption of the design of the Self-Schedule System is that a student's belief in personal control may be an important factor in his or her ability to resist any potentially adverse effects of teacher expectations. It also presupposes that, if learning environments are to effectively foster perceptions of self-responsibility, they need organizational and curriculum structures that allow students to acquire both academic and self-management skills (Wang, 1980, 1981; Wang & Brictson, 1973; Wang, Mazza, Haines, & Johnson, 1972; Wang & Richardson, 1977; Wang & Stiles, 1976a; Weisstein & Wang, 1978, 1980).

The Self-Schedule System has been widely used and field tested by schools. It is currently implemented in a variety of school settings and in conjunction with a range of school improvement programs (Wang, 1983; Wang & Birch, 1984a, 1984b; Wang & Walberg, 1983). The findings of a series of efficacy studies of the Self-Schedule System have consistently shown that (a) it is possible to design intervention programs to foster the development of students' sense of personal control, (b) students can successfully assume self-management responsibilities when learning self-management skills is a major curriculum objective and when students are permitted to manage their learning behaviors and situations, and (c) performance improves as students develop more control over their learning.

Results from studies designed to investigate the implementation and effects of the Self-Schedule System suggest that students' sense of self-responsibility is alterable through intervention. Furthermore, and, perhaps, more important, findings from similar research also suggest that interventions that take into account the social and emotional correlates of failure are likely to facilitate students' schooling success and that successful learning experiences tend, in turn, to foster perceptions of competence and personal control (cf. Madden & Slavin, 1982). In fact, Madden and Slavin (1982), in their review of research on academic and social outcomes for mainstreamed children with academic handicaps, noted that the effectiveness of certain educational approaches in improving the academic progress of students with poor prognoses for achievement may be attributable to the inclusion of program features designed specifically to encourage an internal locus of control and perceptions of self-esteem.

Self-Instructive Skills and Learning

Self-instructive skills, in the context of the research reviewed in this section, are defined as students' ability to gain access to, organize, and use relevant knowledge and skills for new learning. According to this definition, self-instructive learners are knowledgeable about the subject matter related to the criterial task to be learned and about the learning environment and its functional requirements. They are capable of using what they know to learn independently and deliberately through strategy planning, self-monitoring and self-assessment, and self-interrogation and clarification. These two components of self-instructive skills—students' knowledge, and students' ability to use what they know in their learning—are the focus of the review of relevant research discussed in this section of the chapter.

Although classroom process research has focused for some time on the role of the learner, the primary interest has been the learner's management of his or her behavior and/or of the learning environment. For the most part, this research has been undertaken from the perspectives of achievement motivation, learning efficiency, and productivity, and it has concentrated mainly on student outcome variables (see, for example, the discussion in the previous section on research related to student self-responsibility for learning). Little attention has been given to the active role that students may play in the process of knowledge and skills acquisition. This role, as conceptualized here, includes a mediating function in the process of acquiring knowledge and skills and using the acquired knowledge to solve new problems, learn more, and develop new skills. Although the development of students' sense of self-responsibility has significant implications for fostering motivation and achievement, learning does not take place through self-responsibility alone. Students also must utilize self-instructive skills in becoming increasingly efficient and self-sufficient in their learning. Understanding the nature and patterns of the use of self-instructive skills by students in their learning is essential to the building of a knowledge base that increases capabilities for helping students to become more self-instructive in their learning.

Recent empirical research on learning and classroom instruction has provided substantial empirical grounds for systematic analysis of the role of the learner in the learning process. Especially relevant are the research bases from studies of learning and cognition that pertain to the process of learning and the nature and function of metacognitive processes (e.g., Brown, 1978; Brown, Bransford, Ferrara, & Campione, 1983; Flavell, 1976); from investigations of classroom learning and the role of cognitive processes in mediating learning (Doyle, 1977; Humphrey, 1984; Marshall & Weinstein, 1984; Peterson & Swing, 1982; Winne & Marx, 1982); and from studies of innovative educational programs aimed at fostering the effective functioning of students as active learners (Marshall, 1981; Segal, Chipman, & Glaser, 1985; Wang & Walberg, in press).

The linking of findings based on these disparate research bases has resulted in the development of an integrated conceptual model for the study of the self-instructive process in classroom learning contexts. The major components of the model are described below, including an explication of the theoretical and empirical foundations for the design of the model.

Model for the Study of the Self-Instructive Process in Classroom Learning Contexts

Figure 1 is a schematic representation of the model for the study of the self-instructive process in classroom learning contexts. The model is designed to serve as the conceptual framework for analyzing and describing the self-instructive process and its mediating function in enhancing the classroom learning of individual students. Basically, the model includes four clusters of related variables. The first two clusters, learner characteristics and the classroom learning environment, are independent variables. The self-instructive process is considered a dependent variable in relation to learner characteristics and the classroom learning environment but a mediating variable with respect to learner outcomes.

As suggested by Fig. 1, self-instructive skills in the context of the model involve the ability to gain access to knowledge, skills, and strategies and to evaluate and regulate these resources relative to the structure of tasks in particular classroom learning environments. A major premise undergirding the interactive nature of the model is that the self-instructive process plays a mediating role in student learning, and it is likely to be affected by a multiplicity of factors associated with characteristics of individual learners and/or situation-specific characteristics of the learning environment. Variables related to personal and knowledge characteristics of the learner and variables related to the classroom learning environment are hypothesized to have interactive effects, and, together, these two sets of variables are expected to have significant effects on the use of self-instructive skills by students in their learning. The use of self-instructive skills, in turn, is hypothesized to have a direct impact on learner outcomes, which ultimately contribute to the knowledge and motivational characteristics of the learner.

A basic contention of the model is that the individual learner brings to the school learning environment a unique profile of instructionally relevant characteristics, which, in their interaction with particular elements in the classroom learning environment, elicit certain behaviors that may or may not be self-instructive. For example, a profile of learner characteristics might include highly positive perceptions of self-competence in generally being able to complete work with minimal assistance from the teacher, a very low or near-zero knowledge base with respect to a specific new task, and a high degree of motivation to correctly complete the new task. One factor that might influence the extent to which a student with this particular profile would use self-instructive skills in the acquisition of new knowledge and skills, or in the performance of a given familiar or new task, is the situation-specific conditions of the students' learning environment. If the classroom is characterized by a preponderance of teacher-directed activities that involve students working as a whole class at the same pace, the pattern and nature of students' use of self-instructive processes in their learning is likely to be very different from students' use of self-instructive processes in a learning environment with a predominance of flexible instructional-grouping patterns, student responsibility and initiative, the availability of a variety of materials, peer assistance, and adequate time for the teacher to respond to students' requests for assistance.

Distinct patterns of interaction among programming features, student and teacher behaviors, and student outcomes have been noted in studies of differential effects among instructional approaches (e.g., Berliner, 1983; Hedges, Giaconia, & Gage, 1981; Walberg, 1984; Wang & Walberg, in press; Webb, 1982). Findings from a study by Wang and Walberg (in press) of the program implementation and effects of eight, widely implemented, research-based models of instruction suggest, for example, that programs featuring student choice, task flexibility, teacher monitoring, peer tutoring, student-initiated requests for teacher help, a variety of curriculum materials, and task-specific instructions were associated with student self-management, personal interactions between students and teachers, student work in small groups, and substantive interactions between teachers and students. Furthermore, these particular patterns of classroom processes were found to be negatively associated with program features such as whole-class and large-group instruction and teacher-directed instruction.

The validity of using the person-environment-process-product paradigm to investigate the processes of learning and instruction is supported by findings in the contemporary experimental literature on learning and cognition. For example, Brown, Bransford, et al. (1983) pointed to the movement of the field from earlier models that address learner knowledge, the learning process, and learning tasks in isolation toward a more complex and comprehensive model of the interaction of these elements of learning. An example of the latter is Jenkins' tetrahedral model (1979, 1980). The basic premise undergirding the design of the tetrahedral model is that knowledge, skills, thoughts, and actions do not exist in a vacuum, but occur and therefore

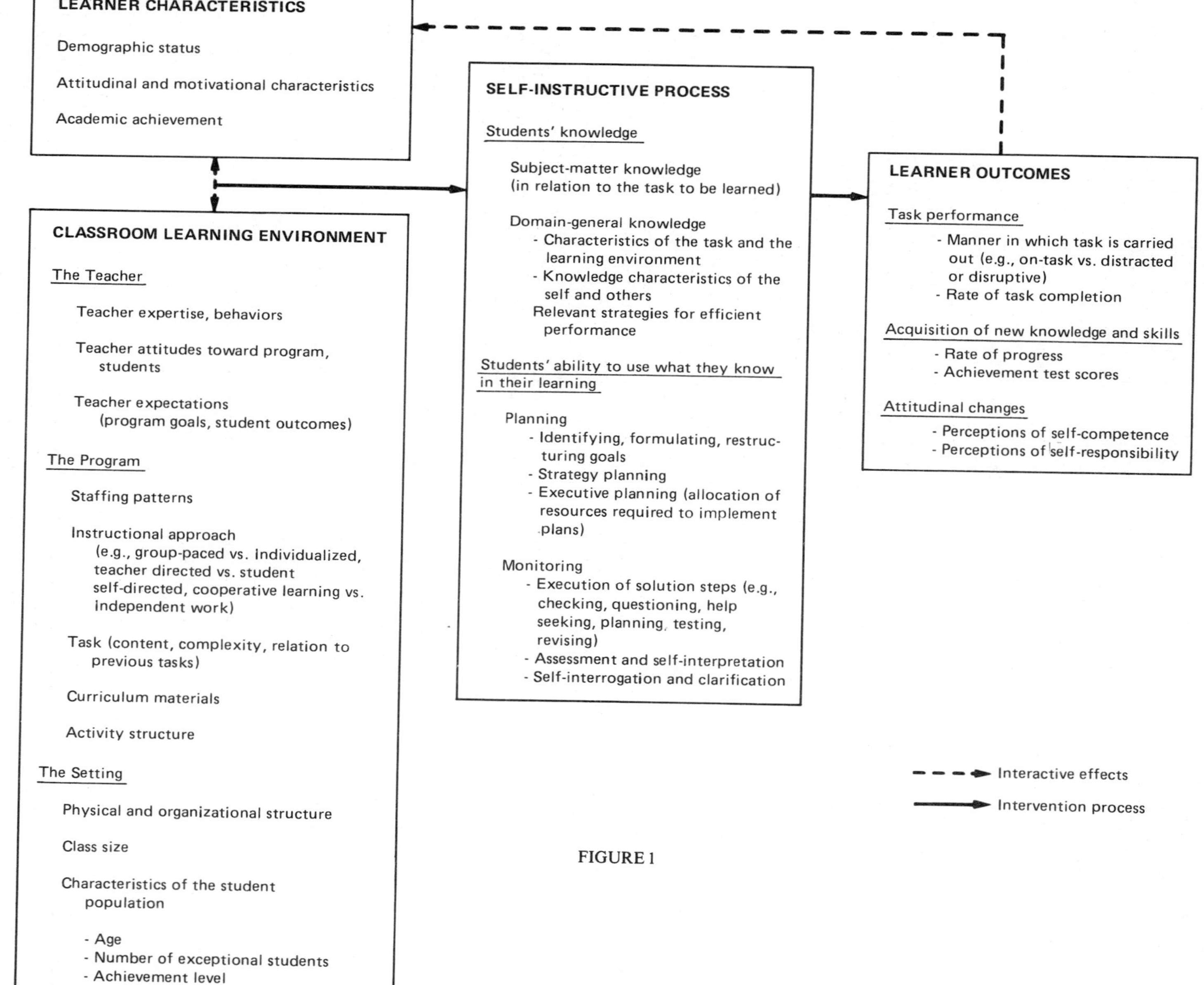
LEARNER CHARACTERISTICS
Demographic status
Attitudinal and motivational characteristics
Academic achievement
CLASSROOM LEARNING ENVIRONMENT
The Teacher
Teacher expertise, behaviors
Teacher attitudes toward program, students
Teacher expectations (program goals, student outcomes)
The Program
Staffing patterns
Instructional approach (e.g., group-paced vs. individualized, teacher directed vs. student self-directed, cooperative learning vs. independent work)
Task (content, complexity, relation to previous tasks)
Curriculum materials
Activity structure
The Setting
Physical and organizational structure
Class size
Characteristics of the student population
- Age
- Number of exceptional students
- Achievement level
SELF-INSTRUCTIVE PROCESS
Students' knowledge
Subject-matter knowledge (in relation to the task to be learned)
Domain-general knowledge
- Characteristics of the task and the learning environment
- Knowledge characteristics of the self and others
Relevant strategies for efficient performance
Students' ability to use what they know in their learning
Planning
- Identifying, formulating, restructuring goals
- Strategy planning
- Executive planning (allocation of resources required to implement plans)
Monitoring
- Execution of solution steps (e.g., checking, questioning, help seeking, planning, testing, revising)
- Assessment and self-interpretation
- Self-interrogation and clarification
LEARNER OUTCOMES
Task performance
- Manner in which task is carried out (e.g., on-task vs. distracted or disruptive)
- Rate of task completion
Acquisition of new knowledge and skills
- Rate of progress
- Achievement test scores
Attitudinal changes
- Perceptions of self-competence
- Perceptions of self-responsibility
Interactive effects
Intervention process

FIGURE 1

should be studied, within a particular context. Context is defined as consisting of individuals (differing in ability, interests, knowledge, purpose); orienting tasks (instructions, directions, activities, apparatus); materials (sensory mode, physical structure, psychological organization, psychological sequence); and criterial tasks (recall, recognition, problem solving, performance). Jenkins' model has been adapted by Bransford (1979) and Brown (1981; Brown, Campione, & Day, 1981) to facilitate the exploration of broader questions concerning learning, understanding, and remembering.

The validity of the person-environment-process-product paradigm is further suggested by findings and recent developments in research on social-psychological processes and attitudes (e.g., Bossert, 1979; Cooper & Good, 1982; Doyle, 1977; Gordon, 1983; Marshall & Weinstein, 1984; Rosenholtz & Wilson, 1980; Stipek, 1981). In a study of high- and low-achieving students' descriptions of their school environment, Marshall, Weinstein, Sharp, and Brattesani (1982) found that students' perceptions of the meaning of the classroom structure and processes could only be understood in terms of multiple interacting classroom factors. Students' understanding of classroom meaning in this context affects how aspects of the classroom are perceived and interpreted and, consequently, how students' learning processes and outcomes are altered. Other research suggests, for example, that the evaluative cues used by students tend to vary as a function of the structure and climate of the classroom (Weinstein, 1983). Furthermore, students' perceptions of the classroom environment consistently have been found to account for variance in learning outcomes beyond that which can be attributed to ability (Haertel, Walberg, & Haertel, 1979), a finding that underscores the importance of classroom context variables.

In a study of the differences in the learning processes of high- and low-achieving students, DeStefano, Wang, and Gordon (1984) found that students' personal characteristics (e.g., temperament, knowledge, motivation) interacted with learning conditions; learner behaviors (e.g., dimensions of task orientation, personal–social flexibility, reactivity); and learning outcomes. This finding supports the hypothesis that students possess unique individual characteristics that interact with learning conditions, such as the physical and organizational structure of the classroom, the nature of task demands, and available instructional-learning resources, and elicit specific learner behaviors, such as time-on-task, energy deployment, task involvement, autonomy, decision making, and resource utilization.

Thus, the findings of psychological and educational research underscore the need to examine the dynamic nature of the interactions of students' personal characteristics, the classroom learning environment, the self-instructive processes used by students, and learner outcomes. Failing to recognize the roles of any (or a set) of these given factors can greatly hamper research and development efforts to mitigate potentially negative effects on learning and to improve classroom learning environments. This possibility is a particularly serious challenge for research that aims to broaden current understanding of how learning takes place for individual students in the classroom and of the reciprocity of individual learning processes and outcomes and the classroom environment. Certain factors may enhance or subvert the influence of other factors and, thus, either reinforce potentially beneficial effects or offset potentially deleterious effects.

Development and Use of Self-Instructive Skills

The discussion of findings from the present review of research related to self-instructive processes focuses on the empirical bases for the constructs and interrelationships suggested in the model shown in Fig. 1, as well as the implications of what the learner knows and how that knowledge influences his or her use of self-instructive skills to increase learning efficiency and to attain intended learning outcomes. In addition, particular consideration is given to the instructional design implications of examining students' ability to learn deliberately on their own as an individual difference variable affecting the provision of instruction and the evaluation of students' functioning in the school learning environment. The discussion is organized under the two major components of the self-instructive process as shown in Fig. 1—students' knowledge, and students' ability to use what they know in their learning.

Students' Knowledge

What students know consistently has been shown to be one of the best predictors of learning performance and outcomes in both the effective-teaching research (e.g., Bloom, 1984; Brophy & Good, 1986; Walberg, 1984) and the related research in social and cognitive psychology (e.g., Bandura, 1981; Covington & Beery, 1976; Glaser, 1984; Larkin, 1981; Nicholls, 1979; Resnick & Ford, 1981). However, detailed analysis of students' knowledge characteristics rarely is considered in the design of school programs or in planning for classroom instruction. Furthermore, when students' knowledge is considered, the focus typically is on gathering information on outcome variables. The use of such information on students' knowledge has tended to be restricted to the classification of students and the selection of students for instruction (or their exclusion from instruction). Very little of this outcomes-oriented information is useful for either designing or improving instruction (e.g., Glaser & Bond, 1981; Reschly, 1984; Reynolds, 1984).

Recent advances in the study of learning and classroom instruction, and, particularly, studies of cognitive processes in learning and their role in mediating learning performance, have not only broadened understanding and characterizations of students' knowledge but also have elucidated the important role of learner knowledge in learning. Prior knowledge has been found to be correlated positively to the performance of a variety of tasks, such as the recall of chess positions (Chase & Simon, 1973); computer programming (Adelson, 1981; McKeithen, Reitman, Rueter, & Hirtle, 1981); and electronics tasks (Egan & Schwartz, 1979); and to the ability to make task-appropriate inferences and elaborations (Marr & Gormley, 1982; Pearson, Hanson, & Gordon, 1979; Voss, Vesonder, & Spilich, 1980). Moreover, evidence suggests that an awareness of incorrect prior knowledge is especially important in planning instruction (Brown & Burton, 1978; Brown & Van Lehn, 1982; Champagne, Klopfer, & Anderson, 1980; Clement, 1979; Siegler, 1981).

Learners' knowledge characteristics are generally described in the experimental and instructional design literature under the rubrics of subject-matter knowledge and domain-general knowledge. Subject-matter knowledge is associated directly with the specific content of the task to be learned. Domain-general knowledge, by contrast, is broad knowledge that does not pertain specifically to a task yet facilitates the learning process. Domain-general knowledge includes knowledge about the characteristics of the task and the learning environment, about the learning characteristics of the self and others, and about strategies that facilitate efficient performance (e.g., study skills and gaining access to such instructional resources as teacher attention and peer help).

Subject-matter knowledge and learning. The relationship between subject-matter knowledge and learning performance in a given domain is well documented. Prior achievement has been found consistently to be an important predictor of students' achievement outcomes (Bloom, 1976; Coleman et al., 1966; Cooley & Leinhardt, 1975; Stallings, 1975; Walberg, 1984), and the role of knowledge has been a central variable in the study of cognition and learning (Brown, Bransford, et al., 1983; Flavell & Wellman, 1977; Glaser, 1984). The findings of research suggest that the quantitative and qualitative aspects of subject-matter knowledge are pervasive and have consistent effects on performance. Furthermore, the research highlights the role of subject-matter knowledge in the acquisition and use of new knowledge in given areas.

Several lines of research on the role of subject-matter knowledge are predominant in the literature on cognition and learning. One line of work in this area is based on the premise that levels (or amounts) of knowledge and performance are relatively isomorphic; that is, differences in knowledge lead to corresponding differences in performance (e.g., Chi, 1985; Chi & Koeske, 1983; Larkin, McDermott, Simon, & Simon, 1980; Lesgold, Feltovich, Glaser, & Wang, 1981). Another line of inquiry, based on a developmental perspective, focuses on the relationship between changes in knowledge and performance over time (e.g., Carey, 1985; Siegler, 1976, 1978; Siegler & Klahr, 1982; Siegler & Richards, 1982). Research from a third perspective examines the correspondence between structures of knowledge and structures of subject matter presented during instruction (e.g., Champagne, Gunstone, & Klopfer, 1983; McCloskey, Caramazza, & Green, 1980).

As might be expected, the findings of research on subject-matter knowledge generally depict successful learners as those who have more knowledge than that possessed by less successful learners. Experts' representations of knowledge domains have been found, for instance, to be more detailed, precise, elaborate, and differentiated than those of nonexperts (Chi, Glaser, & Rees, 1982; Chi & Koeske, 1983). Learning from written material has been found to be easier if the reader already possesses the knowledge structures for organizing new knowledge (Chiesi, Spilich, & Voss, 1979) and if the content of the material coincides with the reader's perspective (Pichert & Anderson, 1977).

Within-age performance differences associated with levels of domain competency have been corroborated by across-age, knowledge-performance trends in the developmental literature. Siegler and his colleagues (1976, 1978; Siegler & Klahr, 1982; Siegler & Richards, 1982), for example, found that age was associated with the complexity of the rules used to judge the relationship between weight and distance on balance-scale tasks, the relative height of water in a glass, and starting and stopping times and speeds in judgments of time. Carey (1985) found, in her study of the reorganization of biological knowledge in 4- to 10-year-old children, that younger children's attributions were organized around human activities, while those of older children centered on biological knowledge. However, as Carey noted, the catalyst for reorganization in this case was the acquisition of biological knowledge in school.

The importance of a knowledge structure to which new information can be related has been emphasized in studies of the acquisition of basic skills such as counting (Greeno, Riley, & Gelman, 1983) and mathematical problem solving (Greeno, 1982); in studies of recall performance in children (Lindberg, 1980); and in studies of skilled performance in college students (Mayer, Steihl, & Greeno, 1975). The identification of initial inadequate conceptions has been suggested to be a significant aspect of the diagnosis of an individual student's learning needs and the starting point for planning instruction that is adaptive to the student's needs (Champagne, Klopfer, & Gunstone, 1982; Clement, 1979). For example, the identification and subsequent correction of misconceptions have been the focus of work on the BUGGY computer program (Brown & Burton, 1978; Brown & Van Lehn, 1981). BUGGY analyzes students' performance on several examples of an arithmetic operation and develops a procedural model for each student that clarifies the incorrect procedures used in specific tasks. In their discussion of the BUGGY program and its use, Goldstein and Brown (1979) pointed to the potential of this type of analysis for testing and tailoring instruction to each student's specific difficulties and needs.

Domain-general knowledge and learning. Domain-general knowledge refers to knowledge that enables individuals to mediate the demands of the learning environment while utilizing their subject-matter knowledge in the performance of specific tasks. Domain-general knowledge encompasses a broad spectrum of knowledge related to learning how to learn efficiently. It has been hypothesized that domain-general knowledge plays a central role in the generalization or transfer of knowledge and skills and, particularly, in the development of strategies or rules for problem solving and the learning of new tasks.

Domain-general knowledge is typically characterized in the research literature as including knowledge of the broad task environment, encompassing classroom structures (Bossert, 1978; Giaconia & Hedges, 1982; Hamilton, 1983; Marshall, 1976; Webb, 1980); classroom ecology (Au, 1980; Doyle, 1981; Kounin & Gump, 1974; Mehan, 1979); and classroom tasks (Doyle, 1979, 1983). Domain-general knowledge also has been described as including students' perceptions and views of the thinking processes involved in classroom learning (Weinstein, 1983; Winne & Marx, 1982) and learning tools such as study skills and knowing when and where to seek help. In the research on cognition and learning, domain-general knowledge is discussed most often under the rubric of metacognition or metacognitive knowledge. That is, it refers to what learners know about their own knowledge characteristics and those of others, what they know about the specific knowledge required for efficient performance of given types of tasks within or across task domains, and how such knowledge influences an individual's learning performance (Flavell & Wellman, 1977).

Domain-general knowledge includes cognitive strategies that effective learners apply to the learning of new tasks (e.g., elaboration, self-questioning, inquiry) as well as understanding of the interaction of a learner's characteristics and the environment. Flavell and Wellman (1977) characterized this aspect of the learner's knowledge as essentially introspective knowledge (insight) about individuals (e.g., cognitive resources, memory capabilities); about tasks (e.g., cognitive requirements); about the environment (e.g., operational constraints, resource supports); and about the interaction of one's learning and outcomes (e.g., necessary adaptations of the learning process to complete a task successfully). Similarly, Bransford (1979) and Brown et al. (1981), based on Jenkins' tetrahedral model, addressed questions of learning, understanding, and remembering by viewing learner behavior as the complex interaction of learner characteristics (e.g., knowledge, attitudes); learning activities (e.g., attention, elaboration); criterial tasks (e.g., recall, transfer); and the nature of materials (e.g., physical and psychological structure).

In the context of the conceptual model for the study of the self-instructive process shown in Fig. 1, domain-general knowledge is discussed here as consisting of three dimensions. They are (a) knowledge about characteristics of the task and the learning environment, (b) perceptions of the knowledge characteristics of the self and others, and (c) knowledge about relevant strategies for efficient task performance.

1. *Knowledge about characteristics of the task and the learning environment*. One of the major premises of research in this area is that knowledge of the task and the learning environment influences students' thinking about the requirements for efficient and successful performance. This knowledge, in turn, influences students' learning, their behavior, and, ultimately, their performance. It provides critical information about expected task goals (problem representation) and procedures (strategies and plans); about what needs to be done in order to complete the task (task criteria); and about the resources required for effective task performance as well as how to obtain them (Campione, Brown, & Ferrara, 1982; Doyle, 1983; Hayes, 1976; Newell & Simon, 1972; Weinstein & Marshall, 1984).

Much research suggests that knowledge of the task enables students to be more self-instructive. This knowledge serves as a framework for organizing and directing attention to a wide variety of information that, subsequently, forms the basis for decisions regarding what must be done as well as how to go about doing it. As noted by Campione et al. (1982),

> If the child is aware of what is needed to perform effectively, then that child can take steps to meet the demands of a learning situation more adequately. If, however, the child is not aware of his or her own limitations as a learner or the complexity of the task at hand, then he or she can hardly be expected to take preventive actions in order to anticipate or recover from problems. (p. 433)

Two complementary lines of research in this area are pertinent to an understanding of the self-instructive process. They are research on what students know about the task and its performance requirements, and research on how knowledge about the task and the learning environment affects learner behavior and new learning.

Research findings suggest that children as young as 6 years of age know that familiarity and perceptual salience make items easier to remember and that increasing the number of items to be remembered makes a task more difficult (Kreutzer, Leonard, & Flavell, 1975). Other evidence indicates, for instance, the importance of the learner's knowledge of the relationship between categorical structure and memorization, the effect of spatial position on recall, the effect of task goals on learning, the relationship between study time and the number of objects recalled, the effects on recall of the time elapsed between storage and recall, and the intervening activities that interfere with recall (Kreutzer et al., 1975; Moynahan, 1973; Rogoff, Newcombe, & Kagan, 1974; Salatas & Flavell, 1976).

Myers and Paris (1978), in their study of 8- and 12-year-old children, noted differences in the children's degrees of awareness of the effects of the length of a passage, the familiarity of story content, and the interest engendered by a story, on reading behavior. In their assessment of the schema for reading among good and poor readers in Grades 2, 4, 6, and 8, Canney and Winograd (1979) found that the better readers at all four grade levels were more aware of the semantic features of reading. Moreover, there were greater increases in this awareness among good readers than among poor readers from one grade level to another. When asked what they thought they needed to learn or to do to become better readers, the good readers in Grades 4, 6, and 8 emphasized relaxing with books as a way to improve their concentration and increasing their general word knowledge and vocabularies. By contrast, the poor readers emphasized reading more as a way to improve the mechanics of their reading. Similarly, Paris and Jacobs (1984) found that metacognitive awareness of the factors of reading was related to reading comprehension, performance on a cloze task, and error detection.

Considerable research conducted in recent years and aimed at defining the cognitive components of learning tasks has resulted in a better understanding of what students need to know in order to learn efficiently. For example, in his review of the nature of academic work as experienced by teachers and students, Doyle (1979) delineated several categories of academic tasks as well as the demands and functions associated with each category. The first category of academic tasks identified by Doyle is memory tasks, in which students are required to recognize or reproduce previously acquired information. The second category of tasks is commonly referred to as procedural tasks, which can be carried out based on students' knowledge of certain routines or standard procedures (e.g., algorithms or heuristics). The third category of tasks involves students' ability to comprehend or understand; it includes the transfer of knowledge, the drawing of inferences, or the selection of appropriate procedures for solving new problems. The final category of tasks identified by Doyle is opinion tasks. Performance of opinion tasks requires that students state a preference.

A focus on analyzing the cognitive components of learning also can be found in the research on problem solving. This research has included examination of the various problems (tasks) encountered in learning and the cognitive processes required to solve them (Greeno, 1973, 1980; Kreutzer et al., 1975; Simon, 1973, 1978, 1980; Simon & Newell, 1971). In his analysis of the cognitive requirements of problem solving, Simon (1978) distinguished between well-structured and ill-structured problems. He concluded that solving well-structured problems (e.g., arithmetic word problems) requires information contained mainly in the problem statements and perhaps other relevant knowledge, such as knowledge of a particular algorithm. Solving ill-structured problems, such as social, political, and economic problems, makes greater information demands on cognitive resources. Greeno (1973) also differentiated two processes of solving problems: productive thinking, and reproductive thinking. According to Greeno, productive thinking is required when problem representation must be recognized or new features must be added. Reproductive thinking, on the other hand, is involved when the solution plan is an algorithm that can be retrieved from long-term memory.

Another area of research in which students' knowledge of the nature and characteristics of the task is of interest is the study of the classroom factors associated with students' thinking and behavior. Perspectives of this research range from the conception of tasks simply as activities to a broad-based view that tasks are comprised of activities, subject-matter content, materials, and goals, which are combined in the presence of teachers and students and are influenced by students' perceptions of the task demands and by the social context of the classroom environment (e.g., Berliner, 1983; Bossert, 1979; Shavelson & Stern, 1981).

Winne and Marx (1982), for example, using a stimulated-recall technique and verbal reports by teachers and students about their thoughts, studied how teachers intended to have students process information in instructions and how students perceived these intentions. They found that (a) the preinstructive activities teachers provided to orient students to a particular task were often not perceived as such and frequently had the effect of focusing students on the wrong task; (b) unless students had a well-established cognitive response to a particular situation, instructions were successful in inverse proportion to the amount of information contained in them; (c) students' perceptions of and responses to instructions depended upon their mastery of content; and (d) students tended to construct a meaning for an exercise whether the teacher intended one or not. The data from a study of student cognition by Leinhardt (1983) also reflect this relationship between students' knowledge of a task and task performance. She found, for example, that students who performed poorly had less of an idea of what was going on in class and less ability to anticipate events than students who performed better. The latter students were more able to anticipate, for instance, the content of a lesson on fractions and to develop strategies for completing the lesson.

Task sequence and the extent and difficulty level of a task have been found to be related to students' opportunities to learn and, consequently, to their learning behaviors and outcomes. Differences in the extent and difficulty level of a task may convey (or be perceived by students as conveying) information about the amount of learning that different students are expected to accomplish (Anderson, Brubaker, Alleman-Brooks, & Duffy, 1984; Good & Beckerman, 1978; Marshall et al., 1982). In their study of high- and low-achieving students' descriptions of the school environment, Marshall et al. (1982) found that students perceived that high achievers were assigned more difficult tasks because the teacher expected these students to be able to do the work. The assignment of fewer or easier tasks to other students was perceived to suggest lesser capabilities than those possessed by students who were assigned more challenging tasks. These findings are also substantiated by data from Anderson et al.'s (1984) study of first-grade students' responses to seat work assignments.

Overall, a substantial body of research suggests that the learner's knowledge of characteristics of the task and the learning environment is significantly related to task performance. This knowledge extends beyond an understanding of the structure of a task. Students also need to know about the nature of the task itself, about the task environment in which they go about learning, and about the requirements for efficient and successful task completion. Thus, recognizing and examining the complexity of task-related interactions in student learning, particularly as they occur in classroom learning situations that typically involve a multitude of interactive factors, may contribute significantly to an understanding of the knowledge characteristics of individual students and of the relationship between these characteristics and the extent to which self-instructive processes are used by students in mediating their learning.

2. *Perceptions of the knowledge characteristics of the self and others.* Increasing recognition of students' role in successful school learning has been paralleled by an interest in students' use of their knowledge and that of others to assess the constraints and resource availability related to the accomplishment of given tasks. A person's knowledge and perception of the task may have much to do with how he or she views it. For example, an experienced or knowledgeable student may view a task as well structured (see the above discussion of knowledge about the task) and accomplish it without additional information, whereas a learner with little or unsuccessful experience with the same task may view it as difficult.

Research related to the knowledge of one's own and others' cognitive functioning typically focuses on memory abilities. Findings suggest that children as young as 5 years of age (or even younger; see Wellman, 1985) have some knowledge of the general characteristics of a person's memory. The 5-year-olds in a study by Markman (1973), for example, knew that people are able to perform certain types of tasks better than other types. There is also evidence that young children know that the ability to perform a task varies from occasion to occasion and from person to person within the same age group (Flavell, Friedrichs, & Hoyt, 1970; Kreutzer et al., 1975; Markman, 1973; Yussen & Levy, 1975). Studies in this area further indicate that children know of their own transient memory processes at an early age (Neimark, Slotnik, & Ulrich, 1971).

In addition to the effects of the awareness of cognitive information stored in memory, learning performance has been shown to be affected by awareness of one's own ability and the ability of others to access affective information stored in memory (Bransford, 1979; Brown, 1978). Of particular importance are an individual's perception of his or her own past experiences (e.g., memory of whether past performances of a similar task was a success or a failure, whether or not the task was interesting, the difficulty level of the experience) and the understanding that this perception can have pervasive effects on his or her performance (Au, 1980; Dweck & Elliot, 1983; McDermott, 1978).

The literature in research on social cognition (e.g., Levine & Wang, 1983) and classroom processes (e.g., Weinstein, 1982) also contains a vast data base on students' knowledge of their own and others' functioning and ability to learn, students' use of this knowledge, and the effect on their behavior and learning. The use of this information and its impact on students' learning and outcomes vary according to a number of interrelated classroom factors (Brophy, 1979; Eder, 1983; Nicholls, 1984; Pepitone, 1982). A case in point is students' interpretation of classroom events (teacher behaviors, peer interactions), which tend to have different meanings for different students'. These meanings, in turn, influence the students' behavior and their learning outcomes. In their study of student's perceptions of teacher interactions, Weinstein and Middlestadt (1979) found a wide range of differences in students' interpretations of teacher behavior. Their student interviews showed, for example, that students viewed teachers' use of the "call-on" technique as a way of giving low-achieving students a chance, relaying the message that a student was "goofing off," calling on "smart kids" because they knew the answer, or not calling on certain students because they were unlikely to know the answer.

Experience with and knowledge of a variety of tasks also have been shown to have a significant impact on how students perceive a particular task. Students working on highly similar tasks, for example, have been found to make more frequent social comparisons of fellow students (Pepitone, 1972; Rosenholtz & Wilson, 1980) than students in multitask environments in which students work on different tasks (Bossert, 1979).

There is research to suggest that the kind of social comparison information discussed above can be either detrimental or positive. In his review of research in this area, Levine (1983) noted that social comparison is likely to produce feelings of inferiority, low aspirations, a lack of motivation, and interpersonal hostility and competitiveness in low-achieving students. Under certain circumstances, however, comparisons with classmates have not been found to have negative effects (Ames, in press; Johnson, Johnson, & Scott, 1978; Marshall et al., 1982). For example, information about one's own performance in relation to that of one's peers may provide a clue as to which students are competent in which areas. Rather than being the cause of social comparison, this information may be construed as a "resource" (e.g., Carter & Doyle, 1982; Marshall et al., 1982; Weisstein & Wang, 1980). In her analysis of the programming requirements for integrating handicapped students in regular classes, Wang (1981) suggested the wisdom of the multiage grouping strategy for maximizing the effective use of instructional resources such as teachers' and students' time and talents. She contended that, in such environments, individual differences tend to be viewed as the norm rather than as exceptions, and that students and teachers alike tend to consider individual differences in learner knowledge as resources.

3. *Knowledge about relevant strategies for efficient task performance.* Knowledge of, and the ability to regulate, cognitive behavior are seminal to cognitive competence. However, in addition to knowledge about the task and one's own cognitive competence, classroom learning requires knowledge about strategies that can facilitate efficient performance. These strategies have come to be generally recognized as "how-to-learn" skills. A variety of such strategies are used routinely by efficient learners to facilitate the encoding and retrieval of information as well as the comprehension and assimilation of new knowledge and skills.

For example, when studying written materials, efficient learners take notes, construct their own outlines, underline key points, and take other steps to make the materials more meaningful. They also are more likely than inefficient learners to relate new information to previously learned material or to use encoding techniques such as verbal elaboration and imagery. In many situations, they also ask questions, seek help from teachers or other students, and study supplementary material. Effective learners know how to learn; they can adopt and adapt a variety of resources in the learning environment to meet their needs. For instance, findings from research suggest that the precision of self-generated elaborations affects cued recall (Stein & Bransford, 1979) and that successful students are more likely to generate precise elaborations (Stein, Bransford, Frank, Owings, Vye, & McGraw, 1982).

Although a great deal has been written about the strategies used by learners (cf., Kail & Hagen, 1977; Ornstein, 1978), and about the relationship between use of the strategies and student performance (cf., Brown, Bransford, et al., 1983; Deschler, Schumaker, & Lenz, 1984), very little research is reported on the learners' introspective knowledge of these strategies. Findings from the few studies in this area point to the prevalence of a developmental trend (Drozdal & Flavell, 1975; Kreutzer et al., 1975; Salatus & Flavell, 1976). Kreutzer et al. (1975) found that, when they were asked how they would remember to take something with them the next day, young children exhibited rudiments of planning ability, but older children showed knowledge of a greater variety of strategies and greater overall planning. Similarly, when subjects in several studies (Drozdal & Flavell, 1975; Kreutzer et al., 1975; Salatas & Flavell, 1976) were asked what they could do to find a lost item, older children were able to think of a greater number of more sophisticated, more indirect, and more logical and methodological strategies, compared with the strategies generated by younger children. In addition, Myers and Paris (1978; Paris & Myers, 1981) found that older and/or better readers were more metacognitively aware of factors that had negative or positive influences on their reading and comprehension.

The effects of knowledge about strategies on performance have been studied with students of different age levels, wide-ranging backgrounds, and different learner characteristics (e.g., Brown, Smiley, & Lawton, 1978; Dunn, Mathews, & Biegler, 1982; Weinstein, 1978). Dansereau et al. (1979) found that college students who had been taught to use a rather detailed set of learning skills showed greater gains in comprehension and retention than did control students. In her work designed to train students to use verbal and imagery elaborations when reading text passages, Weinstein (1978) noted the enhancing effects on students' reading performance. Similarly, Brown and her colleagues (Brown & Day, 1983; Brown, Day, & Jones, 1983), in their cross-sectional investigations, identified four characteristics of the notes and summaries used by competent students to summarize text. These characteristics were (a) the deletion of trivia, (b) the deletion of redundancy, (c) the substitution of superordinate terms or events for subordinate ones, and (d) the selection or development of topic sentences.

Several categories of strategies are prevalant in the literature related to investigations of how to learn more efficiently. These include strategies that learners use to facilitate their comprehension and recall of textual content. Among the strategies that have been found to be effective are constructing and answering questions (Andre & Anderson, 1978–1979; Frase & Schwartz, 1975); developing an outline that requires some reorganization of the given text (Shimmerlik & Nolan, 1976); writing summary statements (Doctorow, Wittrock, & Marks, 1978; Taylor, 1982); and presenting oral summaries (Ross & DiVesta, 1976).

Another category of how-to-learn strategies is associated with remembering. Studies in this area have been conducted to examine the effectiveness of particular strategies. Brown and Barclay (1976) showed that the memory performance of educable mentally retarded children could be improved significantly if they were taught to employ and monitor strategies of anticipation or rehearsal. Work by Salatas and Flavell (1976) with first-grade students indicated that clear instructions to "remember" resulted in the use of effective strategies and improvement in the recall of information.

An often overlooked, but nonetheless important, learning-to-learn strategy or skill is that of help-seeking. Although the ability to obtain and give help, and to recognize when help is needed, has been suggested as an important factor in learning, it has received little systematic attention in the design of school learning environments. In addition to pròviding empirical support for the positive impact of peer tutoring on social development and academic learning, Allen (1983), in a critical review of research related to peer tutoring and student learning, suggested that help-seeking also is an important learning-to-learn skill.

Nelson-LeGall (1981) maintained that the potentially positive consequences of helping and obtaining help in learning situations have important implications for the development of learners' capabilities to make adaptations in the learning environment to accommodate their individual needs. Her research suggests that help-seeking is determined by a complex interaction of age, ability, subject area, and activity structure (Nelson-LeGall & Glor-Scheib, 1983; Nelson-LeGall & Gummerman, 1983; Nelson-LeGall & Scott-Jones, 1981). For example, Nelson-LeGall and Glor-Scheib (1983) found that, in both math and reading, third graders sought help from peers equally as often as they sought help from teachers. Fifth graders, on the other hand, demonstrated an overwhelming preference for seeking help from peers. Similarly, average-ability students requested help from teachers more often than from peers; low- and high-ability students evidenced the opposite trend.

Webb (1982) reported that the negative effect of not getting the help sought can have particular implications for low-ability students. Swing and Peterson (1981) demonstrated that it was possible to train students to be more effective in carrying out task-related interactions with their peers, and that the value of such interations depended on the ability levels of individual students: low-ability students were more positively affected than were students of higher ability. These findings also are supported by the results from a study designed to examine the effects of a cross-age, peer-tutoring program (Fogarty & Wang, 1982) and the results from a study of the social and academic outcomes for students in a mainstreaming program for mildly handicapped students (Weisstein & Wang, 1980).

To summarize, the present review of the extant research identifies a vast knowledge base that suggests the role of both subject-matter and domain-general knowledge in student performance as well as the wisdom of providing instruction that is commensurate with students' entering level of competence. The importance of including analyses of students' knowledge characterisitcs in instructional planning and the monitoring of learning progress is underscored by the findings cited in this section. Despite the research bases discussed here, the various dimensions of students' knowledge rarely are considered in the design and implementation of school programs. Yet, it seems clear that incorporating an understanding of students' knowledge characteristics is essential for the design and improvement of instructional interventions—especially interventions directed toward the large proportion of students who have not been able to benefit from the "outcomes-focused" approach that dominates current practice.

Students' Use of What They Know in Their Learning

The second component of the self-instructive process concerns students' ability to use what they know in learning new tasks and to apply what they know in new situations. Flavell has coined the term "production deficiency" to refer to the lack of spontaneous use of knowledge by those who are aware of certain strategies or behaviors as prerequisites for accomplishing a goal (Flavell, 1970). Production deficiency has particular instructional design implications for increasing the learning efficiency of low-achieving students and students identified as requiring special education and/or compensatory education services such as those provided by Chapter 1. Investigations of students' use of knowledge and learning performance are based on the premise that the learning problems of less successful learners are not the sole result of inadequate prior knowledge (e.g., Bransford, Stein, Shelton, & Owings, 1981; Brown, 1978; Brown & Campione, 1981). Campione et al. (1982) interpreted the finding of knowledge deficits in less successful or mentally retarded learners to be "a symptom of the major underlying problems rather than as a source of them" (p. 435).

It has been argued that, although the lack of relevant knowledge may be a contributing factor in many learning problems, the learner's ability to use (access) relevant knowledge in new learning also is a key factor. For example, in several studies designed to investigate how children approach the learning of new information, Bransford et al. (1981) found that less successful students failed at times to access already possessed knowledge and, consequently, they jeopardized their own chances to learn related new information. It appears that, even though the performance of less successful learners can be improved through explicit instruction, much instruction is needed in order to instill knowledge. Moreover, the initial development of knowledge does not ensure its flexible use. Thus, there seems to be a research base to suggest that knowledge is necessary, but not sufficient in and of itself, for effective learning performance.

Evidence of production deficiency has been noted in investigations with learning disabled students (Kauffman & Hallahan, 1979; Torgensen, 1977); with mentally retarded students (Belmont & Butterfield, 1977; Brown, 1974; Campione & Brown, 1977); and with hyperactive children (Douglas & Peters, 1979). The results from research with handicapped learners, together with data from studies of metacognitive deficits in reading comprehension (Myers & Paris, 1978; Ryan, 1981), suggest that there are children who, despite having difficulty in their learning, nevertheless have an adequate knowledge base, an awareness of the need to use the knowledge base, and an awareness of effective strategies for using the knowledge base. What they lack, however, is the skill to regulate and coordinate what they know about a task with efficient strategies for completing the task. Thus, although they may be potentially competent learners, they do not use the necessary skills to produce intended learning performnance outcomes.

Much of the related work in this area concerns metacognitive skills (e.g., "overseeing" processes in learning such as predicting, planning, monitoring, and checking) that require the use of knowledge about one's own thought process in a given space and at a given time (Brown, 1978). Metacognitive skills are seen as critical for students' ability to self-regulate and to proceed on their own with learning new tasks efficiently and deliberately. Positive correlations between the ability to use what one knows and student achievement have been a consistent finding. The ability of learners to use what they know in learning on their own appears to be a critical component of learning success. Efficient learners are able to access available knowledge and apply it appropriately. Furthermore, students vary as individuals, not only in terms of what they know, but also according to what they do with what they know.

Results from studies designed to compare the learning performance of high- and low-achieving students show that the former tend to demonstrate more spontaneous use of the knowledge and skills they possess (cf. Brown, Bransford, et al., 1983). In addition, the importance of using knowledge in the acquisition of new knowledge is substantiated by findings from studies in a variety of areas that include language acquisition (Bowerman, 1982; Krashen, 1976); writing and composing (Hayes & Flower, 1980; Scardamalia & Bereiter, in press); learning new information (Brown et al., 1981; Camp, Blom, Herbert, & Van

Doornink, 1977; Day, 1980; Kendall & Finch, 1976); cognitive behavior modification (Meichenbaum & Asarnow, 1979); self-instruction (Bornstein & Quevillon, 1976); reading comprehension (Baker & Brown, 1984; Brown, 1980; Capelli & Markman, 1981; Collins & Stevens, 1982; Flavell, 1981; Markman, 1981); and cognitive skills (Markman, 1979; Tobias, 1979; Weinstein & Underwood, 1985).

The findings from research on metacognition in general, and metacognitive skills in particular, have important relevance for clarifying the learner's role in the learning process. Research in this and related areas suggests the importance of the role played by students in making internal adaptations as well as modifying the learning environment in order to adapt to, or accommodate, their individual learning needs. There is a considerable empirical basis for clarifying and furthering understanding of the nature of the changes that take place in learners' internal mental structures as they acquire new knowledge and solve problems (e.g., the self-regulatory process described by Brown, 1978). In addition to internal adaptations,the learner often finds it necessary to make adaptations at several levels in the external environment. Such adaptions may involve the use of a variety of learning-to-learn strategies for enhancing one's ability to self-evaluate, to know when and where to seek help, to plan, to identify specific strategies for improving memory, and to selectively provide relevant information required for learning.

Evidence of the use of knowledge in new learning generally consists of data from studies of learners' activities in planning and self-monitoring of performance. As shown in Fig. 1, planning involves identification, formulation, and restructuring of goals; strategy planning; and executive planning. Monitoring of one's own performance involves execution of solution steps (e.g., questioning, help seeking, checking, testing, revising); assessment and self-interpretation; and self-interrogation and clarification.

Planning. In the context of the conceptual model for the study of the self-instructive process (see Fig. 1), planning is characterized as an interaction of knowledge, task structure, and task demands that is flexible and sensitive to changes in situations over time. Since the beginning of modern cognitive psychology (e.g., Miller, Galanter, & Pribram, 1960), planning has been recognized as a seminal component of cognitive functioning. However, empirical research on development of the processes involved in planning—especially the planning of complex cognitive tasks—is limited. In general, findings from research in this area indicate that planning strategies emerge sporadically when a learner undertakes a new, complex activity. Planning strategies gradually become more stable and systematic as the learner gains experience in the activity or area of knowledge (Brown & Smiley, 1978; Brown, Day, & Jones, 1983; Scardamalia & Bereiter, 1985).

Research suggests that ability and age are factors in competent, flexible, and sensitive planning. Older children have been found to be more flexible planners (Brown & Smiley, 1977). Due in part to their greater knowledge of the structure of text and their greater sensitivity to task demands, older children have been found to use extra study time to improve their recall of important text elements (Brown & Smiley, 1978) and to shift their attention from high-importance to intermediate-importance text elements after experience showed that they could recall the former without further effort (Brown et al., 1978).

Efficient performance also seems to be related to the use of planning strategies as well as to age. A certain amount of spontaneous use of planning strategies has been found for all age levels. Brown, Day, and Jones (1983) found, for example, that, although a greater number of older than younger students used presummary notes, the best predictor of success in composing a competent final product was planning, irrespective of age. Similarly, Owings, Peterson, Bransford, Morris, and Stein (1980) found that more successful fifth graders were more likely than their less successful classmates to adapt study times and reading rates to the difficulty of the material. The work of Flower and Hayes (1981; Hayes & Flower, 1980) indicated that, compared to poor college writers, good college writers not only generated plans that were more responsive to the broader rhetorical problem (the relationship of text, audience, and writer), but they also revised their plans during the writing process.

An ability that is closely associated with efficient planning is the ability to predict outcomes prior to experience. Prediction is characterized in the literature as a complex set of skills that are activated before an attempt to learn or solve a problem. Prediction, as explicated by Brown (1978), essentially is the coordination of various aspects of knowledge to imagine cognitive acts that have not yet occurred. Empirical studies of learners' skills in predicting their performance on a task generally have focused on three types of metacognitive knowledge variables: learners' current feelings about their knowledge of the task, learners' actual knowledge of the task, and learners' knowledge of the appropriate strategy for completing the task.

Brown and Lawton (1977) conducted two studies in which they asked educable mentally retarded children (mental ages [MA] = 6–10) to predict their ability to recognize a familiar picture that they previously had failed to recall. Findings from the studies suggest a trend in the subjects' ability to predict their accurate performance on the basis of their feeling that they knew which pictures they had failed to recall previously. Similar findings were noted by Stein, Bransford, Franks, Vye, and Perfetto (1982) in their investigation of the ability of academically more and less successful fifth-grade students to predict the effects of semantic ambiguity on memory. They found that, in general, more successful students predicted more accurately, were more metacognitively aware of the reasons for their predictions, and were able to benefit from experience. Less successful students demonstrated relatively little skill in these areas.

The relation of knowledge of task difficulty to skill in predicting was examined by Brown (1978) in a study that nvestigated educable mentally retarded children's knowledge about the difficulty of tasks. Brown found a developmental increase in the children's ability to predict, and to justify their prediction of, which of two tasks would be more difficult to accomplish. She concluded, however, that the relationship between awareness of task difficulty and the skills of prediction depended on the complexity of the task being judged. For example, her subjects realized that recognition tasks were easier than recall tasks, but, at the same time, they were unable to judge the effects of retroactive interference on task difficulty.

Monitoring. Although planning involves the coordination of knowledge and strategy variables prior to attempts to learn, monitoring becomes active during the learning process. Thus, monitoring refers to on-line supervision and management of the continually changing interrelationships of knowledge, plans, strategies, and goals en route to the completion of a task.

Studies of learning processes for activities that involve comprehension of written and spoken material have included investigations of monitoring skills (Bransford et al., 1981; Brown, 1980, 1981; Brown & Smiley, 1978; Flavell, 1981; Flavell, Speer, Green, & August, 1981; Markman, 1977, 1979, 1981). Data from studies in which subjects were asked to notice and report inconsistencies or ambiguities in written or spoken text suggest that comprehension monitoring in such situations is a relatively late-developing skill. Research has indicated that young children tend not to be very aware of text structure, and to be more concerned with the truth value of a proposition (i.e., whether the statement corresponds with reality) than with the consistency among propositions (e.g., Brown & Smiley, 1977; Markman, 1976).

Despite the evidence of a developmental trend in the monitoring process, there also is a data base to support the role of task-specific factors, such as task complexity and learner competence, in determining whether monitoring skills are demonstrated by an individual in a particular situation. For example, Garner (1981) found that poor readers in junior high school were less likely to rate inconsistent text as difficult than were good readers, and that poor readers were better at identifying comprehension problems due to vocabulary rather than logical inconsistencies. Subjects have been found to be more likely to notice inconsistencies that were contained within a single sentence (Garner & Krause, 1980) or in adjacent sentences (Markman, 1979), and less likely to notice inconsistencies in disparate parts of the text. The more demanding skill involved in integrating and evaluating information across segments of text also has been shown to cause difficulty, even for college students (Baker, 1979). Thus, there is a data base to suggest that monitoring skills are influenced by task-specific features as well as by the level of cognitive development.

Owings et al. (1980) investigated reactions and adaptability to imprecisely elaborated short stories for more successful and less successful fifth graders. One of the major findings was that the more successful students spontaneously monitored what they read, were aware of having difficulty with the imprecise passages, and could explain why they were having difficulty. By contrast, the less successful students did not demonstrate any of these skills. The more successful students also modified their reading time, studying the imprecise passages longer. The less successful students, on the other hand, studied each type of passage for approximately the same amount of time. As a result, the memory performance of the more successful students was better than that of the less successful students on the cued-recall test for both precise and imprecise passages. Finally, the less successful students could differentiate between stories only when prompted. Overall, the results from the Owings et al. (1980) study suggest that poorer learners do not spontaneously monitor and regulate their learning activities. These results are corroborated by the findings from a series of studies conducted by Bransford, Stein, and their colleagues (Bransford, Stein, et al., 1981; Perfetto, 1982; Franks, et al., 1982; Stein, Bransford, Franks, Owings, Vye, & McGraw, 1982; Stein, Bransford, Franks, Vye, & Perfetto, 1982).

In summary, efficient learners typically are characterized in the research literature as those who are able not only to access available knowledge but also to apply the knowledge appropriately. They are capable of learning independently and deliberately through the identification, formulation, and restructuring of goals; the use of strategy and executive planning; the development and execution of solution steps; and the engagement in self-monitoring, self-assessment, self-interrogation, and clarification. Overall, research seems to suggest that the age-related trend in learners' ability to use their knowledge in new learning (as evidenced in the cross-sectional, developmental research) may be due to a confounding of age with expertise. Studies designed explicitly to investigate the relationship of expertise to performance have found that experts in a particular task area, regardless of age, share adult-like performance characteristics; that is, there are aspects of task performance that are common to experts across age groups. Although there tends to be an overall, age-related increase in the spontaneous use of knowledge in new learning, use of this skill by young learners has been found to be similar to that of adults with equivalent subject-matter knowledge. This finding parallels the recent emphasis on interaction and the concomitant call in the fields of cognitive and developmental psychology for research on multiple rather than isolated variables (e.g., Bransford, 1979; Brown, Bransford, et al., 1983; Jenkins, 1979).

Instructional Interventions for Development and Use of Self-Instructive Skills

Although significant advances are noted in the research aimed at broadening understanding of the role of the learner in general, and the learner's ability to be self-instructive in particular, the development of educational interventions for explicitly fostering students' ability to function as self-instructive learners has been quite limited. The state of practice in this area is summarized in this section under two categories of findings: laboratory-based interventions, and school-based intervention programs.

Laboratory-Based Interventions

Despite the surge of experimental intervention studies in research on cognition and learning, very few of these studies have focused on use of the kinds of self-instructive processes and skills described in this chapter. Although improvement has been noted in cognitive training programs designed to help mentally retarded students use cognitive strategies such as rehearsal, elaboration, and categorization in their learning (Belmont & Butterfield, 1971; Borkowski & Wanschura, 1974; Brown, 1974), the cognitive training studies, for the most part, have failed to produce evidence of long-term maintenance or transfer of learning outcomes (Brown & Campione, 1978; Campione & Brown, 1977; Deschler, Schumaker, & Lenz, 1984). In their review of studies of cognitive instruction for young and retarded children, Belmont and Butterfield (1977) noted no findings of generalized, spontaneous performance results. Findings from the review of recent training studies by Campione et al. (1982), however, point to a more positive trend. Two types of training approaches discussed in their review are especially noteworthy. They are the "informed" and the "self-control" training approaches.

Informed training. In addition to training in cognitive strategies, informed training involves the teaching of aspects of metacognitive knowledge. That is, subjects are taught the utility of particular strategies for reaching specific task goals. Results from several informed training studies suggest that, when learners are told a strategy improves performance, they are more likely to employ the strategy if presented with a task similar to the training task (e.g., Borkowski, Levers, & Gruenfelder, 1976; Burger, Blackman, Holmes, & Zetlin, 1978; Cavanaugh & Borkowski, 1979; Kennedy & Miller, 1976; Lawson & Fuelop, 1980; Paris, Newman, & McVey, 1982; Ringel & Springer, 1980). For example, Kennedy and Miller (1976) found that a rehearsal strategy was more likely to be maintained in the absence of prompts if it was made clear to the subjects during training that using the strategy led to improved recall. Kendall, Borkowski, and Cavanaugh (1980) found similar results using elaboration strategies for paired-associate learning.

Various techniques have been used to develop students' knowledge about the utility of particular strategies for enhancing learning. One method involves providing training in a strategic routine in a variety of contexts. Belmont, Butterfield, and Borkowski (1978) trained subjects to use a strategy in two slightly different contexts so that the rehearsal strategy would have to be varied somewhat in order to take into account response requirements. Greater transfer to a third context was found as a result of this intervention. In another study, feedback after a recall test, combined with presentation of a brief rationale prior to strategy use, resulted in findings of better acquisition performance and longer-term effect (Paris et al., 1982). Based on assessments of learner judgments throughout the latter experiment, it was concluded that knowledge about task goals and knowledge about the usefulness of each component activity in attaining the goals were major factors in the continued, unprompted use of a particular cognitive strategy. Without this awareness, learners exhibited a production deficiency, or a failure to engage in strategic behavior without prompting.

It is important to note here that findings from the informed training studies also suggest that variations in tasks and treatments produce different effects at different ages. Ringel and Springer (1980) found that first graders were unable to benefit from knowledge of strategy effectiveness. For fifth graders, instruction alone was sufficient to produce a transfer. Only third graders were found to benefit from instruction combined with information on strategy utilization. Pressley and his colleagues (e.g., O'Sullivan & Pressley, 1984) found that strategy-utilization knowledge facilitated use of the keyword mnemonic method (the use of imagery techniques to facilitate vocabulary and paired-associate learning) by children in Grades 5 through 7. Adults in the same study were able to independently monitor the effectiveness of the strategies used. (Similar results were noted in the work of Cavanaugh and Borkowski, 1979; Kennedy and Miller, 1976; Kramer and Engle, 1981; and Lawson and Fuelop, 1980.)

To summarize, data from the informed training studies suggest that providing information about the utility of a strategy increases the durability and transfer value of the strategy. However, the effects have yet to be demonstrated for any significant length of time or for tasks other than near-transfer tasks.

Self-control training. In self-control training, subjects not only are informed as to why specific strategies are useful in mastery of a targeted task, but they also are taught the use of skills such as planning, prediction, and monitoring, as well as specific strategies not already in the subjects' repertoire. Although self-control training has not been evaluated extensively, there is some evidence that strategies taught in such training programs are generalized to new tasks (e.g., Brown, Campione, & Barclay, 1979).

Brown and her colleagues have conducted several self-control training studies that have added significantly to the knowledge base on the role of metacognitive processes in enhancing learning outcomes for subjects with learning problems. This work, which has focused on the effects of explicit instruction in skills such as planning, monitoring, and checking, may be viewed as instruction in emulating the activities of spontaneous strategy users. The intervention programs featured training in specific cognitive strategies as well as explicit training in the metacognitive skills required to monitor and regulate strategy usage. The findings of Brown et al. include a differential treatment effect on learning outcomes, depending on the initial competence of individual subjects. In general, this type of training has been found to increase learning performance and the spontaneous use of cognitive strategies. The data also suggest that less skilful and developmentally less mature learners need more explicit instruction in order to spontaneously regulate their performance at a level comparable with that of more competent and older learners.

These general conclusions were derived from a series of empirical studies by Brown and her colleagues. In one set of studies, developmental comparisons were made of mildly retarded children at two different mental ages (MA = 6 and MA = 8) (Brown & Barclay, 1976; Brown et al., 1979). The design of these studies included a readiness-recall task on which the baseline performance for all subjects was poor, as well as strategy instruction that consisted of a rehearsal strategy for one group and an anticipation of items for the second group. (A third group was taught to label stimuli. However, the strategy proved ineffective, regardless of age, and the results for this group have been omitted from this discussion.) Both groups also were taught to engage in self-checking to ensure that they were learning. Significant effects of the strategy-plus-self-regulatory condition were found for the MA = 8 group but not for the MA = 6 group. The results showed that both groups made immediate gains in learning performance after training. However, only the developmentally more mature group showed evidence of spontaneous, self-controlled use of the training strategy in new situations. The MA = 8 group maintained the strategy after one year and transferred the strategy use to different tasks. The MA = 6 group, on the other hand, improved their learning performance only in the prompted, posttest situation. In the absence of prompts, they showed a production deficiency and their performance dropped to baseline level. These results indicate that less mature learners tended to benefit less than more mature learners from instruction in self-regulation of strategic learning behavior. The implication is that learners who are less mature developmentally require more explicit training in order to achieve learning outcomes comparable with those of more mature learners.

Similar results have been found for other populations. Day (1980) taught average and remedial community college students the operations used by experts in summarizing text. Within each ability group, there were four instructional conditions—self-management training (subjects given encouragement and the gist of a good summary); rules (subjects given explicit instruction and modeling in the use of rules); rules and self-management (subjects given both treatments but left to integrate the two sets of information themselves); and rules and self-management, but with explicit connections made between the rules and self-management. Briefly, both groups of subjects (average and remedial) were found to be equally deficient in their use of the different summarization rules. The most effective training for the remedial group was the fourth and most explicit condition. Overall, the average students benefited from all the training procedures and were able to use the training more efficiently than their remedial counterparts.

The findings from the laboratory experiments described above are further supported by the results from a set of investigations by Palincsar and Brown (1984). In these studies, which were carried out in classroom settings, the students were taught four study activities—summarizing, questioning, clarifying, and predicting—through a training procedure called "reciprocal teaching" (informed, self-control training). Overall, their findings were consistent with those from the laboratory studies. Reciprocal teaching was found to be qualitatively better than the alternate intervention of locating information. In the latter strategy, students were taught that the answers to implicit and explicit text questions could be found, with a little work, in the text itself. Palincsar and Brown also found that the target students not only improved dramatically in their comprehension skills but that they also were able to transfer the skills to different environments (resource room, regular classroom) and tasks. Furthermore, and perhaps even more important, reciprocal training was able to be carried out in regular education classrooms by regular classroom teachers with a minimum of training effort (three training sessions).

Other relevant work in this area has been conducted by Franks, Stein, and their colleagues (Franks et al., 1982; Stein, Bransford, Franks, Owings, et al., 1982; Stein, Bransford, Franks, Vye, & Perfetto, 1982). Specifically, their studies attempted to train less successful students to improve their performance on a number of different tasks over baseline measurements. In general, the training emphasized the evaluation of materials, the need to activate prerequisite knowledge in order to make a situation more meaningful, and the reasons why such activities could be helpful in learning new information. In all cases, posttest performance was significantly above pretest performance.

The investigations of laboratory-based interventions also have included cognitive behavior modification research. The work of Meichenbaum (1977), for example, generally has concentrated on impulse control. Studies have shown that, although response latencies tend to increase as a result of such training, concomitant increases in response accuracy are not always demonstrated (e.g., Camp et al., 1977). Evidence of the maintenance and generalization effects of cognitive behavior modification is similarly equivocal (e.g., Meichenbaum & Goodman, 1971). Nevertheless, such training programs seem to produce excellent short-term results for children who lack executive strategies but are proficient in task-specific skills. Some of the cognitive behavior modification research also has provided instruction in task-specific skills (Leon & Pepe, 1978).

Based on results from the training studies discussed here, it seems clear that students need to be fully informed about why and when they should be strategic, and they can be trained in self-directed applications of appropriate strategies. In addition, the degree of explicit training needed for any task depends on the initial ability of a particular learner and his or her speed of learning. Better informed subjects tend to show faster learning and some spontaneous use of self-regulatory skills. Thus, they require less explicit instruction than is required by poorly informed and less able subjects of the same age.

The implications of the findings from the research on laboratory-based interventions are that self-instructive skills as discussed in this chapter can be taught and that academically at-risk students, in particular, require more explicit instruction in the use of self-instructive skills in order to perform at a level comparable with higher ability students. The ideal training package for enhancing learning in children with learning problems would seem to combine task-appropriate, strategy training with metacognitive knowledge about the significance of particular strategies, as well as instruction and practice in the monitoring and self-regulation of strategy use.

School-Based Intervention Programs

School-based programs that include the teaching of self-instructive skills as defined in the context of this chapter most typically are referred to under the general rubric of "thinking skills" programs or "problem-solving skills" programs. Although substantial effort has been devoted to the development and implementation of school-based, thinking skills programs, the data base on the implementation and effects of these programs is scanty at best. A comprehensive description of extant school programs in this area, and a discussion of the implications for instruction and learning, can be found in a recently published book, entitled *Thinking and Learning Skills* (Segal et al., 1985).

Three programs are described here for illustrative purposes. They were selected because of their wide use in schools and because of the availability of data on program effects. The three programs are Feuerstein's Instrumental Enrichment Program (Feuerstein, Jensen, Hoffman, & Rand, 1985; Feuerstein, Rand, Hoffman, & Miller, 1980); Lipman's Philosophy for Children Program (Lipman, 1980, 1985; Lipman & Sharp, 1978; Lipman, Sharp, & Oscanyan, 1980); and Covington's Productive Thinking Program (Covington, 1985; Covington, Crutchfield, Davies, & Olton, 1974).

Instrumental Enrichment Program. The Instrumental Enrichment Program (Feuerstein et al., 1985; Feuerstein et al., 1980) is based on the contention that the below-grade-level functioning of many students with identified learning problems can be improved through sufficient exposure to teacher-mediated interactions aimed expressly at emphasizing the meaningfulness of certain stimuli and de-emphasizing that of others. Referred to as "mediated learning experiences," these interactions incorporate four different activities that students are taught to generalize to academic and other important areas of experience. The first activity involves defining a particular task and selecting and evaluating different strategies for solving the various problems associated with completing the task. The second activity consists of informed practice: Students are encouraged to evaluate strategies while applying them to problems and to generate checking routines. The third activity is an introduction to basic concepts, whereby students are taught concepts such as "model," "rules," and "planning," within the context of problem definitions and solutions. The final activity included among the program's mediated learning experiences involves the provision of specific instruction for students in applying previously learned principles and concepts to other domains.

The Instrumental Enrichment Program is designed to be implemented by teachers in regular classroom settings for 3–5 hours per week over a 2- or 3-year period. Learning materials consist of relatively content-free, paper-and-pencil, problem-solving exercises that focus on concepts such as spatial, temporal, and transitive relationships; categories; and numerical progressions.

Evaluations of the program conducted to date have been limited to assessing its effectiveness with borderline populations of students with certain handicap classifications (behaviorally disordered, culturally different, educable mentally retarded, varying exceptionality), and the findings from these evaluations have been mixed (cf. Segal et al., 1985).

For example, Feuerstein, Rand, Hoffman, Hoffman, and Miller (1979) evaluated the effects of the Instrumental Enrichment Program relative to the effects of a general enrichment program with fifty-seven matched pairs of mentally handicapped students (ranging from borderline to educable mentally retarded as evaluated by the Primary Mental Abilities Test [PMA], Thurstone & Thurstone, 1962, for 2 years). Students spent approximately the same amount of time in either program, and both programs were administered in addition to the standard school curriculum. Multiple criteria were employed: general intellectual functioning (as measured by the PMA); specific cognitive functions (as measured by the Embedded Figures Test, Witkin, Oltman, Raskin, & Karp, 1971); achievement in basic intellectual and scholastic skills (assessed by a battery of nine tests designed for this study and reflective of the school's regular curriculum); classroom interactions (assessed by measures of classroom participation); and self-concept (assessed by measures of self-concept). The Instrumental Enrichment Program group, relative to the control group, evidenced significant increases in IQ, significant improvement on two subtests of the achievement battery, significant improvement on tests of specific cognitive functions, limited gains in classroom participation, and no differences in self-concept.

Haywood and Smith (1979), by contrast, conducted two studies with a more heterogeneous sample (behaviorally disordered, culturally deprived, educable mentally retarded, learning disabled, varying exceptionality) and found significant improvement in IQ for the whole sample in the first study, but only for the varying exceptionality group in the second study. In addition, increases in the General Information Subtest of the Peabody Individual Achievement Test (Dunn & Markwardt, 1970) were evidenced for all Instrumental Enrichment Program students the second study, but only the culturally deprived group showed gains on the Raven's Progressive Matrices (Raven, 1965). The behaviorally disordered students were the only ones to evidence significant gains on the Woodcock–Johnson Psychoeducational Battery (Woodcock & Johnson, 1977–78).

Philosophy for Children Program. The Philosophy for Children Program is a curriculum-based program aimed at teaching the processes of philosophical inquiry (Lipman, 1980, 1985; Lipman & Sharp, 1978; Lipman et al., 1980). It is predicated on the belief that the reliance on curriculum hierarchies—whereby instruction in less complex skills such as reading and math precedes instruction in more complex activities such as philosophical inquiry—has resulted in inadequate instruction in effective thinking and reasoning. The developers of the program contend that instruction in philosophical processes should be included as a seminal component of all elementary and secondary curricula.

The emphasis of the Philosophy for Children Program is on fostering the ability to listen and respond effectively to others by learning to reason during the course of dialogue. Instruction is provided in skills such as abstracting assumptions, drawing inferences, testing for consistency and comprehension, and thinking independently. Activities and materials include stories that feature dialogue between children and adults about issues that arise during the course of everyday situations, the training of teachers to conduct and encourage philosophical discussion among students, and the extensive use of exercises that help students to evaluate their understanding of concepts while also helping teachers to assess student progress.

Experimental evaluations of the Philosophy for Children Program generally provide support for its effectiveness (see Lipman, 1985, for a review of the research). Although findings suggest that there is considerable variation within and between grades, sites, and studies, instruction under the program seems to facilitate formal and creative reasoning skills, reading and math achievement, and, at times, interpersonal skills. Bransford, Arbitman-Smith, Stein, and Vye (1985), while noting that the evaluation data on the Philosophy for Children Program are cause for optimism, also have argued for (a) research aimed at on-line evaluations of students' progress through the program to determine why some students achieve outcomes that others do not (e.g., why some participating students evidence gains in math even though the program has no math exercises); (b) alternative criteria for evaluating program outcomes (e.g., whether, in addition to solving formal reasoning problems, the program might also enhance the ability to evaluate the type of reasoning that occurs in everyday settings); and (c) a greater emphasis on program improvement (e.g., more precisely defined program subgoals and development of feedback mechanisms to improve instructional procedures) rather than focusing almost entirely on proving that the program works.

Productive Thinking Program. The goal of the Productive Thinking Program (Covington, 1985; Covington et al., 1974) is to strengthen students' ability to formulate problems, select strategies, and monitor the relationship between their own individual strengths and weaknesses and their progress toward completing learning tasks and accomplishing learning goals. The design of the program incorporates the belief that academic difficulties can be attributed, at least in part, to individual students' problems in thinking strategically.

The Productive Thinking Program is a 6-week course for students in Grades 5 and 6. Materials include 15 student booklets (each containing a lesson and supplementary problems); a teacher's guide; and auxiliary materials (e.g., visual aids). In each lesson, students are required to use their general world knowledge and a set of 16 thinking guides (general heuristics of the type advocated by Polya, 1973) to solve a mystery (e.g., how some supposedly supernatural tricks are performed). The thinking guides stress ideational fluency, problem restructuring, and the ability to generate a large number of novel ideas (Polson & Jeffries, 1985).

Findings from evaluations of the Productive Thinking Program show benefits for children at all ability levels. For example, Covington (1965) found that students became better able to monitor their comprehension (e.g., to detect inconsistencies and disrepancies in text) and to generate plans of action for dealing with ill-defined, problem-solving situations. In another study, Olton and Crutchfield (1969) evaluated the Productive Thinking Program with 280 fifth- and sixth-grade students who were matched on IQ (mean of 115) and general level of academic achievement. The students were divided into experimental and control groups using a split-class technique. (On average, the students in the sample were 1½ years ahead of grade level as measured by the Stanford Achievement Test, Madden, Gardner, Rudman, Karlsen, & Merwin, 1975). The experimental group received 8 weeks of instruction, 1 hour per day. The control group engaged in other relevant educational activities for the same period of time. All subjects were pretested on measures of productive thinking; they also were tested at the end of the program and 6 weeks after the treatment. The experimental group exhibited significantly better performance on both posttests.

Polson and Jeffries (1985) based their review of the Productive Thinking Program on the Olton and Crutchfield (1969) study. Even though the latter study may be viewed as the most rigorous of a group of studies with results that were found to be "uniformly positive," it exemplifies some of the problems that have been encountered in evaluations of thinking skills programs generally. One of the problems with the Olton and Crutchfield study is that the dependent measure consisted of a broad range of open-ended items that cannot be simply scored as right or wrong. Another problem is that multiple criteria were used in evaluating responses (e.g., number of ideas generated, number of enigmatic facts explained, number of causes listed), with the sum of the resultant scores (after a rather unusual and seemingly laborious scoring procedure) as the main dependent measure. Polson and Jeffries stated, "the justification of such a measure is not clear, nor is its effect on the outcome of the study, if any, apparent" (p. 431). Due to the equivocal nature of the evaluation results to date, further research seems warranted.

Conclusion and Discussion

This chapter has reviewed diverse data bases on how students come to be expert learners through learning from instruction and on their own. The relationship between the role assumed by students in the learning process and learning success is a prevalent finding from research based on various theoretical and practical perspectives. Two major conclusions can be drawn. First, there is a substantial research base for clarifying and extending current definitions of the role of the learner in acquiring and using knowledge and skills. Second, implications can be drawn for treating students' ability to learn deliberately on their own, and from instruction by others, as an individual difference variable in the design and implementation of effective educational interventions. Such interventions could focus in particular on improving the learning efficacy and efficiency of students with poor prognoses for academic success—those generally considered to be academically at-risk and, especially, students classified as mildly handicapped and/or students otherwise identified as requiring compensatory and/or other remedial education services.

Clarifying and Defining the Role of the Learner

The present review of recent research on learning and instruction from varied perspectives has uncovered significant similarities in characterizations of the role of the learner and the patterns of learning processes of more and less effective learners. These similarities can be traced across the work of cognitive-instructional psychologists interested in the cognitive and metacognitive processes underlying knowledge and skills development, social psychologists whose work on social cognition and achievement motivation is tied closely to the learner's perception of self-control and self-competence, and researchers interested in effective schooling and classroom learning. Research in the latter category includes the study of students' mediating function in classroom learning situations and the development of innovative practices that foster student independence and achievement motivation.

Although their work in this area appears to have followed disparate paths, one salient feature in the research of all these groups is the characterization of effective students as cognitively and affectively active participants in the learning process who function as information processors, interpreters, and synthesizers. More precisely, more effective learners are distinguished from less effective learners by their adaptation and use of what they know in the acquisition of new knowledge and skills; by their ability to take responsibility for managing, monitoring, and evaluating their learning; and by their flexibility and skill in making adaptation in their learning environment (e.g., redeploying or obtaining learning resources to fit their needs and goals) and in adjusting themselves to the demands of the learning process. Affectively, more effective learners exhibit greater perceptions of self-competence and stronger motivation to assume responsibility for their own learning. Overall, effective learners commonly are described as knowledgeable, active, and resourceful. They take responsibility for managing their learning environment and behavior, and they know how to learn on their own, from instruction by teachers and/or peers, and through the use and adaptation of a variety of resources in the learning environment.

Implications for Effective Instruction

The changing conception of the role of the learner has been paralleled by a shift of attention in the research on learning and instruction. The focus has moved from analysis of the outcomes of learning toward investigation of the nature and patterns of the process of learning. Learning has come to be seen as necessarily involving both internal and external adaptation on the part of students. External adaptation occurs in the ideas and content that are to be learned and in the modes and forms in which learning is to take place. This type of adaptation can be accomplished by students, or through program design modifications, the curriculum, the teacher, or other external resources. By contrast, internal adaptations take place in the student's mind as new content is assimilated and internal mental structures are modified to accommodate the new content. Thus, the student is seen as the ultimate mediating agent in the learning process, with the primary goal of schooling being the improvement of each student's capability for effectively performing this role in achieving schooling success.

Helping students to become lifelong learners always has been a long-term aspiration of schooling. However, the shorter term goal of ensuring the acquisition of basic academic skills seems to be the predominant thrust—if not the single focus—of schooling practice. Improvement efforts in special education in particular have focused on the study and amelioration of deficits in traditionally defined sets of basic academic skills and social competence. This preoccupation persists despite substantial empirical evidence that the lack of motivation and competence for being self-responsible and self-instructive in learning is a major source of learning difficulty for students in general and for those who are considered academically at-risk and students in special education programs in particular. There have been very few systematic attempts to study and develop instructional interventions that foster the kinds of learning skills described in this chapter as associated with successful students.

In addition to the theoretical and empirical support for investigating the educational implications of the student's role in the learning process and in the effective provision of education, the need to teach self-responsibility and self-instructive skills is supported from the perspective of schooling demands and practicalities. The findings from classroom process research related to time use by students and teachers are a good illustration of a school improvement priority that would seem well-accommodated by effective interventions for fostering the development and use of self-instructive skills. Research in this area suggests close relationships between the use of school time by students and teachers and student learning outcomes (e.g., Fisher & Berliner, 1985), and between student learning and the amount of school time that students are expected to spend working on their own (Anderson, 1983; Denham & Lieberman, 1980).

Data from the California Beginning Teachers Evaluation Study (Fisher et al., 1978), for example, indicate that elementary school students, in general, spend approximately 65–75% of their time on independent seat work (Denham & Lieberman, 1980). Given this statistic, it is not surprising that data from classroom studies repeatedly show teachers' and students' attention being dominated by a concern for maintaining order and for giving and collecting seat work, with very little time being spent on instruction (Anderson, 1981; Blumenfeld, Hamilton, Wessels, & Meece, 1983; Brophy, 1983). In such classrooms, students are held responsible (by default) for understanding the meaning or purpose of assigned work, identifying resources for completing their work, pacing themselves, and checking their work to ensure the correct and timely completion of tasks. Paradoxically, however, students rarely are taught the prerequisite skills for assuming this level of responsibility for their learning. Consequently, teachers often find it necessary to concentrate on explaining directions or procedures for completing and handing in work rather than focusing on the substance of assignments (Blumenfeld et al., 1983; Brophy, 1982).

Thus, findings from the present review suggest that the study and characterization of the role played by students in school learning situations clearly are relevant to the theory and practice of effective schooling. This much needed area of research would increase our understanding and ability to help schools to foster in students the competence and motivation to be self-responsible and self-instructive in their learning and, ultimately, to be effective "learners for life." It would hold particular relevance for increasing schools' capabilities to provide improved chances of schooling success for students with poor academic prognoses, especially those students who are enrolled in the various special and/or compensatory education programs and are identified as requiring greater-than-usual educational support.

A Proposed Agenda for Research and Innovative Program Development

Given the extant research base in this general topic area, as well as the current drive for educational excellence and the targeting of the development of high level learning, thinking, and problem-solving skills as school improvement priorities for the 1990s (e.g., National Commission on Excellence in Education, 1983; Twentieth Century Fund Task Force, 1983), significant implications arise for the design of school learning environments that help students to acquire the knowledge and skills for becoming increasingly self-responsible and self-instructive in their learning. In fact, development of the intellectual and social competence of individual students for mediating their own learning has come to be widely recognized as an ultimate goal of schooling.

An agenda is proposed here for a program of research and innovative program development aimed at fostering students' development and use of self-instructive skills in their school learning. The discussion is organized around the twofold objective of the proposed agenda—to build a descriptive data base that includes findings from investigations in natural classroom environments with students with a wide range of academic standings and other instructionally relevant characteristics; and to conduct instructional design experimentations with the goal of building a knowledge base for creating supportive school environments and identifying effective intervention strategies that foster the development of self-responsibility and self-instructive skills in students.

Building a Descriptive Data Base

Although analysis and description of the role of the learner in the learning process have been major topics of investigation for some time, information on students' knowledge and self-instructive characteristics comes, for the most part, from experimental studies of nonhandicapped populations in laboratory settings. As reflected in the findings from the review of extant research discussed in this chapter, very little empirical work has been carried out in actual school settings. Furthermore, the relevant research base on handicapped learners is sorely lacking.

Theories of planning, for example, generally stem from work in artificial intelligence. The computer models generated within this framework tend to work only in highly refined domains and to be predicated on idealized theories of top-down processing that most typically do not capitalize on the kinds of unforeseen bottom-up events that can benefit human problem solvers (with a few exceptions, such as the work of Hayes-Roth & Hayes-Roth, 1979). Similarly, the testing of theories of comprehension monitoring, which are theoretically more inclusive (e.g., accommodating both top-down and bottom-up processing), usually is carried out in the context of laboratory and memory-task studies. Findings from these studies have few direct implications for practice in the much more complex milieu of natural classroom learning environments.

In cases when research has been aimed at studying the role of the learner in classroom learning situations, as noted earlier in this discussion, the focus usually has been on learners' management of their own behavior and/or the learning environment. Little attention has been given to the active role that students play in the process of knowledge and skills acquisition (Wang & Lindvall, 1984). Moreover, although much of the classroom process research to date has made a significant contribution to the understanding of classroom instruction and schooling practices—an understanding that is noted by Glaser (1979) as being fundamental to the development of macrotheories of instruction—the data base tends to be at too global a level to provide useful information regarding how and what students think as they go about their classroom learning or how they use (and think about) what they know in new learning and apply what they know in new situations. The persistent finding of the relationship between time-on-task and student achievement in research related to the allocation and efficient use of school time is a case in point. The time-on-task data in such research (Denham & Lieberman, 1980; Fisher & Berliner, 1985) tend to be viewed as indicators of student independence or a well-managed class rather than as information that could be used to attribute students' functioning to the time spent on-task or to characterize the nature of the environment (teacher behavior) and the types of activities that occur during observed time-on-task.

Despite the significant advances in contemporary theories of learning and in the empirical data bases from recent research on classroom learning—particularly research on students' mediating processes (DeStefano et al., 1984; Doyle & Carter, 1984; Marshall & Weinstein, 1984)—the linkages among research in the areas of cognition and learning, students' motivation to learn and their perceptions of self-competence, and actual performance in classroom learning situations remain highly inferential. Thus, extending the current, predominantly laboratory-based research to schooling contexts seems to be appropriate as a basic agenda for research and development aimed at improving schools' capabilities to enhance students' ability to influence their own learning. Work in this area can be expected to make a substantial contribution to the data base on what is involved in students' mediating (adaptations) functions in their learning, and how school learning environments can best facilitate the acquisition and use of these functions.

Specifically, we are proposing a program of school-based research aimed at gathering descriptive data for systematic analysis of students' functioning in the role of expert learner, based on the conceptual model for the study of the self-instructive process in classroom learning contexts (see Fig. 1). A particular focus of this research should be the study of handicapped and academically at-risk student populations. A basic contention of the proposed agenda is that, when coupled with subject-matter knowledge, the ability to use self-instructive skills—which we believe are the basics of higher order cognitive skills—to enhance one's own learning differentiates students who succeed in school learning from those who do not. The development of a data base for analyzing the differences between successful and less successful students is critical to providing for those differences.

Among the specific questions that need to be examined, for example, are whether students effectively assess their own capabilities for carrying out given tasks and have good strategies for dealing with negative assessments; whether, and under what circumstances, students use planning strategies in their completion of classroom assignments; whether students monitor and check their own progress as they work; and whether students have a repertoire of backup strategies. Related questions include whether students can determine from the normal presentation of tasks what they are to do, what materials they will need, and the like; whether they determine the criteria for judging their work and then adapt their work to fit the criteria; whether they know the rules and use the resources for getting help in the classroom; and whether they effectively judge situations when persistence alone is not sufficient to overcome difficulty in carrying out school tasks.

Instructional Design Experimentations

As evidenced in the findings from the present review, significant progress has been made, particularly during the past decade, on several fronts. These include a rich array of empirical data bases on the relationship among the active role played by students in their learning and their learning outcomes; the relevance of students' ability to function in this role as an individual difference variable that distinguishes more successful students from less successful students; and the manner in which learners go about learning. The time seems ripe to embark on a program of research and development that can bring this knowledge to bear on improving schooling practice.

Some of the specific foci for the proposed agenda for instructional design experimentations might be (a) determining whether the performance of less successful students can be improved through training in the use of self-instructive skills, (b) delineating particular intervention strategies and classroom conditions that are more or less effective in fostering the use of self-instructive skills in students' learning, (c) identifying specific teacher expertise required to create and maintain classroom learning environments that foster the self-instructive process, and (d) designing teacher training programs and technical assistance activities to help administrators and instructional leaders acquire expertise in supporting the establishment and maintenance of classroom learning environments that foster the development of self-instructive skills in students.

Three lines of research are proposed to address the question, How can student self-responsibility and the use of self-instructive skills be effectively fostered in school learning situations? The first line of research would probe specifically into how, and under what conditions, self-responsibility and self-instructive skills are developed and used. The second proposed line of research would be concerned with the design of classroom environments that ensure opportunities for each student to develop the required competence for being self-responsible and self-instructive in his or her learning. The third line of research would be aimed at developing a systematic implementation delivery system to support the establishment and maintenance of school programs that foster students' development and use of self-instructive processes in their learning.

The concern over the transferability and maintenance of acquired knowledge and skills—a central concern in instructional design research—is the impetus for asking the how, when, where, and who questions related to the development and use of self-responsibility and self-instructive skills. Of particular relevance is the question of whether the development of self-responsibility and self-instructive competencies is tied closely to the acquisition of subject-matter knowledge, or whether these competencies are more or less associated with individual learners and are applied across different task types and subject-matter domains. This same question and the dilemma over the most appropriate approach, whether general or specific, are the subject of much current attention in research on cognition and learning. (For further discussion of the current debate on this and related issues, see Brown, Bransford, et al., 1983; Glaser, 1984; and Segal et al., 1985.) Ongoing development and research in cognitive-instructional psychology have the potential to contribute to the proposed research.

The second focus of this research would be the investigation of whether extant school learning environments are conducive to the development of student self-responsibility and self-instructive skills, as well as the identification of refinements or restructuring that would improve the capabilities of schools toward this end. A key assumption here is that there are reciprocal effects between the learning environment and student learning. The dynamic nature of the interactions among the school learning environment, the development and use of self-instructive skills, and learner outcomes is suggested in the conceptual model for the study of the self-instructive process in classroom learning contexts and underscored by the findings from the present review of extant research in this and related areas. As noted earlier in the discussion, the individual learner brings to the school learning environment a unique profile of instructionally relevant characteristics which, in their interaction with particular elements in the classroom learning environment, elicit certain behaviors that may or may not be self-instructive.

Thus, the identification of specific dimensions of classroom learning environments (e.g., teacher behaviors, staffing patterns, characteristics of student populations in particular classrooms, instructional grouping patterns) that are more or less conducive to (and/or are requirements of) student engagement in the self-instructive process would necessarily be a major thrust of the proposed instructional design research. Specific questions for investigation might include, Does the use of self-instructive skills vary significantly across subject matter and grade level in classrooms that differ along selected dimensions of classroom characteristics? and, Are there significant interactions among differences in dimensions of classroom learning environments and learner characteristics (e.g., high/low knowledge, age level, perceptions of self-competence) that affect students' differential use of self-instructive skills?

The third focus of the proposed instructional design research would be the systematic analysis of implementation requirements and delivery systems that would provide the organizational and resource supports for effective program implementation and maintenance. Schools have encountered major stumbling blocks to the implementation of well-intentioned, innovative practices. These implementation-related problems have a wide variety of sources that include current organizational and staffing patterns; the make-up of student groups (age, ability level, behavioral characteristics, special learning needs); and the motivation and expertise of school and district staff for effecting programmatic changes. Experience in a variety of settings has shown that research and development efforts related to pedagogical concerns tend to have little effect on practice unless serious attention also is given to implementation support needs. Among major tasks in the design of an efficient and effective delivery system for implementing innovative practices and programs are the systematic analysis and consideration of staff development support needs; the identification of ways to effectively redeploy school resources; and the reconstruction of present staffing, classroom structures, and organizational patterns. It is critical that attention to these tasks be incorporated in curriculum design and program implementation delivery systems with the goal of sustaining patterns of self-responsible and self-instructive learning.

In conclusion, the research agenda being proposed here has been conceived within the framework delineated by the model for the study of the self-instructive process shown in Fig. 1. It is intended to incorporate and build upon contemporary theories of learning as well as the diverse research base on cognition, the social-psychological processes of learning, and the process of learning and the school environment. The strong emphasis on the complexity of the classroom environment is intended to highlight three important considerations for future research: the multidimensionality of classroom learning and instruction as a factor in examination of the role that students play in their learning; the need to build a descriptive data base for analysis and description of the classroom learning processes and instructionally relevant characteristics of students' development and use of self-responsibility and self-instructive skills; and the need to further our understanding of individual differences and effective schooling in order to improve the delivery of educational services for students who require greater-than-usual educational and related services.

Author Information

Margaret C. Wang is Professor of Educational Psychology and Director of the Temple University Center for Research in Human Development and Education, and Stephen T. Peverly is Assistant Professor of Psychology and Education at Teachers College, Columbia University.

References

Adelman, H. S., & Taylor, L. (1983). *Learning disabilities in perspective.* Glenview, IL: Scott Foresman.

Adelson, B. (1981). Problem solving and the development of abstract categories in programming languages. *Memory and Cognition*, **9**, 422–433.

Allen, V. L. (1983). Impact of the role of tutor on behavior and self-perceptions. In J. Levine & M. C. Wang (Eds.), *Teacher and student perceptions: Implications for learning* (pp. 367–389). Hillsdale, NJ: Erlbaum.

Ames, C. (1984). Competitive, cooperative, and individualistic goal structures: A motivational analysis. In R. F. Ames & C. Ames (Eds.), *Research on motivation in education. Vol. 1. Student motivation* (pp. 274–318). New York: Academic Press.

Anderson, L. M. (1981, April). *Students' responses to seat work: Implications for the study of students' cognitive processing.* Paper presented at the annual meeting of the American Educational Research Association, Los Angeles, CA.

Anderson, L. M., Brubaker, N. L., Alleman-Brooks, J., & Duffy, G. G. (1984). *Making seatwork work* (Report No. 142). East Lansing, MI: Institute for Research on Education.

Anderson, L. W. (Ed.). (1983). *Time and school learning.* London, England: Croom-Helm.

Andre, M. E. D., & Anderson, T. H. (1978–1979). The development and evaluation of a self-questioning study technique. *Reading Research Quarterly*, **14**, 606–623.

Andrews, G. R., & Debus, R. L. (1978). Persistence and causal perceptions of failures: Modifying cognitive attributions. *Journal of Educational Psychology*, **70**, 2.

Arlin, M., & Whitley, T. (1978). Perceptions of self-managed learning opportunities and academic locus of control: A causal interpretation. *Journal of Educational Psychology*, **70**, 988–992.

Au, K. (1980). *A test of the social organizational hypothesis: Relationships between participation structures and learning to read.* Unpublished doctoral dissertation, University of Illinois, Urbana-Champaign, IL.

Baird, J. R., & White, R. T. (1982). Promoting self-control of learning. *Instructional Science*, **11**, 227–247.

Baker, L. (1979, September). *Comprehension monitoring: Identifying and coping with text confusions* (Tech. Rep. No. 145). Urbana, IL: University of Illinois, Center for the Study of Reading. (ERIC Document Reproduction Service No. ED 177 525)

Baker, L., & Brown, A. L. (1984). Metacognition and the reading process. In P. D. Pearson (Ed.), *A handbook of reading research* (pp. 353–394). New York: Longman.

Bandura, A. (1977). *Social learning theory.* Englewood Cliffs, NJ: Prentice-Hall.

Bandura, A. (1981). Self-referent thought: A developmental analysis of self-efficacy. In J. H. Flavell & L. R. Ross (Eds.), *Social cognitive development: Frontiers and possible futures* (pp. 200–239). New York: Cambridge University Press.

Bandura, A. (1982). The self and mechanisms of agency. In J. Suls (Ed.), *Psychological perspectives on the self* (pp. 3–39). Hillsdale, NJ: Erlbaum.

Bandura, A., & Schunk, D. H. (1981). Cultivating competence, self-efficacy, and intrinsic interest through proximal self-motivation. *Journal of Personality and Social Psychology*, **41**, 586–598.

Belmont, J. M., & Butterfield, E. C. (1971). Learning strategies as determinants of memory deficiencies. *Cognitive Psychology*, **2**, 411–420.

Belmont, J. M., & Butterfield, E. C. (1977). The instructional approach to developmental cognitive research. In R. V. Kail, Jr. & J. W. Hagen (Eds.), *Perspectives on the development of memory and cognition* (pp. 437–481). New York: Wiley.

Belmont, J. M., Butterfield, E. C., & Borkowski, J. G. (1978). Training retarded people to generalize memorization methods across memory tasks. In M. M. Gruneberg, P. E. Morris, & R. N. Sykes (Eds.), *Practical aspects of memory* (pp. 418–426). London, England: Academic Press.

Berliner, D. C. (1983). Developing conceptions of classroom environments: Some light on the T in classroom studies of ATI. *Educational Psychologist*, **18**, 1–13.

Bloom, B. S. (1976). *Human characteristics and school learning.* New York: McGraw-Hill.

Bloom, B. S. (1984). The 2 sigma problem: The search for methods of group instruction as effective as one-to-one tutoring. *Educational Researcher*, **13**(6), 4–16.

Blumenfeld, P., Hamilton, J., Wessels, K., & Meece, J. (1983). Teacher talk and student thought: Socialization into the student role. In J. Levine & M. C. Wang (Eds.), *Teacher and student perceptions: Implications for learning* (pp. 143–192). Hillsdale, NJ: Erlbaum.

Boersma, F. J. & Chapman, J. W. (1981). Academic self-concept, achievement expectations, and locus of control in elementary learning disabled children. *Canadian Journal of Behavioral Science*, **13**, 349–358.

Borkowski, J. G., Levers, S. R., & Gruenfelder, T. M. (1976). Transfer of mediational strategies in children: The role of activity and awareness during strategy acquisition. *Child Development*, **47**, 779–786.

Borkowski, J. G., & Wanschura, P. B. (1974). Mediational processes in the retarded. In N. R. Ellis (Ed.), *International review of research in mental retardation* (Vol. 7, pp. 1–54). New York: Academic Press.

Bornstein, P., & Quevillon, R. (1976). Effects of a self-instructional package on overactive preschool boys. *Journal of Applied Behavior Analysis*, **9**, 179–199.

Bossert, S. T. (1978, January). *Activity structures and student outcomes.* Paper presented at the National Institute of Education's National Invitational Conference on School Organization and Effects, San Diego, CA.

Bossert, S. T. (1979). *Tasks and social relationships in classrooms.* New York: Cambridge University Press.

Bowerman, M. (1982). Starting to talk worse: Clues to language acquisition from children's late speech errors. In S. Strauss (Ed.), *U-shaped behavioral growth* (pp. 101–145). New York: Academic Press.

Bransford, J. D. (1979). *Human cognition: Learning, understanding, and remembering.* Belmont, CA: Wadsworth.

Bransford, J. D., Arbitman-Smith, R., Stein, B. S., & Vye, N. J. (1985). Improving thinking and learning skills: An analysis of three approaches. In J. W. Segal, S. F. Chipman, & R. Glaser (Eds.), *Thinking and learning skills. Vol. 1. Relating instruction to research* (pp. 133–206). Hillsdale, NJ: Erlbaum.

Bransford, J. D., Stein, B. S., Shelton, T. S., & Owings, R. S. (1981). Cognition and adaptation: The importance of learning to learn. In J. H. Harvey (Ed.), *Cognition, social behavior, and the environment* (pp. 93–110). Hillsdale, NJ: Erlbaum.

Bransford, J. D., Stein, B. S., Vye, N. J., Franks, J. J., Auble, P. M., Mezynski, K. J., & Perfetto, G. A. (1982). Differences in approaches to learning: An overview. *Journal of Experimental Psychology: General*, **3**, 390–398.

Brophy, J. (1979). Teacher behavior and its effects. *Journal of Educational Psychology*, **71**, 733–750.

Brophy, J. (1982). Successful teaching strategies for the inner-city child. *Phi Delta Kappan*, **63**, 527–530.

Brophy, J. (1983). Classroom organization and management. *Elementary School Journal*, **83**, 265–286.

Brophy, J., & Good, T. L. (1986). Teacher behavior and student achievement. In M. C. Wittrock (Ed.), *Third handbook of research on teaching* (3rd ed.) (pp. 328–375). New York: MacMillan.

Brown, A. L. (1974). The role of strategic behavior in retardate memory. In N. R. Ellis (Ed.), *International review of research in mental retardation* (Vol. 7, pp. 55–111). New York: Academic Press.

Brown, A. L. (1978). Knowing when, where, and how to remember. In R. Glaser (Ed.), *Advances in instructional psychology* (Vol. 1, pp. 77–165). Hillsdale, NJ: Erlbaum.

Brown, A. L. (1980). Metacognitive development and reading. In R. J. Spiro, B. C. Bruce, & W. F. Brewer (Eds.), *Theoretical issues in reading comprehension* (pp. 453–502). Hillsdale, NJ: Erlbaum.

Brown, A. L. (1981). Metacognition and reading and writing: The development and facilitation of selective attention strategies for learning from texts. In M. L. Kamil (Ed.), *Directions in reading: Research and instruction.* Washington, DC: National Reading Conference.

Brown, A. L., & Barclay, C. R. (1976). The effects of training specific mnemonics on the metamnemonic efficacy of retarded children. *Child Development*, **47**, 70–80.

Brown, A. L., Bransford, J. D., Ferrara, R., & Campione, J. (1983). Learning, understanding and remembering. In J. H. Flavell & E. Markman (Eds.), *Handbook of child psychology. Vol. 1. Cognitive development* (4th ed.) (pp. 77–166). New York: Wiley.

Brown, A. L., & Campione, J. C. (1978). Permissible inferences from cognitive training studies in developmental research. *Quarterly Newsletter of the Institute for Comparative Human Behavior*, **2**, 46–53.

Brown, A. L., & Campione, J. C. (1981). Inducing flexible thinking: A problem of access. In M. Friedman, J. P. Das, & N. O'Connor (Eds.), *Intelligence and learning* (pp. 515–529). New York: Plenum.

Brown, A. L., Campione, J. C., & Barclay, C. R. (1979). Training self-checking routines for estimating test readiness: Generalization from list learning to prose recall. *Child Development*, **50**, 501–512.

Brown, A. L., Campione, J. C., & Day, J. D. (1981). Learning to learn: On training students to learn from texts. *Educational Researcher*, **10**(2), 14–21.

Brown, A. L., & Day, J. D. (1983). Macrorules for summarizing text: The development of expertise. *Journal of Verbal Learning and Verbal Behavior*, **22**, 1–14.

Brown, A. L., Day, J. D., & Jones, R. S. (1983). The development of plans for summarizing texts. *Child Development*, **54**, 968–979.

Brown, A. L., & Lawton, S. C. (1977). The feeling of knowing experience in educable retarded children. *Developmental Psychology*, **13**, 364–370.

Brown, A. L., & Smiley, S. S. (1977). Rating the importance of structural units of prose passages: A problem of metacognitive development. *Child Development*, **48**, 1–8.

Brown, A. L., & Smiley, S. S. (1978). The development of strategies for studying text. *Child Development*, **49**, 1076–1088.

Brown, A. L., Smiley, S. S., & Lawton, S. (1978). The effects of experience on the selection of suitable retrieval cues for studying text. *Child Development*, **49**, 829–835.

Brown, J. S., & Burton, R. R. (1978). Diagnostic models for procedural bugs in basic mathematical skills. *Cognitive Science*, **2**, 155–192.

Brown, J. S., & Van Lehn, K. (1982). Towards a generative theory of "bugs". In T. P. Carpenter, J. M. Moser, & T. A. Romberg (Eds.), *Addition and subtraction: A cognitive perspective* (pp. 117–135). Hillsdale, NJ: Erlbaum.

Burger, A. L., Blackman, L. S., Holmes, M., & Zetlin, A. (1978). Use of active sorting and retrieval strategies as a facilitator of recall, clustering, and sorting by EMR and nonretarded children. *American Journal of Mental Deficiency*, **83**, 253–261.

Camp, B., Blom, G., Herbert, F., & Van Doornink, W. (1977). Think aloud: A program for developing self-control in young, aggressive boys. *Journal of Abnormal Child Psychology*, **5**, 157–169.

Campione, J. C., & Brown, A. L. (1977). Memory and metamemory development in educable retarded children. In R. V. Kail, Jr. & J. W. Hagen (Eds.), *Perspectives on the development of memory and cognition* (pp. 367–406). Hillsdale, NJ: Erlbaum.

Campione, J. C., Brown, A. L., & Ferrara, R. A. (1982). Mental retardation and intelligence. In R. Sternberg (Ed.), *Handbook of human intelligence* (pp. 392–473). Cambridge, MA: Cambridge University Press.

Canney, G., & Winograd, P. (1979). *Schemata for reading and reading comprehension performance* (Tech. Rep. No. 50). Urbana, IL: University of Illinois, Center for the Study of Reading.

Capelli, C. A., & Markman, E. M. (1981). *Improving comprehension monitoring through training in hypotheses-testing.* Unpublished manuscript, Stanford University, Department of Psychology, Stanford, CA.

Carey, S. (1985). Are children fundamentally different kinds of thinkers and learners than adults? In S. F. Chipman, J. W. Segal, & R. Glaser (Eds.), *Thinking and learning skills. Vol. 2. Current research and open questions* (pp. 485–517). Hillsdale, NJ: Erlbaum.

Carter, K., & Doyle, W. (1982, March). *Variations in academic tasks in high and average ability classes.* Paper presented at the annual meeting of the American Educational Research Association, New York.

Cavanaugh, J. C., & Borkowski, J. G. (1979). The metamemory-memory "connection": Effects of strategy training and transfer. *Journal of General Psychology*, **101**, 161–174.

Champagne, A. B., Gunstone, R. F., & Klopfer, L. E. (1983). Naive knowledge and science learning. *Research in Science and Technological Education*, **1**, 173–183.

Champagne, A. B., Klopfer, L. E., & Anderson, J. H. (1980). Factors influencing learning of classical mechanics. *American Journal of Physics*, **48**, 1074–1079.

Champagne, A. B., Klopfer, L. E., & Gunstone, R. F. (1982). Cognitive research and the design of science instruction. *Educational Psychologist*, **17**, 31–48.

Chance, J. (1968). *Mother-child relations and children's achievement* (Terminal Report, Grant No. MHO 5260). Washington, DC: U.S. Public Health Service.

Chapin, M., & Dyck, D. G. (1976). Persistence in children's reading behavior as a function of *n* length and attribution retraining. *Journal of Abnormal Psychology*, **85**, 511–515.

Chase, W. G., & Simon, H. A. (1973). The mind's eye in chess. In W. G. Chase (Ed.), *Visual information processing* (pp. 215–281). New York: Academic Press.

Chi, M. T. H. (1985). Interactive roles of knowledge and strategies in the development of organized sorting and recall. In S. F. Chipman, J. W. Segal, & R. Glaser (Eds.), *Thinking and learning skills: Vol. 2. Current research and open questions* (pp. 457–483). Hillsdale, NJ: Erlbaum.

Chi, M. T. H., Glaser, R., & Rees, E. (1982). Expertise in problem solving. In R. J. Sternberg (Ed.), *Advances in the psychology of human intelligence* (Vol. 1, pp. 7–75). Hillsdale, NJ: Erlbaum.

Chi, M. T. H., & Koeske, R. D. (1983). Network representation of a child's dinosaur knowledge. *Developmental Psychology,* **19**, 29–39.

Chiesi, H. L., Spilich, G. J., & Voss, J. F. (1979). Acquisition of domain-related information in relation to high and low domain knowledge. *Journal of Verbal Learning and Verbal Behavior,* **18**, 257–273.

Clement, J. (1979). Mapping a student's causal conceptions from a problem-solving protocol. In J. Lochhead & J. Clement (Eds.), *Cognitive process instruction* (pp. 211–238). Philadelphia, PA: Franklin Institute Press.

Coleman, J. S., Campbell, E. Q., Hobson, C. J., McPartland, J., Mood, A. M., Weinfeld, F. D., & York, R. L. (1966). *Equality of educational opportunity.* Washington, DC: U.S. Government Printing Office.

Collins, A., & Stevens, A. (1982). Goals and strategies of inquiry teachers. In R. Glaser (Ed.), *Advances in instructional psychology* (Vol. 2, pp. 65–119). Hillsdale, NJ: Erlbaum.

Cooley, W. W., & Leinhardt, G. (1975). *The application of a model for investigating classroom processes* (LRDC Publication Series 1975/24). Pittsburgh, PA: University of Pittsburgh, Learning Research and Development Center.

Cooper, H. M., & Good, T. L. (1982). *Pygmalion grows up: Studies in the expectation communication process.* New York: Longman.

Covington, M. V. (1965, June). *The effectiveness of training for problem-solving efficiency and creative thinking as a function of differing ability levels among children.* Paper presented at the meeting of the Western Psychological Association, Honolulu, HI.

Covington, M. V. (1985). Strategic thinking and the fear of failure. In J. W. Segal, S. F. Chipman, & R. Glaser (Eds.), *Thinking and learning skills. Vol. 1. Relating instruction to research* (pp. 389–416). Hillsdale, NJ: Erlbaum.

Covington, M. V., & Beery, R. (1976). *Self-worth and school learning.* New York: Holt, Rinehart & Winston.

Covington, M. V., Crutchfield, R. S., Davies, L. B., & Olton, R. M. (1974). *The productive thinking program: A course in learning to think.* Columbus, OH: Merrill.

Covington, M. V., & Omelich, C. L. (1979). Effort: The double-edged sword in school achievement. *Journal of Educational Psychology,* **71**, 169–182.

Crandall, V. C. (1966). Personality characteristics and social and achievement tendencies. *Journal of Social Psychology,* **4**, 477–486.

Crandall, V. C., Katkovsky, W., & Crandall, V. J. (1965). Children's belief in their own control of reinforcements in intellectual-academic situations. *Child Development,* **36**, 91–109.

Crandall, V. J., Katkovsky, W., & Preston, A. (1962). Motivational and ability determinants of young children's intellectual achievement behaviors. *Child Development,* **33**, 643–661.

Dansereau, D. F., Collins, K. W., McDonald, B. A., Holley, C. D., Garland, J., Diekoff, C., & Evans, S. H. (1979). Development and evaluation of a learning strategy training program *Journal of Educational Psychology,* **71**, 64–73.

Davis, W. L., & Phares, E. J. (1967). Internal-external control as a determinant of information-seeking in a social influence situation. *Journal of Personality,* **35**, 547–551.

Day, J. D. (1980). *Training summarization skills: A comparison of teaching methods.* Unpublished doctoral dissertation, University of Illinois, Urbana-Champaign, IL.

deCharms, R. (1972). Personal causation training in the schools. *Journal of Applied Social Psychology,* **2**, 95–113.

deCharms, R. (1976). *Enhancing motivation: Change in the classroom.* New York: Wiley.

Deci, E. L. (1975). *Intrinsic motivation.* New York: Plenum.

Denham, C., & Lieberman, A. (Eds.). (1980). *Time to learn.* Washington, DC: National Institute of Education.

Deschler, D. D., Schumaker, J. B., & Lenz, B. K. (1984). Academic and cognitive interventions for LD adolescents: Part 1. *Journal of Learning Disabilities,* **17**, 108–117.

DeStefano, L., Wang, M. C., & Gordon, E. M. (1984, April). Differences in student temperament characteristics and their effects on classroom processes and outcomes. In M. C. Wang (Organizer), *Temperament characteristics and learning.* Symposium presented at the annual meeting of the American Educational Research Association, New Orleans, LA.

Diener, C., & Dweck, C. (1978). An analysis of learned helplessness: Continuous changes in performance, strategy and achievement cognitions following failure. *Journal of Personality and Social Psychology,* **36**, 451-462.

Diener, C., & Dweck, C. (1980). An analysis of learned helplessness: II. The processing of success. *Journal of Personality and Social Psychology,* **39**, 940–952.

Doctorow, M., Wittrock, M. C., & Marks, C. (1978). Generative processes in reading comprehension. *Journal of Educational Psychology,* **70**, 109–118.

Douglas, V. I., & Peters, K. G. (1979). Toward a clearer definition of the attentional deficit of hyperactive children. In G. A. Hale & M. Lewis (Eds.), *Attention and cognitive development* (pp. 173–249). New York: Plenum.

Doyle, W. (1977). Paradigms for research on teacher effectiveness. In L. S. Shulman (Ed.), *Review of research in education* (Vol. 5, pp. 163–198). Itasca, IL: Peacock.

Doyle, W. (1979). Classroom tasks and students' abilities. In P. L. Peterson & H. J. Walberg (Eds.), *Research on teaching: Concepts, findings, and implications* (pp. 183–209). Berkeley, CA: McCutchan.

Doyle, W. (1981, April). *Research on classroom contexts: Toward a knowledge base for policy and practice in teacher education.* Paper presented at the annual meeting of the American Educational Research Association, Los Angeles, CA.

Doyle, W. (1983). Academic work. *Review of Educational Research,* **53**, 159–199.

Doyle, W., & Carter, K. (1984). Academic tasks in classrooms. *Curriculum Inquiry,* **14**, 129–149.

Drozdal, J. G., Jr., & Flavell, J. H. (1975). A developmental study of logical search behavior. *Child Development,* **46**, 389–393.

Dudley-Marling, C. C., Snider, V., & Tarver, S. G. (1982). Locus of control and learning disabilities: A review and discussion. *Perceptual and Motor Skills,* **54**, 503–514.

Dunn, B. R., Mathews, S. R., & Biegler, G. R. (1982). Deviation from hierarchical structure in recall: Is there an "optional" structure? *Journal of Experimental Child Psychology,* **34**, 371–386.

Dunn, L. M., & Markwardt, F. C. (1970). *Peabody Individual Achievement Test.* Circle Pines, MN: American Guidance Service.

Dweck, C. S. (1975). The role of expectations and attributions in the alleviation of learned helplessness. *Journal of Personality and Social Psychology,* **31**, 674–685.

Dweck, C. S., & Elliot, E. S. (1983). Achievement motivation. In P. H. Mussen (Ed.), *Handbook of child psychology. Vol. 4. Socialization, personality, and social development* (pp. 643–692). New York: Wiley.

Eder, D. (1983). Ability grouping and students' academic self-concepts: A case study. *Elementary School Journal,* **84**, 149–161.

Egan, D., & Schwartz, B. (1979). Chunking in recall of symbolic drawings. *Memory and Cognition,* **7**, 149–158.

Felixbrod, J. J., & O'Leary, K. D. (1974). Self-determination of academic standards by children: Toward freedom from external control. *Journal of Educational Psychology,* **66**, 845–850.

Feuerstein, R., Jensen, M., Hoffman, M. B., & Rand, Y. (1985). Instrumental enrichment, an intervention program for structural cognitive modifiability: Theory and practice. In J. W. Segal, S. F. Chipman, & R. Glaser (Eds.), *Thinking and learning skills. Vol. 1. Relating instruction to research* (pp. 43–82). Hillsdale, NJ: Erlbaum.

Feuerstein, R., Rand, Y., Hoffman, M. B., Hoffman, M., & Miller, R. (1979). Cognitive modifiability in retarded adolescents: Effects of instrumental enrichment. *American Journal of Mental Deficiency,* **83**, 539–550.

Feuerstein, R., Rand, Y., Hoffman, M. B., & Miller, R. (1980). *Instrumental enrichment.* Baltimore, MD: University Park Press.

Findley, M. J., & Cooper, H. M. (1983). Locus of control and academic achievement: A literature review. *Journal of Personality and Social Psychology,* **44**, 419–427.

Fisher, C. W., & Berliner, D. (Eds.) (1985). *Perspectives on instructional time.* New York: Longman.

Fisher, C. W., Filby, N. N., Marliave, R. S., Cahen, L. S., Dishaw, M. M., Moore, J. E., & Berliner, D. (1978). *Teaching behaviors, academic learning time and student achievement* (Final report of Phase III-B, Beginning Teacher Evaluation Study). San Francisco, CA: Far West Regional Laboratory.

Flavell, J. H. (1970). Developmental studies of mediated memory. In H. W. Reese & L. P. Lipsitt (Eds.), *Advances in child development and behavior* (Vol. 5, pp. 182–211). New York: Academic Press.

Flavell, J. H. (1976). Metacognitive aspects of problem solving. In L. B. Resnick (Ed.), *The nature of intelligence* (pp. 231–235). Hillsdale, NJ: Erlbaum.

Flavell, J. H. (1981). Cognitive monitoring. In W. P. Dickson (Ed.), *Children's oral communication skills* (pp. 35–60). New York: Academic Press.

Flavell, J. H., Friedrichs, A. G., & Hoyt, J. D. (1970). Developmental changes in memorization processes. *Cognitive Psychology,* **1**, 324–340.

Flavell, J. H., Speer, J. R., Green, F. L., & August, D. L. (1981). The development of comprehension monitoring and knowledge about communication. *Monographs of the Society for Research in Child Development,* **46**(5, Whole No. 192).

Flavell, J. H., & Wellman, H. M. (1977). Metamemory. In R. V. Kail & J. W. Hagen (Eds.), *Perspectives on the development of memory and cognition* (pp. 3–33). Hillsdale, NJ: Erlbaum.

Flower, L., & Hayes, J. R. (1981). The pregnant pause: An inquiry into the nature of planning. *Research in the Teaching of English,* **15**, 229–245.

Fogarty, J. L., & Wang, M. C. (1982). An investigation of the cross-age peer tutoring process: Some implications for instructional design and motivation. *Elementary School Journal,* **82**, 451–535.

Franks, J. J., Vye, N. J., Cribbs, P. M., Mezynski, K. J., Perfetto, G. A., Bransford, J. D., Stein, B. S., & Littlefield, J. (1982). Learning from explicit versus implicit texts. *Journal of Experimental Psychology: General,* **3**, 414–422.

Frase, L. T., & Schwartz, B. J. (1975). Effect of question production on prose recall. *Journal of Educational Psychology,* **67**, 628–635.

Gagné, E. E., & Parshall, H. (1975). Effects of locus of control and goal setting on persistence at a learning task. *Child Study Journal,* **5**, 193–199.

Garner, R. (1981). Monitoring of passage inconsistency among poor comprehenders: A preliminary test of the "piecemeal processing" explanation. *Journal of Educational Research,* **74**, 159–162.

Garner, T., & Krause, C. (1980). *Monitoring of understanding among seventh graders: An investigation of good comprehender–poor comprehender in knowing and regulating reading behaviors.* Unpublished manuscript, University of Maryland, College of Education, College Park, MD.

Giaconia, R. M., & Hedges, L. V. (1982). Identifying features of effective open education. *Review of Educational Research,* **52**, 579–602.

Glaser, R. (1979). Trends and research questions in psychological research on learning and schooling. *Educational Researcher,* **8**(10), 6–13.

Glaser, R. (1984). Education and thinking: The role of knowledge. *American Psychologist,* **39**, 93–104.

Glaser, R., & Bond, L. (1981). Testing: Concepts, policy, practice, and research. *American Psychologist,* **36**, 997–1000.

Goldstein, I. P., & Brown, J. S. (1979). A computer as a personal assistant for learning. In J. Lochhead & J. Clement (Eds.), *Cognitive process instruction* (pp. 201–207). Philadelphia, PA: Franklin Institute Press.

Good, T., & Beckerman, T. (1978). Time on task: A naturalistic study in sixth-grade classrooms. *Elementary School Journal,* **73**, 193–201.

Gordon, E. W. (Ed.). (1983). *Human diversity and pedagogy.* Westport, CT: Mediax.

Gordon, D., Jones, R., & Short, N. (1977). Task persistence and locus of control in elementary school children. *Child Development,* **48**, 1716–1719.

Greeno, J. G. (1973). The structure of memory and the process of solving problems. In R. L. Solso (Ed.), *Contemporary issues in cognitive psychology* (pp. 103–133). Washington, DC: Winston.

Greeno, J. G. (1980). Psychology of learning, 1960–80: One participant's observations. *American Psychologist,* **35**, 713–728.

Greeno, J. G. (1982). *Forms of understanding in mathematical problem solving* (Tech. Rep. UPITT/LRDC/ONR/APS-10). Pittsburgh, PA: University of Pittsburgh, Learning Research and Development Center.

Greeno, J. G., Riley, M. S., & Gelman, R. (1984). Conceptual competence and children's counting. *Cognitive Psychology,* **16**, 94–143.

Haertel, G. D., Walberg, H. J., & Haertel, E. H. (1979, April). *Socio-psychological environments and learning: A quantitative synthesis.* Paper presented at the annual meeting of the American Educational Research Association, San Francisco, CA.

Hamilton, S. (1983). The social side of schooling: Ecological studies of classrooms and schools. *Elementary School Journal,* **83**, 313–334.

Harter, S. (1974). Pleasure derived from cognitive challenge and mastery. *Child Development,* **45**, 661–669.

Harter, S. (1982). The Perceived Competence Scale for Children. *Child Development,* **53**, 87–97.

Hayes, J. R. (1976). It's the thought that counts: New approaches to educational theory. In D. Klahr (Ed.), *Cognition and instruction* (pp. 235–242). Hillsdale, NJ: Erlbaum.

Hayes, J. R., & Flower, L. (1980). Identifying the organization of writing processes. In L. N. Gregg & E. R. Steinberg (Eds.), *Cognitive processing in writing* (pp. 3–30). Hillsdale, NJ: Erlbaum.

Hayes-Roth, B., & Hayes-Roth, F. (1979). A cognitive model of planning. *Cognitive Science,* **3**, 275–310.

Haywood, H. C., & Smith, R. A. (1979, August). *Modification of cognitive functions in slow learning adolescents.* Paper presented at the meeting of the International Association of Mental Deficiency, Jerusalem, Israel.

Heckhausen, H., & Krug, S. (1982). Motive modification. In A. Steward (Ed.), *Motivation and society* (pp. 274–318). San Francisco, CA: Jossey-Bass.

Hedges, L. V., Giaconia, R. M., & Gage, N. L. (1981). *Meta analysis of the effects of open and traditional instruction.* Stanford, CA: Stanford University Program on Teaching Effectiveness.

Humphrey, L. L. (1984). Children's self-control in relation to perceived social environment. *Journal of Personality and Social Psychology,* **46**, 178–188.

Jenkins, J. J. (1979). Four points to remember: A tetrahedral model of memory experiments. In L. S. Cermak & F. I. M. Craik (Eds.), *Levels of processing and human memory* (pp. 429–446). Hillsdale, NJ: Erlbaum.

Jenkins, J. J. (1980). Can we have a fruitful cognitive psychology? In H. E. Howe & J. H. Flowers (Eds.), *Nebraska Symposium on Motivation* (pp. 211–238). Lincoln, NE: University of Nebraska Press.

Johnson, D. W., Johnson, R. T., & Scott, L. (1978). The effects of cooperative and individualized instruction on student attitudes and achievement. *Journal of Social Psychology,* **104**, 207–216.

Kail, R. V., & Hagen, J. W. (Eds.). (1977). *Perspectives on the development of memory and cognition.* Hillsdale, NJ: Erlbaum.

Kauffman, J. M., & Hallahan, D. P. (1979). Learning disability and hyperactivity (with comments on minimal brain dysfunction). In B. B. Lahey & A. E. Kazdin (Eds.), *Advances in clinical child psychology* (Vol. 2, pp. 72–105). New York: Plenum.

Kendall, C. R., Borkowski, J. G., & Cavanaugh, J. C. (1980). Metamemory and the transfer of an interrogative strategy by EMR children. *Intelligence,* **4**, 255–270.

Kendall, P. C., & Finch, A. J., Jr. (1976). A cognitive-behavioral treatment for impulse control: A case study. *Journal of Consulting and Clinical Psychology,* **44**, 852–857.

Kennedy, B. A., & Miller, D. J. (1976). Persistent use of verbal rehearsal as a function of information about its value. *Child Development,* **47**, 566–569.

Keogh, B. K. (1982). Children's temperament and teachers' decisions. In R. Porter & G. M. Collins (Eds.), *Temperamental differences in infants and young children* (pp. 269–285). London, England: Pittman.

Keogh, B. K., & Cahill, C. W. (1971). *Educationally handicapped children's perception of task.* Unpublished manuscript, University of California, Los Angeles, CA.

Kounin, J., & Gump, P. (1974). Signal systems of lesson settings and the task related behavior of preschool children. *Journal of Educational Psychology,* **66**, 554–562.

Kramer, J. J., & Engle, R. W. (1981). Teaching awareness of strategic behavior in combination with strategy training: Effects on children's memory performance. *Journal of Experimental Psychology,* **32**, 513–530.

Krashen, S. D. (1976). Formal and informal linguistic environments in language acquisition and language learning. *TESOL Quarterly,* **10**, 157–168.

Kreutzer, M. A., Leonard, C., & Flavell, J. (1975). An interview study of children's knowledge about memory. *Monograph of the Society for Research in Child Development,* **40** (1, Serial No. 159).

Larkin, J. H. (1981). Enriching formal knowledge: A model for learning to solve textbook physics problems. In J. Anderson (Ed.), *Cognitive skills and their acquisition* (pp. 311–334). Hillsdale, NJ: Erlbaum.

Larkin, J. H., McDermott, J., Simon, D. P., & Simon, H. A. (1980). Models of competence in solving physics problems. *Cognitive Science,* **4**, 317–345.

Lawson, M. J., & Feulop, I. (1980). Understanding the purpose of strategy training. *British Journal of Educational Psychology,* **50**, 175–180.

Lefcourt, H. M. (1982). *Locus of control: Current trends in theory and research* (2nd ed.). Hillsdale, NJ: Erlbaum.

Leinhardt, G. (1983, April). *Student cognitions during instruction.* Paper presented at the annual meeting of the American Educational Research Association, Montreal, Canada.

Leon, T. A., & Pepe, H. (1978). *Self-instructional training: Cognitive behavior modification as a resource room strategy* (Final Report, DHEW, BEH Grant No. G007701991). Washington, DC: U.S. Government Printing Office.

Lesgold, A. M., Feltovich, P. J., Glaser, R., & Wang, Y. (1981). *The acquisition of perceptual diagnostic skill in radiology* (Tech. Rep. PDS-1). Pittsburgh, PA: University of Pittsburgh, Learning Research and Development Center.

Levine, J. (1983). Social comparison and education. In J. Levine & M. C. Wang (Eds.), *Teacher and student perceptions: Implications for learning* (pp. 29–55). Hillsdale, NJ: Erlbaum.

Levine, J. M., & Wang, M. C. (Eds.). (1983). *Teacher and student perceptions: Implications for learning.* Hillsdale, NJ: Erlbaum.

Lindberg, M. A. (1980). Is knowledge base development a necessary and sufficient condition for memory development? *Journal of Experimental Child Psychology,* **30**, 401–410.

Lipman, M. (1980). *Thinking skills fostered by the middle-school philosophy for children program.* Unpublished manuscript, Montclair State College, Upper Montclair, NJ.

Lipman, M. (1985). Thinking skills fostered by philosophy for children. In J. W. Segal, S. F. Chipman, & R. Glaser (Eds.), *Thinking and learning skills. Vol. 1. Relating instruction to research* (pp. 83–108). Hillsdale, NJ: Erlbaum.

Lipman, M., & Sharp, A. M. (1978). *Growing up with philosophy.* Philadelphia, PA: Temple University Press.

Lipman, M., Sharp, A. M., & Oscanyan, F. S. (1980). *Philosophy in the classroom*. Philadelphia, PA: Temple University Press.

Madden, R., Gardner, E. F., Rudman, H. C., Karlsen, B., & Merwin, J. C. (1975). *Stanford Achievement Test*. New York: Psychological Corporation.

Madden, N. A., & Slavin, R. E. (1982). *Count me in: Academic achievement and social outcomes of mainstreaming students with mild academic handicaps* (Report No. 329). Baltimore, MD: Johns Hopkins University, Center for the Social Organization of Schools.

Markman, E. M., (1973). *Factors affecting the young child's ability to monitor his memory*. Unpublished doctoral dissertation, University of Pennsylvania, Philadelphia, PA.

Markman, E. M. (1976). Children's difficulty with word-referent differentiation. *Child Development*, **47**, 742–749.

Markman, E. M. (1977). Realizing that you don't understand: A preliminary investigation. *Child Development*, **46**, 986–992.

Markman, E. M. (1979). Realizing that you don't understand: Elementary school children's awareness of inconsistencies. *Child Development*, **50**, 643–655.

Markman, E. M. (1981). Comprehension monitoring. In W. P. Dickson (Ed.), *Children's oral communication skills* (pp. 61–84). New York: Academic Press.

Marr, M. B., & Gormley, K. (1982). Children's recall of familiar and unfamiliar text. *Reading Research Quarterly*, **18**, 89–104.

Marshall, H. H. (1976). *Dimensions of classroom structure and functioning project: Final report*. Berkeley, CA: University of California.

Marshall, H. H. (1981). Open classrooms: Has the term outlived its usefulness? *Review of Educational Research*, **51**, 181–192.

Marshall, H. H., & Weinstein, R. S. (1984). Classroom factors affecting students' self-evaluations: An interactional model. *Review of Educational Research*, **54**, 301–325.

Marshall, H. H., Weinstein, R. S., Sharp, L., & Brattesani, K. A. (1982 March). *Students' descriptions of the ecology of the school environment for high and low achievers*. Paper presented at the annual meeting of the American Educational Research Association, New York.

Matheny, K., & Edwards, C. (1974). Academic improvement through an experimental classroom management system. *Journal of School Psychology*, **12**, 222–232.

Mayer, R. E., Steihl, C. D., & Greeno, J. G. (1975). Acquisition of understanding and skill in relation to subjects' preparation and meaningfulness of instruction. *Journal of Educational Psychology*, **68**, 331–350.

McCloskey, M., Caramazza, A., & Green, B. (1980). Curvilinear motion in the absence of external forces: Naive beliefs about the motion of objects. *Science*, **210**, 1139–1141.

McCombs, B. L. (1982a, August). *Enhancing student motivation through positive self-control strategies*. Paper presented at the meeting of the American Psychological Association, Washington, DC.

McCombs, B. L. (1982b). Learner satisfaction and motivation: Capitalizing on strategies for positive self-control. *Performance and Instruction*, **21**(4), 3–6.

McDermott, R. P. (1978). *Problem readers and the social order: Some reasons for focusing on classrooms in reading research*. Paper presented at the meeting of the National Reading Conference, New Orleans, LA.

McKeithen, K. B., Reitman, J. S., Rueter, H. H., & Hirtle, S. C. (1981). Knowledge organization and skill differences in computer programmers. *Cognitive Psychology*, **13**, 307–325.

Mehan, H. (1979). *Learning lessons*. Cambridge, MA: Harvard University Press.

Meichenbaum, D. (1977). *Cognitive behavior modification: An integrative approach*. New York: Plenum.

Meichenbaum, D., & Asarnow, J. (1979). Cognitive behavior modification and metacognitive development: Implications for the classroom. In P. Kendall & S. Hollon (Eds.), *Cognitive behavioral interventions: Theory, research, and procedures* (pp. 11–35). New York: Academic Press.

Meichenbaum, D., & Goodman, J. (1971). Training impulsive children to talk to themselves: A means of developing self-control. *Journal of Abnormal Psychology*, **77**, 115–126.

Meyer, W. (1979). Academic expectations, attributed responsibility, and teachers' reinforcement behavior: A comment on Cooper and Baron, with some additional data. *Journal of Educational Psychology*, **71**, 269–273.

Miller, G. A., Galanter, E., & Pribram, K. H. (1960). *Plans and the structure of behavior*. New York: Holt, Rinehart & Winston.

Moynahan, E. D. (1973). The development of knowledge concerning the effect of categorization upon free recall. *Child Development*, **44**, 238–246.

Myers, M., & Paris, S. G. (1978). Children's metacognitive knowledge about reading. *Journal of Educational Psychology*, **70**, 680–690.

National Commission on Excellence in Education. (1983). *A nation at risk*. Washington, DC: U.S. Government Printing Office.

Neimark, E., Slotnick, N. S., & Ulrich, T. (1971). The development of memorization strategies. *Developmental Psychology*, **5**, 427–432.

Nelson-LeGall, S. (1981). Help-seeking: An understudied problem-solving skill in children. *Developmental Review*, **1**, 224–246.

Nelson-LeGall, S., & Glor-Scheib, S. (1983, April). *Help seeking in classrooms*. Paper presented at the annual meeting of the American Educational Research Association, Montreal, Canada.

Nelson-LeGall, S., & Gummerman, R. A. (1983). Children's perceptions of helpers and helper motivation. *Journal of Applied Developmental Psychology*, **4**, 1–12.

Nelson-LeGall, S., & Scott-Jones, O. (1981, April). *Perceptions of work strategies*. Paper presented at the annual meeting of the American Educational Research Association, Los Angeles, CA.

Newell, A., & Simon, H. A. (1972). *Human problem solving*. Englewood Cliffs, NJ: Prentice-Hall.

Nicholls, J. G. (1979). Quality and equality in intellectual development: The role of motivation in education. *American Psychologist*, **34**, 1071–1084.

Nicholls, J. G. (Ed.). (1984). *Advances in motivation and achievement* (Vol. 3). Greenwich, CT: JAI Press.

Nowicki, S., & Barnes, J. (1973). Effects of a structured camp experience on locus of control orientation of inner-city children. *Journal of Genetic Psychology*, **122**, 247–262.

Olton, R. M., & Crutchfield, R. S. (1969). Developing the skills of productive thinking. In P. Mussen, J. Langer, & M. V. Covington (Eds.), *Trends and issues in developmental psychology* (pp. 68–91). New York: Holt, Rinehart & Winston.

Ornstein, P. A. (Ed.). (1978). *Memory development in children*. Hillsdale, NJ: Erlbaum.

O'Sullivan, J. T., & Pressley, M. (1984). Completeness of instruction and strategy transfer. *Journal of Experimental Child Psychology,* **38**, 275–288.

Owings, R. A., Peterson, G. A., Bransford, J. D., Morris, C. D., & Stein, B. S. (1980). Spontaneous monitoring and regulation of learning: A comparison of successful and less successful fifth graders. *Journal of Educational Psychology,* **72**, 250–256.

Palincsar, A. S., & Brown, A. L. (1984). Reciprocal teaching of comprehension-fostering and comprehension-monitoring activities. *Cognition and Instruction,* **1**, 117–125.

Paris, S. G., & Jacobs, J. E. (1984). The benefits of informed instruction for children's reading awareness and comprehension skills. *Child Development,* **55**, 2083–2093.

Paris, S. G., Lipson, M. Y., & Wixson, K. K. (1983). Becoming a strategic reader. *Contemporary Educational Psychology,* **8**, 293–316.

Paris, S. G., & Myers, M. (1981). Comprehension monitoring, memory, and study strategies of good and poor readers. *Journal of Reading Behavior,* **13**, 5–22.

Paris, S. G., Newman, R. S., & McVey, K. A. (1982). Learning the functional significance of mnemonic actions: A microgenetic study of strategy acquisition. *Journal of Experimental Child Psychology,* **34**, 490–509.

Pearl, R. (1982). Learning disabled children's attributions for success and failure: A replication with labeled LD sample. *Learning Disability Quarterly,* **5**, 173–176.

Pearl, R., Bryan, T., & Donahue, M. (1980). Learning disabled children's attributions for success and failure. *Learning Disability Quarterly,* **3**, 3–9.

Pearson, D. P., Hanson, J., & Gordon, C. (1979). The effect of background knowledge on young children's comprehension of explicit and implicit information. *Journal of Reading Behavior,* **11**, 201–209.

Pepitone, E. A. (1972). Comparison behavior in elementary school children. *American Educational Research Journal,* **9**, 45–63.

Pepitone, E. (1982, March). *Social comparison and pupil interaction: Effect of homogeneous vs. heterogeneous classrooms.* Paper presented at the annual meeting of the American Educational Research Association, New York.

Perna, S. J., Jr., Dunlap, W. R., & Dillard, J. W. (1983). The relationship of internal locus of control, academic achievement, and IQ in emotionally disturbed boys. *Behavioral Disorders,* **9**, 36–42.

Peterson, P. L., & Swing, S. B. (1982). Beyond time on task: Students' reports of their thought processes during direct instruction. *Elementary School Journal,* **82**, 481–491.

Phares, E. J. (1968). Differential utilization of information as a function of internal-external control. *Journal of Personality,* **36**, 649–662.

Pichert, J. W., & Anderson, R. C. (1977). Taking different perspectives on a story. *Journal of Educational Psychology,* **69**, 309–315.

Polya, G. (1973). *How to solve it: A new aspect of mathematical method.* Princeton, NJ: Princeton University Press.

Polson, P. G., & Jeffries, R. (1985). Instruction in general problem-solving skills: An analysis of four approaches. In J. W. Segal, S. F. Chipman, & R. Glaser (Eds.), *Thinking and learning skills. Vol. 1. Relating instruction to research* (pp. 417–455). Hillsdale, NJ: Erlbaum.

Raven, J. C. (1965). *Raven's Progressive Matrices.* New York: Psychological Corporation.

Reimanis, S. (1974). Effects of locus of reinforcement control modification procedures in early grades and college students. *Journal of Educational Research,* **68**, 124–127.

Reschly, D. J. (1984). Beyond the IQ test bias: The National Academy Panel's analysis of minority EMR overrepresentation. *Educational Researcher,* **13**(3), 15–19.

Resnick, L. B., & Ford, W. W. (1981). *The psychology of mathematics for instruction.* Hillsdale, NJ: Erlbaum.

Reynolds, M. C. (1984). Classification of students with handicaps. In E. W. Gordon (Ed.), *Review of research in education* (Vol. 11, pp. 63–92). Washington, DC: American Educational Research Association.

Ringel, B. A., & Springer, C. (1980). On knowing how well one is remembering: The persistence of strategy use during transfer. *Journal of Experimental Child Psychology,* **29**, 322–333.

Rogoff, B., Newcombe, N., & Kagan, J. (1974). Planfulness and recognition memory. *Child Development,* **45**, 972–977.

Rosenholtz, S., & Wilson, B. (1980). The effect of classroom structure on shared perceptions of ability. *American Educational Research Journal,* **17**, 75–82.

Ross, S. M., & DiVesta, F. J. (1976). Oral summary as a review strategy for enhancing recall of textual material. *Journal of Educational Psychology,* **68**, 689–695.

Ross, S., & Zimiles, H. (1974). The differentiated child behavior observational system. In M. C. Wang (Ed.), *The use of direct observation to study instructional-learning behaviors in school settings* (LRDC Publication Series 1974/9, pp. 4–21). Pittsburgh, PA: University of Pittsburgh, Learning Research and Development Center.

Rotter, J. B. (1966). Generalized expectancies for internal versus external control of reinforcement. *Psychological Monographs,* **80**(1, Whole No. 609).

Ryan, E. B. (1981). Identifying and remediating failures in reading comprehension: Toward an instructional approach for poor comprehenders. In T. G. Waller & G. E. MacKinnon (Eds.), *Advances in reading research* (Vol. 3). New York: Academic Press.

Sabatino, D. A. (1982). Research on achievement motivation with learning disabled populations. In K. D. Gadow & I. Bialer (Eds.), *Advances in learning and behavioral disabilities* (Vol. 1, pp. 75–116). Greenwich, CT: JAI Press.

Salatas, H., & Flavell, J. H. (1976). Behavioral and metamnemonic indicators of strategic behaviors under remember instructions in first grade. *Child Development,* **47**, 81–89.

Scardamalia, M., & Bereiter, C. (1985). Fostering the development of self-regulation in children's knowledge processing. In S. F. Chipman, J. W. Segal, & R. Glaser (Eds.), *Thinking and learning skills. Vol. 2. Relating instruction to research* (pp. 563–577). Hillsdale, NJ: Erlbaum.

Scardamalia, M., & Bereiter, C. (in press). The development of evaluative, diagnostic, and remedial capabilities in children's composing. In M. Martlew (Ed.), *The psychology of written language: A developmental approach.* London, England: Wiley.

Schunk, D. H. (1981). Modeling and attributional effects on children's achievement: A self-efficacy analysis. *Journal of Educational Psychology,* **73**, 93–106.

Schunk, D. H. (1982). Effects of attributional feedback on children's perceived self-efficacy and achievement. *Journal of Educational Psychology,* **74**, 548–557.

Schunk, D. H. (1984a). Self-efficacy perspective on achievement behavior. *Educational Psychologist,* **19**, 48–58.

Schunk, D. H. (1984b, April). *Self-efficacy and classroom learning.* Paper presented at the meeting of the American Educational Research Association, Montreal, Canada.

Segal, J. W., Chipman, S. F., & Glaser, R. (Eds.). (1985). *Thinking and learning skills. Vol. 1. Relating instruction to research.* Hillsdale, NJ: Erlbaum.

Shavelson, R. J., & Stern, P. (1981). Research on teachers' pedagogical thoughts, judgments, decisions, and behavior. *Review of Educational Research,* **51**, 455–498.

Shimmerlik, S., & Nolan, J. D. (1976). Reorganization and the recall of prose. *Journal of Educational Psychology,* **68**, 799–786.

Shore, M. F., Milgram, N. A., & Malasky, C. (1971). The effectiveness of an enrichment program for disadvantaged young children. *American Journal of Orthopsychiatry,* **41**, 442–449.

Siegler, R. S. (1976). Three aspects of cognitive development. *Cognitive Psychology,* **8**, 481–520.

Siegler, R. (Ed.). (1978). *Children's thinking: What develops?* Hillsdale, NJ: Erlbaum.

Siegler, R. S. (1981). Developmental sequences within and between concepts. *Monographs of the Society for Research in Child Development,* **46**(2, Whole No. 189).

Siegler, R. S., & Klahr, D. (1982). When do children learn? The relationship between existing knowledge and the acquisition of new knowledge. In R. Glaser (Ed.), *Advances in instructional psychology* (Vol. 2, pp. 121–211). Hillsdale, NJ: Erlbaum.

Siegler, R. S., & Richards, D. D. (1982). The development of intelligence. In R. Sternberg (Ed.), *Handbook of human intelligence* (pp. 897–911). New York: Cambridge University Press.

Simon, H. A. (1973). The structure of ill-structured problems. *Artificial Intelligence,* **4**, 181–202.

Simon, H. A. (1978). Information-processing theory of human problem solving. In W. K. Estes (Ed.), *Handbook of learning and cognitive processes. Vol. 5. Human information processing* (pp. 271–295). Hillsdale, NJ: Erlbaum.

Simon, H. A. (1980). Problem solving and education. In D. T. Tuma & F. Reif (Eds.), *Problem solving and education: Issues in teaching and research* (pp. 81–96). Hillsdale, NJ: Erlbaum.

Simon, H. A., & Newell, A. (1971). Human problem solving: The state of the theory in 1970. *American Psychologist,* **26**, 145–159.

Stallings, J. A. (1975). Implementation and child effects of teaching practices in Follow Through classrooms. *Monographs of the Society for Research in Child Development,* **40**(7–8, Serial No. 163).

Stallings, J. A., & Kaskowitz, D. H. (1974). *Follow Through Classroom Observation Evaluation 1972–73.* Menlo Park, CA: Stanford Research Institute.

Stein, B. S., & Bransford, J. D. (1979). Constraints on effective elaboration: Effects of precision and subject generation. *Journal of Verbal Learning and Verbal Behavior,* **18**, 769–777.

Stein, B. S., Bransford, J. D., Franks, J. J., Owings, R. A., Vye, N. J., & McGraw, W. (1982). Differences in the precision of self-generated elaborations. *Journal of Experimental Psychology: General,* **3**, 399–405.

Stein, B. S., Bransford, J. D., Franks, J. J., Vye, N. J., & Perfetto, G. A. (1982). Differences in judgment of learning difficulty. *Journal of Experimental Psychology: General,* **3**, 406–413.

Stipek, D. J. (1981, April). *The development of achievement-related emotions.* Paper presented at the annual meeting of the American Educational Research Association, Los Angeles, CA.

Stipek, D. J., & Weisz, J. R. (1981). Perceived personal control and academic achievement. *Review of Educational Research,* **51**, 101–137.

Swing, S. R., & Peterson, P. L. (1981). *The relationship of student ability and small-group interaction to student achievement* (Tech. Rep. No. 575). Madison, WI: Wisconsin Research and Development Center for Individualized Schooling.

Taylor, B. M. (1982). Text structure and children's comprehension and memory for expository material. *Journal of Educational Psychology,* **74**, 323–340.

Tesser, A., & Campbell, J. A. (1982). A self-evaluation maintenance approach to school behavior. *Educational Psychologist,* **17**, 1–12.

Thomas , J. (1980). Agency and achievement: Self-management and self-regard. *Review of Educational Research,* **50**, 213–240.

Thurstone, L. L., & Thurstone, T. G. (1962). *Primary Mental Abilities Test.* Chicago, IL: Science Research Associates.

Tobias, S. (1979). Anxiety research in educational psychology. *Journal of Educational Psychology,* **71**, 573–582.

Torgensen, J. K. (1977). The role of nonspecific factors in the task performance of learning disabled children: A theoretical assessment. *Journal of Learning Disabilities,* **10**(1), 27–34.

Twentieth Century Fund Task Force. (1983). *Report of the Twentieth Century Fund Task Force on federal elementary and secondary education policy.* New York: Author.

Uguroglu, M., & Walberg, H. (1979). Motivation and achievement: A quantitative synthesis. *American Educational Research Journal,* **16**, 375–389.

Voss, J. F., Vesonder, G. T., & Spilich, G. J. (1980). Text generation and recall by high-knowledge and low-knowledge individuals. *Journal of Verbal Learning and Verbal Behavior,* **19**, 651–667.

Walberg, H. J. (1984). Improving the productivity of America's schools. *Educational Leadership,* **41**(8), 19–30.

Wang, M. C. (Ed.). (1976). *The Self-Schedule System of instructional-learning management for adaptive school learning environments* (LRDC Publication Series 1976/9). Pittsburgh, PA: University of Pittsburgh, Learning Research and Development Center.

Wang, M. C. (1980). Adaptive instruction: Building on diversity. *Theory Into Practice,* **19**, 122–127.

Wang, M. C. (1981). Mainstreaming exceptional children: Some instructional design and implementation considerations. *Elementary School Journal,* **81**, 195–221.

Wang, M. C. (1983). Development and consequences of students' sense of personal control. In J. Levine & M. C. Wang (Eds.), *Teacher and student perceptions: Implications for learning* (pp. 213–247). Hillsdale, NJ: Erlbaum.

Wang, M. C., & Birch, J. W. (1984a). Comparison of a full-time mainstreaming program and a resource room approach. *Exceptional Children,* **51**, 33–40.

Wang, M. C., & Birch, J. W. (1984b). Effective special education in regular classes. *Exceptional Children,* **50**, 391–398.

Wang, M. C., & Brictson, P. (1973, February–March). *An observational investigation of classroom instructional learning behaviors under two different classroom management systems.* Symposium paper presented at the annual meeting of the American Educational Research Association, New Orleans, LA.

Wang, M. C., & Lindvall, C. M. (1984). Individual differences and school learning environments. In E. W. Gordon (Ed.), *Review of research in education* (pp. 161–225). Washington, DC: American Educational Research Association.

Wang, M. C., Mazza, M., Haines, J., & Johnson, M. (1972, April). *Some measured effects of a classroom management model designed for an individualized early learning program.* Paper presented at the annual meeting of the American Educational Research Association, Chicago, IL.

Wang, M. C., Peverly, S., & Randolph, R. (1984). An investigation of the implementation and effects of a full-time mainstreaming program. *Journal of Remedial and Special Education,* **5**(6), 21–32.

Wang, M. C., & Richardson, B. (1977, April). *The Self-Schedule System: Its effects on student and teacher classroom behaviors and attitudes.* Symposium paper presented at the annual meeting of the American Educational Research Association, New York.

Wang, M. C., & Stiles, B. (1976a). Effects of the Self-Schedule System on teacher and student behaviors. In M. C. Wang (Ed.), *The Self-Schedule System for instructional-learning management in adaptive school learning environments* (LRDC Publication Series 1976/9, pp. 7–53). Pittsburgh, PA: University of Pittsburgh, Learning Research and Development Center.

Wang, M. C., & Stiles, B. (1976b). An investigation of children's concept of self-responsibility for their school learning. *American Educational Research Journal,* **13**, 159–179.

Wang, M. C., & Walberg, H. J. (1983). Adaptive instruction and classroom time. *American Educational Research Journal,* **20**, 601–626.

Wang, M. C., & Walberg, H. J. (in press). Exemplary implementation of eight innovative instructional models. *International Journal of Educational Research.*

Webb, N. M. (1980). A process-outcome analysis of learning in group and individual settings. *Educational Psychologist,* **15**, 69–83.

Webb, N. M. (1982). Group composition, group interaction, and achievement in cooperative small groups. *Journal of Educational Psychology,* **74**, 475–484.

Weiner, B. A. (1976). An attributional approach for educational psychology. In L. Shulman (Ed.), *Review of research in education* (Vol. 4, pp. 179–209). Hasca, IL: Peacock.

Weiner, B. A. (1979). Theory of motivation for some classroom experiences. *Journal of Educational Psychology,* **7**, 3–25.

Weiner, B. A. (1983). Speculations regarding the role of affect in achievement-change programs guided by attributional principals. In J. M. Levine & M. C. Wang (Eds.), *Teacher and student perceptions: Implications for learning* (pp. 57–73). Hillsdale, NJ: Erlbaum.

Weinstein, C. E. (1978). Elaboration skills as a learning strategy. In H. F. O'Neil, Jr. (Ed.), *Learning strategies* (pp. 31–55). New York: Academic Press.

Weinstein, R. S. (Ed.). (1982). Students in classrooms [Special issue]. *Elementary School Journal,* **82**, 397–540.

Weinstein, R. S. (1983). Student perceptions of schooling. *Elementary School Journal,* **83**, 287–312.

Weinstein, R. S., & Marshall, H. H. (1984). *Ecology of students' achievement expectations: Final report.* Berkeley, CA: University of California, Department of Psychology.

Weinstein, R. S., & Middlestadt, S. (1979, April). *Learning about the achievement hierarchy of the classroom: Through children's eyes.* Paper presented at the annual meeting of the American Educational Research Association, San Francisco, CA.

Weinstein, C. E., & Underwood, V. L. (1985). Learning strategies: The how of learning. In J. W. Segal, S. F. Chipman, & R. Glaser (Eds.), *Thinking and learning skills. Vol. 1. Relating instruction to research* (pp. 241–258). Hillsdale, NJ: Erlbaum.

Weisstein, W., & Wang, M. C. (1978, March). *An investigation of classroom interactions between the academically gifted and learning disabled children with their teachers.* Paper presented at the annual meeting of the American Educational Research Association, Toronto, Canada.

Weisstein, W., & Wang, M. C. (1980, April). *An investigation of the effects of teacher perceptions on high and low achievers.* Paper presented at the annual meeting of the American Educational Research Association, Boston, MA.

Wellman, H. M. (1985). The child's theory of mind: The development of conceptions and cognition. In S. R. Yussar (Ed.), *The growth of reflection in children* (pp. 169–205). New York: Academic Press.

White, R. W. (1959). Motivation reconsidered: The concepts of competence. *Psychological Review,* **66**, 297–333.

Winne, P. H., & Marx, R. W. (1982). Students' and teachers' views of thinking processes for classroom learning. *Elementary School Journal,* **82**, 493–518.

Witkin, H. A., Oltman, P. K., Raskin, E., & Karp, S. A. (1971). *Embedded Figures Test.* Palo Alto, CA: Consulting Psychologists Press.

Woodcock, R., & Johnson, M. B. (1977–78). *Woodcock–Johnson Psychoeducational Battery.* Allen, TX: DLM Teaching Resources.

Yussen, S. R., & Levy, V. M., Jr. (1975). Developmental changes in predicting one's own span of short-term memory. *Journal of Experimental Child Psychology,* **19**, 502–508.

Zoeller, C. J. (1979). *An attribution training program with mentally retarded adults in a workshop setting.* Unpublished doctoral dissertation, University of California, Los Angeles, CA.

Advances in Improving the Cognitive Performance of Handicapped Students

ANNEMARIE SULLIVAN PALINCSAR

Michigan State University

and

ANN BROWN

University of Illinois at Urbana-Champaign

Abstract—The last decade has seen a burgeoning interest in cognitive strategy instruction to improve the academic achievement of students with mild learning problems. In this chapter, we characterize cognitive instruction as instruction that increases the learner's awareness of task demands, teaches students to use appropriate strategies to facilitate task completion, and prepares the student to monitor the application of these strategies. We review research that has evaluated cognitive strategy instruction in reading, written language, mathematics, and problem solving. Our review suggests that cognitive strategy instruction has resulted in positive academic gains for students. We conclude the chapter by defining a research agenda for the continued exploration of cognitive strategy instruction. In addition, we discuss implications for classroom implementation.

The word *advances* in the title of this chapter suggests a certain air of optimism, and it was in such a spirit that this review was undertaken. It was only a few years ago that Resnick (1981) described cognitive-instructional psychology as "a largely descriptive science, intent upon analyzing performance but not upon making strong suggestions for improving it" (p. 692).

However, cognitive instruction has entered a new era. There is now widespread interest in examining the activity of a learner moving from acquisition toward proficiency and in the role that instruction plays in facilitating this transition. Testimony to this interest includes a new journal, *Cognition and Instruction*; conferences (e.g., The Tri-Services [Air Force, Army, Navy] conference on cognitive science and instruction) (Steicht, Change, & Wood, 1985); and books (e.g., Chipman, Segal, & Glaser, *Thinking and Learning Skills: Research and Open Questions*) devoted to the issue. In this integration effort, we review recent cognitive-instructional endeavors focusing specifically on special populations.

Defining the Boundaries of the Research Integration

There are many avenues by which we can enhance learning. Teachers can be helped to teach better (cf. Duffy et al., in press). Instructional materials can be improved (cf. Armbruster & Anderson, 1984; Omanson, Beck, Voss, & McKeown, 1984), or how a learner interacts with a learning situation can be influenced by identifying and teaching strategic behavior to mediate learning. Although this review focuses on the instruction of strategies, we readily acknowledge the interactive nature of teacher, material, criterial task, and learner in the instructional setting (Bransford, 1979).

A vehicle frequently used in cognitive instruction is the training study. The hallmark of a training study is that it emerges from a theoretical analysis of the components of the task of interest. Once these components have been tentatively identified, they become the object of instruction. The training study, then, serves a multifold purpose (Brown & Palincsar, 1982; Campione, Brown, & Ferrara, 1982): To the extent that it is successful and well designed and executed (these are not synonymous), the training study benefits the learner, confirms the hypothesized analysis, and affirms a given notion of the learner. If the training study fails, such failure prompts a reconsideration of the initial analysis and/or confrontation with the possibility that a component that simply cannot be acquired through training has been encountered.

To clarify the dimensions of this review, we were guided in our search of the literature to locate training studies that addressed academic skill instruction such as reading comprehension, spelling, and mathematical problem solving. In hand with this, the purpose of the instruction examined was to teach strategies to facilitate the acquisition and application of academic skills. Examples of such strategies include looking for main ideas to enhance comprehension, using analogous word parts to identify the spelling of unknown words, and using relationships to solve mathematical problems. Finally, we were particularly interested in those interventions which taught strategies not only for the purpose of improving skills but also for the purpose of increasing learners' metacognition (Brown, 1978, 1980; Flavell, 1970). Metacognition refers to knowledge about cognition and the regulation of cognition. To illustrate, a student who reflects that it is necessary to prepare differently for an essay exam than for a multiple choice test is indicating metacognitive knowledge. The same student who plans his or her approach to studying (e.g., engages in self-questioning, monitors how effectively the approach is working, and evaluates the outcome of such strategy use) is engaging in the regulation of cognition. In our integration, we evaluate the training studies along several dimensions: (a) the extent to which the researchers engaged in in-depth analysis of the task components essential to success; (b) the effort made to assess competence in these components prior to training; (c) whether the researchers evaluated the process of learning and not simply the product of training; (d) whether the researchers measured independent strategy use; and (e) the level of the task, strategy, and metacognitive skill to which the researchers attended.

A taxonomy of training studies proposed by Brown and Palincsar (1982) has facilitated the evaluation of this last dimension and, for this reason, is presented here. The taxonomy suggests three levels of instruction: blind training, informed training, and self-control training. The variables that distinguish one level from the next are the amount of information shared with the trainee and the interaction between the learner and the investigator. In a blind training study, the learner remains naive regarding the role of the strategy to be learned; there is no information regarding why this particular strategy is being used or in what situations its use might be appropriate. The investigator merely tells the student what activity to engage in or leads the learner to do the activity. Although this may be sufficient instruction for some children, for others who fail to spontaneously infer the significance of the strategy, it is not. In informed training, the learner, along with inducements to use the strategy, receives information regarding the strategy's usefulness (e.g., how the strategy enhances performance, with what success, and in what situations). Such instruction leads the learner to an understanding of the significance of the strategy and increases the possibility of continued, unprompted use of the activity.

Finally, in self-control training, the learner receives instruction not only in how to use the strategy but also in how to monitor and evaluate strategy use. In contrast to blind and informed training studies, the student is taught both to produce and to regulate the activity in self-control training through the explicit instruction of planning, checking, and monitoring.

One final parameter of this review is our focus on school-age children. Individuals interested in adult learning have made significant contributions to the cognitive training literature. For example, Dansereau and his colleagues (e.g., Spurlin, Dansereau, Larson, & Brooks, 1984) and Weinstein and her colleagues (e.g., Weinstein & Mayer, 1985) have developed and evaluated strategy training programs to enhance the study skills of college students. As another example, the military has had an abiding interest in teaching strategies, particularly regarding the use of computer-assisted instruction to facilitate strategy acquisition (cf. McCombs, 1984). Space limitations and the overall purpose of the present research integration effort do not allow us to entertain this literature.

Strategy training research has had a long and productive history. It has been almost 20 years since Flavell began his seminal studies of children's strategy use (Keeney, Cannizzo, & Flavell, 1967). The evolution of strategy training research is reflected in the complexity of the problems it has addressed and in the sophistication with which these problems have been addressed. Our review does not focus on a chronology of strategy training research; rather, it presents the research by problem area. Hence, we will review training designed (a) to promote text processing, (b) to foster the skills required for written expression, and (c) to strengthen math/problem-solving skills. We also consider the corpus of study in cognitive instruction related to the training of thinking skills. Following our review of the instructional research, we address the state of practice of cognitive instruction, the role of teachers in and their preparation for conducting cognitive instruction, and directions for future research. We close with a discussion of specific needs and recommendations for future research and practice.

Cognitive Instruction and Special Populations

The concept of strategy training has sparked considerable interest among special educators. This interest stems from a reconceptualization of the learning impaired student as one who requires instruction regarding task-appropriate strategies and the orchestration of their use. Support for this reconceptualization may be found principally in the research on selective attention and memory.

For example, Torgesen (1977) presented good and poor fourth-grade readers with a series of twenty-four pictures that could be grouped into four categories. The students were to study these pictures for later recall. Torgesen observed that the good readers were more likely to organise the pictures into categories than were the poor readers and that the good readers later recalled more of the picture stimuli. However, after a brief training period in which students were instructed in the use of categorization as a mnemonic aid, these good-reader/poor-reader differences were no longer observed. Similar observations regarding the failure of learning impaired students to spontaneously employ effective strategies have been made by Tarver, Hallahan, Kauffman, and Ball (1976) and by Dawson, Hallahan, Reeve, and Ball (1979) in their studies of selective attention.

This focus on strategy instruction contrasts with the focus on underlying ability deficits, which has played a rather significant role in special education. The underlying abilities hypothesis suggests that students do not achieve success in school because the processes they use to execute a strategy are deficient; for instance, a student may experience auditory-reception, auditory figure-ground, or visual-perception problems that impede the acquisition of reading skills. This hypothesis leads to instructional strategies directed either at strengthening these underlying abilities or at circumventing these abilities and teaching to intact abilities.

This instruction has been widely critiqued in special education literature (cf. Arter & Jenkins, 1978; Hammill & Wiederholt, 1983; Vellutino, Steger, Moyer, Harding, & Niles, 1977). It has consistently failed to receive empirical support because of its limited usefulness in planning and xecuting instruction. In contrast to the underlying abilities model, the instructional agenda suggested by the ognitive approach reviewed in this chapter includes ncreasing the learner's awareness of task demands, teaching the student to use appropriate strategies to facilitate ask completion, and instructing the student to monitor the pplication of these strategies. In addition to the disenhantment with the underlying abilities model, further mpetus for the shift to cognitive instruction in special education comes from increased concern about maintenance nd generalization following instructional efforts. This oncern stems principally from the failure of operant procedures to result in the maintenance and/or transfer of social and academic behaviors following intervention.

The emergence of cognitive behavior modification represents perhaps the clearest link between traditional operant procedures and cognitively oriented procedures. Cognitive behavior modification is characterized by the following attributes: (a) a sequence of tasks or steps are identified that lead to successful solutions of problems, (b) the student is instructed to gradually assume responsibility for executing each of these tasks or steps, and (c) this transfer of responsibility from teacher to student is achieved by modeling coupled with verbalization. Initially, verbalizations are teacher generated, but, in time, the students engage in overt verbalization to guide their activity. Finally, these overt verbalizations are faded into covert verbalizations.

Early and most subsequent work in cognitive behavior modification has been directed at impulse control training (cf. Camp, 1977; Meichenbaum & Goodman, 1971), with infrequent measures of the effects of such instruction on academic performance. Those studies which have measured generalization across academic behaviors or across academic settings have yielded equivocal results at best (cf. Robin, Armel, & O'Leary, 1975). Such observations prompt one to recall Stokes and Baer's (1977) admonition that such generalization should be programmed rather than merely hoped for. In the following review of studies, many components of the original work in cognitive behavior modification are evident, including the use of verbalization and modeling to mediate instruction. However, in contrast to the majority of work done in cognitive behavior modification, the focus here is on academic instruction.

Reading

The many skills involved in the task of reading render it a rich domain of study for those interested in cognitive processing. There have been a number of studies that have identified good-reader/poor-reader differences in text processing (see reviews by Golinkoff, 1976; Ryan, 1981). Some of these differences include the failure of poor readers (a) to conceptualize reading as a search for meaning as opposed to a decoding task, (b) to monitor their comprehension to determine if they are deriving meaning, (c) to engage in strategic behavior that will bring meaning to a text or restore meaning if there has been a breakdown in comprehension, and (d) to modify their choice of strategies to meet the variable demands of reading. This profile of poor readers suggests the need for explicit instruction in the use of strategies that can increase awareness of the purposes of reading, provide specific means of achieving meaning, and promote comprehension monitoring.

We now turn to a review of such instructional research. The eight studies selected for review exemplify instruction that attends to the acquisition and control of reading strategies. The eight studies share many instructional features and represent successful endeavors. The first six studies are characterized as laboratory studies in that the interventions were conducted by the investigators in settings other than naturally occurring classrooms and were of relatively short duration. The last two studies are characterized as classroom studies; that is, teachers conducted the interventions with actual reading groups over extended periods of time.

Laboratory Studies

Pflaum and Pascarella (1980) undertook a study to teach disabled readers comprehension-monitoring strategies. There were two components to their training program: The first component was to assist the students in determining when they made an error that disrupted meaning; the second component was to teach methods of correcting errors that altered meaning. There were four treatment groups: one that received both components, a second that received only the first component, a third that received only the second component, and a control group. A total of forty students identified as learning disabled by their schools participated in the study. Their ages ranged from 8 years and 1 month to 13 years. The mean IQ was 89.1 as measured by the Wechsler Intelligence Scale for Children (WISC) (Wechsler, 1974). The mean grade equivalency score on the Gates-MacGinitie comprehension subtest (MacGinitie, 1978) was 2.5. The experimental treatment consisted of twenty-four lessons, each of which was introduced by an explanation of its purpose (to enhance skillful reading) and its relationship to previous lessons. Each concept was modeled through the use of a tape-recorded example of a student exhibiting errors in oral reading. The subjects in the experimental group were to evaluate the errors to determine effects on comprehension. In the second component, the model self-corrected serious errors. In the first component, a procedure was used to gradually transfer responsibility for engaging in this monitoring activity to the student; that is, the subjects initially judged only the errors made by the tape-recorded student. After achieving criterion performance in this skill, they began to record and identify the significance of their own oral reading errors. When receiving instruction in the second component, the students initially marked the self-corrections made on the tape-recording. This was followed by discussion regarding the purpose of the self-correction, practice in using context in a cloze task, and, finally, recording and analysis of their own self-corrections. Materials were developed at two readability levels to accommodate the differing reading levels of the subjects. The control lessons provided practice in oral reading and in the use of phonic cues as aids to word recognition.

The dependent measure was pre- and posttest performance on the Woods and Moe (1981) Analytical Reading Inventory, which assesses word recognition and comprehension. Using regression analysis, Pflaum and Pascarella determined that pretest decoding ability was the best predictor of response to intervention. Those students who were at the highest reading levels (specifically, Grade 3 or above) at pretesting realized the greatest benefit of the treatment. Students who entered with decoding skill and who received both training components indicated greater awareness and use of context in their reading. The variance explained by the treatment was nonsignificant, although the gains earned by each group were consistent with the hypothesis that those students who received both training components would show greater gains on the posttest than those students in the other three groups.

Schumaker, Deshler, Alley, Warner, and Denton (1984) undertook a strategy training study designed to teach students a modification of the traditional Survey, Question, Read, Review, Recite (SQ3R) (Robinson, 1946) procedure that consists of three substrategies: (a) surveying the reading material for the purpose of familiarizing oneself with main ideas and organization of a chapter, (b) reading end-of-chapter questions to determine which facts are most important to learn, and (c) reading the chapter once again to identify key content about which students are to generate questions.

Eight subjects, whose mean IQ was 91, were identified as learning disabled by their schools. Their ages ranged from 14 to 18 years, and their reading achievement scores ranged from 4.3 to 7.3 with a mean of 6.0. Two sets of reading material were provided for each student—one written at the student's reading ability level and another at the student's current grade level.

Instruction followed a series of three steps that were applied to each of the substrategies. First, the teacher assessed the student's approach to reading materials, evaluating specifically the student's use of any of the substrategies. Discussion was held regarding the failure of the student to engage a strategic approach to the task. In the second step, the teacher described the targeted substrategy, contrasting it with the reading approach of the first step and explaining why it would be helpful. In the final step, the teacher modeled the substrategy for the student by "thinking aloud" about each procedure. The student then recited the steps aloud until he or she reached 100% accuracy. This was followed by practice applying each substrategy to reading-ability level material while the teacher provided feedback. The teacher then reassessed (as in the first step) the student's approach to reading-ability level and grade-level material. If the student met the criteria of both sets of materials, instruction was terminated. If the criteria were not met, the student received practice and feedback in material that was written at his or her grade level. Due to the individualized nature of instruction, total instructional time ranged from 4½ to 11½ hours.

There were multiple dependent measures, includi application of the strategies to and accuracy in answeri comprehension questions to chapters (pre- and posttrai ing) that the student studied independently. Although t authors were careful to conduct reliability checks of the observations of strategy use, the individualized nature the materials did not allow for control of passage effects.

The experimental design was a multiple baseline acro the substrategies used by each student. Thus, when the st dent was introduced to the first substrategy, baseline da were collected on the remaining two. The second substra egy was not introduced until the student achieved criteric performance with the first. Finally, to facilitate a measur ment of generalization, measures were taken on both rea ing-ability level and grade-level material.

The results indicate that, while no student used the sul strategies prior to training, each student mastered the sut strategies in ability level material and was able to use ther in grade-level material without further instruction. Th payoff for using the substrategies included improve grades on tests of grade-level material, which rose fror failing or barely passing to a level of C or above.

Wong and Jones (1982) were interested in the effects o instruction in questioning on the comprehension perform ance of learning disabled and normal-achieving students Of the 120 students participating in their study, half wer eighth and ninth graders (whose mean cognitive age [CA was 14 years and 1 month) who had been identified a learning disabled. The other half were normal-achievin sixth graders (whose mean CA was 12 years). As measure by the revised Nelson Reading Skills Test (Hannah Schell, & Schreiner, 1977) the mean reading score of th normal-achieving students was 6.71 and that of the learn ing disabled students was 5.86.

Prior to strategy training, all students received instruction in the concept of a main idea until they achieved 80% accuracy for three consecutive days identifying the main idea. Those subjects in the experimental group then received instruction, modeling, and corrective feedback regarding the following steps: finding and underlining information related to the main idea, thinking of a question about this information, learning the answer to the question, and reviewing the questions and answers to evaluate what information they provide. Students in the control group read the same material for the purpose of evaluating the quality of the writing.

For the purpose of measuring the effectiveness of training, the subjects in the experimental and control groups were randomly assigned to a prediction or no-prediction condition following the two training sessions on self-questioning. All students were then given two passages to read and were asked to answer two sets of comprehension questions from recall. When these tasks were completed, the students were given a third passage. Students in the prediction group were asked to underline those parts of the passage which they thought were so important that they would be included in a test of comprehension. The no-prediction students read the same material for the purpose of evaluating the quality of the writing. Students in both the predicon and no-prediction conditions were asked to record the mount of time spent studying and then to write as much as ey could recall about the passage. This procedure was epeated on 4 test days.

Training worked very well for the learning disabled students, who progressively predicted more important ideanits over the test days. Trained learning disabled students nswered more comprehension questions correctly than id untrained learning disabled students. The recall data uggest that the learning disabled students, regardless of raining, recalled less than the normal-achieving students nd that there was no difference in the recall performance f trained students in the prediction and no-prediction roups. Training did not have the same facilitative effects n the normal-achieving students as on the learning disbled students.

The three studies reviewed thus far generally show an nteraction between the ability of the students and their esponses to interventions. Day's (1980) use of treatment nteraction provides a refined look at this subject (see also Brown, Campione, & Day, 1981). Day trained groups of junior college students in the use of five basic rules of summarization: (a) the deletion of trivia, (b) the deletion of redundancy, (c) the superordination of exemplars of a concept, (d) the selection of topic sentences, and (e) the invention of topic sentences. The students differed in ability (ranging from fifth- and sixth-grade reading and writing skills to no diagnosed reading or writing difficulty) as well as in the type of instruction they received. Students in the control group were given general instructions related to including main idea information and exercising economy with words. A second condition (informed training) involved demonstration and practice with the set of summarizing rules. A third group of students received explicit instruction regarding both the rules and the management and monitoring of the rules (self-control training). Students with no diagnosed learning problems improved with the informed training; however, remedial students required the complete self-control training package before they demonstrated significant improvement.

The findings of Day were supported by a study conducted by Kurtz and Borkowski (1985), who were interested in the relationship between students' metacognition and strategic behavior, specifically in the task of summarizing. Their population consisted of 130 fourth, fifth, and sixth graders who represented both impulsive and reflective approaches to learning. Following assessment of the students' knowledge about memory, reflectivity versus impulsivity, and summarization skills, the students were assigned to one of three conditions. There was a strategy condition, in which students received straightforward instruction on how to summarize, including instruction in the use of superordinates, identification of main idea information, and the invention of topic sentences. In an executive condition, students received, in addition to the summarization instruction, instruction regarding the value of monitoring reading performance, the importance of deliberate strategy selection, the flexibility use of strategies, and the need to work slowly. These metacognitive facets of learning were illustrated using the task of summarizing. There was also an attention control group which read the same experimental material and wrote summaries.

The results indicate that students in the two training conditions performed better than the attention control students when evaluated on paragraph summarization. Furthermore, students who received the metacognitive instruction performed better than those who received instruction in only summarizing. The effect of training on impulsivity versus reflectivity is less clear; fifth-grade students in the executive condition were more reflective than the other fifth graders following training, but this trend did not hold true for fourth and sixth graders. Another important finding of the Kurtz and Borkowski work results from the fact that they had longitudinal data on a number of their subjects' knowledge about memory (the data were collected 3 years prior to the intervention study). They were thus able to determine that a student's extent of metacognitive knowledge plays a significant role in determining responsiveness to strategy training.

Miller (1985) examined the degree to which self-instruction training influences comprehension monitoring during reading. Using an error detection task, a total of 44 fourth graders, whose mean CA was 9 years and 4 months and who were identified as normal readers, were assigned to one of four conditions: specific self-instruction, general self-instruction, didactic instruction, and control. Students in the specific self-instruction condition were taught five statements constructed (a) to define the task ("Does this story have any problems in it?"); (b) to specify an approach to completing the task ("I will ask myself, is there anything wrong with this story?"); (c) to evaluate the approach taken; (d) to self-reinforce ("So far, so good"); and (e) to arrive at task completion ("Did I find any problems in the story?"). Students in this condition were taught the self-statements by means of a fading procedure in which the experimenter first modeled the statements aloud, the students and experimenter then verbalized together, the students then subvocalized the statements independently, and the students finally used the statements covertly. Students in the general self-instruction condition received the same instruction in specific statements and were also taught an additional statement for each component of task completion (self-control training), such as defining the task ("First I need to make sure I know what I am going to do"). The same fading instructional procedure was used to teach these self-statements. In the didactic instruction condition, the same task-specific routines were taught, but they were not posed as self-statements. To illustrate, the task of problem definition was explained by the teacher, who suggested, "You should decide if the story has any problems in it." Students in the control condition simply listened to repeated readings of a passage before determining if there was an error. There were a total of three, 45-minute, individually conducted training sessions for all four groups. Evaluation of the instructional procedure was conducted by a comparison of the accuracy on the error detection task completed prior to instruction with the accuracy on the task immediately following and 3 weeks after instruction. In addition, during this 3-week maintenance check, the students in the experimental groups were asked to recall their instructions.

The results indicate that there was no difference between the performance of students in the didactic instruction condition and that of students in the control condition. On the immediate posttest, there was no significant difference between those students who received the specific self-instruction and those who received didactic instruction on the immediate posttest; however, on the maintenance check, the specific self-instruction group performed significantly better than the didactic instruction group. Students who received instruction in both specific and general statements were significantly more accurate in error detection than students in the didactic condition on both the immediate and delayed checks. Finally, there were no significant differences between the general and specific instructional conditions at either test time. When the recall of instructions was measured at the time of the maintenance checks, there were no differences among the three instructional groups.

The preceding studies represent successful cognitive instructional approaches to improving the reading comprehension skills of students who represent a broad range of chronological ages, cognitive abilities, and achievement levels. Despite the many differences in these studies, such as differences in targeted strategies, instructional modes, and assessment procedures, the studies share many features. Each study endeavored to teach strategies (e.g., identifying main idea information, self-questioning) that could serve both to enhance comprehension and to promote comprehension monitoring. The instructional procedures employed in the different studies share many similarities; they all provided the opportunity for a gradual transfer of responsibility for applying a strategy from the expert (teacher) to the novice (student). Figuring prominently in the instructional procedures was the use of teacher modeling. Generally, the investigators in each study were concerned about criterion-level acquisition of the targeted strategies; that is, even before measuring the independent application of the strategies, they attempted to ensure a degree of mastery with the instructed strategy. The investigators were also careful to control for the readability of the training and assessment materials so that the students were attempting to apply the strategy at their reading-ability level. Each study also attended to students' metacognitive knowledge. Finally, those studies which permitted an examination of aptitude-by-treatment interaction suggest that students with learning problems profit most from interventions that can be described as informed, self-control training. These are exciting findings, made more exciting by the fact that only recently has attention turned from the decoding to the comprehension skills of special populations. We conclude this review of reading studies by describing two series of classroom studies.

Classroom Studies

In a series of instructional studies conducted principally by remedial reading teachers in their natural readi groups, Palincsar and Brown investigated instruction four strategies; summarizing (identifying main idea info mation); question generating (self-testing on informatic identified as important); demanding clarity (noting wh there has been a breakdown in comprehension and resto ing meaning); and predicting (hypothesizing what th author will discuss next) (Brown & Palincsar, 198 Palincsar & Brown, 1984). The instructional procedu investigated, referred to as *reciprocal teaching*, took th form of a dialogue between the teacher and students tha was structured by the four strategies and focused o expository text. Participants in this dialogue took turn assuming the role of teacher. During the initial days o training, the teacher was principally responsible for initiat ing and sustaining the dialogue modeling and for providin instruction in the four strategies. With each day of instruc tion, the teacher attempted to transfer more responsibilit for the dialogue to the students while providing feedbac and coaching. Each day, before beginning the dialogue, th group reviewed the strategies they were learning, th reasons they were learning the strategies, and the situ ations in which the strategies would be helpful.

The students participating in these studies were in middle school (Grades 6, 7, and 8). All of them were identified by their schools as reading at least 1 year below grade level. More typically, their comprehension skills were at least 2 years below grade level. Their decoding skills, in contrast, suggested that their reading-ability levels were grade appropriate. The instructional sizes ranged from groups of four students to groups of eighteen students. There were usually 20 days of instruction, which were preceded by 5-day baseline periods and followed by short- and long-term maintenance checks.

The investigators collected an array of measures to evaluate the effectiveness of the reciprocal teaching procedure. Transcribing and scoring the dialogue that occurred during instruction provided the opportunity to examine the acquisition of the strategies. Consistently, it was observed that, with repeated interaction with an adult model, the students refined their strategies and became increasingly able to implement them independently.

The effect of strategy acquisition on comprehension was measured by having students read expository passages (of about 500 words in length) and answer, from recall, accompanying comprehension questions. These randomly assigned passages were independent of the training materials. The students completed a minimum of five of these exercises prior to intervention and one on each day of intervention. Performance on these exercises was graphed and shared with the students on at least a weekly basis. While normal-achieving readers typically scored 78% correct on the passages, students participating in the studies scored about 40% during baseline. By the end of the first half of training, the experimental group mean approached 60%, and, by the end of training, it approached 80%. These changes represent significant differences when the experimental groups are compared with control groups receiving practice in test taking (Palincsar & Brown, 1984) and instruction in "skill builder" programs (Palincsar, Brown, & Samsel, in preparation). These positive changes have been observed to be maintained for at least 8 weeks following intervention.

In one of the studies (Palincsar & Brown, 1984), generalization probes taken in social studies and science classes indicate that the improvement (as reported by the changes in percentile rankings when compared with those of classmates) demonstrated in the experimental setting generalized to the classroom setting. Finally, transfer measures administered on a pre- and posttest basis indicate that the students in the experimental group made reliable improvements in their ability to use condensation rules for summarizing, to predict questions that a teacher might ask regarding a text, and to detect incongruous sentences embedded in prose passages. These investigators are currently conducting replications across settings and subjects as well as extending reciprocal teaching to the instruction of listening skills with first graders at risk for academic difficulty.

For the past 5 years, Paris and his research team (e.g., Paris et al., 1984) have investigated an instructional program called Informed Strategies for Learning (ISL). Similar to the Kurtz and Borkowski (1985) work, this research addresses the relationship between students' awareness of the metacomponents of reading and their reading skills. In contrast to Kurtz and Borkowski, however, the research of Paris et al. represents classroom instructional research.

Specifically, Paris et al. (1984) were interested in how children's awareness of reading can facilitate their intentional use of reading strategies. The instructional techniques used included the following: (a) teaching what a particular strategy is, how it operates, and when and why it shoud be used; (b) using metaphors and visual displays to render descriptions of the strategies more meaningful (e.g., summarizing is like "round[ing] up" your ideas); (c) group discussion regarding the strategies; (d) guided practice, during which a strategy is applied; and (e) periodically using reading selections from various context areas (science, social studies) to promote the generalization of strategy use across subject matter. The students were introduced to a total of sixteen strategies. The strategies generally addressed constructing text meaning (e.g., through elaborating, activating relevant background knowledge, and summarizing) and comprehension monitoring (through rereading and self-questioning).

Approximately 800 third graders and 800 fifth graders from twenty-eight schools participated in this study. Forty-six teachers provided instruction in the experimental program, and twenty-five provided instruction in control classrooms.

The effectiveness of the ISL program was measured in a number of ways. Extended scaled scores from the Gates–MacGinitie reading comprehension subtest and performance on a cloze task were used to measure comprehension. Comprehension monitoring was assessed through the use of an error detection task. Awareness of reading was evaluated with the use of multiple choice questions that addressed such areas as knowledge of task goals, the use of strategies, and self-evaluation of comprehension. In addition, there were measures of children's self-perception and perceived competence regarding schoolwork and social skills.

For the purpose of analyzing the data, the students were divided into three reading-ability groups (low, medium, and high) based on percentile rankings produced by the Gates–MacGinitie. Other between-subject factors were grade, condition (experimental and control), and sex. The results indicate that students in the experimental rooms increased their reading awareness scores more than twice as much as the students in the control rooms. This effect of training was true for all students regardless of reading ability. The results of both the error detection and the cloze tasks provide evidence that ISL also promoted comprehension.

In addition to information regarding the effectiveness of the instructional program, the data collected by Paris et al. (1984) allow for the examination of the relationship among many interesting variables, including reading attitudes, awareness, and strategy use. Paris et al. observed that the role of comprehension strategies is particularly critical for young and poor readers, while awareness and attitude toward reading correlates with reading achievement more among older students and better readers. The results of these classroom interventions are very encouraging. They suggest that the components typically identified with cognitive instruction lend themselves to application in classroom settings and that such application yields significant benefits to the learner.

Written Communication

Although process may well be as important in the instruction of writing as it is in the instruction of reading, it has received much less empirical attention (Britton, Burgess, Martin, McLeod, & Rosen, 1975). However, emerging from the protocol analysis research of Flower and Hayes (1980, 1981) is one model of processing that illustrates very clearly the various aspects of writing activity.

Flower and Hayes (1980) defined a protocol as "a description of the activities, ordered in time, which a subject engages in while performing a task" (p. 4). Writing protocols are collected by asking subjects to say aloud everything they think and everything that occurs to them while they engage in the task of writing. Analyses of protocols, along with knowledge about the writer and the demands of the writing task, are used to make inferences regarding a model of those processes which facilitate writing. We briefly describe the Flower and Hayes model below to identify those processes to which instruction might attend. We then review the instructional literature to determine which processes have received attention and what success they have had.

Flower and Hayes (1980) proposed three major processes in writing: planning, translating, and reviewing. During the process of planning, writers integrate information they have about the dimensions of a writing task, about what they have already written, and about what they know about a topic. This integration allows the writer to set goals and to establish a game plan that will enable him or her to realize these goals. During the process of translating, the material generated as concepts, relations, and attributes during the planning process is transformed into written text. Collins and Gentner (1980) proposed four levels at which this occurs: the text level; the paragraph level; the sentence level (syntax); and the word level (spelling). Finally, the reviewing process serves to improve the quality of the written text. This process includes evaluating how well the goals have been met and editing to correct mechanical errors such as syntactic and spelling errors.

A review of the instructional literature suggests that research efforts have been directed both at isolated subprocesses and at the orchestration of the set of processes involved in written communication. We first review training studies that have targeted the specific subprocesses of (a) handwriting, (b) correct use of syntax, and (c) spelling. We then discuss more global composition skills. Again, in identifying studies, we were particularly interested in locating research that identified and provided instruction in strategies that could be regulated by the learner to enhance writing performance.

Writing Subprocesses

Handwriting. Since handwriting is a purely mechanical task in writing activity, it has received no attention from cognitive psychologists. However, illegible handwriting was the target of an instructional study conducted by Kosiewicz, Hallahan, Lloyd, and Graves (1982). This within-subject study used a multielement, multiple baseline, across-tasks design to assess the effects of self-instruction, self-correction, and a combination of the two on the handwriting performance of a 10-year-old boy who attended a self-contained class for learning disabled students.

During the self-instruction phase, the subject said the word to be copied aloud, then said the first syllable and named each of the letters in that syllable three times. In addition, the subject named each letter as he wrote it. The teacher initially explained and modeled each step and prompted as necessary. During the next phase, the subject was introduced to self-correction, during which he circled errors made on the previous day's work. This was used along with, or on an alternating basis with, the self-instruction procedure. There were several returns to baseline to observe for maintenance.

The effect of instruction was measured by reports of the percentage of correctly reproduced letters and punctuation marks completed in the process of copying paragraphs and lists. The results indicate that the use of some strategy—self-instruction, self-correction, or a combination of the two—did improve performance over baseline. For instance, accuracy on paragraph writing went from 30% to 76% with the use of self-instruction alone. Although the data are confounded by an order effect, they indicate that self-instruction was more effective on those days when self-instruction and self-correction were alternated. The intervention appeared to generalize across tasks, and maintenance was respectable, although in each case there was some decrement in performance following withdrawal of the intervention(s). This study represents a successful attempt to use fairly simple self-monitoring and guiding strategies to address a skill that has been learned but that needs to be strengthened (e.g., letter formation).

Correct use of syntax. Two studies that targeted the instruction of syntax are included in our review: the first addressed proper syntactic form, while the second was designed to increase the frequency with which particular word classes were used. Using an intervention quite similar to the one reported by Kosiewicz et al. (1982), Stone and Serwatka (1982) endeavored to enhance another subprocess of writing: the use of proper syntactic form. The purpose of this study was to compare the effect of a self-instruction, self-correction program with the effect of a program of teacher correction and feedback. The student, a 14-year-old female, had a full-scale WISC IQ score of 62 and attended a self-contained class for exceptional children. This study also employed a within-subject design. Following baseline, during which the subject's spontaneous writing samples were evaluated to determine the rates of syntactic errors per number of written words in thought units, the investigator marked syntactic errors produced by the student and asked her to read each sentence aloud and note what was wrong with the sentence. If the subject could not self-correct, the investigator explained the error. The student then read the sentence, inserting the correction. Instruction to the student following each of the 5 days of this phase was "read what you write." Baseline conditions were then reinstituted for 5 days. During the second treatment phase, the student wrote one sample daily, read what she had written into a tape recorder, and played it back while simultaneously reading her paper and marking and changing any noted errors. These 5 days were followed by a maintenance phase.

During the initial baseline phase, productivity averaged fifty words daily with a 26% error rate. During the first intervention (teacher correction), productivity averaged fifty-two words daily with a 12% error rate. Return to baseline resulted in a 15% error rate, but the trend during this phase indicated a definite increase in the error rate (e.g., the error rate for the last days of this phase was 23%). When the student engaged in self-monitoring and self-correction, production averaged sixty-two words daily with a 1% error rate, which was maintained throughout the last maintenance phase. In summary, although teacher feedback did result in improved syntactic performance, it was not until monitoring and correction were transferred to the control of the student that the best performance was obtained and maintained. There was apparently no attempt to observe for generalization beyond the experimental setting.

The purpose of a study conducted by Harris and Graham (1985) was to teach students three aspects of compoition that have been identified as positively related to judgments of quality writing: the use of verbs, the use of adverbs, and the use of adjectives. The learning disabled students participating in this study were 12 years of age, were achieving at least 2 years below grade level, and were experiencing significant difficulty with composition. The three targeted skills were introduced one at a time through a sequence of steps in which the students first reviewed their current performance levels. This first step was followed by discussion regarding the significance of each skill. Modeling and thinking aloud were used to introduce each strategy and to describe the development of a good story. This second step was followed by practice, which was accompanied by self-talk regarding deployment of the strategy and by feedback from the teacher. The students monitored their performance by charting the data collected on the use of a targeted skill. Harris and Graham used a multiple baseline design across behaviors (the targeted skills) that was nested within a multiple baseline, across-subjects design.

Evaluation was accompanied by a number of dependent measures, including scores on writing samples completed during training and at the termination of training and scores on generalization probes conducted in the resource room. The results indicate that the instructional procedure positively affected productivity, as well as quality, and that generalization across settings and short-term maintenance occurred. Experimental control is indicated by the fact that there was no transfer across skills: each skill improved only in response to its explicit instruction. On a long-term maintenance check (14 weeks after training), the students were not observed to demonstrate the same treatment effects, even though they could articulate the steps and skills in which they were trained.

Spelling. Spelling is a writing subprocess that poses a significant problem to large numbers of handicapped learners. In fact, the inability to generate correct spelling and detect incorrect spelling has repeatedly been found to characterize the writing performance of mildly handicapped learners (Alley & Deshler, 1979). Two studies in which a strategy training approach was employed to improve spelling are described below.

Englert, Hiebert, and Stewart (1985) investigated the effects of teaching mildly handicapped students to spell new words through the use of spelling patterns from known words, that is, through an analogy strategy. An analogy strategy is one in which developmentally normal learners spontaneously engage but impaired learners do not. Using a group design, Englert et al. compared analogy training to more traditional instruction, in which high-frequency words are isolated and attention is not called to pattern similarities.

Eleven pairs of mildly handicapped students were selected from 11 resource room programs after it was determined that each of the students in the pair performed at about the second-grade reading level and experienced difficulty in reading and spelling basic sight vocabulary (the mean reading levels of both the experimental and control groups was 2.2) but were able to discriminate rhyming words. One student from each pair was randomly assigned to the experimental group; the other was assigned to the control group.

The spelling words targeted for instruction were carefully selected to meet a number of criteria to ensure that they were high-frequency words that represented spelling patterns. Also selected was a set of low-frequency words that represented the same spelling patterns as those of the high-frequency words. Finally, there was a set of practice transfer words used to train the analogy strategy. These were words that rhymed with the common words. The reading stimuli that were used to measure the generalization from spelling to reading were similarly developed to represent high- and low-frequency words.

Pretesting was conducted to identify for each student the spelling words targeted for instruction of the experimental group and the sight word list to be taught to the control group. Instruction was individualized with each teacher instructing both experimental and control students for twelve 10-minute sessions.

The experimental condition included instruction in and demonstration of the analogy strategy, first with known words and then with unknown words. The students (a) identified the known word that rhymed with the unknown word, (b) identified the portions of both words that were spelled the same, and (c) spelled the new word by using the rhyming elements of the known word. In the final instructional phase, the students in the experimental group were given the opportunity to use their new skills in an application task: they were to complete cloze sentences that called upon the use of transfer words. The control students received direct instruction in the reading and spelling of high-frequency words through a model-lead-test format. They also practiced their newly acquired sight vocabulary in a cloze task.

The dependent measures included the results of spelling and reading tests of common and uncommon words. The results indicate significant differences between the spelling test performance of the experimental and control groups with both common and uncommon words. Furthermore, a qualitative analysis of spelling performance indicates that students in the experimental group progressed from lower to higher developmental spelling levels, that is, from prephonemic or early-phonemic to transitional spelling. However, this improvement on the part of the students in the experimental group did not generalize to reading: There was no significant difference between the experimental and control groups when their ability to read common and uncommon words was assessed.

The analogy strategy proved a very effective means of enhancing spelling ability. It is interesting to speculate as to whether or not generalization to the reading domain might have occurred had the students been informed about the appropriateness of applying the analogy strategy acquired in spelling to reading.

In another investigation of spelling instruction, Drake and Ehri (1984) compared the effects of having students prepare for a spelling test by having them pronounce targeted words in one of two ways. In one condition, the students produced careful pronunciation of standard spelling; in the second condition, the students pronounced sound spellings. To illustrate, students in the standard spelling group practiced the word *favorite* by pronouncing *fa-vor-ite*, while those in the phonemic group practiced the same word by enunciating *fa-v-r-t*.

The students were fourth graders who were accustomed to using sound spellings to study spelling words. The subjects were matched to control for spelling ability by means of a developmental spelling inventory. Members of matched pairs were then randomly assigned to the phonetic or conventional group. All students received instruction in decoding the long and short vowel sounds, and the phonetic subjects were also taught the schwa sound until they reached a criterion level. The students then studied twenty words by using one of the two designated procedures. Practice was followed by an immediate posttest and by a delayed maintenance check one week later.

The results of analyses indicate that the students who carefully pronounced conventional spellings spelled more words correctly and correctly remembered more letters than those who used the phonetic spelling technique. The groups did not differ in the recall of letters that were common to both conventional and phonetic spelling. The independent application of these approaches as strategies was neither taught nor tested in this particular study; however, this would seem a very natural and productive next step.

Thus far, our review indicates that the majority of cognitive instructional studies have been conducted at the word and sentence levels. Furthermore, these studies suggest that, although discrete subprocesses in the writing domain are responsive to training that is both explicit and comprehensive, little spontaneous transfer is observed to occur.

Global Composition Skills

A very comprehensive meta-analysis of the instruction of composition was conducted and reported by Hillocks (1984). Included in his analysis were studies that (a) represented a sustained treatment, (b) measured qualitative improvement in spontaneous writing samples, (c) exercised some minimal control for teacher bias, (d) controlled for differences among groups of students, (e) took steps to ensure the reliability and validity of dependent measures, and (f) provided the necessary data to calculate effect sizes. Of the 500 studies screened, sixty-five met these criteria. In his analysis, Hillocks discerned that investigators were typically, more concerned with identifying the focus of instruction rather than the mode of instruction; however, he was able to derive four modes of instruction, the presentational mode, the natural process mode, the individual instructional mode, and the environmental mode, which he characterized and evaluated in the following manner. The presentational mode is one in which the instructor dominates all activity and the learners are passive recipients of rules, advice, and examples of good writing. While this was identified as the most common mode, was also evaluated as the least effective. In the second mode, the natural process mode, the instructor arranges for students to write for one another, to receive comments from their peers, and to make revisions based on the comments of their peers and the instructor. This mode was judged to be 50% more effective than the presentational mode, as was the individual instructional mode in which students receive instruction through such techniques as tutorials and programmed materials.

Hillocks reported that the most effective mode of instruction was the environmental mode, in which the instructor plans and uses activities that encourage high levels of student interaction concerning problems that are central to writing, such as generating assertions and predicting and countering arguments. This mode is characterized by high levels of student involvement in structured problem-solving activities that are designed to transfer to similar problems in composing. The environmental mode was observed to be more than four times more effective than the presentational mode and three times more effective than the natural process mode.

The environmental mode is similar to the type of instruction that occurs in a cognitive approach. For example, consider the following study by Scardamalia, Bereiter, and Steinbach (1984). As in the Flower and Hayes model described earlier, Scardamalia et al. were interested in instructing students in the use of strategies to sustain the reflective thought necessary to the planning phase of composition. Specifically, students were instructed in the use of cues that would stimulate the generation of ideas regarding a topic. For example, when planning an opinion essay one might use the cue, "A whole new way to think about this topic is . . . ." Cues were provided that would aid in expressing new ideas, improving and elaborating on ideas, establishing goals, and integrating the writing effort. Both the instructor and the students engaged in modeling the use of these cues and in follow-up discussion regarding the thinking strategies that were displayed.

This study was conducted in a classroom of 30 sixth-grade students; another sixth-grade class served as the control group. The experimental instruction consisted of two 45-minute periods a week for 15 weeks. The first 10 weeks were devoted to opinion essay writing, while the last 5 weeks were spent on factual exposition.

Evaluation of the instruction was conducted by scoring students' pre- and posttest essays, which were written in response to assigned topics intended to elicit either opinion essays or expositions. In addition, during instruction, all students wrote one topical essay on a subject of their choice. Finally, six students from each group were randomly selected to think aloud while planning their essays. These planning sessions were scored to assess reflective thinking and to determine the specific activities in which the students engaged (e.g., generating, organizing, and goal setting).

The results of evaluation indicated such variability that, with the exception of scores regarding reflectivity, the data were not subjected to traditional analysis of significance.

On this variable, the experimental students were rated as significantly more reflective than the control students. The other dimensions by which writing was measured suggest that the students in the experimental group were more capable of independent planning activity. Although most of this activity was conducted principally at lower levels of the writing process (the experimental students did not, as a group, engage in the reshaping and elaboration of ideas), higher level skills began to emerge.

In summarizing the preceding discussion of research on strategy training in written communication, it is interesting to reflect on the field's apparent concentration on the mechanics and subprocesses of composition with special populations. It is also tempting to draw an analogy between this phenomenon and the virtually exclusive attention that, until recently, was paid to instruction in reading with special populations. The scenario that evolved in reading—the failure of decoding instruction to transfer to improved comprehension for large numbers of students and the responsiveness of learning impaired students to cognitive instruction in comprehension—prompts us to suggest that efforts to provide instruction in the global skills of composition might be in order.

Math Instruction

Resnick and Ford (1981) suggested that the math domain is characterized by the following attributes, which recommend it as an excellent area for the study of cognitive instruction: it is a clearly bounded and well defined area, the subject matter is self-contained and less dependent than other domains on the processing of natural language, and it is readily subjected to task analysis. Despite these attributes, a review of the literature reveals little empirical data on the cognitive instruction of math skills. The preponderance of work we have encountered is devoted to the investigation of those strategies which individuals employ in the solution of math problems (cf. Siegler & Shrager, 1984; Vakali, 1984) rather than to research on instruction in strategies. In this portion of the chapter, we describe the few instructional studies we did encounter that could be characterized as cognitive in nature.

In a study conducted by DeCorte and Verschaffel (1981), the investigators used error analysis and individual interviews to determine the problem-solving activities of first- and second-grade students completing addition and subtraction problems. The errors made by the sample of children were principally of two types, which the investigators categorized as *thinking* (or *algorithmic*) and *technical* (or *computational*). Seventy-eight percent of the errors were judged to be algorithmic, while 13% were computational. The data, which were collected by having the students think aloud or report retrospectively their problem-solving approach, reveal that a number of students did not appear to engage in any thinking whatsoever in their solutions but, rather, performed by rote. More interesting were the thoughts of those students who did engage in mental activity when confronted with an unfamiliar problem type. The investigators observed two different approaches in these students' problem solving. The first approach was categorized as *semantic*. Students using this approach transformed the task into a cognitive scheme available to them. The second approach was characterized as *intelligent trial and error*, a circuitous and less efficient but nevertheless inventive strategy.

Having determined the underlying causes of both success and failure in these tasks, the investigators next sought to instruct students in those processes which lead to successful solutions. The five units that comprised the instructional program were devoted to concepts of equality, part-whole relationships, and the use of relations to solve numerical problems. The focus was on thinking processes and not on technical procedures. In addition, the students were given practice in verifying their answers. Students in the control group continued to receive standard math instruction during the same instructional period.

Posttesting was conducted immediately after and one month after instruction was terminated by means of the same think-aloud procedure. The results indicate that the experimental students made significantly fewer algorithmic errors than those in the control group. There was no difference in the number of technical errors made by each group. The positive results for the experimental group were also indicated on the maintenance check. Furthermore, testing of a sample of the experimental children suggests that they made spontaneous use of the conceptual knowledge they acquired during training in the solution of transfer problems. In summary, this study represents a very successful attempt to identify and teach underlying processes of efficient mathematical problem solving.

A study conducted by Lloyd, Saltzman, and Kauffman (1981) with students identified as learning disabled was also designed to address the rote manner in which large numbers of children solve math problems. The approach, which they labeled *attack strategy training*, was evaluated in two experiments. The dependent measures for Experiment One included problem types in which students were directly trained during the course of the study; problem types that required near-transfer of the instructed attack strategy; and, finally, problem types that required far-transfer.

A multiple baseline, across-subjects design was used to evaluate the effects of teaching students a preskill as well as a strategy. The preskill was rote counting for six numbers, that is, counting by fives, sevens, twos, tens, threes, and fours. This preskill was taught through modeling and drill. When students reached the criterion level with the preskill, they were introduced to strategy training. The purpose of strategy training was to teach the students to apply the instructed preskill to multiplication problems. A final training phase, called *cue training*, was used to instruct students in the use of paper strips that indicated the counting chain for two numbers not taught. The results of daily assessments, including those of the three problem types described earlier, indicate that preskills training resulted in little increase in accuracy. Strategy training resulted in a higher level of performance than that observed during preskills training on both directly trained and near-transfer items. Cue training resulted in more accurate performance on the far-transfer items. Interestingly, strategy training promoted near-transfer, whereas cueing was required to prompt far-transfer.

Experiment Two of the Lloyd et al. study was planned as a replication of Experiment One to investigate the robustness of strategy training when applied to a new class of problems: division. Three of the four students in Experiment One served as the subjects of Experiment Two.

The instructional procedure included teaching discrimination of the multiplication and division signs followed by modeling of the counting off strategy applied earlier in multiplication. The investigators prompted and praised students' application of the strategy. The multiple baseline design with multiple probes across problems indicated that two students, who were unable to do any of the division problems during baseline, achieved and maintained 100% accuracy after a brief intervention period. Only one student indicated variable performance on both the multiplication and division problems when introduced to the strategy; however, his performance did not return to baseline levels. The work of Lloyd et al. supports the importance of explicitly teaching preskills, as well as the strategies for applying preskills, to promote generalization of an academic skill.

The final intervention applied in math instruction that is explored in this discussion is the teaching of heuristic strategies. In a meta-analysis of research on methods of teaching mathematical word-problem solving, Marcucci (1980) classified instructional techniques into four types: (a) modeling, or the use of visual aid manipulatives or models to illustrate relationships in a problem; (b) systematic instruction emphasizing a prescriptive approach to problem solving; (c) guided discovery, in which questions are used to guide a student to discover the solution to a problem; and (d) heuristic instruction stressing the teaching of general problem-solving skills, such as simplifying a problem through the use of fewer variables or smaller numbers. Marcucci concluded that, at the elementary school level, where the clearest conclusions could be drawn, the heuristic approach was the most effective. The systematic approach produced a slightly positive effect while modeling and guided discovery fared no better than the techniques used under the control conditions. Furthermore, each type of technique was most effective for low-ability students.

In the math literature, the words *heuristic* and *strategies* are used virtually synonymously (Schoenfeld, 1980). Heuristics parallel the strategies discussed above to the extent that the use of heuristics characterizes the behavior of experts. Furthermore, the same issues regarding the selection of heuristic strategies, the monitoring of their successful application, and their transfer across problem types apply to this area.

In an investigation of heuristic strategy instruction, Schoenfeld (1980) taught college students five heuristic strategies including the use of diagrams, the establishment of subgoals, and the reduction of variables in problems. Schoenfeld observed that only those students who received explicit instruction in the use of the strategies successfully solved problems analogous to those taught. Schoenfeld cautioned that the use of heuristics requires substantial commitment to an understanding that it is the *process* that must be the focus of instruction. In addition, the role that the teacher assumes is best characterized as that of a coach. This idea is expanded on in our discussion of implications for practitioners.

Instruction in Thinking

There is a growing interest in the explicit teaching of thinking skills independent of specific academic content. The attention that this endeavor is receiving prompts us to include literature in this area in our review. Reviews of this literature have been authored by Nickerson (1984); Nickerson, Perkins, and Smith (1984); and Sternberg, Spurlin, and Dansereau (1983).

Nickerson et al. (1984) proposed five categories of approaches to teaching thinking. The first of these—the cognitive-process approach—assumes that thinking depends upon such fundamental processes as comparing, categorizing, and predicting. Instructional programs with this emphasis provide practice in these processes in a range of contexts. Illustrative of this approach is Feuerstein's Instrumental Enrichment Program (Feuerstein, 1980). This program consists of thirteen types of exercises (e.g., identifying geometric figures embedded in dots, completing number sequences) repeated in cycles. The Feuerstein program has stimulated particular interest among professionals interested in learning disabled populations (cf. Messerer, Hunt, Meyers, & Lerner, 1984), who are enticed by the resemblance between the characteristics of populations for whom Feuerstein designed his program and the characteristics of learning disabled populations (e.g., poor organization and memory skills).

The second approach, heuristics, received attention earlier in this chapter in the description of Schoenfeld's work. Although heuristic strategies were applied in this instance specifically to math instruction, there are certain heuristics that are supported because they are applicable to problem solving independent of the nature of a given problem. Examples include restating or reformulating a problem and breaking it into parts. One program that exemplifies the heuristics approach is the Productive Thinking Program (Covington, Crutchfield, Davies, & Olton, 1974).

The third approach to teaching thinking, reflective of a Piagetian perspective, attends to stages of cognitive development and particularly to the notion that the ability to perform formal or abstract operations is normally acquired only after the ability to perform concrete operations. Consequently, most of the programs using this approach are tailored to post-high school students and emphasize student participation, inquiry, and hypothesizing. An exemplar of such an approach is the program developed at the University of Nebraska (Campbell et al., 1980), entitled Accent on the Development of Abstract Processes of Thought. This program was designed for a number of courses, including economics, math, and history, and focuses not only on presenting material appropriate at the concrete level but also on moving students to the formal stage of cognitive development.

The fourth approach identified by Nickerson et al. is language and symbol manipulation. Those who advocate this approach argue that the planning, organization, and integration required in writing cannot help but enhance the ability to think. Books that promote such instruction include *The Little Red Writing Book* (Scardamalia, Bereiter, & Fillion, 1979) and *Confront, Construct, Complete* (Easterling & Pasanen, 1979). Another example of this approach is the writing of computer programs with a specific emphasis on the use of LOGO (Papert, 1980).

The final approach focuses on the teaching of thinking as subject matter. This approach is grounded in the belief that learning about thinking can improve one's own thinking. Representative of this approach is the Philosophy for Children Program (Lipman, Sharp, & Oscanyan, 1980). In this program, children read texts about characters (children) engaged in thinking about thinking. Specifically, the focus is on such skills as formulating cause–effect relationships, drawing generalizations, and inferring from syllogisms. The situations in which the material is posed are concrete as opposed to abstract (in contrast to the Feuerstein program) and make considerable use of a student's knowledge base.

Data to support the relative effectiveness of these various approaches are sparse—even though there has been fairly widespread adoption of some of the programs. Nickerson (1984) proposed that the developers, convinced of the inherent value of their programs, may not be motivated to evaluate them. Those data which do exist (Feuerstein, 1979, 1980) indicate that, in fact, teachers enjoy and approve of this kind of instruction, noting that it places students in a situation in which they must attend and concentrate. Furthermore, students participating in instruction in thinking have demonstrated improvement on standardized measures of intelligence. A pressing issue is the extent to which the training espoused by any one of the five approaches discussed above can be generalized to enhance the acquisition of academic content and skills. This issue cannot be taken lightly when the instruction of handicapped learners is addressed since we have more than ample data to suggest that generalization and transfer are hard won in the instruction of these individuals.

The State of Practice

Almost without exception, the classic task used in cognitive strategy research is an independent learning task. Furthermore, with the exception of a few studies (e.g., Palincsar & Brown, 1984; Paris et al., 1984) the vast majority of research in cognitive strategy training has not been conducted in natural classroom settings. We are aware of pockets of school activity in various states in which the cognitive-strategy approach to instruction is used. Examples include the Springfield District Schools in Springfield, Illinois; Benchmark School in Media, Pennsylvania; Metcalf School in Bloomington, Illinois; Fairfax County Schools in Virginia; and Montgomery County Schools in Maryland. Many of these examples have been cited in Pearson (1986) as well. The burgeoning interest in staff development to conduct cognitive strategy instruction suggests that the time is coming when it will not be practical to list the schools engaged in this endeavor. However, documentation regarding the efforts in these schools is fairly sparse.

One exemplary program embodying the tenets of cognitive instruction, that has been developed, implemented, and evaluated over several years, is the Kamehameha Early Education Program (KEEP) (Tharp et al., 1984). KEEP principally serves native Hawaiian children from Kindergarten through Grade 3. The principal goal of this program has been the improvement of the language arts curriculum. KEEP classrooms are organized into several centers where students receive practice in and feedback on skills that are emerging but that require refinements before they can be independently applied. In addition to these learning centers, there is time scheduled daily when children and teachers interact in lively discussion. These lessons, which feature reading, listening, speaking, and thinking, are focused on the development of cognitive/linguistic abilities. Specific activities that occur during this time include labeling and word games, cooperatively authored and dictated stories, and group discussion of text, during which comprehension is fostered by bridging existing and new knowledge. Scaffolded instruction plays an important role in these discussions as the teacher (a) evaluates by listening carefully to students, (b) extends students' utterances, (c) paraphrases, (d) makes appropriate adjustments in the level of speech to ensure comprehension, and (e) elicits and provides opportunities for children to talk.

KEEP was initially piloted in laboratory schools and then exported to public schools in rural, economically depressed areas. Evaluation suggests that KEEP students perform significantly better than control students on standardized achievement tests; in fact, they were reported to be at the 50th percentile. This is a remarkable result, considering that native Hawaiians have historically been the lowest achieving minority population in the United States.

If cognitive strategy instruction like that provided by KEEP is to be successfully implemented in classroom settings, certain variables must be considered. Interestingly, the literature that has been generated in this regard has been authored principally by those who conduct research on teaching (e.g., Corno & Rohrkemper, 1984; Peterson & Swing, 1983). The literature suggests that cognitive-instructional psychologists have perhaps not shown enough regard for the character and constraints of classroom settings, but, when they have, such attention has yielded positive results.

One of the most widely recognized characteristics of the classroom is its social nature (Brophy & Evertson, 1974; Good, 1983). Classrooms, perhaps especially traditional special education resource rooms, represent collections of individuals who are heterogeneous in many respects. Consequently, cognitive strategy instruction needs to accommodate this diversity. Diversity in the case of cognitive training is represented by age (cf. Flavell, 1970; Pressley, Heisel, McCormick, & Nakamura, 1982); student ability (cf. Andre & Anderson, 1979); prior knowledge (cf. Baker & Brown, 1984; McGivern & Levin, 1983); and metacognitive knowledge (cf. Baker & Brown, 1984). Furthermore, in addition to this diversity,virtually all the strategy training studies reviewed include feedback components in their programs.

These characteristics suggest the need for such alternatives as small-group instruction or written activities. Norlander, Cherkes-Julkowski, and Gertner (1985) conducted a study in which children with various handicapping conditions worked cooperatively and successfully with one another to generate the best strategy by which stimuli could be recalled. Palincsar, Brown, and Martin (in press) conducted a study in which seventh graders engaged in peer and cross age tutoring in comprehension monitoring strategies. Both of these studies support the usefulness of such small-group activities.

Regarding the use of work sheet activities, Brown and Palincsar (in preparation) conducted a study designed both to analyze the instructional components of reciprocal teaching and to streamline the instructional procedure. To this end, they designed four instructional conditions for teaching the four strategies of summarizing, question generating, predicting, and clarifying, and a fifth condition as a control. The first condition, reciprocal teaching/corrective feedback, replicated their original procedure. Using the dialogue format, teaching initially consisted of instruction and modeling of the four strategies. As the 12 days of instruction proceeded, the students were given more responsibility for the dialogue while the teacher guided their practice by using modeling and feedback specific to each student.

The second condition, reciprocal teaching/practice, was, for the first 4 days of instruction, identical to the reciprocal teaching procedure. However, after these 4 days, practice continued by having the students write their summaries, questions, points to be clarified and predictions, to which the teacher gave feedback by starring the best of the students' responses. Hence, feedback was fairly minimal after the initial days of instruction.

The third condition, demonstration, permitted very little opportunity for interaction or practice. Each day, the teacher demonstrated the four strategies, and student participation was restricted to answering the questions posed by the teacher.

In the fourth condition, treated control, the students were given work sheet activities that introduced them to the strategies one at a time. In this condition, there was plenty of opportunity for practice and, because the work sheets were completed with teacher assistance, for student–teacher interaction. However, there were were no opportunities to integrate and practice these strategies in the context of reading. Finally, there was an untreated control group, which completed only the assessment associated with this study.

The results of this study by Brown and Palincsar (in preparation) suggest that the most effective of the four instructional interventions was traditional reciprocal teaching, followed, but not closely, by reciprocal teaching with practice and work sheet activity. Demonstration was the least effective of the instructional conditions. These results support the role of teacher–student interaction in achieving guided practice. Although this is interesting from a theoretical perspective, the practical implications are worth noting as well. In this study, the investigators were unable to identify a more economical means than the labor-intensive reciprocal teaching procedure by which the same comprehension gains could be achieved.

We also are aware of school programs that include 15 minutes daily of problem-solving activity in their curricula—time when youngsters are to put on their "metacognitive caps." The literature suggests that such isolated practice, which has been analogized to "exercising the muscles of the brain," offers slim hope of being transferred to general academic content. This seems particularly true for special-needs students. The features of successful cognitive instruction identified throughout this review suggest that cognitive instruction is probably best when it is used either in isolation or in a situation dependent solely on the use of adjunct material. Some of these features include (a) careful analysis of the task at hand; (b) the identification of strategies that will promote the successful completion of the tasks; (c) the explicit instruction in the strategies, accompanied by metacognitive information; (d) provision of feedback on the usefulness of the strategies and the success with which they are being acquired; and (e) instruction regarding the generalization of such strategies. It seems appropriate to conceptualize instruction with these features as an integral part of teaching activity.

Lest we appear extremely naive, we hasten to add that considerably more work will be needed to define the role of cognitive instruction in the classroom. The role that the classroom teacher plays as mediator in this form of instruction is a particularly demanding one. This role requires a reconceptualization on the part of those teachers who have traditionally assumed principally managerial responsibilities. It has been our experience that teachers are more able to assume the role of mediator if they have collaborated on an instructional activity. We regard cognitive-instructional research as an excellent opportunity for researchers to collaborate with classroom teachers.

Needs and Recommendations

Our review of the literature indicates that cognitive strategy instruction yields positive academic gains. Despite this fact, cognitive strategy instruction has not received widespread implementation in educational practice. To address this disparity, it is helpful to propose further directions for research and to explore practical as well as policy issues regarding classroom implementation.

Research Efforts

There are many reasons why the needs and recommendations portion of this paper must begin with a discussion f research efforts. Several topical journals in the early 980s devoted issues to the application of cognitive strat-gy training with special populations (e.g., *Topics in Learning and Learning Disorders* [Wong, 1982]; and *Exceptional Education Quarterly* [Hallahan, 1980]). Authors contributing to these issues were virtually unani-nous in urging that we exercise reasoned caution before outing such interventions (cf. Keogh & Glover, 1980; O'Leary, 1980). Their enthusiasm for cognitive strategy training was tempered by a number of issues that remain largely unexplored. Examples include the issue of which components are prerequisite to the success of cognitive strategy training interventions and the extent to which such interventions result in generalization and mainten-ance. The studies cited in this chapter suggest that (a) researchers have been increasingly attentive to these issues, and (b) continued exploration in this area is warranted.

It would seem that now, in contrast to the turn of the decade, we are ready to ask more specific questions and to engage in more refined research. The following are examples (not a comprehensive list) of questions that might define a research agenda in this domain and the implications of conducting such research:

1. What is the relationship among such subject factors as chronological age, prior knowledge, cognitive skill, language skill, and motivation when responsiveness to cognitive strategy training is evaluated? This is a particularly important question when related to special-needs populations, who are characterized by hetereogeneity, if nothing else. The attentiveness of researchers to a careful description of their populations will facilitate generalization from the training literature. The call to incorporate motivational factors in metacognitive theory is fairly recent (Brown, Palincsar, & Purcell, 1985; Paris & Oka, in press) and should not go unheeded.

2. How can advances in cognitive-instructional research be used to inform assessment procedures? As related chapters in this integration effort suggest, assessment in special education is in a worrisome state. In the introduction to this chapter, we refer to the emphasis of the cognitive approach on the interaction of the learner and the learning situation. Wixson and Lipson (1986) and Johnston (1984) have presented sound arguments supporting the reconceptualization of assessment as a process of finding the patterns of interactions that facilitate the identification of a match between the learner and instruction. As applied specifically to the area of reading, Wixson and Lipson have proposed that assessment should address the interaction of *reader* (e.g., background knowledge), *text* (e.g., organization and structure), and *task* (e.g., writing summaries versus responding to questions). This model of assessment encourages attention to the student's awareness of the learning task as well as the available strategies to be employed. Furthermore, the model shares the desirable features of curriculum-based assessment (Blankenship & Lilly, 1981; Ysseldyke et al., 1983), which relates assessment activity directly to instructional content and activity. In research endeavors, we need to be more cognizant of the manner in which we assess students for the purposes of tapping information about the strategies students currently use and for achieving a more comprehensive evaluation of the effectiveness of the interventions.

3. How can we ensure that strategy training receives a fair but critical evaluation? Recommendations include (a) continuing the analysis of components of strategy training programs—an analysis that is driven by theory; (b) structuring the lengths of interventions based on performance criteria rather than on the number of days of training; (c) investigating the usefulness of strategy training in applied settings with an array of teachers; (d) recognizing the need to compare strategy training with other modes of intervention, such as reinforcement programs, that are currently in popular use; and (e) continuing to gather evidence on those features of training which promote generalization and transfer.

These questions suggest that many diverse approaches to designing and conducting research are in order. For example, studies that are ethnographic in nature provide rich opportunities to observe natural strategy choice and application; comparative studies are necessary to evaluate the relative merits of various components of intervention procedures; and within-subject design, which is characterized by a careful description of subjects and repeated measures to observe strategy acquisition, has the potential to supply valuable missing data.

Finally, many issues in the area of cognitive instruction would be served by a merger between cognitive researchers and researchers in the area of teacher effectiveness. Presently, there does not seem to be much dialogue between these two groups—despite the fact that they address many of the same issues. For example, Duffy et al. (in press) explored the relationship between explicit teacher explanation in the instruction of reading strategies and student awareness and achievement. They observed teacher explicitness to be a significant determiner of student awareness. In the early 1970s, cognitive instruction researchers determined that the more severe the deficit displayed by the learner, the greater the need for explicitness in instruction.

School Implementation

The likelihood of the success of cognitive instruction in classroom practice is significantly influenced by one's conceptualization of learning, teaching, and curriculum. In a cognitive-instructional model, learning assumes many dimensions, including (a) planning an approach to the task at hand, (b) applying appropriate strategies that enable the acquisition of new knowledge and/or skills, (c) monitoring and evaluating the strategies to determine their effectiveness, and (d) revising the approach as appropriate. Unfortunately for students identified as low abilitied or disabled, it appears that this notion of learning has been reserved for the more capable students. If we can extrapolate from the reading literature and the observations of Collins (1980) and Brophy and Good (1974), it appears that, although good learners are encouraged to engage in critical evaluation and other thinking skills while reading, teachers focus the attention of poor learners on decoding and pronunciation. This differential treatment has many interesting and startling repercussions. The good learner identifies the goal of reading as constructing meaning, while the poor learner believes the purpose of reading is to say words correctly. In turn, the good learner employs an array of strategies for the purpose of comprehending text while the poor learner seems unaware of the need to engage in such activities as predicting, self-questioning, skimming, and rereading. The good learner receives instruction (although certainly not extensive amounts [cf. Durkin, 1984]), while the poor leaner receives little or none. The dilemma emerging from this scenario is a gross mismatch between the profile of the learner and the instruction he or she receives. The teacher and the curriculum can play leading roles in addressing this mismatch.

The focus of cognitive instruction is to assist students in identifying and enlisting strategies that promote and monitor learning. The final measure of the effectiveness of this instruction is the independent application of these strategies. The role that the teacher plays in cognitive instruction has been compared to the role of an expert providing the support necessary to nudge the novice from acquisition, through various levels of competence, to eventual mastery of skills. Characteristics of this model of instruction, which has been labeled *expert scaffolding* (Bruner, 1975; Cazden, 1979; Rogoff, Ellis, & Gardner, 1984), have figured prominently in much of the cognitive instruction reviewed in this chapter. Specifically, the teacher initially assumes responsibility for leading the instruction by modeling and providing explanations that render the strategies explicit, concrete, and overt. The responsibility for learning is then shifted gradually to the student through guided practice. At this point, the teacher's involvement is focused on evaluation and encouragement. Evaluation may lead the teacher to provide further instruction (providing ample support); to prompt (providing moderate support); or simply to praise (providing minimal support). In this model, instruction is not complete until independent application of the strategies is ascertained.

There are several important variables that contribute to the success of scaffolded instruction. One is, naturally enough, the comfort and skill with which the teacher undertakes this form of instruction. Teachers observed by Palincsar and Brown have expressed, virtually without exception, some initial uneasiness with this form of instruction. For most teachers, it represents a far more interactive form of instruction than that to which they are accustomed. In addition, in scaffolded instruction, teachers de-automatize skills that, for them, have become automatized, and they must make overt what they generally do covertly. However, with experience, the discomfort passes, and the majority of teachers become skilled advocates of scaffolded instruction. To date, Palincsar and Brown have involved eighteen regular and developmental classroom teachers in the use of scaffolded instruction to teach reading and/or listening comprehension strategies. All but two of the teachers, at the conclusion of 20 days of experienc were achieving proficiency with this instruction.

A second variable influencing the success of scaffolde instruction is instructional group size. Scaffolded instruc tion is, in fact, individualized instruction to the extent tha the amount of support provided by the teacher is deter mined by each student's need. The concept of individual ized instruction is one to which special educators have bee wedded for many years. It has been our experience tha such individualized instruction with ample opportunity fo interaction between teachers and students and among stu dents can occur in groups as large as ten (one teacher did a outstanding job with eighteen!); however, it is certainl more easily managed in groups of six and eight. There ar fewer implications of this variable for special educator since small group size is generally the norm in special edu cation programs.

The role that curriculum plays in cognitive instructio could have interesting implications for special educators A cognitive-instructional approach must be embedded i the existing curriculum. Instruction focuses simul taneously on the content to be mastered and the thinking processes that promote mastery. This requires that specia educators become very knowledgeable about curriculum and that they work in a far more collaborative relationship with the classroom teacher than they presently do.

Policy Issues

In hand with a reconceptualization of the role of the teacher and the focus of the curriculum, there are policy issues germane to providing teachers with the incentive to conduct cognitive instruction. A frequently cited aphorism suggests that assessment drives instruction. Assessment, to date, has generally focused on the recall of rote facts as the product of learning but seldom on measuring the process of learning. Just as we have argued that instruction must be two-pronged, so also must assessment become two-pronged, evaluating both declarative knowledge, or knowledge of content, and procedural knowledge, or knowledge of skill and process. The adoption of cognitive instruction and the close interplay between cognitive instruction and curriculum support the call for curriculum-based assessment (Ysseldyke et al., 1983). School psychologists, special educators, and teachers would determine where a student fits in the school's curriculum, what strategies the student brings to bear in an academic task, and how responsive the student is to strategy training, that is, how extensive the scaffold must be to ensure learning. The work conducted by Vye, Burns, Delclos, and Bransford (in press), Budoff (1972), Hall and Day (1984), and Brown and Ferrara (1980) provide interesting prototypes for this type of assessment.

Because cognitive instruction does not currently enjoy widespread use and is not the focus of textbooks or basal materials, there will be a need for extensive staff development to prepare teachers to use it. Palincsar and Brown are currently investigating a staff development model that has many of the same attributes as scaffolded instruction.

teachers who have been involved in the investigation of cognitive strategy training are serving as leaders in staff development, modeling for their colleagues, gradually transferring responsibility for leading instruction to their colleagues, and generating new strategies when attempted ones fail. Support for this model is found in the work of Wang, Vaughan, and Dytman (1985) and Joyce and Showers (1980). Interestingly, teachers who have been prepared to conduct strategy training in reading/listening have spontaneously generalized such instruction to other content areas, such as history and science.

Perhaps the most critical element, however, in promoting classroom implementation of cognitive instruction is the continued pursuit of a vigorous program of research that will advance our understanding of how learners learn, how teachers teach, and how compatibility between these two processes can be achieved.

Author Information

Annemarie Sullivan Palincsar is Assistant Professor of Education at Michigan State University. Ann Brown is Professor at the Center for the Study of Reading, University of Illinois at Urbana-Champaign.

References

Alley, G. R., & Deshler, D. D. (1979). *Teaching the learning disabled adolescent: Strategies and methods.* Denver, CO: Love.

Andre, M. E. D., & Anderson, T. H. (1979). The development and evaluation of a self-questioning study technique. *Reading Research Quarterly*, **14**, 606–623.

Armbruster, B. B., & Anderson, T. H. (1984). *What did you mean by that question? A taxonomy of American history questions* (Tech. Rep. No. 308). Urbana, IL: University of Illinois, Center for the Study of Reading.

Arter, J., & Jenkins, J. (1978). *Differential diagnosis-prescriptive teaching: A critical appraisal* (Tech. Rep. No. 80). Urbana, IL: University of Illinois, Center for the Study of Reading.

Baker, L., & Brown, A. L. (1984). Metacognitive skills of reading. In P. D. Pearson, M. Hamil, R. Barr, & P. Mosenthal (Eds.), *Handbook of reading research* (pp. 353–394). New York: Longman.

Blankenship, C., & Lilly, M. S. (1981). *Mainstreaming students with learning and behavior problems: Techniques for the classroom teacher.* New York: CBS.

Bransford, J. D. (1979). *Human cognition: Learning, understanding and remembering.* Belmont, CA: Wadsworth.

Britton, J., Burgess, T., Martin, N., McLeod, A., & Rosen, H. (1975). *The development of writing abilities.* London: Macmillan.

Brophy, J., & Evertson, C. M. (1974). *Process product correlations in the Texas Teacher Effectiveness Study: Final report.* Austin, TX: University of Texas, Research and Development Centre for Teacher Education. (ERIC Document Reproduction Service No. ED 091 394)

Brophy, J. E., & Good, T. (1974). *Teacher-student relationships: Causes and consequences.* New York: Holt, Rinehart & Winston.

Brown, A. L. (1978). Knowing when, where, and how to remember: A problem of metacognition. In R. Glaser (Ed.), *Advances in instructional psychology* (Vol. 1, pp. 77–165). Hillsdale, NJ: Erlbaum.

Brown, A. L. (1980). Metacognitive development and reading. In R. J. Spiro, B. C. Bruce, & W. Brewer (Eds.), *Theoretical issues in reading comprehension* (pp. 453–482). Hillsdale, NJ: Erlbaum.

Brown, A. L., Campione, J. C., & Day, J. D. (1981). Learning to learn: On training students to learn from texts. *Educational Researcher*, **10**, 14–21.

Brown, A. L., & Ferrara, R. A. (1980, October). *Diagnosing zones of proximal development: An alternative to standardized testing.* Paper presented at the Conference on Culture, Communication and Cognition: Vygotskian Perspectives, Center for Psychological Studies, Chicago, IL.

Brown, A. L., & Palincsar, A. S. (1982). Inducing strategic learning from texts by means of informed, self-control training. *Topics in Learning and Learning Disabilities*, **2**(1), 1–17.

Brown, A. L., & Palincsar, A. S. (in preparation). *Unpacking a multicomponent instructional program.*

Brown, A. L., Palincsar, A., & Purcell, L. (1985). Poor readers: Teach don't label. In U. Neisser (Ed.), *The academic performance of minority children: New perspectives* (pp. 105–143). Hillsdale, NJ: Erlbaum.

Bruner, J. S. (1975). From communication to language—A psychological perspective. *Cognition*, **3**, 255–287.

Budoff, M. (1972). *Measuring learning potential: An alternative to the traditional intelligence test.* Cambridge, MA: Research Institute for Educational Problems. (ERIC Document Reproduction Service No. ED 085 962)

Camp, B. W. (1977). Verbal mediation in young aggressive boys. *Journal of Abnormal Psychology*, **86**, 145–153.

Campbell, T. C., Fuller, R. G., Thornton, M. C., Peter, J. L., Peterson, M. Q., Carpenter, E. T., & Narveson, R. D. (1980). A teacher's guide to the learning cycle: A Piagetian-based approach to college instruction. In R. G. Fuller (Ed.), *Piagetian programs in higher education* (pp. 27–46). Lincoln, NE: University of Nebraska-Lincoln.

Campione, J. C., Brown, A. L., & Ferrara, R. A. (1982). Mental retardation and intelligence. In R. J. Sternberg (Ed.), *Handbook of human intelligence* (pp. 392–490). Cambridge, MA: Cambridge University Press.

Cazden, C. B. (1979). Peekaboo as an instructional model: Discourse development at home and at school. *Papers and Reports on Child Language Development*, **17**, 1–29.

Chipman, S., Segal, J., & Glaser, R. (1985). *Thinking and learning skills: Research and open questions* (Vol. 2). Hillsdale, NJ: Erlbaum.

Collins, A., & Gentner, D. (1980). A framework for a cognitive theory of writing. In L. W. Gregg & E. R. Steinberg (Eds.), *Cognitive processes in writing* (pp. 51–72). Hillsdale, NJ: Erlbaum.

Collins, J. (1980). Differential treatment in reading groups. In J. Cook-Gumperz (Ed.), *Educational discourse* (pp. 127–143). London: Heinemann.

Corno, L., & Rohrkemper, M. M. (1984). The intrinsic motivation to learn in classrooms. In C. Ames & R. E. Ames (Eds.), *Research on motivation in education: The classroom milieu* (pp. 53–90). Orlando, FL: Academic Press.

Covington, M. V., Crutchfield, R. S., Davies, L., & Olton, R. M. (1974). *The productive thinking program: A course in learning to think.* Columbus, OH: Merrill.

Dawson, M. M., Hallahan, D. P., Reeve, R. E., & Ball, D. W. (1979). *The effect of reinforcement and verbal rehearsal on selective attention in learning disabled children* (Tech. Rep. No. 164). Charlottesville, VA: University of Virginia, Virginia Research Institute on Learning Disabilities.

Day, J. D. (1980). *Training summarization skills: A comparison of teaching methods.* Unpublished doctoral dissertation, University of Illinois, Urbana, IL.

DeCorte, E., & Verschaffel, L. (1981). Children's solution processes in elementary arithmetic problems: Analysis and improvement. *Journal of Educational Psychology,* **73**, 765–779.

Drake, D. A., & Ehri, L. C. (1984). Spelling acquisition: Effects of pronouncing words on memory for their spellings. *Cognition and Instruction,* **1**, 297–320.

Duffy, G. G., Roehler, L. R., Meloth, M. S., Vavrus, L. G., Book, C., Putnam, J., & Wesselman, R. (in press). The relationship between explicit verbal explanations during reading skill instruction and student awareness and achievement: A study of reading teacher effects. *Reading Research Quarterly.*

Durkin, D. (1984). Teachers' manuals in basal reading programs. In J. Osborn, P. T. Wilson, & R. C. Anderson (Eds.), *Reading education: Foundations for a literate America* (pp. 3–10). Lexington, MA: Lexington Books.

Easterling, J., & Pasanen, J. (1979). *Confront, construct, complete.* Rochell Park, NJ: Hayden.

Englert, C. S., Hiebert, E. H., & Stewart, S. R. (1985, April). *Spelling unfamiliar words by an analogy strategy.* Paper presented at the annual meeting of the American Educational Research Association, Chicago, IL.

Feuerstein, R. (1979). *The dynamic assessment of retarded performers: The learning potential assessment device, theory, instruments, and techniques.* Baltimore, MD: University Park Press.

Feuerstein, R. (1980). *Instrumental enrichment: An intervention program for cognitive modifiability.* Baltimore, MD: University Park Press.

Flavell, J. H. (1970). Developmental studies of mediated memory. In H. W. Reese & L. P. Lipsitt (Eds.), *Advances in child development and behavior* (Vol. 5, pp. 182–213). New York: Academic Press.

Flower, L., & Hayes, J. R. (1980). The cognition of discovery: Defining a rhetorical problem. *College Composition and Communication,* **31**, 21–32.

Flower, L., & Hayes, J. R. (1981). A cognitive process theory of writing. *College Composition and Communication,* **32**, 365–387.

Golinkoff, R. (1976). A comparison of reading comprehension in good and poor comprehenders. *Reading Research Quarterly,* **11**, 623–659.

Good, T. L. (1983). Classroom research: A decade of progress. *Educational Psychologist,* **18**, 127–145.

Hall, L. K., & Day, J. D. (1984, April). *Intelligence and cognitive control as predictors of generalization of learning.* Paper presented at the annual meeting of the American Educational Research Association, New Orleans, LA.

Hallahan, D. P. (Ed.). (1980). Teaching exceptional children to use cognitive strategies [Special Issue]. *Exceptional Education Quarterly,* **1**(1).

Hammill, D. D., & Wiederholt, J. L., (1973). Review of the Frostig Visual Perception Test and the related training program. In L. Mann & D. A. Sabatino (Eds.), *The first review of special education* (Vol. 1, pp. 33–48). Philadelphia, PA: JSE Press.

Hannah, G., Schell, L. M., & Schreiner, R. (1977). *The Nelson Reading Skills Test.* Los Angeles, CA: Houghton Mifflin.

Harris, K. R., & Graham, S. (1985). Improving learning disabled students' composition skills: A self-control strategy training approach. *Learning Disability Quarterly,* **8**, 27–36.

Hillocks, G. (1984). What works in teaching composition: A meta-analysis of experimental treatment studies. *American Journal of Education,* **93**, 133–170.

Johnston, P. H. (1984, April). *A Vygotskian perspective on assessment in reading.* Paper presented at the annual meeting of the American Research Association, New Orleans, LA.

Joyce, B., & Showers, B. (1980). Improving in-service education: The messages of research. *Educational Leadership,* **37**, 379–385.

Keeney, T., Cannizzo, S., & Flavell, J. (1967). Spontaneous and induced verbal rehearsal in a recall task. *Child Development,* **38**, 953–967.

Keogh, B. K., & Glover, A. T. (1980). The generality and durability of cognitive training effects. *Exceptional Education Quarterly,* **1**(1), 75–82.

Kosiewicz, M. M., Hallahan, D. P., Lloyd, J., & Graves, A. W. (1982). Effects of self-instruction and self-correction procedures on handwriting performance. *Learning Disability Quarterly,* **5**, 71–77.

Kurtz, B. E., & Borkowski, J. G. (1985, March). *Metacognition and the development of strategic skills in impulsive and reflective children.* Paper presented at the meeting of the Society for Research on Child Development, Toronto, Canada.

Lipman, M., Sharp, A. M., & Oscanyan, F. S. (1980). *Philosophy in the classroom* (2nd ed.). Philadelphia, PA: Temple University Press.

Lloyd, J., Saltzman, N. J., & Kauffman, J. M. (1981). Predictable generalization in academic learning as a result of preskills and strategy training. *Learning Disability Quarterly,* **4**, 203–216.

MacGinitie, W. (1978). *Gates-MacGinitie Reading Tests.* Boston, MA: Houghton Mifflin.

Marcucci, R. J. (1980). A meta-analysis of research on methods of teaching math problem solving. *Dissertation Abstracts International,* **41**, 2485A.

McCombs, B. L. (1984). Processes and skills underlying continuing intrinsic motivation to learn: Toward a definition of motivational skills training. *Educational Psychologist,* **19**, 199–218.

McGivern, J. E., & Levin, J. R. (1983). The keyword method of vocabulary learning: An interaction with vocabulary knowledge. *Contemporary Educational Psychology,* **8**(1), 46–54.

Meichenbaum, D., & Goodman, J. (1971). Training impulsive children to talk to themselves: A means of developing self-control. *Journal of Abnormal Psychology,* **77**, 115–126.

Messerer, J., Hunt, E., Meyers, G., & Lerner, J. (1984). Feuerstein's instrumental enrichment: A new approach for activating intellectual potential in learning disabled youth. *Journal of Learning Disabilities,* **17**, 322–325.

Miller, G. E. (1985). The effects of general and specific self-instruction training on children's comprehension monitoring performances during reading. *Reading Research Quarterly,* **20**, 616–628.

Nickerson, R. S. (1984). *Teaching thinking: What is being done and with what results?* Cambridge, MA: Bolt, Beranek & Newman.

Nickerson, R. S., Perkins, D. N., & Smith, E. E. (1984). *Teaching thinking.* Cambridge, MA: Bolt, Beranek & Newman.

Norlander, K., Cherkes-Julkowski, M., & Gertner, N. (1985, April). *Differences in strategy usage among MR, LD, and average children: A social cognition approach.* Paper presented at the annual meeting of the American Educational Research Association, Chicago, IL.

O'Leary, S. (1980). A response to cognitive training. *Exceptional Education Quarterly*, **1**(1), 89–94.

Omanson, R. C., Beck, I. L., Voss, J. F., & McKeown, M. G. (1984). The effects of reading lessons on comprehension. A processing description. *Cognition and Instruction*, **1**(1), 45–67.

Palincsar, A. S. & Brown, A. L., (1984). Reciprocal teaching of comprehension fostering and comprehension monitoring activities. *Cognition and Instruction*, **1**(2), 117–175.

Palincsar, A. S., Brown, A. L., & Martin, S. (in press). Peer interaction in reading comprehension instruction. *Educational Psychologist.*

Palincsar, A. S., Brown, A. L., & Samsel, M. (in preparation). *From "skill builders" to building skills: The adoption of reciprocal teaching by a school district.*

Papert, S. (1980). *Mindstorms.* New York: Basic Books.

Paris, S., Cross, D., DeBritto, A., Jacobs, J., Oka, E., & Saarnio, D. (1984, April). *Improving children's metacognition and reading comprehension with classroom instruction.* Paper presented at the annual meeting of the American Educational Research Association, New Orleans, LA.

Paris, S. G., & Oka, E. R. (in press). Children's reading strategies, metacognition and motivation. *Developmental Review.*

Pearson, P. D. (1986). The comprehension revolution: A twenty year perspective on changes in process and practice. In T. E. Raphael (Ed.), *Contexts of school-based literacy* (pp. 43–62). New York: Random House.

Peterson, P. L., & Swing, S. R. (1983). Problems in classroom implementation of cognitive strategy instruction. In M. Pressley & J. R. Levin (Eds.), *Cognitive strategy research: Educational applications* (pp. 267–286). New York: Springer-Verlag.

Pflaum, S. W., & Pascarella, E. T. (1980). Interactive effects of prior reading achievement and training in context on the reading of learning disabled children. *Reading Research Quarterly*, **16**, 138–158.

Pressley, M. G., Heisel, B. E., McCormick, C. B., & Nakamura, G. V. (1982). Memory strategy instruction with children. In C. J. Brainerd & M. G. Pressley (Eds.), *Verbal processes in children* (pp. 125–159). New York: Springer-Verlag.

Resnick, L. (1981). Instructional psychology. In M. R. Rosenzweig & L. W. Porter (Eds.), *Annual review of psychology.* (Vol. 3, pp. 659–704). Palo Alto, CA: Annual Reviews.

Resnick, L. B., & Ford, W. W. (1981). *The psychology of mathematics for instruction.* Hillsdale, NJ: Erlbaum.

Robin, A. L., Armel, S., & O'Leary, D. (1975). The effects of self-instruction on writing deficiences. *Behavior Therapy*, **6**, 178–187.

Robinson, F. P. (1946). *Effective study.* New York: Harper Brothers.

Rogoff, B., Ellis, S., & Gardner, W. (1984). Adjustment of adult-child instruction according to child's age task. *Developmental Psychology*, **20**, 193–199.

Ryan, E. B. (1981). Identifying and remediating failures in reading comprehension: Toward an instructional approach for poor comprehenders. In T. G. Waller & G. E. MacKinnon (Eds.), *Advances in reading research* (Vol. 2, pp. 223–261). New York: Academic Press.

Scardamalia, M., Bereiter, C., & Fillion, B. (1979). *The little red writing book: A source book of consequential writing activities.* Ontario, Canada: Ontario Institute for the Study of Education, Pedagogy of Writing Project.

Scardamalia, M., Bereiter, C., & Steinbach, R. (1984). Teachability of reflective processes in written composition. *Cognitive Science*, **8**, 173–190.

Schoenfeld, A. H. (1980). Teaching problem-solving skills. *American Mathematical Monthly*, **87**, 794–805.

Schumaker, J., Deshler, D., Alley, G., Warner, M., & Denston, P. (1984). Multipass: A learning strategy for improving reading comprehension. *Learning Disability Quarterly*, **5**, 295–304.

Siegler, R. S., & Shrager, J. (1984). Strategy choices in addition and subtraction: How do children know what to do? In C. Sophian (Ed.), *Origins of cognitive skills* (pp. 229–293). Hillsdale, NJ: Erlbaum.

Spurlin, J. E., Dansereau, D. F., Larson, C. O., & Brooks, L. W. (1984). Cooperative learning strategies in processing descriptive text: Effects of role and activity level of the learner. *Cognition and Instruction*, **1**, 451–463.

Steicht, T. G., Change, F. R., & Wood, S. (Eds.). (1985). *Proceedings of the Tri-services Cognitive Science Synthesis Conference.* Monterey, CA: Navy Postgraduate School.

Sternberg, R., Spurlin, J. E., & Dansereau, D. F. (1983). *How can we teach intelligence?* Philadelphia, PA: Research for Better School, Inc.

Stokes, T., & Baer, D. (1977). An implicit technology of generalization. *Journal of Applied Behavior Analysis*, **10**, 349–367.

Stone, A. K., & Serwatka, T. S. (1982). Reducing syntactic errors in written responses of a retarded adolescent through oral patterning. *Education and Training of the Mentally Retarded*, **17**, 71–74.

Tarver, S. G., Hallahan, D. P., Kauffman, J. M., & Ball, D. W. (1976). Verbal rehearsal and selection attention in children with learning disabilities: A developmental lag. *Journal of Experimental Child Psychology*, **22**, 375–385.

Tharp, R. G., Jordan, C., Speidel, G. E., Au, K. H., Klein, T. W., Calkins, R. P., Sloat, K. C., & Gallimore, R. (1984). Product and process in applied developmental research: Education and the children of a minority. In M. E. Lamb, A. L. Brown, & B. Rogoff (Eds.), *Advances in developmental psychology* (Vol. 3, pp. 91–141). Hillsdale, NJ: Erlbaum.

Torgesen, J. K. (1977). Memorization processes in reading-disabled children. *Journal of Educational Psychology*, **69**, 571–578.

Vakali, M. (1984). Children's thinking in arithmetic word problem solving. *Journal of Experimental Education*, **52**, 106–113.

Vellutino, F., Steger, B. M., Moyer, S. C., Harding, C. J., & Niles, J. A. (1977). Has the perceptual deficit hypothesis led us astray? *Journal of Learning Disabilities*, **10**(6), 375–385.

Vye, N. J., Burns, M. S., Delclos, V. R., & Bransford, J. D. (in press). Dynamic assessment of intellectually handicapped children. In C. S. Lidz (Ed.), *Dynamic Assessment: Foundations and fundamentals.* New York: Guilford Press.

Wang, M. C., Vaughan, E. D., & Dytman, J. A. (1985). Staff development: A key ingredient of effective mainstreaming. *Teaching Exceptional Children*, **17**, 112–120.

Wechsler, D. (1974). *Wechsler Intelligence Scale for Children—Revised.* New York: Psychological Corporation.

Weinstein, C. E., & Mayer, R. E. (1985). The teaching of learning strategies. In M. C. Wittrock (Ed.), *Handbook of research on teaching* (3rd. ed.) (pp. 315–327). New York: McMillan.

Wixson, K. K., & Lipson, M. Y. (1986). Reading (dis)ability: An interactionist perspective. In T. E. Raphael (Ed.), *The contexts of school-based literacy* (pp. 131–148). New York: Longman.

Wong, B. (Ed.). (1982). Metacognition and learning disabilities [Special issue]. *Topics in Learning and Learning Disorders*, **2**(1).

Wong, B., & Jones, W. (1982). Increasing metacomprehension in L.D. and normally achieving students through self-questioning training. *Learning Disability Quarterly*, **5**, 228–238.

Woods, M. L., & Moe, A. J. (1981). *Analytical Reading Inve tory*. Columbus, OH: Merrill.

Ysseldyke, J. E., Thurlow, M., Graden, J., Wesson, C., Algozzin B., & Deno, S. (1983). Generalizations from five years research on assessment and decision making: The Universi of Minnesota Institute. *Exceptional Education Quarterl* **4**(1), 75–93.

Effective Educational Practices and Provisions for Individual Differences

HERBERT J. WALBERG

University of Illinois, Chicago

and

MARGARET C. WANG

Temple University Center for Research in Human Development and Education

Abstract—Research in psychology and education has made great strides, particularly during the last decade, in delineating the characteristics of special needs students, and this progress has been paralleled by the development of educational provisions that effectively adapt to student differences. Several aspects of these provisions and their efficacy in addressing individual student differences are addressed in this chapter. The results of a large-scale meta-analysis of educational effects, which is the first of four studies that are discussed, indicate that there are certain factors of student aptitude, instruction, and environment that have been consistently identified as influential in student learning. The remainder of the discussion focuses specifically on various aspects of learning environments that effectively provide for students' individual needs, such as the salient features that are characteristic of adaptive instruction and various models of adaptive instruction, which range from traditional models, such as enrichment and acceleration, to more recent models. The finding of three syntheses of quantitative research on adaptive education both support the value of instructional programs with features that are adaptive to students' individual learning needs and also contribute significantly to the formation of a data base for future research on effective educational provisions for individual learning differences.

Helping schools to create effective and practical learning environments that meet students' individual needs has been a continuing challenge in the history of school improvement efforts. In fact, the development of educational innovations that maximize the chances of learning success for students with unique learning needs has been the hallmark of special education: it is, essentially, what makes special education "special." Thus, special education can be defined as instructional interventions that are adaptive to the special learning needs of individual students. In this context, effective special education, by definition, incorporates alternative strategies for instruction and resource utilization as well as built-in flexibility to permit various routes to and amounts of time for learning. One premise of this approach is that individual students learn in different ways and at varying rates, and a major task for schools is to provide educational experiences that accommodate these differences in order to optimize each student's education.

Information on the learning characteristics of special needs students and the practical use of such information have undergone significant changes, particularly during the past decade. (For further discussion of the research on these and related topics, see the Wang and Peverly chapter in this volume.) Wang and Peverly have noted that teachers are now able to obtain a broad range of information on student characteristics and learning differences for use in planning instruction. This information includes a focus on the wide variability in the ways that students acquire, organize, retain, and generate knowledge and skills. Thus, learner differences are less likely to be identified through traditional ability tests than through the manner in which students process information and display knowledge of and competence in specific subject-matter content. Furthermore, individual learner characteristics and differences have come to be considered alterable rather than static.

The evolution of psychological concepts and educational principles has been paralleled by the growing prominence of educational provisions that aim to be adaptive to student learning characteristics. This instructional approach has received increasing attention in efforts to ensure high-quality educational opportunities for every student, including students with poor prognoses for schooling success and students identified as learning handicapped. The state of the art and the integration mandate of the Education for All Handicapped Children Act of 1975 (PL 94-142) (i.e., the "least restrictive environment" principle regarding the placement of special needs students) are examples of such efforts (Gilhool, 1985).

Thus, there seems to be growing interest, as well as stepped-up activity, in the development of innovative programs and practices that improve schools' capabilities to adapt instruction to student diversity. This approach, which is commonly referred to as *adaptive instruction,* combines specific assessment of student capabilities with specific instruction that builds each student's competence. The purpose of this chapter is to discuss the research findings on instructional effectiveness that have direct implications both for current theories of learning, instruction, and individual differences and for the improvement of each student's chances for success through instruction that adapts to individual needs.

The syntheses of research discussed in this chapter focus on practices in general education that effectively adapt to student differences. The rationale for centering the present research review on general education practices is threefold. First, other chapters in this volume include comprehensive reviews of effective special education practices. Second, one of the premises of the discussion in this chapter is that, just as disabled students are no longer isolated in the schools, effective practices for meeting the learning needs of special education students should no longer be examined outside the context of the entire educational enterprise. Finally, the focus on general education practices recognizes the significant progress that has been made during the past decade both in research on effective teaching (cf. Good, 1983) and in the provision of effective schooling for diverse student populations (cf. Wang & Lindvall, 1984; Wang & Walberg, 1985). The findings of the research in these areas have important implications for identifying the kinds of regular classroom settings that can accommodate special needs students—one of the crucial conditions for the implementation of the integration mandate of PL 94-142.

The discussion of research centers on the findings of four recently completed research integration studies. All four studies were designed to identify the critical features of widely implemented educational programs or practices and to determine the resulting impact on classroom processes and a variety of student outcomes. Considered collectively, the studies represent a comprehensive analysis of the state of the art and the state of practice in topics related to effective schooling and student differences. The findings of the studies illustrate the research bases for identifying features of school learning environments that provide greater-than-usual educational support to accommodate the diverse learning needs of individual students in regular classes. The first study involved compiling and summarizing the findings of more than 2,500 studies of educational effects on learning (Walberg, 1984). It was conducted to identify major causal influences on educational productivity. The second, third, and fourth studies were designed to identify characteristic features of programs that provide for student differences. The second was a quantitative synthesis of research on features and outcomes of instructional programs aimed at adapting to student differences (Waxman, Wang, Anderson, & Walberg, 1985). The third was a quantitative synthesis that focused on the features and efficacy of mainstreaming, the integration of handicapped students in regular classes (Wang & Baker, 1985–1986). The final study was a large-scale, classroom observation study of the program features, classroom processes, and outcomes of exemplary classes of eight instructional models (Wang & Walberg, in press).

In the next section, the findings of Walberg's (1984) synthesis of research on educational effects are summarized. Then, a set of theories and a body of evidence on adaptive instruction that hold particular relevance for the learning progress of special needs students are described, and the findings of the three studies that synthesize research on effective adaptive instruction programs and practices are summarized. The discussion in the concluding section draws implications from the current research base for future practice and further development.

Productivity Factors in Learning

The discussion in this section addresses two major topics: the findings of a major synthesis of research on the educational effects of selected factors and a consideration of the general effectiveness of autonomous learning.

Synthesis of Research on Educational Effects

The results of Walberg's (1984) analysis of estimated educational effects identified nine factors that generally have been found to be consistent and influential causes of learning. Evidence of the efficacy of these educational productivity factors was derived from experimentally and statistically controlled field studies as well as large-scale studies. The most notable of the latter studies are the High School and Beyond study, the study by the International Association for the Evaluation of Educational Achievement, the National Assessment of Educational Progress, and the National Longitudinal Study (see Walberg & Shanahan, 1983).

As shown in Fig. 1, the nine educational productivity factors fall into three groups: student aptitude, instruction, and environment. The three factors in the student aptitude group are ability or prior achievement, as measured by the usual standardized tests; development, as indexed by chronological age or state of maturation; and motivation or self-concept, as indicated by personality tests or a student's willingness to persevere in learning tasks. Instruction consists of two factors: the amount of time students engage in learning; and the quality of instructional experiences, including psychological and curricular aspects. Finally, the environmental factors found to consistently affect learning are the educational and psychological climates of the home; the classroom social group; the peer group outside of school; and the use of out-of-school time (specifically, the amount of leisure time spent on television viewing). As illustrated by Fig. 1, the major causal influences on student learning flow from aptitude, instruction, and the environment to learning. The three groups of factors also influence each other, and, in turn, they are influenced by how much students learn: students who begin well learn faster.

The five factors of student aptitude and instruction are prominent in the educational models of Benjamin Bloom, Jerome Bruner, John Carrol, Robert Glaser, and others (see Haertel, Walberg, & Weinstein, 1983, for a comparative analysis). Each factor appears necessary for learning in schools; without at least a small amount of each, students can learn little. Large amounts of instruction and high degrees of ability, for example, may count for little if students are not motivated or if the instruction is unsuitable. It is important to note that the five factors are only

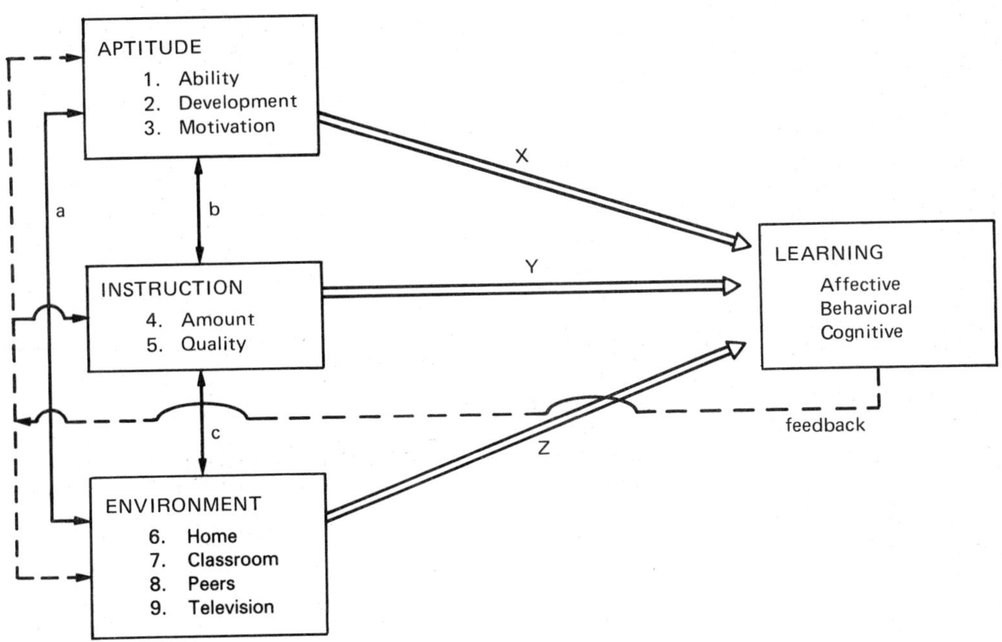

FIGURE 1. Casual Influences on Student Learning.

Aptitude. instruction, and the psychological environment are major direct causes of learning (shown as double arrows X, Y, and Z). They also influence one another (shown as arrows a, b, and c), and are in turn influenced by feedback on the amount of learning that takes place (shown as broken arrows).

Note: From "Improving the Productivity of America's Schools" by H. J. Walberg, 1984, *Educational Leadership,* **41**(8), 23. Copyright by *Educational Leadership.* Reprinted by permission.

partly alterable by educators. For example, the curriculum, or the length of time devoted to various subjects and activites, is determined to a great extent by diverse economic, political, and social forces. Ability and motivation, moreover, are influenced by parents, by prior learning, and by students themselves. Thus, educators are unlikely to raise achievement substantially by their own efforts alone.

Three of the environmental factors—the psychological climate of the classroom group; enduring affection and academic stimulation from adults at home; and an out-of-school peer group with learning-related interests, goals, and activities—influence learning in two ways: First, students learn from them directly, and, second, these factors indirectly benefit learning by raising student ability, motivation, and responsiveness to instruction. Thus, the powerful influences of out-of-school factors, especially the home environment, must be considered. The 180 six-hour days in each of the 12 years of elementary and secondary school add up to only about 13% of the waking, potentially educational time during the first 18 years of a student's life.

If a large proportion of the student's waking, out-of-school time that is nominally under the control of parents were spent in academically stimulating conditions in the home and with the peer group, then the total amount of learning time could be expected to rise dramatically beyond that found in conventional American schools. For example, high school students might draw on some of the 28 hours per week they spend viewing television (Walberg & Shanahan, 1983) to increase from a mere 4 to 5 hours a week the amount of time they typically spend on homework. Europeans and the Japanese believe that homework helps learning; this belief is supported by the empirical results of American research summarized in this section.

Tables 1 through 3 show Walberg's compilation of the numerical results of his synthesis of more than 2,500 studies of academic learning that were conducted during the past half-century. These estimates are based upon quantitative synthesis, or meta-analysis, of these studies. Interested readers and those who wish technical details may examine Walberg's (1984) detailed reporting of findings and methods, which includes references to the original studies. (In several instances, synthesis projects funded by the National Science Foundation have yielded separate estimates of correlates and effects in math and science.) Tables 1 through 3 present both the effects and correlations (the correlations made on the assumption of a 1-standard-deviation rise in the independent variable) of the three categories of educational productivity factors—aptitude, instruction, and environment. The results for each category are described briefly below.

TABLE 1
Summary of Findings on the Influence of Aptitude on Learning

Aptitude factors	Effect size	
Ability		
IQ	.71	XXXXXXX
IQ (Science)	.48	XXXXX
Development		
Piagetian Stage	.47	XXXXX
Piagetian Stage (Science)	.40	XXXX
Motivation		
Motivation	.34	XXX
Self-Concept	.18	XX

Note: The "X" symbols represent the sizes of the correlation coefficients in numbers of tenths.

From "Improving the Productivity of America's Schools" by H. J. Walberg, 1984, *Educational Leadership*, **41**(8), 23. Copyright by *Educational Leadership*. Adapted by permission.

Student Aptitude

Table 1 summarizes the findings regarding the influence of aptitude on instruction. As shown in Table 1, IQ is a strong correlate of general academic learning but only a moderately strong correlate of science learning. A student's Piagetian stage of development correlates moderately with both general and science learning. By contrast, motivation and self-concept are weaker correlates of either type of learning. Overall, the results suggest that the three factors of student aptitude are powerful correlates of learning, and, therefore, they should be included in theories of educational productivity. It should be noted that student aptitude may be less alterable than instruction. Yet positive home environments and good instruction have been shown to have some effect on aptitude (see Fig. 1).

Instruction

The results of the synthesis of findings on the effects of instruction on learning are summarized in Table 2. The results are grouped according to the two factors of instruction noted in Fig. 1—quality and amount.

Quality of instruction. The findings on the learning effects of the quality of instruction delineate specific instructional methods or features that have the largest effects, other large effects, and moderate or small effects.

TABLE 2
Summary of Findings on the Influence of Instructional Methods and Instructional Time on Learning

Aspects of instruction	Effect size	
Instructional Method		
Reinforcement	1.17	XXXXXXXXXXXX
Acceleration	1.00	XXXXXXXXXX
Reading Training	.97	XXXXXXXXXX
Cues and Feedback	.97	XXXXXXXXXX
Science Mastery Learning	.81	XXXXXXXX
Cooperative Learning	.76	XXXXXXXX
Reading Experiments	.60	XXXXXX
Personalized Instruction	.57	XXXXXX
Adaptive Instruction	.45	XXXXX
Tutoring	.40	XXXX
Individualized Science	.35	XXXX
Higher Order Questions	.34	XXX
Mainstreaming	.33	XXX
Diagnostic Prescriptive Methods	.33	XXX
Individualized Instruction	.32	XXX
Individualized Mathematics	.32	XXX
New Science Curricula	.31	XXX
Teacher Expectations	.28	XXX
Computer Assisted Instruction	.24	XX
Sequenced Lessons	.24	XX
Advance Organizers	.23	XX
New Mathematics Curricula	.18	XX
Inquiry Biology	.16	XX
Homogeneous Groups	.10	X
Class Size	.09	X
Programmed Instruction	−.03	−.
Instructional Time	.38	XXXX

Note: The "X" symbols represent the sizes of effects in tenths of standard deviations.

From "Improving the Productivity of America's Schools" by H. J. Walberg, 1984, *Educational Leadership*, **41**(8), 24. Copyright by *Educational Leadership*. Adapted by permission.

1. *Largest instructional effects.* Of all the methods listed in Table 2, the psychological components of mastery learning rank first and fourth in terms of effects on educational outcomes. Skinnerian reinforcement or reward for correct performance has the largest overall average effect—1.17 standard deviations; the method involving instructional cues, engagement, and corrective feedback has effects equal to approximately 1 standard deviation. A separate synthesis of the effects of mastery learning programs in science shows an average effect of 0.81 standard deviation.

Acceleration programs, ranked second in effect, provide advanced activities for elementary and high school students who have outstanding test scores. Students in these programs evidence academic gains much greater than those of students in comparable control groups.

Reading training, ranked third in instructional impact, refers to programs that coach learners in adjusting their reading speed and provide techniques for skimming, comprehension, and finding answers to questions. The usual criterion for evaluating this instructional method is the learner's adaptability to the method.

2. *Other large effects.* As shown in Table 2, several other instructional methods have large effects ranging from 0.76 to 0.33. These include cooperative-team learning, in which some autonomy over the means and pace of learning is delegated to students who help each other in small groups. Personalized and adaptive instruction, tutoring, and diagnostic-prescriptive methods, and mainstreaming also have large effects. Personalized instruction is similar to mastery learning in that it eliminates lectures and recitations for the most part. Students are guided through the use of entry tests, written lessons, and individual help (see Walberg, 1984). Adaptive instruction uses similar techniques, in addition to work in small groups and differentiated staffing, to increase learning. Tutoring and basing lesson prescriptions on diagnosed individual needs are similar ways of adapting instruction to learners that do not "batch process" them. All these related methods seem to succeed by helping students to concentrate on their individual, specific goals, or by freeing students from the pervasive seat work and group recitation strategies that might be effective with only the middle third of students.

3. *Moderate or small effects of instruction.* Although many schools no longer use the science and math curricula created in the 1960s after Sputnik, several of the syntheses of evaluation results suggest that such curricula (referred to in Table 2 as Individualized Instruction, Individualized Mathematics, and New Science Curricula) have moderate effects on learning. Table 2 shows that teacher expectations for student performance also have a moderate effect, as do advance organizers. The latter essentially are "cognitive maps" that show the relationship of material to be learned in a lesson to concepts learned in previous lessons.

Some highly touted methods or programs have small or even negative effects, on average. Reducing class size, for example, has small positive effects, but it is expensive and draws money and effort away from instructional methods with demonstrably large effects. The effect reported for programmed (computer-assisted) instruction is deceptively small. Most of the research included in the synthesis for this instructional method focused on the effects of drill-and-practice or "page-turning" computer programs rather than the instructional effectiveness of more psychologically sophisticated programs. Because future computer programs will be able to adapt to learner interests and abilities, it is likely that they will show large effects (Walberg, 1983). (However, educators may have to wait a decade or two before such effects are demonstrated. The accumulation of unused or minimally usable computers today may deter valid and efficient use of much better ones later.)

Quantity of instruction. As shown in the last row of results in Table 2, the overall correlation of instructional time with learning outcomes is approximately .4. It is neither the chief determinant nor a weak correlate of learning; rather, it appears to be a necessary ingredient but insufficient by itself to produce learning.

For at least two reasons, time is a particularly interesting factor. First, national reports have called attention to the need for lengthening the school day and year to the levels of other countries, particularly Japan and Western Europe (National Commission on Excellence in Education, 1983; Walberg, 1983). Second, time is the only educational productivity factor that can be roughly measured on a ratio scale that contains a true zero-point and equal intervals between scale points. When it is measured on an absolute scale in a way that is analogous to measurements of capital and labor inputs to production processes in agriculture and industry, increases in time after a certain point show diminishing returns (Fredrick & Walberg, 1980); that is, after an optimal point, additions of time, with the quality of instruction held fixed, yield ever smaller gains in learning. This finding suggests that neither time alone nor any other factor by itself can solve the problem of how to achieve greater educational productivity.

It is reasonable to assume that a zero amount of time results in a zero amount of learning, regardless of the level of other factors. Likewise, it may be generalized that the other essential factors of educational productivity, if well measured, would prove necessary but insufficient by themselves and would show diminishing returns. Although there may be a danger in concentrating on time as a single factor, this remains a matter for speculation, since the other factors are not measured either as universally or as precisely as time.

Therefore, it may be concluded that learning is produced jointly by several factors rather than by any one factor alone. A preliminary estimate suggests that if all nine factors indicated in Fig. 1 are optimized simultaneously, an effect of about 3.7 would result. This effect is approximately three times the 1.2 effect of reinforcement, the most powerful instructional method listed in Table 2, and nearly fifteen times the effect of socioeconomic status (SES) (Horn & Walberg, 1984).

Environment

Table 3 shows the major results of the synthesis of research findings on the effects of the four environmental or support factors. Although they have been ignored by several national reports and by instructional theories, these factors have strong influences on learning. The psychological morale or climate of the classroom group, for example, strongly predicts end-of-course measures of affective, behavioral, and cognitive learning. (Morale refers to the cohesiveness, satisfaction, goal direction, and related

TABLE 3
Summary of Findings on the Influence of Home, Peers, Class Morale, and Media Effects on Learning

Environmental factor	Effect size	
Graded Homework	.79	XXXXXXXX
Class Morale	.60	XXXXXX
Home Interventions	.50	XXXXX
Home Environment	.37	XXXX
Assigned Homework	.28	XXX
Socioenconomic Status	.25	XXX
Peer Group	.24	XX
Television	.05	X

Note: The "X" symbols represent the sizes of effects in tenths of standard deviations or correlations.

From "Improving the Productivity of America's Schools" by H. J. Walberg, 1984, *Educational Leadership,* **41**(8), 24. Copyright by *Educational Leadership.* Adapted by permission.

social-psychological properties or climate of the classroom group as perceived by students.)

Table 3 shows that the influence of the peer group outside of school is moderate and comparable to the influence of SES. It also shows that homework that has been graded or commented upon has three times the effect of SES. By contrast, homework that is merely assigned but not commented upon has an effect comparable to that of SES. Perhaps because it displaces more educationally constructive home activities, leisure-time television viewing in excess of 12 hours per week has a weak negative or deleterious influence on school learning. These findings suggest that increasing the amount of supervised homework and reducing the amount of television viewing are likely to have positive effects on educational productivity.

School–parent programs aimed at improving academic conditions in the home also have an outstanding record of success in promoting achievement. As indicated in Table 3, what might be referred to as "the alterable curriculum of the home" (Home Interventions) is twice as predictive of academic learning as family SES. This curriculum includes informed parent–child conversations about school and everyday events; encouragement and discussion of leisure reading; monitoring and joint critical analysis of television viewing and peer activities; deferral of immediate gratifications to accomplish long-term, human-capital goals; expressions of affection and interest in the child's academic and other progress as a person; and, perhaps, among these unremitting efforts, smiles, laughter, caprice, and serendipity.

Cooperative efforts by parents and educators to modify the alterable academic conditions in the home have strong, beneficial effects on learning. In twenty-nine controlled studies conducted during the past decade, 91% of the comparisons favored children whose families participated in school–parent programs over children in nonparticipating control groups. Although the average effect was twice that of SES, some school–parent programs had effects ten times as large, and the programs appeared to benefit older and younger students alike. Even though few of the programs included in the studies reviewed by Walberg (1984) were longer than a semester, the potential effectiveness of programs that are sustained over the years of schooling seems great. At the same time, it should be recognized that educators cannot carry out school–parent programs by themselves; effective implementation requires the concerted cooperation of parents, students, and other agents in the community.

Autonomous Learning

In nearly all the studies cited in the previous section, it is assumed that knowledge is a given to be inculcated and that achievement on standardized or teacher-made tests is the criterion for effectiveness. Yet educators, parents, and students aim for something more than this. In democratic societies, learners should become autonomous, critical thinkers, able to continue their learning independently beyond the classroom door. From the start, proponents of open education have upheld the importance of educational outcomes that reflect teacher, parent, student, and school board goals. These goals include cooperation, critical thinking, self-reliance, constructive attitudes, life-long learning, and other goals that are seldom measured by technically oriented psychometrics. Raven's (1981) summary of surveys in Western countries, including England and the United States, showed that, when given a choice, educators, parents, and students rank these goals above standardized test scores and grading.

Moreover, a synthesis of the relation between grades and adult success conducted by Samson, Graue, Weinstein, and Walberg (1984) showed only a slight association. Thirty-three post-1949 studies of the college and professional school grades of physicians, engineers, civil servants, teachers, and other groups showed an average correlation of .155 between grades in school and life-success indicators such as income; self-rated happiness; work performance and output indexes; and self-, peer-, and supervisor-ratings of occupational effectiveness.

These results should challenge educators and researchers to seek a balance between students' autonomy, motivation, responsibility, and skills in learning new tasks as individuals or group members on the one hand, and memorization of teacher-selected, textbook knowledge that may soon be obsolete or forgotten on the other. Since the time of Socrates, however, these two views have remained so polarized that educators find it difficult to stand firmly on the high middle ground of a balanced or cooperative teacher–student determination of the goals, means, and evaluation of learning. Progressive education, the Dalton (Parkhurst, 1925) and Winnetka (Washburne, 1925) plans, team teaching, the ungraded school, and other innovations in this century all were born of similar ideals but eventually drifted into authoritarianism, permissiveness, or confusion. They were difficult to sustain as they had been conceived.

Although open education, like its precursors, faded from view, it was massively researched by dozens of investigators whose work generally has been given little notice. Syntheses of this research may be useful to educators who are interested in basing practice on synthesized knowledge rather than on fads, or to those who will evaluate future descendants of open education.

Hedges, Giaconia, and Gage (1981) synthesized 153 studies of open education, including ninety dissertations. The average effects were near zero for achievement, locus of control, self-concept, and anxiety (suggesting no difference between open education and control classes on these criteria); about 0.2 for adjustment, attitude toward school and teachers, curiosity, and general mental ability; and about a moderate 0.3 for cooperativeness, creativity, and independence. Thus, students in open classes seem to do no worse on standardized achievement tests than students in conventional classes, and they do slightly to moderately better on several outcomes that educators, parents, and students consider of great value.

Giaconia and Hedges (1982) recently took another constructive step in synthesizing the research on open education. In order to distinguish more effective program features from less effective features, they identified those studies from the Hedges et al. synthesis (1981) which had the largest positive and negative effects on several outcomes. They found that programs that were more effective in producing positive nonachievement outcomes in areas such as attitude, creativity, and self-concept tended to sacrifice academic achievement on standardized measures. These programs emphasized the importance of the student's role in learning, the use of diagnostic rather than norm-referenced evaluation, the provision of individualized instruction, and the use of manipulative materials. However, they did not include three components that are thought by some to be essential to open education programs—multiage grouping, open space, and team teaching. Giaconia and Hedges (1982) speculated that students in the more extreme open education programs may have done somewhat less well than the control groups on conventional achievement tests because they had had little experience with the tests. The findings of the two comprehensive research syntheses described above suggest that open education may be able to enhance several nonstandard outcomes without detracting substantially from academic achievement.

Summary

The findings on productivity factors in learning can serve as one of the bases for educational reform in the area of identifying practices and programs that are demonstrably effective in improving the chances of schooling success for diverse student populations. Although Walberg's (1984) estimates of the effects indicated by a large body of extant research require replication and further study, they do yield a substantial knowledge base for efforts to increase educational effectiveness and productivity. Admittedly, the educational productivity factors found for regular education may not yield identical results for special student populations, instructional treatments, learning conditions, and educational contexts. Nevertheless, the findings discussed in this section comprise a sound empirical data base for designing further investigations of relative educational effects under such special circumstances.

Learning Environments That Effectively Provide for Student Differences

One of the basic assumptions of this chapter is that the design and implementation of school learning environments that enable each student to achieve desired educational outcomes are at the core of effective schooling. Instructional experimentation and innovative program development and implementation over the past decade have produced a substantial research base to support the improvement of school effectiveness through the provision of adaptive instruction. This research base has made it possible to derive a rather consistent list of salient features of programs that are adaptive to individual differences.

Discussion in this section is intended (a) to define adaptive instruction and touch upon the psychological theories and models of instruction from which it draws, and (b) to summarize the findings of research related to the school implementation of adaptive instruction.

Theories and Models of Adaptive Instruction and Individualization

Adaptive instruction programs make use of a variety of techniques that have been found to be effective in different classroom settings. These techniques include mastery learning, cooperative teamwork, and individualized instruction (Wang & Lindvall, 1984). They are used in ways that seem most suitable for each teacher, class, and student, and there is considerable variety in their use among different adaptive instruction programs.

Despite varying applications of certain instructional techniques, a core set of features seems to distinguish adaptive instruction from traditional or nonadaptive education. Unlike rigorous Boolean logical descriptors, these features can be compared to family facial features that collectively set one group noticeably apart from another. Wang and Lindvall (1984) delineate the following distinguishing features of adaptive instruction:

1. Instruction is based on the assessed capabilities of each student.
2. Materials and procedures permit each student to make progress in the mastery of instructional content at a pace suited to his or her abilities and interests.
3. Periodic evaluations of student progress serve to inform individual students of their mastery.

4. Each student assumes responsibility for diagnosing his or her needs and abilities, for planning individual learning activities, and for evaluating his or her mastery.
5. Alternative activities and materials are available to aid students in the acquisition of essential academic skills and content.
6. Students have choices in determining their individual educational goals, outcomes, and activities.
7. Students assist each other in pursuing individual goals, and they cooperate in achieving group goals.

Theoretical models of individualized instruction, which are discussed in this section, can be characterized as adaptive in certain respects. Although traditional and contemporary theories and practices of individualization are intended to suit lessons to groups or to individual students, they are more appropriately viewed as only elements or components of the more comprehensive approach that has come to be known as adaptive instruction. Nevertheless, individualization is often portrayed as being synonymous with adaptive instruction. The following discussion of various models of individualization identifies some principles and practices that have influenced the design of extant adaptive instruction programs.

Traditional Individualization Models

Enrichment and acceleration are the most common instructional methods employed by traditional models of individualized learning. Both methods require a series of activity units and tests and, generally, a final examination. All students in a class move through the same course of instruction in the same sequence; in most cases, failure in one or more units means that a student must repeat the entire course.

Enrichment has been the dominant method of American schooling since the turn of the century. In programs that focus on enrichment, all students spend the same amount of time on learning. Individual variability, to the distress of radical egalitarians, is evidenced by normally distributed scores on unit tests and final examinations that correlate with measures of aptitude and home environment. Enrichment often is combined with whole-group lessons, recitation, and seat work.

In the acceleration method, the criterion for satisfactory performance is fixed at a particular level (e.g., correct responses to 80% of questions). Each student is expected to attain the specific performance criterion, and students are expected to require different amounts of time to meet the criterion. A major assumption of the acceleration method is that time can compensate for deficiencies in the quality of instruction, student aptitude, and home environment. This assumption is in sharp contrast with the conclusions of two extensive reviews of early classroom research by Strang (1937) and Stephens (1968). These investigators concluded that there is little correlation between time spent on instruction and achievement. Recent quantitative syntheses, however, show consistently positive correlations between time spent and amount learned (Anderson, 1984; Denham & Lieberman, 1980; Fisher & Berliner, 1985; Walberg, 1984).

Recent Diagnostic Models

In two contemporary models of individualized learning—the hierarchical model and the profile model—diagnostic tests are given before students begin courses of instruction. The hierarchical model is based on the belief that it is necessary to learn the content elements of one unit of instruction before going on to the next and that students will have mastered certain units before beginning a new course. Pretests serve to place each student at the most appropriate point in the sequence of instruction. Progress is measured upon the student's completion of each unit; if a student fails a unit, it must be repeated before the student proceeds to the next unit.

One assumption of the profile model is that instructional units need not be presented in a hierarchy or sequence; rather, students have unique profiles of prior knowledge of subject matter or skills. Another assumption is that different students are likely to need instruction in different, selected units. Diagnostic pretests are used under the profile model to determine the specific units to be assigned to individual students. The goal is to ensure that students master the corpus of units and avoid studying those they have already mastered.

Thus, the hierarchical and profile models have in common the notion that children vary in their prior skills or knowledge; they differ in that the hierarchical model assumes a fixed sequence of learning, and the profile model assumes that units of learning do not necessarily precede one another. Both are somewhat theoretical in the sense that it has been difficult in practice to diagnose the levels of the profiles of prior learning and then to prescribe the most suitable lesson for each child.

Yet such diagnosis and prescription must be taken more seriously today for several reasons. We now recognize that these models would, in principle, enable teachers to teach children efficiently what they need to know rather than what they already know or cannot learn yet. The computer, moreover, holds out the prospect of routinizing diagnosis, prescription, and record keeping, which are not possible for a teacher to accomplish under normal circumstances. In addition, adaptive systems of education (discussed in subsequent sections) already allow the incorporation of such increased flexibility.

Multimodal and Multivalent Models

Two recent experimental models of individualized instruction—the multimodal model and the multivalent model—require multiple courses of instruction. In the multimodal model, several different courses of instruction or sequences of lesson units lead to the same achievement goals. Pretests are administered to determine the aptitude levels of individual students (which may be measured in terms of prior achievement, learning styles, and/or motivational preferences) and, subsequently, an appropriate course of instruction is assigned to each student. In this model, students also may be allowed to select their own courses.

One assumption of multimodal individualization is that aptitudes interact with educational treatments, that is, that some forms of instruction are better than others for particular students or groups. Despite much research in this area in the last few years, however, aptitude-by-treatment interactions have been difficult to replicate. In a 231-item review, Bar-Yam (1969) found some replicated evidence that bright, flexible, and assertive students perform better with instructional methods that are flexible and require independence, compared to students with the opposite aptitude, who may do better in more structured settings. Nevertheless, aptitude-by-treatment interactions appear to account for little replicated variance in achievement compared to the main effects of aptitude, instruction, and environment (see the previous discussion of "Productivity Factors in Learning"), and it is likely that, if such interactions were indeed powerful, their influence would have been uncovered by now. Nevertheless, much of the theorizing about individualization seems to be based on the premise of aptitude-by-treatment interactions (Cronbach & Snow, 1974), and, therefore, they may deserve further research.

The multivalent model assumes not only that there should be a variety of sequences of instruction but also that there should be different instructional goals for different students. The Project Physics Course (1970) is an example of an individualized program that is deliberately based on these premises. This program maintains that teachers and students might elect to pursue different goals in physics, such as mastery in math or understanding the nature and history of scientific methods. To permit cooperative planning, guides for teachers and students describe the course organization, various objectives, and alternate instructional activites. Open education is an even more radical multivalent model: students are expected to find or create learning materials that suit their individual educational goals (Walberg, 1984).

The success of contemporary models of individualized learning may depend on efficient monitoring as well as an effective system for the quick summarization of data for making instructional decisions and providing feedback to students. The continuing pervasiveness of enrichment with whole-group lessons and recitations and, to a lesser extent, acceleration with seat work, may be attributable to the lack of well-developed management systems for more suitable instruction. Feasible adoption and maintenance of comprehensive adaptive instruction programs over the long term may require school reorganization, extensive staff support, and computer processing of data on student progress so that lessons can be effectively and conveniently tailored to individual needs.

The Findings of Research Related to School Implementation of Adaptive Instruction

The development of practical educational interventions that provide greater-than-usual educational support to accommodate the learning needs of individual students has been a central concern both of effective schooling in general (cf. Brandt, 1985) and of special education services in particular. (For further discussion, see the chapters in this volume by Reschly and by Reynolds and Lakin.) During the past decade, the development and implementation of instructional programs with the goal of providing for individual student differences have resulted in a proliferation of research investigating the relative impact of such programs on student learning (cf. Wang & Walberg, 1985). The findings of three recently completed research studies on the design and related outcomes of adaptive instruction are discussed below to provide an overview of developments in this area. Two of the studies were quantitative syntheses of the findings of empirical studies of adaptive instruction; the third study was an observational study of exemplary classrooms of eight contemporary educational models that have the common objective of accommodating student differences. All three studies were designed to identify critical features of widely implemented educational approaches or interventions as well as to investigate the relationship of the program features to a variety of desired student learning processes and outcomes. The findings of the studies represent a substantial data base for analyzing the state of the art and the state of practice in topics related to schooling and student diversity.

A Quantitative Synthesis of the Findings of Research on Adaptive Instruction

Research on full-scale systems of adaptive instruction that meet the seven criteria set forth by Wang and Lindvall (1984) was recently synthesized by Waxman et al. (1985). Each study had to have been conducted in an ordinary elementary or secondary school classroom, have used either contrasted groups or correlational results, and have had sufficient quantitative data to calculate effect sizes (Glass, McGaw, & Smith, 1981). In addition, the programs studied had to contain at least one of the seven characteristics of adaptive education discussed by Wang and Lindvall (1984) and listed above in the discussion under "Theories and Models of Adaptive Instruction and Individualization."

Waxman et al. calculated 309 effects from statistical data on approximately 7,200 students in Kindergarten through Grade 12. The data were derived from thirty-eight studies of adaptive instruction programs. Of all the comparisons included in the quantitative synthesis to determine positive effects on learning outcomes, 77% were favorable to adaptive instruction; the average weighted effect was .45, which suggests that, under adaptive instruction programs, the average student scored at the 67th percentile of the control group distribution.

It is noteworthy that the average overall effect of adaptive instruction, as suggested by the effect sizes, is substantial and positive; the effect sizes, however, were not found to be as large as those of some of the component features that were included in most adaptive instruction programs. Reinforcement is one such component (Walberg, 1984). However, reinforcement and related components are often used with a few learners in very special circumstances and have short-term consequences. Evaluations of these components, moreover, are typically based on narrow measurements that directly reflect immediate lessons rather than on more general learning and nationally standardized achievement tests. Adaptive instruction programs, by contrast, tend to be evaluated according to multiple, comprehensive criteria. Thus, in their selection of specific strategies for adapting to the learning needs of individual students, educators may be faced with a trade-off between components that efficiently maximize the attainment of a few, narrow goals under special circumstances and full-scale systems that produce a substantially greater variety of outcomes.

Another trade-off educators may face is that between traditional or group-paced, teacher-directed instruction, which provides whole-group lectures, discussion, and seat work geared to the average child and which may raise the average of a class, and instruction that is adaptively differentiated to make it suitable for each child. Since research on group-paced, teacher-directed instruction has not been quantitatively synthesized, the efficacies of instructional approaches that are to be adaptive to individual differences and of group-paced, teacher-directed instruction cannot be objectively compared. Reviews of group-paced, teacher-directed instruction, moreover, have been extremely selective and suffer a great many methodological flaws (see Waxman & Walberg's, 1982, analysis of nineteen reviews).

Proponents of group-paced, teacher-directed instruction have ardently argued for the efficacy of their recommendations, but much of their research is correlational, without adequate statistical controls or randomized experimental assignment of alternative methods. Group-paced, teacher-directed instruction undoubtedly remains the dominant practice in regular education, yet special educators who are particularly aware of individual differences and concerned about children at the ends of the ability distributions must be cautious about accepting this approach. More research and synthesis are obviously necessary to determine the relative efficacy of direct instruction.

A Quantitative Synthesis of the Features and Efficacy of Mainstreaming Programs

Wang and Baker (1985–1986) conducted a study to synthesize, weigh, and analyze the empirical data base developed from the mid-1970s to the mid-1980s on the practice of integrating students with special needs in regular classes, which is commonly termed *mainstreaming*. Meta-analysis was used to summarize the relevant data of empirical studies that were published in 1975 or later and were concerned with the effects of mainstreaming on identified "exceptional" children. Eleven studies met the selection criteria and were included in the meta-analysis.

The analysis focused on studies that included in their designs one or both of two types of analysis: analysis comparing the performance, and/or attitudinal, and/or process outcomes of disabled students in integrated (mainstreamed) environments with those of disabled students in segregated, special education program; and a pre- and post-analysis of program effects on disabled students in mainstreaming programs. Performance effects included measures of achievement in academic subject areas such as math, language arts, reading, and social studies, as well as measures of the quality of play for preschoolers. Attitudinal effects included measures of students' self-concept and/or their attitudes toward learning and schooling, the attitudes of mainstreamed handicapped students toward their nonhandicapped classmates, the attitudes of nonhandicapped students toward mainstreamed handicapped students, and the attitudes of teachers and parents toward mainstreaming. Process effects included measures of classroom processes such as the types of interactions between teachers and students and among students.

In general, the results of empirical studies reported in this synthesis support claims for the effectiveness of mainstreaming in improving the performance, attitudinal, and process outcomes of handicapped students. This is a particularly noteworthy finding, one that surpasses the general finding of previous reviews (Carlberg & Kavale, 1980; Leinhardt & Pallay, 1982; Madden & Slavin, 1982; Semmel, Gottlieb, & Robinson, 1979) that only the academic outcomes of disabled students in mainstreaming programs reflect the positive effects of mainstreaming. The data from these studies also suggest that mainstreaming is effective only with students with certain special education classifications. Carlberg and Kavale (1980) found, for instance, that the placement of educable mentally retarded students in regular classes contributed to superior achievement and that learning disabled and emotionally disturbed students profited more than other students from placement in special education classes. Leinhardt and Pallay (1982) concluded similarly that high-IQ disabled students were more effectively placed in regular than in segregated classes and that low-IQ educable mentally retarded students were more effectively placed in special education classes than in regular classes. Other studies have also indicated that the social outcomes of mainstreaming were generally negative (Heller, 1981; Madden & Slavin, 1982; Meyers, MacMillan, & Yoshida, 1980).

Although the findings of this synthesis seem positive, there are limitations in the research base and problems in research designs that are inherent in studying mainstreaming effects. The fact that only eleven studies from a pool of 264 studies met the criteria of the Wang and Baker (1985–1986) meta-analysis underscores the need for improved studies focusing on programming factors and their related effects on mainstreamed special education students.

Despite these limitations, several of the findings from the Wang and Baker meta-analysis of mainstreaming studies seem noteworthy. They suggest the feasibility of implementing mainstreaming programs on a full-time basis, that is, of offering a more inclusive regular education program that can effectively serve students with special needs and disabled students of various special education categories. They also indicate the need to develop a descriptive data base on the specific program features and instructional practices of effective mainstreaming programs. Although the use of continuous assessment, alternative routes and a variety of curriculum materials, individualized progress plans, student self-management, peer assistance, instructional teaming, and consulting teachers were among the most frequently mentioned features of the mainstreaming programs reported in the literature, few studies provided data that directly addressed their impact on student outcomes in those mainstreaming programs. The impact of these practices has been noted in the effective teaching literature, however, particuluarly in the Waxman et al. (1985) and the Wang and Walberg (in press) studies, which are discussed in this chapter.

A Large-Scale, Observational Study of Features and Effects of Adaptive Instruction

As noted throughout the preceding discussion in this chapter, there has been much research on individual differences and learning, and instructional provisions that are adaptive to student differences have been included as a central component of many school improvement programs. However, neither research nor program development efforts have yielded much of a data base on the relationship among program design features, implementation conditions and delivery systems, and program effects on classroom processes and student outcomes. A recent survey was initiated by Wang and Walberg (in press) to (a) characterize features of exemplary adaptive instruction approaches, and (b) increase understanding of how different combinations of features are integrated into working programs to produce the kinds of classroom processes and outcomes widely associated with effective instruction and learning. Aspects of the design and selected findings of the study are discussed below.

A number of current instructional programs or models of instruction are aimed at providing school learning experiences that are adaptive to individual student needs (Wang & Lindvall, 1984; Wang & Walberg, 1985). Several of the programs are considered prototypes, and some have been widely adopted by schools (Jeter, 1980; Rhine, 1981; Talmage, 1975). Eight such programs were included in the Wang and Walberg study. These eight programs were the Adaptive Learning Environments Model (Wang, Gennari, & Waxman, 1985); The Bank Street Model (Gilkeson, Smithberg, Bowman, & Rhine, 1981); The Behavior Analysis Model (Ramp & Rhine, 1981); the Direct Instruction Model (Becker, Engelmann, Carnine, & Rhine, 1981); Individually Guided Education (Klausmeier, 1972); the Mastery Learning approach (Bloom, 1968); Team-Assisted Individualization (Slavin, 1983); and the Utah System Approach to Individualized Learning (U-SAIL) (Jeter, 1980). Classrooms that represented exemplary implementations of these programs were identified by the program developers and served as the sample pool for the study.

Data from a total of sixty-five second-, third-, and fourth-grade classrooms provided information on contextual characteristics of the programs and the implementation sites, the critical features of adaptive instruction as they were implemented, and the nature and patterns of classroom processes. The findings described here were derived from two types of analyses: analyses aimed at identifying, comparing, and contrasting salient program design features; and analyses of data across the eight programs on classroom processes, student perceptions of self-responsibility, and student achievement.

Characteristic design features of the programs. Wang and Walberg analyzed the designs of the programs to determine common instructional features and to characterize the salient differences among the features of the programs. The three sources of information for the analyses were the program design documents on each program, the ratings of program features by the program developers, and observations of the sample classrooms.

1. *Program design documents.* Overall, analysis of the documents on program design features suggests that a diagnostic-prescriptive component is part of the core of adaptive instruction across all the programs. Differences were found among the programs in terms of how frequently diagnostic tests are used, whether or not such tests are the only type of assessment used in prescription, how directly prescriptions follow from diagnoses, and how specific prescriptions are. Nevertheless, each program emphasizes the importance of prescribing tasks that are appropriate to the learning needs of individual students. Similarly, each of the programs uses assessment procedures to determine whether students have achieved objectives and are ready to move on or whether they need further instruction or practice. Finally, all the programs stress the need to maintain current and accurate records of each student's placement and progress, information that is also used in instructional planning. Thus, a diagnostic-prescriptive component that facilitates appropriate adjustments in instruction seems to be central to the adaptive instruction programs.

Beyond this common component or feature, the eight programs were found to incorporate a wide variety of strategies and classroom processes for accommodating student differences. These range from teacher-led, group instruction to student-initiated, individualized activities; from peer tutoring to student-cooperative work; and from the use of contingency contracts to student choice and scheduling of activities. None of the programs claims to be a panacea for all educational problems. Instead, each provides a core of instructional practices (which are not unlike certain practices cited in the effective teaching literature) that are implemented in various ways to meet the goals and improvement needs of schools where the programs are adopted.

2. *Developers' ratings of program features.* In addition to analyzing the program design documents, the investigators asked the developers of each program to rate the extent to which items on the Observation Rating Scale for Adaptive Instruction (Waxman, Wang, Lindvall, & Anderson, 1983) were important to the design of their respective programs.

With respect to differences among specific programs in the physical design of classrooms, the developers' ratings showed that the use of learning centers was considered important to the designs of the Bank Street Model, U-SAIL, Team-Assisted Individualization, and the Direct Instruction Model. The Mastery Learning approach was rated as making the least prevalent use of learning centers. Classroom arrangement was rated high in importance for the Bank Street Model, U-SAIL, and the Direct Instruction Model and lowest in importance for the Mastery Learning approach. With regard to curriculum materials, clear delineation of task-specific directions was rated most important to the Direct Instruction Model and least important to the Adaptive Learning Environments Model, the Behavior Analysis approach, and Individually Guided Education.

On variables related to the provision of adaptive instruction, diagnostic testing was most important to Team-Assisted Individualization and the Direct Instruction Model and least important to the Bank Street Model. The developers rated student choice as most important to the Bank Street Model, the Adaptive Learning Environments Model, and U-SAIL and least important to the Mastery Learning and Behavior Analysis approaches. With respect to the student and teacher behavior variables, peer tutoring was rated most important to U-SAIL and Team-Assisted Individualization and least important to the Behavior Analysis approach.

3. *Observed program features.* Data obtained through several rating scales and observation forms were analyzed to address two questions: What were the adaptive instruction features observed in the exemplary classrooms for each program? and Were certain of these features more prevalent for some programs than for others?

The findings of the analysis of observed program features showed that the Bank Street Model was tightly clustered around the mean T-score of 50 and appeared to be the most typical or representative of the adaptive instruction programs; that is, it was neither positively nor negatively distinct from the other programs. The Mastery Learning approach, although slightly above the mean in other respects, was notable for scores below the mean on the features of learning centers and materials in order. The Adaptive Learning Environments Model was sharply above the mean in all physical design features. The Behavior Analysis approach, Individually Guided Education, and Team-Assisted Individualization were clustered close to the mean in most respects. U-SAIL had notably high scores on all features but classroom arrangement, on which it was two standard deviations below the mean. The Direct Instruction Model was fairly low in all physical design features.

In terms of the inclusion of a variety of curriculum materials and the clear delineation of task-specific directions, classrooms under the Adaptive Learning Environments Model scored high and classrooms under the Direct Instruction Model scored low. Individually Guided Education also was quite low on these variables.

There were patterns of high adaptivity for the Adaptive Learning Environments Model and relatively low adaptivity for Individually Guided Education and the Direct Instruction Model, as reflected by the distributions of the program features, student choice, individualized prescriptions, diagnostic testing, and task flexibility among the eight programs. These patterns were repeated for the variables of informal evaluation, self-management, record keeping, peer tutoring, seeking adult help, and teacher monitoring. In all these distributions, the Adaptive Learning Environments Model was high, and Individually Guided Education and the Direct Instruction Model were generally much lower. In addition, the Bank Street Model was somewhat lower than average and the Mastery Learning and Behavior Analysis approaches were somewhat higher than average on variables related to the provision of adaptive instruction. The Bank Street Model also was lower than average in all three student and teacher behavior variables, and Team-Assisted Individualization was extremely high in peer tutoring.

Summary of findings on classroom processes, student perceptions of self-responsibility, and student achievement. The observers' ratings of classroom processes were used to address two questions: What were the classroom processes observed in the exemplary classrooms for each of the eight programs? and Were certain of the classroom process variables more relevant for some of the programs than for others?

The results of the analysis of classroom process data show that the Bank Street Model was highest in personal interactions with teachers. The Mastery Learning approach was highest in teachers' use of explaining and demonstrating/modeling. The Adaptive Learning Environments Model was highest in students working on independent tasks in group-parallel settings, use of exploratory materials, student interactions with adults, teachers giving managerial instructions to students, one-to-one tutoring, teachers encouraging student self-responsibility, and teachers having contact with students in exploratory activities; the Adaptive Learning Environments Model was lowest in small-group instruction and teacher interactions with students focusing on specific content. The Behavior Analysis approach was highest in ponding, praising behavior, and cueing or prompting; it s lowest in student/constructive interactions.

Under the category of subject-matter area, Individually ided Education was highest in the amount of time allo-ted to reading. U-SAIL was highest in language arts d whole-class instruction. Team-Assisted Individualiza-n was highest in student/constructive interactions, stu-nts working alone on independent tasks, students taking ts and quizzes, written assignments, students assisting classroom management, and students' assessment of sk difficulty. The Direct Instruction Model was highest small-group instruction, teacher time spent on reading, d communicating criteria; it was lowest in explaining.

With respect to differences in classroom processes, the daptive Learning Environments Model and Team-ssisted Individualization were most prominent and dis-ctive among the eight programs. Adaptive Learning nvironments Model classrooms, on the one hand, were served to have the most indicators of adaptive instruc-on. These included constructive, student-to-student teractions and students working on independent tasks in oup-parallel settings; encouragement of self-manage-ent, student choice, and exploration; and the teacher ting as manager and consultant rather than as a sciplinarian or lecturer to the whole class or small oups. Team-Assisted Individualization, on the other and, was prominent and distinctive with respect to nother pattern of classroom processes. Students often ere observed to work individually on written assignments, sts and quizzes, and other seat work; the teacher's role as to diagnose and assist.

Differences also were found across the eight programs in e degree of responsibility that students assumed for their wn positive and negative learning outcomes. Students nder the two programs that, by design, delegate more utonomy to students, Team-Assisted Individualization nd the Adaptive Learning Environments Model, were bserved to assume the greatest amount of responsibility or both types of outcomes. Students in the Individually Guided Education classes assumed the least responsibility or negative outcomes, and students under the Direct nstruction Model assumed the least responsibility for ositive outcomes.

Finally, significant differences were found across the rograms in math achievement but not in reading achieve-ment. The Mastery Learning approach, the Adaptive Learning Environments Model, and the Behavior Analysis pproach were superior in regression-adjusted achieve-ment. The Bank Street Model, Individually Guided Edu-cation, and the Direct Instruction Model were lower than verage in both reading and math achievement.

Comment. The large-scale survey of adaptive instruc-tion features and effects of exemplary implementations of eight widely used instructional models conducted by Wang and Walberg (in press) provides useful descriptive infor-mation. Overall, the findings from exemplary implemen-tations of the various instructional approaches, each with its own characteristic features and pedagogy, make it poss-ible to delineate relationships between specific program features and classroom processes and student learning outcomes. The results show that, when they are well implemented, features such as the allocation of available class time for curriculum-related activities, a variety of instructional strategies, a variety of materials and activi-ties, and learning tasks that are appropriate for students' learning needs and achievement levels can produce superior classroom processes and achievement results that are not unlike those associated with ideal realizations of traditional, teacher-directed, and group-paced instruc-tion, such as those portrayed in the effective teaching literature (cf. Brophy & Good, 1986). Moreover, features such as student choice, which is suggested in the effective teaching literature to be an ineffective feature of adaptive instruction programs, actually were found to facilitate stu-dent learning.

It cannot be assumed that adaptive instruction pro-grams always show such superior results with respect to achievement, student perceptions of self-responsibility, and constructive classroom activities. Moreover, some variations in the socioeconomic levels of students in the classrooms of programs included in the study may have been overadjusted or underadjusted in the analysis. Of course, no study, no matter how large, can be considered completely definitive. Nevertheless, the results described above do seem to suggest that adaptive instruction pro-grams can be validly implemented and that classrooms with well-implemented features of adaptive instruction can lead to classroom processes that have been noted in effective teaching research as effective.

Conclusion and Implications

Implications of the Research Findings

The findings of the synthesis of educational productivity factors (Walberg, 1984) and the syntheses of adaptive instruction (Wang & Baker, 1985–1986; Waxman et al., 1985), combined with the findings of the large-scale, observational study (Wang & Walberg, in press), produce a scenario that contrasts sharply with the predominant portrayal in the effective teaching literature of educational programs that are designed to adapt instruction to student differences. A common core of program features is dis-tinguishable across the studies of adaptive instruction reviewed by Waxman et al. (1985). These features include (a) instruction based on the assessed capabilities of each student; (b) materials and procedures that permit each student to make progress in mastering instructional con-tent at a pace suited to his or her abilities and interest; (c) periodic evaluations to inform each student of his or her progress toward skills mastery; (d) students' assumption of responsibility for diagnosing their needs and abilities, planning individual learning activities, pursuing the planned activities, and evaluating mastery; (e) alternative activities and materials for aiding each student's acqui-sition of essential academic skills; (f) student choice in selecting educational goals, outcomes, and activities; and (g) students assisting one another in pursuing individual goals and cooperating to achieve group goals.

Similar features were found to be prominent in the data from studies included in the quantitative synthesis of the features and effects of instructional programs for effective mainstreaming of handicapped students (Wang & Baker, 1985–1986). The design features cited most frequently among the mainstreaming programs were continuous assessment, the use of alternative routes and a variety of materials, individualized progress plans, student self-management, peer assistance, and instructional teaming. The common features of programs that aim to provide adaptive instruction—the features found in the Waxman et al. (1985) and the Wang and Baker (1985–1986) quantitative syntheses of extant empirical studies—were also noted in the results from the observational study of design features, processes, and outcomes of eight widely used contemporary educational programs (Wang & Walberg, in press). Many of the programs included in the Wang and Walberg study are identified by descriptors such as individualized instruction, mastery learning, and adaptive education, and they incorporate program features such as cooperative learning, differentiated staffing, and computer-assisted management and instruction.

It is noteworthy that the findings of all four studies discussed in this chapter suggest that it is not the inclusion of single, specific, instructional features that distinguishes effective from ineffective programs. Instead, it is the combination and coordination of certain critical features in well-implemented programs—including adaptive instruction programs—that produce positive classroom processes and student outcomes.

The conditions of the current educational climate seem to make it critical to begin accumulating evidence that either verifies or contrasts with the extant literature supporting the efficacy of teacher-directed, group-paced instruction. These conditions include the push to achieve educational excellence for the increasingly diverse student populations our schools are challenged to serve, the recognition of the critical need to ensure students' acquisition of higher level thinking and problem-solving skills in addition to basic skills, and the growing interest in the development of students' motivation and ability for lifelong learning. One of the main arguments of the effective teaching literature is that programs that make allowances for individual differences, student initiative, and student self-responsibility for learning tend to be ineffective in increasing time-on-task and basic skills acquisition as well as impractical for wide-scale implementation in regular classroom settings (Bennett, 1976; Brophy, 1979; Hedges et al., 1981).

The findings of the four studies reported in this chapter are a counterpoint to this argument. In particular, the results of the Wang and Walberg study are pertinent for two important reasons. First, they illustrate that high degrees of implementation of adaptive instruction features in regular classrooms can be established and maintained in a variety of school settings. Second, they show that, although different instructional programs were in use, there seemed to be a close resemblance in observ classroom processes between the exemplary classrooms programs featuring adaptive instruction and classroo portrayed as instructionally effective in the effecti teaching research literature. Moreover, features such student choice and student initiative, which have be suggested in the effective teaching literature to be ineffe tive program features, actually were found to facilitate st dent learning. Other specific features described in t effective teaching literature as generic to "good" instru tion (Brophy & Good, 1986) include a variety of materia and activities, allocation of available class time for curric lum-related activities, and learning tasks that are appr priate for students' learning needs and achievement level

Thus, the research described in this chapter represen an important step toward accumulating a data base th currently is sorely lacking, that is, a data base on the fe tures and effects of instructional programs that provide f individual differences. The findings make it possible delineate relationships between specific program featur and classroom processes and desired student learning ou comes like those described in the extant effective teachin literature. The results of the Waxman et al. (1985) stud and the observational study by Wang and Walberg (i press) suggest that exemplary implementations of adap ive instruction programs can produce classroom process and achievement results that are superior to those achieve under ideal realizations of traditional or convention instruction. (Ideal realizations of traditional instructio include features such as whole-group explanation, reci tation, and repetition; individual seat work; and, in shor teacher-directed, group-paced instruction.) The Wan and Walberg observational study may be unique in it analysis of exemplary versions of adaptive instruction pro grams. It shows that adaptive instruction programs, on th average, tend to raise achievement and student self responsibility to greater levels than programs that provid little tailoring to group and individual differences. In addition, several of the adaptive instruction program included in this study were found to produce superior class room process outcomes that many students, parents, an educators greatly value. These include constructive stu dent interactions, independent work, individual diagnosis and prescription, cooperative learning, and student exploration.

Although reviews of the literature seem to indicate that traditional instruction can produce greater-than-ordinary classroom achievement (Brophy, 1979; Rosenshine, 1979), quantitative syntheses and meta-analyses of research also indicate that components of adaptive instruction produce superior results. Even so, it should be acknowledged that nonexemplary adaptive instruction and individualized programs do not, as a matter of course, show process and outcome results superior to ordinary or direct instruction. Because they tailor education to individual students, adaptive instruction programs are complicated and difficult to manage. Because more things can go wrong, these programs require close attention. To show superior results, adaptive instruction programs seem to equire valid implementation and good management. ;ince direct instruction is closer to traditional methods and equires little collaboration among instructional staff, it nay be more convenient and easier for ordinary teachers to mplement and sustain. The choice seems to lie between the lifficulty of attaining the best and the convenience of ;ettling for the good. The following discussion identifies ɔositive steps toward overcoming this difficulty.

Recommendations for Future Research

More research is required on the comparative effectiveness of alternative programs as they are implemented over the long term in regular and special education settings. Programs and practices need to be even more sharply defined and tested if they are to establish precedents for providing effective and efficient education for regular and special populations; optimizing affective, behavioral, and cognitive learning; and incorporating educational alternatives into schools without excessive disruption and expense.

Research studies must be larger in scale than much previous work—larger with respect to special populations, measures, and programs sampled—yet closely monitored, as in pilot implementation studies of special programs and methods, to ensure the authenticity of treatments. In both research and practice, staff development and monitoring will be essential.

The considerable evidence reviewed in this chapter shows that several programs work effectively for both regular and special education. Moreover, a synthesis of thousands of studies indicates that a variety of old and new programs and techniques work much more effectively than the traditional, predominant methods now used in schools. What was previously lacking was a knowledge of the comparative effects of traditional and innovative techniques, methods, and programs, but this is now available.

Past research and program development efforts also lacked sufficient information about management systems that incorporate selected effective components into an integrated, well-managed system of education that also provides for individual differences among children. The large-scale studies reviewed in this chapter show that such adaptive systems of education can indeed be widely implemented in a variety of school settings to provide for individual differences and to lead to superior affective and cognitive outcomes.

Author Information

Herbert J. Walberg is Research Professor of Education at the University of Illinois at Chicago. Margaret C. Wang is Professor of Educational Psychology and Director of the Temple University Center for Research in Human Development and Education.

References

Anderson, L. W. (1984). *Time and school learning.* London, England: Croom Helm.

Bar-Yam, M. (1969). *The interaction of student characteristics with instructional strategies: A study of students' performance and attitudes in a high school innovative course.* Unpublished doctoral dissertation, Harvard University.

Becker, W. C., Engelmann, S., Carnine, D., & Rhine, W. R. (1981). Direct Instruction Model. In W. R. Rhine (Ed.), *Making schools more effective: New directions from Follow Through* (pp. 95–154). New York: Academic Press.

Bennett, S. N. (1976). *Teaching styles and pupil progress.* London, England: Open Books.

Bloom, B. S. (1968). Learning for mastery. *Evaluation Comment,* **1**(2), 74–86.

Brandt, R. S. (1985). Success through adaptive education. *Educational Leadership,* **43**, 3.

Brophy, J. (1979). Teacher behavior and its effects. *Journal of Educational Psychology,* **71**, 733–750.

Brophy, J., & Good, T. L. (1986). Teacher behavior and student achievement. In M. C. Wittrock (Ed.), *Handbook of research on teaching* (3rd ed.) (pp. 328–375). New York: MacMillan.

Carlberg, C., & Kavale, K. (1980). The efficacy of special versus regular class placement for exceptional children: A meta-analysis. *Journal of Special Education,* **14**, 295–309.

Cronbach, L. J., & Snow, R. E. (1974). *Instructional methods and aptitudes.* New York: Appleton-Century-Crofts.

Denham, C., & Lieberman, A. (Eds.). (1980). *Time to learn.* Washington, DC: National Institute of Education.

Fisher, C., & Berliner, D. (Eds.). (1985). *Perspectives on instructional time.* New York: Longman.

Fredrick, W. C., & Walberg, H. J. (1980). Learning as a function of time. *Journal of Educational Research,* **73**, 183–194.

Giaconia, R. M., & Hedges, L. V. (1982). *Identifying features of open education.* Stanford, CA: Stanford Center for Educational Research.

Gilhool, T. K. (1985, January). *Constitutional basis of LRE.* Keynote address presented at the conference on Least Restrictive Environment and Parent Training and Information Projects, sponsored by the Technical Assistance for Parent Programs (TAPP) Project of the National Network of Parent Centers, Washington, DC.

Gilkeson, E. C., Smithberg, L. M., Bowman, G. W., & Rhine, W. R. (1981). Bank Street Model: A developmental-interaction approach. In W. R. Rhine (Ed.), *Making schools more effective: New directions from Follow Through* (pp. 249–288). New York: Academic Press.

Glass, G. V., McGaw, B., & Smith, M. L. (1981). *Meta-analysis in social research.* Beverly Hills, CA: Sage.

Good, T. L. (1983). Classroom research: A decade of progress. *Educational Psychologist,* **18**, 127–144.

Haertel, G. D., Walberg, H. J., & Weinstein, T. (1983). Psychological models of educational performance: A theoretical synthesis of constructs. *Review of Educational Research,* **53**, 75–92.

Hedges, L. V., Giaconia, R. M., & Gage, N. L. (1981). *Meta-analysis of the effects of open and traditional instruction.* Stanford, CA: Stanford University Program on Teaching Effectiveness.

Heller, K. (1981). Secondary education for handicapped students: In search of a solution. *Exceptional Children,* **47**(8), 582–598.

Horn, A., & Walberg, H. J. (1984). Achievement and attitude as functions of quantity and quality of instruction. *Journal of Educational Research,* **77**, 227–232.

Jeter, J. (Ed.). (1980). *Approaches to individualized education.* Alexandria, VA: Association for Supervision and Curriculum Development.

Klausmeier, H. J. (1972). *Individually Guided Education: An alternative system of elementary schooling* (Harlan E. Anderson Lecture). New Haven, CT: Yale University, Center for the Study of Education.

Leinhardt, G., & Pallay, A. (1982). Restrictive educational settings: Exile or haven? *Review of Educational Research,* **52,** 557–578.

Madden, N. A., & Slavin, R. E. (1982). *Count me in: Academic achievement and social outcomes of mainstreaming students with mild academic handicaps* (Rept. No. 329). Baltimore, MD: Johns Hopkins University, Center for the Social Organization of Schools.

Meyers, C. E., MacMillan, D. L., & Yoshida, R. K. (1980). Regular class education of EMR students: From efficacy to mainstreaming. In J. Gottlieb (Ed.), *Educating mentally retarded persons in the mainstream.* Baltimore, MD: University Park Press.

National Commission on Excellence in Education. (1983). *A nation at risk.* Washington, DC: U.S. Government Printing Office.

Parkhurst, H. (1925). The Dalton Laboratory Plan. In A. M. Whipple (Ed.), *Twenty-fourth yearbook of the National Society for the Study of Education* (pp. 83–94). Chicago, IL: University of Chicago Press.

The Project Physics Course. (1970). New York: Holt, Reinhart & Winston.

Ramp, E. A., & Rhine, W. R. (1981). Behavior Analysis Model. In W. R. Rhine (Ed.), *Making schools more effective: New directions from Follow Through* (pp. 155–200). New York: Academic Press.

Raven, J. (1981). The most important problem in education is to come to terms with values. *Oxford Review of Education,* **7**(3), 253–272.

Rhine, W. R. (Ed.). (1981). *Making schools more effective: New directions from Follow Through.* New York: Academic Press.

Rosenshine, B. V. (1979). Content, time, and direct instruction. In P. L. Peterson & H. J. Walberg (Eds.), *Research on teaching: Concepts, findings, and implications* (pp. 28–56). Berkeley, CA: McCutchan.

Samson, G., Graue, M. E., Weinstein, T., & Walberg, H. J. (1984). Academic and occupational performance: A quantitative synthesis. *American Educational Research Journal,* **21,** 311–321.

Semmel, M. I., Gottlieb, J., & Robinson, N. M. (1979). Mainstreaming: Perspectives on educating handicapped children in the public school. In D. C. Berliner (Ed.), *Review of research in education* (Vol. 7, pp. 223–279). Washington, DC: American Educational Research Association.

Slavin, R. E. (1983). *Team-Assisted Individualization: A co-operative learning solution for adaptive instruction in mathematics.* Baltimore, MD: Johns Hopkins University Center for the Social Organization of Schools.

Stephens, J. M. (1968). *The process of schooling: A psychological examination.* New York: Holt, Rinehart & Winston.

Strang, R. (1937). *Behavior and background of students in college and secondary school.* New York: Harper & Row.

Talmage, H. (Ed.). (1975). *Systems of individualized education.* Berkeley, CA: McCutchan.

Walberg, H. J. (1983). Scientific literacy and economic productivity in international perspective. *Daedalus,* **112,** 1–28.

Walberg, H. J. (1984). Improving the productivity of America's schools. *Educational Leadership,* **41**(8), 19–30.

Walberg, H. J., & Shanahan, T. (1983). High school effects on individual students. *Educational Researcher,* **12**(7), 4–9.

Wang, M. C., & Baker, E. T. (1985–1986). Mainstreaming programs: Design features and effects. *Journal of Special Education,* **19,** 503–525.

Wang, M. C., Gennari, P., & Waxman, H. C. (1985). The Adaptive Learning Environments Model: Design, implementation, and effects. In M. C. Wang & H. J. Walberg (Eds.), *Adapting instruction to individual differences* (pp. 191–235). Berkeley, CA: McCutchan.

Wang, M. C., & Lindvall, C. M. (1984). Individual differences and school learning environments: Theory, research, and design. In E. W. Gordon (Ed.), *Review of research in education* (Vol. 11, pp. 161–226). Washington, DC: American Educational Research Association.

Wang, M. C., & Walberg, H. J. (Eds.). (1985). *Adapting instruction to individual differences.* Berkeley, CA: McCutchan.

Wang, M. C., & Walberg, H. J. (in press). Exemplary implementation of eight innovative instructional models. *International Journal of Educational Research.*

Washburne, C. N. (1925). *Twenty-Fourth yearbook of the National Society for the Study of Education: Adapting the schools to individual differences.* G. M. Whipple (Ed.). Chicago, IL: University of Chicago Press.

Waxman, H. C., & Walberg, H. J. (1982). The relation of teaching and learning: A review of reviews. *Contemporary Education Review,* **2,** 103–120.

Waxman, H. C., Wang, M. C., Anderson, K. A., & Walberg, H. J. (1985). Adaptive education and student outcomes: A quantitative synthesis. *Journal of Educational Research,* **78,** 228–236.

Waxman, H. C., Wang, M. C., Lindvall, M. C., & Anderson, K. A. (1983). *The Observation Rating Scale for Features of Adaptive Instruction.* Pittsburgh, PA: University of Pittsburgh, Learning Research and Development Center.

SECTION 2

Effectiveness of Differential Programming in Serving Handicapped Students

Introduction

KENNETH A. KAVALE

University of Iowa

ecial education represents the conjunction of two dis- ct but related components: the instruction of students h special needs and the use of special instruction. The us of this topic area is on the second component and con- ns the questions of what, how, when, and where it is best teach handicapped students. It may be argued that cial education has taken the adjective *special* too seri- sly, as evidenced by its large repertoire of programming hniques that are unique and different. The history of cial education is literally filled with divination, leger- main, and sorcery in its interventions. Much faith has en placed in these methods, even though many are mar- d by an egregious absence of supportive evidence. though special education has developed a more critical sture about such methods, differential programming for ndicapped students does, in fact, exist and is often pre- red over regular education programming for handi- pped students. One concern then is the nature of these fferences and the question of whether these differences e either necessary or desirable. These problems rep- sent a basic philosophical concern about the relationship tween special and regular education.

One means of approaching this problem is to examine e programming alternatives that are unique to special ucation and evaluate their efficacy. If these program- ing alternatives are found to be effective, then special ucation can be justified. If, however, the differential pro- amming alternatives in special education are found to ssess a variety of difficulties, then their usefulness for rving the needs of handicapped students should be estioned.

The concerns about differential programming in special lucation are not easily addressed. The programming ternatives span a wide continuum and offer no natural amework for investigating the primary issues. Therefore, framework needs to be imposed upon the general topic of ifferential programming in order to delimit the bound- ries and allow for investigation of primary issues. To this nd, five topics were chosen for review in this section. They re (a) the relationship among academic, social, and areer education in programming for handicapped udents; (b) diagnostic-prescriptive teaching; (c) the pplication of cognitive-behavioral training methods to aching basic skills to mildly handicapped elementary hool students; (d) programming independent living skills r handicapped learners; and (e) placement options and structional programming. Although these topics are onexhaustive, they provide a comprehensive perspective bout the nature of special education practices in provid- ng service to handicapped students. As a group, the topics present an overview of primary concerns related to differential programming for handicapped students and allow for conclusions to be drawn with respect to the present state of the art as well as the state of practice.

In the first chapter in this section, "Relationship Among Academic, Social, and Career Education in Programming for Handicapped Students," Gale Morrison explores the role that social (behavioral) and career education should play in programming for handicapped students in relation to the role of academic remediation (which may be considered primary, at least for mildly handicapped students). She examines the form and function of social and career education in total planning; the options available for remediating social behavior, such as behavior modification and psychoeducational approaches, and their efficacy; and how and when career education should be incorporated into program planning.

In the chapter entitled "Diagnostic-Prescriptive Teaching," by Ronald Colarusso, theoretical and empirical issues as well as philosophical and ideological issues that have polarized a portion of the special education community are addressed. Diagnostic-prescriptive teaching has been conceptualized as incorporating two distinct models—the process (or ability) model and the behavioral (or skill) model—but the validity and efficacy of these models continue to be an area of much debate. The process model's assumptions about the testing and training of underlying abilities remain in contention. It is not certain that process tests are a reliable and valid foundation for programming. Nor can it be stated assuredly that process training (i.e., perceptual-motor and psycholinguistic training) is efficacious for improving both process functions and learning ability in the transfer to academic areas. With respect to the behavioral model, its value in academic remediation and the effectiveness of direct instruction approaches for improving academic areas continue to be major issues. A related question involves the validity of task analysis and skill hierarchies as the foundation for academic programming. Finally, the nature of diagnostic-prescriptive teaching as two distinct models is a focus of debate. Colarusso discusses each of these issues and synthesizes the available literature in an attempt to bring perspective to the diagnostic-prescriptive model.

In the third chapter, entitled "Application of Cognitive-Behavioral Training Methods to Teaching Basic Skills to Mildly Handicapped Elementary School Students," Michael Gerber discusses conceptual problems associated with cognitive-behavioral training methods. He then assesses the validity of applying theoretically derived constructs about cognitive-behavioral methods to the practical concern of teaching basic academic skills to handicapped students. The outcome is a comprehensive review suggesting the value of methods aimed at recruiting the assistance of students in their own behalf and the teaching of a learning competency curriculum as opposed to a skill-sequenced curriculum.

"Programming Independent Living Skills for Handicapped Learners" is the topic of discussion in the fourth chapter. Authors Larry Irvin, Daniel Close, and Robert Wells examine how well we prepare handicapped students for adult roles, including domestic and community roles. Irvin and his colleagues focus on what is termed generally as "career education," in which handicapped students are assumed to pursue a variety of careers (e.g., learner, consumer, citizen, family member, worker) requiring a combination of basic academic, vocational, personal-social, and daily living skills. How these facets are best incorporated into a curriculum package and delivered to handicapped students is explored. The authors also demonstrate clearly that, although the state of the art is commendable, there exists a variety of research and development needs, specifically the building of large data bases from coordinated and programmatic research efforts. Irvin and his associates provide a state-of-the-art document that should alert us to the necessity of closing the gap between the state of the art and the state of practice with respect to instructional programs designed to prepare handicapped students for independent living.

In the fifth chapter of this section, Susan Epps and Gerald Tindal focus on "The Effectiveness of Differential Programming in Serving Students with Mild Handicaps: Placement Options and Instructional Programming." They conclude that little supportive evidence exists for either the efficacy of special education or the development of differential programs as a result of the assessment-placement process. Their comprehensive review include historical analysis of the research as well as a methodolo cal critique and suggests clearly that programming optio are all too often implemented without regard to assessm information. The difficulties appear to surround the mea ures used, the lack of precision in instructional strategi and the failure to evaluate the integrity of delivery system

To summarize, the topic area concerned with the eff tiveness of differential programming attempts to assess t overall efficacy of special education practices. A major d ficulty in such a broadly defined area was delineating fi topics that would provide a comprehensive overview. Th was accomplished by organizing the five topics arou three levels of specificity. One level assesses specific co cerns (i.e., cognitive-behavioral training for basic skil programming independent learning skills), while t second level deals with general theoretical and philosoph cal concerns embodied in special education practices (i. diagnostic-prescriptive teaching). Finally, the third lev focuses on general concerns about the manner in whi intervention practices are best integrated and coordinat (i.e., instructional programming and placement option the relationship among academic, social, and care education).

The authors of these five chapters have produced com prehensive syntheses of the literature that both inform an instruct the reader about each topic with respect not only content but also to the associated theoretical, philosoph cal, and methodological issues. Each chapter can stan alone as an important document with a full and comple rendering of the literature describing the primary issu and concerns. But even more important, the set of chapter provides an inclusive perspective about both the state of th art and the state of practice in the area of delivering speci education services to handicapped students.

Relationship among Academic, Social, and Career Education in Programming for Handicapped Students

GALE M. MORRISON

University of California at Santa Barbara

Abstract—The relationship between academic, social, and vocational programming for handicapped children in the schools is explored through the use of curriculum as a framework for analysis and discussion. Several perspectives are chosen for the examination of this relationship. These perspectives include the following influences on curriculum decisions and products: (a) historical, philosophical, and policy trends, (b) theoretical and empirical contributions, (c) state-of-the-art practices, and (d) decision-making processes. Recommendations are made for future directions in research, development, and personnel training in the area of curriculum decisions for handicapped children.

In order to answer the question posed by the topic of this chapter (i.e., what is the relationship among academic, social, and career education in program planning for handicapped students of different age and severity levels?), one must first find a blueprint for this program planning process. The concept of curriculum may be considered a blueprint for program planning (Mori & Neisworth, 1983). Definitions of curriculum vary in nature and scope. One very broad definition is that "curriculum is what a learner experiences in a learning situation" (Meyen & Horner, 1976, p. 268). In further explicating what it is that a learner experiences, we encounter a myriad of complex influences on a child's learning experience. A more narrow definition of curriculum has been chosen to guide the discussion in this chapter; that is, curriculum is "a series of planned, systematic learning experiences organized around a particular rationale or philosophy of education (Wood & Hurley, 1977) that includes goals and objectives in particular content areas (i.e., language, cognitive, perceptual, etc.)" (Mori & Neisworth, 1983, p. 2). By considering curriculum as a blueprint for content, we are able to examine curricula, curriculum models, and strategies for curriculum decision making to illuminate the nature of the relationship between content areas and the way decisions are made in reference to this relationship. Thus, the focus of discussions about curriculum is on *what to teach* as opposed to *how to teach;* that is, it is on content as opposed to strategies of instruction.

The decision to focus the discussion of this chapter on the *what* of programming, although partially one of the pragmatics of covering a vast literature base in programming, was reinforced for this author upon discovering the apparent neglect of this topic in the last 10–15 years. As Poplin (1979) appraised the situation, "We do not know what we are teaching [in special education]" (p. 1). Tawney and Sniezek (1985), as well, have noted that, in reference to the education of severely handicapped children, "If the field is lacking in content descriptions, it is blessed with explicitly described instruction procedures" (p. 84). Although this state of affairs could be partially due to the diversity of special education populations (Bricker & Filler, 1985) and to present policy emphases (e.g., a focus on *individualized* educational plans), it seems that, in order to ensure the best and most appropriate education for handicapped children, we must ensure that enough thought has been given to *what* we are teaching these children. If we have a firm ground for the content of programs, then instructional strategies can be matched and applied appropriately.

The title of this chapter refers to the *relationship* among academic, social, and career programming efforts. In order to focus the discussion on this relationship, the programming and curricular efforts that apply solely to any one of these areas is not to be reviewed in depth. Other chapters within the general topic area cover academic and social programming in a more thorough fashion (see the Irvin and Gerber chapters). An examination of the relationship between these areas implies that several sources of information are appropriate to consider. An orientation to these sources will be given in the following paragraphs.

Philosophical Trends

One important influence on curricular offerings is philosophical trends in educating handicapped children. Influential philosophies can originate from within our profession; for example, different beliefs exist about what content should be emphasized (academic vs. social) for severely handicapped individuals (Rago & Cleland, 1978; Sontag, Certo, & Button, 1979). Philosophical influences can also come from general public opinion trends such as the recent emphasis on teaching the basics to children in the schools (Smith & Dexter, 1980). These trends and influences affect the kinds of decisions that are made about what to teach and how to prioritize offerings to handicapped children.

Government Policies

The active development and implementation of government-based policies in relation to the education of handicapped children in this country have had a tremendous impact on the nature of the curriculum offered to these children in our schools (Meyen & Horner, 1976). The least restrictive environment mandate of the Education for All Handicapped Children Act of 1975 (PL 94-142) has affected where these children are educated and, thus, ultimately has had an effect on what they are taught. The Individualized Educational Program (IEP) mandate has resulted in a specific process for determining the content of individual programs that involves input from both school personnel and parents of handicapped children. Additionally, the appropriate education aspect of the law has implied that there are certain qualitative standards of education that must be met. The nature of these standards has been debated in several precedent-setting court cases. Thus, policy influences cannot be ignored in our examination of what is being taught to handicapped children.

Theoretical and Empirical Contributions

We hope to find some guidance from theoretical approaches to and empirical findings about the combinations of content offerings that are the most likely to produce desired outcomes for handicapped children. General theoretical approaches to the education of children with various handicaps do exist. Although they have served as guides for program development, little proof of the efficacy of singular approaches is available. Further, as is examined later in this chapter, help from empirical investigations is limited at this point due, in part, to our inability to agree upon desired outcomes and the inherent difficulty of isolating pure approaches to the education of handicapped children.

State-of-the-Art Practices

Another approach to answering questions about emphases on academic, social, and career goals in the education of handicapped children is simply to examine what is being done in the field in this regard. That is, what are the state-of-the-art practices that are currently being implemented in classrooms for handicapped children? Although this approach to the problem certainly provides a solid basis for an examination of this question, it involves looking at an accumulation of work that has been influenced by a number of critical factors. For example, there have been certain historical developments in the field of the education of handicapped individuals that have had a great impact on classroom practices. In terms of curriculum development, the use of the unit method in classes for mentally retarded students (Ingram, 1935; Meyen, 1972) has provided a guide for teachers in the offering of instruction in content and skill areas. This method was very popular in the beginning years of the special day class arrangement. Even as the administrative structures of special education have changed, this method has provided a structure for curricular offerings in classrooms for handicapped children.

Decision-Making Processes

Finally, an answer to the relationship question is pursued through a review of the decision-making processes that result in differential foci on the academic, social, and career content areas. The generalizable nature of these processes may provide a logical means for answering similar questions in the future of the education of handicapped children.

In summary, there are many sources of influence on the state of the art in the field. It is the intent of this chapter to examine closely the assumptions, biases, and beliefs that specifically affect the prioritization of academic, social, and vocational content within the programs for handicapped children.

The range and variability in the nature of handicaps are vast and, naturally, add to the complexity of the issues discussed in this chapter. Age level is another critical variable in the process of prioritizing content areas. The discussion addresses a sample of issues that are pertinent to handicapped children in the mild-, severe-, and low-prevalence categories along the range of school age levels from preschool to postsecondary. A major part of the professional literature on curriculum content concentrates on the mild and severe handicaps from the preschool through secondary school years. Efforts in those areas which have received less attention (e.g., visual and hearing impairments) have generally been adapted from work in the areas that have been more fully developed (e.g., mild and severe handicaps).

Historical and Philosophical Bases for Determining Goal Priorities

The determination of curriculum content typically has been made with three major considerations: (a) a consideration of the characteristics and needs of the individual students who will be exposed to the curriculum, (b) a determination of useful content for these individuals, and (c) an examination of the needs and values of the society in which these individuals will be participating (Klein, Pasch, & Frew, 1979; Willoughby-Herb, 1983). The third of these is perhaps the most complex and, potentially, the most influential. The influences of society can include the input of parents, teachers, concerned citizens, and other educational personnel at school sites or institutions that have a vested interest in the education of handicapped children. The values and biases of these parties must be considered in the curriculum development process, despite the fact that the biases may often be in conflict. For example, Elkind (1983) described the potential discrepancy between a content-centered as opposed to child-centered curriculum. The curriculum that experts agree upon (content centered) may differ from that preferred by teachers (child centered), who interact with children in groups and individually on a day-to-day basis. Despite the potential for bias, some overall agreement on curriculum parameters is critical.

Perhaps the first place to start in terms of agreement is at the level of general goals for handicapped individuals. Stemming from the report of the National Commission on Excellence in Education in 1983 and subsequent discussions of this document (Council for Exceptional Children [CEC] Ad Hoc Committee, 1983; Will, 1984), the consensus seems to be that the goals for handicapped children should be the same as those for children without disabilities; that is, students should be allowed to develop to the maximum degree possible to become productive adults. Although this goal seems straightforward, the various means to this end are certainly topics for debate. Relevant to the present discussion is the question, Which content areas should students master to what degree to enable them to reach this goal?

The complexity of arriving at agreement about these means is captured by Reynolds and Birch (1982), who described the distinction between cultural imperatives and cultural electives in the consideration of educational programming. Cultural imperatives are those skills which should be required of all students, whereas cultural electives are those skills which are not absolutely essential. Reynolds and Birch (1982) considered this consensus as related to the following curricular areas:

1. Language: speaking, listening, comprehending, reading, and writing for everyday personal and social needs.
2. Mathematics: at least those basic skills required in the marketplace and for daily life.
3. Health and safety: the knowledge of self-care, health, and protection for community living, if possible.
4. Social skills: for acceptable behavior in citizenship and in group life (non-destructive, cooperative, etc.).
5. Career education: preparation for employment, an economically useful life, and other life roles. (p. 101)

Of the above areas, those involving academic subjects traditionally have received greater emphasis in the overall curriculum plan (Polloway, Payne, Patton, & Payne, 1985). As exemplified by the court case *Lau v. Nichols* (1947), parents, in particular, want their children to be prepared to compete successfully in the society in which they live. Academic skills are considered to be critical to gaining this success. Smith and Dexter (1980) defined basic academic skills as "those fundamental skills which are considered prerequisite for the effective functioning of any individual in the every day life of our society" (p. 72). However, given this broad definition of basic academic skills, one is forced to consider social and career education as a key to "effective functioning" for handicapped individuals. It may be that the social and personal competencies of handicapped individuals are a key support to other more academic talents.

Influence of Administrative Arrangements

The degree of emphasis placed on the acquisition of academic skills changes with the passage of time and the zeitgeist of an era. In the case of mildly mentally retarded individuals, the movement in the 1920s and 1930s to place these students in special classrooms was, in part, intended to remove them from high expectations for academic achievement and allow for a more well-rounded program, including social and vocational skills training. As a result of a philosophical movement away from the potentially stigmatizing effects of segregating these students and a failure to document the academic benefits of special class placement (Kirk, 1964), a range of less restrictive placement alternatives became available. Two of these alternatives, placement in regular classrooms and placement in resource room programs, represent returns to an emphasis on academic skills training by the very nature of the programming option. Although program emphasis is not always clearly delineated, the issue is further clouded in efficacy studies that do not match program priorities with the weighting of emphasis on outcome variables (MacMillan & Semmel, 1977). However, the main point here is that the prioritization of the content goals of curricula for handicapped students is influenced significantly by the programming philosophies and subsequent administrative arrangements of the time.

Influence of the Minimum Competency Testing Movement

The movement of the 1980s in general education toward an emphasis on the basics is stimulating a reopening of the discussion about the emphasis on academic content for mildly handicapped children. Smith and Dexter (1980) feared the return to a sink-or-swim policy, which would once again exclude mildly retarded students from certain educational opportunities. They noted that the exclusion of nonacademic skills from curricular emphasis is not realistic for this population. Cohen, Safran, and Polloway (1980) also questioned the relationship between adult success and emphasis on academic skills training, noting the importance of interpersonal skills in job success. However, they stated on a more positive note, that the imposition of minimum criteria for graduation might provide (or force) a standard for educational outcomes and encourage the early identification of and attention to students with problems in these areas. Such an imposition of standards in the academic area would necessitate a larger emphasis on academic skills than another that might occur given the professional assumption of some that social and vocational skills are critical for the successful postschool adjustment of mildly handicapped children.

However, the struggle between teaching the basics and teaching functional skills is especially apparent at the practitioner level, where local school personnel are faced with the day-to-day decisions of how much to emphasize each set of skills. On the one hand, school districts have certain requirements for graduation, achieving a minimum competency being only one of these. On the other hand, teachers can readily see that these requirements may not be realistic or functional for their secondary-level handicapped students. Additionally, there is the moral or ethical consideration of when to cease spending time on academic skills that may not be directly pertinent to the future daily lives of the students (especially in the case of mildly disabled students). These issues have no easy answers, yet their resolution is absolutely critical for decision making in the major content areas.

Academic Versus Self-Help and Socialization Skills for Severely and Profoundly Retarded Students

A parallel debate over the emphasis on content area in curricular plans occurs in discussions concerning severely and profoundly retarded students. Burton and Hirshoren (1979) and Rago and Cleland (1978) supported an emphasis on teaching self-help, social, and leisure skills to severely and profoundly retarded individuals, contending that efforts to teach these individuals higher level cognitive skills have either failed or resulted in highly mechanistic behaviors. Sontag et al. (1979) took issue with this position and cited improvements in the technology of training and the potential contribution of setting improvements in the education and treatment of this population. In addition to the need to determine the effect on training efforts of variables such as level of retardation (Hotte, Monroe, & Philbrook-Scarlata, 1984), competence of personnel, level of technology, and setting in which the services are delivered, philosophical differences remain on the educability of severely and profoundly retarded students and on the content emphasis of education and treatment efforts.

General Perspectives on the Balance of Academic, Social, and Vocational Goals

The examples given above involving mildly and severely mentally retarded individuals are specific instances in which academic goals and objectives have been placed in competition with social or vocational goals and objectives. These examples are indicative of the more general debate about curricular content emphasis. In support of emphasizing the teaching of cognitive skills, Elkind (1983) encouraged giving up the "clinical bifurcation" of cognitive and affective instruction. He contended that a good curriculum does not need an affective component. Learning, if properly arranged, is naturally socially motivated. However, another perspective taken by some professionals is that social and affective development in handicapped children cannot be taken for granted given the extra challenges that these individuals face in adapting to their life settings (Dil,1983; Strain, Cooke, & Apolloni, 1976). These researchers emphasized understanding handicapped children as they function both cognitively *and* socially in environments inside and outside of school. This more ecological view of the child is grounded in the assumption that progression or regression in one realm (cognitive or social) of a child's functioning affects his or her functioning in the other realm. However, acceptance of the need to spend time on the teaching of social and affective skills has been slow, perhaps because of the generally sensitive and inherently more complex nature of these skills (Childs, 1979).

Although the struggle in prioritization more commonly takes place between the academic and social areas of the curriculum, advocates for vocational and career education have been more vocal in the last 10 years (Brolin, 1982). On the one hand, calls are heard for focus on vocational skills in educational planning for handicapped students, especially during the adolescent years, as these individuals prepare to enter the job market or postschool job placements (Greenan, 1982; Muraski, 1982). On the other hand, a more comprehensive argument exists for incorporating career education goals and objectives into the curriculum throughout students' tenure in the education system (Brolin, 1982; Mori, 1982; Muenster, 1982). This more comprehensive view of career education defines it as a "lifelong developmental process that allows individuals to acquire the attitudes, habits, values, and skills to prepare for a successful and personally satisfactory work life" (Mori, 1982, p. 41). This kind of curriculum incorporates academic and social skills as part of the preparation for the work world. Thus, career education does not imply a concentration on one content area at the expense of another but advocates the integration of all areas toward the achievement of career success.

Although the previous paragraphs describe conflicts and struggles between parties emphasizing different content areas, a reminder is necessary that these content areas are not mutually exclusive (Polloway et al., 1985). Emphasis on particular content areas will vary according to the nature of the population being served (including age level and the nature of the handicap) and the sources of input into the decision-making process. The discussion in the following section describes some of the forces behind such decision making as well as some of the resulting curricular trends in the field.

The Role of Policy in Curriculum Decisions

The intent of PL 94-142 is to provide an "appropriate" education for all handicapped children. At the heart of appropriate education are decisions about curriculum and programming. The issue of what constitutes appropriate education, as well as two other major components of PL 94-142 (the least restrictive environment mandate and IEPs) are being discussed here in terms of their impact on decision making regarding the content of special education programming.

Appropriate Education

The appropriate education component of PL 94-142 has been the focus of several landmark cases in the courts. Even before the passing of this law, the decisions in *Brown v. Board of Education* (1954) and the *Pennsylvania Association for Retarded Children v. the Secretary of Education, Pa.* (1972) paved the way for appropriate education by stating that education is a basic right that cannot be denied to either nonhandicapped or handicapped individuals. Given this basic right, the content of education and treatment comes into focus with the decision of the *Wyatt v. Stickney* (1972) case, which ensured "realistic opportunity to lead a more useful and meaningful life and return to society"; the standards declared in *Pennhurst State School and Hospital v. Halderman* (1981) of "appropriate habilitation in the least restrictive environment"; and the decision more recently in *Youngberg v. Romeo* (1982), which ensured "minimally adequate training" (Turnbull, 1982). The interpretation of these decisions is related to content issues in the sense that they indicate a level of quality that must be adhered to. Issues of quality can be related to the prioritization of goals; for example, questions have been raised about whether to concentrate on leisure-related rather than skill-related interventions with severely and profoundly retarded residents (Ellis et al., 1981). Another issue of quality suggesting a specific nature of intervention strategies was raised in the *Youngberg v. Romeo* case, in which there were differences of opinion on whether minimally adequate training included prevention of a person's skills from deteriorating from preinstitutionalized levels (Reynolds, 1985; opinion of dissenting judges in *Youngberg vs. Romeo*). These issues are related to the cultural imperative versus cultural elective distinction made by Reynolds and Birch (1982). Reynolds (1985) argued that cultural imperatives should include the enhancement as well as maintenance of one's skills.

Thus, the courts have found it necessary to specify not only the right to education but also the beginnings of what might be construed to be the right to a certain quality (implying type) of education. The implications of the latter involvement could have significant effects on what is to be taught to handicapped individuals.

Least Restrictive Environment

The least restrictive environment component specified that a handicapped child must be educated, to the maximum extent that is appropriate, with children who are not handicapped. The major vehicle for compliance with this mandate has been the availability of a continuum of placements for handicapped students that vary in extent of restrictiveness (Deno, 1970). Although basically administrative in nature, these placements have a critical impact on the nature of the curriculum offered to students within them (Meyen & Horner, 1976). Meyen and Horner described the curriculum-related consequences of alternative placement models that vary according to (a) the teacher who has responsibility for instruction; (b) the amount of time a child spends in each setting; (c) the focus of the total instructional program; (d) the locus of administrative control (i.e., in regular or special education); and (e) the heterogeneity of pupil characteristics.

With reference to the balance of content offerings in these settings, a resource room arrangement usually offers instruction in specific academic areas to a child for a few hours per day. The mildly handicapped children who are in this setting might receive social and vocational instruction in their regular classroom setting. Alternatively, in a special day class setting, the handicapped child is offered a total (and, one hopes, a well-rounded) program encompassing all of his or her educational needs. Thus, the curricular emphases are likely to vary vastly from setting to setting for handicapped children, as are the desired individual outcomes for these children (Morrison & MacMillan, 1983). Meyen and Horner (1976) warned that "unless the curriculum dimension of mainstreaming is successfully dealt with, like the special class, mainstreaming will become an additional administrative model rather than an instructional delivery system" (p. 268).

Another issue related to curriculum content and the placement of handicapped children in the least restrictive environment is that of preferred child outcome. The move to mainstream handicapped children was based on philosophy and value rather than evidence, as the research on the issue is contradictory and fraught with methodological problems (MacMillan & Semmel, 1977). However, the dichotomy between academic versus social skills emphases arises once again in tentative conclusions that are based on mainstreaming efficacy studies. The best studies indicate that the outcomes for academic skills in the two settings do not differ but that the outcomes in the personal–social area are better in the special class setting (Semmel, Gottlieb, & Robinson, 1979). Thus, depending on the priority of content emphasis, one would pick different settings for the placement of handicapped children. Alternatively, if the decision were whether or not to place a child in a mainstreamed setting, evidence suggests that special attention should be given to the social and affective status of the child.

IEPs

The mandate for IEPs for all handicapped children has also had a great impact on the nature of curriculum decision making. Decisions about the goals and objectives of a program for an individual child must be made with the input of a multidisciplinary team, which includes the parents of the child and, when appropriate, the child himself or herself. The institutionalization of the IEP team has made the input of parents much more salient than it was in the past. Although the amount of influence that parents have on an IEP team is being called into question (Gilliam & Coleman, 1981), the opportunity is there for parents to directly influence the prioritization of the goals and objectives for their child.

Given the impact that the IEP mandate has had on programming for individual handicapped children, the distinction should be made between individualized programming and comprehensive programming. Individualized programming was defined by Mercer and Mercer (1981) as "an instructional program in which the student works on appropriate tasks over time under conditions that are motivating. It may occur within various instructional arrangements . . ." (p. 4). In contrast, comprehensive programming, as used in this chapter, refers to the consideration of curriculum decisions in terms of an overall program for handicapped students as groups. The danger that exists in special education today is ignoring comprehensive programming in favor of creating numerous individual plans.

Theoretical Approaches to Curriculum Development

When one considers what content should be taught to which children, one source of guidance may be theories about this topic that have been formulated and tested. Ideally and theoretically, we should be able to make predictions about the efficacy of practices based on information about aptitude-by-treatment interactions. Although such exact information is not available at this time, researchers and educators have developed approaches to educating handicapped children that are based on philosophical notions of what these interactions should be. Three major approaches are described below: those used in the instruction of severely handicapped students, mildly handicapped students, and low-prevalence populations of handicapped children.

Theoretical Approaches to the Instruction of Severely Handicapped Students

Three major approaches to curriculum development for severely handicapped students are described here. They are the developmental, behavioral, and functional approaches.

Developmental Approach

The developmental approach includes approaches that subscribe to the following assumptions:

> (a) normal development constitutes the most logical ordering of the behaviors in a curriculum; (b) many behaviors within normal development are prerequisite behaviors; and (c) behaviors acquired at a particular age by a normal child are appropriate objectives for a severely handicapped student at the same level of development. (Guess & Noonan, 1982, p. 1)

The implication of this approach for the selection and emphasis of content is that selection is governed primarily by analyses of sequences of behavior that would be expected to occur in the normal development of a child. Numerous assessment instruments and curricula have been developed based on this model (see Guess & Noonan, 1982). The major drawbacks of this approach to program planning for severely handicapped students focus on questions of the invariability of sequences of behavior, the inappropriateness of some tasks for a given age level, and the ultimate functioning of severely handicapped students.

Behavioral Approach

Another major approach to curriculum development with this group of students is the behavioral, "how-to-teach", orientation. This school of thought essentially provides a powerful technology based on behavioral principles to facilitate skill acquisition by severely handicapped students. The major assumption is that, if a skill is broken down into small enough units of behavior (through task analysis), it can be taught to even very low-functioning students. Although the behavioral approach has provided a much needed technology for teaching handicapped students, as a whole, the approach has little to offer in terms of making decisions about what to teach these students.

Functional Approach

A functional approach to programming for severely handicapped students is exemplified by the use of the "criterion of ultimate functioning" (Brown, Nietupski, & Hamre-Nietupski, 1976). This concept is based on the premise that the curriculum content for severely handicapped students should evolve around teaching skills that will be needed in their various life settings. The criteria outlined by Brown et al. (1976) for judging emphasis on curriculum content include the following:

> 1. Why should we engage in this activity?
> 2. Is this activity necessary to prepare students to ultimately function in complex heterogeneous community settings?
> 3. Could students function as adults if they did not acquire the skill?
> 4. Is there a different activity that will allow students to approximate realization of the criterion of ultimate functioning more quickly and more efficiently?
> 5. Will this activity impede, restrict, or reduce the probability that students will ultimately function in community settings?
> 6. Are the skills, materials, tasks, and criteria of concern similar to those encountered in adult life? (p. 9)

The above criteria provide a process for making decisions about the curriculum content to be delivered to severely handicapped students. The advantages of this pproach lie in its ability to offer a program that is age ppropriate and functional for the ultimate adaptation of :s target students.

Theoretical Approaches to the Education of Mildly Handicapped Children

Parallel to the theoretical orientations for severely handicapped children are four major schools of thought hat guide the education of mildly handicapped children, specifically learning disabled and behaviorally disordered children. These theoretical orientations have had a major mpact on methods of assessment and general programming. MacMillan and Morrison (1979) described them as the psychoeducational, the sensory-neurological, the ecological, and the behavioral approaches. Each approach is described briefly, as are the implications of each for decision making about curricular emphasis.

Psychoeducational Approach

The psychoeducational approach stems from the assumption that a child is experiencing some emotional conflict and that working through this conflict should be the focus of the remediation. Program characteristics might include the teacher establishing a warm, accepting, and trusting relationship with the child within a classroom environment that has been arranged to enable the management of conflicts as soon as they occur (see Aichorn, 1965; Morse, 1965). MacMillan and Morrison (1979) noted that there are few specific content suggestions stemming from psychoeducational approaches and that they rely "heavily on the flexibility and resourcefulness of the teacher to integrate the social, emotional, and academic curriculums" (p. 419).

The development of specific programming for handicapped children in the affective realm that is emphasized by the psychoeducational approach has been limited, probably due to one or all of the following reasons: disagreement about the school's role in dealing with the affective development of students, difficulty in measuring significant change in this area, and difficulty in defining and conceptualizing the constructs of importance related to the affective development of children. The last reason is exemplified by the difficulties that psychologists and educators have had in conceptualizing self-concept and self-esteem (Wylie, 1974). Existing curriculum content for affective development tends to adapt programs that were originally developed for nonhandicapped populations, such as Developing an Understanding of Self and Others (Dinkmeyer, 1970), or it tends to combine affective and social development in a unified approach (Elias & Maher, 1983).

Sensory-Neurological Approach

The sensory-neurological approach views the cause of behavioral and learning disorders as stemming from neurological impairment (Hewett, 1968). Neurological impairment manifests itself in, among other things, perceptual deficits. These deficits become the focus of remediation, which proceeds on the assumption that improvements will be seen in perceptions as well as related learning tasks. Curricular suggestions have included arranging the environment to reduce distractibility (Cruickshank, Bentzen, Ratzeburg, & Tannhauser, 1961) as well as direct attempts to ameliorate the specific perceptual process (Frostig, Lefever, & Whittlesey, 1961; Kephart, 1960). Given this orientation to learning and behavioral problems in children, one might assume that curricular emphasis would be weighted in favor of cognitive-oriented programming.

More recently, the cognitive processing theme has been represented by the cognitive-behavioral training approach (see the chapter in this volume by Gerber) and by an approach developed by Feuerstein (1979), called Instrumental Enrichment, which provides "mediated learning experiences" that directly reinforce the processes that are suspected of being deficient in retarded learners. The approaches mentioned above have been highly developed as instructional strategies and generally are not considered in terms of the role that they play in the overall curriculum for handicapped students.

Ecological Approach

The ecological orientation to programming assumes the existence of some discordance between the child and some aspect of his or her environment, such as peers, teachers, or parents. Thus, programming consists of providing a therapeutic school situation for the child and preparing the child and discordant others for more positive interpersonal relationships (as exemplified by Project Re-Ed, Hobbs, 1965, and Lewis, 1970). This orientation is similar to the psychoeducational approach in its emphasis on social content and interpersonal strategies.

One example of a program that could be considered as ecological in nature and that has received more attention in recent years is the social problem-solving approach to personal and social adjustment (Elias & Maher, 1983; Spivack, Platt, & Shure, 1976). This type of approach systematically teaches the steps to solving problems that children encounter in their various social environments. A curriculum entitled AWARE—Activities for Social Development (Elardo & Cooper, 1977) is an example of a series of classroom activities that are designed to stimulate discussion and practice with problem-solving skills. It should be noted that programs of this type usually do not come with suggestions about the way they can fit into existing curricula or about the emphasis they should receive.

Behavioral Approach

Finally, the behavioral approach for mildly handicapped children represents the same orientation described for the severely handicapped population. The approach is based on behavioral principles and provides a strong technology for bringing the behavior of handicapped students under the control necessary for their positive functioning in school environments. Specific examples of programs based on this approach are abundant and have been imitated widely, in part or wholly, in the field (Glavin, Quay, Annesley, & Werry, 1971; Haring & Phillips, 1962; Hewett, 1968; Hewett, Taylor, & Artuso, 1969). Although very effective in bringing a child to attention and to a given task, programming in this area does not have an overall orientation to decision making concerning the academic, social, or vocational content areas.

In contrasting the approaches to programming for mildly handicapped children just described, it is apparent that these approaches differ in their contribution to the question of *what* to teach these children. Although the focus of the sensory-neurological approach is clearly on cognitive, or perceptual remediation, the other three approaches contribute more to the determination of the processes and climate for teaching. That is, the psychoeducational approach encourages the provision of a warm, accepting environment to encourage the development of the self, the ecological attempts to facilitate interpersonal relationships, and the behavioral provides a technology for ensuring appropriate behavior in students. Overlooking the problems that might exist in prioritizing and comparing the outcomes of these approaches, few studies have attempted to determine the efficacy of the various approaches as total programs in which questions might arise concerning an overall curriculum balance. Behavioral programs have been empirically tested more often than the others, resulting in the following conclusion; these programs have been effective in controlling social behaviors in special class settings but have shown less success in effecting changes in academic achievement (MacMillan & Morrison, 1979). Thus, although they provide guidance for the individual components of a program, the theoretical approaches just described may be limited to their contribution to overall curriculum content decisions. Educators of children with mild handicaps might benefit from considering some of the more functional approaches being adapted for use with severely handicapped children, such as doing an in-depth analysis of what functional skills a student needs to succeed in future environments.

Curriculum Content Balance for Low-Prevalence Populations

The information compiled so far in this chapter has focused primarily on the handicaps included in the mild and severe ranges of handicapping conditions. Pertinent literature for low-prevalence populations, such as the visually impaired, hearing impaired, and physically impaired populations, is scant. Fewell and Sandall (1983) noted that teachers of these handicapped children are often forced to adopt a curriculum that has initially been constructed for a more generic population of handicapped children. They noted that these curricula rarely meet the "specific and unique" needs of the low-prevalence handicapped children. These investigators suggested strategies for adapting existing curricula according to the developmental differences of these handicapped children.

Arkell (1982) analyzed the suitability of developmental, remedial, functional, and adaptive and/or prosthetic models of curriculum development for use with multiply involved, hearing impaired students. The developmental, functional, and remedial models parallel respectively the developmental, functional, and behavioral models described previously for severely handicapped students. Arkell (1982) concluded that the functional model is the most appropriate for multiply involved, hearing impaired students because of its broad consideration of other environments (living and working) in which the students will be functioning. This preference is in keeping with a curricular emphasis that balances the academic, social, and vocational content areas for the maximum adaptation of students to their ultimate environments. Cunningham (1983) provided a similar analysis for educating visually impaired, severely-to-profoundly retarded children.

White (1982) considered the weighting of competencies within the social content area for hearing impaired students. White reported the results of a series of workshops intended to establish a comprehensive definition of personal and social competencies and to determine the priorities for teaching these competencies to hearing impaired students. The strategy (described in detail later in this chapter) used in the workshops to pool the information from 281 participants is a promising example of how the prioritization of content goals might be accomplished in future attempts of this kind.

Empirical Studies of Program Effectiveness

This review has focused on theoretical and professional orientations that provide guidance for making decisions regarding program content emphasis. Very little empirical research has been conducted to verify the outcomes of differential weighting of content areas. In fact, in regard to an empirical base for programming with severely handicapped children, Tawney and Sniezek (1985) stated, "the field lacks an empirical data base to document its effectiveness. . . . It is not unreasonable for the individual parent to ask, 'Is my child learning? Show me the data'" (p. 88). It would be reasonable to say that evidence for mildly handicapped children is even harder to find. Perhaps the attempts that have come closest to providing this empirical documentation have been made by evaluators of early childhood education programs that are designed to prevent the occurrence of mild retardation.

Program efficacy studies in the early childhood area generally fall into three major categories (Gotts, 1983): (a) demonstrations of the overall effects of providing a program versus not providing one, (b) examinations of the differential effects of models based on varying philosophies, and (c) specifications of the effects of specific program features within various models. Of interest to the present iscussion are the last two of these approaches to evalu-tion because of their implications for differential empha-s of program content.

Several major early childhood projects throughout the ountry have compared programs utilizing different cur-iculum models (Karnes, 1973; Miller & Dyer, 1975; Wei-art, Epstein, Schweinhart, & Bond, 1978). The programs ompared generally fall under three kinds of curriculum pproaches: (a) a cognitive approach based on Piaget's heory emphasizing mental growth occurring through hildren's active exploration and manipulation of their nvironment; (b) a structured-language approach based n the work of Bereiter and Engelmann (1966), which pro-ides children with specific preacademic skills in an atmos-here of high structure and positive reinforcement; and (c) traditional, child-centered approach focused on the ocial and emotional growth of the child. These three pproaches have definite implications for balance between he academic and social realms. The cognitive and tructured-language approaches reflect an emphasis on cademic growth, whereas the traditional approach ncourages growth in the social area. Weikart (1981) eviewed the results of the studies that compared these rientations and concluded that "major differences etween curricula simply are not obtained" (p. 33). Rather han program philosophy being of major significance, Weikart suggested that successful programming was related to the quality of program implementation. Thus, parties claiming program efficacy based on the emphasis of one content area as opposed to another may be begging the question; the key to program efficacy may be located in other issues.

The Stallings (1975) investigation represents an evalu-ation approach designed to compare specific program features rather than overall models. The focus of this in-vestigation was on Project Follow Through. A "planned variation" research design was utilized to examine the dif-ferential effectiveness of various program procedures. The results revealed that different instructional procedures led to different child outcomes. For example, procedures that emphasized time spent, practice, and reinforcement in reading and mathematics led to higher scores in these areas. In contrast, a more open and flexible approach to engaging children with tasks was associated with higher nonverbal problem-solving scores and lower absence rates. The implication of this study for the academic- and social-skills debate is that one's preference for outcomes is critical to conclusions about the efficacy of different programming models.

The relationship between programming emphasis and child outcomes is not a simple one either in terms of what we know or of what we can agree upon about prioritization. The outcome variable that has been utilized as a measure of cognitive development more often and with greater emphasis than any other is IQ. However, our ability to change IQ in a permanent or significant way is not as impressive as the success that has been achieved in affect-ing more molar variables, such as the prevention of grade retention or placement in special education (Rescorla & Zigler, 1981). Zigler and Trickett (1978) argued cogently for the broadening of evaluation criteria to include gains in social competence rather than IQ. Thus, it seems that there is little consensus about what professionals consider to be the major criteria for program efficacy. Agreement on the prioritization of outcome variables for program effective-ness is critical to our ability to sensibly discuss program emphasis in specific or general terms.

Another issue in need of clarification for program effi-cacy discussions is that of the allocation of time for pro-gram components. Reith, Polsgrove, and Semmel (1981) warned against the polarization of academic and affective content in terms of time allocation. They noted that treat-ment of these areas as separate components in the curricu-lum has been shown to have a negative impact on academic achievement. As an alternative, teachers should incorpor-ate the affective content areas within the framework of academic tasks, allowing the development of skills in both realms. The question of integrated versus separate treat-ment of content delivery is in need of further investigation. However, eventual conclusions reached about this ques-tion will be qualified by decisions about the prioritization on outcome variables.

Organization and Emphasis of Curriculum Content: Current Guides

The what-to-teach decisions in curriculum planning for handicapped students are generally focused on three broad areas: academic, social, and vocational. The selection of specific skills within these areas and the emphasis placed on skills in the various areas differ according to the age of the targeted students, the nature of their handicapping conditions, and the general philosophy and values of those in decision-making positions (parents, teachers, and other pertinent school personnel). The following paragraphs provide a description of what is available in our field to serve as guides or examples for the organization and emphasis of curriculum content. These examples represent what would be considered state-of-the-art practices or guidelines in the education of handicapped students.

Age × Instructional Emphasis × Content Interaction

Campbell (1968) has captured graphically the relation-ship between age (level of schooling) and instructional emphasis for various content areas and nature of handicap (see Figs. 1 and 2). Content areas are charted according to the degree of instructional emphasis they receive at different levels of schooling. The differences between pro-gramming for educable and trainable mentally retarded students in overall emphasis between content areas can be seen in the two figures as can the variation in specific skills taught. It should be noted that the two charts represent a program as it would be presented in a special day class for-mat. Skill emphasis is expected to change according to the administrative arrangement associated with the content presentation.

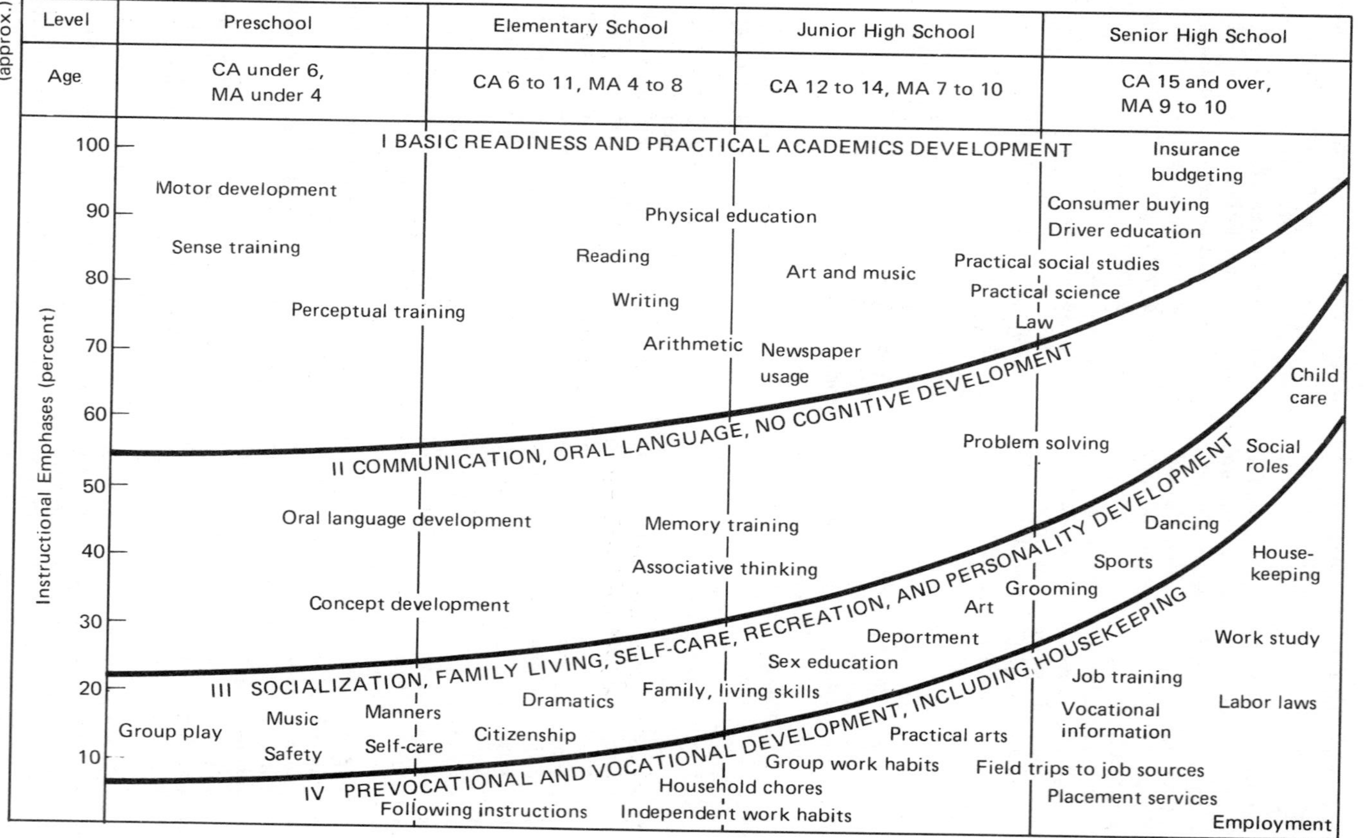

Level
Preschool
Elementary School
Junior High School
Senior High School
Age
(approx.)
CA under 6, MA under 4
CA 6 to 11, MA 4 to 8
CA 12 to 14, MA 7 to 10
CA 15 and over, MA 9 to 10
Instructional Emphases (percent)
100
90
80
70
60
50
40
30
20
10
I BASIC READINESS AND PRACTICAL ACADEMICS DEVELOPMENT
Motor development
Sense training
Perceptual training
Physical education
Reading
Writing
Arithmetic
Art and music
Newspaper usage
Insurance budgeting
Consumer buying
Driver education
Practical social studies
Practical science
Law
II COMMUNICATION, ORAL LANGUAGE, NO COGNITIVE DEVELOPMENT
Oral language development
Concept development
Memory training
Associative thinking
Problem solving
Child care
Social roles
III SOCIALIZATION, FAMILY LIVING, SELF-CARE, RECREATION, AND PERSONALITY DEVELOPMENT
Group play
Music
Safety
Manners
Self-care
Dramatics
Citizenship
Family, living skills
Sex education
Deportment
Art
Grooming
Sports
Dancing
House-keeping
IV PREVOCATIONAL AND VOCATIONAL DEVELOPMENT, INCLUDING HOUSEKEEPING
Following instructions
Independent work habits
Household chores
Group work habits
Practical arts
Field trips to job sources
Placement services
Vocational information
Job training
Work study
Labor laws
Employment

FIGURE 1

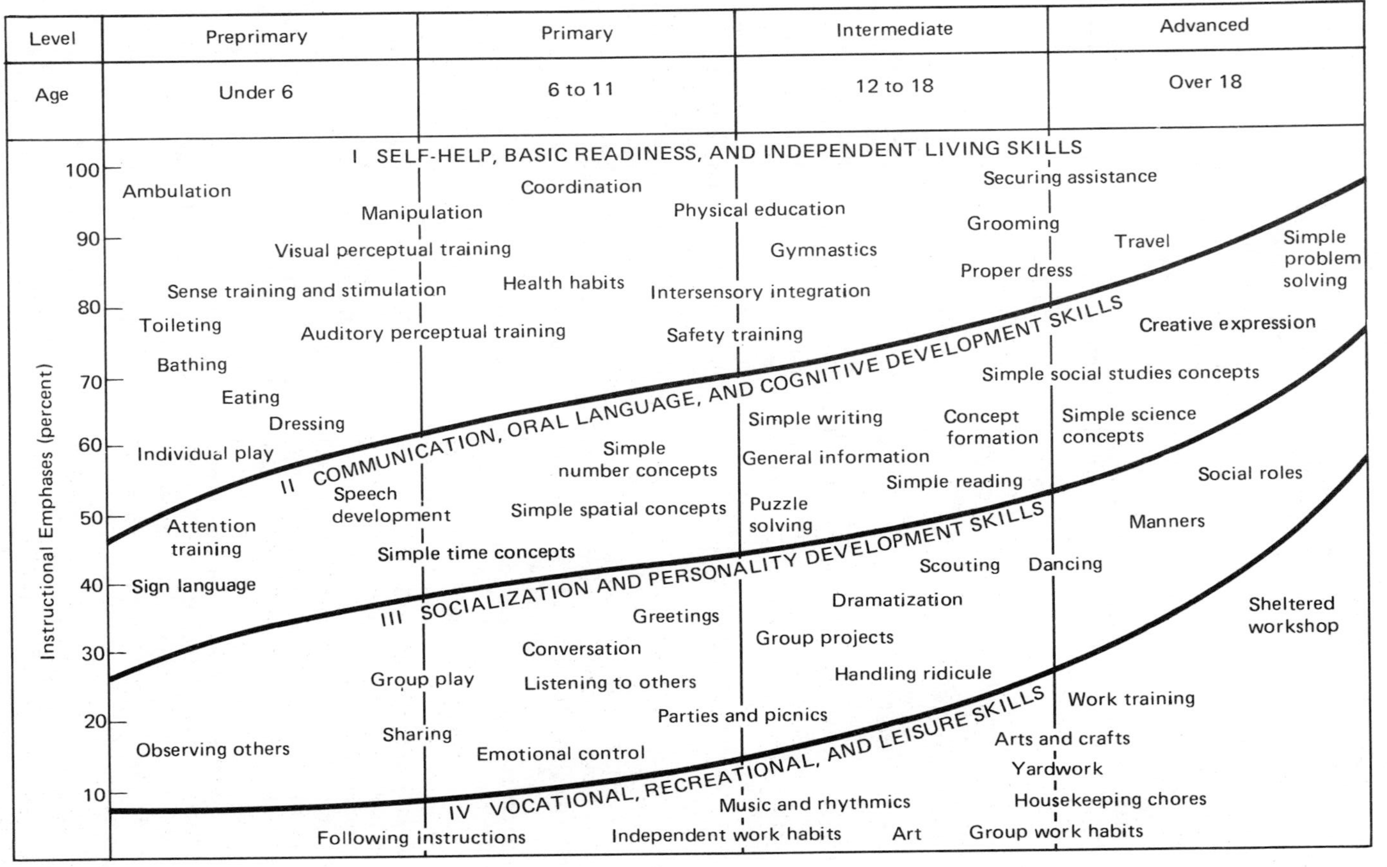
Level
Preprimary
Primary
Intermediate
Advanced
(approx.)
Age
Under 6
6 to 11
12 to 18
Over 18
Instructional Emphases (percent)
100
90
80
70
60
50
40
30
20
10
I SELF-HELP, BASIC READINESS, AND INDEPENDENT LIVING SKILLS
Ambulation
Manipulation
Coordination
Physical education
Securing assistance
Grooming
Travel
Simple problem solving
Visual perceptual training
Gymnastics
Proper dress
Sense training and stimulation
Health habits
Intersensory integration
Toileting
Auditory perceptual training
Safety training
Bathing
Eating
Dressing
Individual play
II COMMUNICATION, ORAL LANGUAGE, AND COGNITIVE DEVELOPMENT SKILLS
Creative expression
Simple social studies concepts
Simple writing
Concept formation
Simple science concepts
Simple number concepts
General information
Simple reading
Social roles
Speech development
Simple spatial concepts
Puzzle solving
Attention training
Simple time concepts
Manners
Sign language
III SOCIALIZATION AND PERSONALITY DEVELOPMENT SKILLS
Scouting
Dancing
Dramatization
Greetings
Sheltered workshop
Conversation
Group projects
Group play
Listening to others
Handling ridicule
Work training
Parties and picnics
Observing others
Sharing
Emotional control
IV VOCATIONAL, RECREATIONAL, AND LEISURE SKILLS
Arts and crafts
Yardwork
Music and rhythmics
Housekeeping chores
Following instructions
Independent work habits
Art
Group work habits

FIGURE 2

Perhaps the greatest utility of a model like this, which charts the changes in instructional emphasis across age levels, is as a guide for curriculum development efforts. Similar models have been used for emotionally disturbed children (McDowell & Brown, 1978) and for demonstrating the developmental aspects of career education (Muenster, 1982). This model could also be used as a guide for critiquing and adjusting existing programs, such as those represented by the curriculum guides described in the remainder of this section.

Cautions are necessary, however, against the uncritical use of this kind of model. First, empirical verification of changing emphases across age levels is nonexistent. Although one could argue convincingly that empirical verification may not be as critical as agreement by experts and consumers (parents and children), documentation about this agreement is usually lacking as well. For example, the Campbell charts describing programs for educable mentally retarded children show a definite decrease in the emphasis on academic development. Despite the fact that most professionals might agree to this trend, there may be some individuals (e.g., parents or professionals still looking for a cure) who might strongly question the merit of giving up on academic skills at any stage. Therefore, the assumptions and philosophies behind the use of any guide should be examined for their pertinence to the ultimate consumers of the resulting curriculum.

Curriculum Guides

The type of charting described above may be useful for other handicaps as well. A similar organization of content is available in less succinct and more detailed form in the array of curriculum guides throughout local school systems. The development of these guides was especially prevalent during the initial days of special day classes for handicapped children, when the assumption of a different set of goals was new. However, as a survey conducted by Cegelka (1978) indicates, the majority of curriculum guides available have been developed specifically for use with mildly and moderately retarded students at the primary and intermediate levels.

In an evaluation of 250 curriculum guides, Simches and Bohn (1963) found that most curriculum guides were merely a "rephrasing and reemphasizing of available courses of study used for normal children that do not even have the benefit of form, structure, and sequence connected with standard curriculum development" (p. 115). Their objections were partly based on the contention that mentally retarded children originally were put in special classrooms to provide them with a distinct curriculum, only to be presented with a watered-down version of curricula encountered in regular classroom settings.

One of the more popular guides, developed by Goldstein and Seigle (1958), was the Illinois Curriculum Guide, which emphasized social and vocational skills. Basic tool subjects were presented in a context similar to that in which students would be expected to apply the skills. Cegelka's (1978) analysis also revealed a content redundancy in guides that he examined, and he noted that t content reflected the pioneering work of the 1940s in s cial education.

Although representing extensive efforts by profession to compile curricula with recommended scopes a sequences of tasks to teach mentally retarded children, resulting guides need to be critically examined a updated in light of recent developments in instructio technology as well as changing philosophies of what teach these students. Periodic review of existing school d trict guides for curriculum is critical, not only to ensu that there is some coherence in what the students are bei exposed to in the curriculum, but also to give teachers a others who are presently involved in the educational s tem the sense that they are active contributors to t decision making about as well as the implementation curriculum goals.

Unit Method

The unit method is a curricular approach that empha izes content that has been utilized mainly for menta retarded students in special class settings (Ingram, 193 It was developed in the early days of the use of this admini trative arrangement. In the unit method, content is stru tured or organized in units. The units are based on t areas of interests of retarded children, and skill areas a incorporated into activities that reflect these areas of inte est. In other words, reading, writing, language, arithmet social studies, and so forth are taught in the context some unit topic such as "Playing House" or "Life on Farm". Basic-tool subjects are taught in situations whe actual applications can be made. Ingram (1935) suggeste a number of criteria for effective units of experience. Uni should include a variety of experiences that span the se tings where a student is expected to function (e.g., schoo home and community). The units created should empha ize activities that utilize basic-tool subjects as well provide an opportunity for the development of soci participation skills. Finally, the selection of units should b based on the level of mental, social, and physical functio ing of the students for whom the instruction is intended.

Thorsell (1961) criticized the topics being used for unit as haphazard selections from regular education. Othe criticisms of the unit method include the isolation of ind vidual units, the lack of a developmental sequence of con cepts and content, and the lack of a uniqueness of conten for the problems of mentally retarded students.

In response to some of these criticisms, Meyen (1972 developed an organizational framework within which unit can be developed. His Life Experience Unit approach i based on six core areas of learning experience: arithmet concepts, communication skills, social competencies safety, health, and vocational skills. Skills and concept from all core areas are included in each unit. Meye (1972) outlined developmental steps and guidelines fo writing Life Experience Units to ensure that the units ar comprehensive and integrated and that they provide fo the teaching of necessary academic and social skills.

Thus, the unit method presents a definite bias toward esenting content in an integrated manner to accommo-te the special learning characteristics of the intended nsumers, mentally retarded students. Emphasis is aced on the teaching of functional life skills, which cessitates the inclusion of skills from the academic, cial, and vocational areas. Skills from these areas are not aced in competition with each other for emphasis; rather, cisions are based on the usefulness of skills for the life nctioning of the students. The unit method may be seen the forerunner of more recent efforts in the career devel-ment area and emphasis of functional skills for curricu-m development projects.

urriculum Development Projects

Before 1965, there were few major efforts to systemati-lly develop curricula for handicapped children. Curricu-r efforts were mainly reflected in the curriculum idelines that were compiled by state and local agencies. leyen and Horner (1976) attributed this lack of emphasis 1 systematic curriculum development to several factors. irst, despite the original reason for separating special lucation students (i.e., to provide them with a specialized urriculum), emphasis was placed on other aspects of spe-al education, such as assessment of student character-tics and evaluation of the efficacy of administrative rrangements. Curriculum development often followed urrent trends in conceptualizing disabilities. For exam-le, Strauss and Lehtinen (1947) recommended curricular odifications according to the etiology of learning prob-ms (e.g., brain injury). This led to an approach developed ccording to a perceptual model. The mainstreaming iovement also represented a movement motivated by hilosophical, conceptual, and political reasons that had ast implications for curriculum planning. Again, curricu-um played an accommodating rather than a leading role.

Another reason for lack of emphasis on formal curricu-um development was the paucity of special educators rained in curriculum development for special education. 'his lack of professional commitment accompanied a ninimal availability of funds to develop systematic curri-ula. However, to reverse this trend, there was an increased ommitment of federal monies in the 1970s specifically for he purpose of developing curricula for educable mentally etarded students.

One major contribution of the curriculum projects that ame out of the 1970s was their example of how curricula an be constructed in a systematic and scholarly manner. leyen and Horner (1976) presented a model of the influ-nces that should be systematically used in the curriculum levelopment process. The model conceptualized child ariability, material, institutional setting, and teacher haracteristics as critical influences on the curriculum ontext that need to be specified. Consideration of these ariables takes place in the context of curriculum dev-lopment, which consists of the following stages: (a) speci-ication of the target population, needs, and objectives; (b) description of rationale and instructional design; (c) devel-opment and testing; (d) evaluation and revision; and (e) dissemination and implementation. The curriculum devel-opment process has been described in great detail by Mayer (1982) and others associated with the specific pro-jects described below. The process is highly complex if quality products are to be produced. An appreciation of the complexities involved in curriculum development is not always forthcoming when local systems take on the process by themselves. Thus, an issue to be considered is the weigh-ing of the trade-offs between having a well-developed cur-riculum that local professionals do not feel ownership of, versus one to which they can relate but which is not appro-priately documented or tested.

One example of one of these early curriculum projects is the Social Learning Curriculum (Goldstein, 1975). The focus of the curriculum is on the development of social competence in primary-level school children. Integrated into the instructional experiences are emphases on skills and concepts related to language, math, and motor devel-opment. The development of this curriculum was based on models representing the retarded child's need areas (physi-cal, social, and psychological) and expanding environment (self, home and family, neighborhood, and community). The overall scheme of the curriculum is represented in phase books covering the following topics: perceiving individuality, recognizing the environment, recognizing interdependence, recognizing the body, recognizing and reacting to emotions, recognizing what the senses do, com-municating with others, getting along with others, identi-fying helpers, and maintaining bodily functions. The design of activities in these books encourages the use of inductive teaching strategies. This curriculum represents an effort to integrate the critical content areas into a presentation of topical material.

Other curricula developed for educable mentally retarded students include the Biological Science Study Committee's Me Now, Me and My Environment, and Me and My Future (Mayer, 1975); Project Math (Cawley et al., 1976); I Can (physical education) (Wessel, 1975); Pacemaker Primary Curriculum (total habilitation) (Ross & Ross, 1972); and Portage Project (cognitive, self-help, motor, language, and socialization behaviors) (Shearer & Shearer, 1972). (See Meyen & Horner, 1976 for more thorough descriptions of these curricula.)

Some of the more recent curriculum development efforts have focused their efforts on the education of mod-erately and severely retarded children. For example, Tawney, Knapp, O'Reilly, and Pratt (1979) developed the Programmed Environments Curriculum to guide the teaching of skills acquired during the first 3 years of life. It provides a profile of instructional objectives that a teacher may utilize in teaching severely handicapped children dur-ing these years. Fredericks et al. (1976) provided a similar skills approach to teaching older and higher functioning students. (Other such efforts are described in more detail in the Irvin chapter of this volume.)

Integration of Content Within a Career Education Program

Advocates for the implementation of a comprehensive career education program argue convincingly that career education can become a vehicle for the teaching of academic and social skills as well as vocational skills (Brolin, 1982; Leggett, 1978; Muenster, 1982). Leggett (1978) described the significant overlap of the programming goals of special education and career education. Such overlapping characteristics include (a) the development of self-awareness in terms of interests, attitudes, and capabilities; (b) a commitment to the development of the whole child that capitalizes on strengths and remediates deficits; (c) the development of an awareness of others and ways of facilitating interpersonal interactions: and (d) an awareness of careers and the competencies necessary to succeed in these careers. Given this overlap, Leggett (1978) called for an expansion of the "friendship of commitment" into a true partnership of the two types of educational orientations.

A generic definition of career education, consistent with the overlap just described, was offered by the Council for Exceptional Children in 1978:

> Career education is the totality of experiences through which one learns to live a meaningful, satisfying work life . . . providing the opportunity to learn, in the least restrictive environment possible, the academic, daily living, personal-social, and occupational knowledges and skills necessary for attaining their highest levels of economic, personal and social fulfillment. This can be obtained through work (both paid and unpaid) and in a variety of other societal roles and personal life styles . . . student, citizen, volunteer, family member and participant in meaningful leisure-time activities. (Brolin, 1982, p. 3)

Consistent with the concepts in this definition, Brolin (1982) described a Life Centered Career Education (LCCE) model, which was developed to combine the goals of special and career education. LCCE is designed to promote the acquisition of three major categories of competencies (daily, personal-social, and occupational skills) through four stages of career development (awareness, exploration, preparation, and placement/follow-up/continuing education), which start early in elementary school and span a student's educational career. The teaching of the targeted skills takes place within the contexts of the student's school, family, and community. Brolin emphasized that

> career education is not intended to replace traditional education but, rather, to redirect it to be more relevant and meaningful for the student and to result in the acquisition of attitudes, knowledges, and skills one needs for successful community living and working. (p. 3)

Although career education offers a seemingly logi organization and weighting of competencies in the ac demic, social, and vocational content areas, such progra have not been adopted extensively to this point. Burton a Bero (1984) surveyed junior and senior high school teac ers and local employers and found that there were lar gaps between teachers' and employers' perceptions of wh skills and abilities are necessary to prepare students for li and work. Although teachers focused on isolated jo related tasks and basic academic skills, employers empha ized the need for personal-social and coping skills. The was little recognition of the relationship between the ac demic and career education competencies that are outlin in programs such as Brolin's (1982). Thus, it seems th the viability of a career education method of integrati content awaits the increased awareness of educational pe sonnel of how it fits with existing programming (see Ellin ton & Winkoff, 1982) and of what its potential may for providing a comprehensive, relevant organization curriculum content.

Determination of Program Content Emphasis Through Structured Decision-Making Processes

The models and orientations described to this point a all contributors to final decisions concerning progra content. If one of these models and the accompanyin products or guides for products are not adopted intact by consumer group, the decisions regarding curriculum co tent will be critically influenced by the decision-makin process itself. Mayer (1982) described curriculum deve opment as a process and a legacy, noting the "startling lac of papers dealing with curriculum development" (p. 1 The documentation of a decision-making process in th development of a curriculum may be a more valuable con tribution, in the long run, than the curriculum produc itself. Although personal and professional philosophie and state-of-the-art knowledge change with time decision-making models can always be adapted for use i new curriculum development efforts.

Two components of the decision-making process ar discussed here. They are the prioritizaticn of goals an objectives, and the matching of goals and objectives t individual needs.

Prioritization of Goals and Objectives

Although comprehensive curriculum development models have been described in the literature (see Mayer, 1982), few of them deal specifically with the process of weighting the emphasis of content areas. Isolated attempts have been made to prioritize the importance of teaching skills to specified groups of handicapped children. For example, Geiger, Brownsmith, and Forgnone (1978) sampled 122 teachers to determine the relative importance of 550 skills and twenty-six skill areas in the instruction of trainable mentally retarded students. Teachers ranked nese skills on a 5-point rating scale, which ranged from *ssential* (1) to *very unimportant* (5). There was strong greement between the relative rankings of the general kills areas and specific skills, despite the fact that these ankings were done independently. The investigators mphasized the importance of this consensus of skill nportance as a first step toward improving the quality of rogramming for these students.

White (1982) used a modified Delphi technique to rioritize personal and social competencies that are needed y hearing impaired students. First, definitions were btained for 24 competency areas. These competency reas were then rated by workshop participants (representing a cross-section of school personnel) from six chools (total n = 281) on a scale from *very little or no mprovement needed* (1) to *critical improvement needed* 5). The ratings were summarized and averaged for each competency area, discussed by small groups, and then erated according to the same scale. Finally, the participants were asked to choose, based on the following criteria, our areas in which the hearing impaired students at their espective schools most urgently needed improvement:

1. What is the probability of success in improving an area of competency?
2. What is the cost?
3. Is it the school's responsibility to provide programs and experiences that will foster improvement in the given area?
4. How are the different areas of competency related?

The resulting ratings indicated that there was consistency in prioritization of skill areas across age level and a high degree of consensus on which skill areas were most urgently in need of improvement. The authors emphasized the value of these data in guiding schools as they develop and refine programs for the hearing-impaired. (p. 269)

The efforts cited above to prioritize goals focused on the input of teachers and other school personnel. Input from parents, people from the community, and other professionals who are concerned about quality education for handicapped children should also be considered. A system could conceivably be constructed to include and weight the input from these other sources.

Matching of Goals and Objectives to Individual Needs

The decision-making processes described to this point are concerned with the prioritization of goals and objectives for groups of handicapped youngsters. One key to making any curricular approach relevant and effective is to match it to the critical characteristic of the consumers, that is, the handicapped children themselves. Poplin and Gray (1980) noted that

> the danger of using a predetermined curriculum as the basis for assessment and instructional programming, no matter how sound its rationale, is that the curriculum becomes the master; the child's needs are seen only in terms of what the curriculum has to offer. The only content suitable as a basis for effective assessment and instruction results from a comparison of the child's present abilities and the abilities and understanding necessary for a satisfying, self-fulfilling life. (p. 78)

This passage reinforces the need to link child characteristics with the determination and prioritization of specific goals and objectives. This theme is realized in the mandate of PL 94-142 for IEPs. The requirements of the IEPs themselves and the process surrounding their construction ensures the link between child characteristics and program goals.

Specific to the topic of differential emphasis of program content for individuals is the aspect of the IEP procedure that requires the prioritization of goals and objectives for each child. Dardig and Heward (1981) described a procedure for prioritizing IEP goals. The procedure includes the following steps:

1. Team members introductions
2. Listing and discussing many possible goals
3. Determining criteria for prioritizing goals
4. Individual team members ratings
5. Synthesizing individual responses
6. Prioritized list of annual goals. (p. 8)

The following criteria are suggested by Dardig and Howard for prioritizing annual goals:

1. Will the child be able to use the skill in his/her immediate environment?
2. Is it a functional, useful skill?
3. Will the child be able to use the skill often?
4. Has the child demonstrated an interest in learning this skill?
5. Is success in teaching this skill likely?
6. Is the skill a prerequisite for learning more complex skills?
7. Will the child become more independent as a result of learning this skill?
8. Will the skill allow the child to qualify for improved or additional services, or services in a less restrictive environment?
9. Is it important to modify this behavior because it is dangerous to self or others? (p. 8)

Each team member rates the list of goals according to each criterion (from *lowest priority* (1) to *Highest priority* (5)). The ratings of each team member are synthesized into a group rating, which serves as the final prioritization. The suggested procedure provides for a systematic process of goal prioritization that should contribute to the productivity and ease of working of IEP teams. Additionally, it provides a sound basis for decisions about the emphasis of various content areas for individual children.

Brown et al. (1980) suggested a strategy for generating comprehensive, longitudinal, and chronological-age-appropriate IEPs for severely handicapped students. This strategy consists of six phases: (a) a strategy for organizing curricular content, (b) ecological inventory strategies, (c) student-repertoire inventory strategies, (d) parent/guardian inventory strategies, (e) strategies for putting curricular content in priority order, and (f) the design and implementation of instructional programs. Of specific interest to this discussion are those strategies dealing with curricular content. For organizing curricular content, Brown et al. suggested organizing curricula for severely handicapped students into five, nonmutually exclusive, curricular domains: (a) the domestic domain, (b) the vocational domain, (c) the recreational/leisure domain, (d) the general-community-functioning domain, and (e) the interaction-with-nonhandicapped-persons domain. In order to systematically assign priorities to these content areas, Brown et al. listed 16 dimensions that a teacher should consider:

— teacher preferences
— ancillary-staff preferences
— student preferences
— commercial-publisher preferences
— number of environments
— social significance
— minimization of physical harm
— chronological-age-appropriate nature of skill
— administrator preferences
— parent/guardian preferences
— unique student characteristics
— presumed logistical and practical realities
— number of occurrences
— probablility of skill acquisition
— functional nature of a skill
— relevant research (p. 209)

Brown et al. (1980) recognized that "It is one thing to compile a list of dimensions to consider when designing an IEP; far more complex and difficult is the task of designing a strategy that elicits the agreement of all persons involved with regard to the final characteristics of an IEP" (p. 212). However, consideration of these dimensions is critical to the ultimate quality and relevance of the resulting IEP for a severely handicapped child. In order to evaluate the decisions made about the content of IEPs, Brown et al. (1976) outlined six questions to consider as the criterion of ultimate functioning (detailed earlier in this chapter). In summary, these suggestions provide the structure for a decision-making procedure for defining the content of programs for individual severely handicapped students.

The strategy of developing curriculum content goals through an individualized process of determining the critical skills needed in environments of ultimate functioning has gained popularity in its use with severely handicapped children and young adults. One model program being utilized throughout California is the Individualized Critical Skills Model (ICSM) (California State Department of Education, 1985). Critical skills are defined as "those relevant, essential skills that are deemed important by all significant individuals in the student's life, and the student if appropriate, and that increase the student's participation in chronological age-appropriate activities in present and future natural environments" (California State Department of Education, 1985, p. 2). The program involves a nine-phase procedure that essentially analyzes the significant environments in a given child's life and determines the appropriate targets for instruction on critical skills. Similar approaches have been developed for postschool environments (Rusch & Chadsey-Rusch, 1985; Wilcox & Bellamy, 1982). The critical distinction between this community-based approach to curriculum development and traditional approaches is that, as opposed to organizing a curriculum along traditional academic sequences (e.g., language, math, and job skills), this approach delineates the basic demands of an individual's life (e.g., community and school participation, leisure, employment). Thus, rather than being necessarily exhaustive, the curriculum content is tailored to the individual's specific needs.

Along the same line of aligning curriculum development procedures with individual needs, but emphasizing the more traditional approach, Poplin (1979) outlined a three-step procedure for coordinating curriculum and IEP development procedures:

1. Delineate goals or constructs of a given special education area (e.g., academic or self-help skills).
2. Delineate general objectives.
3. Break down general objectives into short-term instructional goals.

The resulting curricular maps are then used as a source for the selection of goals and objectives as well as a structure for monitoring and evaluating student progress. Poplin (1979) emphasized that "special educators should never be forced to use a set of curriculum objectives that they have not had an active part in developing" (p. 5) and that the disadvantages of time-consuming processes are outweighed by the advantages of having an original and relevant set of curriculum objectives.

The decision-making procedures outlined above represent considerations of handicapped children as members of groups and as individuals. Voeltz, Evans, Freedland, and Donellon (1982) analyzed the decision-making patterns of teachers in the process of prioritizing goals for educational programming. These investigators found that teachers considered both general professional education practices and the individual characteristics of handicapped children. Thus, it is likely that the group and individual perspectives for prioritizing content areas are both necessary for consideration in the provision of appropriate programs to handicapped children.

Conclusions, Needs, and Recommendations

Recognition of the numerous historical, philosophical, policy, theoretical, and empirical influences that affect existing and potential programs for handicapped children is a first step toward answering questions about the relationship among academic, social, and career content emphases. In reviewing these factors, one gets the sense hat some are more controllable than others (e.g., policy and the philosophies of the time being less controllable than practice originating from practitioners) and that some influences result in more relevant applications than others (e.g., theoretical influences having less direct application than actual delineations of usable decision-making processes). Given the trends in the field as they have occurred in an historical context, predictions can be made about which influences will be critical in the future development of knowledge, expertise, and practice in this area of programming interest.

With the advent of PL 94-142 and its mandates (including least restrictive environment, IEPs, due process, and nondiscriminatory assessment), process has become a very critical variable in the determination of educational programming. That is, a structure has been established for making decisions about the education of handicapped children. The process remains constant across children, but the content of what is recommended for each child differs as a result of the contributors to the process. In other words, contributors to the construction of overall curriculum patterns in the past, such as parents and educational personnel, are now determining similar patterns at individual levels.

From one perspective, it makes sense to define process variables for the determination of the presentation of content because process variables are more generalizable than specific patterns of curricular content, which are matched with individual characteristics. Process variables can be expected to last through time as well, in contrast to content emphasis, which may vary according to the zeitgeist.

However, there are dangers in relying too heavily on process guidelines for the determination of *what* to teach handicapped children. One danger is that a focus on individual decision making might devalue the development of an overall curricular plan for handicapped children as a group. Despite the variability in these groups, there are certain needs that these individuals have in common that can be addressed by a systematic, organized approach to the prioritization and presentation of content. Further, a singular individualized approach cannot take advantage of the accumulated knowledge that the profession as a whole has amassed on how best to educate children with certain characteristics. Therefore, it seems wise to recommend a balance between the individualized approach inherent in the IEP process and a global approach guided by verified practices.

Another trend that will influence future programming efforts in the education of handicapped children is that of accountability. Accountability is critical at all levels, from research and development projects to the implementation of individual programs for handicapped children. The underlying intent of the push for accountability is to provide proven practices for use in the education of handicapped children. Pertinent to the present topic is the question of the integration and emphasis of the various content areas. As noted earlier, at this point, there is very little hard evidence on the effects of differential emphasis on academic, social, or vocational programming. This status is likely to remain until a clarification of desired outcomes is achieved. Perhaps a logical (but not necessarily obtainable) goal is to determine answers to the possible combinations in the equation, aptitude-by-treatment = outcome. Such a determination would be the ultimate example of accountability.

The recommendations with which this chapter concludes address two general points: the focus of continuing and future efforts by research and development professionals and recommendations for personnel preparations.

Focus for Research and Development Professionals

Questions about the relationship between academic, social, and career goals for programming effectiveness have not been satisfactorily answered. The nature of these questions is threefold: (a) Should one content area be preferred to the others? (b) What should the order of prioritization be? and (c) Are the content areas best taught in concert in an integrated curriculum? Of course, the answers to these questions vary according to the nature of the handicapped students in question as well as their age.

Although the logical impulse may be to say that these questions need to be answered through vigorous and well-controlled research studies, there are several cautions to be noted about this kind of strategy. First, we may be asking the wrong questions. A parallel situation can be found in the classic question behind efficacy studies on mainstreaming, Does it work? The error of our ways has been primarily in asking such a simplistic question for such a complex situation. However, as Forness and Kavale (1984) have suggested, the question of proven procedures has been mixed up with a question of policy. Applied to the topic being discussed here, there are both procedural and philosophical issues at hand. The question of the prioritization of the content areas of a curriculum might be answerable given an agreement on what the desired outcomes should be (foregoing for the moment the complexity of determining the aptitude-by-treatment interaction, given the multitude of levels of each side of the interaction). However, given the necessity of considering the opinions of many involved individuals, it is unlikely that a solid agreement on preferred outcomes can be obtained. Therefore, research-documented answers to these questions would be accepted as valid by some but not others . . . and we are once again in the fact-versus-philosophy bind.

Another problem associated with answers to the questions posed earlier is the inherent conflicts of interest that exist between researchers and practitioners. On the one hand, educators who are working with children in the schools need answers and solutions right now. The questions to which they need answers are broad and involve numerous variables. They need answers to these questions within the contingencies of administrative systems that cannot change for the sake of a well-controlled study. On the other hand, researchers are committed to answering questions according to a certain methodology to get valid and reliable answers. The nature of many methodologies typically used in the social sciences is such that questions need to be answered in small bits and pieces, ideally with as much control over the environment as possible. Therefore, the situation is usually reduced to the question, How much control can be compromised in order to answer some of the pressing questions related to practice? In order to change these inherent conflicts between research and practice, further examination of both systems will be needed to identify where compromises can most effectively be made.

Despite the conflicts described above, there are some avenues in which research and development efforts can provide some leadership. These efforts could focus on decision-making processes and how different patterns of influence within these processes affect educational outcomes for handicapped children. Morrison, MacMillan, and Kavale (1985) have noted that the procedures utilized in referral, assessment, and identification processes significantly affect where a child is placed and therefore what the overall focus of his or her program will be. Ysseldyke and Algozzine (1982) and others (Yoshida, Fenton, Maxwell, & Kaufman, 1978) have documented the numerous influences that determine the decisions made by multidisciplinary teams. If these processes are a major factor in the determination of educational programming for handicapped children, then the development of effective exemplary practice is critical.

The discussions of the nature of system identification of handicapped children (MacMillan, Meyers, & Morrison, 1980; Morrison, MacMillan, & Kavale, 1985) bring to mind an important factor in the research and development of curriculum for these students. That is, the populations that are of concern as well as their situations in the school system are subject to change over time, particularly in association with policy changes. For example, Polloway and Smith (1983) and Forness and Kavale (1984) have noted that the group of students who now may be identified as educable mentally retarded are a much more delayed group of students than educable mentally retarded students who were being educated 15–20 years ago, when much of the research and development on curricular issues for this group was being done. Further, the administrative arrangement for these students, although most likely to be the special day class (MacMillan & Borthwick, 1980), may in fact involve a variety of options that may imply a different curricular or instructional approach. The point to be emphasized here is that any research or development effort needs to be carried out with the realization that changes in populations and educational contexts need to be considered.

Ultimately, the consideration of educational programming for handicapped children should include a consideration of the relationship of this programming to the larger context of schools in general or regular education in particular. Quality education for handicapped students would be more likely if this relationship were clearly defined. Perhaps the vehicle for considering this larger issue is one in which regular education is now heavily involved, such as the effective schools movement (Averch, Carroll, Donaldson, Kiesling, & Pincus, 1984). Some of the indicators of effective schools are a clear school mission, instructional leadership, high expectations, an emphasis on academic skills, frequent monitoring of student progress and its utilization in curriculum planning, and productive home-school relations. These variables are logically related to effective programming for handicapped children as well. Some questions about programming that might be raised and considered in depth are: (a) How do school-wide curriculum development efforts relate to those specifically geared to handicapped children? (b) Is the same set of goals and objectives pertinent for handicapped children? How do they differ? In what ways are they the same? (c) What is the responsibility of school-wide personnel for involvement in the education of handicapped children? and What is the administrative and instructional relationship between regular and special education? The answers to these questions seem to be critical to the resolution of the more critical issues of effective programming for handicapped students.

Recommendations for Personnel Preparation

The preparation of personnel who work with handicapped children in the schools is an important vehicle for the communication and dissemination of effective, quality practices in the field of special education. This knowledge can be transmitted at several levels. Competent professionals need a solid knowledge base. In this case, the knowledge base would provide answers to the question, What content should be taught to children of various handicaps and age levels based on the accumulated knowledge in the field to this date? Additionally, professionals need to be exposed to exemplary practices of the processes and procedures that are used in the field to determine educational programming for handicapped children. However, perhaps of greater urgency is the goal of teaching special education personnel to be critical consumers of what is available and what is being practiced in the schools to educate handicapped children.

Until concrete answers to the questions raised on the previous pages are available, we must depend on quality, informed decision making by personnel who plan and implement programs for handicapped children. For example, the availability of "canned" curricula is increasing. Professionals who are potential consumers of these curricula need to be able to discriminate those packages which are quality programs from those which are not. Meyen and Horner (1976) recommended the following questions to guide the analysis or review of a curriculum:

1. What was the project's organizational structure?
2. Which individuals were responsible for conducting the curriculum development activities?
3. What model or body of research formed the basis for the curriculum?
4. What curriculum products have been produced, and how are they being disseminated?

5. Who are the individuals who are expected to use the curriculum products?
6. Who are the individuals who are expected to be taught with the curriculum products?
7. Does the curriculum design specify a particular organizational structure, that is, classroom, resource room, one-to-one, and so forth?
8. What is the content of the curriculum products?
9. Does the curriculum specify a particular teaching format?
10. What procedure was used to evaluate the curriculum products? (p. 271)

    As implementers of programs for handicapped children, teachers hold a great deal of power in, as well as have responsibility for, guiding the planning of effective programs for these children.

In addition to being critical consumers of existing curricula, educational personnel should also have the competencies and motivation to become more personally involved in curriculum development efforts. As Poplin (1979) emphasized, this involvement has the advantage of facilitating increased teacher competence and confidence as well as increasing the effectiveness of educational programming. Ferguson (1985) noted that, without the effort of teachers of severely handicapped children to implement the spirit of a policy-backed philosophy of training functional skills, the reform and development efforts in this area are threatened. Thus, it may be critical to get the involvement and commitment of teachers not only in the implementation but also in the development of programming structures and guidelines. One way of facilitating this situation is to provide some level of training in curriculum development at the pre-service level.

Another of the key competencies that a teacher might have for curriculum development efforts is the ability to work in a collaborative manner with other professionals. Personnel preparation efforts in training teachers have typically focused on teaching skills for working with handicapped children as opposed to those for working with adults. An investigation by Morrison, Lieber, and Morrison (1986) revealed that regular and special education teachers viewed situations in which they needed to meet with other teachers and professionals as anxiety-provoking events with which they were ill-equipped to deal. This being the case, group process and leadership skills might be an important target for emphasis in future training efforts. If, as suggested earlier in this chapter, decision-making processes are critical to the development of effective programming, then training key personnel in these processes is one step toward ensuring effective programs for handicapped children.

In conclusion, this chapter has included descriptions of a number of major influences on what is taught in the schools to handicapped children of different ages and handicapping conditions. It should be noted that some of the contributing factors are dated in terms of their major impact. Further, none of the avenues to development of curriculum approaches is systematic or comprehensive. Thus, it is obvious that special education professionals must renew their interest in and commitment to the development of strong curricular structures for the education of handicapped individuals. Further, any efforts in this direction should include a careful examination of the historical, philosophical, political, theoretical, and empirical factors that have existed in the past and those that are now pertinent in order to ensure a sound, cohesive structure for what to teach handicapped individuals now and in the future.

Author Information

Gale M. Morrison is Associate Professor at the Graduate School of Education, University of California at Santa Barbara.

References

Aichorn, A. (1965). *Wayward youth*. New York: Viking.

Arkell, C. (1982). Functional curriculum development for multiply involved hearing-impaired students. *Volta Review*, **84**, 198–208.

Averch, H. A., Carroll, S. J., Donaldson, T. S., Kiesling, H. J., & Pincus, J. (1984). *How effective is schooling? A critical review and syntheses of the research*. Englewood Cliffs, NJ: Educational Technology.

Bereiter, C., & Engelmann, S. (1966). *Teaching disadvantaged children in preschool*. Englewood Cliffs, NJ: Prentice-Hall.

Bricker, D., & Filler, J. (1985). The severely mentally retarded individual: Philosophical and implementation dilemmas. In D. Bricker & J. Filler (Eds.), *Severe mental retardation: From theory to practice* (pp. 2–10). Lancaster, PA: Division on Mental Retardation of the Council for Exceptional Children.

Brolin, D. E. (1982). Life-centered career education for exceptional children. *Focus on Exceptional Children*, **14**(7), 1–15.

Brown v. Board of Education, 347 U.S. 483 (1954).

Brown, L., Falvey, M., Vincent, L., Kaye, N., Johnson, F., Ferrara-Parrish, P., & Gruenewald, L. (1980). Strategies for generating comprehensive, longitudinal, and chronological-age-appropriate individualized education programs for adolescent and young-adult severely handicapped students. *Journal of Special Education*, **14**, 199–215.

Brown, L., Nietupski, J., & Hamre-Nietupski, S. (1976). Criterion of ultimate functioning. In M. A. Thomas (Ed.), *Hey, don't forget about me!* (pp. 2–15). Reston, VA: Council for Exceptional Children.

Burton, L., & Bero, F. (1984). Is career education really being taught? *Academic Therapy*, **19**, 389–395.

Burton, T. A., & Hirshoren, A. (1979). Some further thoughts and clarifications on the education of severely and profoundly retarded children. *Exceptional Children*, **45**, 618–625.

California State Department of Education. (1985). *Overview to the Individualized Critical Skills Model (ICSM)*. Sacramento, CA: Author.

Campbell, L. (1968). *Study of curriculum planning*. Sacramento, CA: California Department of Education.

Cawley, J. F., Fitzmaunce, A. M., Goodstein, H. A., Lepore, A. V., Sedlak, R., & Althaus, V. (1976). *Project MATH*. Tulsa, OK: Educational Development Corporation.

Cegelka, W. J. (1978). Educational materials: Curriculum guides for the mentally retarded: An analysis and recommendations. *Education and Training of the Mentally Retarded*, **13**, 187–188.

Childs, R. E. (1979). A drastic change in curriculum for the educable mentally retarded child. *Mental Retardation*, **17**, 299–301.

Cohen, S. B., Safran, J., & Polloway, E. A. (1980). Minimum competency testing and its implications for retarded students. *Education and Training of the Mentally Retarded*, **15**, 250–255.

Council for Exceptional Children. (1978). *Position paper on career education*. Reston, VA: Author.

Council for Exceptional Children Ad Hoc Committee. (1983). Reply to "A Nation at Risk." *Exceptional Children*, **50**, 484–494.

Cruickshank, W. M., Bentzen, G. A., Ratzeburg, F. H., & Tannhauser, M. T. (1961). *Teaching methodology for brain injured and hyperactive children*. Syracuse, NY: Syracuse University Press.

Cunningham, D. (1983). Educating the visually impaired severely-to-profoundly retarded child: A long range perspective. *Education of the Visually Handicapped*, **15**, 95–100.

Dardig, J. C., & Heward, W. L. (1981). A systematic procedure for prioritizing IEP goals. *The Directive Teacher*, **3**, 6–8.

Deno, E. (1970). Special education as developmental capital. *Exceptional Children*, **37**, 229–237.

Dil, N. (1983). Affective curricula: Theory, models and implementation. *Topics in Early Childhood Special Education*, **2**(4), 25–33.

Dinkmeyer, D. (1970). *Developing an understanding of self and others (DUSO)*. Circle Pines, MN: American Guidance Service.

Dunn, L. M. (1973). *Exceptional children in the schools: Special education in transition*. New York: Holt, Rinehart & Winston.

Elardo, P., & Cooper, M. (1977). *AWARE: Activities for social development*. Menlo Park, CA: Addison-Wesley.

Elias, M. J., & Maher, C. A. (1983). Social and affective development of children: A programmatic perspective. *Exceptional Children*, **50**, 339–346.

Elkind, D. (1983). Viewpoint: The curriculum disabled child. *Topics in Learning and Learning Disabilities*, **3**, 71–78.

Ellington, C., & Winkoff, L. (1982). Low cost implementation of a career education program for elementary school children with handicaps. *Journal of Career Education*, **8**, 246–255.

Ellis, M. R., Balla, D., Estes, O., Warren, S. A., Meyers, C. E., Hollis, J., Isaacson, R. L., Palk, B. E., & Siegel, P. S. (1981). Common sense is the habilitation of mentally retarded persons: A reply to Menolascino and McGee. *Mental Retardation*, **19**, 221–226.

Ferguson, D. C. (1985). The ideal and the real: The working out of public policy in curricula for severely handicapped students. *Remedial and Special Education*, **6**(3), 52–60.

Feuerstein, R. (1979). *Instrumental enrichment: Redevelopment of cognitive functions of retarded performers*. Baltimore, MD: University Park Press.

Fewell, R. R., & Sandal, S. R. (1983). Curricula adaptations for young children: Visually impaired, hearing impaired, and physically impaired. *Topics in Early Childhood Special Education*, **2**, 51–66.

Forness, S. R., & Kavale, K. A. (1984). Education of the mentally retarded: A note on policy. *Education and Training of the Mentally Retarded*, **19**, 239–245.

Frederick, H., Riggs, C., Forey, T., Grove, D., Moore, W., McDonnell, J., Jordan, E., Hanson, W., Baldwin, V., & Wadlow, W. (1976). *The teaching research curriculum for moderately and severely handicapped*. Springfield, IL: C. Thomas.

Frederick, H., Toews, J., Petersen, J., Templeman, T., Bunse, C., Trecker, N., Egan, I., Hendreckson, K., & Muthersbaugh, S. (1984). *The secondary data based classroom for the severely handicapped*. Monmouth, OR: Instructional Development Corporation.

Frostig, M., Lefever, D., & Whittlesey, D. J. (1961). A developmental test of visual perception for evaluating normal and neurologically handicapped children. *Perceptual Motor Skills*, **12**, 383–394.

Geiger, W. L., Brownsmith, K., & Forgnone, C. (1978). Differential importance of skills for TMR students as perceived by teachers. *Education and Training of the Mentally Retarded*, **13**, 259–264.

Gilliam, J. E., & Coleman, M. C. (1981). Who influences IEP committee decisions? *Exceptional Children*, **47**, 642–644.

Glavin, J. P., Quay, H. C., Annesley, G. R., & Werry, J. S. (1971). An experimental resource room for behavior problem children. *Exceptional Children*, **38**, 131–137.

Goldstein, H. (1975). *The social learning curriculum*. Columbus OH: Merrill.

Goldstein, H., & Siegle, D. (1958). *A curriculum guide for teachers of the educable mentally handicapped*. Springfield, IL: Department of Public Instruction.

Gotts, E. E. (1983). Broad impacts of early childhood curriculum models on nonintellective processes. *Topics in Early Childhood Special Education*, **2**(4), 43–50.

Greenan, J. R. (1982). Problems and issues in delivering vocational education instruction and support services to students with learning disabilities. *Journal of Learning Disabilities*, **15**, 231–235.

Guess, D., & Noonan, M. (1982). Curricula and instructional procedures for severely handicapped students. *Focus on Exceptional Children*, **14**(5), 1–12.

Haring, N. G., & Phillips, E. L. (1962). *Analysis and modification of classroom behavior*. New York: McGraw-Hill.

Hewett, F. (1968). *The emotionally disturbed child in the classroom*. Boston, MA: Allyn and Bacon.

Hewett, F., Taylor, G. D., & Artuso, A. A. (1969). The Santa Monica Project: Evaluation of an engineered classroom design with emotionally disturbed children. *Exceptional Children*, **35**, 523–529.

Hobbs, N. (1965). How the Re-Ed plan developed. In N. J. Long, W. C. Morse & R. G. Newman (Eds.), *Conflict in the classroom*. Belmont, CA: Wadsworth.

Hotte, R. A., Monroe, H. J., Philbrook, D. L., & Scarlata, R. W. (1984). Programming for persons with profound mental retardation: A three-year retrospective study. *Mental Retardation*, **22**, 75–78.

Ingram, C. P. (1935). *Education of the slow-learning child*. Yonkers, NY: World Books.

Karnes, M. B. (1973). Evaluation and implications of research with young handicapped and low-income children. In J. C. Stanley (Ed.), *Compensatory education for children, ages 2 to 8* (pp. 109–144). Baltimore, MD: Johns Hopkins University Press.

Kephart, N. (1960). *The slow learner in the classroom*. Columbus, OH: Merrill.

Kirk, S. A. (1964). Research in education. In H. A. Stevens & R. Heber (Eds.), *Mental retardation: A review of research* (pp. 57–99). Chicago, IL: University of Chicago Press.

Klein, N. K., Pasch, M., & Frew, T. W. (1979). *Curriculum analysis and design for retarded learners.* Columbus, OH: Merrill.

Lau v. Nichols, 414 U.S. 563 (1974).

Leggett, C. L. (1978). Special education and career education: A call for a new partnership. *Education and Training of the Mentally Retarded,* **13**, 430–431.

Lewis, W. W. (1970). Ecological planning for disturbed children. *Childhood Education,* **46**, 306–310.

MacMillan, D. L., & Borthwick, S. (1980). The new EMR population: Can they be mainstreamed? *Mental Retardation,* **18**, 155–158.

MacMillan, D. L., Meyers, E., & Morrison, G. M. (1980). System identification of mildly mentally retarded children: Implications of interpreting and conducting research. *American Journal of Mental Deficiency,* **85**, 108–115.

MacMillan, D. L., & Morrison, G. M. (1979). Educational programming. In H. C. Quay & J. S. Werry (Eds.), *Psychopathological disorders of childhood* (2nd ed., pp. 411–450). New York: Wiley.

MacMillan, D. L., & Semmel, M. I. (1977). Evaluation of mainstreaming programs. *Focus on Exceptional Children,* **9**(4), 1–14.

Mayer, W. V. (1982). Curriculum development: A process and a legacy. *Focus on Exceptional Children,* **14**(6), 1–12.

McDowell, R. L., & Brown, G. B. (1978). The emotionally disturbed adolescent: Development of program alternatives in secondary education. *Focus on Exceptional Children,* **10**, 1–16.

Mercer, C. D., & Mercer, A. R. (1981). *Teaching students with learning problems.* Columbus, OH: Merrill.

Meyen, E. L. (1972). *Developing units of instruction: For the mentally retarded and other children with learning problems.* Dubuque, IA: W. C. Brown.

Meyen, E. L., & Horner, R. D. (1976). Curriculum development. In J. Wortis (Ed.), *Mental retardation and developmental disabilities* (Vol. 3, pp. 258–296). New York: Brunner/Mazel.

Miller, B., & Dyer, J. (1975). Four preschool programs: Their dimensions and effects. *Monographs of the Society for Research in Child Development,* **40**, (5–6, Serial No. 162).

Mori, A. A. (1982). School-based career assessment programs: Where are we now and where are we going? *Exceptional Education Quarterly,* **3**(3), 41–47.

Mori, A. A., & Neisworth, J. T. (1983). Curricula in early childhood education: Some generic and special considerations. *Topics in Early Childhood Special Education,* **2**, 1–8.

Morrison, G. M., Lieber, J., & Morrison, R. L. (1986). A multidimensional view of teacher perceptions of special education episodes. *Remedial and Special Education,* **7**(2), 15–23.

Morrison, G. M., & MacMillan, D. L. (1983). Defining, describing, and explaining the social status of mildly handicapped children: A discussion of methodological problems. In J. M. Berg (Ed.), *Prospectives and progress in mental retardation. Vol. 1. Social, psychological, and educational aspects* (pp. 51–60). Baltimore, MD: University Park Press.

Morrison, G. M., MacMillan, D. L., & Kavale, K. (1985). System identification of learning disabled children: Implications for research sampling. *Learning Disability Quarterly,* **8**, 1–10.

Morse, W. (1965). The crisis teacher. In N. Long, W. Morse, & R. Newman (Eds.), *Conflict in the classroom: The education of emotionally disturbed children* (pp. 251–253). Belmont, CA: Wadsworth.

Muenster, G. E. (1982). The career development process at the elementary level. *Journal of Career Development,* **8**, 238–245.

Muraski, J. A. (1982). Designing career education programs that work. *Academic Therapy,* **18**, 65–71.

National Commission on Excellence in Education. (1983). *A nation at risk.* Washington, DC: U.S. Government Printing Office.

Pennhurst State School and Hospital v. Halderman, 451 U.S. 1 (1981).

Pennsylvania Association for Retarded Children v. Commonwealth of Pennsylvania, 343 F. Supp. 279 (E.D. Pa. 1972).

Polloway, E. A., Payne, J. S., Patton, J. R., & Payne, R. A. (1985). *Strategies for teaching retarded and special needs learners* (3rd ed.). Columbus, OH: Merrill.

Polloway, E. A., & Smith, J. D. (1983). Changes in mild mental retardation: Population, programs, and perspectives. *Exceptional Children,* **50**, 149–159.

Poplin, M. (1979). The science of curriculum development applied to special education and the IEP. *Focus on Exceptional Children,* **12**(3), 1–16.

Poplin, M., & Gray, R. (1980). A conceptual framework for assessment of curriculum and student progress. *Exceptional Education Quarterly,* **1**(3), 75–86 .

Rago, W. V., & Cleland, C. C. (1978). Future directions in the education of the profoundly retarded. *Education and Training of the Mentally Retarded,* **13**, 184–185.

Reith, H. J., Polsgrove, L., & Semmel, M. T. (1981). Instructional variables that make a difference: Attention to task and beyond. *Exceptional Education Quarterly,* **2**(3), 61–72.

Rescorla, L. A., & Zigler, E. (1981). The Yale child welfare program: Implications for social policy. *Educational Evaluation and Policy Analysis,* **3**, 5–14.

Reynolds, M. C. (1985). *Emergence of the cultural imperatives: Biological vs. cultural imperatives.* Manuscript in preparation, University of Minnesota, Minneapolis.

Reynolds, M. C., & Birch, J. W. (1982). *Teaching exceptional children in all America's schools.* Reston, VA: Council for Exceptional Children.

Ross, D. M., & Ross, S. A. (1972). *An intensive training curriculum for the education of young educable mentally retarded children.* (Project No. 142106 and H939106A). Washington, DC: Bureau of Education for the Handicapped.

Rusch, F. R., & Chadsey-Rusch, J. (1985). Employment for persons with severe handicaps: Curriculum development and coordination of services. *Focus on Exceptional Children,* **17**(9), 1–8.

Semmel, M. I., Gottlieb, J., & Robinson, N. (1979). Mainstreaming: Perspectives on educating handicapped children in the public schools. In D. C. Berliner (Ed.), *Review of research in education* (pp. 223–279). Washington, DC: American Educational Research Association.

Shearer, M., & Shearer, D. (1972). The Portage project: A model for early childhood education. *Exceptional Children,* **39**, 210–217.

Simches, G., & Bohn, R. (1963). Issues in curriculum: Research and responsibility. *Mental Retardation,* **1**, 84–87.

Smith, J. D., & Dexter, B. L. (1980). The basics movement: What does it mean for the education of the mentally retarded students? *Education and Training of the Mentally Retarded,* **15**, 72–74.

Sontag, E., Certo, N., & Button, J. E. (1979). On a distinction between the education of the severely and profoundly handicapped and a doctrine of limitations. *Exceptional Children,* **45**, 604–616.

Spivack, G., Platt, J. J., & Shure, M. B. (1976). *The problem-solving approach to adjustment.* San Francisco, CA: Jossey-Bass.

Stallings, J. (1975). Implementation and child effects of teaching practices in Follow Through classrooms. *Monographs of the Society for Research in Child Development,* **40**, 7–8.

Strain, P. S., Cooke, T. P., & Apolloni, T. (1976). *Teaching exceptional children: Assessing and modifying social behavior.* New York: Academic Press.

Strauss, A. A., & Lehtinen, L. E. (1947). *Psychopathology and education of the brain-injured child.* New York: Grune & Stratton.

Tawney, J. W., Knapp, D., O'Reilly, C., & Pratt, S. (1979). *The programmed environment curriculum.* Columbus, OH: Merrill.

Tawney, J. W., & Sniezek, K. M. (1985). Educational programs for severely mentally retarded elementary-age children: Progress, problems, and suggestions. In D. Bricker & J. Filler (Eds.), *Severe mental retardation: From theory to practice* (pp. 76–96). Lancaster, PA: Division on Mental Retardation of the Council for Exceptional Children.

Thorsell, M. (1961). Organizing experience units for the educable mentally retarded. *Exceptional Children,* **27**, 177–185.

Turnbull, H. R. (1982). Youngberg v. Romeo: An essay. *The Association for the Severely Handicapped Journal,* **8**, 3–6.

Voeltz, L. M., Evans, I. M., Freedland, K., & Donellon, S. (1982). Teacher decision making in the selection of educational programming priorities for severely handicapped children. *Journal of Special Education,* **16**, 179–198.

Weikart, D. P. (1981). Effects of different curricula in early childhood intervention. *Educational Evaluation and Policy Analysis,* **3**, 25–35.

Weikart, D. P., Epstein, A. S., Schweinhart, L., & Bond, J. T. (1978). The Ypsilanti preschool curriculum demonstration project. *Monographs of the High/Scope Foundation* (No. 4).

Wessel, J. A. (1975). *Project I Can: Individualized curriculum design for mentally retarded.* East Lansing: Michigan State University, Department of Health, Physical Education and Recreation.

White, K. R. (1982). Defining and prioritizing the personal and social competencies needed by hearing-impaired students. *The Volta Review,* **84**, 266–274.

Wilcox, B., & Bellamy, G. (1980). *Design of high school programs for severely handicapped students.* Baltimore, MD: Paul Brookes.

Will, M. C. (1984). Let us pause and reflect—but not too long. *Exceptional Children,* **51**, 11–16.

Willoughby-Herb, S. J. (1983). Selecting relevant curricular objectives. *Topics in Early Childhood Special Education,* **2**(4), 9–14.

Wood, M. M., & Hurley, O. L. (1977). Curriculum and instruction. In J. B. Jordan, A. H. Hayden, M. B. Karnes, & M. M. Wood (Eds.), *Early childhood education for exceptional children: A handbook of ideas and exemplary practices* (pp. 132–157). Reston, VA: Council for Exceptional Children.

Wyatt v. Stickney, 325 F. Supp. 781 (M.D. Ala. 1972).

Wylie, R. C. (1974). *The self-concept: A review of methodological considerations and measuring instruments.* Lincoln NE: University of Nebraska Press.

Yoshida, R. K., Fenton, K. S., Maxwell, J. P., & Kaufman, M. J. (1978). Group decision making in the planning team process: Myth or reality? *Journal of School Psychology,* **16**, 237–244.

Youngberg v. Romeo, 102 S.Ct. 2452 (1982).

Ysseldyke, J. E., & Algozzine, B. (1982). *Critical issues in special and remedial education.* Boston MA: Houghton Mifflin.

Zigler, E., & Trickett, P. K. (1978). IQ, social competence, and evaluation of early childhood intervention programs. *American Psychologist,* **33**, 789–798.

Diagnostic-Prescriptive Teaching

RONALD P. COLARUSSO
Georgia State University

Abstract—Diagnostic-prescriptive teaching has been the center of controversy in special education. The process training model, a widely used model of diagnostic-prescriptive teaching in special education programs, assumes that psychological processes such as perceptual and psycholinguistic abilities underlie academic learning. Examination of the cumulative research in the area of process training leads to the conclusion that training has been ineffective. Although it has been established that the majority of assessment devices and teaching materials are ineffective and should not be employed in the planning and implementation of special education programs, it cannot be concluded that research in the process area should be completely disregarded or discontinued. Programs and materials developed for process training do not meet minimal standards of adequacy, and, in general, the quality of research on process training has been poor. However, research has supported the existence of the process constructs on which the process training model is based.

The term diagnostic-prescriptive teaching has been the center of controversy and discussion during the 1970s and 1980s within the field of special education. The controversy focuses not on diagnostic-prescriptive teaching as it is used in a broad sense by many educators to describe intervention models but on the narrow definition often used by special educators to describe the process training model.

In general education, the term diagnostic-prescriptive teaching is used to describe intervention models emphasizing assessment of learning behaviors and prescription of instructional strategies based on the assessment. For example, Peter (1965), in his diagnostic-prescriptive teaching model, specified that, in translating diagnostic data into teaching techniques, individual problems, situational factors, and school environment variables must be considered. Numerous and varied diagnostic-prescriptive teaching models of this nature can be found in most general and regular education methods textbooks.

In special education, the term diagnostic-prescriptive teaching is indicative of a more specific model that developed out of the medical model. This model developed out of the need for intervention methods that would be effective with children experiencing problems in learning through traditional teaching and remedial strategies. The special educator's role in the teaching process is to first diagnose the learning problem and its underlying cause(s) and then prescribe appropriate intervention teaching techniques to correct the underlying problem. This model gained prominence in special education beginning in 1963, when Kirk suggested the educational term learning disabilities in place of etiological terms such as minimal brain dysfunction, dyslexia, and perceptual handicaps. Leaders in the field of learning disability at that time emphasized the assessment and training of underlying psychological processes of academic abilities such as perceptual-motor and psycholinguistic training (Frostig, 1963; Johnson & Myklebust, 1967; Kirk, 1963). The process training model, which concentrates on the diagnosis of disabilities that impede academic learning, assumes that psychological processes such as perceptual and psycholinguistic abilities underlie academic learning. Therefore, intervention strategies are focused on the assessment and intervention of the underlying processes.

During the 1970s, a number of researchers began to question the value of process training as an effective intervention strategy. Numerous research studies were found in the literature addressing the effectiveness of process training while sometimes calling it diagnostic-prescriptive teaching. Therefore, the term diagnostic-prescriptive became synonymous in usage with the term process training.

Within special education, there remains much controversy about the effectiveness of the process training model. Until there is some closure as to the effectiveness and appropriateness of this model, the field of special education will continue to function as a contentious and directionless field, its legitimacy open to question. This chapter attempts to objectively synthesize the research that addresses the issues surrounding diagnostic-prescriptive teaching.

Integration of the Research

The research reviewed in this chapter was identified through an Educational Resources Information Center literature search as well as an individual search of current periodicals. After a thorough review of the literature, it became evident that the vast majority of research studies performed in the area of process training was completed during the 1970s. Attention in this chapter is focused on the findings of previous literature reviews rather than individual studies. Some of the more comprehensive literature reviews on the topic of process training that are used in this chapter are those conducted by Arter and Jenkins (1979); Goodman and Hammill (1973); Hammill (1972); Hammill and Larsen (1974a, 1974b); Kavale (1981a, 1981b, 1982a, 1982); Kavale and Mattson (1983); Keogh (1974); and Larsen and Hammill (1975).

The psychological ability areas most frequently associated with the process training model are visual perception, auditory perception, and psycholinguistics. It is assumed that failure to develop appropriate abilities in these areas will lead to failure in academic subject areas such as reading. This model has been discussed in the literature under several names (e.g., the diagnostic-remedial model, the diagnostic-prescriptive model, prescriptive teaching, ability training). In this chapter, the term process training model is used.

Ysseldyke and Salvia (1974) identified the steps in the diagnostic-prescriptive process that include diagnostic delineation of learner strengths and weaknesses and prescriptive intervention in light of these strengths. In specifying critical assumptions for effective diagnostic-prescriptive teaching, they clearly addressed the process training model. The assumptions are that (a) children enter a teaching situation with strengths and weaknesses; (b) these strengths and weaknesses are causally related to the acquisition of academic skills; (c) these strengths and weaknesses can be reliably and validly assessed; and (d) there are well-identified links between children's strengths and weaknesses and the relative effectiveness of instruction.

Researchers have questioned the existence of some of the psychological constructs included in the process training model and they believe that support of this model is dependent on the reliability and validity of the instruments that purport to measure its underlying constructs. Support also relies on a demonstration that deficits can be remediated or academic performance can be improved through training ability strengths (Arter & Jenkins, 1979). Discussion of this topic is organized in this chapter to address the following main questions.

1. How should the psychological, or process, constructs of the process model be defined?
2. Can these process constructs be assessed?
3. Can deficits in the process areas be remediated or trained?

Definition of the Process Constructs

The problem with drawing conclusions about the existence of the process constructs begins with their definition. The problem is exemplified by the confusion surrounding the definition of visual perception. Volumes have been written on the definition of perception. In reviewing the literature, Colarusso (1971) found that the definition of perception ranged anywhere from sensation to cognition and, in some cases, included an affective component. Colarusso (1971) also found motor involvement to be a confusing variable in visual perception studies. As exemplified by problems related to the coexistence of various definitions of perception in research purporting to study this area, it is difficult and/or doubtful validity to compare or classify the research and draw unitary conclusions from it. Still, in the face of contending approaches to effectively educating students with learning problems, the issue c hardly be dropped on a technicality.

Assessment of the Process Constructs

In a model that focuses on the diagnosis of abilities in given construct with the intent of prescribing appropria intervention based on assessment, an appropriate prescri tion is possible only if the diagnosis is correct. Therefor the reliability and validity of the assessment device employed to diagnose a particular construct are critica The reliability of a test refers to the consistency of score obtained from one administration to another. The validit of a test refers to the extent to which a test measures what i is intended to measure. The following discussion addresse reliability and validity separately, but it is important t remember that they are interrelated. Validity indicate whether a test is measuring the construct it is intended t measure; reliability provides a degree of consistency tha limits validity (Gronlund, 1976).

Although there are numerous tests in the process area the more frequently researched tests are the Bender Gestalt (Bender, 1938); the Developmental Test of Visua Motor Integration (Beery & Buktenica, 1967); the Illinois Test of Psycholinguistic Abilities (ITPA) (Kirk, McCarthy, & Kirk, 1968); the Marianne Frostig Developmental Test of Visual Perception (DTVP) (Frostig, Maslow, Lefever, & Whittlesey, 1964); and the Purdue Perceptual Motor Survey (Roach & Kephart, 1966).

Reliability of Assessment Devices

To determine whether a test score can be considered accurate, authorities in psychological testing have tried to establish standards of reliability, but they have disagreed on what levels are acceptable. In their comprehensive literature reviews on instruments that assess processes, investigators have assigned different cutoff reliability scores (e.g., Arter & Jenkins, 1979, 0.85; Hammill & Wiederholt, 1973, 0.80). For psychological testing, Anastasi (1968) suggested a minimum reliability coefficient of 0.80 as acceptable for assessment purposes. However, Salvia and Ysseldyke (1981) made the argument for a higher minimum reliability quotient of 0.90 when making individual decisions. Arguments concerning the choice of an appropriate reliability are similar to arguments concerning the choice of a cutoff score for inclusion in a program for handicapping conditions (e.g., to be included in a mental retardation program, a student must have an IQ lower than 70). Rather than establishing a minimum reliability for all purposes, perhaps a realistic approach would be to demand relatively higher reliabilities as fewer sources of data for decision making are used and relatively more serious decisions are being made.

Comprehensive reviews addressing the reliability of process tests have been completed by Arter and Jenkins (1979); Colarusso (1971); Colarusso and Gill (1975); Hammill and Wiederholt (1973); Sedlack and Weener

1973); Waugh (1975); and Ysseldyke (1973). There are several types of reliability that are more related than other types to interconsistency and test construction (i.e., split-half, Kuder-Richardson, and Hoyt's) (Anastasi, 1968). Reliability research is usually focused on test–retest, which addresses temporal consistency, and interscorer, which addresses consistency between scorers.

In reviews of the ITPA, Sedlack and Weener (1973), Waugh (1975), and Ysseldyke (1973) reported test–retest reliability for the total test score ranging from 0.66 to 0.95. Subtest reliabilities were consistently low, with Auditory Association the highest (0.62 to 0.90).

The DTVP demonstrated test–retest reliability similar to the ITPA. Total test score reliability ranged from 0.69 to 0.98, with the highest subtest reliability of 0.67 to 0.80 for Form Constancy (Colarusso & Gill, 1975; Hammill & Wiederholt, 1973; Ysseldyke, 1973).

Validity of Assessment Devices

Validity is the extent to which a test measures what it is supposed to measure. The issue of validity is much more complicated than that of reliability because validity is dependent upon reliability as well as variables outside the actual test, such as achievement and performance in other areas. The American Psychological Association (1966) identified three types of validity: content, criterion-related, and construct.

Content validity. This type of validity determines whether a test includes a representative sample of items in the behavior domain being measured. It is more appropriate for achievement tests and has limited value in aptitude and personality testing, where it may even be misleading. Although relevance of content must be considered in the test construction, establishment of validity should be directed to criterion-related and construct validity (Anastasi, 1968).

Criterion-related validity. This type of validity indicates the effectiveness of a test in predicting behavior in a specific situation. There are two types of criterion-related validity: concurrent and predictive. Concurrent criterion-related validity focuses on the current status of the individual, while predictive criterion-related validity is concerned with future outcomes. In determining criterion-related validity for processing tests, both concurrent and predictive criterion-related validity should be evaluated. In the following paragraphs, a discussion of research on these types of criterion-related validity is presented.

Concurrent criterion-related validity establishes whether a construct currently predicts academic abilities. Several reviews of criterion-related validity appear in the literature and focus mainly on the ITPA and the DTVP. Other tests of visual perception and auditory perception have also been the focus of some research.

Comprehensive literature reviews have been conducted to determine the concurrent relationship between the ITPA and academic abilities (Arter & Jenkins, 1979, Haring & Bateman, 1977; Larsen & Hammill, 1975; Newcomer & Hammill, 1976; Proger, Cross, & Burger, 1973; Sedlack & Weener, 1973). Analyzing the results of the various studies and the individual correlational results comparing the ITPA and its subtests with scores from various achievement tests shows that the Total Test Score, Grammatic Closure, Auditory Association, and Sound Blending were consistent in correlating significantly with at least one area of achievement across studies. Newcomer and Hammill (1976) concluded that, when the intelligence variable is controlled for, only Grammatic Closure maintains an acceptable correlation above 0.35. These researchers question the use of this subtest because of possible racial and social class bias.

There are also comprehensive literature reviews on the concurrent criterion-related validity of visual perception tests when related to measures of achievement (Arter & Jenkins, 1979; Hammill, 1972; Hammill & Wiederholt, 1973; Larsen & Hammill, 1975; Silverston & Deichmann, 1975; Ysseldyke, 1973). The cumulative summary of research does not support visual perception tests as concurrent predictors of academics. Hammill and Wiederholt (1973) contended that the DTVP correlates significantly with reading achievement at the first- and second-grade levels but not at the third-grade level. Although the results of the Larsen and Hammill review (1975) indicate significant relationships between the DTVP and arithmetic, IQ was not controlled for in the studies reviewed.

Although there are not as many studies reported that compare auditory perception with achievement, overall, the results have been nonsupportive (Arter & Jenkins, 1979; Hammill, 1972; Hammill & Larsen, 1974b; Haring & Bateman, 1977; Sabatino, 1973; Silverston & Deichmann, 1975). As in the area of visual perception, a few studies were found that showed significant relationships between auditory perception abilities and achievement. In summary, Arter and Jenkins (1979) stated, "Lack of evidence for concurrent validity is particularly striking within those studies that control for IQ" (p. 529). Kavale (1981b) performed meta-analysis on the findings of 106 studies and concluded that auditory perception is an important correlate of reading ability.

Concurrent criterion-related validity is also assessed by comparing on a construct (e.g., perception) two groups that differ on a criterion (e.g., achievement). Most of the studies found in the literature compared the performance of groups who were contrasted by reading achievement on a process variable. Four reviews (Arter & Jenkins, 1979; Newcomer & Hammill, 1975; Proger et al., 1973; Sedlack & Weener, 1973) summarized twenty-seven studies that compared good and poor readers on the ITPA. The Grammatic Closure and Sound Blending subtests correlated significantly in more than half the correlations performed. However, when IQ was controlled, no subtest differentiated more than 33% of the time (Arter & Jenkins, 1979).

Seven reviews addressed visual perception (Arter & Jenkins, 1979; Hammill, 1972; Hammill & Larsen,

1974b; Larsen & Hammill, 1975; Sabatino, 1973; Silverston & Deichmann, 1975; Ysseldyke, 1973). About half of the studies (51%) reported significant results in the ability of various tests to discriminate between good and poor readers. Arter and Jenkins (1979) noted that this figure dropped to 32% when IQ was taken into consideration.

The ability of auditory perception tests to distinguish between good and poor readers is more impressive. After reviewing the work of Hammill (1972), Hammill and Larsen (1974b), and Sabatino (1973), Arter and Jenkins (1979) reviewed fifteen primary sources and found that, in the majority of cases (88%), significant differences were found between good and poor readers. In addition, in all studies in which auditory-visual integration was assessed, significant differences were found between reading groups (Arter & Jenkins, 1979). The results of these studies indicate that some auditory tests, auditory-visual tests and subtests, and some auditory-type subtests of the ITPA (Grammatic Closure and Sound Blending) do discriminate between good and poor readers.

Fewer studies involving the second type of criterion-related validity, predictive criterion-related validity, were performed on the process tests. This is probably due to the time factor (i.e., time required between original testing and later follow-up testing). Most of the studies examined psycholinguistic abilities as measured by the ITPA and perceptual abilities as measured by various visual and auditory perception tests. Again, studies focused on the ability of the tests to predict academic achievement. Seven major reviews (Arter & Jenkins, 1979; Barrett, 1965; Hammill & Larsen, 1974b; Larsen & Hammill, 1975; Newcomer & Hammill, 1976; Sedlack & Weener, 1973; Silverston & Deichmann, 1975) examined a total of twenty-nine studies that had intervals of up to 3 years between ability and achievement testing. The results of these comprehensive reviews are at best ambiguous, with different studies reporting conflicting findings. However, the ITPA Total Test Score did appear to be a useful predictor of later academic achievement, and the Auditory Association subtest predicted reading ability. Clear-cut conclusions could not be made in some cases because so few studies were reported, and, in other instances, no studies were available for some instruments.

Construct validity. Finally, construct validity is the extent to which a test measures a theoretical construct such as perception. It may be determined by (a) comparing a test with other tests of the same construct to determine a relationship, (b) comparing the performance of contrasted groups on the test, and (c) doing a factor analysis. Each of these steps is appropriate and necessary to determine the construct validity of tests in the process area.

Most of the construct validity studies found were factor analytic and were performed on the ITPA and the DTVP. Factor analytic support is especially important in tests that have subtests. If a test has a number of subtests, a factor analysis should support the existence of the separate constructs that each subtest is purported to measure.

In their literature reviews of factor analytic studies of the ITPA, Proger et al. (1973) and Sedlack and Weener (1973) concluded that the factors necessary to support the ITPA and its twelve subtests were not found. However, a later study by Newcomer, Hare, Hammill, and McGettigan (1974) and a review by Waugh (1975) supported the constructs of the ITPA. It should be noted, however, that none of the studies showed a high degree of matching between the ITPA subtests and the factors found.

In reviewing factor analytic studies performed on the DTVP, Hammill & Wiederholt (1973) found no support for the five separate subtests. Only two of the nine studies reviewed reported two separate factors, while the remaining studies found only one general perceptual-motor factor. Later, more sophisticated studies were more supportive.

Summary

In summarizing the results of many studies, it is apparent that the reliability of most tests in this area is very limited. Although a few tests do demonstrate acceptable reliability, the more popular tests mentioned above do not have acceptable reliability. Subtests in general were not found to be reliable.

In summarizing validity research findings, the majority of the research is nonsupportive of the concurrent criterion-related validity of process tests as predictors of academic achievement. However, in all areas, some studies were found that support the validity of the various process tests. Devices that assessed auditory perception abilities and auditory–visual integration were found to consistently discriminate between good and poor readers, except when controls for intelligence were introduced. Predictive criterion-related validity studies have conflicting results and are at best inconclusive. The majority of results are nonsupportive.

Construct validity studies focused on the subtest constructs of the DTVP and ITPA. Results of these studies were unanimously nonsupportive of the DTVP. There are conflicting findings for the ITPA. However, the most recent factor analysis studies *did* support the constructs of the ITPA.

Although there is some evidence to support the validity of some assessment devices in the process area, the conclusion is that tests in this area do not demonstrate acceptable validity. Although some support has been found for the construct validity of these tests, support is lacking for predictive criterion-related validity. In addition, the low reliability of most of the tests adds to the lack of validity support in this area.

Remediation and Intervention in the Process Domain

The basic premise behind the diagnostic-prescriptive teaching model is that deficits in perceptual, perceptual-motor, or psycholinguistic abilities will produce negative effects on the ability to perform academic tasks. The objece of process training programs is to develop skills and/or nediate specific weaknesses in a process area. This is ne with the intent of enhancing skills necessary to perm academic tasks such as reading, writing, and mathatics. Some of the better known training programs in process area are the Frostig Program for the Development of Visual Perception (Frostig & Horne, 1964); the DAL Program: Language Development (Karnes, 1972); MWM Program for Developing Language Abilities Minskoff, Wiseman, & Minskoff, 1972); Patterning oman, Delacato, & Doman, 1964); the Physiology of adiness: An Action Program for the Development of rception for Children (Getman & Kane, 1964); and the ow Learner in the Classroom (Kephart, 1960).

RCEPTUAL-MOTOR TRAINING

Numerous research reviews have been compiled to termine the effectiveness of perceptual-motor training ograms and general intervention techniques (Arter & nkins, 1979; Goodman & Hammill, 1973; Hallahan & uickshank, 1973; Hammill, 1972; Hammill, Goodman, Wiederholt, 1974; Haring & Bateman, 1977; Kavale, 82a; Kavale & Mattson, 1983; Keogh, 1974; Kleisius, 72; Krippner, 1973; Larsen & Hammill, 1975; Proger et ., 1973; Robinson, 1972; Sabatino, 1973; Sedlack & eener, 1973; Ysseldyke, 1973). Although all of the views examined perceptual-motor training, they differ om each other because they examined different areas of rceptual-motor training and classified studies by differt criteria. Some review articles evaluated each study to termine whether each was acceptable or unacceptable in sign (Hallahan & Cruickshank, 1973; Hammill, Goodan, & Wiederholt, 1974). Early reviewers tallied results individual studies, while Kavale and Mattson (1983) ed meta-analysis to analyze the same basic set of studies.

Regardless of the procedure employed in analyzing the search studies, the findings of the reviews were generally e same: (a) there is little or no support for the premise at perceptual-motor training improves perceptual bility, and (b) there is little or no support for the premise at perceptual-motor training has a positive transfer fect on academic achievement. The conclusions are summarized in the two most comprehensive reviews, which mployed different statistical strategies (Arter & Jenkins, 979; Kavale & Mattson, 1983).

Arter and Jenkins (1979) compared the results of inety-two studies that were rated as poor or good, and hey found that 88% of the forty-one poor studies were suportive of the intervention technique, whereas only 24% of he fifty-one studies rated good supported intervention. In ummarizing reviews by specific training programs, the ame nonsupportive results were found. The only program hat had support in more than half of the studies (55%) was he Frostig Program for the Development of Visual Perception. However, when only studies that were rated good were considered, support dropped to 12.5%.

Kavale and Mattson (1983) used a statistical procedure, meta-analysis, as a means to statistically combine the results of several independent research studies. Using this technique, which gives equal weight to all included studies, regardless of the quality of their design, they statistically analyzed 180 studies on perceptual-motor training and concluded that perceptual-motor training is ineffective.

The combination of the information in these two exhaustive studies leads to the conclusion that intervention and training in the area of perception have been unsuccessful in improving perceptual-motor abilities or in improving academics.

PSYCHOLINGUISTIC TRAINING

Psycholinguistic training has received as much or more attention as has perceptual-motor training in educational practice, but it has not had as voluminous a number of research studies performed to determine its effectiveness. The major literature reviews have been performed by Hammill and Larsen (1974a) and Kavale (1982b). These reviewers came to different conclusions. In the earlier study, Hammill and Larsen (1974a) reviewed thirty-nine research studies and grouped them by three criteria: type of subjects, type of approach, and type of intervention. By determining the percentage of studies that found psycholinguistic training to be successful, they concluded that the effectiveness of such training is not supported.

The conclusions drawn by Hammill and Larsen (1974a) led to a response by Minskoff (1975), who expressed concern that their analyses compared studies that were different and/or inadequate. In her criticism, Minskoff (1975) specified guidelines for research on psycholinguistic training in three areas: nature of subjects, nature of treatment, and experimental design. In response to Minskoff, Newcomer, Larsen, and Hammill (1975) argued that, if the error sources in the studies reviewed were corrected, the results would be even less supportive of psycholinguistic training.

Lund, Foster, and McCall-Perez (1978) reanalyzed twenty-four of the thirty-nine studies reviewed by Hammill and Larsen (1974a), and, after finding both supportive and nonsupportive studies, stated that no clear-cut conclusion could be drawn for nonsupport of psycholinguistic training. Hammill and Larsen (1978) reinterpreted this conclusion as an indication that "the overwhelming consensus of research evidence concerning the effectiveness of psycholinguistic training is that it remains essentially nonvalidated" (p. 412).

Kavale (1982b) employed meta-analysis to statistically analyze thirty-four studies that used the ITPA as the dependent variable. The results of the meta-analysis are supportive of psycholinguistic training. In summarizing the results, Kavale (1982b) concluded the following.

> Although some subtests and constructs appear more amenable to intervention, all areas of psycholinguistic functioning were enhanced by various training programs. Most encouraging were the receptiveness to

> intervention of the Expressive constructs, particularly Verbal Expression, and the Representational Level subtests since they embody the "language" aspects of the ITPA and, ultimately, produce language behavior. (p. 507)

Kavale's conclusions (1982b), which were supportive of psycholinguistic training, led to a response by Larsen, Parker, and Hammill (1982), who performed a meta-analysis on their data and concluded that psycholinguistic training remains nonvalidated. Sternberg and Taylor (1982) also questioned the findings of Kavale and, in cautioning the practitioner, stated, "While these findings can shed light on general trends, they do not necessarily have applicability to the classroom or other settings" (p. 256).

Modality Matching

Modality matching, the process of identifying a child's strong and weak modalities and then planning academic instruction through the strong modality, has been advocated as a method of process training (Johnson & Myklebust, 1967). For example, if a child were diagnosed as an auditory learner, reading instruction would be provided through an approach that emphasizes auditory skills. Arter and Jenkins (1977) identified fifteen studies in the research literature that addressed this topic. Reading instruction was provided to correspond with each child's preference of modality in auditory, visual, or kinesthetic approaches. In all but one study, the results were not supportive of such an approach in the teaching of reading.

Summary

Present research is nonsupportive of the intervention strategies employed to train the perceptual area. Using meta-analysis and factor analysis to analyze the results of 161 studies, Kavale (198lb, 1982a) determined that visual perception is an important correlate related to reading achievement. Employing the same technique, he found auditory perception to be an important correlate of reading. However, it should be pointed out that significant relationships between perception and reading do not provide support for the training programs in perception that presently exist. There is no clear evidence of a causal relation or transfer effects. Also note that, although other reviewers found the majority of the studies they reviewed to be nonsupportive, each reviewer found some studies that were supportive of intervention in the perceptual-motor training area. The current literature also does not support the teaching of academics by modality matching (Arter & Jenkins, 1977). In addition, the value of training the psycholinguistic abilities and the relationship of this training to academics still shows conflicting conclusions.

State of the Practice

After more than a decade of synthetic research debate, the diagnostic-prescriptive teaching model is advocated by some special educators. The survivabilit the model stems, at least in part, from the use of this te to mean different things. The term diagnostic-prescript teaching is frequently used in the literature, especiall textbooks, to describe a variety of teaching strategies, c cepts, and philosophies (Cartwright & Cartwright, 19 Cartwright, Cartwright, & Ysseldyke, 1973; Lern 1981; Peter, 1965).

To some extent, a diagnostic-prescriptive teachi model is endemic to special education because of the re lations and requirements that govern the procedures identification, assessment, and program planning exceptional children. An Individualized Educational P gram (IEP) is required for every child identified as exc tional who is receiving a special education. A diagnost prescriptive teaching model is required to the extent th in most states, students must be diagnosed into a categ of exceptionality and prescribed a special education p gram. Therefore, it is assumed that intervention in spec education takes some form of a diagnostic-prescripti approach. In fact, to many, the term is almost synonymo with special education itself.

On the other hand, process training is a special subset the wide range of diagnostic-prescriptive activities that a implemented in special education. However, despite a de ade of criticism and nonsupportive research findings, t process training model is still a major component of spec education. This seems evident in contemporary textboo in special education (especially in the learning disabili area) that include the different components of this mod as an intervention strategy (Kirk & Gallagher, 197 Lerner, 1981). The endurance of the process traini model is also evident in surveys of professionals.

In a survey of special education teachers in Illinois du ing 1977, Arter and Jenkins (1979) found that:

> . . . 82% of special education teachers believed th they could, and should, train weak abilities, 99 thought that a child's modality strengths and weak nesses should be a major consideration when devisin educational prescriptions, and 93% believed that the students had learned more when they modifie instruction to match modality strengths. (pp 549–550)

In a more recent survey, Noel, Valdivieso, and Full (1985) conducted personal interviews with sixty-eig special education faculty from twenty-five colleges an universities in five states. One hundred percent of thos interviewed believed that federal policy and legislatio have perpetuated the child deficit model. When asked the orientation of their training program favored a chil deficit or a social environment orientation, one-thir strongly supported a child deficit model that include assessing weaknesses and strengths and then plannin

.ining. One-third felt that the child deficit model per-des in theory and training but that they need to look at ıer models. The remaining one-third were noncommit-. The results of this survey indicate that some broad ·m of the diagnostic-prescriptive teaching model is still ing supported and/or used to train special education ıchers today. Even those opposed to the child deficit odel felt that the evidence against the process training odel is not strong enough to completely eliminate its con-leration for use in special education.

Although the Illinois survey (conducted by Arter and nkins almost a decade ago) suggests wide acceptance of e process perspective among special educators, the task ıalytic model has been increasingly used in special edu-tion in recent years. This is evident from reviewing ethods texts in special education that include strategies r skill and task analysis. The task analytic viewpoint fers a different approach to diagnostic-prescriptive aching. The premise behind the task analytic approach is at mastery of a general skill (e.g., division) derives from astery of component subskills and that intervention to neliorate academic difficulties should be focused on the bskills(s) impending progress rather than on the pre-mption that the difficulties derive from deficiencies that ust be reduced before mastery of an academic task can be tained (Bijou, 1970; Cohen, 1969; Mann, 1971).

Researchers have demonstrated that a "hierarchy of arning skills/task analytic approach" can be used suc-ssfully to enhance student progress (Resnick, 1973; esnick, Wang, & Kaplan, 1973; Wang, 1973; Wang, esnick, & Boozer, 1971). However, Prescott (1971) cau-oned against too literal an acceptance of the hierarchy oncept, questioning that a sequence of skills in mastering task will be found to be discrete and definite. He used ading as an example for the argument that there is no stablished hierarchy of skills. Furthermore, the studies at demonstrated the usefulness of hierarchical ordering f skills in teaching (Resnick, 1973; Wang, 1973; Wang et l., 1971; White, 1973) did not address the effectiveness of is model in special education settings.

In addressing the diagnostic-prescriptive teaching odel, Smead (1977) argued that neither the process raining model nor the task analytical model is complete. he felt that a combination of the two models is needed hen identification of abilities within the learner is natched to the teacher, setting, and task variables.

Although intervention programs that are combinations f process and task analytic approaches have not emerged, ariations on each theme are being used in practice. Semel nd Wiig (1981) have demonstrated the effectiveness of anguage programs that are broadly designed. Although he intervention strategies are not strictly process training nodels, they are developmental in nature and include ctivities to develop prerequisite language skills such as uditory memory.

In other instances, knowledge about attending abilities as been combined with behavioral strategies, such as self-nonitoring, to develop cognitive-behavior modification rocedures. Cognitive-behavior modification is based on the premise that students with learning problems often fail to adequately employ learning strategies such as rehearsal and attention. Campione and Brown (1977) addressed the need to train mentally retarded students in cognitive strategies. Self-monitoring of on-task behavior has been effective in increasing attention to academic tasks with learning disabled children (Hallahan, Lloyd, Kosiewicz, Kauffman, & Graves, 1979; Rooney, Polloway, & Hallahan, 1985). These approaches attend to the information processing skills of individuals without presuming physiologically or psychologically pathological deficiencies that must be corrected.

Similarly, adaptive instruction models assume that, although students learn in different ways and at different rates, these differences can be accommodated in the regular classroom setting. However, instead of attempting to diagnose students' processing skills and prescribing remediation, assessment activities focus on appropriate placement of students in hierarchical curricula with intensified instruction for students exhibiting difficulty. Two programs based on this model are the Adaptive Learning Environments Model (Wang, 1980; Wang & Birch, 1984a, 1984b) and the Bank Street Model (Gilkeson, Smithberg, Bowman, & Rhine, 1981).

These models and the specific programs based on them show great promise for the use of a diagnostic-prescriptive approach. This approach is required by PL 94-142 for meeting the needs of handicapped students without presuming differences in psycholinguistic processing which, as indicated in this chapter, has not been shown to be reliably and validly measured, consistently improved by training, or, if improved, related to improved academic performance of students. However, the majority of research support for these models is theoretical or basic in nature. Empirical data that demonstrate the effectiveness of the alternatives through improvement in academic achievement of exceptional students in programs using these models is still lacking.

Conclusions and Recommendations

Examination of the cumulative research in the area of process training leads to the conclusion that this approach to special education has been, to date, generally ineffective. However, although research has shown that the majority of assessment devices and teaching materials are ineffective, it cannot be concluded with surety that the process area is doomed to failure and should be completely disregarded. Although the existing programs and materials developed in this area have been shown to be of little substantive benefit, the same cannot be concluded about the constructs themselves. It is certainly within the realm of plausible hypothesis that the empirical status of process training derives from the quality of assessment instruments, training activities, or even the nature and quality of research examining it, rather than from the bankruptcy of the entire notion.

There would appear to be strong justification for the

movement away from process training to more direct forms of instruction in applied special education. However, within the author's role of a reviewer of the state of knowledge and art in the process area, it seems important to summarize what can be learned from the research in this area. The remaining portion of this chapter is devoted to a discussion of the research methodology employed in this area and includes recommendations for future process training research. In no way is this discussion intended to justify continued use of process training under the premise that its effectiveness has not been discredited with well-diagnosed research; obviously, although it occurs too rarely, the justification for an alternative therapeutic approach (in this case, as an alternative to regular school curricula and direct instruction) should be demonstrated before introduction into applied settings.

Assessing Process Abilities

The results of numerous research studies indicate that the reliability of most process ability tests is unacceptable. When considering the reliability of total test scores, support can be found for some of the tests because they approach conventionally accepted reliability quotients. Perhaps more important to the process training approach is the fact that reliability for almost all subtests is below conventionally accepted standards.

Poor subtest reliability may be a function of the test construction rather than a function of the construct to be measured. The small number of items included in subtests most likely contributes to low reliabilities. Subtests are usually kept short because of the time constraints of the testing situation. Lengthening a test by including more items will generally increase its reliability. If student assessments within specific constructs are to be conducted, longer and more reliable instruments will need to be developed. This, in turn, would require considerably longer and more costly assessments or *a priori* hypotheses about the particular processes in which a student should be examined.

Validity is more complicated than reliability and has reliability as an additional "error factor" since reliability is a necessary condition in establishing validity (Gronlund, 1976). Because a test instrument with low reliability automatically has questionable validity, most, if not all, of the subtests in the process areas are automatically invalidated. The low reliability of subtests may be a contributing factor in the variability of findings among validity studies. The makeup of the samples tested and the accuracy of their scores are significant factors affecting the results of validity testing. For example, Auditory Association, the subtest of the ITPA with the highest reliability, was found to consistently predict reading ability across studies.

Basically, two general types of validity studies were performed on the tests in this area: criterion related and construct. Criterion-related studies, whether concurrent or predictive, in most cases used achievement as the criterion variable. Although most of the research performed to determine the validity of the assessment devices produced results that are nonsupportive, the results are not clear-c Concurrent validity studies tended to be somewhat s portive at younger ages when readiness tests were used the criterion and less supportive at older ages wh achievement tests were used. These findings may be int preted in different ways.

One interpretation is that the items on readiness te are similar in nature to the items on ability tests, especia in the area of visual perception. Therefore, one wo expect significant relationships between perceptual te and readiness tests. Another interpretation relates to t age of the subjects and the development of process abiliti If a process ability is usually developed by a certain a one would expect a ceiling effect on a process ability te that would create low correlations between the process te score and the achievement test score. This also raises t possibility that violations of the required assumptions the computation of Pearson product-moment correlati coefficients exist in the validity studies performed on pr cess ability tests. Two important assumptions are that t form of the relationship is linear and uniform througho the range and that homoscedasticity exists throughout t range (Anastasi, 1968). A strong argument can be ma that the relationship between visual perception a achievement is not linear and uniform throughout t range. Achievement may require a minimum level ability in visual perception. Once this minimum is met, fu ther increments in visual perception ability may be unr lated to achievement. Therefore, a rise in visual percepti scores might show a relationship between the two up to point and then level off. This is a strong argument becau there is general acceptance that visual perception is large developed by age 8. A large number of research studies this area include subjects 8 years of age or older. Th developmental leveling might have particular effect on th results of these studies.

The results of validity studies comparing contraste groups indicate that auditory and auditory-visual inte gration measures differentiated between good and poc readers. No support was found for the ITPA or visual per ception tests in their ability to discriminate between goo and poor readers. Most of the studies were performed wit a variety of types of subjects. However, there is an absenc of studies performed with children identified as havin specific process ability deficits. The groups were con trasted by criterion (e.g., reading achievement) rathe than by ability. The study that comes closest to a con trasted group study, in which the subjects were grouped b ability, was conducted by Larsen, Rogers, and Sowel (1976). In this study, learning disabled students were con trasted with normal learners on the ITPA. Even in thi situation, psycholinguistic ability deficits could not b assumed simply because the subjects were labeled as learning disabled. Appropriate contrasted groups would includ an experimental group identified as having a specific process deficit and a control group with no process deficiency as classified by an acceptable authority.

Construct validity also leads to questionable conclusions. There is little or no support for construct validity y the determination of age differentiation, although most st norms show increases in scores with age. In most of the onstruct validity studies, factor analyses were performed n the DTVP and the ITPA. Although no support was ound for the DTVP in measuring five separate factors, the TPA studies have mixed results. Arter and Jenkins 1979) grouped these studies into early and later studies. lthough the earlier studies were nonsupportive, the later tudies showed support for the separate variables of the TPA. The later studies have more weight from a procedural viewpoint because they included other variables imilar to the subtests in their analyses.

Several of the researchers who have questioned the validity of the process ability tests have pointed out that IQ is confounding factor. When IQ is partialed out, support or validity of many process ability tests is decreased Arter & Jenkins, 1979). Kavale (1982a) found that, when Q is partialed out, the relationship between reading and isual perception decreases in magnitude. However, Kavale also found that the relationship between visual perception and reading still exists exclusive of IQ.

Some conclusions can be drawn about the measurement characteristics of process ability tests: (a) there is evidence strongly suggesting that individuals possess conceptually and diagnostically differentiable process abilities; (b) the reliability and validity of current instruments to measure these abilities are inadequate and should not be used for decision making about individual subjects; (c) tests that demonstrate reliability and validity in measuring process abilities are absolutely essential to determining whether further study in the process areas is likely to be productive (e.g., studies of auditory perception and its relationship to reading appear to warrant further attempts to develop valid and reliable tests in this area); and (d) research on process training programs that used unreliable and/or invalid assessment instruments must be considered questionable.

Training Process Abilities

After reviewing the most current, largely nonsupportive literature on the issue of process training, it still cannot be argued that the process training hypothesis is untenable. Clearly, the majority of research studies fail to support process training (Arter & Jenkins, 1979). However, those reviews (Hammill & Larsen, 1974a) in which the majority of the studies contained negative results also included studies that met the criteria of acceptable research and showed positive effects of process training.

The current research literature does not support the teaching of academics by modality matching (Arter & Jenkins, 1977). A limited amount of research was found addressing this concept, but the overwhelming conclusion was that selecting an academic teaching approach based on a student's strength in a process area is not empirically supported.

An abundance of research literature has been generated addressing the trainability of perception and its effect on academics. The overwhelming results are nonsupportive of training in this area (Arter & Jenkins, 1979). However, there is evidence that a relationship exists between reading and both visual and auditory perception (Kavale, 1981b, 1982a).

The question of training the psycholinguistic abilities and their relationship to academics still shows conflicting conclusions. Hammill and Larsen (1974a) tallied the results of the studies they reviewed and drew nonsupportive conclusions based on the results of the majority of the studies. Kavale (1981a) generated his results in the form of correlations and drew supportive conclusions based on the significance of the relationships generated. If one chooses to draw conclusions by majority, Hammill and Larsen's conclusions would be supported. However, although in most of their analyses, the majority of results were nonsupportive, there were areas where support was found (e.g., the prescriptive approaches in visual association, verbal expression, and manual expression). For all psycholinguistic areas, some studies demonstrate positive results.

The relationship found between auditory perception and reading (Arter & Jenkins, 1979; Kavale, 1981b) should not be ignored. Because this relationship has been determined, researchers might want to explore whether training in auditory perception might improve reading for children with auditory perceptual deficits. Semel and Wiig (1981) demonstrated some positive effects from auditory process training. However, a major shortcoming of process training research in this and other areas is the absence of controlled research showing longitudinal academic attainment by students in process training programs and students in alternative educational programs (e.g., direct instruction).

The lack of soundness of the methodological procedures employed in research studies on process training has been noted frequently (Hallahan & Cruickshank, 1973; Minskoff, 1975). Hallahan and Cruickshank (1973) argued that so many studies in perception are unsound in their methodological procedures and include faulty reporting that no conclusions can be drawn regarding the efficacy of perceptual-motor training. Kavale and Mattson (1983) took exception with Hallahan and Cruickshank and stated, "By statistically integrating the perceptual-motor training literature, it was possible to uncover information not tapped in previous reviews, which led to reliable and reproducible conclusions suggesting that perceptual-motor is not an effective intervention for learning disabled children" (p. 172).

However, two arguments made by Hallahan and Cruickshank (1973)—length of intervention time and selection of subjects—cannot be dismissed by choice of statistical procedure. The average intervention time for the studies they reviewed was 31 hours, which they believed to be insufficient for the adequate assessment of the merits of an intervention approach. They also criticized the population selection of many studies in which the subjects varied in classifications from mentally retarded to normal. They suggested that studies need to use children who exhibit significant perceptual-motor deficits. Minskoff (1975) made similar critical comments about the research performed on psycholinguistic training.

In addition to these limitations, the ages of the subjects have received too little attention, especially when the subjects have not been identified as having deficits in the process area. The method of intervention should also be considered. For example, if the intent of process training is to be diagnostic-prescriptive in nature, the intervention method used in a study should be individualized according to the need of the individual subjects (Wang, 1980).

Although many arguments can be made relating to research methodology, one aspect of research that is easy to evaluate is the number of subjects in the sample. When employing inferential statistics, at least thirty subjects per group should be included in order to use large sample statistics (Ary, Jacobs, & Razavieh, 1985).

These criteria can be applied to studies of psycholinguistic training. The studies reviewed by Hammill and Larsen (1974a) are evaluated here because they consider similar criteria. Most of these studies were also included in Kavale's (1981a) review.

Hammill and Larsen (1974a) presented the characteristics of thirty-nine psycholinguistic training studies, taking into consideration the limitations of number of subjects, type of subjects, age of subjects, approach used, and training time. In reviewing the Hammill and Larsen findings, it becomes evident that the studies examined do not meet criteria specified to qualify as being based on acceptable research methodologies. At least eighteen of the thirty-nine studies had inadequate sample sizes to perform inferential statistics. Not one study identified its subjects specifically as having language deficits or psycholinguistic disabilities. In addition, twenty of the thirty-nine studies used disadvantaged samples and, therefore, they do not necessarily represent exceptional subjects or subjects who already are in need of specific individualized instruction. Only eight of the studies employed diagnostic-prescriptive or individualized techniques. In about half of the studies, data was collected over a period of more than 50 hours. It should also be pointed out that sixteen of the thirty-nine studies used the Peabody Language Development Kits (Dunn & Smith, 1966), which provide a general language development program, not specific process training. Not one of the thirty-nine studies satisfied all of the criteria for number, approach, age, and length of training. A concluding statement drawn from the results of the studies reviewed might be: taking a nonindividualized approach to training language for a short intervention period, overall improvement of psycholinguistic functioning, as measured by unreliable instruments of questionable validity, was not found for disadvantaged or retarded subjects.

Due to the inadequacies of past research, even those who have taken strong positions against the use of process training in school programs have left the door open for further research. For example, Hammill and Larsen (1974a) made the following statement.

> Whether some of the subtests are unresponsive to instructional efforts because they are basically impossible or extremely difficult to teach, because th[e] training programs do not provide sufficient attentio[n] to them, or because the ITPA subtests are not appro[-]priate measures of these constructs, we cannot say. This is a matter for future research to clarify. (p. 12)

Ysseldyke and Salvia (1974), while arguing that ther[e] are clearly better present choices for current special education interventions, did not categorically deny the potential of process training when they stated the following.

> Some time in the future educators may be able t[o] demonstrate reliable and valid identification of processes or abilities which underlie academic skill development and demonstrate empirical links betwee[n] these processes or abilities and particular instructional strategies. To arrive at this point will requir[e] extensive experimentation. To engage in experimentation is science; to bypass experimentation and t[o] implement unvalidated ability training programs i[n] educational settings is both unscientific and premature. (p. 184)

Having focused on evaluating the contemporary research base on the process training approach to special education interventions, which identifies little to support its continued use, this author feels compelled to caution against the tendency to see the discredit of one approach as establishing the credibility of alternative approaches. As Tindal (1985) recently noted, methodological flaws abound in the available research throughout the field of special education. For too long, the popularity of theories has had far more influence than efforts to determine their tenability empirically.

As a field, special education must become much more unwilling to accept assessment devices and teaching programs that have not been field tested and validated before commercialization. And just as important, the field must provide a vehicle for support of researchers in performing the quality of in-depth comprehensive studies necessary to adequately evaluate theories, rather than continuing to rely on the kinds of inadequate, piecemeal studies that, in the past, have brought more confusion and contradiction than closure to important issues in the education of children with mild handicaps.

Author Information

Ronald P. Colarusso is Professor of Special Education at Georgia State University in Atlanta.

References

American Psychological Association. (1966). *Standards for educational and psychological tests and manuals.* Washington, DC: Author.

Anastasi, A. (1968). *Psychological testing.* New York: Macmillan.

Arter, J. A., & Jenkins, J. R. (1977). Examining the benefits and prevalence of modality considerations in special education. *Journal of Special Education* **11**, 281–298.

Arter, J. A., & Jenkins, J. R. (1979). Differential diagnostic-prescriptive teaching: A critical appraisal. *Review of Educational Research*, **49**, 517–555.

Ary, D., Jacobs, L. C., & Razavieh, A. (1985). *Introduction to research in education* (3rd ed.). New York: Holt, Rinehart & Winston.

Barrett, T. C. (1965). The relationship between measures of prereading visual discrimination and first grade reading achievements: A review of literature. *Reading Research Quarterly*, **1**, 51–76.

Beery, K. E., & Buktenica, N. (1967). *Developmental Test of Visual Motor Integration*. Chicago, IL: Follett.

Bender, L. (1938). A visual-motor Gestalt and its clinical use. [Monograph]. *American Orthopsychiatric Association*, **3**.

Bijou, S. W. (1970). What psychology has to offer education—now. *Journal of Applied Behavior Analysis*, **3**, 65–71.

Campione, J. C., & Brown, A. L. (1977). Memory and metamemory development in educable retarded children. In R. V. Kail & J. W. Hagen (Eds.), *Perspectives on the development of memory and cognition*. Hillsdale, NJ: Erlbaum.

Cartwright, G. P., & Cartwright, C. A. (1972). Gilding the lily: Comments on the training based model for special education. *Exceptional Children*, **39**, 231–234.

Cartwright, G. P., Cartwright, C. A., & Ysseldyke, J. E. (1973). Two decision models: Identification and diagnostic teaching of handicapped children in the regular classroom. *Psychology in the Schools*, **10**, 4–11.

Cohen, S. A. (1969). Studies in visual perception and reading in disadvantaged children. *Journal of Learning Disabilities*, **2**, 498–507.

Colarusso, R. P. (1971). *The development of a motor-free test of visual perception*. Unpublished doctoral dissertation, Temple University, Philadelphia, PA.

Colarusso, R. P., & Gill, S. (1975). Selecting a test of visual perception. *Academic Therapy*, **11**, 157–167.

Doman, G., Delacato, C. H., & Doman, R. (1964). *The Doman—Delacato Developmental Profile*. Philadelphia, PA: Institute for the Achievement of Human Potential.

Dunn, L. M., & Smith, J. O. (1966). *The Peabody Language Development Kits*. Circle Pines, MN: American Guidance Service.

Frostig, M. (1963). Visual perception in the brain-injured child. *American Journal of Orthopsychiatry*, **33**, 665–671.

Frostig, M., & Horne, D. (1964). *The Frostig Program for the Development of Visual Perception: Teacher's guide*. Chicago, IL: Follett.

Frostig, M., Maslow, P., Lefever, D. W., & Whittlesey, J. R. (1964). The Marianne Frostig Developmental Test of Visual Perception: 1963 standardization. *Perceptual and Motor Skills*, **19**, 463–499.

Getman, G. N., & Kane, E. R. (1964). *The physiology of readiness: An action program for the development of perception for children*. Minneapolis, MN: Programs to Accelerate School Success.

Gilkeson, E. C., Smithberg, L. M., Bowman, G. W., & Rhine, W. R. (1981). Bank Street Model: A developmental-interaction approach. In W. R. Rhine (Ed.), *Making schools more effective: New directions from Follow Through* (pp. 104–132). New York: Academic Press.

Goodman, L., & Hammill, D. (1973). The effectiveness of the Kephart-Getman activities in developing perceptual-motor cognitive skills. *Focus on Exceptional Children*, **9**(3), 1–9.

Gronlund, N. E. (1976). *Measurement and evaluation in teaching* (3rd ed.). New York: Macmillan.

Hallahan, D. P., & Cruickshank, W. M. (1973). *Psychoeducational foundations of learning disabilities*. Englewood Cliffs, NJ: Prentice–Hall.

Hallahan, D. P., Lloyd, J., Kosiewicz, M. M., Kauffman, J. M., & Graves, A. W. (1979). Self-monitoring of attention as a treatment for a learning disabled boy's off-task behavior. *Learning Disability Quarterly*, **2**, 24–32.

Hammill, D. (1972). Training visual perceptual processes. *Journal of Learning Disabilities*, **5**, 39–44.

Hammill, D., Goodman, L., & Wiederholt, J. L. (1974). Visual-motor processes: Can we train them? *The Reading Teacher*, **27**, 470–479.

Hammill, D., & Larsen, S. C. (1974a). The effectiveness of psycholinguistic training. *Exceptional Children*, **41**, 5–14.

Hammill, D., & Larsen, S. C. (1974b). The relationship of selected auditory perceptual skills and reading ability. *Journal of Learning Disabilities*, **7**, 40–46.

Hammill, D., & Larsen, S. C. (1978). The effectiveness of psycholinguistic training: A reaffirmation of position. *Exceptional Children*, **44**, 402–414.

Hammill, D., & Wiederholt, J. L. (1973). Review of the Frostig Visual Perception Test and the related training program. In L. Mann & D. A. Sabatino (Eds.), *The first review of special education* (Vol. 1, pp. 33–48). Philadelphia, PA: JSE Press.

Haring, N. G., & Bateman, B. (1977). *Teaching the learning disabled child*. Englewood Cliffs, NJ: Prentice-Hall.

Johnson, D. J., & Myklebust, H. R. (1967). *Learning disabilities: Educational principles and practices*. New York: Grune & Stratton.

Karnes, M. B. (1972). *GOAL Program: Language Development*. Springfield, MA: Milton Bradley.

Kavale, K. (1981a). Functions of the Illinois Test of Psycholinguistic Abilities (ITPA): Are they trainable? *Exceptional Children*, **47**, 496–510.

Kavale, K. (1981b). The relationship between auditory perceptual skills and reading ability: A meta-analysis. *Journal of Learning Disabilities*, **14**, 539–546.

Kavale, K. (1982a). Meta-analysis of the relationship between visual perceptual skills and reading achievement. *Journal of Learning Disabilities*, **15**, 42–51.

Kavale, K. (1982b). Psycholinguistic training programs: Are there differential treatment effects? *Exceptional Children*, **29**, 21–30.

Kavale, K., & Mattson, P. D. (1983). One jumped off the balance beam: Meta-analysis of perceptual-motor training. *Journal of Learning Disabilities*, **16**, 165–173.

Keogh, B. K. (1974). Optometric vision training programs for children with learning disabilities: Review of issues and research. *Journal of Learning Disabilities*, **7**, 219–231.

Kephart, N. C. (1960). *The slow learner in the classroom*. Columbus, OH: Merrill.

Kirk, S. A. (1963). Behavioral diagnosis and remediation of learning disabilities. In *Proceedings of the Conference on Exploration Into the Problems of the Perceptually Handicapped Child* (Vol. 1, pp. 3–32). Chicago, IL: The University of Illinois Press.

Kirk, S. A., & Gallagher, J. J. (1979). *Educating exceptional children* (3rd ed.). Boston, MA: Houghton Mifflin.

Kirk, S. A., McCarthy, J. J., & Kirk, W. D. (1968). *Illinois Test of Psycholinguistic Abilities: Revised edition*. Urbana, IL: University of Illinois Press.

Kleisius, S. E. (1972). Perceptual-motor development and reading—A closer look. In R. C. Aukerman (Ed.), *Some persistent questions on beginning reading* (pp. 132–163). Newark, DE: International Reading Association.

Krippner, S. (1973). Research in visual training and reading disability. In B. Bateman (Ed.), *Reading performance and how to achieve it*. Seattle, WA: Bernie Straub.

Larsen, S. C., & Hammill, D. (1975). The relationship of selected visual-perceptual abilities to school learning. *Journal of Special Education*, **9**, 281–291.

Larsen, S. C., Parker, R. M., & Hammill, D. D. (1982). Effectiveness of psycholinguistic training: A response to Kavale. *Exceptional Children*, **49**, 60–66.

Larsen, S. C., Rogers, D., & Sowell, V. (1976). The use of selected perceptual tests in differentiating between normal and learning disabled children. *Journal of Learning Disabilities*, **9**, 85–90.

Lerner, J. W. (1981). *Learning disabilities: Theories, diagnosis, and teaching strategies* (3rd ed.). Boston, MA: Houghton Mifflin.

Lund, K., Foster, G., & McCall-Perez, F. (1978). The effectiveness of psycholinguistic training: A re-evaluation. *Exceptional Children*, **44**, 310–319.

Mann, L. (1971). Psychometric phrenology and the new faculty psychology: The case against ability assessment and training. *Journal of Special Education*, **5**, 3–65.

Minskoff, E. (1975). Research on psycholinguistic training: Critique and guidelines. *Exceptional Children*, **42**, 136–144.

Minskoff, E., Wiseman, D. E., & Minskoff, J. G. (1972). *The MWM Program for Developing Language Abilities*. Ridgefield, NJ: Educational Performance Associates.

Newcomer, P. L., & Hammill, D. (1975). ITPA and academic achievement: A survey. *The Reading Teacher*, **28**, 731–741.

Newcomer, P. L., & Hammill, D. (1976). *Psycholinguistics in the schools*. Columbus, OH: Merrill.

Newcomer, P., Hare, B., Hammill, D., & McGettigan, J. (1974). Construct validity of the ITPA subtests. *Exceptional Children*, **40**, 509–510.

Newcomer, P., Larsen, S. C., & Hammill, D. (1975). A response. *Exceptional Children*, **42**, 144–148.

Noel, M. M., Valdivieso, C. H., & Fuller, B. C. (1985). *Determinants of teacher preparation: A study of departments of special education*. College Park, MD: University of Maryland, Institute for the Study of Exceptional Children.

Peter, L. J. (1965). *Prescriptive teaching*. New York: McGraw-Hill.

Prescott, G. A. (1971). Criterion-referenced test interpretation in reading. *The Reading Teacher*, **24**, 347–354.

Proger, B. B., Cross, L. H., & Burger, R. M. (1973). Construct validation of standardized tests in special education: A framework of reference and application to ITPA research (1967–1971). In L. Mann & D. A. Sabatino (Eds.), *The first review of special education* (Vol. 1, pp. 165–202). Philadelphia, PA: JSE Press.

Resnick, L. B. (1973). Hierarchies in children's learning: A symposium. *Instructional Science*, **2**, 311–349.

Resnick, L. B., Wang, M. C., & Kaplan, J. (1973). Task analysis in curriculum design: A hierarchically sequenced introductory mathematics curriculum. *Journal of Applied Behavior Analysis*, **6**, 679–710.

Roach, E. G., & Kephart, N. C. (1966). *Purdue Perceptual-Motor Survey*. Columbus, OH: Merrill.

Robinson, H. M. (1972). Perceptual training—Does it result in reading improvements? In R. C. Aukerman (Ed.), *Some persistent questions on beginning reading*. Newark, DE: International Reading Association.

Sabatino, D. A. (1973). Auditory perception: Development, assessment, and intervention. In L. Mann & D. A. Sabatino (Eds.), *The first review of special education* (Vol. 1, pp. 49–82). Philadelphia, PA: JSE Press.

Salvia, J., & Ysseldyke, J. (1981). *Assessment in special and remedial education* (2nd ed.). Boston, MA: Houghton Mifflin.

Sedlack, R. A., & Weener, P. (1973). Review of research on the Illinois Test of Psycholinguistic Abilities. In L. Mann & D. A. Sabatino (Eds.), *The first review of special education* (Vol. 1, pp. 113–164). Philadelphia, PA: JSE Press.

Semel, E. M., & Wiig, E. H. (1981). Semel Auditory Processing Program: Training effects among children with language-learning disabilities. *Journal of Learning Disabilities*, **14**, 192–197.

Silverston, R. A., & Deichmann, J. W. (1975). Sense modality research and the acquisition of reading skills. *Review of Educational Research*, **45**, 149–172.

Smead, V. S. (1977). Ability training and task analysis in diagnostic/prescriptive teaching. *Journal of Special Education*, **11**, 113–125.

Sternberg, L., & Taylor, R. L. (1982). The insignificance of psycholinguistic training: A reply to Kavale. *Exceptional Children*, **49**, 254–256.

Tindal, G. (1885). Investigating the effectiveness of special education: An analysis of methodology. *Journal of Learning Disabilities*, **18**, 101–112.

Wang, M. C. (1973). Psychometric studies in validation of an early learning curriculum. *Child Development*, **44**, 54–60.

Wang, M. C. (1980). Adaptive instruction: Building on diversity. *Theory Into Practice*, **19**, 122–127.

Wang, M. C., & Birch, J. W. (1984a). Comparison of a full-time mainstreaming program and a resource room approach. *Exceptional Children*, **51**, 33–40.

Wang, M. C., & Birch, J. W. (1984b). Effective special education in regular classes. *Exceptional Children*, **50**, 391–398.

Wang, M. C., Resnick, L. B., & Boozer, R. (1971). The sequence of development of some early mathematics behaviors. *Child Development*, **42**, 1767–1788.

Waugh, R. P. (1975). ITPA: Ballast or bonanza for the school psychologists. *Journal of School Psychology*, **13**, 201–208.

White, R. T. (1973). Learning hierarchies. *Review of Educational research*, **43**, 361–375.

Ysseldyke, J. E. (1973). Diagnostic-prescriptive teaching: The search for aptitude-treatment interactions. In L. Mann & D. A. Sabatino (Eds.), *The first review of special education* (Vol. 1, pp. 5–32). Philadelphia, PA: JSE Press.

Ysseldyke, J. E., & Salvia, J. (1974). Diagnostic-prescriptive teaching: Two models. *Exceptional Children*, **41**, 17–31.

Application of Cognitive-Behavioral Training Methods to Teaching Basic Skills to Mildly Handicapped Elementary School Students

MICHAEL M. GERBER

University of California, Santa Barbara

Abstract—Methodological and conceptual problems in current special education research seriously limit the ability to establish an empirical basis for differentially programming traditionally defined groups of mildly handicapped students. It may be more pragmatic to seek integration of findings pertinent to needs that are common across the range of mildly handicapping conditions. This chapter, therefore, reviews an emerging body of research on cognitive-behavioral training (CBT) methods for training more self-directed learning. Although impressive evidence has accumulated supporting the use of CBT techniques to induce self-monitoring of attention and comprehension, many applications tend to focus either on practice activities involving too little new learning or on more complex tasks (e.g., comprehension monitoring) that obscure how various subskills must be efficiently coordinated. The chapter reviews the development of CBT-related research and its implications for the acquisition of basic skills (e.g., decoding, spelling, simple arithmetic) for younger or less able learners. It is recommended that practitioners and researchers pursue such CBT applications more vigorously.

The fuzzy professional boundaries demarcating special education as a scholarly discipline encompass a vast and diffuse literature ranging from medicine to sociology, from classical laboratory experimentation to testimonial, from focus on infants to focus on adults, from ambiguously defined but seemingly ubiquitous "slow learners" to children with rare and highly circumscribed pathology. Even in the relatively delimited area of research on learning disabilities, formidable barriers are quickly encountered. For example, in a review of 3 years of research (1976 to 1978), Torgesen and Dice (1980) estimated that only 24% of reported studies were the "second or more study in a series by the same author on the same topic" (p. 534). Thus, it is extraordinarily difficult to extract useful knowledge from this unwieldy body of fact and informed speculation to improve special education practice.

In addition to the general unwieldiness of special education literature, there are a number of specific conceptual problems that should be explicitly discussed before presuming to try to make this research useful for practitioners. If classification of elementary students as mildly handicapped is to make pedagogical sense, rather than being merely an administrative convenience, it has long been thought necessary to first show that something resembling "aptitude-treatment interactions" exists for some discriminable category of students such that classification, when it occurs, implies some set of reliable and unambiguous instructional programming options. Indeed, the desire to summarize and integrate knowledge about effectiveness of differential programming in serving handicapped students rests on the assumption that a basis for differential programming exists.

However, over this first decade of national public policy for handicapped children, both theoretical and practical obstacles have been encountered that seriously impede progress toward discovering and empirically validating such aptitude-treatment interactions. Inability to gain consensus on definition, for example, presents obstacles that more seriously impede ability to inform practice by reviewing research than do the inevitable methodological and experimental design flaws that are often noted (e.g., see Hallahan, 1975; Torgesen, 1975; Torgesen & Dice, 1980). Teachers are likely to be less concerned than their research counterparts with threats to internal and external validity of findings for groups than they are concerned with ambiguity in how learners can be usefully characterized.

Enormous variability in service rates—across states, across districts within states, and across school sites within districts—has been interpreted as evidence that a markedly heterogeneous group of children continues to be classified into categories intended to describe discrete, mildly handicapping conditions (e.g., see Algozzine & Korinek, 1985; Algozzine & Ysseldyke, 1983; Gerber, 1984a; Kauffman, 1980; Meyen & Moran, 1979; Ysseldyke, Algozzine, & Epps, 1983). Several authors have attributed this variability to systematic and structural constraints on schools, classrooms, and teachers (Gerber & Semmel, 1984, 1985; MacMillan, Meyers, & Morrison, 1980; Shepard, Smith, & Vojir, 1983) and, as a consequence, have argued that it will be extremely difficult to integrate and draw appropriate inferences for instructional practice from research that relies on school identification procedures for obtaining and describing subjects.

Even if definitional and identification problems were somewhat ameliorated, it has been argued that theoretical discreteness in categorical labels need not imply correspondingly discrete instructional interventions. In a frequently cited paper, Hallahan and Kauffman (1977) drew attention to the practically significant overlap in instructionally relevant behavioral characteristics that are attributed to different categories of mildly handicapped students. Similarly, Lloyd (1975, 1980) argued for direct and powerful instructional techniques that will yield reliable gains independent of categorical and individual differences.

Thus, efforts to distill practical, instructional, or programmatic guidance from research are severely hampered by (a) persistent variability in characteristics of school-identified samples of students classified under various categories of mild handicaps; and (b) uncertainty, or at least lack of persuasive evidence, that researchers are indeed able to identify category-specific aptitudes that readily and clearly suggest educational treatments. For teachers who must respond to problem learners one at a time, these problems make research less usable than it would be hoped.

However, the outlook for identifying empirically valid instructional practices may not be as gloomy as these problems appear to indicate. Despite conceptual fuzziness regarding categories and the resulting confusion over generalizations drawn from the central tendencies of ad hoc experimental groups, the past decade has seen a dramatic shift toward instructional research that may yield information that is more accessible as well as more relevant for practitioners. This research is evolving from cognitive or cognitive-behavioral models of performance and has increasingly been applied to both differentiated and non-differentiated groups of students who share common characteristics of poor response to conventional methods of instruction.

Given the resistance of much of special education's professional literature to simple summary and integration this review veers somewhat from a traditional review of the literature. The purpose of this review is to assess the impact of a set of evolving, theoretically derived, cognitive and cognitive-behavioral training (CBT) methods on the development of academic programming for elementary school children believed to have mildly handicapping conditions.

Having stated this purpose, it is also necessary to caution the reader that the literature reviewed here presents an emerging instructional strategy rather than a single transportable program or packaged curriculum. Although more than 40% of currently published studies may deal with cognitive issues, training, and academic tasks (Torgesen & Dice, 1980), only a small percentage as yet directly address the issue of CBT for academic skills acquisition. More than 30% of studies reported in the earliest issues of the *Journal of Educational Psychology* were concerned with "pedagogy or structure of content areas" (Farnham-Diggory & Nelson, 1984, p. 35). However, in the 71-year history (1910–1981) of this journal, 1981 was the first year since 1914 in which school task articles outranked (by about 30%) articles on tests and measurements. In 1984, a major new journal appeared, *Cognition and Instruction,* also reflecting new and growing interest in relating cognitive research to instructional methods.

Despite these developments, professional literature in special education may lag, as it traditionally has don somewhat behind developments in psychology. Neverth less, although work in CBT is still being done by relativel few special education researchers, review of the sma amount of CBT literature is justified. First, unlike much c special education research, these studies can be theoret cally, not merely thematically, related. Second, th methods and content of most CBT experiments may b more readily interpreted and applied by practitioners tha other research in this field. Third, CBT represents a prom ising conceptual advance in special education that appear to have important practical implications for some of th more intractable instructional dilemmas (i.e., generaliza tion and maintenance) confronted by teachers of mildl handicapped children. Finally, CBT may represent a mor rational basis for differential programming for student with mild learning handicaps than is currently represente by any other method.

Brief Sketch of an Emerging Literature

CBT research with students identified as mildly handicapped represents a confluence of several independent scholarly pursuits, not a clearly circumscribed effort with common concepts, motives, or methods. It is difficult to pinpoint precisely those critical events or studies which instigated a shift of research paradigms away from traditional mental deficiency, perceptual processes, or psychodynamic models of mental retardation, learning disabilities, or emotional disturbance, respectively, and toward an interest in cognitive-behavioral methods. Clearly, issues arising from civil rights and educational equity concerns forced a reconsideration of some assumptions underlying many identification and instructional practices, particularly assumptions about the degree to which educational programming of children identified as mildly handicapped ultimately could or should be normalized. These issues, first raised with respect to the development of and educational responsibility toward ethnolinguistic minorities, ultimately broadened to include even severely and profoundly retarded individuals.

Against this backdrop of social change, evidence from behaviorally oriented therapies, evaluation studies of teacher effectiveness, cognitive and developmental psychology, and social learning research converged in similar conceptualizations of the mildly handicapped learner as cognitively "inactive" (Torgesen, 1977) and lacking in the type of cognitive self-regulation that is adaptive in school settings (Loper, 1980). Moreover, real advances in instructional technology based upon application of operant principles most certainly helped to undermine those assumptions and concepts about educability which comprised special education dogma in the late 1960s.

For example, rapid accumulation of evidence of the effectiveness of applied behavior analysis approaches to skills training for severely handicapped individuals not only impressed practitioners working with mildly handicapping conditions (e.g., see Lovitt, 1975) but also began to reorient special education practice to a new instructional pragmatism. This pragmatism emerged from impatience with diagnostic-prescriptive approaches based on medical models of disability and was anchored in the firm belief that observable classroom learning behavior was directly modifiable. Indeed, demonstration of the power and conceptual simplicity of teaching methods derived from behavioral perspectives, now collectively known as direct instruction procedures, achieved among researchers a rough consensus about specific teacher behaviors that appeared to be critical for effective instruction of underachieving students (Good, 1983; Rosenshine, 1983; Stevens & Rosenshine, 1981).

Insights From Direct Instruction

Generally speaking, techniques derived from these pragmatic, intervention-oriented perspectives emphasize active effort by the teacher to elicit as many correctable or reinforceable responses from students as possible within instructional time constraints. Moreover, these techniques typically require careful attention to the amount and type of environmental structuring necessary to assure controlled and consistent student achievement. Some of the features of such structuring include (a) grouping by immediate instructional needs; (b) careful sequencing (i.e., programming) of academic skills to be taught; (c) modeling; (d) rapid pacing to achieve high-density response opportunities; (e) use of response signals to control attention and pace; (f) use of choral as well as independent responding; (g) immediate corrective feedback, including adequate, contingent reinforcement; and (h) frequent, teacher-monitored practice.

There has been ample demonstration and review elsewhere in the literature of the power, utility, and broad applicability of these techniques in all aspects of curriculum and across a range of learner characteristics (e.g., Becker, 1977; Becker & Carnine, 1981; Carnine, 1983; Engelmann, 1969; Lloyd, 1975; Lloyd, Cullinan, Heins, & Epstein, 1980). Therefore, they will not be discussed further here.

It is necessary to point out, however, that successful demonstration of these and related active, or "hot," teaching techniques, particularly with students presumed to have mild handicaps, generally has not been derived from theoretical models of learning specific to exceptional children. Cognitive processes are subsumed for instructional purposes under one of three categories of knowledge: basic concepts (i.e., "forms"); relationships (i.e., "joining forms"); and cognitive "routines" (Carnine, 1983, p. 23). Although Becker (1977) and Carnine (1983) argued that there are cognitive, as well as behavioral, reasons for the observed effectiveness of direct instruction procedures, in practice application has been largely atheoretical and relegated by some to the status of an engineering problem.

Specifically, teachers are advised to control events that have empirically demonstrated relationships to desirable child outcomes. Insight into individual differences among learners is considered interesting but not necessary for programming instruction. Instead, there is a conscious pragmatism in selecting techniques that are so economical and potent that reliable, though perhaps not optimal, gains are achieved independent of individual differences. Consequently, it has become common to treat these techniques as instances of good, or effective, teaching, without analysis of how they, as educational treatments, may uniquely interact with specific learning characteristics (i.e., aptitudes) of students prone to be identified as mildly handicapped. However, it is common experience that some students require little more than a verbal hint, while others require the full panoply of highly structured techniques, to acquire the same knowledge or display the same level of skilled behavior. As in making many other inferences from educational research, there is great risk in evaluating the evidence of universal effectiveness of direct instruction too casually or in confusing group and individual responsiveness to instructional variables.

Contributions From Cognitive Research

Possibly rich sources of theory have been suggested from cognitive and developmental research concerned with human memory and having applied implications for individual difference research (Atkinson & Shiffrin, 1968; Craik & Lockhart, 1972; Flavell, Friedrichs, & Hoyt, 1970; Tulving, 1972). Researchers who choose to approach learning problems of mildly handicapped students from a cognitive, or information-processing, perspective have begun to develop descriptive and explanatory models of learning failure that, while not clearly demarcating classical categories of exceptional learners, could nevertheless be used both to differentiate the needs of and to design instructional interventions for individual students (Farnham-Diggory & Nelson, 1984).

Seminal work with mentally retarded children by Belmont and Butterfield (1969, 1971) and by Brown and her colleagues (e.g., Brown, 1974) created an impressive foundation literature on the relationship between intentional and purposeful mnemonic effort and intelligent performance on a variety of laboratory tasks. Once the theoretical, as well as practical, importance of this and other accumulating evidence regarding differences in memory, selective attention, encoding, and verbal mediation was recognized, there was a rapid, unmistakable, paradigmatic shift away from neurogenic, perceptual defect models and toward inefficient or ineffective information-processing models of mental retardation and learning disabilities (Campione & Brown, 1977; Hall, 1980b; Kavale & Forness, 1985; Torgesen 1982; Torgesen & Kail, 1980).

Impulsivity and Distractibility: Prototypical Applications of CBT

To briefly characterize the nature of this shift, it is useful to consider what teaching problems are encountered with students who display unusual impulsivity and distractibility—two characteristics that have long been associated with learning behavior of mildly handicapped students (e.g., see Gerber, 1983; Harris, 1982). These characteristics present a double-edged sword that threatens to reduce the effectiveness of most conventional classroom instruction. First, to the extent that impulsivity and distractibility are global and pervasive within and across all learning tasks, mildly handicapped students will require more general monitoring and management from teachers than normal-achieving peers. Second, to the extent that impulsivity and distractibility have peculiar and task-specific manifestations, learning based on particular problems or lessons is constantly threatened by misunderstood explanations, ineffective or inefficient selection or manipulation of task information, and insufficient error monitoring and repair.

These undesirable learner characteristics can be addressed through the use of two related but distinct remedial approaches. One approach is to search for a means of reducing global impulsivity and distractibility in the hope that normal teaching techniques will be more effective. The other is to impose reinforcement or punishment contingencies on a task-by-task or response-by-response basis. It has proven difficult, however, with the present level of instructional technology, to address both global and specific impulsivity and distractibility simultaneously. For example, behavior modification techniques have been used to help students increase their response latencies so that their behavior superficially resembles that of their more reflective peers. Usually, though, it has been the case that inaccuracy has to be remediated separately. Moreover, even when simple manipulation of incentives and corrective feedback can increase attention and accuracy, the effects tend to be task specific and fail to engender generalized improvements in approach and performance on all academic tasks likely to be encountered.

This was essentially the problem confronting researchers in the early part of the last decade when Meichenbaum and Goodman (1971) successfully combined techniques implied by social learning theory (i.e., modeling) and language development (i.e., self-statement) into a training package that increased both appropriate reflection and accuracy on a laboratory task. Their training paradigm consisted mainly of modeling and eliciting successively better and more subvocal imitations of four self-questions designed to control attention and guide students through a broad range of problem situations. The self-questions generally reduce to the following:

1. What is my problem?
2. What is my plan?
3. Am I using my plan?
4. How am I doing?

Unfortunately, global impulsivity was not clearly reduced by training children on the specific tasks used in the study. Egeland (1974), however, was able to train impulsive children in general "search-and-scan" rules that led to improved performance on several laboratory tasks and appeared to improve performance on a test of reading comprehension 5 months after training. Finally, Kendall and Wilcox (1980) created a more elaborate training program that resulted in practical (not merely statistically significant) improvements for a group of impulsive children. Their training program was unique because it combined but differentiated, concrete (task-specific) and conceptual (generalized) training targets and procedures. Children were trained in a range of actual behavior and academic problem situations. Six components used in both types of training consisted of modeling and practice in using verbal self-instructions. These components were made problem or task specific during concrete training, while they were presented more abstractly for application to problems in general during conceptual training. The six components were (a) problem definition, (b) problem approach, (c) focusing attention, (d) problem solution, (e) self-reinforcement, and (f) coping with errors.

These behaviorally oriented studies paralleled in logic and time a number of more theoretically grounded developments in cognitive psychology. Therefore, a not entirely arbitrary selection of a year to demarcate a major paradigmatic shift and in which to expect changes in research literature might be 1977. In that year, an important paper by Torgesen (1977) appeared, which in describing learning disabled students as cognitively inactive, began to draw together various strands of research on the development of cognitive processes. Also, in the same year, Brown and her colleagues published a number of equally important, theoretical, and empirical reviews of their programmatic investigations of cognitive strategy training with mentally retarded students (e.g., Campione & Brown, 1977).

Subsequently, special education research on cognitive and behavioral training methods for children with mildly handicapping conditions has burgeoned. Reviews of the latest experimental findings and speculations about their applied implications have appeared in unusually rapid succession (Abikoff, 1979; Harris, 1982; Sheinker, Sheinker, & Stevens, 1984).

To avoid confusion with any specific, formally defined theory, procedure, or school of thought, the present review concentrates on research using what will be collectively referred to as CBT methods. The review takes the form of an assessment that has two, relatively limited goals. One, obviously, is to better inform those who might effect emerging instructional and programmatic practices. A second and related goal is to begin development of an integrated perspective on promising strands of CBT research that can be applied to teaching basic academic skills.

Review of CBT Research

Boundaries of the Review

The criteria used for defining student subgroups of interest and for sampling CBT literature are described in the following paragraphs.

Student Subgroups of Interest

In this review, *children with mild handicaps* refers chiefly to students classified by special education policy as earning disabled. School-identified learning disabled students comprise the largest single group of students classified as handicapped under current special education public policy, numbering over 1.7 million students in 1983 Gerber, 1984a)—somewhat more than 4% of kindergarten through twelfth-grade enrolment.

However, the review also includes literature from three other, presumably discriminable subgroups under the generic label mildly handicapped: students considered mentally retarded whose classification as handicapped is based largely on tests interpreted to indicate low learning potential (e.g., IQ less than 80); students whose academic difficulties are thought to result from chronically inappropriate classroom behavior and who, thus, may be considered emotionally disturbed; and, finally, those who may not have been formally declared handicapped but whose learning problems, nevertheless, are considered severe due to their apparently unusual difficulty in acquiring basic reading skills. Brown and Palincsar (1982) have suggested that these three groups are part of a continuum, varying in extent and severity of learning disability.

The rationale for such a broad view of mild handicaps rests on two observations. First, operationalized criteria for distinguishing discrete categories of mildly handicapped students in current public policy are sufficiently vague and arbitrary so as to diminish their importance for the purposes of reviewing instructional and programmatic literature. Second, for practical purposes, there is increasingly convergent belief that these subgroups of learning problems represent a continuum of cognitive and adaptive inefficiency and ineffectiveness in classroom learning situations, rather than discretely different disabilities (Algozzine & Ysseldyke, 1983; Brown & Palincsar, 1982; Hallahan & Kauffman, 1977). That is, even if subgroups of poor learners can be rigorously identified, evidence from applied research seems to support the use of highly similar instructional principles and methods. In this review, therefore, instructional differences are assumed to be most usefully characterized as differences in how intensively or extensively methods must be applied to achieve reliable academic gains.

Sampling CBT Literature

The present review made use of all the approaches described by Cooper (1982) to track recent studies and reports concerned with the application of CBT methods to basic academic skills. An attempt was made to establish criteria for studies and reports that represent (a) direct applications from coherent, definable CBT models or theoretical positions; (b) examples of programmatic research on CBT applications; or (c) demonstration or development projects linked to this research either directly by citation or indirectly by explicit statements revealing commonly held assumptions about the basis for CBT methods. Thus, a highly circumscribed sample was sought from a wider "population" of topically related studies and reports; that is, no attempt was made to critique or comprehensively summarize all current discussion nominally relevant to cognitive-behavioral interventions used with students thought to be mildly handicapped. Rather, the population of studies sampled, those in which CBT methods were applied to the teaching of basic academic skills, must be viewed as representing a new and emerging literature. Specific selection criteria were: (a) the procedure described was applied to training basic academic skills in reading, writing, mathematics, or independent study; (b) the procedure described was explicitly described as cognitive, cognitive-behavioral, behavior strategy, or some other logically related synonym; and (c) the procedure described included formal or informal evaluation of effects.

Focus of CBT Interventions

If mildly handicapped students can be characterized by the fact that they learn at a slower rate than their normal-achieving peers, can CBT methods be used to address specific obstacles encountered during acquisition of basic academic skills, resulting in generally accelerated learning? In the first case, CBT might be applied as needed whenever acquisition roadblocks were confronted; in the second case, CBT might need to be a formal part of the everyday curriculum (Borkowski & Cavanaugh, 1979; Borkowski & Konarski, 1981).

Corno and Mandinach (1983) have recently suggested that work on CBT methods has underscored the need to develop better conceptualizations of "self-regulated" learning on applied tasks in natural classroom settings, not only on analogue or even applied tasks in laboratories. It is in actual day-to-day teaching of mildly handicapped learners that an ongoing need for guidelines in modifying or adapting CBT methods is likely to become apparent. That is, self-regulated learning implies that students have the abilities to be efficient and effective on specific learning tasks as well as some sort of general competence to learn cumulatively, independent of task content, over time. Emergence of such generalized learning competence would manifest itself as ability to shift attention between tasks in a fluid, deliberate, and cognitively engaged fashion. The puzzle, from both a theoretical and applied point of view, is whether there can be a unified CBT approach that can be applied simultaneously to specific and general learner competence, that respects individual and content differences, and that can be implemented with reasonable economy of time and effort in real classrooms.

Approaches to Self-Monitoring

To illustrate the theoretical and practical dilemma arising from the application of CBT methods to specific training tasks as a means of enhancing global learning behavior, recent programmatic studies conducted at the University of Virginia's Learning Disabilities Research Institute are briefly considered. These studies focused on demonstration of the effectiveness of CBT techniques for training elementary learning disabled students to monitor and record their attention to task. Clearly, in light of empirical research on the importance of "academic learning time" (e.g., see Gettinger & White, 1979; Stallings, 1980), using methods aimed at increasing self-regulation of on-task behavior is a worthwhile objective. Training students to pay attention to task (here *attention* means cognitive engagement with task content as well as resistance to distraction) should result in generalized improvement in learning, independent of task.

In a number of systematically developed studies (e.g., see Hallahan et al., 1983), it was shown that training similar to that used by Meichenbaum and Goodman (1971) resulted in learning disabled students learning how to regulate their task-orientation behavior to match a behavioral model of appropriate attention to task. Moreover, these studies found that students trained to self-monitor and record attention showed marked improvements over baseline in academic productivity (i.e., number of observable, correct, or appropriate responses per minute), making it logical to infer that observed changes in attention were associated with desirable cognitive activity and not merely its behavioral concomitants.

However, this research was conducted almost entirely during independent practice or other drill activities involving known responses. In fact, the investigators observed that

> the self-recording procedure works best with students whose primary problem is attentional. In other words, it does not seem appropriate for children who do not have the skills to do the work they have been assigned. Instead, it seems most appropriate for children who, while they have skills to perform the work, are unable to do so because they have difficulty staying on-task. (Hallahan et al., 1983, p. 104)

The inference that self-monitoring training of this type might need to be restricted to overt attention difficulties presents some conceptual and practical disappointments. First, it certainly reduces the breadth of application of the technique, however easy to implement, for helping students acquire new skills. It might be argued that increasing cognitive engagement during drill makes more efficient use of that time, thereby freeing time for direct instruction of new skills. Presumably, though, during direct instruction of new material, students would be as difficult to teach, relative to their normal-achieving peers, as ever. Instructional efficacy would seem not to be strongly, if at all, influenced by use of the CBT methods in this case. Cognitive self-regulation during learning of new material, of the kind and quality expected from normal-achieving students, would only be partially achieved; successful learning would still depend more on externally provided structuring, as opposed to internally controlled processing, of information.

However, a practical and theoretical dilemma exists regarding how to design CBT interventions to induce more internally directed learning of specific material. In a recent review of twenty-seven studies of the effects of self-questioning training on students' processing of prose, Wong (1985b) differentiated three approaches to designing such interventions that were generally based on three different conceptual frameworks. These frameworks were loosely classified as active processing, metacognitive, and schema theories. She noted that active processing theories have resulted in interventions that use higher order self-questions to induce deeper, more thorough processing of material. Self-questioning routines based on metacognitive theories, on the other hand, tend to emphasize self-monitoring of discriminable aspects of prose material or response that can be compared to an optimizing model or set of guidelines. This type of self-questioning, when applied to monitoring of attention to task, was used in the Virginia studies. The final theoretically driven model of self-questioning, taken from what Wong labels "schema theory," emphasizes self-statements designed to help students access prior knowledge that might be relevant for completing their present task.

Although using CBT to induce self-questioning cannot replace some form of instruction when students simply do not possess relevant or sufficient knowledge, it would be helpful to systematically test the University of Virginia's studies concerning the potential of the self-questioning version of CBT for reducing the amount of external structure required during teaching by using self-questions that were more schematizing and less metacognitive. For example, in an exploratory attempt to extend the findings from the University of Virginia's line of research, Gerber and Niemann (1983) applied the same CBT methods in a multiple baseline design to train a distractible learning disabled student to monitor the quality of his performance on three tasks: reading comprehension, listening comprehension, and expository writing. However, the self-monitoring question used in previous work (i.e., "Was I paying attention?") was replaced with questions for each task that specifically directed the student's attention to the criterion performance expected (e.g., "Will I be able to answer the questions at the end?"; "Am I checking capitals, punctuation, and spelling?"). In addition, the student was provided with materials that were judged to be at his instructional level—not practice material.

CBT was experimentally compared with a no-intervention baseline and a contingent reinforcement condition. Results indicated practically meaningful improvement above levels achieved at baseline or during reinforcement on measures of reading comprehension and writing accuracy in addition to increases in on-task behavior. The relative failure of listening comprehension to show a meaningful improvement was interpreted to mean that the verbal self-monitoring induced by training was itself distracting during a listening activity. However, the findings from the other two tasks were interpreted as indications that CBT could enhance the quality of performance on difficult material as well as increase on-task behavior and productivity during practice.

What Are Appropriate Goals for CBT?

Practitioners studying these exemplars of early CBT research inevitably confront the following dilemma: are students to be taught individual skills in a more or less linear fashion in the hope that greater generalized competence will emerge from a sufficient repertoire? Stated differently, could one expect a qualitative shift in learner competence to occur as a function of incremental changes in the number of discrete skills acquired? Or, similar to Zeno's Paradox, is there an infinity of definable skills, or subskills within skills, to be learned, making it practically hopeless to tailor some new version of CBT for each item in the curriculum? From a cognitive perspective, this problem translates into a need for an instructional decision about whether to teach students what they must learn as opposed to teaching students how they can approach learning generally (Brown, Campione, & Day, 1981; Sternberg, 1981). Brown et al. (1981) proposed that "training studies aimed at improving students' academic performance can succeed by adding substantially to the students' knowledge; or they can succeed by instructing students in ways to enhance their own knowledge (i.e. in promoting learning to learn activities)" (p. 14).

From the perspective of behaviorists or instructional technologists, the same issue is expressed as a need for "specifying procedures needed to teach general cases and to cumulatively build knowledge within sets of related concepts" (Becker, 1977, p. 531). This approach avoids becoming tediously additive because it "seeks to identify the smallest set of rote memory items and set of rules for combining these items that will provide skills for attacking problems of a given type while also developing the basis for attacking related problems" (Lloyd et al., 1980, p. 11).

Role of Cognitive Strategies

The pivotal concept in contemporary discussion of these issues by both cognitivists and behaviorists is the concept of a *strategy*. The idea of a strategy has become a kind of conceptual placeholder that helps investigators infer links between covert and overt events. It is a theoretical entity that helps to bridge partially understood mental operations, like memory, and more obscure phenomena, such as motivation, attribution, and intention. Unfortunately, the concept has also allowed researchers to be less than rigorous in inferring the specificity or generality of putative strategies.

Recently, it has been argued that strategies are often invoked uncritically to explain experimental results related to a host of different theoretical positions and applied purposes. Gerber (1983) warned that the concept would become progressively obscured and lose its apparent explanatory power unless its meaning were clarified. Lloyd (1980), for example, described strategies as "a series of steps . . . through which students proceed in order to solve a problem" (p. 53). According to Lloyd, these steps can be abstracted as general plans for any task, or they can be very task specific. Related discussion in the literature concerning differentiation of cognitive from metacognitive activity does little to clarify the central notion of a strategy. Rather, the concept appears to drift in response to the conceptual needs of the writer, sometimes describing an overt behavior, sometimes a presumptive self-verbalization, sometimes mental activity presumed to relate to information handling and transformation, the precise parameters of which are not known. Are strategies collections of rote-memorized rules or abstract algorithms for reading, writing, or doing computation? Are strategies organized, problem-related thoughts or thoughts about organizing problem-related thoughts? Are they plans to control thinking, or are they the controls themselves? The answers are unclear and often contradictory, but they are nonetheless critical to how CBT methods are designed and implemented (e.g., for extensive discussion of these issues see special issues of *Exceptional Education Quarterly*, Hallahan, 1980; *Topics in Learning and Learning Disabilities*, Swanson, 1982; Wong, 1982).

Hall (1980) suggested that concern for organization and reduction of information load is common to cognitively and behaviorally oriented interventions. Researchers of both orientations wish to discover ways in which mildly handicapped students can be taught to approach learning tasks in a more structured and, thus, more efficient, manner. Structure, in Hall's argument, implies organization. It would also seem to imply a transactional relationship between operations devoted to searching a knowledge base for relevant information and the structure of that knowledge base. For example, how quickly and efficiently one can reduce uncertainty by using what is known may determine to some degree both the reliability and future accessibility of newly appended knowledge. Conversely, the degree of organization with which knowledge has accumulated in the past may severely constrain the possible speed and efficiency of search procedures selected in response to learning problems in the present.

To the extent that strategies impose structure by controlling the organization and sequencing of information and the timing and rate of response demand, it is a matter of pedagogical indifference whether they are defined as overt behaviors or as internalized, cognitive habits. Moreover, understood in this sense, it becomes somewhat clearer how teaching can be optimal or suboptimal for different learners. For mildly handicapped students particularly, effective teaching, as in direct instruction, provides a highly constraining structure that serves as an environmental proxy for absent or ineffective strategies (e.g., see Corno & Mandinach, 1983).

Cognitive Elements of Effective Instruction

The work reviewed thus far, as a body of evidence, provides a strongly unifying and theoretical basis for applying more behaviorally derived techniques to promote self-regulatory behavior. There has been impressive success in demonstrating the effectiveness of such techniques for decreasing impulsivity and increasing self-control of attention during performance of academic tasks. Most important, though, CBT methods seem to have captured and organized for student use what appear to be the critical features of effective instructional techniques. This section briefly considers some of the elements of effective instruction that emerge as self-regulatory tools in many CBT experiments.

In Walberg's (1984) summary of data on a variety of general teaching approaches across student types and subject matter, his analyses showed that manipulations of reinforcement contingencies (interventions providing minimal structure by linking some pattern of antecedent and consequent events to responses) produced an average effect size of 1.20. Individualized tutoring, on the other hand, produced an average effect size of 2.00. That is, the performance of students in experimental groups in which tutors monitored ongoing attention to task and needs for explanation, guidance, or modeling achieved levels that averaged 2 standard deviations above the mean performance of students in control groups.

Because individualized tutoring may not be feasible, Bloom (1984) compared Walberg's data to data from mastery learning studies in which teachers provided each student with sufficient time and corrective feedback over trials to assure performance at some targeted level. Although conventional approaches to instruction resulted in estimated effect sizes of about 0.50, or 0.76 when enhanced by methods to assure "cognitive entry prerequisites," mastery learning alone resulted in an effect size of 1.00 and an effect size of 1.60 when it was enhanced by cognitive entry prerequisites.

Determination of cognitive entry prerequisites was operationalized by pretraining assessment measures that were used to ascertain students' cognitive preparedness for a particular unit of instruction. These data are particularly interesting in light of Palincsar and Brown's (1984) conclusion from a long series of studies that, to be successful, cognitive training must force students to be cognitively active (i.e., engaged) during learning tasks; provide corrective feedback on appropriate use of trained tactics or strategies; and provide "instruction in why, when, and where such activities should be applied" (p. 122). Similarly, Bloom (1984) argued that, as effort is made to assure that students possess ideas or skills necessary for learning new material, "they become more positive about their ability to learn the subject, and they put in more active learning time than do control students" (p. 7).

Carnine (1983) reported two studies using direct instruction techniques with similar implications for structuring thinking during learning. In the first study, systematic preskills training of simple multiplication was compared with a no-preskills training condition in which each error was corrected and retaught as it occurred. It took more than 30% more teaching time to reach criterion levels of performance without preskills training. Moreover, those students trained in preskills transferred their knowledge more readily to a new set of items. In a second study of the effects of overt versus covert procedures for learning to read lists of phonetically simple words, the group that received instruction in component skills, including a "sounding out" operation, reached criterion minutes faster than a group that received only "look–sa practice. On a transfer task, the component skills gro averaged over three times as many correct responses.

These general investigations of teaching effectivene support the general thesis that good instruction provides elicits the amount of structure most likely to maximal reduce response uncertainty. Moreover, the amount structure that must be provided by teaching metho appears to relate inversely to the cognitive maturity prospective learners. These various techniques—overt controlling incentives and attention to informati environmental cues (e.g., reinforcement); intensively gui ing and monitoring attention to task and responding (e.g tutoring); presenting sufficient response and feedba opportunities (e.g., direct instruction, mastery learning assuring that necessary preskills are available and useab (e.g., some forms of direct instruction, mastery learnin cognitive training); or direct teaching of demonstrab useful overt behaviors related to task-specific performan (e.g., sounding out unknown words)—find commo ground in their capabilities for making correct respondin on a target task more probable by reducing or organizin information for students.

How CBT Research Methods Relate to Instructional Methods

Owing to the group focus of much of the instructiona research just discussed, we are able to distill only relativel general principles for designing educational programmin for mildly handicapped students. Without methods an approaches that inform teachers about how to make desig modifications for individual learners, it will be difficult t prescribe differential programming components fron much extant research literature.

As might be expected, shifts in major paradigms fo research with mildly handicapped students have led to a intense and continuing search for better experimenta methods and designs (e.g., see Belmont & Butterfield 1977; Brown & Campione, 1978; Brown & Palincsar 1982; Kendall & Wilcox, 1980). Because researchers wishing to investigate cognitive processes were implicitly and necessarily confronted with the need to systematically attend to instructional issues, their methodologica descriptions of general models of training also serve as appropriately pragmatic schema for teachers. In terms used by Belmont and Butterfield (1977), instruction means

> calculated models, suggestions, rules, or injunctions that have a known influence on the way a child thinks about the materials with which he must work. . . . The definition rules out instructions and demonstrations that simply define the criterion task's information-processing requirements, and . . . variables relating to the materials, such as choices, arrangements, modes, and rates or rhythms of presentation. (p. 446)

lthough these other kinds of instruction are important, elmont and Butterfield wished to emphasize methods at induce solving problems that are created by a grasp of sk requirements, not merely methods that facilitate that rasp.

'elected Experimentations in CBT nterventions

In conducting their research, Brown et al. (1981) pproached the issue of appropriate methods of CBT omewhat differently. These researchers identified three ypes of intervention methods that have been used expernentally to influence cognitive-behavioral competence. 'he types of intervention identified were (a) blind rule folowing, (b) informed rule following, and (c) controlled rule ollowing. They are described in the paragraphs below.

3LIND RULE FOLLOWING

The first, and most common, type of intervention was abeled *blind training*. In this approach, task, environnent, and instructions are arranged to induce a certain ype of appropriate behavior, but students are never told explicitly why the behavior is being induced or what potenial benefit such behavior might have for them as learners n other circumstances. Performance under this training approach amounts to a kind of blind (or unregulated) rule following that mimics the competent, spontaneously strategic behavior of normal-achieving students but almost always requires that external prompts and cues (i.e., "the executive work," Brown & Palincsar, 1982) be provided to elicit or maintain desired levels of responding.

This approach is analogous to typical classroom teaching, in which learning tasks, often derived from commercially produced material, are the major vehicle for academic rule learning. The learning task becomes both the unit of instructional planning and the focus of learning activity. Within the context of these tasks, independent of learner characteristics, often independent of teachers, problems are posed, information is organized, and rule-following responses are prompted. Teacher behavior during these learning tasks is often aimed at modal, normal-achieving students who are spontaneously strategic in solving problems, able to access or extract relevant information for solving target problems, and capable of discovering or inventing underlying rules for generalizing solutions to other problem situations.

For example, nonhandicapped students given a list of similarly spelled homophonic words to decode (e.g., ball, call, fall, hall) can be induced by the learning material and accompanying instructions to (a) note each initial consonant, (b) recall the previous or model word's pronunciation, and (c) voice as a unit the new consonant together with the rhyming string. For atypical learners, however, this approach is dramatically unsuccessful. Although normal-achieving students may rapidly come to understand on their own the principle of initial consonant substitution without further explanation, learning handicapped students often do not.

Even when the major goal of academic learning tasks is to teach such rules and their use, learning handicapped students neither combine nor coordinate such rules strategically or spontaneously, nor will they necessarily understand the general usefulness of such strategic behavior. Therefore, when applied to classroom teaching, blind training might more aptly be labeled *double blind training* since teachers as well as students often lack awareness and knowledge of how particular rules can be strategically and effectively applied or of what long-term benefits might be obtained by individual handicapped learners.

INFORMED RULE FOLLOWING

The second type of training was referred to by Brown and her colleagues (1981) as *informed training*. In using this approach, students are induced to use a strategy and are given some information about its general relevance and possible utility. In teaching practice, this approach may provide information about the general utility of a particular, overt procedure such as sounding out. Students may be taught to sound out as a general strategy whenever words are not recognized while reading. However, sounding out has as its goal fast as well as accurate word identification. As noted above, mildly handicapped students in particular will generally have difficulty in recalling and coordinating the use of this tactic and in spontaneously knowing when employment of this problem-solving tactic is failing to to facilitate recognition (e.g., labored, fruitless vocalizing, guessing, or frank errors) or operating so slowly that some other tactic might more productively be applied.

CONTROLLED RULE FOLLOWING

Brown's third training type is referred to as *self-control training* because it intends not only to train strategies and inform students about the probable learning benefits derived from use of these strategies, but also tries to teach students "how to employ, monitor, check, and evaluate" (Brown et al., 1981, p. 15) these strategies. She and her colleagues have suggested (Brown & Palincsar, 1982) and demonstrated (Palincsar & Brown, 1984) an ideal training strategy that combines features of all three of these training approaches. According to Brown and Palincsar (1982), such an approach minimally includes (a) practice using a task-appropriate strategy, (b) instruction on the significance of this activity, and (c) instruction on how to monitor and control strategy use.

In a recent study, Ghatala, Levin, Pressley, and Lodico (1985) taught second graders how to use a "strategy-monitoring" strategy for assessing the utility or effectiveness of their plans for solving a set of simple performance tasks. The students were then given a paired associate task involving pairs of words and were instructed to do as well as they could. Following this task, a second paired word task was given, but this time half of the subjects were taught an effective mnemonic strategy, while the remaining half were instructed in a strategy that was actually known to be detrimental to recall. Performance of all of these students was compared with that of students who were initially taught to self-monitor how much fun they were having during tasks, and a control group of students who were merely taught that there were different ways of performing these tasks.

Students who were taught to monitor strategy effectiveness were more strategic overall in their task performance than students in the other two groups. That is, strategy-monitoring students who also had been taught an effective mnemonic strategy used it more effectively, and strategy-monitoring students who had been taught a detrimental mnemonic routine abandoned this technique more readily than did students in either of the other experimental groups. This and previous studies by these researchers are important in at least two regards. First, the results illustrate that young children with relatively little school experience can indeed be taught to be more self-regulating during task performance in addition to being more effective at performing specific tasks. Second, this research illustrates how generalized and content-specific training can be systematically organized and presented in a sequence of instruction.

Instructional Guidelines From Researchers

Major contributors to both the theory and method of CBT (e.g., Belmont & Butterfield, 1977; Brown, 1974; Brown & Palincsar, 1982; Ghatala et al., 1985; Meichenbaum, 1982; Wong, 1985b) have agreed upon a general set of procedural guidelines for research purposes. These same guidelines may also serve as a framework for implementing CBT methods for teaching. The guidelines can be construed as having three components: first, how to design an intervention; second, what general instructional methods should be used; and third, what task-specific rules, algorithms, or manipulations should be taught. The following paraphrase of the compact set of principles proposed by Belmont and Butterfield (1977) addresses the first, or the planning and design, component.

1. Observe as directly as possible how students are thinking while performing specific learning tasks.
2. Know as accurately as possible how normal-achieving students should be thinking while performing this task.
3. Specify what task students must complete or how well students must complete a task to permit conclusions that instruction worked successfully.

Based on commonalities of CBT methods described in the literature, the second, or general methods, component can be described for teachers as follows.

1. Reduce efficient and effective problem-solving procedures to a series of discrete, usually overt, steps.
2. Model problem solving for students by "thinki aloud" as well as by demonstrating physic manipulation of task materials.
3. Prompt and reinforce students for imitating ove (gradually faded to covert) use of verbalizations f guide and control behavior during each step.
4. Prompt and reinforce students for delayi responses until self-instruction or other self-ma aged consideration of alternative responses h occurred.
5. Prompt and reinforce effective use, as well as effe tive procedures for self-evaluation of utility (e.g see Ghatala et al., 1985), of trained strategies in series of exemplar tasks or situations.

The third, or task-specific rules, component is obvious more difficult to specify since it depends upon teachers' (understanding of the information-processing requir ments for each discrete task; (b) knowledge of rules manipulations that are ecologically valid, reliably effe tive, and relatively efficient in terms of time, knowledg base, and cognitive effort; and (c) ability to design stru tured, overt behavior routines that represent, induce, an constrain desired types or levels of cognitive activity (e.g see Carnine, 1983).

Use of CBT to Enable Academic Learning

Basic skills are minimally necessary basic "facts" academic life for elementary school students that includ knowledge of alphabet, phoneme/grapheme relationship sight vocabulary, pronunciation, orthographic and othe writing conventions, syntax, simple addends, difference products, quotients, and a lexicon of sufficient size an scope, as well as the ability to use such knowledge in lear ing more complex material. Such baseline knowledge transformed into a set of enabling skills to the exten that items can be rapidly retrieved with no conscious atten tion and near-perfect reliability. Moreover, to truly b enabling, passive knowledge must be transformed into usa ble cognitive tools that permit active exploration o each new academic problem as it occurs. This transform ation appears to be accompanied by students' acquisitio of additional knowledge about how to use the knowledg they possess. This knowledge about use minimally consist of a set of coded environmental features that are strongl associated with the range of task situations for whic retrieval of particular fact knowledge is necessary. Knowl edge about use of basic facts must also be retrievable auto matically and accurately for skilled performance to b enabled in any meaningful sense.

Although many studies have now been done to describ mnemonic (Torgesen & Kail, 1980), metacognitiv (Wong, 1985a), and other information-processing diffi culties of mildly handicapped students (Brown, 1974 Hall, 1980), little direct attention has been given to the use of CBT methods to promote the acquisition of basic enabling skills. From a pragmatic standpoint, teachers' orts to foster students' development of a high level of omaticity of these skills will likely be rewarded by uction in students' need for extraordinary instructional ources over the long term. Laborious decoding of words structs, in a very concrete sense, comprehension of text limiting the amount of time available for consideration meaning. It is logical, then, to hope that CBT methods ght facilitate the teaching of basic skills and their use as rt of more general operations and strategies.

However, Torgesen has raised some guardedly pessistic questions about the applicability of CBT methods teaching basic enabling skills (e.g., see Torgesen's coments in Meichenbaum, 1982). First, he pointed out that hough learning disabled students differ from normalhieving peers in reading more on the basis of slow and reliable decoding skills than on the basis of global ategic behaviours for comprehending text, strategic ficiencies do not seem to account for the failure of learng disabled students to develop automaticity in decoding. cond, Torgesen raised the possibility that innate prossing-speed limitations may underlie inefficient task rformance, not only because such limitations impose sic constraints on cognitive efficiency, but also because a story of learning failure associated with these limitations ay produce an overlay of maladaptive affect, attribution, d motivation.

However, it is extremely difficult to demonstrate absole limitations of the type to which Torgesen alluded. In search, failure of an experimentally trained group to ow predicted improvement does not necessarily lead to e conclusion that students have limited capacity. This is pecially true when it is conceded that representation of gnitive strategies as overt behavior is always risky from oth a theoretical and an engineering perspective. The ppropriateness or power of putative strategies is always uch in question.

Application of CBT techniques to basic skills instruction as been viewed as insurmountably difficult because of a ndency to view basic knowledge as a set of items and elationships that must be rote memorized to some stanard of reliable accuracy. This view leads to the use of brute force" (Brown et al., 1981, p. 14) approaches that ssume basic skills learning is fostered most economically y structure that is completely external to students, egardless of potentially important learner characteristics uch as age, IQ, and previous learning history. These pproaches (e.g., direct instruction) try to bulldoze tudents with the sheer controlling power of teachers' nstructional behavior (e.g., see Lloyd, 1980; Lloyd, pstein, & Cullinan, 1979).

Such methods are undoubtedly effective for inducing rbitrarily targeted levels of accurate responding indepenlent of learner differences. It is not as clear, however, that hey also result in optimal development of automaticity or nowledge of use. Gettinger and White (1979) and Getinger (1984a), for example, have demonstrated that diferences in students' ability to benefit from instruction are manifested by differences in time required to master responses. This can be interpreted to mean that there is a unique number of trials necessary for each student to achieve automaticity as well as reliable accuracy. Thus, teachers who teach only to an accuracy criterion create a surface homogeneity of responses that disguises actual variance in cognitive efficiency.

The practical consequences are straightforward (e.g., see Ackerman & Dykman, 1982; Chi & Gallagher, 1982; Sternberg & Wagner, 1982). From an information-processing point of view, suboptimal speed of processing elemental information, however accurate the ultimate response, impedes future development of new knowledge and learning strategies because requirements for cognitive management of any constituent, basic information will be inordinately effortful and distracting (i.e., attention demanding). When decoding fails to become effortless, comprehension suffers (Stanovitch, 1983a, 1983b). If handwriting (i.e., remembering and executing motor patterns for letter drawing) fails to become automatic, attention is withdrawn from attempts to spell; likewise, if spelling is slow and laborious, written expression will be truncated. If simple arithmetic combinations cannot be rapidly retrieved, multistep word problems will be more difficult, and so on.

What seems to be the simplest solution—namely repeated practice until speed of accurate responding reaches a maximum—may not eliminate the practical problems associated with teaching mildly handicapped students more complex academic material. Their observed response speed maximums may, as Torgesen (i.e., in Meichenbaum, 1982) suggested, represent absolute limitations under conventional teaching conditions and not merely unfavorable ratios of "time spent learning to time needed to learn" (Chi & Gallagher, 1982; Gettinger, 1984a). But it has been suggested that these limitations can be caused by specific constraints on any of four component stages of processing: encoding; decision (i.e., mental manipulation); response selection; or execution (Chi & Gallagher, 1982). How tractable any or all of these components are to specific interventions is not known with certainty, and that question, in fact, forms part of the basis for much of the current interest in CBT methods. Although much has been learned about facilitating memory generally, very little research has focused on memory for and use of foundation knowledge in basic academic tasks such as word recognition, spelling, and simple arithmetic. Therefore, in the next section of this review, evidence of the effectiveness of CBT methods in the acquisition of basic academic enabling skills is presented.

CBT Methods Applied to Reading

Of the academic subjects in the elementary school curriculum, reading probably has been studied longest and most intensively of all. Leinhardt, Zigmond, and Cooley (1981) recently studied the effects of several reading instruction variables on the reading performance of learning disabled students in a natural, self-contained special class. They found that 59% of the variance in observable classroom reading behaviors was attributable to previous learning (i.e., represented by a pretest); amount of teacher-led instruction (e.g., modeling, explanation, feedback, cueing, monitoring); incentives to learn (i.e., reinforcement and "cognitive press"); and planned productivity (i.e., "pacing"). Promotion of classroom reading behavior, in turn, was related to posttest reading scores. An increase in approximately 5 minutes of silent reading per day would be expected to result in about a 1-month gain in tested achievement. These data can be interpreted to suggest that directive teacher behaviors are effective if (a) students have adequate preskills (i.e., represented by a pretest), and (b) time allocated for learning is structured and paced for learning disabled students.

Using methods borrowed from Leinhardt et al. (1981), Haynes and Jenkins (1984) looked at effects of instructional variables on reading performance for slightly older learning disabled students in part-time resource classrooms. In their sample of classrooms, Haynes and Jenkins found great variability in instruction unrelated to student characteristics, overall low levels of reading instruction, and no reliably predictive relationship between instructional process variables and achievement. Pretest scores, representing previous learning and level of preparedness, were most predictive of posttest performance. However, teachers' directive teaching behavior was once again found to be significantly related to students' reading behaviors. That is, teachers could increment engagement by providing task monitoring, feedback, explanation, and so forth, but the reduced amount of instructional time permitted in resource classrooms also reduced the ability of teacher-mediated structure alone to effectively transfer executive work to students.

In short, it appears that one or both of two conditions must exist for even conventional teaching to succeed with learning disabled students. First, students must have sufficient preparation or preskills to be able to learn to use teacher-provided structure (e.g., see Pflaum & Pascarella, 1980; Pflaum, Pascarella, Auer, Augustyn, & Boswick, 1982). Second, intensive and directive teacher attention must force an increase in information-handling efficiency. Evidently, the environmental arrangements that force efficiency can transfer to student control if instruction occurs over sufficiently long (i.e., extensive) periods of time.

An interesting question is raised, however, by the potency of these variables, summarized by what Leinhardt et al. (1981) referred to as cognitive press. Cognitive press was described as "the degree to which the target student was focused on academic material and the degree to which the teacher was supporting or encouraging that orientation" (p. 348). Although sufficient time and press appear to facilitate internalization of external task structure, it would clearly be desirable to encapsulate the extensive and intensive effort of such teacher-generated structure into self-regulatory routines that could be directly trained and modified. Were this possible, teachers, as part of ongoing instruction, would also begin to be relieved of a cognitive burden by shifting the executive work of response organization away from themselves and onto learning han capped students.

Decoding

Although much has been written about the use of CB methods to enhance reading comprehension (e.g., s Wong, 1985b) virtually no research is available for guidi teachers in overlapping task-specific and strategic instru tional goals when teaching basic decoding skills. Revie ing the first 13 years of *Reading Research Quarter* Pflaum, Walberg, Karegianes, and Rasher (1980) fou 665 investigations of instructional methods in reading. T researchers found that about 75% of experimental co trasts favored experimental over control groups. Me effect sizes ranged from −0.05 for one comparison (synt training) to 1.62 in three comparisons (sound-symb blending, individualized mastery training, and compr hension instruction). (It is important to note that of the 1 studies randomly selected for meta-analysis, 50% we found deficient due to an inadequate period of treatme [i.e., less than five sessions, no comparison control grou lack of inferential statistics]. In Pflaum et al.'s final san pling of ninety-seven studies, only thirty-one reporte means and standard deviations necessary for calculation effect size.)

The power of sound-symbol training, generally sun marized as phonics instruction, is noteworthy in light of large body of evidence that learning handicapped studen often experience enormous difficulty learning an developing automaticity at the level of word identificatio (Ackerman & Dykman, 1982; Stanovitch, 1983a). More over, in CBT studies of comprehension strategies, studen who are not able to decode rapidly (i.e., the less able an younger students) seldom demonstrate the same impres ive gains in comprehension as peers who are fast decoders

Palincsar and Brown (1984), for example, required tha students who were nominated by teachers for comprehen sion training could in fact read grade-appropriate words a better than 80 words per minute with fewer than two error before attempting to train them to monitor their compre hension. Conversely, gains in comprehension can some times be obtained by training mildly handicapped student to identify words more rapidly. Presumably, as decodin becomes more automatic, attentional resources can b allocated for establishing executive control of comprehen sion, as well as for processing of semantic information.

One interesting approach to teaching faster decoding the "repeated readings" technique, involves a cluster o similar techniques for promoting reading speed i deficient readers (e.g., for a brief review, see Bos, 1982) Several investigators have studied the use of this tech nique, and their research converges on the finding tha repeating reading of passages until criterion speeds ar achieved results in improved comprehension as well a greater passage fluency. Initial readings of each new passage tend to be faster than initial readings of previou passages, and performance reaches criterion levels o speed sooner on each successive trial (Samuels, 1979) lthough repeated readings and related techniques are milar to blind instructional interventions as defined by rown and her colleagues (1981), repeated readings do lustrate procedures that might lend themselves to a CBT ffort.

For example, in none of the repeated-readings studies eviewed by Bos (1982) did researchers specifically nstruct students about the significance of faster word lentification or about how to monitor their reading rates nd to compensate accordingly when they were reading too lowly to allocate sufficient attention to comprehension. nowledge about rate-comprehension and sound-symbol elationships and about how to use such knowledge while eading constitutes part of a necessary repertoire of nabling skills that, when purposefully and efficiently oordinated, can become the basis for a self-regulated trategy to assist reading comprehension. How potentially menable such a strategy might be to instruction using BT methods is unknown at the present time but deserves reater attention.

BT Methods Applied to Writing

Learning to write, perhaps more clearly than learning to ead, requires learning a hierarchy of skills, each becoming nore automatic and subordinate in turn to newly emerg-ng, more complex skills. Hence, unless letter drawing ecomes effortless, acquisition of spelling skills is impeded; ikewise, if adequate speed of processing during spelling ails to develop, cognitive resources will be unavailable to nanage ideation, narrative, and theme. A significant body of non-CBT research has accumulated to support these views (e.g., see Graham & Miller, 1979, 1980, 1982).

HANDWRITING

An early study by Robin, Armel, and O'Leary (1975) attempted to assess the effects of training kindergarten children who were having problems learning to write to verbally guide their own efforts. However, the procedure proved somewhat cumbersome and time-consuming. Overt verbalization did not correlate with handwriting performance, and even though treated children improved, there was no evidence of generalization to untrained letters. The researchers even allowed that self-verbalization may have interfered with task performance.

In another study, Kosiewicz, Hallahan, Lloyd, and Graves (1982) trained an older learning disabled student in a self-instruction procedure to be used during a paragraph copying exercise. The task-specific strategy that was taught consisted of naming each world, each syllable, and each letter within syllables before copying. A self-correction procedure in which errors from previous work were marked before copying was also investigated. Performance was best when both procedures were used simultaneously. The superior results reported in this study compared to those of Robin et al. (1975) might be attributable to the ages of students involved. The older student obviously possessed a knowledge base that included information about handwriting, such as letter names, appearance, and even an approximate, though inadequate, motor program to guide production. Also, it has often been suggested that older students are more capable metacognitively to constructively manage the potential interference of overt verbal self-instruction. However, a recent attempt to replicate Robin et al.'s CBT method with older learning disabled students failed to demonstrate large or generalized effects (Graham, 1983).

SPELLING

Although researchers have long suspected that poor spelling was in some way a window on mental activity, it is only recently that modern information-processing paradigms have been applied to the development of models of skilled spelling behavior (e.g., see Farnham-Diggory & Nelson, 1984; Frith, 1980). Gerber and Hall (1981; also see Gerber, 1984c, 1985) compared misspellings of attention disordered, learning disabled students with those of normal-achieving students with the hypothesis that similar kinds of errors could be interpreted to mean similar information processing. They found that learning disabled students produced errors that were similar to those of younger, normal-achieving peers. Evidently, learning disabled students accessed a knowledge base and problem solving processes similar to those accessed by younger, non-learning disabled students. Moreover, learning disabled students appeared to develop the same strategies for solving spelling problems in the same invariant sequence as normal-achieving students. The following general strategy stages were identified and described by Gerber and Hall.

1. An initial "preliterate" strategy recognizes that spelling requires written placeholders but demonstrates a limited knowledge base that may not include all of the alphabet or may not differentiate between the alphabet and other written symbols (e.g., DIODUFOS/dog; 8T/eighty).
2. A "prephonetic" strategy is based upon sufficient alphabet knowledge but lacks the power to rapidly encode a stable representation of the entire phonemic string (i.e., word). This may be because cognitively immature individuals do not yet understand that retrieval (i.e., recognition) of a whole word permits a more reliable representation of a phonemic string than does trying to encode the acoustical string in a serial fashion as it is perceived. Moreover, the knowledge base of children who use a prephonetic strategy also lacks stable, reliably accessible rules for obtaining a conventional parsing of each phonemic string. Consequently, some phonemes are represented, but some are not (e.g., SR/start; TP/type).
3. A "phonetic" strategy is based upon a stable representation of the phonemic string. In using this strategy, every phonemic position is matched with the name of a letter whose articulation position is as

close as possible to the articulation position of the target phoneme. Thus, all phonemes are represented by using letter names for vowels or by collapsing certain adjacent phonemes (e.g., UMN/human; LATR/latter; AT/ate).

4. A "transitional" strategy is based on a large knowledge base, consisting of an extensive lexicon, some orthographic rules and conventions, and routines for monitoring and correcting some types of errors. However, breadth of word knowledge, knowledge about less frequently used spelling conventions, and alternative problem-solving routines are still limited (e.g., TIPE/type; YOUMAN/human; BERD/bird).
5. A fifth strategy produces correct spellings. However, variability can be observed in the speed, rhythm, and efficiency of self-monitoring that accompanies correct spelling.

It was reasoned that older learning disabled students must have had much more experience with written language than younger students and, therefore might be susceptible to a CBT approach. Therefore, in a subsequent study (Gerber, 1982), effects of self-monitoring training using self-questioning procedures similar to those suggested by Meichenbaum and Goodman (1971) were assessed for younger and older learning disabled students as well as for a comparison group of normal-achieving students. Following two, 20-minute training sessions, error quality improved for older, but not for younger learning disabled students, to a level equivalent to that of untrained, non-learning disabled students. Interestingly, training also enhanced performance of normal-achieving students. These findings were interpreted to mean that older disabled students and normal-achieving students had "excess capacity" that could be recruited as a function of overt self-monitoring. However, it was observed that normal-achieving students were often disrupted by requests to self-verbalize and never imitated the modeled self-questioning as accurately as learning disabled students.

In a new series of training studies using external structure (Gerber, 1984b, 1984d; Nulman & Gerber, 1984), learning disabled students received a spelling dictation test of difficult words. Following each incorrect attempt, the trainer first imitated the error and then modeled the correct spelling. A new trial was repeated every day until all words were spelled correctly. In the first study (Nulman & Gerber, 1984), a student was presented with a second, rhyming list of words to assess transfer. Although numbers of correct spellings increased only by one word, correct spellings of specific orthographic features apparently generalized from the previous list. In the second study (Gerber, 1984c), students continued with the second list until they achieved mastery, at which time a third list was presented. Before attempting the third list, however, students were told that what they had learned about the previous lists would help them to spell the worlds in the new list. Results showed that students reached mastery in fewer trials and spelled more words correctly on the first trial of each successive list. The third study (Gerber, 1984d) replicated previous findings but assessed transfer with a nonrhyming list of words that contained some orthographic features in common with the first list. Results showed enhanced spelling of these features even though numbers of correctly spelled words remained the same.

Graham and Freeman (1984) conducted a CBT study in which learning disabled students were trained in use of a spelling study procedure. A self-choice condition was compared to three strategy-use conditions: teacher directed, teacher monitored, and student controlled. Students in all strategy-trained groups recalled more spellings than students in the self-choice condition but did not differ significantly among themselves. Graham and Freeman concluded that learning students lack and can benefit from either externally or internally controlled organization and task regulation.

Results from these studies can be interpreted to suggest that basic spelling acquisition by older elementary school learning disabled students may potentially benefit from comprehensive self-control training, including task-specific and more global self-regulatory strategies. As with other areas of academic skills training, substantial evidence exists to support instruction based upon externally provided structure (e.g., see Graham & Miller, 1979). Particularly well-researched procedures, such as limiting the number of items to be learned in a session, providing sufficient distributed practice, and sequencing and juxtaposing items to encourage generalization (Gettinger, 1984b), lend themselves to self-control training, and each has a potential parallel in an imaginable CBT design.

Composition

An early study by Ballard and Glynn (1975) used applied behavioral intervention techniques to train third graders to assess and appropriately reinforce their composition attempts. If self-monitoring was indeed induced by the self-assessment behaviors taught in this study, it did not result in clearly improved composition skills. Yet, some evidence was presented to indicate that self-assessment procedures and self-reinforcement together resulted in increased productivity (i.e., more sentences, more words). However, it is likely that self-administered reinforcement of objectively described composition behaviors was responsible for these changes, just as teacher-controlled reinforcement has similarly improved writing behavior. The fact that reinforcement was self-administered was an innovation, but the study falls short of being the type of self-control CBT study recommended by Brown et al. (1981).

In fact, CBT studies of composition with mildly handicapped students are still relatively rare. Recently, however, Harris and Graham (1985) reported an investigation in which a seven-part procedure was used to train awareness, appreciation, and effective use of various self-regulatory behaviors during composition. Students were taught hree task-specific strategies (i.e., use of action words, ction "helpers," describing words) and a five-step, self-questioning/self-statement, general strategy for story writing. Adult modeling, reinforced practice to criterion, nd self-assessment were then used to assure mastery. Results of the nested, multiple baseline experiment clearly howed that students' use of targeted word classes ncreased above baseline, as did number of words and overall quality of compositions. Follow-up probes after 14 weeks showed that training-induced changes in writing products were maintained.

CBT Methods Applied to Arithmetic

As with other academic skills, simple arithmetic has proven susceptible to direct, behavioral intervention (Carnine, 1983; Lloyd, 1980; Lloyd, Saltzman, & Kauffman, 1981). An early study with CBT implications was done by Lovitt and Curtiss (1968), who trained a student to verbalize arithmetic problems (e.g., "Some number minus two equals six") before attempting to solve them and write answers. This relatively simple, straightforward intervention resulted in an increased rate of correct responding on similar arithmetic problems that was maintained despite attempts to reverse this effect by giving instructions not to verbalize. However, effects did not spontaneously generalize to a different, but very similar, class of arithmetic problems. Nevertheless, when each new set was separately trained, results were similarly positive. An attempt by independent researchers to replicate these results failed, according to Lloyd (1980), raising questions about relationships among learners' knowledge base, instructional experience, and task-specific, problem-solving rules or algorithms.

A related study by Grimm, Bijou, and Parsons (1973) found that reinforcing overt steps in number concept tasks resulted in improvements in match-sample performance. In this study, two handicapped children were given special stimulus materials (i.e., three types of match-to-sample cards: numeral to countables, countables to numerals, countables to countables) and taught overt counting and circling of answers. This research successfully used contingent social and token reinforcement of a behavioral chain (i.e., pointing, verbal identification of sample, verbal counting, circling) to teach both students basic number concept. Despite its unequivocal behavioral paradigm, this study is notable because both intermittent and continuous teacher attention (i.e., explanation, corrective feedback) had previously failed to produce any observable effect on correct responding. Moreover, treatment effects were maintained even after withdrawal of teacher monitoring and reinforcement.

Despite a researcher's intuition that overt verbalization might improve performance on simple arithmetic, these early studies lacked a theoretical model of how students process information during simple arithmetic. Such models are beginning to emerge and may prove useful for designing CBT interventions (e.g., see Baroody, 1984; Carpenter, Moser, & Romberg, 1982; Russell & Ginsberg, 1984; for a more behavioral perspective on intervention design, see Carnine, 1983; Cullinan, Lloyd, & Epstein, 1981). Emerging models have emphasized developmental changes in mnemonic processes specific to learning simple arithmetic to a high level of automaticity. For example, certain strategies for handling arithmetic information appear to emerge in a predictable sequence as a function of normal cognitive development, such as the following strategies inferred from children's behavior during simple addition.

1. A "counting all with objects" strategy consists of representing each addend in concrete form using objects or fingers and then counting the combined group of objects. Example: 2 + 3 becomes // + /// becomes /////, which is counted as 5.
2. A "counting on" strategy involves transforming an addend into a paused count and then counting forward the number of counts indicated by the second addend. Example: 2 + 3 becomes 1, 2 + (3) becomes 1, 2 /// becomes 1, 2, 3, 4, 5.
3. "Counting on from largest" is similar to a counting on strategy but includes a step in which the largest of the two addends is selected and used for the paused count. This reduces the memory demand in the counting-forward step by minimizing the size of the counting associated with the second addend.
4. "Pattern recognition" represents awareness that sums are stable regardless of task, setting, or order of addends; and recognition of addend combinations for which alternative names (i.e., sums) are recalled from memory (e.g., simple identities, like 4 + 0 = 4; simple count-forwards pairs in which 1 or 2 is the second addend; simple doublets, such as 3 + 3; and all remaining combinations with 0 to 9 addends).

Although normal-achieving students learn to use such strategies spontaneously and flexibly, students with learning handicaps do not (Russell & Ginsburg, 1984). Moreover, a body of knowledge concerning abstract mathematical concepts and nonalgorithmic procedures (e.g., ordinality) is acquired sooner and more readily by nonhandicapped learners. There is obvious need for more research that evaluates the effectiveness of CBT techniques for enhancing strategy development and modifying chronically slow acquisition of arithmetic skills.

Needs and Recommendations

The purpose of this review was to assess the potential for applying a set of theoretically derived cognitive and CBT methods to the teaching of basic academic enabling skills to a generic group of mildly handicapped students. Lack of clear discrimination among existing categories of mildly handicapped and other slow learning or remedial students on instructionally relevant variables has led to the pragmatic conclusion that teachers should use powerful, direct instruction methods for teaching elemental academic responses. However, one of the foremost goals of special education for mildly handicapped students is to enhance students' abilities to be independent and successful learners, over and above training of discrete, task-specific responding. Therefore, it may prove to be useful for teachers to learn, customize, and use new instructional research models of CBT. These models appear to hold great promise for simultaneously addressing general learning competence as well as specific task performance.

Guidelines for Practitioners

Information helpful for implementing CBT approaches is unusually accessible to teachers compared to other educational interventions. This is because CBT research has developed several methodological standards that make translation into practice more intuitive and direct than most other educational research. Translation is facilitated primarily because much of this research focuses on relationships among instructional arrangement, instructor behavior, and associated changes in student performance on applied learning tasks—relationships that also form the core professional concern of classroom teachers.

Also, this research literature is perhaps more self-conscious in its concern for demonstrating internal validity of effects associated with experimentally manipulated instructions than other types of educational research (e.g., Belmont & Butterfield, 1977; Brown & Campione, 1978). In part, this self-consciousness arises from difficulties inherent in attempts to change cognitive processes by manipulating task environments and observable behavior. As a result, precise and detailed explanations of instructional manipulations have become more common. There has also been an accompanying tendency for more direct and systematic replication of findings than has been typical of research with mildly handicapped individuals in the past. Consequently, research has also tended to be more programmatic than one would otherwise expect in special education literature (e.g., see Torgesen & Dice, 1980). For practitioners, these factors have combined to make available an emerging body of literature that directly investigates academic tasks; attempts to fuse concern for content and general learning competence into instructional designs; explicitly describes how instructors (i.e., teachers) should behave and what instructional arrangements must exist to achieve what outcomes; and specifies measures and measurement tactics that are both practical and appear to have a least face validity.

Although the theoretical underpinnings of this work may be forbidding, its application would not seem to require a special background to mediate between research findings and their practical implications. The use of small-N designs, especially when accompanied by qualitative and graphical analysis, helps to make this research more understandable to lay readers, compared to typical group contrast studies in which sophisticated statistical analyses and statistically significant findings often support non-intuitive inferences. The practical significance of demonstrated effects in instructional research, when they can be documented, is more readily grasped and appreciated by practitioners. In-service and pre-service training programs should acquaint teachers with examples from the impressive body of ongoing work done by researchers like Brown, Borkowski, Farnham-Diggory, Graham, Hallahan, Torgesen, Wong, and their students and colleagues.

However, it would be wrong to leave the impression that this scant literature provides a panacea for planning differential programming for handicapped students. Quite to the contrary, this literature has not congealed into any universally applicable, easily transportable, well-documented curriculum package. In fact, teachers should be wary of the exaggerated claims being made for a new wave of commercial packages that advertise themselves as cognitive interventions and promise cognitive benefits for handicapped students. Normal professional prudence and knowledge of special education's past flirtations with cure-all treatments make it mandatory that teachers become familiar with the principles underlying CBT and not merely specific applications.

Moreover, it is likely that it is teachers who, when given appropriate in-service or pre-service training, will be best equipped and situated to create and empirically validate specific applications. Although further developments will likely come from formal research, there is a need for more diverse experimentation in a wider variety of situations than reasonably can be expected over the next several years. Therefore, teacher training programs and school in-service planners should take the initiative to empirically evaluate the general principles described in this review when applied to types of students and areas of curriculum that are systematically varied. Such an effort requires planfulness as well as a commitment to development and dissemination of objective evidence, but it might easily be included as part of ongoing curriculum and staff development and evaluation processes in local schools. Relevant state and federal policy-makers might encourage this type of application-development process by providing technical assistance and by soliciting competitive proposals from local and state educational agencies.

Future Directions

Although research that investigates effects of cognitive, cognitive-behavioral, and metacognitive variables on attention, memory, and self-regulation tasks has accumulated steadily since the mid-1970s, many laboratory analogue tasks used for training bear little resemblance to learning tasks typically observed in classrooms. Furthermore, studies have rarely focused on the acquisition of simple foundation skills, because it has been suggested that mnemonic and metacognitive abilities of cognitively immature learners are too limited to permit simultaneous attention to discrimination of specific responses and to rules, algorithms, and other procedural knowledge necessary to monitor and regulate performance. Therefore, it has been concluded by some researchers that basic skills are not amenable to cognitive self-control strategy training. Instead, researchers have gravitated to complex cognitive skills associated with learning independence, such as reading comprehension (e.g., see Wong, 1985b).

It is unfortunate that CBT methods have not been fully explored for influencing acquisition of basic reading, writing, and arithmetic skills. Unless students develop high degrees of automaticity in using these skills, the ability to use more complex learning strategies will likely be less attainable. In fact, researchers conducting experiments aimed at inducing these higher level skills have reported almost uniformly that prerequisite skills must be verified or directly taught before strategy training can proceed. A related finding has been that older students, who presumably possess adequate basic skills, are generally more responsive to self-regulation strategy than younger or less mature peers. However, a sufficient empirical test has not yet been conducted of the susceptibility of handicapped learners to CBT methods for teaching basic academic skills. In particular, work by Ghatala and her colleagues (Ghatala et al., 1985; Lodico, Ghatala, Levin, Pressley, & Bell, 1983; Pressley, Ross, Levin, & Ghatala, 1984) on using CBT techniques to teach strategy monitoring as part of a training sequence that includes task-specific strategies provides the research paradigm and evidentiary basis for pursuing research in this area more vigorously.

Reasons to Be Hopeful

Results from the few studies of effects of CBT on basic skill acquisition can be interpreted to suggest that initial attempts to learn alphabet, sound-symbol associations, number concept, simple arithmetic, spelling, and word identification are special instances of problem solving. In these cases, a knowledge base, albeit limited, transacts with invented or improvised tactics for deciding upon an appropriate response. When viewed in this way, situational demands to read individual words, add numbers, or spell induce response uncertainty at a level of recognizable alarm sufficient to motivate action. Cognitively immature children then attempt to reduce uncertainty by a combination of rote and improvised behaviors. Although their responses often reveal limited knowledge and hasty decisions, they also reveal some knowledge and some decision making—indicators of emerging competence even in mildly handicapped students, rather than signs of deficit. Also, when mildly handicapped students are observed using basic academic skills, their performance is similar, but not identical, to that of normal-achieving, younger peers. Their longer experience with schooling makes them cognitively distinct from younger children and, therefore, more likely candidates for use of CBT methods.

It has been clearly demonstrated that instructions to verbalize specific or general task-orientation questions often helps control attention, maintain task-orientation, and improve quality of response (e.g., see Hallahan et al., 1983; Gerber & Niemann, 1982). Attempts at error repair and self-correction, however ineffective, are also observed following such training (Gerber, 1982). Even young students can be taught to actively evaluate and select strategies for effectiveness (e.g., Ghatala et al., 1985). These should be taken as hopeful signs, rather than as disappointingly narrow findings.

None of this should be construed as an argument against active, directive teaching or as an unqualified endorsement of CBT methods. Rather, this discussion poses two, enduring questions about how teaching can ever hope to facilitate cognitive development and accelerated academic achievement in handicapped children. First, to what degree should or could teaching aim to recruit the assistance of learners on their own behalf? Second, to what extent should teaching methods reflect a learning competency curriculum as opposed to a curriculum composed of arbitrary, fragmented skills, subskills, and discrete, task-specific responses? These questions address two related, but different, concerns. The first question is concerned with instructional efficiency as much as with strategy. To some extent, at least, the power of various direct instruction or behavior management techniques can be attributable to the fact that these techniques provide external structure to replace or supplement deficiences in student-generated, cognitive structure. However, external management of students' learning behavior must occur in real classrooms comprised of heterogeneous groups of students who vary on many instructionally relevant dimensions. Managing a learning environment optimally for each student requires enormous knowledge, skill, and effort. Under these circumstances, there is an obvious and clear economic need to transfer control of learning to students as quickly as possible. Students who have been identified as mildly handicapped merely accentuate this need regardless of placement status or administrative arrangement for their instruction.

The second question posed in this discussion really addresses theoretical and curricular issues regarding instructional effectiveness rather than efficiency, instructional purpose as well as practice. The question implies a need to design instructional approaches that will accelerate the academic progress of mildly handicapped students. Such approaches, perhaps embedded in new technologies of instruction, will be necessary if special educators are to have any hope of narrowing the achievement gap between mildly handicapped students and their normal-achieving peers. The explicit promise associated with emergence of CBT theory and methods is that global as well as particular levels of achievement, performance, and ability can be addressed in a unified manner. That is, CBT may enable students to learn not only discrete responses to academic tasks but also general procedures for managing their own cognitive resources across a range of potential problems. Thus, a curriculum goal that may be superordinate to the normal scope and sequence of discrete academic skills is implied. Moreover, this superordinate curriculum goal—training generalized problem-solving competence—may lead to greater clarity in differentiating special from regular education.

Author Information

Michael M. Gerber is Associate Professor at the Graduate School of Education, University of California at Santa Barbara.

References

Abikoff, H. (1979). Cognitive training interventions in children: A review of a new approach. *Journal of Learning Disabilities,* **12**(2), 65–77.

Ackerman, P. T., & Dykman, R. A. (1982). Automatic and effortful information-processing deficits in children with learning and attention disorders. *Topics in Learning and Learning Disabilities,* **2**(2), 12–22.

Algozzine, B., & Korinek, L. (1985). Where is special education for students with high prevalence going? *Exceptional Children,* **51**, 388–394.

Algozzine, B., & Ysseldyke, J. (1983). Learning disabilities as a subset of school failure: The oversophistication of a concept. *Exceptional Children,* **50**, 242–246.

Atkinson, R. C., & Shiffrin, R. M. (1968). Human memory: A proposed system and its control processes. In K. W. Spence & J. T. Spence (Eds.), *The psychology of learning and motivation* (Vol. 2, pp. 7–113). New York: Academic Press.

Ballard, K. D., & Glynn, T. (1975). Behavioral self-management in story writing with elementary school age children. *Journal of Applied Behavior Analysis,* **8**, 387–398.

Baroody, A. J. (1984). The case of Felicia: A young child's strategies for reducing memory during mental addition. *Cognition and Instruction,* **1**, 109–116.

Becker, W. C. (1977). Teaching reading and language to the disadvantaged—What we have learned from field research. *Harvard Educational Review,* **47**, 518–543.

Becker, W. C., & Carnine, D. W. (1981). Direct instruction: A behavior theory model for comprehensive educational intervention with the disadvantaged. In S. W. Bijou & R. Ruis (Eds.), *Behavior modification: Contributions to education.* Hillsdale, NJ: Erlbaum.

Belmont, J. M., & Butterfield, E. C. (1969). The relations of short-term memory to development and intelligence. In L. Lipitt & H. Reese (Eds.), *Advances in child development and behavior* (Vol. 4). New York: Academic Press.

Belmont, J. M., & Butterfield, E. C. (1971). Learning strategies as determinants of memory deficiencies. *Cognitive Psychology,* **2**, 411–420.

Belmont, J. M., & Butterfield, E. C. (1977). The instructional approach to developmental cognitive research. In R. Kail & J. Hagen (Eds.), *Perspectives on the development of memory and cognition* (pp. 437–481). Hillsdale, NJ: Erlbaum.

Bloom, B. S. (1984). The 2 Sigma Problem: The search for methods of group instruction as effective as one-to-one tutoring. *Educational Research,* **13**, 4–16.

Borkowski, J. G., & Cavanaugh, J. C. (1979), Maintenance and generalization of skills and strategies by the retarded. In N. R. Ellis (Ed.), *Handbook of mental deficiency: Psychological theory and research* (2nd ed.) (pp. 569–617). Hillsdale, NJ: Erlbaum.

Borkowski, J. G., & Konarski, E. A. (1981). Educational implications of efforts to train intelligence. *Journal of Special Education,* **15**, 289–305.

Bos, C. S. (1982). Getting past decoding: Assisted and repeated readings as remedial methods for learning disabled students. *Topics in Learning and Learning Disabilities,* **1**(4), 51–57.

Brown, A. L. (1974). The role of strategic behavior in retardate memory. In N. R. Ellis (Ed.), *International review of research in mental retardation* (Vol. 7, pp. 55–111). New York: Academic Press.

Brown, A., & Campione, J. (1978). Permissible inferences from the outcome of training studies in cognitive development research. *Quarterly Newsletter for the Institute for Comparative Human Development,* **2**, 46–53.

Brown, A. L., Campione, J. C., & Day, J. D. (1981). Learning to learn: On training students to learn from texts. *Educational Researcher,* **10**(2), 14–21.

Brown, A. L., & Palincsar, A. S. (1982). Inducing strategic learning from texts by means of informed, self-control training. *Topics in Learning and Learning Disabilities,* **2**(1), 1–18.

Campione, J. C., & Brown, A. L. (1977). Memory and metamemory development in educable retarded children. In R. V. Kail & J. W. Hagen (Eds.), *Perspectives on the development of memory and cognition.* Hillsdale, NJ: Erlbaum.

Carnine, D. (1983). Direct instruction: In search of instructional solutions for educational problems. In *Interdisciplinary voices in learning disabilities and remedial education* (pp. 1–66). Austin, TX: Pro-Ed.

Carpenter, T., Moser, J., & Romberg, T. (Eds.). (1982). *Addition and subtraction: A cognitive perspective.* Hillsdale, NJ: Erlbaum.

Chi, M. T. H., & Gallagher, J. D. (1982). Speed of processing: A developmental source of limitation. *Topics in Learning and Learning Disabilities,* **2**(2), 23–32.

Cooper, H. M. (1982). Scientific guidelines for conducting integrative research reviews. *Review of Educational Research,* **52**, 291–302.

Corno, L., & Mandinach, E. B. (1983). The role of cognitive engagement in classroom learning and motivation. *Educational Psychologist,* **18**, 88–108.

Craik, F. I. M., & Lockhart, R. S. (1972). Levels of processing: A framework for memory research. *Journal of Verbal Learning and Verbal Behavior,* **11**, 671–684.

Cullinan, D., Lloyd, J., & Epstein, M. H. (1981). Strategy training: A structured approach to arithmetic instruction. *Exceptional Education Quarterly,* **2**(1), 41–49.

Egeland, B. (1974). Training impulsive children in the use of more efficient scanning techniques. *Child Development,* **45**, 165–171.

Engelmann, S. (1969). *Preventing failure in the primary grades.* Chicago, IL: Stanford Research Associates.

Farnham-Diggory, S., & Nelson, B. (1984). Cognitive analyses of basic school tasks. *Applied Developmental Psychology,* **1**, 21–74.

Flavell, J. H., Friedrichs, A. G., & Hoyt, J. D. (1970). Developmental changes in memorization processes. *Cognitive Psychology,* **1**, 324–340.

Frith, U. (1980). *Cognitive processes in spelling.* London: Academic Press.

Gerber, M. M. (1982, April). *Effects of self-monitoring training on the spelling performance of learning disabled and normally achieving students.* Paper presented at the annual meeting of the American Educational Research Association, New York.

Gerber, M. M. (1983). Learning disabilities and cognitive strategies: A case for training or constraining problem solving? *Journal of Learning Disabilities,* **16**, 255–260.

Gerber, M. M. (1984a). The Department of Education's Sixth Annual Report to Congress on P.L. 94–142: Is Congress getting the full story? *Exceptional Children,* **51**, 209–224.

Gerber, M. M. (1984b, April). *Generalization of spelling strategies by LD students as a result of contingent imitation/modeling and mastery criteria.* Paper presented at the annual meeting of the American Educational Research Association, New Orleans, LA.

Gerber, M. M. (1984c). Investigations of orthographic problem-solving ability in learning disabled and normally achieving students. *Learning Disability Quarterly,* **7,** 157–164.

Gerber, M. M. (1984d). Techniques to teach generalizable spelling skills. *Academic Therapy,* **20**(1), 49–58.

Gerber, M. M. (1985). Spelling as concept-driven problem solving. In B. Butson (Ed.), *Advances in reading/language research* (Vol. 3, pp. 39–75). Greenwich, CT: JAI.

Gerber, M. M., & Hall, R. J. (April, 1981). *The development of orthographic problem solving strategies in learning disabled children.* Paper presented at the annual meeting of the American Educational Research Association, Los Angeles, CA.

Gerber, M. M., & Niemann, C. (1983). *Self-monitoring and acquisition of new academic skills.* Unpublished manuscript.

Gerber, M. M., & Semmel, M. I. (1984). Teacher as imperfect test: Reconceptualizing the referral process. *Educational Psychologist,* **19,** 137–148.

Gerber, M. M., & Semmel, M. I. (1985). The microeconomics of referral and integration: A paradigm for evaluation of special education. *Studies in Educational Evaluation,* **11,** 13–29.

Gettinger, M. (1984a). Achievement as a function of time spent in learning and time needed for learning. *American Educational Research Journal,* **21,** 617–628.

Gettinger, M. (1984b). Applying learning principles to remedial spelling instruction. *Academic Therapy,* **20**(1), 41–48.

Gettinger, M., & White, M. A. (1979). Which is the stronger correlate of school learning? Time to learn or measured intelligence? *Journal of Educational Psychology,* **71,** 405–412.

Ghatala, E. S., Levin, J. R., Pressley, M., & Lodico, M. G. (1985). Training cognitive strategy-monitoring in children. *American Educational Research Journal,* **22**(2), 199–215.

Good, T. L. (1983). Classroom research: A decade of progress. *Educational Psychologist,* **18,** 127–144.

Graham, S. (1983). The effect of self-instructional procedures on LD students' handwriting performance. *Learning Disability Quarterly,* **6,** 231–234.

Graham, S., & Freeman, S. (1984). *Strategy training and teacher vs. student-controlled study conditions: Effects of learning disabled students' spelling performance.* Unpublished manuscript.

Graham, S., & Miller, L. (1979). Spelling research and practice: A unified approach. *Focus on Exceptional Children,* **12**(2), 1–16.

Graham, S., & Miller, L. (1980). Handwriting research and practice: A unified approach. *Focus on Exceptional Children,* **13**(2), 1–16.

Graham, S., & Miller, L. (1982). Composition research and practice: A unified approach. *Focus on Exceptional Children,* **14,** 1–16.

Grimm, J. A., Bijou, S. W., & Parsons, J. A. (1973). A problem solving model for teaching remedial arithmetic to handicapped young children. *Journal of Abnormal Child Psychology,* **1,** 26–39.

Hall, R. J. (1980). cognitive behavior modification and information-processing skills of exceptional children. *Exceptional Education Quarterly,* **1**(1), 9–15.

Hallahan, D. P. (1975). Comparative research studies on the psychological characteristics of learning disabled children. In W. Cruickshank & D. P. Hallahan (Eds.). *Perceptual and learning disabilities in children—Research and theory* (Vol. 2, pp. 29–60). Syracuse, NY: Syracuse University Press.

Hallahan, D. P. (Ed.). (1980). Teaching exceptional children to use cognitive strategies [special issue]. *Exceptional Education Quarterly,* **1**(1).

Hallahan, D. P., & Kauffman, J. M. (1977). Labels, categories, behaviors: ED, LD, and EMR reconsidered. *Journal of Special Education,* **11,** 139–149.

Hallahan, D. P., Hall, R. J., Ianna, S. O., Kneedler, R. D., Lloyd, J. W., Loper, A. B., & Reeve, R. E. (1983). Summary of research findings at the University of Virginia Learning Disabilities Research Institute. *Exceptional Education Quarterly,* **4**(1), 95–114.

Harris, K. R. (1982). Cognitive-behavior modification: Application with exceptional students. *Focus on Exceptional Children,* **15**(2), 1–16.

Harris, K. R., & Graham, S. (1985). Improving learning disabled students' composition skills: Self-control strategy training. *Learning Disability Quarterly,* **8,** 27–36.

Haynes, M. C., & Jenkins, J. R. (1984). *Reading instruction in special education resource rooms.* Unpublished manuscript.

Kauffman, J. M. (1980). Where special education for disturbed children is going: A personal view. *Exceptional Children,* **46,** 522–527.

Kavale, K., & Forness, S. (1985). *The science of learning disabilities.* San Diego, CA: College-Hill Press.

Kendall, P. C., & Wilcox, L. E. (1980). Cognitive-behavioral treatment for impulsivity: Concrete versus conceptual training in non-self-controlled problem children. *Journal of Consulting and Clinical Psychology,* **48,** 80–91.

Kosiewicz, M. H., Hallahan, D. P., Lloyd, J. W., & Graves, A. W. (1982). Effects of self-instruction and self-correction procedures on handwriting performance. *Learning Disability Quarterly,* **5,** 71–78.

Leinhardt, G., Zigmond, N., & Cooley, W. W. (1981). Reading instruction and its effects. *American Educational Research Journal,* **18,** 343–361.

Lloyd, J. (1975). The pedagogical orientation: An argument for improving instruction. *Journal of Learning Disabilities,* **8**(2), 74–78.

Lloyd, J. (1980). Academic instruction and cognitive behavior modification: The need for attack strategy training. *Exceptional Education Quarterly,* **1**(1), 53–63.

Lloyd, J., Cullinan, D., Heins, E. D., & Epstein, M. H. (1980). Direct instruction: Effects on oral and written language comprehension. *Learning Disability Quarterly,* **3,** 70–76.

Lloyd, J., Epstein, M. H., & Cullinan, D. (1979). *Direct teaching for learning disabilities* (Project ExCEL Working Paper 1). DeKalb, IL: Northern Illinois University, Department of Learning and Development.

Lloyd, J. W., Saltzman, N. J., & Kauffman, J. M. (1981). Predictable generalization in academic learning as a result of preskills and strategy training. *Learning Disability Quarterly,* **4,** 203–216.

Lodico, M. G., Ghatala, E. S., Levin, J. R., Pressley, M., & Bell, J. A. (1983). The effects of strategy-monitoring training on children's selection of effective memory strategies. *Journal of Experimental Child Psychology,* **35,** 263–277.

Loper, A. B. (1980). Metacognitive development: Implications for cognitive training. *Exceptional Education Quarterly,* **1**(1), 1–8.

Lovitt, T. (1975). Specific research recommendations and suggestions for practitioners. *Journal of Learning Disabilities,* **8**(8), 504–517.

Lovitt, T. C., & Curtiss, K. A. (1968). Effects of manipulating an antecedent event on mathematics response rate. *Journal of Applied Behavior Analysis,* **1,** 329–333.

MacMillan, D. L., Meyers, C. E., & Morrison, G. M. (1980). System-identification of mildly retarded children: Implications for integrating and conducting research. *American Journal of Mental Deficiency,* **85,** 108–115.

Meichenbaum, D. (1982). Cognitive behavior modification with exceptional children: A promise yet unfulfilled. *Topics in Learning and Learning Disabilities,* **2**(1), 83–87.

Meichenbaum, D., & Goodman, J. (1971). Training impulsive children to talk to themselves: A means of developing self-control. *Journal of Abnormal Psychology,* **77,** 115–126.

Meyen, E. L., & Moran, M. R. (1979). A perspective on the unserved mildly handicapped. *Exceptional Children,* **45,** 526–530.

Nulman, J. H., & Gerber, M. M. (1984). Improving spelling performance by imitating a child's errors. *Journal of Learning Disabilities,* **17**(6), 328–333.

Palincsar, A. S., & Brown, A. L. (1984). Reciprocal teaching of comprehension-fostering and comprehension-monitoring activities. *Cognition and Instruction,* **1**(2), 117–175.

Pflaum, S. W., & Pascarella, E. T. (1980). Interactive effects of prior reading achievement and training in context on the reading of learning disabled children. *Reading Research Quarterly,* **16,** 138–158.

Pflaum, S. W., Pascarella, E. T., Auer, C., Augustyn, L., & Boswick, M. (1982). Differential effects of four comprehension facilitating conditions in LD and normal elementary school readers. *Learning Disability Quarterly,* **5,** 106–116.

Pflaum, S. W., Walberg, H. J., Karegianes, M. L., & Rasher, S. P. (1980). Reading instruction: A quantitative analysis. *Educational Researcher,* **9**(7), 12–18.

Pressley, M., Ross, K. A., Levin, J. R., & Ghatala, E. S. (1984). Increasing the use of strategy-utility knowledge in children's strategy decision making. *Journal of Experimental Child Psychology,* **38,** 491–504.

Robin, A. L., Armel, S., & O'Leary, K. D. (1975). The effects of self-instruction on writing deficiencies. *Behavior Therapy,* **6,** 178–187.

Rosenshine, B. (1983). Teaching functions in instructional programs. *Elementary School Journal,* **83,** 335–351.

Russell, R. L. & Ginsburg, H. P. (1984). Cognitive analysis of children's mathematics difficulties. *Cognition and Instruction,* **1**(2), 217–244.

Samuels, S. J. (1979). The method of repeated readings. *The Reading Teacher,* **32,** 403–408.

Sheinker, A., Sheinker, J. M., & Stevens, L. J. (1984). Cognitive strategies for teaching the mildly handicapped. *Focus on Exceptional Children,* **17**(1), 1–15.

Shepard, L. A., Smith, M. L., & Vojir, C. P. (1983) Characteristics of pupils identified as learning disabled. *American Educational Research Journal,* **20,** 309–331.

Stallings, J. (1980). Allocated academic learning time revisited, or beyond time on task. *Educational Researcher,* **9,** 11–16.

Stanovitch, K. E. (1983a). Individual differences in the cognitive processes of reading: I. Word decoding. *Annual Review of Learning Disabilities,* **1,** 57–65.

Stanovitch, K. E. (1983b). Individual differences in the cognitive processes of reading: II. Text-level processing. *Annual Review of Learning Disabilities,* **1,** 66–71.

Sternberg, R. J. (1981). Cognitive-behavioral approaches to the training of intelligence in the retarded. *Journal of Special Education,* **15,** 165–183.

Sternberg, R. J., & Wagner, R. K. (1982). Automatization failure in learning disabilities. *Topics in Learning and Learning Disabilities,* **2**(2), 1–11.

Stevens, R., & Rosenshine, B. (1981). Advances in research on teaching, *Exceptional Education Quarterly,* **2**(1), 1–9.

Swanson, H. L. (Ed.). (1982). Controversy: Strategy or capacity deficit [Special Issue]. *Topics in Learning and Learning Disabilities,* **2**(2).

Torgesen, J. (1975). Problems and prospects in the study of learning disabilities. In E. M. Hetherington, J. W. Hagen, R. Kron, & A. H. Stein (Eds.), *Review of child development research* (Vol. 5, pp. 385–440). Chicago, IL: University of Chicago Press.

Torgesen, J. K. (1977). The role of nonspecific factors in the task performance of learning disabled children: A theoretical assessment. *Journal of Learning Disabilities,* **10**(1), 27–35.

Torgesen, J. K. (1982). The learning disabled child as an inactive learner: Educational implications. *Topics in Learning and Learning Disabilities,* **2**(1), 45–52.

Torgesen, J., & Dice, C. (1980). Characteristics of research on learning disabilities. *Journal of Learning Disabilities,* **13**(9), 531–535.

Torgesen, J. K., & Kail, R. V. (1980). Memory processes in exceptional children. In B. Keogh (Ed.), *Advances in special education* (Vol. 1, pp. 55–99). Greenwich, CT: JAI.

Tulving, E. (1972). Episodic and semantic memory. In E. Tulving & W. Donaldson (Eds.), *Organization of memory.* New York: Academic Press.

Walberg, H. J. (1984). Improving the productivity of America's schools. *Educational Leadership,* **41,** 19–27.

Wong, B. Y. L. (Ed.). (1982). Metacognition and learning disabilities [Special Issue]. *Topics in Learning and Learning Disabilities,* **2**(1).

Wong, B. Y. L. (1985a). Metacognition and learning disabilities. In T. G. Walker, D. Forrest, & E. MacKinnon (Eds.), *Metacognition, cognition, and human performance* (pp. 137–180). New York: Academic Press.

Wong, B. Y. L. (1985b). Self-questioning instructional research. *Review of Educational Research,* **55,** 227–268.

Ysseldyke, J., Algozzine, B., & Epps, S. (1983). A logical and empirical analysis of current practice in classifying students as handicapped. *Exceptional Children,* **50,** 160–166.

Programming Independent Living Skills for Handicapped Learners

LARRY K. IRVIN

Oregon Research Institute, and University of Oregon

DANIEL W. CLOSE and ROBERT L. WELLS

University of Oregon

Abstract—We have addressed five major topics in this review. First, the state of the art of program development in independent living skills was determined to be substantial for both mildly and severely handicapped learners. Second, the state of the science, or empirical validation of components of curriculum and instruction in independent living skills, was characterized as lacking. Current research on teaching generalization of skills was highlighted as exemplary. Third, the state of practice of program implementation was found to be largely undocumented. Existing model programs were described for both mildly and severely handicapped students. Fourth, the evidence on the impact of school programs was interpreted as showing that handicapped students do not develop optimal independent living skills during school years. Finally, the implications of these conclusions were detailed for policy developers, state and local agencies, and researchers.

Handicapped children grow older and become adults just like the rest of us. For many, the process is simply a function of age and is indistinguishable from that experienced by nonhandicapped youngsters. For some, though, much purposeful instruction and practice are required for adult roles to be assumed successfully. For a few others, instruction must be precisely focused, sequenced, and guided; rehearsal must be repeated; and other conditions for learning and performing must be optimal if even small elements of adult roles are to be assumed.

Increasing professional effort has been directed toward developing, delivering, and evaluating the impact of instruction in independent living skills for handicapped students. It derives primarily from an ideological commitment to enabling these young people, as they grow older, to function successfully in as many valued adult roles as possible. The principle of normalization (Wolfensberger, 1972) is the major foundation of this commitment. PL 94-142 and various federal court determinations regarding "appropriate education" are its legal operationalization (e.g., *Battles v. Commonwealth of Pennsylvania,* 1980).

The intent of this chapter is to review the nature and impact of curriculum and instruction in independent living skills in school programs for handicapped children and youth. Severity of handicap is the primary dimension along which the differential aspects of such programming are examined. The major focus is on programs for students with mild mental retardation or severe handicaps. It is largely within these efforts that development of independent living skills instruction has occurred, if it has occurred at all. Relevant programs for students with learning disabilities are addressed as appropriate.

Severely Handicapped Learners

Recent and commonly used definitions of *severely handicapped* learners have all been referenced to education in one way or another, primarily to document the perceived need for differential educational programming for such learners (Wilcox & Bellamy, 1982). The definition that seems most consistent with the individual programming requirements of PL 94-142 is one in which level of handicap is determined by the focus of needed educational programming (Sontag, Smith, & Sailor, 1977). This definition allows for important distinctions between impairments or disabilities and their effect (i.e., handicap) in any context (Wood, 1978). And it accounts for the fact that level of handicap is not a unitary concept—one can experience a severe handicap with respect to vocational development concomitantly with a less severe handicap regarding home living.

Most of the recent definitions also stress that one characteristic of most severely handicapped school-age individuals is severe intellectual impairment—IQ scores lower than four standard deviations below the mean on a standardized individualized IQ test (Bricker & Filler, 1985). This consensus is reflected in this review. Distinctions in home and community living programming needs are *not* made here on the basis of whether retardation is or is not accompanied by other disabilities.

Mildly Handicapped Learners

As Gerber and Semmel (1984) emphasized, "psychometric-based identification procedures for children thought to be learning disabled, mildly mentally retarded, and emotionally disturbed are inappropriate as a basis for public policy and irrelevant to program development efforts" (p. 137). The current push toward declassification of students with mild mental retardation is clear (Polloway & Smith, 1983). The emphasis is on identifying similarities between students with learning disabilities and mild mental retardation because both of these groups of students experience academic and social problems in school and in independent living after leaving school.

Treatment of youth with learning disabilities or mild mental retardation is an educational responsibility. Thus, we define learning disability and mild mental retardation as "mildly handicapping" conditions. McLeod (1983) noted that, whatever the terminology, the first necessity is to define clearly, defensibly, and in an educational context those in need of specialized help. After identification, intervention should begin on an individual basis. We propose to address the problem of how to intervene with these individuals so that school failure does not seriously limit their opportunities to assume meaningful life roles.

Content of Independent Living Skills

As Vogelsberg, Williams, and Bellamy (1982) noted, the content of the independent living domain is limitless. It includes any skills needed for integrated home and community living. For severely handicapped learners, independence is a relative concept—it is a function of environmental opportunities and demands, modifications of those demands, individual skills, and daily application of those skills. Students' access to and participation in activities of daily living, as well as students' and parents' values about environments in which participation is desired, are important determinants of adequacy of independent living.

For learners with mild handicaps, content is focused on "the important knowledge, skills and attitudes" necessary for "various life roles and settings" (Kokaska & Brolin, 1985, p. 43). In this "career education" approach, individuals are viewed as pursuing a multiplicity of careers during their lifetimes: learner, consumer, family member, citizen, worker. Foundation in basic academics, vocational preparation, and personal–social and daily living skills is required if competence is to be achieved in life roles (Bender & Valletutti, 1982; Kokaska & Brolin, 1985).

A useful context is provided by these perspectives. Direct implications exist for the content *and* the rationale of instruction in independent living. The dual emphasis on skills and participation, and on adult roles within current programming for handicapped learners, provides a rationale and definition, even on an individual student basis, for *what* to teach and for *why* that content is appropriate.

Because the domain of independent living is potentially so large, it is somewhat narrowly defined here in terms of the "general domestic" and "general community living" roles and related skills commonly identified as essential for handicapped students. Relevant research on program development and instructional technology has been concentrated in the areas of home living (cooking, cleaning, telephone use); use of community facilities (restaurants, grocery stores); mobility in the community (bus riding, street crossing); personal appearance (dressing, laundry, grooming); use of money (coin summation, change computation, banking); and health care (medication, first aid) (Cuvo & Davis, 1983).

The roles and related skills involved in work, leisure, and purely social–interpersonal pursuits are not emphasized here. Clearly, they are components of the larger framework of independent living, and there is overlap among home, community, and work roles and skills, especially in domains such as social skills and mobility. However, each of these components of work, leisure, and social skills has been the focus of a substantial body of program development and research literature in its own right. In the present review, home and community living components of independent living are emphasized. Thus, social, vocational, and adult development are treated as boundary issues here and are addressed when relevant. In addition, the role(s) of parents, peers, or significant others are treated as boundary issues in this review. The nature of parental and peer involvement has been delineated in a variety of program design criteria (see Kokaska & Brolin, 1985; Rose, 1984; Wilcox & Bellamy, 1984).

Policy Trends

Several clear trends exist in public policy—judicial, legislative, and programmatic—to provide a context for this review. Programs for severely handicapped students are themselves in transition—from permissive to entitlement (Noel, Burke, & Valdivieso, 1985), and from school based to community based. "The task of preparing severely handicapped persons to function in community-based settings is becoming the responsibility of local public school systems" (Schutz, Williams, Iverson, & Duncan, 1984, p. 16).

The determination of *appropriateness* of educational experience for handicapped youth has emerged as a major policy question. Where judicial determinations have been made, especially with reference to learners with severe handicaps, it is clear that the domains of independent living that comprise home and community living have been identified as *the* appropriate educational emphases (Laski, 1985).

Transition from school to adult roles is another focus of much recent policy development and implementation effort, as addressed by Halpern (1985) and Will (1984). The "future orientation" identified as essential in educational programming by Williams, Vogelsberg, and Schutz (1985) and others provides additional impetus to efforts that address transition issues.

Finally, policies to guide integration of handicapped students into school and community environments (including continuing and higher education) are and will continue to be the foundation for a variety of interrelated program developments (Brolin, 1984; Noel et al., 1985; Polloway, 1984). PL 94-142, and its "least restrictive environment" provision, provide the necessary policy framework for accomplishing integration (Peck & Cooke, 1983). The ideological foundation, an expansion of the normalization principle for school-age youth, is provided by Brown, Branston, et al. (1979) and others.

merging Issues

ISPARITY BETWEEN PROGRAM EVELOPMENT AND EMPIRICAL VALIDATION

The "state of the art" of curriculum and program evelopment is evident in home and community living nstruction for severely handicapped learners. A substanal program development effort has occurred in the last 5 ears (e.g., Sailor & Guess, 1983; Wilcox & Bellamy, 982). endent living needs of mildly handicapped learners (e.g., Halpern, Close, & Nelson, 1985; Schalock, Harper, & arver, 1981). A number of curriculum packages have een developed to address independent living skills for mildly handicapped learners in school settings (e.g., Brolin, 1978; Clark, 1979; Taylor, Close, Carlson, & Larrabee, 1981; Wimmer, 1981).

The empirical validation of the effects of differential pplications of programming components is not so evident, however, nor is it clearly focused and structured for either mildly or severely handicapped learners (Polloway & Epstein, 1985; Switzky & Haywood, 1985). The "state of he science" of curriculum and instructional technology in home and community living for school-age handicapped youth is lacking. The disparity between the development and the programmatic validation of program, curriculum, and instructional technology is a major focus of this eview. The evidence on the nature and effectiveness of program design, curriculum, and instructional technology s examined and interpreted.

ACCESS

Access to appropriate educational programs for home and community living in the least restrictive environment is another issue explored here. The "state of practice," that is, the nature and extent of translation of curriculum and program development into existing educational practices for handicapped youth, is examined. A clear foundation is provided for such access by PL 94-142 and various federal court determinations of appropriateness (e.g., *Battles v. Commonwealth of Pennsylvania,* 1980; *Campbell v. Talladega County Board of Education,* 1981). Answers to the question, Access to what? are not equally unequivocal. To the extent that descriptions and evaluations of the state of practice are available, they are reviewed here.

IMPACT OF INSTRUCTION

A number of well-known, follow-up studies were conducted before 1980 to examine the postschool adjustment of disabled persons (e.g., Baller, Charles, & Miller, 1967; Kennedy, 1966). Most were focused on individuals with mild or moderate handicaps. Several recent postschool follow-up efforts also have been reported (e.g., Mithaug, Horiuchi, & Fanning, 1985). Part of the increasing interest in their results appears to be motivated by current questions regarding the effects of special education services. In addition, the recent federal priority regarding the transition from school life to working life has served to sharpen the focus on this issue (Will, 1984). The results and implications of these recent follow-up studies are examined in this review. Issues related to social validity are included (e.g., Kazdin & Matson, 1981).

A Roadmap for the Reader

The evaluation of relevant research and professional practice that is presented in this review is organized in the following manner. First, an evaluative summary is presented of the state of the art of program development in independent living domains for handicapped learners. A clear distinction is made between programs developed for severely handicapped learners and those developed for learners with mild handicaps. After this review of the state of the art, an analysis of the state of the science is presented. In this analysis, the research foundation for curricular and instructional technology is evaluated. Current research emphases are then described separately for efforts relevant to mildly and severely handicapped learners. Following the state of the science review is an examination of the state of practice of implementation efforts related to programming independent living skills instruction for handicapped learners. Examples and characteristics of model programs are identified separately for mildly and severely handicapped learners. Relevant evaluation data are presented. Following this state of practice review is an evaluative summary of evidence regarding the impact of school programs on independent living skills of handicapped learners. Finally, the implications of the conclusions that result from the review are presented for future research, policy development, and state and local program development.

Curriculum and Instructional Technology: State of the Art—Program Development

Program Development for Severely Handicapped Learners

Three major curricular approaches have emerged in applications for severely handicapped students: the *developmental*, or *normative/developmental*; the *behavioral* or *operant*; and the *ecological*, or *community adaptation.*

DEVELOPMENTAL CURRICULAR APPROACH

The developmental, or normative/developmental, approach is based on three assumptions: normal developmental sequence as the most logical ordering of behaviors;

the prerequisite nature of some behaviors; and the appropriateness of behaviors acquired at a certain age by nonhandicapped children as objectives for severely handicapped students who are at the same level of development, regardless of age (e.g., Baldwin, 1976). Curricula take the form of developmentally sequenced behavior checklists (e.g., Hanson, 1977); task-analyzed developmental sequences (e.g., Fredericks et al., 1980); and/or task-analyses of developmental activities *and* their consequences in other developmental tasks, as well as descriptions of integrated activities to achieve multiple objectives (Connor, Williamson, & Siepp, 1978).

The conceptual relevance of normative scales for development of severely handicapped children has been challenged (e.g., Switzky, Rotatori, Miller, & Freagon, 1979; Vincent et al., 1980). Additionally, the developmental model has been taken to task for emphasizing "curriculum objectives which are often disassociated from each other, as well as from usual behavior and environmental contexts in which youngsters (or adults) with severe handicaps are engaged" (Brinker, 1985, p. 217). The relevance of the developmental model for independent living skills instruction can also be questioned. Severely handicapped students are likely to progress slowly through early prerequisite sequences. They may not be provided with opportunities to learn community survival skills.

Behavioral Curricular Approach

The behavioral, or operant, model includes several major elements: experimental (functional) analysis of the relationships between specific behaviors and specific antecedents and consequences; task analyses of content (behavior) into teachable and measurable components; and use of prompting, shaping, and feedback (Brinker, 1985). Curricula incorporating this approach combine task-analyzed components of behaviors and systematic applications of instructional procedures such as cues and prompts (e.g., Project MORE [Lent & McLean, 1976]; Community Living Assessment and Teaching System [CLATS] [Close, Halpern, Slentz, & Irvin, 1984]).

The utility of behavioral curricula has been criticized for too great an emphasis on detailed task analyses at the possible cost of slowing down some learners by training through unnecessary steps (Liberty & Wilcox, 1981) and for too often producing only results specific to the training setting. This latter problem has been the focus of a substantial research effort during the past 5 years and is addressed in more detail later in this review. There are two additional shortcomings of many behavioral curriculum applications. First, skills are often taught in an isolated fashion, even though in everyday life they are needed simultaneously (e.g., the communication skills often needed during preparation of meals and while eating). Second, nonfunctional skills have often been instructional targets, largely because they are the most amenable to the formats of behavioral technology (e.g., massed trial instruction of hand raising for imitation training [Guess & Noonan, 1982]).

Ecological Curricular Approach

The ecological, or community adaptation, model plac emphasis upon functional, chronological-age-appropria skills for successful integration into home, community, a work settings. In a paper that has had enormous impact program design for severely handicapped learners, Brow Nietupski, and Hamre-Nietupski (1976) proposed t "criterion of ultimate functioning" as the basis for curric lum applications. In this "top-down" model, the importa tasks in current and future (adult) environments are t focus of instruction. The logical justifications for th approach include increases in independent participation postschool integrated environments (Brown, Falvey, e al., 1979; Voglesberg et al., 1982), and optimal use of t "relatively little time" for students with significant pe formance deficits "to develop those skills necessary to su port independent living" (Wilcox & Bellamy, 1982, p. 30 It is also emphasized that "changing the quality of life" fo learners with severe handicaps "requires direct instructio on important tasks of adult life" (Wilcox & Bellam 1982, p. 30).

Several related approaches to program design hav emerged from this general framework. In a recent revie of education for severely handicapped elementary-ag children, Tawney and Sniezek (1985) described thre foundations that serve to shape present and futur program design: a functional curriculum for independen living for adulthood, public education in communit placements, and maximum interaction with non handicapped persons. Similarly, Williams et al. (1985 described a model for secondary education based on post school environmental demands as a curriculum base, wit a "focus on reducing individual dependencies on other and enhancing the quality of environments to which learners have access" (p. 104). The major elements include *adaptation of performance objectives* to enable at leas partial participation; *community-based instruction,* that is, teaching skills under conditions that exist in the natura environment by in-school simulation and/or in vivo instruction; *social integration* of students with and without severe handicaps; *facilitating transitions to postschool environments* via coordinated planning with service providers in residential, work, leisure, and educational agencies; and *parental involvement* in school-based planning and program implementation, as well as in postschool planning.

A variation based on these foundations, which involves teaching skill clusters, has been proposed by Guess and colleagues (e.g., Guess & Noonan, 1982). In this variation, critical skills and skill clusters are identified. These are behaviors essential to successful performance within and across content domains. They are taught as functional clusters to enable more learner interaction with elements of current and next environments. For example, a child might be taught to look at an object (toy for young child, radio or hairbrush for older child); raise his or her head; produce a sound; reach out and grasp the object; and then use it in an appropriate manner (Guess & Noonan, 1982).

This "individualized curriculum sequencing" (ICS) model is certainly compatible with the criterion of ultimate functioning. Older students can be involved in skill cluster instruction, such as counting money, making purchases in a cafeteria, and carrying food to a table. This model is one way to combine the skill deficiency assessment strength of the developmental tradition, with appropriate behavioral technology aimed at functional skills instruction across multiple content domains (Guess & Noonan, 1982).

Other recent examples of program design for severely handicapped learners have similar emphases. The criterion of ultimate functioning and its various corollaries—the "criterion of the next educational environment" (Vincent et al., 1980), integration, community-based instruction, and functional content—make up the well-defined philosophical foundation for all of these efforts (e.g., Baumgart et al., 1982; Ford & Mirenda, 1984).

For all of its apparent utility in applications regarding independent living skills instruction (particularly its emphasis on participation and integration), the ecological model has historically lacked an empirical basis. Its premises—increases in independence, optimal use of instructional time, necessity of direct instruction for changing quality of life, community-based instruction, parental involvement—have not been tested widely or validated in any programmatic sense. Its appeal and promise are large, but its relative utility with respect to valued criteria (post-school quality-of-life indicators such as participation and independence) has not been documented.

Program Development for Mildly Handicapped Learners

One major approach has emerged for programming independent living skills for learners with mild handicaps: career education. This concept has had great influence on special education programs for mildly handicapped students. Although much confusion exists concerning the precise definition of career education, many career education activities are common in school districts throughout the United States (Hoyt, 1982).

Life Skills Education

A key component of career education, as opposed to vocational education, is life skills education. On this topic, Super (1977) noted that "career education must take into account . . . the numerous roles which can constitute a career, and the non-occupational roles that acquire prominence in society as that of occupation diminishes" (p. 42). Implicit in this concept is the notion that life skills maintain and complement work activity. It has long been recognized that disabled persons often succeed or fail in work in large part due to competence in personal–social or independent living skills (Baller et al., 1967; Cobb, 1972). Kokaska and Brolin's (1985) recent definition attempted to clarify career education by emphasizing the various roles a person must perform in society. Thus, the current definition appears to be moving toward an integration of life skills, personal–social skills, and work or vocational skills to promote satisfactory adult adjustment.

Brolin (1973, 1978, 1983) defined career education from the perspective of what students need to know to be able to function after leaving school. The curriculum model developed by Brolin and his associates is the Life-Centered Career Education Model (LCCE) (Brolin, 1978). The LCCE curriculum is a competency-based model to help students acquire twenty-two major competencies that are critical to the successful community adjustment of handicapped persons. The twenty-two major competencies are organized into three major curriculum areas: (a) daily living skills; (b) personal–social skills; and (c) occupational skills. Kokaska and Brolin (1985) noted that these twenty-two competencies represent what research, practitioners' experience, and expert opinion have deemed essential for successful career development.

The LCCE model requires that instructional programs for handicapped students be designed in partnership with parents and community resources. As Kokaska and Brolin (1985) stated,

> The LCCE competency-based approach does not advocate elimination of current courses or change in the structure of education. Instead, it recommends that educators change the form of instructional content to serve career needs of students and that family and community resources be used to a greater extent in helping students gain experience. (p. 64)

With such a cooperative relationship, parents and community members can help students learn new skills while becoming more aware and supportive of the adult adjustment needs of students.

Role of Work

As the definition of career education has evolved, the role of work has alternately been emphasized or diminished. Hoyt's (1975) initial definition clearly emphasized the primacy of work; a later definition indicated that "it includes many parts of one's total lifestyle in addition to activities performed within the world of paid work" (Hoyt, 1982, p. 10). Clark (1974) asserted that career education should facilitate "the process of living" and that it is "not limited to facilitating the process of making a living" (p. 10).

Career Development

Another key component of career education is the concept of career development. Clark (1976) noted that career education has much to offer students and teachers in the elementary school. He argued persuasively that mildly retarded and learning disabled students would benefit from career education during the primary years. Concerning the nature of career education curricula in elementary school (Grades K-6) and in junior high school (Grades 7–9), Clark noted that,

> the curricula would be based around the mutually important elements of (a) attitudes, values, and habits; (b) human relationships; (c) occupational information; and (d) acquisition of job and daily living skills. These four elements change in their nature as pupils progress through the grade hierarchy and as the sequence of objectives is accomplished. (1976, p. 20)

Clark further noted that much of the career education curriculum during the elementary school years should occur in the regular classroom rather than in special classrooms and learning centers. However, he presented no evidence, and none was identified in the course of this review, to document empirically the value of career education programming in elementary schools, regardless of the type of classroom.

Summary

Clearly, the career education movement has many positive elements. There is direct correspondence between the twenty-two competencies and skills deemed critical for adult adjustment of mildly handicapped students (Halpern et al., 1985; Schalock, Harper, & Carver, 1981). Further, by design, career education has succeeded in strengthening the link between school system efforts and community resources (Hoyt, 1982). In addition, career education curricula are available from a variety of sources (Brolin, 1978; Clark, 1979). Unfortunately, the promise of the career education movement has not been documented with program evaluation data.

Career education is at a crossroads. The instructional goals set forth have included both life skills and employability. Although the career education movement has attempted to influence the whole of education, its primary influence remains in secondary-level programs for persons with mild disabilities. Career education exists in many schools, but with questionable overall quality (Halpern & Benz, 1984). In Hoyt's (1982) summary of the accomplishments of career education during the 1970s, he noted that additional research is needed to fully explain or document present success or failure. Specifically, he criticized the data base for career education as largely lacking in areas such as "practising good work habits, and making productive use of leisure time" and as being inconclusive in such areas as "improvement in basic academic skills, and job seeking/finding/getting/holding skills" (p. 6). He noted that successes for career education have occurred largely via a recognition and support for such programs by the general education system.

A major problem of the Clark (1979) and Brolin (1978) curricula is a lack of specification of instructional procedures necessary to produce acquisition, maintenance, and generalization. The primary career education curricula are precise on *what* to teach, but very imprecise *how* to teach. Instruction of career education ski requires a detailed set of instructional procedures th address both cognitive and applied behavioral content f the learner. Wimmer (1981) noted a lack of cognitive based content in career education curricula. T combination of imprecise instructional strategies a inadequately sequenced materials makes it difficult f practitioners to teach adequately and to acquire quali measurements of student gains in career educati programs.

Proponents of career education have not yet deliver the necessary efficacy or comparative research to demo strate empirically the effectiveness of career educati content and instruction. The research is encouraging special class placement with precise instructional focus relevant, functional content with certain mildly hand capped students (Polloway, 1984). But few credib studies have been conducted to document the effectivene of career education instruction for mildly handicapp students. Research on the effectiveness and efficiency career education programming must be conducted wi quality evaluative instruments, high fidelity of instructic in field-tested curricula, and longitudinal emphases. Wit out this careful documentation, the career educatic approach, like many program models, may simply disa pear and be another victim of good intentions an inadequate evaluation.

State of the Science: Research on Instructional Procedures

A general instructional strategy, which derives from th behavioral, or operant, tradition, has been applied with wide range of handicapped students across a variety of cur ricular approaches. The major components, summarize from Cuvo and Davis (1981) and Wilcox and Bellam (1982) are:

1. Defining what is to be taught (objectives).
2. Precise behavioral assessment.
3. Instructional sequencing: cues, prompts, correctio procedures, and reinforcers.
4. Data-based instruction (immediate decision mak ing based on student performance [correct o erroneous responses]).
5. Empirical determination of effects of instruction.
6. Direct and frequent measurement of studen responses.
7. Defined decision rules for program modification.
8. Systematic programming through all phases o learning: acquisition, proficiency, maintenance, and generalization.

Two additional components are used by many, but deemphasized by ecologically oriented practitioners: (a) careful analysis of prerequisite skills, and (b) precise skills or content task analysis.

The utility of these basic instructional procedures has

een validated across a wide array of content, including dependent living domains, and with a variety of learners f all ages. They are accepted as effective and are widely romoted and used. The thrust of this section is twofold: a) to summarize the general empirical basis (or the lack hereof) for these curricular and instructional ideologies nd technologies; and (b) to identify existing and needed rogrammatic research foundations.

A number of comprehensive recent reviews are available egarding research on curricula and instruction for handiapped persons. They are structured by content domain e.g., Marchetti & Matson, 1981; Reid, Wilson, & Faw, 983; Whitman, Scibak, & Reid, 1983) or by curricular pproach and/or instructional technique (Cuvo & Davis, 981, 1983; Huguenin, Weidenman, & Mulick, 1983; Williams et al., 1985). It is clear from the similar conlusions in these reviews that variations on the behavioral model of instruction are reliably effective for teaching ome and community living skills to youth with mild to evere handicaps.

There are few unifying features regarding instructional echnology in the various research efforts (and in reviews of that research) that focus on content of independent living skills. Some studies involve only mildly handicapped earners, others include mildly and severely handicapped earners. Settings for the research vary from laboratoryype to natural environments. Learners of different ages are grouped together in subject groups. Sequence of training procedures is not controlled.

It is clear that handicapped persons acquire a variety of independent living skills when structured instruction is provided. What is not clear, however, is the effect of severity of handicap, age, training setting, sequence of training procedures, and differential instructional components (e.g., prompts, consequences, fading). Empirically validated assessment systems for surveying these important factors are lacking. We do not know, with any degree of certainty, the relative effectiveness or efficiency of different approaches for implementing independent living skills instruction, especially with *individual* school-age learners with severe handicaps.

Review of Research on Instructional Technology

The effectiveness of standard behavioral-instructional techniques for retarded learners, such as behavior shaping, task analysis, chaining, stimulus fading, stimulus shaping, delayed cue presentation, and generalization techniques, has been reviewed by Huguenin et al. (1983). Each of these procedures has been demonstrated to be effective with certain retarded learners in certain training settings. Programmatic analyses have not been made of the role(s) of important variables such as age; training setting; nature of target behavior (vocational, social, independent living); and severity of handicap. Mental retardation often has been treated as a unitary characteristic. The dynamics of behavioral instruction with retarded learners are understood only in the most general sense: Certain strategies work with some retarded learners some of the time. When, where, and why they work with some and not other handicapped learners is not clear.

The research on "Behavior Therapy and Community Living Skills" was reviewed through 1982 by Cuvo and Davis (1983). They structured their review in a most useful manner: it was organized to be consistent with the step-by-step sequence of issues that must be considered when developing behavior therapy programs to teach community living skills to developmentally disabled clients (e.g., assessing functioning environment and learner skills, setting goals, task analysis, systematic training, evaluation). Several of these steps have been the focus of a fair amount of research attention: training settings—simulated versus in vivo (e.g., van den Pol et al., 1981); individual versus group training (e.g., Reid & Favell, 1984); sequence of training (forward versus backward chaining, etc.) (e.g., Walls, Dowler, Haught, & Zawlocki, 1984); distributed versus massed versus spaced practice (e.g., Mulligan, Lacy, & Guess, 1982); prompting—verbal, visual, modeling, physical (e.g., Johnson & Cuvo, 1981); fading of prompts (e.g., Billingsley & Romer, 1983; Snell & Gast, 1981); maintenance (e.g., Matson, 1981); generalization (e.g., Horner, McDonnell, & Bellamy, 1985); and social validation (e.g., Matson, 1981).

Space limitations preclude a detailed description of Cuvo and Davis's (1983) review. It is a comprehensive and noteworthy contribution to the research literature on independent living skills instruction for handicapped learners. Of special interest in the review is the observation that social validation of the results of community living skill training programs has been the focus of some research effort. In order to have criteria with which to judge the adequacy of community living skills, standards must be determined. Social comparison is one approach—for example, comparison of the behavior of retarded persons with that of a sample of community members on restaurant skills (van den Pol et al., 1981) and grocery shopping skills (Matson, 1981). Another approach is subjective evaluation—for example, rating of edibility of cooked food by observers before and after training (Johnson & Cuvo, 1981) or rating of adequacy of retarded children's fire escape responses by firefighters (Haney & Jones, 1982).

The contributions of behavior therapy techniques to development of community living skills for handicapped youth have been chronicled and evaluated (Cuvo & Davis, 1983). The relevant research points unequivocally to the conclusion that, when instruction is properly structured, persons with developmental disabilities can learn and perform a variety of home and community living skills. However, the dynamics of that learning and performing are not so clear. In many of the studies, both wide age ranges and several levels of severity of handicap are represented in small numbers of subjects. Questions remain as to which subjects of which ages with which severity levels of handicaps are acquiring and performing which skills via which instructional procedures?

Instructional Technology: Severely Handicapped Learners

Of the forty-four studies reviewed by Cuvo and Davis (1983), only three focused exclusively on school-age severely retarded children, with *N*s of 1, 1, and 3: Coon, Vogelsberg, and Williams (1981) on transportation; Sowers, Rusch, and Hudson (1979) on transportation; and Vogelsberg and Rusch (1979) on pedestrian skills; respectively. No systematic strands of research have addressed impact of task difficulty; impact of learners' level of prerequisite skills (especially such learning operations as imitation, responsiveness to prompts, and receptive language); or impacts of requirements of and training in the community where individuals live and learn. These questions about context(s) for learning and performing are crucial to resolve if we are to know the *utility* of the behavioral and ecological curriculum and instructional models.

handicapped youth (Tawney & Sniezek, 1985) adds some weight to the questions posed above. To identify the existing data base on progress of severely retarded students in public schools, they reviewed, through 1983, the nine major professional periodicals in which mental retardation and behavior therapy research is published. They identified only 11 studies meeting their criteria, of which nine involved only one, two, or three subjects. Only three of the eleven studies focused on independent living for severely handicapped individuals (i.e., the Hill, Wehman, & Horst, 1982 [*N* = 3] study of leisure skills; the Sowers et al., 1979 [*N* = 1] study of transportation skills; and the Vogelsberg & Rusch, 1979 [*N* = 3] study of pedestrian skills). Tawney and Sniezek proposed that a "national data base of educability of severely retarded persons" (p. 93) be developed.

In conducting the present review, we updated Tawney and Sniezek's (1985) review through December, 1984. In addition to updating their review of the nine professional periodicals, we searched three major data bases and reviewed all issues of two relatively new mental retardation research journals. We identified five additional data based descriptions of research focusing on independent living instruction with severely handicapped school-age youth (i.e., grocery shopping: Aeschleman & Schladenhauffen, 1984; toilet training: Dunlap, Koegel, & Koegel, 1984; functional community skills: Heal, Colson, & Gross, 1984; grocery purchasing: McDonnell, Horner, & Williams, 1984; eating: Sobsey & Orelove, 1984). This update is described here to document the validity of the Tawney and Sniezek (1985) review and to demonstrate that the data base on community living skills of severely handicapped youth has not grown much in a year. The contributions of these recent studies are detailed in a section on current research later in this chapter.

Instructional Technology: Mildly Handicapped Learners

A variety of factors, such as mainstreaming, efforts to decertify persons with mental retardation, and the emergence of the learning disability classification, has shift resources away from persons with mild retardation (Pol way, 1984). This situation led Haywood (1979) to lame the difficulty of obtaining funds for research or servi delivery for persons with mild retardation, despite prev lence figures that showed them to be significantly larger numbers than severely handicapped learners. One result this situation has been a paucity of recent research and cu riculum development to promote instruction in indepe dent living skills for persons with mild retardation (Clos Irvin, Taylor, & Agosta, 1981; Halpern & Benz, 1984). addition, many special education programs continue rely on academic curricula or on programming strategi devised for more severely handicapped learners (Pollowa & Smith, 1983). The legacy has been continued poor tra sition from school to work and independent living f mildly retarded persons.

A major reason for the poor transition from school work and adult life is the lack of sophistication in instru tional procedures to teach independent living skills (Clos Sowers, Halpern, & Bourbeau, 1985). Educational pr grams for mildly disabled students rarely provide instru tion that specifically programs for generalization an maintenance. Instead, an assumption is made that skil learned in the classroom will automatically transfer t home, community, or work settings. This assumptio occurs despite the fact that mildly retarded persons hav difficulty making generalizations without carefull designed instruction. This overall lack of generalizatio training led Stokes and Baer (1977) to describe muc instruction as the "train and hope" method of teaching.

Recently, special educators have recognized the importance of programming for generalization and maintenance Polloway and Epstein (1985) noted that the high rating o these issues by an internationally known group of scholar and teachers reflects the apparent importance of the issue in the evaluation of intervention procedures.

A major problem in analyzing research on instructiona procedures is that studies include persons with differen levels of severity of handicap. Given the potential differences between individuals of varying levels of competence it is difficult to interpret the results of such studies. The few studies that have controlled for this problem are reviewed here.

During the mid-1970s and early 1980s, a productive line of research occurred in the application of the principles of behavior analysis to teach independent living skills to mildly retarded secondary and postsecondary individuals. In the Cuvo and Davis (1983) review described earlier, a number of studies were examined. Their results clearly indicate that verbal instruction and modeling procedures were effective in teaching social/independent living skills to mildly retarded adolescents in classroom settings (e.g., Lowe & Cuvo, 1976; van den Pol et al., 1981). This line of research indicates that carefully sequenced verbal instructions and modeling procedures produced criterion performance in the classroom setting but not necessarily in the natural environment.

The lack of positive results in teaching generalization

as stimulated calls for active programming to facilitate eneralization in instructional design research in general Stokes & Baer, 1977) and in independent living research ith mildly retarded persons in particular (Close et al., 981; Cuvo & Davis, 1983). Another line of research volves efforts to teach generalized skills that maintain ver extended periods of time. These endeavors are escribed later in the section on current research with ildly retarded learners.

)THER RELATED RESEARCH

To be sure, other related data-based studies exist. They ave focused on adults, though, or on vocational/social lomains, or on mixed levels of severity of handicap (e.g., ask analysis: Crist, Walls, & Haught, 1984; vending nachine use: Nietupski, Clancy, & Christiansen, 1984). Also, sources other than scientific and professional journals exist. Several such studies are described in the next ections in order to highlight trends and emphases that ppeared to exist in 1985. Though the focus of current efforts has not departed radically from those just described, it is important to describe contemporary emphases in order to identify implications for policy and practice.

Relevant Current Research: Severely Handicapped Learners

Recent research on instruction for severely handicapped youth has been designed to address the effects of specific contextual variables associated with learning and performing. Three major themes emerge: (a) behavioral assessment to account for impacts of task difficulty, learner age, severity of handicap, and extent of intact learning skills (learning potential: imitation, receptive language, responsiveness to physical prompts) for optimum curricular placement (Close & Halpern, 1984; Close et al., 1985); (b) experimental program validation of the general ecological curricular approach and some of its component parts, which include functional content, community-based instruction, social integration, and parental involvement (Brinker & Thorpe, 1984; Heal et al., 1984; Rose, 1984); and (c) development of a specific technology for producing generalized performance from training to natural settings (e.g., Bates & Cuvo, 1984–1985; Horner, McDonnell, & Bellamy, 1985).

The results of current efforts in these three areas are addressed here, with an emphasis on their implications. A fourth theme exists in the current literature: analysis of the effects of instructional strategies such as task analysis, prompting, and chaining procedures on acquisition variables (Crist et al., 1984; Spooner & Spooner, 1984; Walls et al., 1984). It has developed primarily, though, with adult learners with varying handicaps in vocational settings, or with samples of mixed age and handicaps across cognitive, motor, vocational, and community living domains.

GENERALIZATION

The current research on generalization of severely handicapped persons' acquired behavior from training to community settings is summarized by Bates and Cuvo (1984–1985); Horner, McDonnell, and Bellamy (1985); and White (1983). The "general case methodology" (Becker & Engelmann, 1978) is acknowledged as an effective and efficient approach for programming generalization. Effectiveness refers to extent of reliable learner acquisition or performance, and efficiency refers to the resources required to reach the training criterion. The general case methodology comprises five major elements: (a) defining the instructional universe or the sets of stimuli across which the skills should be performed; (b) selecting teaching and testing examples that adequately sample the range of relevant stimulus variation and that include positive examples (stimuli to which learners are to respond) and negative examples (stimuli to which learners are not to respond); (c) sequencing teaching examples to include multiple components of an activity within each training session, maximally similar positive and negative examples one after the other, and to review examples from previous sessions; (d) teaching with applications of prompting, fading, shaping, reinforcing, and pacing, as appropriate; and (e) testing with a new and untrained set of examples.

The effectiveness and efficiency of the general case approach has been demonstrated with severely handicapped learners in many home and community living domains, for example, street crossing (Horner, Jones, & Williams, 1985), and vending machine use (Sprague & Horner, 1984). The general case approach was recommended by Bates and Cuvo (1984), in part because it directly addresses the impact of task-related and other important learning context variables. In addition, Horner, McDonnell, and Bellamy (1985) noted that it produces functional, socially valid lifestyle changes (e.g., generalized street crossing of untrained local neighborhood streets: Horner, Jones, & Williams, 1985). Presenting multiple examples within training has been documented to be more effective than training with a single example (Horner & McDonald, 1982), and sampling the range of relevant stimulus variation during acquisition training is more effective than unsystematic "multiple instance" training (Sprague & Horner, 1984).

The efficacy of simulation versus natural environment (in vivo) training has become the focus of part of the research literature on generalization. Some studies have demonstrated the efficacy of simulation for prompting generalization of behavior, while others have shown that in vivo training is required (e.g., Coon et al., 1981; McDonnell, 1984; Sowers et al., 1979). Some variation in results appears to be due to severity of handicap: Mildly and moderately retarded learners have demonstrated more generalized behavior (e.g., van den Pol et al., 1981). Some difference in results, though, is understood best in terms of the general case model. Effectiveness of simulation training may well depend on how well variation in range of relevant stimuli is sampled. Important task-related, interpersonal and other variables (environmental features such as sights and sounds) must be considered (Bates & Cuvo, 1984).

A functional definition of simulation, and guidelines for its use to promote generalization based on the general case model, have been developed by Horner, McDonnell, and Bellamy (1985). Previous studies with conflicting results can be analyzed regarding the extent to which they conform to general case programming principles within simulation training. Such an analysis reveals that, when simulation incorporates examples that are the same or nearly the same relevant stimuli found in the natural environment, generalization performance by severely handicapped learners is enhanced.

Comparative studies are needed to determine the relative contributions of isolated in vivo, isolated simulation, general case simulation, and general case simulation plus in vivo approaches. Three such studies addressing grocery shopping provide an intriguing start. In the Aeschleman and Schladenhauffen (1984) study, a multiple probe design was used to demonstrate that role-playing contributed most significantly to acquisition of shopping skills and that in vivo training was not essential for acquisition. In fact, no in vivo training was presented because all participants reached training criteria with role-playing instruction. The results were interpreted by the authors as also demonstrating generalization of acquired shopping behaviors to novel stores ("the majority of skills components generalized . . ." p. 255). However, analysis of correct responding on key steps (item selection and accurate amount of money) reveals that only 69% and 50% of the responses were correct on these steps in novel stores. In another study, neither in-classroom role-playing combined with isolated in vivo training nor role-playing with stimuli similar and dissimilar to natural stimuli were shown to promote effective generalization (McDonnell et al., 1984). And, in a third study, combined simulation (with slides) and in vivo training produced almost twice the number of correct behaviors (target item selection in grocery store) in untrained stores than did isolated in vivo instruction in one store (McDonnell & Horner, 1985).

In a study focused on toilet training, Dunlap, Koegel, and Koegel (1984) used a multiple baseline design to demonstrate that training in multiple community settings facilitates successful performance of toileting skills in multiple settings. This approach involving continuity of treatment across settings was clearly superior to training in only some environments. An analysis of the relevant stimulus features across performance settings, and an implementation of a general case training approach, might well increase the efficiency of such training so that training might not be necessary in all performance environments.

All of the research on generalization—general case approach, simulation, continuity of training—contributes to an understanding of the efficacy and efficiency of elements in the behavioral and ecological curricular models. Community-based training, for example, is not only ideologically preferred (Brown, Nietupski, & Hamre-Nietupski, 1976) but has been demonstrated to be feasible and even necessary for effective instruction generalization. Likewise, increases in independence learners are achievable. Finally, to be consistent with t criteria proposed by Williams et al. (1985), the requi ments of local settings have been addressed systematical

Learning Potential Model

Another emphasis has emerged in recent research. It h centered on how best to make decisions about which trai ing formats to use with which severely handicapp learners. To accomplish this goal, Close and colleagu have developed the Community Living Assessment a Teaching System (CLATS) (Close & Halpern, 198 Close et al., 1985). This system is an integrated assessme and curriculum package that employs a learning potenti assessment format to make curriculum placeme decisions. In this format, assessment is accomplished v measurement of the effects of systematic teachin Students are taught in standardized sequences of verba modeled, and physically prompted instructions and corre tions in order to assess their responsiveness to: (a) differe modes of instruction and correction, and (b) tasks of diffe ent length and difficulty. Discrimination complexity an manipulation difficulty are varied systematically.

A study of the validity of using such assessment resul to make curriculum placement decisions has been com pleted (Close & Halpern, 1984). Sex, age (14–21 and ove 21), functioning level (high and low as measured by criterion-referenced behavioral instrument), and livin setting (institution and community) were experimentall controlled via sampling and research design. The curricu consisted of 140 task-analyzed tasks in the communit living domain. Some tasks involved only single core skil (e.g., grasp, place, turn). Others involved multiple cor skills in "functional" units that could be taught as a singl instructional step ("Pull zipper up"). Still other tasks wer "extended functional units" of two to three steps that coul be taught as a single sequence or chain of behavior ("Plac zipper parts together at bottom and pull zipper up"). Cor relational analyses demonstrated relationships of $r = 0.7$ to 0.74 for two different forms of the assessment instru ment with subsequent trials-to-criterion on curriculu tasks identified by assessment results as appropriate train ing targets for individual learners.

This approach has also been applied successfully i vocational assessment of severely retarded adults and ado lescents. Criterion-related validity has been demonstrate for the learning potential scores on the Trainee Perform ance Sample (TPS) (Irvin, Gersten, Taylor, Close, & Heiry, 1981), a twenty-five item test of severely retarde persons' responsiveness to instruction on vocationally rel evant tasks. The validity coefficients were $r = -0.60$ t -0.75 for predicting training time and trials-to-criterio on actual vocational assembly and sorting tasks (highe TPS scores predict lower training time on trials).

The learning potential assessment research has demon strated that important contextual variables for learning and performing (task difficulty and learning skills such a imitation, responsiveness to verbal instructions and/or prompts) can be measured reliably. Further, the results of such assessments can be used to make data-based decisions about which training formats to employ and/or which learning skills to teach to enhance the impact of subsequent training. A unique feature of this approach is that functioning levels of learners are conceptualized as learning operations or competencies and are operationalized into variables that can be addressed by instruction. An important implication is that functioning level is not static but can be increased with properly focused instruction.

Validation of the Ecological Curricular Approach

Several interesting studies have been reported recently that aim at validating, in one way or another, the ecological curricular model. In one study, Heal et al. (1984) examined the efficacy of community-based training using an ecological inventory to select content with the help of parents and teachers. The instructional procedures involved task analysis of skills into teachable units, standard correction procedures, and data-based instruction with thirty-five severely handicapped students 15–21 years of age. Students were trained in a variety of community and domestic skills. While community-based training proceeded, classroom training focused on parallel content. With crossover, and crossover/cross-group designs with two sets of tasks, it was demonstrated that community-based training was effective (postscores on task-analysis measures for trained tasks were higher than pretraining scores). Significantly greater gain was produced for trained tasks than for untrained tasks. The results are a unique demonstration of an effective instructional technology applied in the service of a least restrictive, normalized ideology. This research represents the first experimental test of the effectiveness of a training package both of instructional procedures (task analysis, error correction) and of curricular elements (ecological inventory, community-based training, social integration), which are the substance of the ideological and curricular foundations for the ecological approach.

The impact of instructional components (task analysis, pacing, reinforcement, prompting procedures) was not addressed by the study. In fact, the instructional procedures were described only in a most general fashion and appear to have been implemented as a treatment package. Clearer specification of the utility of the various procedures for teaching acquisition and subsequent performance would be useful to those who apply variations of the general community adaptation curricular approach.

In another study of components of the ecological model, Brinker and Thorpe (1984) examined the impact of integration of severely handicapped youth and nonhandicapped peers on an educationally relevant outcome —proportion of Individualized Educational Program (IEP) objectives achieved. A total of 245 severely handicapped students, 3–22 years of age, from thirteen school districts, were observed in the study. With functioning level controlled, rate of interaction with nonhandicapped students accounted for 2% of the variance ($p < 0.025$). Though the proportion of variance accounted for was small, it was non-chance and demonstrated a relationship between integration and educational achievement. Interaction with handicapped peers did not account for a significant proportion of the variance in IEP objectives achieved.

The contribution of this approach is its focus on potential *educational* outcomes of integration. Previous studies have focused on social variables. Additionally, the study contributes a piece of evidence, however small, for the efficacy of the ecological educational model for severely handicapped youth.

The drawback, of course, is that we do not know the nature and quality of the IEP objectives used as criteria in the study. Use of an index to measure IEP quality would lend such results more credibility. Such an index has been developed recently by Hunt, Goetz, and Anderson (1985).

In another study, Rose (1984) attempted to increase severely retarded adolescents' participation in home and community activites by intervening with their parents in an experimental/control, pretest/posttest design. Data were collected for thirty-four students from nine classrooms. The intervention included three training and information meetings for parents over a 7-week period, one telephone follow-up prompt, and information sent home regarding home and community activities. Results were that: (a) the majority of students were in the two lower quartiles with respect to participation in numbers of activities; (b) parental assistance consisted primarily of transportation and telling youths to do the desired activity; and (c) experimental treatment participants did not participate more actively in home and community activities than did control group participants.

This study is presented here because of its rationale and focus. Parental roles are viewed as crucial with respect to participation of students in home and community activities (Brown, Falvey, et al., 1979; Wilcox & Bellamy, 1982). The outcomes of Rose's (1984) study demonstrate that parents will likely require some systematic assistance and resources beyond information and planning if their roles are to be effective. Simple interventions with parents, though desirable from ideological (least intrusive) and pragmatic (feasibility) perspectives, do not appear to produce quality-of-life changes for severely handicapped youth.

Summary

Current research with school-age severely handicapped learners documents the first steps in an empirical foundation for curricular approaches that combine behavioral and ecological principles and methods. Increased independence of performance has been demonstrated in a variety of natural environments (e.g., grocery stores, banks, and family homes). Several of the premises for the ecological approach to instruction—increased independence, community-based instruction, effectiveness of direct instruction, functional skill emphasis, social integration, and social validity—have been supported by educationally relevant, programmatic, and empirical studies. Other premises—parental involvement, efficiency of instruction (optimal use of time), quality-of-life changes (participation)—either have not been addressed empirically or have not been validated in efforts to date. Current research also has demonstrated that learning skills possessed by severely handicapped learners, and effects of task difficulty and other task-related features, can be effectively assessed by learning potential procedures. Thus, decisions regarding effective and efficient training formats can be made more reliably. Clearly, innovative curriculum and instructional technologies are being put to the test and are emerging as effective tools.

Relevant Current Research: Mildly Handicapped Learners

Special educators have become aware of the need to teach functional independent living skills. Additionally, it is clear that simple acquisition of skills in a classroom setting is insufficient for handicapped students. To be functional, new skills must generalize to the criterion environment in which they will occur naturally. Research on instructional technology with mildly handicapped learners has focused on efficiency and effectiveness of teaching procedures for facilitating such generalization. The emphasis has been on understanding how to make naturally occurring cues and events more meaningful to students. A key factor in this process is a well-designed and sequenced set of instructional materials. Two techniques have emerged as most useful: (a) training via simulation, and (b) training via general case programming. Each of the available studies of these two approaches combines basic applied behavior analysis and a technology of programming for generalization.

Some studies have demonstrated that community-based instruction is superior to simulation training for mentally retarded persons (Cuvo & Davis, 1981; Schalock, Harper, & Carver, 1981). On the other hand, the advantages of such in vivo instruction may be outweighed by concerns for resources needed to plan, implement, and evaluate such programs. This is especially true in the case of mildly handicapped learners who have competencies in basic academic skills, and who respond to verbal and visual instructions in the learning process. For these students, the cost of transportation, scheduling, and staffing to teach skills in the natural environment are substantial. Concerns regarding expense and efficiency justify research efforts to identify instructional procedures for use with groups of students in simulated classroom environments.

Simulation Training

In the simulation approach, the training environment is designed systematically to approximate the characteristics of the natural setting (Baine, 1982). The student receives training in the simulated setting (typically a classroom) and generalization to the natural environment is probed after initial skills acquisition in the simulated setting. Studies described earlier clearly demonstrate the value of simulation technologies (e.g., van den Pol et al., 1981). But, unequivocal interpretation is impossible because of lack of experimental control of students' functioning levels, students' prior history with tasks or settings, and uncontrolled relative complexity of tasks or settings. The overall effectiveness of these procedures has not been clearly established across the broad range of skills needed by mildly handicapped learners.

Two main features of simulation training are (a) direct instruction to teach skill acquisition, and (b) appropriately sequenced stimuli to increase the likelihood that learners will attend to relevant cues (Close et al., 1985). The nature of the visual-spatial displays required for effective instruction is a focus of research (Engelmann & Carnine, 1982). Visual displays incorporate pictures, symbols, line drawings, and sequenced scripts to present facts and their interrelationships.

A recent study by Bourbeau, Sowers, and Close (1985) was designed to investigate the extent to which two banking skills that were taught using direct instruction procedures and visual displays in a simulated setting at school generalized to two different banks in the community. One bank was the target from which instructional materials (deposit and withdrawal forms) were obtained. When the student reached criterion in the simulated setting in the classroom, a series of probes were conducted. These included probes with novel stimulus materials in simulated setting; target materials in the target setting; and novel materials in novel setting (a second bank in the community). The results indicate that subjects generalized their performance from the simulation setting to both the target and novel banks with both target and novel deposit and withdrawal slips. In addition, subsequent probes indicate that performance of criterion behavior maintained after 3 months.

The Bourbeau et al. (1985) study has made clearer the importance of the design of instructional materials to teach generalized banking skills to mildly retarded students in a simulated classroom study. Additional research is needed to analyze the stimulus features of other functional tasks so that teachers can predict where errors are most likely to occur and adjust their teaching efforts accordingly.

Bates and Cuvo (1984–1985) reported on a series of studies that examined the effectiveness of two levels of instruction (pictorial simulations and community training) across two levels of retardation (mild and moderate) for two independent living skills (grocery shopping and laundry). Preliminary results suggest that simulated instruction in the form of pictorial training did not result in significant generalization to the community for either the mildly or moderately retarded students in the grocery shopping domain. Community training did result in generalization for both groups. On the laundry task, mildly etarded students generalized more from school to the natural environment than did moderately retarded students. The community instruction was the superior training method.

These results led to two conclusions. First, level of retardation is a factor to consider in designing simulated instructional environments and simulation materials. Students with mild retardation are able to generalize better from abstract instructional formats than are moderately retarded students. Second, generalization responses involve a complex combination of stimulus and response generalization, and skill maintenance. "The nature and degree of generalization that students might evidence depends on the correspondence between the stimulus features and response requirements in the training environment and subsequent community environment" (Bates & Cuvo, 1984, p. 15). Increased specificity is needed in research on instructional design to clearly delineate the effects both of the skills of students and of the demands of the criterion environments.

General Case Programming

As defined earlier, general case programming refers to initial training across a set of stimuli so that performance will occur ultimately in the presence of different, untrained stimuli in different environments (Horner & McDonald, 1982). To date, the primary application of these procedures with mildly retarded students has been in academic content (Maggs & Maggs, 1980).

In a recent study by Ho, Close, Sowers, and Keating (1985), a general case instructional approach was used to teach generalized cooking skills to mildly retarded high school students. The study investigated the extent to which a sample of cooking skills (specifically, boiling, frying, and baking) that were trained using visual displays (recipe cards) generalized to untrained cooking tasks. The results indicate that subjects generalized their performance from the general case instruction to untrained recipes. The key elements of the instructional design were a clear delineation of the range of cooking tasks, selection of a representative sample of the stimulus features associated with ultimate performance, and the use of carefully sequenced visual materials to reduce the complexity of visual discriminations required by the tasks.

An analysis of skills that can be taught via this strategy is now in order. Skills such as banking and use of laundromats are performed most often in a single setting with a restricted range of required responses. They may not be the appropriate skills to teach via general case approaches. Tasks such as cooking, grocery shopping, or bill paying, which vary over time and settings, may be the most appropriate targets for application of these procedures.

State of Practice: Implementation

For severely handicapped youth, PL 94-142 has served as *the* catalyst for provision of relevant educational services. For mildly handicapped youth, the change has been from segregated educational settings and watered-down academic skills instruction to an emphasis on integrated settings (Polloway, 1984). Determination of what constitutes appropriateness of such educational programs—programmatically, legislatively, or judicially—is underway.

The Pennsylvania Association for Retarded Citizens enforcement cases (e.g., *Battles v. Commonwealth of Pennsylvania,* 1980; *Campbell v. Talladega County Board of Education,* 1981) have established independent living as *the* appropriate educational focus for severely handicapped youth. These and other cases have provided guidelines indicating that educational programs must yield real educational benefits. The courts have ruled that the avenue to educational benefit is independent living skills instruction for severely handicapped learners. Likewise, the Vocational Education Act amendments of 1968, and the Career Education Incentive Act of 1978 (PL 95-207) emphasize the appropriateness of independent living skills instruction for mildly handicapped youth (Hoyt, 1982).

These judicial, legislative, and professional directions notwithstanding, there simply is not enough evidence to determine the extent of implementation of independent living skills instruction programs in public schools throughout the country. Some evidence is described here.

State of Practice: Severely Handicapped Learners

In a review of three data bases (ERIC, PSYCHINFO, and Exceptional Child), and of four professional journals (*Journal of the Association for Persons with Severe Handicaps* [*JASH*], *Education and Training of the Mentally Retarded, Exceptional Children,* and *Mental Retardation*), for 1980 through 1984, we located seven local or state education agency descriptions of independent living skills instruction programs for severely handicapped students. Interestingly, five of the seven descriptions are from locales where well-known university training programs exist to prepare professionals to work with severely handicapped youth.

The descriptions range from task-analyzed curriculum content with discussion of relevant issues (e.g., least restrictive environment, adult living, data collection), through narrative teachers' guides and case examples for a variety of content areas, to the comprehensive papers associated with Brown and colleagues in Madison, Wisconsin (Brown, Certo, Belmore, & Crowner, 1976; Brown, Falvey et al., 1979). Two descriptions are from *JASH*. They address program history, rationale, logistics, standards, procedures, and common problems and their solutions for domestic training (Freagon et al., 1983) and community-based training (Hamre-Nietupski, Nietupski, Bates, & Maurer, 1982). None of the descriptions are data based; no evaluative outcomes are discussed.

So, although access to educational services is in place for severely handicapped youth, the nature of the educational programs and the extent to which their focus is on independent living skills are largely unknown. No systematic survey of such implementation was identified.

Two existing programs are described briefly below. One of the programs serves secondary-level students, and the other serves students over 21 years old in a community college setting. These programs are presented because they are known to the authors, they are consistent with the models employed by Brown et al. (1976), and they are examples of the state of practice for which evaluation data exist. They are also presented as examples of the most likely types of contemporary translation of ideology and research foundations into practice.

Oregon High School Model

One program that has been developed through federal funding and evaluated throughout the State of Oregon is the Oregon High School Model (OHS) (Bellamy & Wilcox, 1984). The eleven major outcome elements of the OHS model are: integrated, age-appropriate, noncategorical, percentage of total time in instruction, percentage of total time in community instruction, number of contacts with nonhandicapped peers, progress in instructional programs, progress in IEP goals, percentage of scheduled weekly tasks completed, number of contacts with parents, and instructional delivery. Other model elements are operationalized in such areas as curriculum development, administration and program support, and transition planning. Each element is associated with stated criteria by which achievement is measured and judged. The OHS model was validated in eight classrooms for severely handicapped learners throughout the state.

Evaluation results after 3 years demonstrate that (a) 80%+ of model elements (outcome as well as others) were in place in all sites after 3 years; (b) classroom teachers rated the utility of OHS as quite high and rated the overall effort required in the medium range for supporting a community-based program; (c) effectiveness of the OHS was established by data showing that students in the seven replication sites spent 90% of their school day in instruction, about half of that in community settings, and had contact with nonhandicapped peers at least thirty-eight times per week; (d) public school staff and parents' satisfaction with the OHS was high; and (e) students achieved 83% of targeted IEP objectives after one year.

Over-21 Project

Another program is the Over-21 Project, which provides full-time continuing education for severely handicapped young adults living near San Francisco, California (Sailor & Goetz, 1983). The program is located on a community college campus, and is described as occurring "in a variety of age-appropriate, socially integrated, natural environments," and as providing "ongoing systematic, data-based instruction that results in measurable acquisition of functional age-appropriate skills" (p. 1).

For the initial group of twenty learners, evaluation results demonstrate that:

1. Learners acquired an average of 66% per 6 months of their annual instructional objectives as listed on IEPs.
2. Parents/guardians were actively involved in their young adults' continuing education; over 50% were directly involved on-site in the program.
3. Regular documentation of learner performance was used successfully to guide ongoing community-based instruction and to provide summative evaluation data.

The point of these brief summaries is to demonstrate exemplary practices with severely handicapped students. Other local and state education agencies undoubtedly have implemented similar programs. Wilcox and Bellamy (1980) noted that, in the late 1970s, federal funding supported such applications via other statewide systems change efforts. Examples are not referenced, nor have they been disseminated in a manner so as to surface for this review. Nonetheless, the OHS and Over-21 models serve as useful examples of what can be accomplished.

State of Practice: Mildly Handicapped Learners

Although career education has not met with the success that many of its advocates have hoped for, the impact of the movement is clearly evident. In a statewide study in Oregon, Halpern and Benz (1984) reported that (a) secondary special education teachers identified curriculum in prevocational and vocational education skills for independent living and interpersonal skills as particularly valuable for their students; (b) career education content was cited by half of the respondent teachers as an area in need of improvement; (c) 40% of the respondent secondary teachers studied were not trained to teach career education content; and (d) many parents were dissatisfied with the career education offerings provided by the schools.

The emerging role of career education for individuals with mild disabilities is further documented by a recent survey conducted with special education authorities. Polloway and Epstein (1985) reported that the highest rated issues were vocational and career education, and postschool adjustment. As Halpern (1985) noted, career education programs that promote transition to work and adult life are cost-effective because of their emphasis on marketable postsecondary skills.

What follows is a review and discussion of current career education program models that have been implemented in local education agencies and postsecondary settings. Evaluation data exist only for some. The program descriptions have been selected to represent what can be accomplished. The initial models presented are based on Brolin's LCCE model.

LCCE Programs

The LCCE curriculum (detailed earlier) has been implemented in many schools and adult service agencies throughout the United States (Kokaska & Brolin, 1985). The foundation of the LCCE program is a curriculum guide, *Life Centered Career Education: A Competency-Based Approach* (Brolin, 1978), which assists teachers in training the twenty-two major competencies in the three content domains. Emphasis is placed on using community and family resources in teaching the competencies. Hence, students are provided with exploration experiences in and out of school to learn and practice skills.

Brolin (1978, 1983) described several school districts that have implemented the LCCE. In addition, Kokaska and Brolin (1985) described "best practice" career education programs. In each of the programs, the emphasis is placed on local variations of the basic LCCE model.

> Daily living skills are taught through survival skills in the community, a class offered to clients as they make final preparations prior to learning the program. Students take weekly field trips to those organizations that they must rely upon. . . . Weekly class discussions help students to conceptualize the information that students obtained on the field trips. (Kokaska & Brolin, 1985, p. 312)

An extension of the LCCE curriculum to community colleges was reported by Brolin (1984). Three community colleges in the Midwest participated in the Lifelong Career Development (LCD) Project. The LCD Project was designed to provide postsecondary education services to handicapped adults in a community college setting. Brolin described the components of the LCD Project as a program of career assessment, planning, instruction, advocacy, information, and guidance to disabled persons. Instruction is focused on the twenty-two life-centered competencies. Advocacy and information are provided to assist the student in maintaining skills and in connecting with existing agencies or resources.

The LCCE and LCD programs represent instructional programs designed to teach life roles to disabled persons. Unfortunately, no comparative or evaluative information is provided in support of the basic elements of the models. Clearly, applications of the LCCE and LCD models are providing services to the students in their school districts and college campuses. Data on the effects of different elements in the models are now required to validate the utility of these systems.

Community College Component

The Lane Community College Adult Skills Development Program (ASDP) (Auty & Close, 1986) in Eugene, Oregon is designed to provide education and training to mildly handicapped young adults at a community college campus. Course work is organized into three broad areas relating to home, community, and vocational adjustment. A substantial component of the curriculum is directed toward the generalization and maintenance of newly acquired skills, since attention to these skills is essential if mildly disabled persons are to perform adequately after learning new skills.

The instructional program of the ASDP is planned, designed, and evaluated via functional assessment practices (Halpern, 1984). In this approach to assessment, information is collected with the goal of producing a profile of the relevant skills that have not been mastered by each student. The assessment also addresses the students' process of learning in order to identify best instructional strategies. Each course in the ASDP utilizes both *knowledge* tests (e.g., the Social and Prevocational Information Battery [SPIB], Halpern, Raffeld, Irvin, & Link, 1975) and individually designed *performance* tests that measure the student's response to carefully selected examples of the course content. Thus, the assessment program is program-related and is designed to assist in planning, monitoring, and evaluating student progress toward instructional goals.

The instructional program of the ASDP is organized into 10-week modules, following the regular college schedule. Instruction takes place in both classroom and community settings. Small group and individual instruction is provided to each student. Emphasis is placed on systematically combining direct instruction principles (Engelmann & Carnine, 1982) into a comprehensive instructional package designed to facilitate efficient learning, generalized performance, and long-term maintenance of independent functioning.

Evaluation results after 18 months demonstrate that (a) 250 mildly disabled students completed course work successfully in twelve different courses (given the 40–50% dropout rate of special education students in high school programs [Edgar, 1985], this is a noteworthy result); (b) over 95% of the students made significant skill gains in money management and cooking and nutrition, based on preknowledge/postknowledge and performance-based testing; (c) 75% of the students were "very satisfied" and 25% were "satisfied" with course work, as rated on a student satisfaction scale; and (d) public school, community college, and adult service satisfaction was high based on satisfaction measures provided by agency personnel.

Impact of Instruction

Special education programs must yield real educational benefits for handicapped learners. Independent living skills have been posited as the appropriate educational emphasis in such school programs. What are the benefits realized to date? What real benefits are reasonably to be expected? How skilled in independent living domains are postschool young adults who were labeled as handicapped during school years? These questions have guided the development of the following review. Attention is directed to overall adjustment (success) of the persons studied, and to specific problem areas that have been noted. Due to the difficulty of establishing precise relationships with data that are correlational in nature, no firm conclusions are drawn. The current data base on the postschool adjustment of disabled persons is not extensive.

Follow-up Studies of Special Education Students

There are four recently reported follow-up studies that shed some light on the impact of post-PL 94-142 school programs to date in preparing handicapped youth for home and community living roles. In all of them, results were summarized in a manner that makes it difficult to relate outcomes specifically to graduates with severe or mild handicaps.

In one study, Hasazi, Gordon, and Roe (1985) presented data related to employment status of a sample of 460 handicapped youth exiting high school from nine districts in Vermont between 1979 and 1983. The sample was designed to be representative of population demographics in Vermont. A total of 129 of the 462 subjects were in "special class" placements during school years. Most of the remainder were in resource room programs. Thus, educable mentally retarded and trainable mentally retarded students were all considered to be the relatively most severely handicapped students in this study. In fact, Bellamy (1985) noted a personal communication from the first author that indicated that "*no* severely handicapped school learners were in the sample" (p. 475). Major employment-related outcomes for the young adults with the more severe handicaps (educable and trainable mental retardation) during school years were that (a) they were less employed than others; (b) vocational education had no statistically significant effect on employment status; and (c) work experience in school years did not enhance employment after leaving school. Given the trends in the data, and since mildly and severely handicapped students cannot be separately identified from the data summaries, we can only assume that the most severely handicapped students probably demonstrated the least impact of school programs upon employment status. That would have to be very little or no impact at all, given the overall outcomes detailed above.

A statewide study from Colorado was also reported recently (Mithaug et al., 1985). A total of 234 graduates in 1978 were identified. Some thirty-six districts were involved. The sample was described as approximating the state's population characteristics of age, sex, handicap, and location of school district. There were, however, several major discrepancies reported between the sample and population characteristics: overrepresentation of physically handicapped and rural respondents, and underrepresentation of young adults who were labeled as emotionally/behaviorally disordered during school years. The closest identification that can be made of the severity of students' handicaps is that approximately 29% of the sample had been in self-contained programs. The overall outcomes related to independent living domains were that (a) 68% of the sample reported ongoing needs in preparation for independent living; (b) 58% reported current needs in preparation for participating in social and community life; and (c) all respondents reported relatively little social life outside the home. As with the Vermont study, it is impossible to identify separately the students with mild and severe handicaps. We can only infer from the data that needs and general negative social status are greatest for severely handicapped young adults. It is not clear what differential impact, if any, school programs in Colorado have had on the postschool independent living needs of students with varying levels of handicap severity.

Another follow-up study in which impact of severity of handicap cannot be determined directly was conducted in four communities in Virginia (Kregel, Wehman, & Seyfarth, 1985). Approximately 40% of the 300 handicapped students who left school in these communities during the years 1979 through 1983 were from classes for students with moderate and severe mental retardation. Outcomes related to independent living were that, within the whole sample of 300, (a) 86% lived at home; (b) 90%+ performed basic self-help skills; (c) 75% cooked or prepared snacks; (d) 67% did household chores; (e) 75% walked around in the community; (f) 65% did shopping activities; (g) 40–50% did laundry, bought clothes, or went to restaurants; and (h) 57% were unemployed. From the results of this study, it appears likely that school programs are having a positive impact, even for some severely handicapped persons, on certain skill and performance domains: basic self-help, food preparation at home, getting around the community, participation in household chores, and shopping activities.

Finally, a follow-up study of 108 special education students graduating from 10 school districts in Nebraska from 1974 through 1984 has been reported (Schalock et al., 1985). Only eleven of the 108 were classified as severely handicapped. The study involved a multiple regression design with nineteen predictor and eleven outcome variables. The methodological problems associated with sample size/variables ratios notwithstanding, the outcomes related to independent living and employment for severely handicapped young adults were that (a) 75% lived in supervised settings, and (b) 75% received all income from parents or public sources. In addition, those with severe handicaps were least likely to be employed, least likely to live with minimal supervision, and least likely to be self-sufficient. Though one or two of the severely handicapped young adults demonstrated some independent living skills and performance (earned some money, lived in semi-supervised settings), the impact of the Job Exploration and Training Model (see Schalock et al., 1985) used during school years was not substantial for most. Patterns of totally dependent lifestyles were the norm for young adults with severe handicaps. Of those with milder handicaps, approximately one third lived away from home and were employed.

Follow-up Studies of Severely Handicapped Students

An early post-PL 94-142, follow-up study was reported by Van Deventer et al., 1981). Fifty-three severely handicapped graduates of Madison, Wisconsin's public school program from 1971 through 1978 were identified. A total of seventeen of these fifty-three were actually followed up in depth. "Problematic observations," supported by confirming anecdotal data, were that (a) school-based vocational programs did not prepare graduates for a variety of work environs; (b) many severely handicapped students did not demonstrate appropriate work attitudes; (c) independent mobility typically was not demonstrated, even by graduates who had learned those skills; (d) shopping skills were not demonstrated, even when graduates had learned them; (e) money-related skills were poor; and (f) there were a restricted number and type of domestic environs in which graduates functioned. It should be kept in mind that many of these graduates attended school before PL 94-142 was enacted and/or before its impact was realized.

In the only available recent evaluation focused exclusively on trainable mentally retarded and other severely handicapped young adults (Brodsky, 1983), there were several outcomes worthy of special note. Only thirteen of the 234 trainable mentally retarded graduates between 1977 and 1981 were employed in 1983. Though 64% had been involved in some type of transition planning for post-school roles, there was no apparent effect of such planning on graduates' eventual time on waiting lists for service. Only eight graduates were living in independent or semi-independent settings, though forty-one of the 234 did live in group homes. The large majority of services needed were related to independent living domains.

Follow-up Study of Mildly Handicapped Students

The transition from high school to adult life is typically a traumatic event for mildly disabled persons. Many of their experiences in high school produce little success and much failure. Often these students remain in academically oriented programs longer than is meaningful for their life goals (Halpern, 1979). Consequently, when mildly disabled persons graduate from high school, they usually experience less success than their abled peers. This tendency toward failure in the transition from high school to adulthood has been well documented over the past half-century (Baller, 1967; Kennedy, 1966).

Recently, the postschool adjustment of mildly disabled persons has gained increased attention. Part of this interest is a result of the current debate on the impact of special education services. In addition, the current federal priority to improve the transition from school to working life has served to sharpen the focus on this issue (Will, 1984).

Halpern et al. (1985) recently reported a study of the status of mildly disabled persons in unsupervised residential settings. In-depth interviews by trained interviewers were conducted in eight major metropolitan areas in the western United States. A stratified random sample of clients being served in semi-independent living settings was drawn. Location, age, sex, and length of time in setting were the stratifiers.

The mean age of the sample was 28, with approximately 50% of the subjects between the ages of 16 and 25. The IQ distribution of the subjects was 50% mildly mentally retarded and 33% learning disabled, with the remainder having IQs below 55. More than 90% of the subjects had attended special education programs. Some of the oldest subjects had never attended public schools.

Information was sought from multiple sources in order to obtain several perspectives on the adjustment of the clients. These sources included administrative and direct service staff in the semi-independent living programs and, most important, the clients themselves. Multiple types of information were also collected, ranging from data that could be treated as quantitative variables, such as employment status, income, independent living skills, and number of social contacts, to more subjective data such as self-reported estimates of satisfaction, interpersonal competence, and social support.

Results were as follows. Subjects varied greatly in their ability to perform in the eight content areas comprising independent living skills. Consistent with findings from other research (e.g., Schalock, Harper, & Gerung, 1981), the areas of money management, apartment cleanliness, and interpersonal communication were problematic for many subjects. Approximately one third of the population was employed; of those working, over half were employed in sheltered workshop settings. On the whole, few of the subjects had behavioral problems and less than 2% of the sample had been arrested the previous year. Interestingly, most demonstrated motivation to improve their lives: Almost 90% of the sample desired to be totally independent, and 80% desired to learn new skills in home and money management and sex education. When asked if they were satisfied with their lives, the vast majority reported enjoying their lives in the community but noted the desire to be more "on my own."

Summary

One of the most surprising findings from all of the follow-up studies is the large number of students still living with parents 4–6 years after graduation. The percentages range from 86% of the young adults living at home in Virginia to two-thirds living at home in Nebraska and Colorado. Approximately two-thirds of the subjects in the Colorado and Nebraska studies were employed, while approximately two-fifths of the Virginia subjects had full-time work. In spite of the relative financial dependence on parents, the graduates in the Colorado and Virginia studies were relatively satisfied with their lives.

Not much benefit, if any in some cases, is being realized from school programs by severely handicapped students.

Most live at home with parents, receive all support from family or public sources, are unemployed, and have limited involvement in community activities. It is not clear whether this is due to ineffective school programs (trying to teach independent living skills but not succeeding) or to nonexistent school programs (not attempting to teach independent living skills on any scale). In any case, severely handicapped students seem to have benefited most from instruction in skills related to functioning in the home: basic self-care, food preparation, household chores, and mobility.

A debate exists currently among professionals regarding whether such outcomes are due to limits on educability of some individuals—a "doctrine of limitations." (See, in particular, various articles in Volume 1, Number 1 of the journal *Analysis and Intervention in Developmental Disabilities* for a lively and cogent debate on these issues. Also relevant are various articles in Volume 45 of *Exceptional Children* [1979].)

Data such as are reported for the OHS model by Bellamy and Wilcox (1984), and for a study by Close (1977), demonstrate the fallacy of the doctrine of limitations. In Close's (1977) study, five randomly selected severely and profoundly retarded young adults were placed from a state institution into community-based residential and behavioral training programs. Their acquisition and maintenance of a variety of independent home, vocational, and community living skills demonstrate what can be done. For whatever reasons, current school programs are not, in general, accomplishing the reasonably to be expected outcomes with severely handicapped youth.

Implications

The basic premise underlying programming for independent living skills is that, just like the rest of us, handicapped students need to learn to function effectively in adult roles. An unmistakable conclusion from the foregoing review is that a clear and consensual vision regarding the nature of those roles, and how best to prepare handicapped students for them, has not been established. The efforts of parents, professional educators, research and development specialists, and policy developers are not necessarily motivated by shared goals. Recent policy has emphasized the importance of the transition from school to the world of work. Parents are concerned with decisions about quality of life for their children. Educators have focused their efforts on content domains; instruction in cooking, dressing, mobility, and so on has been emphasized, often outside of the context of the actual skills needed in a student's life. Research and development specialists have documented the applicability of a variety of behavioral-instructional strategies, and have organized content into appealing frameworks by developing scope and sequence of curriculum content.

The results of the recent impact studies are clear: most handicapped young adults live at home, do not have jobs, and do not participate much in activities outside the home. These results appear to derive, in part, from the lack of a shared "future-oriented" vision among parents and pr fessionals during students' school years. School progran in independent living have not been guided, on a wid spread basis, by perceptions of the nature and demands c the next environments in which handicapped youngste are likely to function.

Many of the conclusions and recommendations th emerge as reasonable from this review—need for focus o elementary-level programs, need for concerted effort i postschool planning, need to identify effective roles fo parents—are related to this apparent lack of a cohesiv foundation for determining the necessary contributions c all concerned. An orientation toward current and nex environments would serve as a foundation from which shared vision could be developed. The recent emphasis a the federal level on transitions to the world of work is timely example of a necessary building block.

Policy Development

Much interest has emerged during the past few years concerning transition from school to work. The transition initiative was stimulated in large part through funding priorities set by the Office of Special Education and Rehabilitative Services (OSERS) of the U.S. Department of Education (Will, 1984). The goal of transitional activities, in the view of Will (1984), is to facilitate "the transition from school to working life" (p. 1). This view incorporates concern for other aspects of adult adjustment (such as leisure, social, and personal competence), but gives employment the top priority. Will (1984) noted though, that "independent living enhances opportunities both to obtain employment and enjoy its benefits" (p. 1).

The OSERS has identified three bridges for transition from school to adult life. One bridge, "transition without special services," refers to the use of generic services available to all citizens in a given community (e.g., the postsecondary program available in most community colleges). A second bridge, labeled "transition with time-limited services," refers to specialized, short-term services typically restricted to disabled persons (e.g., the state vocational rehabilitation programs). The final bridge, "transition with ongoing services," refers to services that disabled persons need to succeed in adult life (Will, 1985, p. 4). Will (1984) noted that few examples of this type of service are available, and that new federal research funding is dedicated to the development of this final bridge.

The focus on transitional services for disabled persons is a bold and timely move on the part of the federal government. The lack of quality services available to handicapped students at the secondary level has been documented (Brodsky, 1983; Vogelsberg, Williams, & Friedl, 1980), as has the need for ongoing support services for adults after leaving school (Close, Taylor, & Pickett, 1982; Schalock, Harper, & Carver, 1981).

One concern noted with the new federal initiative from OSERS is the lack of attention to personal, social, and leisure skills domains, which are needed to facilitate independent living. Halpern (1985) suggested the addition of two mensions to complete the OSERS transition model. ..iving successfully in one's community should be the pri-ary target of transitional services. The dimension of com-unity adjustment includes the quality of a person's resi-ntial environment and the adequacy of social and terpersonal network" (p. 480). Empirical support exists r such a revision of Will's (1984) model. Research by alpern et al. (1985) demonstrates that the effects of pro-ammatic efforts aimed at a single dimension of adjust-ent are not correlated with improvements along the other imensions of adjustment. To be successful, transition pro-rams will require multiple components that are directed ecifically toward all important dimensions of adult djustment (e.g., employment, residential environments, nd social and interpersonal networks).

Research is needed to document the impact of the initial cus on employment for transition services. Likewise, esearch is needed to document the roles of independent ving components for successful transition to adult life. tudies are required of the vocational, independent living, nd personal/social status of handicapped graduates *at he time of graduation* if we are to understand fully their eeds for postschool services and the impact of differential ostschool services on their adult adjustment. Establishing he characteristics of successful graduates (and successful rograms) at the time of graduation *and* at intervals there-fter should help to direct subsequent policy development vith respect to programmatic emphasis. Finally, policy esearch and development efforts are needed on the third ridge in the OSERS model, transition with ongoing ser-ices, in the areas of employment and independent living kills. Documenting the utility of the transition emphasis n these ways would enhance the likelihood of better lives or disabled persons.

tate and Local Program Development

Special education services should be directed toward reparing handicapped students for successful adult djustment. A key question is, When should training and rogram development efforts begin? Unfortunately, the mplications of graduation often are perceived only as that vent draws near. Furthermore, given the appalling stat-stics on dropout rates of special education students with nild disabilities (Edgar, 1985), it is clear that many tudents do not receive the training needed to enhance their abilities to function as adults.

It has been argued that a focus on traditional academics in special education is unsatisfactory at both the elemen-tary and secondary levels for some mildly disabled students (Clark, 1979; Wimmer, 1981). There is simply a lack of correspondence between the skills needed for adult adjust-ment and such an "educational foundations" notion of special education. This lack of content-appropriate edu-cation has led many to embrace the career education model for special education as a needed reform in general edu-cation (Brolin, 1978, 1983; Hoyt, 1982).

A clear emphasis within the career education movement is the provision of functional content in the elementary school years (Clark, 1979). This early emphasis on developing appropriate functional skills is not without controversy. Some have noted that emphasis on functional skills in the elementary years unnecessarily differentiates mildly handicapped students from their nonhandicapped peers and limits their ability to be assimilated into the mainstream of educational programming (Edgar, 1985). These criticisms may be valid for many mildly disabled students. However, the lack of success of special education programs in preparing handicapped youngsters for adult roles is apparent (Edgar, 1985). Given that proper assess-ment and curricular choices are made, it is necessary both to teach functional content in the elementary schools (Clark, 1979) and to plan concretely for transition to adult life throughout the student's school years (Brolin, 1983).

This is especially true for severely handicapped students. It is clear from recent reviews that such programs for elementary-level students often are based largely on curriculum that emphasizes normal developmental mile-stones (Brinker, 1985; Guess & Noonan, 1982). With such preparation, these severely handicapped students are not prepared for secondary-level programs in which the focus is on transitions to adult roles.

A curriculum focus on current and next environments would help to address these concerns. Transition from elementary- to secondary-level programs is just as import-ant a program emphasis as is transition from secondary-level programs to adult life. Elementary students become secondary students just as surely as secondary students become young adults. If all levels of programming are coordinated and guided by a shared vision of desired out-comes, the likelihood of achievement of those valued results is enhanced. In addition to identifying the require-ments of the ultimate settings in which learners will func-tion as adults, we must ask, What are the requirements of (specific) secondary programs for handicapped learners? in order to determine effective curriculum and instruction for elementary students. The "curricula without recipes" approach recommended by Brinker (1985) is especially relevant here. In this approach, curriculum content is determined by identifying desired participation in school, home, and community environments. Teaching environ-ments that encourage development of functional skills are used. Student activities within these environments, and students' existing knowledge and skills, are used as starting points for instruction.

State and local education agencies need to develop mechanisms to plan concretely for various transitions that handicapped students must accomplish as they grow. Basic elements of this transitional model should include (a) clear specification of the desired goals and products of special education; (b) use of functional assessment instruments and methodology to identify the level of educational resources needed to meet individual goals in all adolescent and adult roles; (c) functional curricula to teach indepen-dent performance of the entire range of personal and daily living skills; and (d) evaluation criteria and methodology to determine the effectiveness of special education services for secondary-level and adult adjustment of handicapped students.

Planning for postschool functioning of handicapped students is essential. Educators and parents must identify the likely and possible postschool roles of individual learners in residential, vocational, leisure, and continuing education environments. This is especially true for severely handicapped learners who require continued services and support throughout postschool years (Williams et al., 1985). Postschool service providers must be identified and specific plans developed for facilitating access to necessary services (Van Deventer et al., 1981). Determination of available services, identification of anticipated performance levels, and value negotiation with parents are the major elements of such planning. Educators must be knowledgeable about postschool environments and services and must provide relevant information to parents (Sailor & Guess, 1983).

An instructive model effort in this direction was reported recently by the Board of Cooperative Educational Services of Nassau County, New York (1984). An "aging-out" study was undertaken to identify the status and needs of all 17–21-year-old handicapped students (N = 1,200) on a number of dimensions relevant to postschool functioning. The key dimensions (for purposes of our review here) were basic self-help skills, mobility skills, residential setting, supervision required in residence, long-term plan with parents, and recommended postschool residential placement. Based on 884 returns (74% return rate) selected results were as follows. Essentially, all students with IQs of 50+ were independent performers of basic self-help skills; only 60–76% of severely handicapped students could do the same. In the area of travel skills, 60% of the mildly handicapped students "used transportation in and away from their neighborhood"; 55% of the severely handicapped students "cannot go anywhere unsupervised." Only 50% of all parents had been involved with educators in long-term planning. And, the recommended postschool placements for all severely handicapped students were with their families or in structured and/or supervised environments. Interestingly, the same was true for 88% of the mildly handicapped students.

The implications of these findings for postschool and longer term planning were emphasized. In fact, the study was initiated for those purposes. This seems an especially appropriate model for state and local education agencies to use to facilitate postschool adjustments of their handicapped students.

Research and Development

Program development efforts aimed at appropriate education of handicapped learners in independent living domains have been reviewed here. The state of the art is commendable. Career education models are well-developed for mildly handicapped learners. Program models designed to provide instruction in home and community living skills to more severely handicapped learners are increasingly comprehensive and well articulated, especially at the secondary level.

A variety of research and development needs are st apparent. The lack of previous emphasis on the nature effective elementary programs is striking. Certainly shared future-oriented vision implies the importance coordinated elementary-secondary programming, and focus on transitions therein. The effective role(s) parents in helping handicapped learners to develop ind pendent living skills are not yet clear. And, how to enhan parents' functioning in those roles is still not establishe Finally, the impact of school programs on performance independent living skills, and of postschool plannir efforts for transition to adult life, has not been we documented.

In a general sense, even though much research on pr gramming independent living skills for handicappe learners has been conducted and reported, meaningf data bases do not appear to exist. Inclusion of learners different ages and different handicap severity levels withi individual studies, as well as lack of documentation effects of task and setting characteristics, make interpre ation difficult. The differential nature and sequence effective instructional strategies has not been clear developed for mildly versus severely, younger versus olde or community- (school-) versus institution-based handi capped learners. Research on school-based programmin is still not common. Coordinated and *programmatic* effor is clearly required to address these research and develop ment needs. The suggestions by Tawney and Sniezel (1985) for establishing national-, state-, and local-leve data bases are timely.

Future Directions

Disabled students require instructional programs to pre pare them for independent performance of a wide range o independent living skills. This emphasis on independen performance clearly implies the need to focus instructio on what Stokes and Baer (1977) refer to as generalizatio and maintenance of skills. The focus on training for generalization and maintenance is a high priority in specia education (Horner, McDonnell, & Bellamy, 1985; Polloway & Epstein, 1985). In addition, a number of studies have been conducted to begin the development of a technology for teaching independent performance of community living skills (Cuvo & Davis, 1983; Horner, Jones, & Williams, 1985). What is needed now is a *model development* approach in which progress is made from research development and validation activities into full-scale replication efforts across multiple sites (Paine, Bellamy, & Wilcox, 1980). The initial stage is the *development* of techniques that are used to teach or change the behavior of students. These techniques utilize advances in instruction and service delivery in their development. The second stage is *validation* of the techniques and procedures in a *field-based service setting* controlled by the developers. During the final *replication* phase, the developers provide assistance to sites and carefully evaluate the outcomes of instruction.

This model development approach to research has distinct advantages over the small-case, single-instance, nonprogrammatic research that has typically been conducted in special education. Knowledge is improved through rigorous evaluation of efforts at each stage in the process. Once the model is properly evaluated, dissemination efforts can be enhanced through systematic replication of the model. Finally, standardization of assessment procedures, instructional methodology, and evaluation criteria allow for the development of larger data bases for ultimate integration and analysis.

A comprehensive list of references on independent living skills for handicapped learners is available from the first author at Oregon Research Institute, 1899 Willamette, Eugene, Oregon 97401. The references at the end of this chapter represent an abbreviated version of those reviewed.

Author Information

Larry K. Irvin is Adjunct Associate Professor at the University of Oregon and Research Scientist at the Oregon Research Institute. Daniel W. Close is Associate Professor and Research Associate, and Robert L. Wells is a doctoral candidate, both at the University of Oregon, Division of Special Education and Rehabilitation, Rehabilitation Research and Training Center in Mental Retardation.

References

Aeschleman, S., & Schladenhauffen, J. (1984). Acquisition, generalization and maintenance of grocery shopping skills by severely mentally retarded adolescents. *Applied Research in Mental Retardation,* **5**, 245–258.

Auty, B., & Close, D. (1986). *The adult skills development program.* Unpublished manuscript, University of Oregon, Rehabilitation Research and Training Center in Mental Retardation, Eugene, OR.

Baine, D. (1982). *Instructional design for special education.* Englewood Cliffs, NJ: Educational Technology Publications.

Baldwin, V. L. (1976). Curriculum concerns. In M. A. Thomas (Ed.), *Hey, don't forget about me!* (pp. 64–73). Reston, VA: Council for Exceptional Children.

Baller, W. R., Charles, D. C., & Miller, E. L. (1967). Mid-life attainment of the mentally retarded: A longitudinal study. *Genetic Psychology Monographs,* **75**, 235–239.

Bates, P., & Cuvo, A. J. (1984). *The effect of school (simulated) versus community based instruction on the acquisition, transfer of training, generalization, and maintenance of independent living skills by mildly and moderately retarded adolescents* (84.023EH30027). Transition research project, U.S. Department of Education.

Bates, P., & Cuvo, A. (1984–1985). Simulated and naturalistic instruction of community functioning skills with mentally retarded learners. *Association for Direct Instruction News,* **4**(2), 14–15.

Battles v. Commonwealth of Pennsylvania. 629 F. 2d, 275 (3rd Cir. 1980).

Baumgart, D., Brown, L., Pumpian, I., Nisbet, J., Ford, A., Sweet, M., Messina, R., & Schroder, J. (1982). Principle of partial participation for severely handicapped students. *Journal of the Association for Persons With Severe Handicaps,* **7**(2), 17–27.

Becker, W. C., & Engelmann, S. (1978). Systems for basic instruction: Theory and applications. In A. C. Catania & T. A. Brigham (Eds.), *Handbook of applied behavior analysis: Social and instructional process* (pp. 225–377). New York : Irvington.

Bellamy, G. T. (1985). Transition progress: Comments on Hasazi, Gordon and Roe. *Exceptional Children,* **51**, 474–478.

Bellamy, G. T., & Wilcox, B. (1984). *Oregon High School Model Project final report.* Eugene, OR: University of Oregon, Specialized Training Program.

Bender, M., & Valletutti, P. J. (1982). *Teaching functional academics: A curriculum guide for adolescents and adults with learning problems.* Baltimore, MD: University Park Press.

Billingsley, F., & Romer, L. (1983). Response prompting and the transfer of stimulus control: Methods, research and a conceptual framework. *Journal of the Association for Persons With Severe Handicaps,* **8**(2), 3–12.

Board of Cooperative Educational Services of Nassau County, New York. (1984). *Survey of Youth Aging-Out.* Westbury, NY: Board of Cooperative Educational Services of Nassau County, New York, Division of Special Education.

Bourbeau, P., Sowers, J., & Close, D. (1985). *Generalization of banking skills from the classroom to trained and untrained bank settings in the community.* Unpublished manuscript, Oregon Research Institute, Eugene, OR.

Bricker, D., & Filler, J. (1985). *Severe mental retardation: From theory to practice.* Washington DC: Council for Exceptional Children.

Brinker, R. P. (1985). Curricula without recipes. In D. Bricker & J. Filler (Eds.), *Severe mental retardation: From theory to practice* (pp. 208–229). Washington, DC: Council for Exceptional Children.

Brinker, R. P., & Thorpe, M. (1984). Integration of severely handicapped students and the proportion of IEP objectives achieved. *Exceptional Children,* **51**, 168–175.

Brodsky, M. (1983). *Post high school experiences of graduates with severe handicaps.* Unpublished doctoral dissertation, University of Oregon, Eugene, OR.

Brolin, D. (1973). Career education needs of secondary educable students. *Exceptional Children,* **39**, 619–624.

Brolin, D. E. (1978). *Life centered career education: A competency based approach.* Reston, VA: Council for Exceptional Children.

Brolin, D. E. (1983). Career education: Where do we go from here? *Career Development for Exceptional Individuals,* **6**, 3–15.

Brolin, D. E. (1984). Refocusing special education for career development. *The Journal for Special Educators,* **19**(4), 55–60.

Brown, L., Branston, M., Hamre-Nietupski, S., Johnson, F., Wilcox, B., & Gruenewald, L. (1979). A rationale for comprehensive longitudinal interactions between severely handicapped students and nonhandicapped students and other citizens. *American Association for Education of the Severely and Profoundly Handicapped Review,* **4**, 3–14.

Brown, L., Certo, N., Belmore, K., & Crowner, T. (1976). *Madison's alternative for zero exclusion: Papers and programs related to public school services for secondary age severely handicapped students* (Volume VI, Part 1), Madison, WI: Madison Public Schools.

Brown, L., Falvey, M., Baumgart, D., Pumpian, I., Shroder, J., & Gruenewald, L. (Eds.). (1979). *Strategies for teaching chronological age-appropriate functional skills to adolescent and young adult severely handicapped students.* Madison, WI: Madison Metropolitan School District.

Brown, L., Nietupski, J., & Hamre-Nietupski, S. (1976). Criterion of ultimate functioning. In M. A. Thomas (Ed.), *Hey, don't forget about me!* (pp. 2–15). Reston, VA: Council for Exceptional Children.

Campbell v. Talladega County Board of Education, 518 F. Supp. 47 (N.D. Ala. 1981).

Clark, G. M. (1974). Career education for the mildly handicapped. *Focus on Exceptional Children,* **9**, 110.

Clark, G. M. (1976). Career exploration: An integral part of the career education program. In G. Blackburn (Ed.), *Colloquium series on career education for handicapped adolescents.* West Lafayette, IN: Purdue University.

Clark, G. M. (1979). *Career education for the handicapped in the elementary classroom.* Denver CO: Love.

Close, D. (1977). Community living for severely and profoundly retarded adults: A group home study. *Education and Training of the Mentally Retarded,* **81**, 256–262.

Close, D. W., & Halpern, A. S. (1984). Measuring the learning potential of severely mentally retarded adults. In A. Halpern & M. Fuhrer (Eds.), *Functional assessment in rehabilitation* (pp. 159–170). Baltimore, MD: Paul H. Brookes.

Close, D. W., Halpern, A. S., Slentz, K. I., & Irvin, L. K. (1984). *Community living assessment and teaching system: Assessment manual.* Omro, WI: Conover Company.

Close, D. W., Irvin, L. K., Taylor, V. E., & Agosta, J. M. (1981). Community living skills instruction for mildly retarded persons. *Exceptional Education Quarterly,* **2**(1), 75–85.

Close, D. W., Sowers, J., Halpern, A. S., & Bourbeau, P. (1985). Programming for transition to independent living for mildly retarded persons. In R. Bruininks & C. Lakin (Eds.), *Living and learning in the least restrictive environment* (pp. 161–176). Baltimore, MD: Paul H. Brookes.

Close, D. W., Taylor, V. E., & Pickett, M. (1982). Training and support for independent living. *Community Services Forum,* **2**(3), 2–3.

Cobb, H. (1972). *The forecast of fulfillment: A review of research on predictive assessement of the adult retarded for social and vocational adjustment.* New York: Teachers College Press.

Conner, F. P., Williamson, G. G., & Siepp, J. M. (1978). *Program guide for infants and toddlers with neuromotor and other developmental disabilities.* New York: Teachers College Press.

Coon, M. E., Vogelsberg, R. T., & Williams, W. (1981). Effects of classroom public transportation instruction on generalization to the natural environment. *Journal of the Association for the Severely Handicapped,* **6**(2), 23–29.

Crist, K., Walls, R. T., & Haught, P. (1984). Degree of specificity in task analysis. *American Journal of Mental Deficiency,* **89**, 67–74.

Cuvo, A., & Davis, P. (1981). Home living for developmentally disabled persons: Instructional design and evaluation. *Exceptional Education Quarterly,* **2**(1), 87–98.

Cuvo, A., & Davis, P. (1983). Behavior therapy and community living skills. In M. Hersen, R. Eisler, & P. Miller (Eds.), *Progress in behavior modification* (Vol. 14, pp. 125–171). New York: Academic Press.

Dunlap, G., Koegel, R., & Koegel, L. K. (1984). Continuity of treatment: Toilet training in multiple community settings. *Journal of the Association for Persons With Severe Han[dicaps,* **9**(2), 134–141.

Edgar, E. (1985). How do special education students fare af[ter] they leave school? A response to Hasazi, Gordon and R[oe]. *Exceptional Children,* **51**, 470–473.

Engelmann, S., & Carnine, D. (1982). *Theory of instructic[on]: Principles and applications.* New York: Irvington.

Ford, A., & Mirenda, P. (1984). Community instruction: A nat[u]ral cues and corrections decisions model. *Journal of t[he] Association for Persons With Severe Handicaps,* **9**(2[)], 79–88.

Freagon, S., Wheeler, J., Hill, L., Brankin, G., Costello, D., [&] Peters, W. (1983). A domestic training environment f[or] students who are severely handicapped. *Journal of t[he] Association for Persons With Severe Handicaps,* **8**(4[)], 49–61.

Fredericks, H. D., Baldwin, V. L., Heyer, M., Alrick, B., Bans[...] C., & Samples, B. (1980). *TR curriculum for severe[ly] handicapped adolescents and adults.* Springfield, Il[:] Charles C. Thomas.

Gerber, M. M., & Semmel, M. I. (1984). Microeconomics o[f] referral and reintegration: A paradigm for evaluation [of] special education. *Studies in Educational Evaluation,* **2**(1[)], 13–29.

Guess, D., & Noonan, M. (1982). Curricula and instructiona[l] procedures for severely handicapped students. *Focus o[n] Exceptional Children,* **14**(5), 1–12.

Halpern, A. (1979). Adolescents and young adults. *Exceptiona[l] Children,* **45**, 518–525.

Halpern, A. (1984). Functional assessment and mental retar[]dation. In A. Halpern & M. Fuhrer (Eds.), *Functiona[l] assessment in rehabilitation* (pp. 61–78). Baltimore, MD[:] Paul H. Brookes.

Halpern, A. (1985). Transition: A look at the foundation. *Excep[]tional Children,* **51**, 479–486.

Halpern, A., & Benz, M. (1984). *Toward excellence in secondar[y] special education.* Unpublished manuscript, University o[f] Oregon, Rehabilitation Research and Training Center ir[n] Mental Retardation, Eugene, OR.

Halpern, A., Close, D., & Nelson, D. (1985). *On my own: The impact of semi-independent living programs on adults with mental retardation.* Baltimore MD: Paul H. Brookes.

Halpern, A., Raffeld, P., Irvin, L., & Link, R. (1975). *Social and Prevocational Information Battery.* Monterey, CA: CTB/McGraw-Hill.

Hamre-Nietupski, S., Nietupski, J., Bates, P., & Maurer, S. (1982). Implementing a community-based educational model for moderately/severely handicapped students. *Journal of the Association for Persons With Severe Handicaps,* **7**(4), 38–43.

Haney, J. I., & Jones, R. T. (1982). Programming maintenance as a major component of a community-centered preventative effort: Escape from fire. *Behavior Therapy,* **13**, 47–62.

Hanson, M. (1977). *Teaching your Down's syndrome infant.* Baltimore, MD: University Park Press.

Hasazi, S. B., Gordon, L. R., & Roe, C. A. (1985). Factors associated with the employment status of handicapped youth exiting high school from 1979 to 1983. *Exceptional Children,* **51**, 455–469.

Haywood, H. C. (1979). What happened to mild and moderate retardation? *American Journal of Mental Deficiency,* **83**, 429–431.

Heal, L., Colson, L., & Gross, J. (1984). Evaluating adult skill training for severely mentally retarded secondary students. *American Journal of Mental Deficiency,* **89**, 146–155.

ill, J., Wehman, P., & Horst, G. (1982). Toward generalization of appropriate leisure and social behavior. *Journal of the Association for the Severely Handicapped,* **6,** 38–44.

o, S., Close, D. W., Sowers, J., & Keating, T. (1985). *Teaching generalized boiling skills to mildly handicapped adolescents.* Unpublished manuscript, University of Oregon, Rehabilitation Research and Training Center in Mental Retardation, Eugene, OR.

orner, R. H., Jones, D., & Williams, J. A. (1985). Teaching generalized street crossing to individuals with moderate and severe mental retardation. *Journal of the Association for Persons With Severe Handicaps,* **10**(2), 71–78.

orner, R. H., & McDonald, R. S. (1982). A comparison of single instance and general case instruction in teaching a generalized vocational skill. *Journal of the Association for the Severely Handicapped,* **7,** 7–20.

Iorner, R. H., McDonnell, J. J., & Bellamy, G. T. (1985). Teaching generalized skills: General case instruction in simulation and community settings. In R. H. Horner, L. Meyer, & H. Fredericks (Eds.), *Education of learners with severe handicaps: Exemplary service strategies* (pp. 289–314). Baltimore, MD: Paul H. Brookes.

Ioyt, K. B. (1975). *Career education and the handicapped person.* Unpublished manuscript, U.S. Office of Education, Washington, DC.

Ioyt, K. B. (1982). Career education: A new beginning? *Career Development for Exceptional Individuals,* **5,** 3–12.

Iuguenin, N., Weidenman, L., & Mulick, J. (1983). Programmed instruction. In J. Matson & J. Mulick (Eds.), *Handbook of mental retardation* (pp. 443–454). New York: Pergamon Press.

Iunt, P., Goetz, L., & Anderson, J. (1985). *The quality of IEP objectives.* Unpublished manuscript, San Francisco State University, Department of Special Education.

rvin, L. K., Gersten, R., Taylor, V., Close, D., & Heiry, T. (1981). Vocational skill assessment of severely mentally retarded adults. *American Journal of Mental Deficiency,* **85,** 631–638.

ohnson, B. F., & Cuvo, A. J. (1981). Teaching mentally retarded adults to cook. *Behavior Modification,* **5,** 187–202.

Kazdin, A., & Matson, J. (1981). Social validation in mental retardation. *Applied Research in Mental Retardation,* **2,** 39–53.

Kennedy, R. F. (1966). *A Connecticut community revisited: A study of the social adjustment of a group of mentally deficient adults in 1948 and 1960.* Hartford, CT: Connecticut State Department of Health, Office of Mental Retardation.

Kokaska, C. J., & Brolin, D. E. (1985). *Career education for handicapped individuals* (2nd ed.). Columbus, OH: Merrill.

Kregel, J., Wehman, P., & Seyfarth, J. (1985). *Community integration of young adults with mental retardation: Transition from school to adulthood.* Unpublished manuscript, Virginia Commonwealth University, School of Education, Research and Training Center, Richmond, VA.

Laski, F. (1985). Judicial address of education for students with severe mental retardation. In D. Bricker & J. Filler (Eds.), *Severe mental retardation: From theory to practice,* (pp. 36–48). Washington, DC: Council for Exceptional Children.

Lent, J. R., & McLean, B. M. (1976). The trainable retarded: The technology of teaching. In N. G. Haring & R. L. Schiefelbusch (Eds.), *Teaching special children* (pp. 197–231). New York: McGraw-Hill.

Liberty, K., & Wilcox, B. (1981). Slowing down learning. *Association for the Severely Handicapped Newsletter,* **1**(2), 1–2.

Lowe, M. L., & Cuvo, A. J. (1976). Teaching coin summation. *Journal of Applied Behavior Analysis,* **9,** 483–489.

Maggs, A., & Maggs, R. (1980). Direct instruction in Australia. *Journal of Special Education Technology,* **3**(3), 26–34.

Marchetti, A., & Matson, J. L. (1981). Training skills for community adjustment. In J. Matson & J. McCartney (Eds.), *Handbook of behavior modification with the mentally retarded.* New York: Plenum Press.

Matson, J. L. (1981). Use of independence training to teach shopping skills to mildly mentally retarded adults. *American Journal of Mental Deficiency,* **86,** 178–183.

McDonnell, J. (1984). Teaching generalized community skills to students with severe handicaps. *Association for Direct Instruction News,* **4**(1), 5–6.

McDonnell, J., & Horner, R. H. (1985). *Effects of in vivo versus simulation—plus in vivo training of high school students with severe handicaps.* Unpublished manuscript, University of Oregon, Specialized Training Program, Eugene, OR.

McDonnell, J., Horner, R. H., & Williams, J. (1984). Comparison of three strategies for teaching generalized grocery purchasing to high school students with severe handicaps. *Journal of the Association for Persons With Severe Handicaps,* **9**(2), 123–133.

McLeod, J. (1983). Learning disability is for educators. *Journal of Learning Disabilities,* **16,** 23–24.

Mithaug, D. E., Horiuchi, C. N., & Fanning, P. N. (1985). A report on the Colorado statewide follow-up survey of special education students. *Exceptional Children,* **51,** 397–404.

Mulligan, M., Lacy, L., & Guess, D. (1982). Effects of massed, distributed, and spaced trial sequencing on severely handicapped students' performance. *Journal of the Association for the Severely Handicapped,* **7**(2), 48–61.

Nietupski, J., Clancy, P., & Christiansen, C. (1984). Acquisition, maintenance and generalization of vending machine purchasing skills by moderately handicapped students. *Education and Training of the Mentally Retarded,* **19,** 91–96.

Noel, M. M., Burke, P. J., & Valdivieso, C. H. (1985). Educational policy and severe mental retardation. In D. Bricker & J. Filler (Eds.), *Severe mental retardation: From theory to practice.* Washington, DC: Council for Exceptional Children.

Paine, S., Bellamy, G. T., & Wilcox, B. (1980). *Human services at work: From innovation to standard practice.* Baltimore, MD: Paul H. Brookes.

Peck, C., & Cooke, T. (1983). Benefits of mainstreaming: How much can we expect? *Analysis and Intervention in Developmental Disabilities,* **3,** 1–22.

Polloway, E. A. (1984). The integration of mildly retarded students in the schools: A historical review. *Remedial and Special Education,* **5**(4), 18–28.

Polloway, E. A., & Epstein, M. H. (1985). Current research issues in mild mental retardation: A survey of the field. *Education and Training of the Mentally Retarded,* **20**(3), 171–174.

Polloway, E. A., & Smith, J. D. (1983). Changes in mild mental retardation: Population, programs, and perspectives. *Exceptional Children,* **50,** 149–159.

Reid, D., & Favell, J. (1984). Group instruction with persons who have severe disabilities: A critical review. *Journal of the Association for Persons With Severe Handicaps,* **9**(3), 167–177.

Reid, D., Wilson, P., & Faw, G. (1983). Teaching self-help skills. In J. Matson & J. Mulick (Eds.), *Handbook of mental retardation* (pp. 429–442). New York: Pergamon Press.

Rose, H. E. (1984). *Non-instructional interventions: Affecting the way adolescents with severe handicaps spend their time outside school.* Unpublished doctoral dissertation, University of Oregon, Department of Special Education and Rehabilitation, Eugene, OR.

Sailor, W., & Goetz, L. (1983). *Over-21 final report* (Contract #81-68120). Sacramento, CA: California Department of Developmental Services.

Sailor, W., & Guess, D. (1983). *Severely handicapped students: An instructional design.* Boston, MA: Houghton Mifflin.

Schalock, R. L., Harper, R. S., & Carver, G. (1981). Independent living placement: Five years later. *American Journal of Mental Deficiency,* **86**, 170–177.

Schalock, R., Harper, R., & Gerung, T. (1981). Community integration of mentally retarded adults: Community placement and program success. *American Journal of Mental Deficiency,* **85**, 478–488.

Schalock, R., Wolzen, B., Ross, I., Elliot, B., Werbel, G., & Peterson, K. (1985). *Post-secondary community placement of handicapped students: A five-year follow-up analysis.* Unpublished manuscript, Mid-Nebraska Mental Retardation Services, Hastings, NE.

Schutz, R., Williams, W., Iverson, G., & Duncan, D. (1984). Social integration of severely handicapped students: A review of the literature. In N. Certo, N. Haring, & R. York (Eds.), *Public school integration of severely handicapped students: Rationale, issues, and progressive alternatives* (pp. 15–42). Baltimore, MD: Paul H. Brookes.

Snell, M. E., & Gast, D. L. (1971). Applying time delay procedure to the instruction of the severely handicapped. *Journal of the Association for the Severely Handicapped,* **6**(3), 3–14.

Sobsey, R., & Orelove, P. (1984). Neurophysiological facilitation of eating skills in severely handicapped children. *Journal of the Association for Persons With Severe Handicaps,* **9**(2), 98–110.

Sontag, E., Smith, J., & Sailor, W. (1977). The severely/profoundly handicapped: Who are they? Where are they? *Journal of Special Education,* **11**, 5–11.

Sowers, J., Rusch, F. R., & Hudson, C. (1979). Training a severely retarded young adult to ride the city bus to and from work. *American Association for Education of the Severely and Profoundly Handicapped Review,* **4**, 15–23.

Spooner, F., & Spooner, D. (1984). A review of chaining techniques. *Education and Training of the Mentally Retarded,* **19**, 114–124.

Sprague, J. R., & Horner, R. H. (1984). The effects of single instance, multiple instance, and general case training on generalized vending machine use by moderately and severely handicapped students. *Journal of Applied Behavior Analysis,* **7**, 349–367.

Stokes, T. F., & Baer, D. M. (1977). An implicit technology of generalization. *Journal of Applied Behavior Analysis,* **10**, 349–367.

Super, D. (1977). Vocational maturity in mid-career. *Vocational Guidance Quarterly,* **24**, 294–301. (ERIC Document Reproduction Service No. EJ 160 267)

Switzky, H., & Haywood, H. C. (1985). Perspectives on methodological and research issues concerning severely mentally retarded persons. In D. Bricker & J. Filler (Eds.), *Severe mental retardation: From theory to practice* (pp. 264–284). Washington, DC: Council for Exceptional Children.

Switzky, H., Rotatari, A., Miller, T., & Freagon, S. (1979). The developmental model and its implications for assessment and instruction for the severely/profoundly handicappe *Mental Retardation,* **17**, 167–170.

Tawney, J. W., & Sniezek, K. (1985). Educational programs f severely mentally retarded elementary-age children: Pr gress problems and suggestions. In D. Bricker & J. Fill (Eds.), *Severe mental retardation: From theory to practi* (pp. 76–96). Washington, DC: Council for Exception Children.

Taylor, V. E., Close, D. W., Carlson, C. A., & Larrabee, (1981). *Independent living skills teachers' manual.* Eugen OR: University of Oregon, Rehabilitation Research an Training Center in Mental Retardation.

van den Pol, R. A., Iwata, B. A., Ivancic, M. T., Page, T. J., Nee N. A., & Whitley, F. P. (1981). Teaching the handicapped eat in public places: Acquisition, generalization, and mair tenance of restaurant skills. *Journal of Applied Behavic Analysis,* **14**, 61–69.

Van Deventer, P., Yelinek, N., Brown, L., Schroder, J., Loomis R., & Gruenewald, L. (1981). A follow-up summation c severely handicapped graduates of the Madison Metrc politan School District from 1971–78. In L. Brown, D Baumgart, I. Pumpian, J. Nisbet, A. Ford, A. Donnellan, M Sweet, R. Loomis, & J. Schroder (Eds.), *Education prc grams for severely handicapped students* (Vol. 11, pp 1–178). Madison, WI: Madison Public Schools.

Vincent, L., Salisbury, C., Walter, G., Brown, P., Gruenewald, L. & Powers, M. (1980). Evaluation and curriculum in earl childhood/special education: Criteria of the next environ ment. In W. Sailor, B. Wilcox, & L. Brown (Eds.), *Method of instruction for severely handicapped students* (pp 303–328). Baltimore, MD: Paul H. Brookes.

Vogelsberg, R. T., & Rusch, F. R. (1979). Training severel handicapped students to cross partially controlled intersec tions. *American Association for Education of the Severel and Profoundly Handicapped Review,* **4**, 264–273.

Vogelsberg, R., Williams, W., & Bellamy, G. (1982). Preparatior for independent living. In B. Wilcox & G. Bellamy (Eds.) *Design of high school programs for severely handicappe students* (pp. 153–174). Baltimore, MD: Paul H. Brookes.

Vogelsberg, R. T., Williams, W., & Friedl, M. (1980). Facilitating systems change for the severely handicapped: Secondary and adult services. *Journal of the Association for the Severely Handicapped,* **5**, 78–85.

Walls, R. T., Dowler, D., Haught, P., Zawlocki, R. (1984). Progressive delay and unlimited delay of prompts in forward chaining and whole task training strategies. *Education and Training of the Mentally Retarded,* **19**, 276–284.

White, O. (1983). Descriptive analysis of extant research literature concerning skill generalization and the severely/profoundly handicapped. In M. Boer (Ed.), *Investigating the problem of skill generalization: Literature review I* (pp. 1–20). Seattle, WA: University of Washington, Washington Research Organization.

Whitman, T., Scibak, J., & Reid, D. (1983). *Behavior modification with the severely and profoundly retarded.* New York: Academic Press.

Wilcox, B., & Bellamy, G. T. (1980). *Oregon High School Project proposal to U.S. Office of Special Education.* Eugene, OR: University of Oregon, Specialized Training Program.

Wilcox, B., & Bellamy, G. (1982). *Design of high school programs for severely handicapped students.* Baltimore, MD: Paul H. Brookes.

Wilcox, B., & Bellamy, G. T. (1984). *Community Participation Project*. Proposal to U.S. Office of Special Education, University of Oregon, Specialized Training Program, Eugene, OR.

Will, M. (1984). *Bridges from school to working life. Programs for the handicapped*. Washington, DC: The Office of Special Education and Rehabilitative Services, Office of Information and Resources for the Handicapped.

Will, M. (1985). Bridges from school to working life. Programs for the handicapped. In R. W. English (Ed.), *Preparation of leadership personnel: School to community transitions doctoral program* (84–029 D, p. 4) Eugene, OR: University of Oregon, Rehabilitation Research and Training Center in Mental Retardation.

Williams, W., Vogelsberg, R. T., & Schutz, R. P. (1985). Programs for secondary-age severely handicapped youth. In D. Bricker & J. Filler (Eds.), *Severe mental retardation: From theory to practice* (pp. 97–118). Washington, DC: Council for Exceptional Children.

Wimmer, D. (1981). Functional learning curricula in the secondary schools. *Exceptional Children*, **47**, 610–613.

Wolfensberger, W. (Ed.), (1974). *The principle of normalization in human services*. Downsview, Toronto, Canada: National Institute on Mental Retardation.

Wood, F. H. (1978). Accepting the challenge to provide educational alternatives for secondary level students with special needs. In J. B. Jordan (Ed.), *Exceptional students in secondary schools* (pp. 1–8). Reston, VA: Council for Exceptional Children.

The Effectiveness of Differential Programming in Serving Students with Mild Handicaps: Placement Options and Instructional Programming

SUSAN EPPS AND GERALD TINDAL

University of Oregon

Abstract—The issues addressed in this chapter concern the development of effective alternative programs for students served in special education. The research conducted to date, including the latest efforts using meta-analyses, is reviewed and interpreted. Caution is urged in the interpretation of the results, primarily on the basis of the poor methodology employed in the original research and the serious lack of definition of treatments. The conclusion from this research is that placement setting is not the appropriate variable for investigating the efficacy of special education programs. The second section of the paper is an analysis of the content of special education programs. The data indicate few substantive differences in the manner in which special and regular education programs are defined. Given this impasse—the lack of differences either in program outcomes or content—the broader issue that is addressed is whether any effective educational practices can be considered in the delivery of programs to students with mild handicaps. The effective teaching research and three model programs are then described: the Adaptive Learning Environments Model, Active Mathematics Teaching, and Direct Instruction. Finally, implications and conclusions are considered from three different perspectives: practice in the schools, training programs, and the development of social policy.

An underlying assumption in special education is that all students do not prosper under identical educational programs. In the past, the purpose of extensive assessment and classification procedures has been to match students and interventions so that each student received optimal treatment. Hence, appropriate and effective instruction was viewed as being dependent on the category of students involved. Generally, special education practice has followed a categorical model (although there is a growing trend toward noncategorical placement), in which students are divided into distinct groups, such as behaviorally disordered, learning disabled, or mildly mentally retarded students (Heller, Holtzman, & Messick, 1982), and treated in settings removed from the regular classroom. Thus, it is important to examine the efficacy of differential instruction in the context of classification decisions.

Do separate categories of students profit from distinctly different educational programs, or do common components of effective instruction apply to multiple categories? This question focuses on whether students receive different types of instruction as a result of their classification. At present, most special education programs operate with specially certified staff, often reflecting the nature of the classifications of students. The relevant issue is whether these certifications have any functional implications for the classroom and for the development of individualized education programs (IEPs).

These components, the classification of students into disability groups, the certification of teachers through specialized endorsements reflecting the classifications, and the development of IEPs, all may be considered within the aptitude-by-treatment paradigm (Cronbach & Snow, 1977). Instead of asking simply whether an intervention is effective, one should ask, Which types of interventions work with which kinds of students? Use of this paradigm leads to an examination of how individual differences of special students interact with program processes to yield differential outcomes (Burnstein & Guiton, 1984). One basic issue to be addressed, then, is whether placement settings mediate instructional decisions. Do students profit more when they receive instruction in regular or mainstreamed settings or when they are placed in resource room or self-contained settings?

Mainstreaming

Providing equal educational opportunities for special education students requires designing and delivering high quality, comprehensive, and least restrictive educational services. In response to this goal, the concept of mainstreaming evolved. Mainstreaming refers to multiple service levels at which a range of administrative and instructional options as well as a variety of staff utilization patterns are available. These multiple service options are in contrast to the initial conceptualization and organization of special education as distinct from general education (Kaufman, Gottlieb, Agard, & Kukic, 1975). Although the term mainstreaming is pervasive in much of the recent literature in special education, there has been less than consistent agreement regarding the salient features that define a mainstreaming program (Kaufman et al., 1975; MacMillan & Semmel, 1977).

One common component in definitions of mainstreaming is the provision that special education students be educated, at least in part, in general education settings. In general, discussions of mainstreaming have focused more on administrative arrangements, such as the amount of time students spend in general education settings, than on instruction variables, such as the type of goal structure (e.g., cooperative vs. individualistic) in the regular classroom. Such attention to the administrative aspects of integrating special education students into general education has led to the predominant view of mainstreaming as a temporal dichotomy in which students spend an arbitrarily established portion of their school time in regular classes. Frequently, a determination of the least restrictive environment for a given student is inextricably tied to the student's classification (Heller, 1982). Temporal integration, which refers to the amount of time a student spends in regular classrooms with nonhandicapped peers, is one of the characteristics of mainstreaming programs that is most frequently noted in efficacy studies. Therefore, in a review of the effects of special education programs, temporal integration might be considered a necessary, but not sufficient, criterion for a mainstreaming program (Semmel, Gottlieb, & Robinson, 1979).

Cascade Model

The most common scheme for organizing special education programs along a continuum of instructional arrangements has been the cascade model. General education settings such as the regular classroom may represent the least restrictive setting for some students; settings such as residential schools or hospitals may represent the most restrictive placements (Cartwright, Cartwright, & Ward, 1984). Reynolds and Birch (1982) outlined several positive features of the cascade model. First, it proposes that one means of meeting the needs of special education students is to provide support in regular classes. Second, it provides a framework for placing students in more restrictive settings only when necessary and for moving them to less restrictive settings as soon as feasible. Third, it proposes that the demarcation between special and general education be opened so that adjustments in level can be made easily, as dictated by students' educational needs. Fourth, it suggests that special and general educators collaborate by sharing responsibilities for students. And fifth, the cascade model proposes that substantial justification be required to remove a student from a regular classroom.

The regular classroom represents the base of the model in which students with special needs have been either unrecognized or instructed by general educators who received no additional assistance. This level is immediately appealing since students avoid special labels and remain in regular settings with their nonhandicapped peers. The disadvantage, however, is that, without support services, they may struggle and fall further behind other students.

There are four levels in the cascade model at which students may receive services while still remaining in a regular class with their nonhandicapped peers. First, they may receive indirect services, such as consultative assistance that is provided to the general education teacher by professionals such as resource room teachers, special education consultants, or school psychologists. These consultative services might include suggestions about program modification or the preparation of special materials to supplement regular class assignments (Cartwright et al., 1984). At this level, students receive no direct instruction from the consultant. Second, students might receive direct instruction from an itinerant specialist, such as a speech and hearing therapist. Third, students may receive up to one half of their instruction from special education personnel in resource rooms (Sindelar & Deno, 1978). A resource room teacher typically offers direct instruction and also may offer consulting services to general educators. Increasingly, resource room teachers are being employed for multicategorical placements or for a more generic noncategorical model (Reynolds & Birch, 1982). Fourth, students may have a part-time special class placement that still enables them to participate in some general education activities. For example, students with mild mental retardation may attend a regular homeroom and nonacademic school activities, but go to a special class for academic instruction (Cartwright et al., 1984). One advantage of at least partial regular classroom placement is that students are not entirely segregated from general education students. In addition, part-time special education is intended to remediate areas in which students are demonstrating difficulties.

At the most restrictive end of the continuum of services in the cascade model is full-time special education with no integration into general education. One level is placement in a special class within a regular school. Even more restrictive arrangements include full-time special education in completely separate day or residential schools.

In the cascade model, attention is focused on the setting or place in which special education is provided. Because setting is a macrovariable with discernible parameters, it has received considerable attention with respect to policy decisions (Leinhardt & Pallay, 1982). In efficacy research, setting also has been viewed as a form of treatment for students experiencing difficulty in the regular classroom. Hence, because it is a salient feature that has been examined as an independent variable, it is necessary to investigate the extent to which setting itself directly influences student achievement.

Need to Examine Efficacy of Special Education

Since the intent of special education has been to provide needed services to students experiencing difficulty in general education, the establishment of special education generally has been viewed as a positive event. It was presumed that an accepting environment, modified instructional goals and techniques, and teachers with special training in areas of exceptionality would lead to more effective educational programs for handicapped individuals. Since the assumption was that special programs were beneficial, they characteristically received little systematic scrutiny; data regarding the efficacy of special education programs typically were unavailable. This lack of data did not imply that these programs were ineffective but, rather, that the impact of certain programs was unknown. Therefore, it has not been possible to determine the relative effectiveness of various instructional programs with particular students (Sheehan & Keogh, 1984).

Recently, a number of economic and professional influences have made evaluating and demonstrating program impact a high priority for special education personnel. Both governmental and private funding agencies are requesting evidence of program impact. Instructional accountability also has become an important factor for special educators who now are compelled to document how and in what ways their interventions are effective. This emphasis is fortunate, because evaluation data are needed to improve educational practice. Given the present economic climate, data on program evaluation will continue to be of paramount importance as special programs compete for tighter funds. The systematic collection of data to evaluate program effectiveness thus has become a salient concern (Sheehan & Keogh, 1984).

In reviewing the literature on the efficacy of special versus general education placement for exceptional students, two issues need to be addressed. First, there is the question of setting: do students experiencing difficulty in school fare better when placed in special education settings, such as resource rooms and self-contained classes, or when allowed to remain in regular classrooms? Second is the issue of instructional components: what is the content of instruction in special settings, and how is it different from the content offered in regular classrooms? This chapter systematically examines these two related issues: (a) the extent to which separate categorical labels facilitate the process of providing appropriate and effective education for exceptional students, and (b) whether specific instructional features appear in the delivery of specialized programs.

An imporant issue in examining the efficacy of special education programs, however, is the methodology used to generate findings. This topic, which is reviewed first, includes a focus on the types of populations that are served in the specialized programs; the design of the research, including the assignment of students to treatments; the measurement of outcomes, including both the types of measures used and the metric for analyzing these outcomes; and, finally, the independent variables or content of the special education programs. Given this framework for critically analyzing the research base, exemplary studies are then presented and critiqued in a review of the literature on the efficacy of special education. In this section, specialized programs are reviewed in more detail, and a series of studies are reviewed that systematically document the content and context of instruction in the resource room setting. Rather than viewing setting as the macrovariable of import in the evaluation of program efficacy, these more recent studies provide considerable detail on the nature of instruction in that setting. Finally, in the last section of the chapter, conclusions and implications are considered from three different perspectives: practice, training, and policy. In all three areas, a major issue is the need for better designed research with more precise focus.

Threats to the Validity of Efficacy Research

Before reviewing studies that have examined the efficacy of special education for students, there is an important caveat: the research reported in the literature is plagued by serious methodological flaws. Therefore, the results of special education efficacy studies must be interpreted cautiously for two reasons. One is that attention has been focused largely on the setting in which special instruction has been provided rather than on the particular components of the instruction. (This limitation is discussed in a subsequent section.) The second reason pertains to the serious threats to internal validity that characterize much of the evaluation literature.

Much of the special education efficacy research suggests that a number of special programs may be of questionable value to students because there may be no advantages over regular class placement, or worse, because special education placements may have a detrimental effect on student progress. Two possible explanations may account for this rather disappointing finding: (a) special education intervention indeed may be ineffective, and (b) the methodology for measuring the treatments and program outcomes may be questionable and/or insensitive. In the rush to answer questions about the effectiveness of special education, both researchers and those offering summary reviews of the literature often have neglected to consider, or have dismissed, some of the methodological problems that plague research in general and applied research in particular. More attention has been focused on results than on the method of producing these findings. Because of these problems, it has been difficult to find a definitive answer in efficacy research. Consideration of the potential sources of confounding is absolutely critical in providing an accurate evaluation of the effectiveness of special education. When threats to internal validity are not controlled, there can be little confidence in data suggesting either that special class placement was more effective than regular class placement or the reverse.

When evaluating empirical data regarding the effectiveness of special education services, there are at least five methodological concerns that need to be examined. The extent to which studies have considered each of these concerns and controlled for experimental confounding determines the validity of the results. A discussion of these concerns is presented below, drawing in part from a review by Tindal (1985).

Populations Served

Before students are eligible to receive special services, assessments typically are completed to classify the students into certain categories of exceptionality. These classifications span a wide range and include such groups as learning disabled, educationally handicapped, mentally retarded (educable, mildly, moderately, trainable, severely, profoundly), emotionally disturbed, chronically disruptive, behaviorally disordered, neurologically handicapped, and reading disabled students, and students with perceptual problems.

Variability Among Definitions

A major problem in attempting to evaluate the efficacy of special education for a particular category is that each category represents a heterogeneous group of students who have been classified according to diverse and often ambiguous criteria that may vary from district to district as well as from state to state. This lack of agreement about how to define a special education category has had a significant impact both on research literature and on school classification procedures. Researchers and educational personnel have selected dissimilar samples based on diverse definitional criteria and have used different psychoeducational devices. Students classified into one category in one setting are very likely to be different from those similarly identified in another setting. Even if diagnostic personnel were able to reach a consensus on a definition, differences would be almost certain to remain in the way the definition is operationalized. For example, if learning disability is defined as a discrepancy between ability and achievement, a decision still needs to be made about how to operationalize this definition (i.e., Which specific devices or techniques are to be used?). The selection of one operational definition over another will not necessarily result in the identification of the same group of students (Epps, Ysseldyke, & Algozzine, 1985) or even the same number of students (Epps, Ysseldyke, & Algozzine, 1983). The classification of students into a certain area of exceptionality not only depends on pupil characteristics but is also a function of the formula and the specific tests that are used to derive scores that are entered into the formula. Hence, a classification that is made when one group of tests is used is not always generalizable to an identical classification that is based on other instruments.

Additional complications are encountered when attempts are made to operationalize the definition of a category of exceptionality. Not only are there differences among operationalizations of a single definition due to the use of different tests, but results may also be differentially biased depending on the match between curriculum and test (Jenkins & Pany, 1978). In addition, operationalizations of definitions are influenced by the amount of decision making required of diagnostic personnel. For example, some professionals compute estimated true scores and confidence intervals rather than rely on obtained scores. Such a practice certainly influences classification decisions, particularly when tests having low reliability are used (see Salvia & Ysseldyke, 1985).

In sum, efficacy studies with various categories of exceptionality are difficult to interpret because of the variability among definitions even for the same category. Students may or may not be classified in a given category depending on the definition that is selected, the way it is operationalized, the idiosyncratic approach to assessment by the diagnostician, the degree of curriculum bias, and the extent to which information on exclusionary criteria is used (Epps et al., 1983). Considering the variation in the definition of exceptionality and the subsequent heterogeneity of student populations, and since effective instruction for a student is more likely to depend on his or her actual characteristics as a learner than on a particular special education classification, the reliance on categorical labels to characterize students clearly limits the kinds of conclusions that can be drawn from much of the efficacy research (Heller et al., 1982).

Historical Changes in Classification

An additional difficulty in interpreting efficacy research regarding certain categories concerns historical changes in classification practices in the schools. In the past decade, there has been a significant decrease in the number of students classified as educable mentally retarded as well as a sharp increase in the number of students identified as learning disabled (Tucker, 1980; U.S. Department of Education, 1980). Consequently, students who currently are classified as educable mentally retarded, particularly those who have not been mainstreamed and are placed in self-contained settings, may very well be more disabled than their counterparts who were classified as educable mentally retarded in previous years. The results of efficacy studies on this older cohort may not be generalizable to the current group of educable mentally retarded students (Heller et al., 1982).

Placement Histories

Cegelka and Tyler (1970) and White (1984) pointed out a common methodological weakness in much of the efficacy research: different placement histories of exceptional students potentially might interact with their current program placement. The possibility therefore exists that the apparent effect of each successive intervention might be confounded by its order in the sequence. The net result would be that the confounded effects of multiple treatments would seriously limit the generalizability of experimental findings (Campbell, 1969). It seems likely that long-term studies are less likely to be subjected to this threat to internal validity introduced by confounded placement histories (Sindelar & Deno, 1978).

The characteristics of students within a given category are more diverse than the single label suggests. Therefore, it is possible, perhaps even probable, that some students in the category may profit more from instruction in the regular classroom while others may benefit more from special classes. An example of such a situation was found in a study by Goldstein, Moss, and Jordan (1965), in which students with IQs in the range of 81–85 who were instructed in regular classrooms had slightly, although not significantly, higher achievement test scores than did students within the same IQ range in self-contained classes. For students with IQs of less than 80, the opposite pattern was found: students in the special classes had higher math achievement test scores than did those served in regular classes.

Myers (1976) also found varying results depending on IQ level. Eight months after placement, the low-IQ group (Slosson IQ of 49–70) in classes in a special school demonstrated significantly higher grade-level gain scores on the reading and math subtests of the Wide Range Achievement Test (Jastak & Jastak, 1965) (WRAT) than students in self-contained or regular classes. In contrast, the high-IQ group (Slosson IQ of 71–85) in regular classes achieved significantly greater grade-level gain scores on the WRAT reading subtest than students in self-contained classes. Because heterogeneous samples may mask such an outcome, it may be difficult to glean accurate information from many efficacy studies. In addition to analyzing the effectiveness of special education by dividing samples into high- and low-IQ groups, Myers suggested that other possible divisions might include racial and cultural subgroups, groups divided by sex, and urban, rural, and suburban subgroups.

Assignment to Treatment

Of particular importance in controlling many variables, such as history, maturation, testing, instrumentation, regression, selection, mortality, and the interaction of selection and maturation (Cook & Campbell, 1979), is the manner in which subjects are assigned to treatments. These variables may threaten internal validity so that the effects on outcome data actually are unrelated to the treatment. When sampling is not a randomized process, comparison groups are not likely to be comparable. In many efficacy studies, particularly the earlier ones, randomness was not achieved. Often the procedure for subject selection included the use of preexisting groups. The main objection to using already existing groups is that these groups are not placed into alternate forms of educational intervention on a random basis. Instead, some schools transfer the most educationally problematic children into segregated classes while retaining other students who are less problematic in regular classes. Hence, students most disturbing to general educators may be disproportionately represented in special classes. Indeed, the complex referral and identification process contains considerable potential for bias (Ysseldyke & Algozzine, 1982; Ysseldyke & Thurlow, 1983). In addition, the school and adjustment histories of students in special education may not be similar to those of students who remain in regular classes. Therefore, it may be that any differences between the groups are due to antecedent conditions rather than to the effects of educational intervention (Kaufman & Alberto, 1976). Such biases in sample selection are serious enough to render the results suspect.

The issue of random assignment is an inherent limitation of applied research in the schools. Ethical and legal issues dictate that schools serve those students identified as in need. For example, given the spirit of the law that program decisions be made on an individual basis, the random assignment of a student to an alternative placement could be considered a possible violation of the student's right to placement in the most appropriate setting (Polloway, 1984). Given the difficulty of randomization, a more frequently used procedure is to match students on various characteristics such as IQ, sex, and age. As Campbell and Stanley (1963) noted, however, "matching on background characteristics other than [outcome measure] is usually ineffective and misleading" (p. 12). For instance, if the primary interest is in the effect of special versus regular class placement on reading, experimental and control subjects need to be matched on reading skill. There have been few studies in which students have been matched on the outcome measure (e.g., Franklin & Sparkman, 1978; Vacc, 1968; Walker, 1974).

Appropriateness of Measuring Devices

Another factor contributing to the inconsistency of the results of special education studies involves dependent variables. Standardized tests used to document students' progress have limited power because they provide only relatively gross summarizing scores rather than fine-grained clinical data. Considering that the rate of growth is often slow and inconsistent for many handicapped students and that the magnitude of treatment effects may be small, test data may not reveal change even in successful treatment programs (Sheehan & Keogh, 1981, 1984).

The ways in which dependent variables are operationalized is particularly important since these variables must provide accurate and generalizable data that enable program evaluators to make valid inferences. A variety of tests, rating forms, and observation systems has been used in efficacy studies. Although these instruments may purport to measure the same skill, results are not likely to be interchangeable because the instruments may sample different student behaviors (e.g., they may sample different content due to differences in test items). For instance, some devices sample the domain of oral reading more thoroughly than others. Therefore, studies in which tests are used whereby students are required merely to read a list of words in isolation may not yield results that reflect students' true oral reading skills. One group in one setting may achieve superior scores; however, the same results may not be generalizable to the oral reading of a passage from a story. Furthermore, tests differ in their technical adequacy (Salvia & Hunt, 1984). Hence, a mathematics score on the Key Math Diagnostic Arithmetic Test (Connolly, Nachtman, & Pritchett, 1971) is not equal to a score on the Peabody Individual Achievement Test (PIAT) (Dunn & Markwardt, 1970), and, due to the problem of curriculum bias, both might have low content validity. Even if the same test were used to measure change in student performance resulting from special or regular class placement, a differential match between program and test content would be expected because students in each setting may be exposed to different curricula. As a result, differences in test performance would be expected simply because of this unequal match (Jenkins & Pany, 1978). Diagnostic personnel may be led to radically different conclusions about a student's performance depending upon the selection of achievement test and the student's previous academic curriculum.

To evaluate educational programs, clear statements must be specified about the academic goals and objectives that students are expected to attain (Jones, Gottlieb, Guskin, & Yoshida, 1978). If the primary purpose is to improve academic performance, students' skill levels in academic subjects should be the dependent variables. If the primary goal is to develop appropriate social behaviors, measures should be taken on social skills. As Stanton and Cassidy emphasized (1964), "In order to decide the effectiveness of special classes . . ., we must first answer the critical question—effective for what?" (p. 12).

Determining appropriate measures in efficacy research is difficult because it is possible that two different types of educational programs with nonoverlapping goals may be compared. For instance, one may consider the utility of a standardized achievement test to assess students' mathematics skills. There may be more emphasis on this academic subject in regular classrooms than in special classes. Differences in test performance between students served in special and general education settings may, in part, reflect a lack of emphasis placed on traditional academic subjects in special classes (Heller, 1982). It is probably more valid to judge the effectiveness of special education for moderately mentally retarded populations, for example, by conducting functional assessments of how students use math skills in the natural environment, such as in community and vocational settings.

The variability of instrumentation is particularly problematic when social behaviors are the dependent variables; the measures used to evaluate social behaviors are even less reliable than the instruments used to measure academic achievement (Brown, 1970). Although direct observation of social skills in the classroom can help resolve the issue of technical limitations, problems still remain about what to do with different target behaviors, different observation techniques (e.g., partial interval recording vs. momentary time sampling), and differences across settings in the discriminative stimuli that serve to occasion various student behaviors. Hence, even when careful behavioral assessment is done and interobserver agreement is high, the resulting data still may not be comparable.

One variable that has not been considered much in efficacy research is the differing expectancy levels held by regular and special education teachers for the academic achievement and social behaviors of special education students. Teacher expectancy is of particular concern when teacher-completed checklists are used. Especially when such checklists lack an objective standard, and given that teachers have different frames of reference, identical behaviors exhibited by exceptional students in special and regular classes may very likely be rated differently (Kaufman & Alberto, 1976).

Metric of Analysis for Dependent Measures

By far, the majority of studies investigating the effectiveness of special education have reported in grade equivalent scores (Tindal, 1985). However, there are serious problems with such a metric. A major limitation in the use of grade (and age) equivalent scores is that they fail to take into account the variation in curves (lines relating the number of correct answers to the various grades or ages). In general, when the correlation between grade and test score is low, students' scores are perceived to be more extreme, that is, more advanced or more retarded, than when the correlation is high. The difficulty is that grade equivalent scores can give a distorted and exaggerated impression of an individual's level of advancement or retardation, particularly if the test is unreliable (Angoff, 1971).

Flanagan (1951) reported other problems with grade equivalent scores. First, one assumption of grade equivalent scores is that growth is uniform throughout the school year and that either no growth takes place during the summer or that growth during the summer is equal to 1 month of growth during the school year. Second, grade equivalent scores for low and high grades often are impossible to establish from available data and have to be obtained by extrapolation from existing observations. Similarly, grade equivalent scores are estimated from scores that fall butions. This interpolation occurs despite the fact that no students between these two grades were tested (Salvia & Ysseldyke, 1985). Both extrapolation and interpolation procedures are extremely unreliable. And third, the use of grade equivalent scores, in general, tends to exaggerate the significance of small differences. Because of large within-grade variability, it is possible, for instance, for a student who is only moderately below the median for his or her grade to appear to be as much as 1 year or even 2 years deficient on the grade equivalent scale.

In addition to statistical shortcomings, there is a serious problem of interpretation from an educational point of view. For example, to say that a sixth grader's performance has a grade equivalent of 8 is not to say that he or she performs at the level of a student in the eighth grade. In fact, the sixth grader probably has been instructed and tested with the type of material that is appropriate to his or her grade and has not been formally exposed to the kind of educational material in school that normally is given to an eighth grader. In general, the student also has not had the opportunity to demonstrate proficiency in eighth-grade material.

Independent Variables

A basic question being asked in efficacy research is whether a program is doing what it purports to be doing. Presumably, this goal has been incorporated into the curriculum that is being used. A basic tenet in special education is that students to be served need the content and/or rate of instruction to be different from that found in regular classes. To compensate, a specialized curriculum is established. Hence, exceptional students in special versus regular classes are compared on the basis of what may be two sets of curricular content and objectives and different rates of presentation. The problem is that conclusions about program effectiveness still are made. The majority of efficacy studies make no mention of curriculum content. If such components are not specified, the set of criteria against which student achievement is measured is unknown, and it is not possible to make an informed appraisal of achievement (Kaufman & Alberto, 1976).

Assessing the efficacy literature is problematic because of the necessity of evaluating often complex field-based studies in which several independent variables may not have been adequately controlled or defined. Clearly, there is a very wide range of different service delivery models that have been investigated, with little consistency found among common features (Lakin, 1983). Although groups of students in special and general education programs are compared on various outcome measures, the components of these programs typically are not delineated or analyzed. When there is a failure to control for teaching procedures and curricula, treatment names may imply differences in instruction that either do not exist or are inconsistently applied (Cegelka & Tyler, 1970).

Measuring independent variables entails assessing the nature of treatment (which should be described in detail) and verifying the integrity of its delivery (i.e., that it was delivered as intended) to determine whether program components are implemented as planned (Peterson, Homer, & Wonderlich, 1982). It is necessary to obtain descriptive information about the content of instructional activities to assess the extent to which ongoing lessons are consistent with stated educational goals. Educational programs often may be highly complex. A thorough explication of interventions might include specifying staff qualifications and special training, the nature of teacher–student interactions, ancillary services, parental involvement and training, materials, and duration of program (Jones et al., 1978; Salvia & Hunt, 1984). Yet, as Tindal (1985) noted, very few studies describe the major components of a program, and "without this type of information, the special versus regular education dichotomy is not a replicable or identifiable independent variable" (p. 102).

Review of the Literature

Until recently, efficacy research generally focused on determining the type of administrative setting associated with the greatest treatment gains for exceptional students. Many researchers attempted to determine the effects of mainstreaming by comparing the performance of students in special classes with that of students placed in a variety of integrated settings. These settings spanned the range of service options from treatment in full-time special education settings to regular class placement with resource room support to regular class placement with supportive services offered within the regular classroom. Many of the earlier studies, from the 1930s to about 1970, hypothesized that separate classes were more effective (Heller et al., 1982). From the late 1960s to early 1970s, however, the mainstream was regularly touted as the most efficacious placment (Polloway, 1984).

It is useful to consider a historical framework when so-called efficacy studies of special education placement are examined. Polloway (1984) examined the past 50 years of placement efficacy (focusing on educable mental retardation) and identified five historical stages. The major question associated with each stage and an approximation of the time span associated with each are discussed briefly below to provide a context for conceptualizing the nascence and development of efficacy research.

1. 1930 to 1940s: Do handicapped students profit more from an opportunity to be in school together with or apart from their nonhandicapped peers? This question is associated with the birth of the efficacy question.
2. 1950s to mid-1960s: Are students' needs best met in regular or special class programs? This stage represents the zenith of research on efficacy. The studies on placement options reviewed in the first half of this chapter address this question.
3. Late 1960s to early 1970s: Can special classes present a viable program for handicapped students in light of the inherent legal, sociological, and political concerns that their existence raises and in light of the absence of research supportive of their benefits? This question shifted the focus to a broader issue as the concept of the special class was attacked at the national level (although, paradoxically, the number of special classes continued to grow at the local level). This issue is addressed in the general discussion section at the end of the chapter.
4. Late 1960s/early 1970s to 1980s: Which alternative is most appropriate for the individual student? In this stage, which represents a thematic, not a temporal, difference from stage three, consideration was given to the expanding variety of placement options within the cascade of services. Based on studies reviewed to examine the second question, this question is addressed by documenting the need to shift the focus from placement alternatives to instructional programs.
5. Mid-1980s: Can the population of special education students remaining after the legal and sociological turmoil of the early 1970s be successful in the integrated placements inspired by PL 94–142? This question converges on a reanalysis of appropriate placements that has been undertaken due to cohort

differences. The implications of this issue are examined in the closing section in this chapter.

The search for pertinent research articles comprised three steps. First, multiple descriptors were generated from key topic-related terms. For example, *instructional methods* also was keyed in as *instructional design/activities/decisions, teaching techniques/methods/processes,* and *curriculum.* Second, these terms facilitated a computer search of a data base of educational materials from the Educational Resources Information Center consisting of abstracts from *Research in Education* and *Current Index to Journals in Education.* And third, the references in the articles generated by these efforts were explored for additional studies. Using this approach, two literature searches were conducted on (a) program effectiveness as a function of setting and placement option, and (b) instructional programming as a function of classification and levels of services. The latter search considered only those studies that used direct observation in the classroom and described the content and context of instruction in specific low-inference terms.

The task of reviewing the literature on special education placement options and instructional programming is monumental, and the present review is not intended to be exhaustive of the extant data base. Academic achievement in mildly handicapped populations receives primary emphasis. Since the major focus in efficacy research has been on the category of educable mental retardation, many of the studies reviewed examine this group. Attention also is given to students classified as learning disabled or behaviorally disordered/emotionally disturbed and to those receiving Chapter 1 services.

Special Education Placement Options

In this section, the performance of students served in different settings is compared. Contrasts are made between regular and self-contained settings, resource and self-contained rooms, and resource rooms and regular classes. The review emphasizes academic achievement. More comprehensive reviews can be found elsewhere on students with mental retardation (Carlberg & Kavale, 1980; Corman & Gottlieb, 1978; Kaufman & Alberto, 1976; Leinhardt & Pallay, 1982; Semmel et al., 1979); behavior disorders (Carlberg & Kavale, 1980; Leinhardt & Pallay, 1982; Semmel et al., 1979); and learning disabilities (Carlberg & Kavale, 1980; Leinhardt & Pallay, 1982; Semmel et al., 1979). Semmel et al. (1979) also reviewed efficacy studies with hearing and visually impaired students. Sindelar and Deno (1978) and Tindal (1985) have provided reviews of students with mild handicaps.

Regular Versus Self-Contained Settings

Studies comparing the performance of students in regular versus self-contained settings can be divided into two periods of time: (a) prior to 1970 and (b) after 1970. This point of division is made due to some major changes in designs and results. After 1970, more attention was given to the problem of subject selection bias. Some of the later studies involved comparisons of newly developed demonstration programs, and more information was reported about program description (Leinhardt & Pallay, 1982).

Pre-1970. Although there were numerous efficacy studies conducted during this time, because significant methodological problems make it unwise to place much emphasis on their results, only a few are reviewed here. Elenbogen (1957) compared the academic and social adjustment of two groups of educable mentally retarded students whose mean chronological age was 13.46. During the 2 years prior to the study, one group was placed in special classes, while the other group remained in regular classes. Groups were matched on chronological age (CA), sex, IQ, and school district. The results in reading and arithmetic, as measured by the Stanford Achievement Test (SAT) (Madden, Gardner, Rudman, Karlsen, & Merwin, 1975), indicated significantly higher mean scores for students in regular classes. In contrast, rating scales completed by teachers indicated significant differences in favor of students in special classes. Since achievement, as operationalized by reading and arithmetic SAT scores was higher for students who remained in regular classrooms, one might conclude that general education placement was superior to special education. Although such a conclusion may be correct, this interpretation is not warranted considering several significant methodological shortcomings. Students who were placed in special classes were not selected randomly from a pool (with the remaining students serving as control subjects). Instead, students were matched on several characteristics, which did not include achievement level. Hence, the two groups were not equivalent; the subject selection bias gave the regular class group the advantage. Students who were not placed in special classes probably were superior on other school-related characteristics. Furthermore, the study provides no information about the curriculum used in each setting.

Mullen and Itkin (1961) conducted a 2-year study using 140 pairs of educable mentally retarded students in special and regular classes who were matched for age (CA range = 7–13 years), IQ (range = 50–74), sex, socioeconomic status, foreign language spoken at home, and reading achievement. Although these two groups still may not have been equivalent, one positive feature of the study is that they were matched on outcome measure. At the end of the first year, the students in regular classes had significantly greater gains in arithmetic, but not on any other achievement measure. However, there was no maintenance of this effect after 2 years, where there were no significant differences.

These studies are two examples of pre-1970 research in which regular class students who received no special help performed academically better than or as well as special class students (see also Blatt, 1958; Stanton & Cassidy, 1964). Leinhardt and Pallay (1982) reviewed numerous other studies during this period and found that regular class students who received no special help did better than or as well as special class students in academic subjects. One problem with concluding that the special instructional setting itself had a negative impact is that students in the more segregated environments often received curricular content that was severely watered down, leading to a general reduction in the intensity of instruction with little systematic modification of instructional technique (Guskin & Spicker, 1968). These studies also were plagued by biases in subject selection, indicating that groups were being compared that were not equivalent, thus stacking the deck against students in special classes.

Only one of these earlier studies attempted to eliminate the problem of subject selection bias by randomly assigning pupils to classrooms. Because it controlled for many of the methodological flaws that have plagued efficacy research, it will be reviewed in detail. Goldstein et al. (1965) screened 2,000 students entering first grade in 20 Illinois school districts with the Primary Mental Abilities Test (Thurston & Thurston, 1962). Those who scored below 85 were tested with the Standford–Binet Intelligence Scale (Terman & Merrill, 1960). The 129 students who scored between 56 and 85 on both measures were assigned randomly either to self-contained classes that had specially designed curricula and trained teachers (with bachelor's degrees in the education of mentally retarded students) or to regular classes. At the end of 4 years, there were no differences in IQ gains between the two groups, although both showed significant IQ increases, which occurred primarily in the first year of school (students in special classes gained 7 points; those in regular classes gained 8 points). Since some children had obtained IQs above 85, which at that time was the upper limit of the commonly accepted range for educable mental retardation, separate analyses were made for a low-IQ group (80 or below) and a high-IQ group (81 and above). Since the special curriculum was intended for educable mentally retarded students, the investigators considered the results for the low-IQ group to be more meaningful than those for either the total sample or the high-IQ group in evaluating the efficacy of special classes.

Various achievement tests were administered to students at the end of each of the 4 years of the project. For the total sample, there were significant differences between the experimental group (students in special classes) and the control groups (students in regular classes) in reading after the first 2 years, with the control group scoring 0.5 and 0.3 grade equivalent scores higher. In math, there was a significant difference between groups only after the first year, again with the control group scoring 0.3 grade equivalent scores higher. For the total sample, then, students in regular classes outscored those in special classes in both reading and math, but this advantage was not maintained.

For the high-IQ group, significant differences were apparent both in reading and in math at the end of the first year and in reading at the end of the second year, with control students outscoring experimental students by 0.6 and 0.4 grade equivalent scores in reading and 0.5 grade equivalent scores in math. The same pattern of results was apparent for the high-IQ group as it was for the total sample, with students served in regular classes scoring higher, but only during the first 2 years of the project.

For the low-IQ group, there were no significant differences in reading. Experimental and control groups scored within 0.2 grade equivalent scores of each other. However, significant differences were apparent in math during the last 3 years of the project, with the experimental group outscoring the control group by 0.5 (year 2), 0.7 (year 3), and 1.0 (year 4) grade equivalent scores.

The Goldstein et al. (1965) study represented a significant contribution to the literature at the time because of its control for certain methodological inadequacies of previous investigations, which had not assigned subjects randomly to treatment conditions, had not controlled for varying school experiences prior to special class placement, and had left the special class educational program unspecified. Although important information was gained about a differential effect of special classes depending on students' IQ levels, the data did not provide overwhelming support for the superiority of special class placement. After all the extra programming efforts of instructional personnel with a 15–1 student–teacher ratio, academic gains were minimal. One possible reason for the lack of greater academic gains may be that the special class curriculum placed a greater emphasis on practical knowledge, social skills, and emotional development than did the regular class curriculum. Therefore, curriculum–test overlap was reduced significantly (Jenkins & Pany, 1978; Leinhardt & Seewald, 1981).

Although general interpretations have been made that the high-IQ students, who probably were above the educable mental retardation range in academic ability, were better off in mainstreamed settings without special support and that special classes seemed to be beneficial to students whose IQs were 80 or below, these conclusions must be examined within the context of the methodological issues discussed in an earlier portion of this chapter. A serious weakness of the study is that children were placed in self-contained or regular classrooms on the sole basis of an IQ score; this feature reduces the project's external validity. Students typically are not placed in special classes unless they have been referred because they are experiencing difficulty in school. Therefore, the experimental group in the Goldstein et al. (1965) project may not be comparable to students typically served in special classes, particularly since a sizable portion of those placed in special classrooms later (e.g., after the first year of the project) had IQ scores above 85. Information was not obtained in this project about the effects of special class placement on students who were placed when they were older than 6 years or the effects on pupils who were placed using selection criteria other than fairly high IQ scores (Heller, 1982).

A second shortcoming of the project pertains to the appropriateness of the measuring devices. Standardized achievement tests were used as summative evaluation measures to document students' progress. These measures may have been insensitive to detecting changes that may have occurred regardless of setting. In addition, a variety of tests was used. Although experimental and control groups received the same tests at any point in time, they were not tested with the same devices throughout the course of the project. For example, the New York Test of Arithmetical Meanings (Wrightstone, Justman, Pincus, & Lowe, 1956) was used at the end of the first year, whereas the Primary II of the Metropolitan Achievement Test (MAT) (Bixler, Hildreth, Lund, & Wrightstone, 1965) was used after the second year, and the MAT Elementary Battery was used after the third and fourth years. This variable instrumentation may have affected the pattern of results across time.

The metric of analysis for the dependent variables was a third shortcoming. Grade equivalent scores were used that tended to exaggerate the significance of small differences. Despite the fact that there were some statistically significant differences between the experimental and control groups, it is questionable whether these differences are clinically significant. For the total sample, there was a statistically significant difference in reading of 0.3 grade equivalent scores at the end of the second year. This difference is probably trivial in its overall effect on school success.

Semmel et al. (1979) noted that data from numerous investigations, including the Goldstein et al. (1965) study, indicate that, regardless of class placement, mentally retarded pupils read poorly. The low-IQ students in the Goldstein et al. project earned scores of 2.7 (for the experimental group) and 2.8 (for the control group) at the end of their fourth year. These scores do not suggest that students in either setting had acquired a functional set of reading skills. Since a mainstreamed setting may be at least as effective (or ineffective) as a segregated setting, instructional alternatives that have focused on setting may not be focusing on the critical variable. Perhaps attention should be shifted to instructional variables and to more appropriate instructional delivery systems.

In summary, the pre-1970 literature examining the performance of students in regular versus self-contained settings strongly suggests that segregated settings are either negative in their effects or unsuccessful. In many of the studies, regular class students who received no special help did better than or as well as special class students, although neither environment is necessarily effective, since students often remained below grade-level expectations.

1970 to 1980. A trend toward less segregation of handicapped students began in the early 1970s, perhaps fueled in part by the disappointing results of earlier efficacy studies. With an increase in interest in the mainstreaming philosophy, a new series of studies tested the hypothesis that exceptional students would benefit if they spent at least part of their school time with their nonhandicapped peers (Heller et al., 1982).

As in the earlier research, the results concerning the academic benefits derived from self-contained and regular settings have been inconsistent. Some studies have favored self-contained special classes. Myers (1976) examined the efficacy of a special day school, self-contained classes, and regular classes for educable mentally retarded students (N = 30 for each group). When the WRAT was used as a measure of academic achievement, there were no significant differences in grade-level gain scores among the three settings. However, when the three groups of students were divided into low-IQ (Slosson IQ of 49–70) and high-IQ groups (Slosson IQ of 71–85), there were significant differences in grade-level gain scores. In both reading and spelling, low-IQ students in the special school (N = 13) demonstrated significantly greater gains than either the special class (N = 14) or regular class group (N = 13). A different pattern of results was apparent for the high-IQ group, in which students remaining in regular classes (N = 17) made significantly greater gains in reading than students in self-contained classes (N = 16). These data suggest that at least for this sample, low-IQ students made more academic gains in a segregated setting, while high-IQ students made more gains in the regular class (but not significantly more than gains made in the special school). It must be noted, however, that, in arithmetic, there were no significant differences among the three treatment conditions for either low-IQ or high-IQ students.

There is a limitation to the Myers (1976) study. Subjects were selected from preexisting groups in rural Alabama. Although there apparently were no significant differences in IQ among the three treatment groups (this analysis was not reported), the groups may have differed on other important variables; pretest academic achievement scores were not reported.

Sabatino (1971) also found support for preferring self-contained classes to regular settings. Students classified as learning disabled made more academic gains in reading than control students served in regular classes. This study is discussed in more detail in the following section on resource rooms.

Although Haring and Krug (1975) did not contrast self-contained and regular classes, they did examine the effects of special class instruction on subsequent achievement in regular classes. Forty-eight educable mentally retarded students were randomly assigned to four special classes (twenty-four to two experimental classes and twenty-four to two control classes) for a 1-year controlled study of the effect of precision teaching and token reinforcement on academic achievement. Experimental treatment consisted of contingency management, daily measurement and graphing of students' academic performance, and the use of plan sheets that described specific operations for teaching. Students in the control classes were exposed to whatever programs their teachers specified. After 8 months, WRAT reading gain scores of 13.5 months for the experimental group and 4.5 months for the control group were apparent. In arithmetic, experimental students gained 16.1 months; control students gained 4.8 months.

By the fall of the academic year following the experimental program, thirteen of the twenty-four experimental students (54%) were placed in regular classes. In contrast, none of the control group pupils had been transferred to general education settings. The criteria for returning upils to regular classes were clearly specified. The cri-rion in reading was met when a student read orally at a inimum rate of 70 words per minute with two or fewer rrors in a reading book selected by the receiving regular lassroom teacher. The criterion in math was achieved hen a student correctly computed arithmetic drill prob-ms at a rate of 30 written answers per minute with two or wer errors.

The year following the experimental program, 1 month fter school had started, the thirteen students who were hen in regular classes were matched, without the teacher's nowledge, with students already in the class whose read-ng scores most nearly resembled their own. This pro-edure allowed for a comparison of special students who ad been in a highly structured experimental setting and tudents already functioning in a regular class. At the end f this second year, WRAT gain scores indicated 13 nonths' improvement in reading for the students who had een in the experimental special classes and 7 months' for heir matched controls. In arithmetic, experimental tudents gained 9 months, and the control students gained months.

The Haring and Krug (1975) study indicates that the pecial class (or a precision teaching model) may be effec-ive in preparing exceptional children for placement in reg-ılar classes. Although the special students continued to nake academic gains in their first year back in regular classes, and ten of them (77%) were viewed by their teach-ers as being able to remain in general education without special help (as compared to eight of the matched group), the study did not answer the question about whether these students could make progress in regular classes for an extended period of time without additional support services.

Although Sabatino (1971) and Myers (1976) reported favorable results regarding self-contained classes, regular class placement tended to be favored when Myers' high-IQ group was considered. Two other studies have indicated no significant differences between the two settings. Bersoff, Kabler, Fiscus, and Ankney (1972) examined the effec-tiveness of a self-contained classroom, regular class place-ment with tutoring 2–5 hours per week from certified teachers, and regular class placement with no additional help for children who had been identified as neurologically handicapped. Since students differed on pretreatment scores, an analysis of covariance was done and revealed no significant differences among the three treatment groups on WRAT reading or arithmetic measures. Neither spe-cial class placement nor individual tutoring increased the academic performance (as measured by this standardized test) of neurologically handicapped students beyond what was obtained in regular classrooms. The limitations of the study include a lack of random assignment of subjects to treatment conditions (preexisting groups were used) and a lack of specificity regarding the independent variable. Stu-dents in the special classes received "a highly structured and individualized academic and behavioral program"; programs for students being tutored were "determined by the individual tutor"; and students in regular classes had a daily program "like that of other children in medium-sized (25–30) classrooms" (p. 159).

O'Leary and Schneider (1977) examined the effect of special and regular class placement on conduct problem (highly disruptive) first graders and found that those in special classes essentially did no better when returning to regular classes than those who attended regular classes for the entire year. Subjects were randomly assigned to groups. Teaching methods in the regular classes varied from traditional structured programs to informal individ-ualized instruction. Students who spent 8 months in special classes received 15 minutes per day of individualized reading tutoring and token reinforcers for appropriate academic and social behavior (the remainder of the instructional program was vague).

A positive feature of this study is that posttreatment assessment was conducted in the regular classes after spe-cial children had been reintegrated for one month. To assess the relative gains for each group, repeated analyses of variance were conducted for the Behavior Problem Checklist (Quay & Peterson, 1967) factors and for each category of the Classroom Observation Code (O'Leary, Kaufman, Kass, & Drabman, 1970). Gains were not sig-nificantly greater for one group than another. Three subte-sts from the WRAT and six subtests from the California Achievement Test (CAT) (Tiegs & Clarke, 1976) were administered to students as posttests. Only on the WRAT reading subtest was there a significant difference between the two groups, with the special group outscoring the con-trol group. Although there were no significant differences between groups at preassessment on the Metropolitan Readiness Test (Nurss & McGauvran, 1976), differences might have been found if the WRAT had been adminis-tered as a pretest. Children in both groups showed improvement in several classroom behaviors, but the spe-cial class children appeared to lose many of these gains in the transition back into regular classes. Presumably, the authors were suggesting that behavioral gains were not maintained, although the data to support this statement were not presented.

In summary, the results on the academic benefits of self-contained versus regular classroom contrasts after 1970 have been inconsistent. Some studies favor self-contained special classes, while others indicate no significant differ-ences between the two settings or an advantage of regular classes. Both Goldstein et al. (1965) and Myers (1976) suggested that students at the high end of the mildly handi-capped range may be better off in mainstreamed settings. In general, most of these studies do not clearly describe the nature of the independent variable.

Resource rooms. When self-contained and regular class-room settings are compared with resource rooms, results are not definitive. For mildly retarded populations, the small body of research has afforded conflicting findings. Carroll (1967) compared a resource room program (of half-day special class, half-day regular class students, $N =$ 19) with a full-time special class and found that, after 8 months, there was a statistically significant but only moderate increase in students' performance on the WRAT for both groups. The integrated group, however, made significantly greater gains on the reading subtest. The relative equivalence of these two groups is questionable, though. The resource room students had higher initial scores on all three subtests and may have been better students. There may have been other significant differences between the groups as well. The assignment of subjects to treatment conditions was vague and "depend[ed] upon the operation of each school system" (p. 94).

Walker (1974) also found that students in a resource room program outperformed students in a special class on the word reading and vocabulary (but not arithmetic) subtests of the SAT. When a resource room program was compared with regular class placement (Smith & Kennedy, 1967) and a resource room program with special class placement (Budoff & Gottlieb, 1976), there were no significant differences in achievement.

Findings are inconclusive on the resource room versus self-contained contrast with nonretarded populations. Leinhardt and Pallay (1982) reported only one such study. Sabatino (1971) evaluated the academic achievement of children who were identified as having learning disabilities but who received no special form of classroom management (N = 11) and those who were placed in a self-contained special class (N = 11), a resource room (Plan A) for 1 hour each day (N = 27), or a resource room (Plan B) for ½ hour each week (N = 48). Subjects were matched on chronological age, sex, IQ, and perceptual impairment, but not on achievement. On the reading subtest of the WRAT, there were highly significant differences in academic gain. Students in the Plan A resource room gained 1.9 age equivalents compared to 1.4 for self-contained, 1.2 for Plan B, and approximately 0.1 for control pupils. A different pattern of results was obtained when the reading comprehension subtest of the Gilmore Oral Reading Test (Gilmore & Gilmore, 1968) was used. Students in the self-contained class gained 2.0 age equivalents; gains of 1.5 for Plan A, 1.0 for Plan B, and approximately 0.3 for control students were apparent.

Sabatino's (1971) work can be cited as a study in which students in self-contained and resource room classes performed better academically than regular class control subjects. It also can be cited as support for a special class over a resource room or a resource room over a special class, depending on which outcome measure is used. One major problem with the study is that there was a poor selection of dependent variables. Only two of the fourteen variables were measures of academic achievement. One of these (the WRAT) represents a limited sample of word recognition in that students are merely required to read a short list of words in isolation. Such a measure is not likely to be sensitive to changes in pupils' reading recognition skills. The other achievement measure, the Gilmore reading comprehension subtest, has extremely low reliability (Salvia & Ysseldyke, 1985).

Although the advantage of resource rooms over self-contained classes is uncertain, studies (such as Sabatino, 1971) contrasting resource rooms with regular prograr suggest that resource room programs may be superic Glavin, Quay, Annesley, and Werry (1971) examined t performance of behavior problem children in resource pr grams and regular classes. Subjects were selected by inve tigators asking elementary school teachers to complete t Behavior Problem Checklist for students they viewed either extremely disruptive or overly withdrawn. Half these students, the experimental group (N = 27), we selected randomly for part-time participation in a resour room, while the other half (N = 34), remained in the re ular class. In the experimental group, fourteen studen attended the resource room for two periods a day ar received instruction in both reading and arithmetic, eleve attended for one period per day and were instructed only reading, and two attended one period a day and receive instruction in arithmetic only. Students participated resource room programs from 5 to 6.5 months, for a mea of 5.8 months. Poker chips were used to reinforce startin maintaining, and completing assigned work. Accuracy an speed also were reinforced. Observation data were co lected on deviant behavior, on-task behavior, and teache pupil contact. The control group was observed in a regula classroom; the experimental group was observed both i regular classrooms and in resource rooms. Achievemer gains were assessed with the CAT.

Based upon the investigators' analysis of the behavior data (they made a pre- vs. postsplit by date of admission fc the experimental group and by median date of admissio for the control group, then conducted a two-way analysis c variance), they concluded that the groups showed an equa amount of significant improvement (reduction in devian behavior and increase in on-task behavior) across the dur ation of the program. When the experimental group' behavior in the resource room was compared with the con trol group's behavior in the regular classroom, there wer significant differences in all three classes of behavior. Thi difference was not apparent when each group's behavior i the regular class situation was considered. In academi achievement, the experimental group had significantl higher gain scores (the type of score was unspecified) i reading comprehension (0.74 vs. 0.21) and arithmetic fun damentals (1.55 vs. 0.61). There were no significant differ ences in reading vocabulary and arithmetic reasoning This superiority of the resource room program is particu larly impressive, since the mean IQ of the experimenta group was significantly lower (by 7 points) than the contro group's.

Quay, Glavin, Annesley, and Werry (1972), in a study of the second year of the program described by Glavin et al (1971), also found the resource room group scoring significantly higher than the regular class group on CAT reading vocabulary, total reading, arithmetic fundamentals, and total arithmetic, but not in reading comprehension. The first-year postcheck following the termination of this 2-year program indicated a continued significant difference only on arithmetic fundamentals (Glavin, 1973). At the second-year postcheck, there were no significant differences between the two groups (Glavin, 1974).

In summary, although it has not been clearly established at resource room programs in general are effective in proving the academic performance of all populations, in me studies they have been found to be superior to full-ne placement in regular classes. An additional issue may ed to be addressed when resource rooms are evaluated. oes the effectiveness of resource rooms vary depending whether students have repertoire or motivational oblems?

Repertoire versus motivational problems. Threats to the lidity of the efficacy studies discussed earlier in this apter characterize many studies that have investigated source rooms. Random assignment to treatment, propriateness of measuring devices, and unspecified dependent variables are chief among the methodological oblems. A potentially important area that has been glected in the literature on the effectiveness of self-ntained and resource room programs is the type of prob-ms students have. If students do not seem to be able to erform a behavior, they probably have a skill deficiency repertoire (can't do) problem. If they can perform the ehavior but do not, they probably have a motivational von't do) or reinforcement problem. Because of general-ation issues, this distinction is a crucial one to consider in e planning of interventions, which includes the determi-ation of the treatment setting (see Epps, Thompson, & ane, 1985, and Wood, Duncan, & Hansell, 1983, for ore detail).

In evaluating special education programs, it is import-nt to examine the extent to which they are successful with oth repertoire and motivational deficiencies. Some of the consistencies in the literature may have resulted, in part, rom the lack of differentiation between these two types of roblems. For studies in which students exhibited skill eficits, such as in reading, and were instructed in multiple ettings, such as a regular classroom and a resource room, pecial education may well have been effective. Similarly, pecial classes may have produced significant improve-nents over general education in studies in which students ad motivational problems, but only when target behaviors vere measured in the special setting. However, when neasurements of students' motivational deficiencies were aken in general education settings (where reinforcement ontingencies are different), after special services had een provided, the result may have been that special edu-ation was not found to be effective since behavior in the egular classroom did not improve.

The Glavin et al. (1971) study provides an example of his situation. Students were viewed by their teachers as either extremely disruptive or overly withdrawn. The researchers stated that 90% were academically retarded. In resource room programs, half of the students received academic instruction, token reinforcement for work-related behaviors (previously described), and exclusionary time out for persistent violation of classroom rules. Although there was not enough detail provided in the study to conduct a performance analysis to determine if students had repertoire or motivational deficiencies, it appears that students' academic achievement reflected a skill problem, whereas on-task behavior and refraining from deviant behavior were motivational problems. For the skill problem, the resource room program led to significant improvements over the regular class setting on two of the four CAT subtests administered. For the motivational problem, however, the resource room could not be viewed as effective, since the real significance of the improved behavior of the students was not apparent in situations outside the resource room, such as the regular class.

Thus, when the question about whether students experiencing difficulty in school fare better when placed in special education settings than when allowed to remain in regular classrooms is addressed, the extent to which the students have repertoire or motivational deficiencies may be a relevant variable. To date, the literature has not addressed this distinction.

Meta-Analysis of Efficacy Research

The purpose of a meta-analysis is to draw conclusions about a certain topic by systematically analyzing and integrating the results of a large number of studies (see Glass, 1976, 1977). It provides a standardized estimate of a treatment group's standing relative to the control group distribution. Two major meta-analyses were conducted to analyze the efficacy of special education. Carlberg and Kavale (1980) examined studies from 1932 to 1977. A more recent article by Wang and Baker (1985–1986) reviewed research articles published between 1975 and Spring 1984. According to Wang and Baker, 45% of the studies in their meta-analysis had not been included in previous reviews.

1932 to 1977. In their review of the literature on the efficacy of special versus regular education placement for exceptional students, Carlberg and Kavale (1980) concluded that there was little convincing evidence that special education either facilitated or hindered the educational development of exceptional students. Hence, they embarked on a meta-analysis in which they integrated and reanalyzed primary data. Out of a pool of approximately 860 documents, fifty met the inclusion criteria for their meta-analysis. Their unit of analysis was effect size, which is a quantification of the magnitude of the effect of a given experimental intervention. In this particular meta-analysis, a positive effect size favored the special class; a negative effect size favored the regular class. Their overall result was a mean effect size of −0.12, which translates into a one-tenth of a standard deviation inferiority of the special class. This value indicates that the average student in a special class ranks at appromimately the 45th percentile of students in a regular class. The effect, then, of special class placement is to reduce the relative standing of the typical special education student by 5 percentile ranks. According to Carlberg and Kavale, this reduction represents 1–2 months on most standardized tests used in the elementary grades. When an approximate 95% confidence interval was placed around the mean effect size, the lower and upper bounds were −0.18 and −0.06. Therefore, the mean effect size of −0.12 is significantly different from zero at the 0.05 level.

When effect size was calculated for each special education category, differential effects did emerge. According to the meta-analysis, special class placement was not disadvantageous for students with "lowered IQ." When compared to general education counterparts, students with IQs of 75–90 lost 13 percentile ranks. Educable mentally retarded students with IQs of 50–75 lost 6 percentile ranks. On the other hand, students who had been classified as learning disabled or behaviorally disordered/emotionally disturbed evidenced an improvement of 11 percentile ranks over the level they had achieved in their special class placement. A 99% confidence interval around the mean effect size for learning disabled and behaviorally disordered/emotionally disturbed students ranged from 0.07 to 0.75, suggesting that these students did benefit more from special education than their counterparts who remained in regular classes.

Overall, Carlberg and Kavale (1980) concluded that "special class placement is an inferior alternative to regular class placement in benefiting children removed from the educational mainstream" (p. 304). When the category of exceptionality was considered, however, students whose IQs were 50–75 or 75–90 experienced negative consequences as a result of special class placement, while learning disabled and behaviorally disordered/emotionally disturbed students had positive effects.

1975 to 1984. From a total pool of 264 studies, Wang and Baker (1985–1986) selected eleven that had empirical data adequate for quantitative synthesis. In their meta-analysis, they set out to examine the efficacy of mainstreaming and to identify program design characteristics and implementation processes that were likely to lead to effective mainstreaming. Analyses focused on three types of program effects: performance, attitudes, and classroom processes. *Performance effects* included measures of academic achievement and the quality of play for preschoolers; they represented 13% of the total number of the comparisons done across the studies. *Attitudinal effects* (75% of the comparisons) included measures of self-concept, attitudes toward schooling, attitudes toward classmates, and attitudes of teachers and parents toward mainstreaming. *Process effects* (12% of the comparisons) included measures of interactions between teachers and students and among students. The programs reported in the meta-analysis were categorized into two mainstreaming approaches. Information about a particular mainstreaming approach was reported for 84% of the comparisons. Of these approaches, 48% used a part-time approach (involving pull-out special education in resource rooms); 52% used a full-time approach (providing special education in regular classes on a full-time basis).

A total of 541 students served as subjects in the studies included in the meta-analysis. Grade levels from preschool through middle school were represented. Approximately 39% of the comparisons involved students in Grades 1 through 6; 16% were with students Grades 7 through 9; and 1% were with preschool children. Grade-level information was not provided in 44% of the studies reviewed. A variety of special education categories was represented: 53% of the students were classified as mentally retarded, 3% as learning disabled, 19% as hearing impaired; 25% had mixed classifications. Classifications were unspecified in 17% of the comparisons.

1. *Overall mainstreaming effect.* A total of 115 effect sizes was calculated; 65% of these were positive. The strongest mainstreaming effect was found in process outcomes, with a mean weighted effect size of 0.55 and a percentile rank of 71. The mean weighted effect size for performance outcomes was 0.44, with a percentile rank of 67. The mean weighted effect size for attitudinal outcomes was 0.11, with a percentile rank of 54. The overall mean weighted effect size across all eleven studies and all three types of outcome measures was 0.33. The corresponding percentile rank was 63, which indicates that the mean weighted effect size for mainstreamed handicapped students across all three measures was 13 percentile ranks higher than the percentile rank of 50 for the comparison group, who were special education students in self-contained classes. This gross summary statistic suggested that, overall, mainstreaming appeared to have had somewhat higher positive performance, attitudinal, and process effects for handicapped students when compared with non-mainstreaming approaches for handicapped students with similar classifications.

2. *Relationship between independent variables and mainstreaming outcomes.* Within each cluster of independent variables, none of the F tests of differences in weighted effect sizes was statistically significant. No statistically significant differences in effect sizes were apparent as a function of background (e.g., grade level, classification), program features (e.g., subject matter, part- or full-time approach), or type of research design. This finding suggests that the positive impact of mainstreaming on student outcomes (the main effect) was not likely to have resulted from any one, specific, independent variable other than the treatment variable of mainstreaming.
attitudinal outcome measures showed noticeably higher effect sizes for handicapped students in full-time (as opposed to part-time) mainstreaming programs. The percentile ranks for the mean weighted effect size of performance outcomes were 64 compared to 53, and for attitudinal outcomes, 67 versus 53.

3. *Summary and conclusions.* Wang and Baker (1985–1986) offered several interpretations of the findings from their meta-analysis:

- The meta-analysis provides empirical evidence supporting mainstreaming. Handicapped students in mainstreaming programs consistently outperformed those with comparable special education classifications who were in self-contained settings.
- Since none of the independent variables by themselves contributed significantly to the mainstreaming effects (except for comparison type: mainstreamed vs. self-contained settings), attributing the statistically significant and positive effects on student outcomes to mainstreaming itself appears appropriate.
- Although the findings from this meta-analysis of mainstreaming effects indicate some variation in effect sizes among students with different classifications in mainstreaming programs, there is no discernible pattern to suggest that mainstreaming is differentially effective for certain special education classifications. Regardless of exceptionality, the mean effect sizes for mainstreamed handicapped students were consistently higher than those for students in self-contained settings. This result is contrary to the conclusions drawn by Carlberg and Kavale (1980), who suggested that learning disabled and behaviorally disordered/emotionally disturbed students benefited from special class placement.

Qualifications in the use of meta-analysis. Although eta-analysis has been proposed as a method that obviates rtain problems of integrating divergent research findgs, it is not uniformly accepted as appropriate. Eysenck 984) suggested that it is a pseudo-objective computered technique that essentially treats all studies as equals, ıms them up, and arrives at some form of statistical conusion without taking into account the quality of the data. onsidering the threats to the internal validity of many pecial education efficacy studies, particularly those prior 1970, a cogent argument can be made that some studies ith empirical data should not be included in a metanalysis. A threat associated with a particular design in the rimary research also applies to the results of an integrate review (Cooper, 1982).

An unfortunate limitation of meta-analyses is that they an only assess if a variable design feature relates to outomes. Although the effects of matching subjects can be etermined, a meta-analysis cannot compare studies that se more and less appropriate achievement measures since few studies use appropriate devices). For instance, if egative achievement outcomes for special classes are argely the result of using instruments that measure reglar class but not special class achievement objectives, it is ot possible to correct for this shortcoming in a metanalysis (Guskin, 1984).

Carlberg and Kavale (1980) did examine the influence f a number of threats to the validity of effect sizes in pecial class/regular class comparisons and found low ositive correlations, none of which was reliably nonzero. Because smaller effect sizes were associated with more valid studies, they suggested that there was some credibility in the assertion that, when groups were randomly assigned, the effect of special class placement was smaller. Conversely, the greater the threat was to validity, the greater was the superiority of special to regular classes (Guskin, 1984).

Setting as a Macrovariable

Efficacy research generally has addressed the issue of the type of placement option in which special education students would benefit the most, but treating setting as the independent variable has provided little insight into what constitutes effective education. Studies examining the differential effectiveness of self-contained, resource room, and general education placements have produced contradictory results. Neither separate classes nor full-time mainstreaming clearly appears most efficacious, although the meta-analysis by Wang and Baker (1985–1986) does lend empirical support for mainstreaming. Resource room placement has shown, but not consistently, positive effects when compared with self-contained and regular classroom placements. It also must be noted that students sometimes perform best when they remain in regular classes and their own teacher is assisted in providing special instruction (Heller et al., 1982). Clearly, a certain placement option does not guarantee the presence of effective instructional practices. It may be possible that setting provides the occasion for teachers to engage in different behaviors; however, this indirect influence has not been systematically investigated. Alternatively, variables that promote positive student outcomes may occur in many settings.

Two interpretations are therefore possible from the research on the efficacy of special education. First, it can be concluded that special education settings are more effective than regular education settings, but the poor methodology of the research has obfuscated the emergence of any clear and consistent findings. As noted in the critique of the research, many studies investigating special-education settings have used such poor methodology (e.g., weak experimental designs, poor measures of outcome, inappropriate analyses) that the findings must be interpreted with caution. Efforts must be directed at the use of appropriate methodology for generating internally valid findings.

In contrast, a second interpretation is that the lack of consistent support for special education settings may accurately reflect a lack of differences between special and regular education. Components of effective instructional practices are not situation specific and confined to special education settings, but, rather, appear consistently in regular education classrooms. Furthermore, educational setting, as a global unit, is not the salient variable that determines the success of instruction. Rather, certain features of educational interventions systematically affect outcomes but are not unique to one setting in particular. For studies in which different instructional settings are compared and significant differences are found, it may be a certain component of a treatment package rather than the setting per se that is responsible for a positive effect. Unfortunately, many efficacy studies (almost all of those presented in the present review) have not provided sufficient detail to allow researchers to delineate those instructional components that led to positive change in the performance of special education students (Heller et al., 1982). Accordingly, efforts should be directed toward the precise specification of effective programs for the education of students with mild handicaps.

It is not the setting itself, then, but instructional variables within these settings that largely influence student achievement. Although setting may not operate directly on student achievement, it remains a relevant consideration, because it indirectly influences other important variables, such as instructional and affective processes. For instance, certain structured and highly systematic programs *may* be implemented and monitored more tightly in self-contained than in mainstream settings, and a restrictive setting makes it more difficult for rapid pacing and high expectation to occur (Leinhardt & Pallay, 1982). Issues of stimulus generalization (cf. Epps, Thompson, & Lane, 1985; Stokes & Baer, 1977) are also critical considerations when instruction is provided outside general education settings.

Reschly (1984) has suggested that the issue of setting is probably more complex than appreciated by Finn and Resnick (1984) or Leinhardt and Pallay (1982) because the chronological age of students needs to be considered. In the early grades, setting may be less of a problem because the discrepancy between educable mentally retarded students, for example, and those with average achievement is not large. These two groups are often close enough that supplemental assistance through peer tutoring or part-time special education, particularly considering the child-oriented attitudes of most elementary grade teachers, is sufficient. However, a much larger discrepancy between functional educational levels is apparent in the upper grades, certainly by high school, when many teachers are far more subject-matter oriented than child oriented. Hence, Reschly argued that the effects of setting interact with students' ages.

Differential Programming Options for Students with Mild Handicaps

The next section of this chapter examines the efficacy research from a second perspective, in which special and regular education settings are contrasted in terms of content. Each environment is described more specifically in terms of the amount and type of instruction offered. The focus of this research, then, is primarily on input descriptions and comparisons of the independent variables that define treatment(s) rather than on outcome. This research addresses the question of whether differential *programming* occurs as a result of the assessment–placement process. This area has only recently been developed and lacks the breadth of coverage that appears in the efficacy research. To date, much of the focus has been on the detailed description of classrooms, with no direct attention to special education, and has been reported under the rubric of process-product research (Brophy & Good, 1986). Recently, however, the same focus has been extrapolated to the differential comparison of special versus regular education classrooms.

Given this comparison between two settings, several issues must be addressed in the actual development of differential programs for handicapped students. The next section reviews three of these issues as they affect current conceptions of effective instructional environments. The concern in this review is, first, the development of effective programs and, second, the analysis of setting as a controlling variable. Since so much of the efficacy research has not supported the direct analysis of setting as a functional variable, this approach may be more fruitful.

The first issue involves the identification of *any* instructional behaviors that have portents for improving student achievement. Although the history of this line of research is relatively new, many studies are converging in their findings that certain teacher behaviors are related to student achievement. This support is in direct contrast to much of the earlier research, which was summarized by Durkin and Biddle (1974), in which the focus was less specific and the findings less supportive. Further analysis is then needed to determine whether these behaviors are situation specific (i.e., having relevance only for special or regular education).

The second issue concerns the integrity of the implementation of educational treatments. Increasingly, the content of instruction is being scrutinized with more and more precision, including analysis of curriculum materials and the interactive behaviors of teachers. All too often, program implementation is assumed and never really checked (Hall & Loucks, 1977). Unfortunately, in many cases, naturalistic observation has revealed a serious lack of definition of instructional behaviors that has serious consequences regarding the reliable implementation of educational programs.

The third issue, then, becomes one of assembling effective instructional variables into a program of instruction for use with low-achieving and mildly handicapped students. Although important principles are emerging from this line of research, the actual practice of such principles is heavily dependent upon the development of model programs, with the instructional materials developed and all of the components fully described. This integration of instructional components is an important step, from the points of view both of attaining widespread adoption in the field and of achieving reliable implementation.

Descriptions of Special Education Settings

Although systematic research on effective teaching has existed for the past 15–20 years, only recently have efforts been expended to apply the process–product methodology o special education environments (Englert, 1983; Leinhardt, Zigmond, & Cooley, 1981). In this paradigm of research, classroom processes are observed and student achievement is measured to determine how instruction relates to student performance outcomes. In these studies by Englert (1983) and Leinhardt et al. (1981), special education settings were observed for an extended period of time, and student achievement was measured following a period of instruction. In neither of the studies, however, was instruction experimentally manipulated.

The study by Leinhardt et al. (1981) investigated reading instruction in self-contained classrooms for primary children classified as learning disabled. Three questions were addressed: (a) What did reading instruction in classes for learning disabled students comprise?; (b) What was the relationship between various reading activities and student achievement?; and (c) What instructional situations provided the appropriate opportunity for these activities? A total of 105 students in eleven classrooms was included in the final sample. The design of the study included pretesting the students, observing the classrooms over a 20-week period, and posttesting them. The observation focused on the following teacher variables: model presentations, explanations, feedback, cueing, montitoring, frequency of reinforcement, and the "cognitive press" exerted by the teacher on the student. Two major student behaviors were observed: involvement in direct and indirect reading and five different nonreading activities. Although considerable variation was present across the classrooms, the researchers did find that posttest reading performance was significantly influenced by the amount of time students spent reading silently and by the use of reinforcers by the teacher.

Englert (1983) attempted to determine specific instructional practices that are associated with pupil achievement during direct instruction in special education settings. The subjects for this study included seventeen teacher trainees, each working with approximately twelve students. A low-inference observation system was employed to record direct instruction teacher behaviors (Englert & Sugai, 1981) and student responses. A significant relationship was found between student achievement and the amount of content covered, though none was found between achievement and holding pupils to a high success criterion, the use of teacher feedback, or task involvement by the student.

These studies are significant for two reasons: (a) they apply the process-product paradigm to special education settings, and (b) they operationalize an observation system that is precise and systematic. Both of these considerations are important in the definition of individualized programs for students with mild handicaps.

Comparative Descriptions of Regular and Special Education Settings

To move to a more precise analysis of differential programming requires the use of more than special education populations and the use of the same process–product paradigm in an investigation of both regular and special education students. Very little comparative research has been conducted in this area. At present, most of the research has focused on context variables, with only minor attention devoted to interactive instructional variables. Of primary concern has been the amount of time that students and teachers are engaged in various activities, particularly those with an academic focus. *Academic engaged time* is the term employed in this research, which has become the major dependent variable of many studies (Denham & Lieberman, 1980; Fisher & Berliner, 1985). Generally, it has been used to refer to the amount of time a student is actively engaged in an academic response. Because the definition requires some overt (academic-related) response, it is different from *on-task,* which encompasses more passive (attending only) responses.

As part of the observation studies on academic responding time, several other classroom processes have also been investigated, including type of activity, task, teaching structure, teacher position and activity, and, finally, student response. A description of the major studies that focus on these issues as they relate to the differential programming of instruction as a function of assessment placement decisions follows.

One of the earliest studies conducted on classroom processes using a systematic observation system (Code for Instructional Structure and Student Academic Response [CISSAR], Stanley & Greenwood, 1980) was done by Greenwood, Delquadri, Stanley, Terry, and Hall (1982). Two samples of Chapter 1 and regular education students were compared in terms of instructional contexts, student responses, and academic achievement. In all, ninety-three fourth-grade students from four different schools were observed, two of which were Chapter 1 schools and two non-Chapter 1 schools. Observations were conducted for each of the students over an entire school day.

The major finding of this study was that, with IQ controlled, context variables (e.g., teaching structure, tasks, teacher position) contributed unique variance to the prediction of reading and mathematics achievement. That is, with the differences among students' IQs partialed out, classroom practices were significantly related to achievement outcomes on measures of reading and math. Student behavior interacted differentially with classroom contexts in predicting achievement in the two environments. That is, the same teacher and student behaviors resulted in different relationships with achievement in the Chapter 1 and non-Chapter 1 rooms. In general, the number of teacher–student relationships was lower in the Chapter 1 rooms. Chapter 1 students scored significantly lower than their non-Chapter 1 cohorts in total reading achievement; amount of time receiving instruction in language, mathematics, and handwriting; amount of time the teacher was in front of or among students; and amount of time spent talking to the teacher. The Chapter 1 teachers were more engaged in direct teaching behaviors than the non-Chapter 1 teachers. One final significant difference was in the total amount of academic responding time, with Chapter 1 students actually engaged an average of 14 minutes less per day than the students in the non-Chapter 1 settings. The major similarity between the Chapter 1 and non-Chapter 1 environments was in the time allocated to academic activities, approximately 180 minutes, with only 67 minutes in which the students were engaged actively in academic work.

In summary, the assumption that placement in a Chapter 1 setting will provide more structure and opportunity for students to engage in reading and math may not be completely accurate. Though different structures may be directly provided in these more restricted settings, the effect on students' opportunities to practice and improve may not be as direct. More important, the total amount of engaged time is significantly less than the amount allocated, with a considerable amount of time devoted to task management, regardless of setting. In this study, students were engaged only 67 minutes, out of a total of 250 minutes devoted to academic work. Three times more time was involved in task management than in engagement with academic work (Stanley & Greenwood, 1981).

This study, though conducted with a limited sample of schools, did include the use of an extensive observation system, in which the classroom environment was very precisely described. In addition, the research included a focus both on the process of classroom practices and on the product of student achievement. One obvious limitation, however, is in the population studied. The findings may not be generalizable for special education populations served in different settings. Although the measurement of the independent variables involving instructional classroom processes appears adequate, the measurement of student achievement is less rigorous, particularly in math, for which the WRAT, Level 1 was used. This test has been seriously criticized by Salvia and Ysseldyke (1985) as a measure with poor technical adequacy.

In extending this work and applying its methodology to resource room classes, investigators at the Institute for Research on Learning Disabilities at the University of Minnesota have conducted a series of studies. These investigators also have focused on the differences between special and regular education in the time allocated to various classroom processes. These studies were done on thirty-four students in Grades 3 and 4 (representing seventeen different classrooms in nine elementary schools) for 2 full days during the last half of the school year, from January through March. At the end of the year, all of the students were tested on the PIAT. Three different studies are pertinent to the concern of this chapter that differential program plans emanate from the assessment-placement process.

Comparing learning disabled students with non-learning disabled students on a variety of classroom process variables, including activity, task, structure, teacher position and behavior, and, finally, student response, Thurlow, Graden, Greener, and Ysseldyke (1982) found very few significant differences. Not a single significant difference was found in the time allocated to any of the classroom activities for either the composite of academic or nonacademic activities or the types of student responses. The only significant differences included the type of tasks involving the use of other media (e.g., films, games, crafts), teacher position (e.g., beside the student) and teacher activities (e.g., giving approval). Another consistent distinction between the two environments involved the administrative arrangements, with resource room delivering more individual instruction and regular room delivering more entire group instruction. In total, only six of twenty-eight student responses were significant across the two environments. The final summary of the academic time used across different activities and tasks, teacher behaviors, and student responses revealed approximately 180 minutes engaged for learning disabled students and 185 minutes engaged for non-learning disabled students out of a total of 360 minutes during the school day, a non-significant difference.

The relationship between the various classroom process variables and student achievement was somewhat inconsistent within both the learning disabled and non-learning disabled groups. In general, it was found that academic activity positively correlated with achievement and that task management negatively correlated with achievement. An analysis of the change in achievement over the year was conducted on a small subset of the students, and it revealed some positive relationships between academic responses and gain in achievement.

The findings from this study must be qualified by the limited observation data that were available for analysis. Given the large variation that was found, both within the groups of students over the 2 days of observation and especially between the groups, any statements made about general trends must be qualified. In addition, the analyses relating classroom process variables to achievement are highly tenuous, given the small sample size.

Within the group of learning disabled students from this study, the data from a subsample were analyzed to determine if academic responding time was related to the level of service (Thurlow, Ysseldyke, Graden, Greener & Macklenberg, 1982). For this study, twenty-six learning disabled students from twenty-five classrooms and eleven schools served as subjects. The five levels of service were defined in terms of the amount of specialized help received by the student and reflect the levels described earlier in the chapter. Level 1 students received all of their instruction on the regular classroom, with consultation from the resource teacher; Level 2 students received more direct help, including tutoring, from the resource teacher in the regular classroom; Level 3 students were served part-time (less than 50%) in the resource room; Level 4 students were served primarily (more than 50%) in the resource room; and Level 5 students received all of their instruction in a full-time, self-contained resource room. Three students were randomly selected from each of Levels 1, 2, 3, 4 and 5, and fourteen from Level 3.

Again, the results indicate very few significant differences in classroom practices between the various levels of service. No significant differences were found for any activities or teacher positions, while one significant difference was found for each of the following: type of task (listening to lecture); teacher activity (giving approval); and student response (looking around). The two major differences between the five levels of service consisted of teaching structure and total academic time. Students in Levels 4 and 5 received significantly less instruction within an entire group structure than in the other three levels, with students in Level 4 receiving more instruction in a one-to-one format. When total allocated times were summed up, a significant difference in the amount of academic time appeared across the levels of service. Contrary to the predicted direction (i.e., more time allocated for more severely disabled students), the students in Levels 4 and 5 received significantly less time than those in Level 3.

The data from this study reveal very inconsistent findings regarding the relationship between classroom process variables and achievement. Academic activity was negatively correlated with achievement, while inappropriate student responses were positively correlated with achievement. Task management was, however, found to be negatively correlated with achievement.

In another analysis of this same data base, change in services was investigated as a function of the placement process (Ysseldyke, Thurlow, Mecklenberg, Graden, & Algozzine, 1984). This focus differs from that of the previous analysis in that the critical variable was not the absolute level provided but the change in level from pre- to postplacement. The subjects for this study included four students from four classrooms in Grades 1, 2, and 3. At the time of the first observation, all students had been enrolled in regular education. For the second and third observations, three of the students were receiving learning disability services, and one was in a Chapter 1 program.

The results of the observations conducted during the referral-to-placement process indicate that the students did not recieve more intensive services in special education than they received in the regular education environment. Generally, amounts of academic instruction and responding time diminished 2 months after placement in special education. Again, these findings must be qualified due to the extreme variability between students. The researchers cite as an example the findings on one student, for whom the amount of academic responding time dropped by half during the referral-to-placement process and then doubled over the next 2 months. Basically, placement in special education did not necessarily result in increases in student academic responding. The referral-to-placement process served to alter some aspects of the daily routine; nevertheless, with time, patterns remarkably similar to those observed prior to intervention were found.

The findings from the three studies conducted at the University of Minnesota Institute for Research on Learning Disabilities must be qualified. Although students were observed for a very extended period of time in terms of total minutes, the number of days of observation was very limited. Therefore, the data may or may not be stable enough to generalize the findings to special education practices in general. In addition, the number of students and classrooms was somewhat constricted, again limiting the generalizability of the findings. Finally, the analyses of the achievement data were based on severely limited samples, precluding a sensitive or generalized assessment of the relationship between the classroom processes and their effect on achievement.

Although the research conducted by the investigators at the University of Minnesota Institute for Research on Learning Disabilities provides valuable data on the process of the differential programming of students in special versus regular education, very few data are available on the product, that is, student outcomes. In all of the analyses, achievement data were available from too few students to provide a meaningful analysis. The obvious inference, however, from these studies is that, when students are given essentially the same environment and opportunities in special education that they are provided in regular education, it is unlikely that they will achieve any more. The teacher–student ratio, the only consistent contribution appearing in special education settings, may, however, account for some differential gain.

An Investigation of Differential Programming and Outcome Determination

The last study to be reviewed was an investigation of special education using the process–product paradigm, in which classroom practices were observed and student achievement was measured (Haynes & Jenkins, 1984). This study was one of the most direct investigations of differential programming based on the placement of students into special education. Because of its immediate relevance to this issue, this study is extensively discussed.

In this study, observations were conducted in resource rooms with mildly handicapped students from fourth through sixth grade to identify teacher behaviors and student activities related to reading achievement. In this description of the programs, the focus was on three major issues in the definition of educational programming: (a) to assess the degree to which programs were standardized and represented a relatively uniform delivery system, (b) to determine the comparability of reading programs between regular and special education environments, and (c) to assay the relationship between teacher behaviors and student achievement.

A total of 133 students was studied in this investigation, comprising three groups of students. The largest group was an urban sample of 117 fourth-, fifth-, and sixth-grade students from twenty-three resource rooms. The second group, representing a subset of the 117 students, was observed not only in the resource room but also in the regular education classroom along with nonhandicapped peers. The third group consisted of sixteen fourth-grade students from five resource rooms in an adjacent suburban district, which used a direct instruction approach to teaching (Englemann et al., 1978).

The investigators pretested all students, using several published achievement measures (CAT, Slossen Oral Reading Test [Slosson, 1963], and WRAT). From January through May, classroom observations were conducted using a time sampling system that cumulates the time spent on specific activities: student activities (both reading and nonreading); proximity to teacher; statements (positive and negative); and teacher activities. Each student was observed for five to eight scheduled reading periods in the responses room on different days of the week.

To create a subsample, students from regular classrooms were matched and observed for 2 entire school days; the students included eighteen mildly handicapped students from the larger group of 117 and six randomly selected nonhandicapped peers. Given the first objective, to describe reading instruction in the resource and regular classrooms, Haynes and Jenkins computed the average time spent on various activities. For example, they found that 47 minutes per day were scheduled in the resource room, though considerable variation existed among the students. Although this variation was not surprising, they further assessed whether the time scheduled was related to "student need," which was operationalized as grade-placement/achievement-level discrepancy, by using the WRAT pretest to correlate student need with scheduled hours. A weak correlation was found between student need and the amount of remedial service scheduled, accounting for only 4% of the variance in the scheduling of students for instruction. That is, students were scheduled in classes, not on the basis of need but of other issues. Further analyses using multiple linear regression and various student factors revealed no significant predictors, suggesting that scheduling practices were more a function of teacher and school context factors than any kind of pupil characteristics.

Additional descriptions of the enviroment included time spent in reading and in independent seatwork. Students spent 10 minutes on direct reading activities and 8.5 minutes on indirect reading. Of the total 47 minutes scheduled for reading, only 19 minutes (40%) were actually spent on reading activities. Nonreading activities consumed most of the time in the resource room. The analysis of proximity indicated that students spent 25 minutes (52%) of their time on individual seatwork. Very little time was spent on either teacher reading instruction in the form of cognitive explanations (5%) or on monitoring (17%). Reading instruction in these resource rooms can be best described as involving students in independent seatwork; giving minimum feedback, explanations, or demonstrations; and engaging students in reading only 25% of the time. Furthermore, the relationship between scheduled time and the actual time engaged in instruction was low, and the amount and type of instruction offered was more a function of the teacher or school than student characteristics.

A comparison of the urban sample with the suburban sample (using direct instruction) revealed great differences in the amount of time scheduled, with more than three times as much allocated for the suburban sample. Similar discrepancies were found on eleven other variables dealing with student and teacher behaviors (e.g., out-of-room, off-task, individual seatwork, engaged time, one-to-one instruction, teacher–student interactions). Based c these findings, Haynes and Jenkins (1984) concluded th assignment to the resource room is not a standardize intervention that is highly related to individual stude needs. Rather, extreme variation in the amount of sche uled time and in the type of reading instruction was prese in a nonsystematic manner across students and resour rooms.

Comparisons of the regular classroom with the resourc room revealed that students spent significantly more tim reading (17 minutes vs. 13 minutes of total reading time and had more indirect reading instruction (27 minutes v 12 minutes) in the regular classroom than in the resourc room. Furthermore, they were on-task significantly mor in the regular classroom than in the resource room. Thi finding is counterintuitive, given the lower teacher–stu dent ratio that is afforded in resource rooms. Indeed, th students in the resource room received more teacher read ing instruction during a greater proportion of their tim and spent more time working one-to-one or in small group with the teacher than students in the regular classroo (40% vs. 3%). However, more than half of the time spent i the resource room was devoted to independent seatwor with no direct instruction. It is this component that ma explain why students were more off-task in the resourc room. Finally, little continuity existed between the readin programs in the two settings. Not only did the resourc room typically supplant reading instruction in the regula classroom, but when reading was offered in both settings they were rarely coordinated with each other. In fact several resource room teachers were not aware of reading programs in the regular classroom.

A major finding of the Haynes and Jenkins (1984) study was the great variability in the time students spent in direct reading and total reading time. Reading in the regular classroom for special education students ranged from 0 minutes to 32 minutes. This variation in time spent reading was also true for the nonhandicapped peers, which ranged from 6 minutes to 49 minutes of direct reading. The great amount of variability serves not only to limit the generalizability of the findings but also, more importantly, to underscore the lack of a relationship between the students' needs and the programs' offerings. The correlation between need (operationalized as the discrepancy between achievement level and grade level, and reading time) and program offering was close to zero and nonsignificant.

A comparison between the regular and resource rooms on several process variables involving teacher proximity, instruction, activities, and statements resulted in few significant differences between the two environments. The only two dissimilar variables were time spent reading letters or isolated words and time spent on one-to-one instruction. As these researchers noted, a major conclusion of this research is that the similarity between regular and resource rooms is so great as to defy any serious attempts to have handicapped students catch up to their nonhandicapped peers.

Finally, several regression analyses were conducted to determine which variables best predicted achievement.

fter controlling for the effects of pretest preformance and Q, no significant time variables of reading activity were ound to predict achievement significantly. Reading time vas, however, related to pretest performance, in which tudents with higher pretest scores also had higher rocess scores and posttest achievement.

Haynes and Jenkins (1984) concluded that student haracteristics, in particular, achievement level, are only veakly linked to scheduling and the amount of reading nstruction received. This finding is in direct contradiction o the fundamental premise of special education programs being designed for individual student needs.

The methodology of this study is stronger than the methodologies of the other studies reviewed above, primarly in terms of the measurement of achievement. Not only were multiple measures conducted, but the timing of their administration was also coordinated with observation schedules and applied to more students. Limitations similar to those in the study by Ysseldyke et al. (1984) exist for this study in the measurement of the classroom process. Given the great amount of variability, the limited number of days of observation may not be sufficient to allow generalizations of the findings to other special and/or regular education environments. The large sample size in this study at least partially compensates for this problem.

In summary, the research that has been done comparing program definitions across various educational settings reveals few substantive differences. Setting as a macrovariable does not appear to be highly related to functional differences in the delivery of instruction, including context variables and interactive teaching variables. This is true in the research comparing Chapter 1 and non-Chapter 1 settings, as well as in the research conducted in resource rooms with mildly handicapped students and in regular classrooms with nonhandicapped peers.

Analysis of Instructional Variables

The two major areas of research that have been reviewed to this point provide little definitive support for the differential programming of students in special environments. In the discussion of the findings of efficacy research in the first section of the review of the literature, inconsistent support was found favoring special education settings in improving student achievement, though most of the studies had major methodological flaws. In the second section, the focus was directed toward the definition of the independent variables within special education settings. This more specific review addressed the content of instruction, including observation of major process and context variables. Again, little support was found favoring special education environments over the environment that is found in regular education classes.

Studies comparing different placement options have addressed the differences in the components of instruction in these different settings and have provided little support for considering setting as a macrovariable of importance on its own. Only indirectly can educational setting be considered influential in the development of program options. For example, given the teacher–student ratio as the major difference between special and regular education, it is possible that this variable provides differential opportunity for teachers to engage in various behavior.

In the third section of the review of literature, then, more specific issues of effective instruction are addressed: (a) the identification of those teacher behaviors, independent of setting, which are effective in improving the achievement of students; (b) an analysis of the issues of implementing instruction in the classroom; and (c) a discussion of effective teaching practices within the context of instructional models that have been field tested and empirically supported. In this review of the literature, the important consideration is whether these teacher behaviors can be implemented in special education classrooms.

Effective Teaching Research

In reviewing and integrating the research on effective teaching that has been accumulating over the past 15 years, Good (1983) noted that the literature on basic skills instruction has moved from a state of confusion to a point at which consistent findings are emerging. A major contention of his review is that many specific teacher behaviors can have a significant and practical effect upon student achievement. Waxman and Walberg (1982) provided a review of reviews of the process–product research published from 1970 to 1979. These authors included reviews that summarized at least three different primary studies and considered at least two teaching variables. In their review, nineteen different summary articles were included, and thirty-five different variables were clustered into four major constructs: (a) cognitive and motivational stimulation, (b) student engagement, (c) reinforcement, and (d) management and climate. Although Waxman and Walberg noted that serious problems exist in terms of the lack of systematicity in study selection and analysis, they nevertheless concluded that the results seemed to be strong and robust enough to emerge with a fair amount of consistency and that they certainly deserved attempts at replication.

All the teacher variables that appear highly related to student achievement appear to be applicable across educational environments. For example, a general finding from the Medley (1979) review indicates that student achievement is highly related to an environment exhibiting the following characteristics: teacher-directed structure in a large group, in which an academic focus prevails and high rates of approval and low rates of disapproval are present; the use of low-level questions, with few pupil-initiated questions, little feedback, and little amplification of pupil comments; and little time engaged in seatwork, which is, however, closely monitored. The findings from other reviews are consistent with this outcome (Borich, 1979; Brophy, 1979; Brophy & Good, 1986; Rosenshine, 1979). The most current review, by Brophy and Good, encompasses all other reviews and includes a breakdown of all the major studies conducted in the past decade. A major conclusion from this review is that effective instruction varies with classroom context. The findings are not so clear and definitive that they may be applied without consideration of setting. Nevertheless, specific findings are beginning to emerge that are consistent across investigators, methods, and populations.

Both regular and special education encompass environments enabling instructional programs to be implemented based on the premise that the effectiveness of instruction varies with setting. Nevertheless, such a description of educational environments is far from prescriptive enough to be useful in differentially developing programs for use with handicapped students. Many of the variables that have been included in the process–product research lack sufficient specificity to become components within a comprehensive educational program. This lack of detail has great effect on the implementation of any instructional program.

Integrity of Independent Variables

As Good (1983) noted, teachers vary widely not only in their utilization of time but also in their classroom management strategies, their selection and design of classroom learning tasks, their level of active teaching and communication, and their expectations and academic standards. In relating these issues, he proposed a relatively simple but straightforward explanation: many teachers do not actively teach content or concepts. Rather, instruction consists of brief explanations followed by long periods of seatwork. Brief explanations of seatwork do not provide sufficient opportunities for meaningful and successful practice of the concepts taught; furthermore, the conditions necessary for students to discover or use principles on their own are rarely present.

This same issue has been addressed by Durkin (1979), whose classroom observations revealed a near total lack of instruction in comprehension. In her observation of thirty-six classrooms, she found that very few teachers actively engaged in instructional behaviors related to comprehension in reading. Her definition of instruction included components of description, modeling, and demonstration. However, simply asking whether students understood a passage was not included as an instructional behavior but, rather, as comprehension assessment. She coined the term *mentioning* to refer to a nearly tangential presentation and an almost exclusive use of questioning without feedback in the presentation of instructional material related to comprehension.

Brophy (1982) has conceptualized a model in which the content of instruction is transformed further from that which appears in the curriculum to that which is applied in the classroom, including the deletions, additions, and incorrect applications of the intended curriculum to the actual content. He noted that direct distortion due to teacher misconceptions is more typical than indirect distortion occurring because of incomplete or inadequate teaching. Furthermore, such distortions often have the most undesirable effects on low-achieving students, in particular in classrooms where students are grouped according to ability. The material presented to these studen often results in content fragmentation, mystification, re etition, little theory, and limited exposure to integratir concepts (Confrey & Good, 1981). In this study, studen in general mathematics class spent most of their time o repetitive drill and practice, with inadequate attentio paid to the foundations underlying concepts.

In summary, although the research on effective teachin has provided a basis for improving instructional practice the generalizations are far from prescriptive. The greate problem lies in the lack of sufficient specificity fo implementation. To date, the content of most instructiona programs has not been delineated with enough precision t enable movement beyond correlational research to th next step of experimental research (Rosenshine & Furst 1973). The development of robust aptitude-by-treatmen interactions—the essence of differential programmin —is even more undeveloped. As Berliner (1983) has noted most of the research in classrooms has lacked any precisio in the description of environments or treatments. "Relatively speaking, we have measured aptitude witl micrometers and treatments with divining rods" (p. 1). To overcome this problem, then, more effort must be exerted in the detailed description of both context variables (i.e., activity structures, as described by Berliner) and interactive teacher behaviors (Stevens & Rosenshine, 1981).

Models of Replicable Instructional Programs

Three models of instruction have been developed recently that do represent a significant departure from traditional, ill-defined conceptions of treatments and provide the field of education with a first step toward the development of specific, prescriptive environments that are not only highly related to achievement but also capable of experimental manipulation. These three programs have been under development and investigation over the past decade, each having accumulated enough of an empirical basis to warrant serious consideration. Though not exhaustive of the possibilities, they represent the kind of programs that are needed—not only in terms of their content but also, more importantly, in terms of their replicability. The first is the Adaptive Learning Environments Model (ALEM) from the University of Pittsburgh's Learning Research and Development Center (Wang, 1980a, 1981; Wang, Gennari, & Waxman, 1985). The second is Active Mathematics Teaching from the University of Missouri (Good, Grouws, & Ebmeier, 1983). The third is Direct Instruction from the University of Oregon (Becker, Engelmann, Carnine, & Rhine, 1981; Carnine & Silbert, 1979; Engelmann, 1980; Engelmann & Carnine, 1982; Silbert, Carnine, & Stein, 1981).

These three programs have been selected on the basis of two criteria: (a) the degree of specificity and capability for evaluating implementation, and (b) the empirical support that has been generated to date regarding their impact on student achievement. Therefore, the important issue in all three of these programs is the high attention to detail that not only provides direction for implementation but also allows the experimental verification of effects.

ALEM. The ALEM is an educational program designed to make instructional provisions that are effective in meeting the diverse social and academic needs of individual students in regular classes. As described by Wang and her associates (Wang & Birch, 1984a; Wang, Gennari, & Waxman, 1985), the model is designed to create school learning environments in which all students can learn basic academic skills and increase their confidence in their ability to learn and cope with the social and intellectual demands of schooling. The curriculum combines direct instruction, which has been proven effective in fostering students' mastery of basic skills (Bloom, 1976; Glaser, 1977; Rosenshine, 1979), with aspects of informal or open education that generate attitudes and processes of inquiry, self-responsibility, and social cooperation (Johnson, Maruyama, Johnson, Nelson, & Skon, 1981; Marshall, 1981).

The design of the ALEM includes five major components: (a) a basic skills curriculum consisting both of highly structured, hierarchically organized prescriptive learning activities and of more open-ended exploratory learning activities; (b) an instructional/learning management system designed to maximize the use of classroom and school resources such as curricular materials and time; (c) a family involvement component designed to increase communication and to integrate school and home learning experiences; (d) a flexible grouping and instructional team system aimed at increasing the use of teachers' and students' talents, time, and educational resources; and (e) a data-based staff development program for increasing staff members' capabilities to initiate and monitor ALEM implementation.

The data from research on the implementation and effects of the ALEM in schools suggest that, when these components are well implemented, they promote a unique classroom learning environment for students (Wang & Birch, 1984b; Wang, Nojan, Strom, & Walberg, 1984; Wang & Walberg, 1983). Physically, the ALEM classroom is organized to facilitate movement and simultaneous activities. Students work in small and large groups and alone while teachers circulate among them, providing individual feedback and tutoring, and organizing and providing instruction to small groups of students or the entire class. Instruction is individually planned, and each student is expected to progress through the curriculum at his or her own pace. Learning tasks are broken down into small steps, affording frequent opportunities for evaluation. Thus, small successes are easily recognized and acknowledged, and momentary difficulties can be pinpointed and addressed before they become learning problems. When a learning problem does occur, it is viewed not as a failure on the part of the student but as a signal to the teacher to use an alternative instructional method.

Students in ALEM classes are taught to plan and monitor their own learning and are held responsible for planning, managing, and completing teacher-prescribed and self-selected learning tasks within time limits jointly decided on with the teacher. Students often collaborate in teaching and testing one another, but all activity is observed closely by teachers, who work alone or in teams to provide the instructional and management assistance students require. Special educators and support personnel are available to help provide diagnostic services, offer the intensive instruction some students require, and consult with general education teachers and parents.

Implementation of the program is monitored and refined through an ongoing staff development delivery system that is data-based and individually tailored to individual teachers. Information on the degree of implementation is gathered periodically through systematic checks with the Implementation Assessment Battery for Adaptive Instruction (Wang, 1980b). This instrument consists of a series of performance indicators for determining the presence or absence of twelve critical dimensions of the program: (a) creating and maintaining instructional materials, (b) record keeping, (c) diagnostic testing, (d) prescribing, (e) monitoring and diagnosing, (f) interactive teaching, (g) instructing, (h) motivating, (i) arranging space and facilities, (j) establishing and communicating rules and procedures, (k) managing aides, and (l) developing student self-responsibility.

The results from research examining the implementation and effects of the ALEM in a variety of school settings show consistent, positive trends regarding the feasibility of implementation and the effects of the program both on students' achievement in basic skills and on their social behavior and attitudes. Evidence has been provided that supports establishing and maintaining the program in schools with differing demographic characteristics in a variety of geographic locations (Wang, Nojan, Strom, & Walberg, 1984). The findings also suggest that, over time, improvement in the degree of implementation is possible through the data-based approach to the provision of systematic staff development support (Wang & Gennari, 1983; Wang, Vaughan, & Dytman, 1985). In addition, the data suggest that program implementation leads to concomitant changes in classroom processes and student achievement.

Analyses of standardized achievement test results show that students in ALEM classes participating in the National Follow Through Program not only scored above estimated population norms but also tended to score above national norms (Wang & Walberg, 1983). Positive student achievement and attitudinal outcomes have been found in ALEM classrooms, where mildly to moderately handicapped and gifted students are integrated on a full-time basis. The results include increased perceptions of self-competence and peer acceptance, as well as significantly increased decertification rates (Wang & Birch, 1984a, 1984b; Wang, Peverly, & Randolph, 1984). Achievement and attitudinal data show favorable performance by regular students in the mainstream classes as well.

Active Mathematics Teaching. This program was developed initially on the basis of a naturalistic study of effective classrooms (Good & Grouws, 1975). On the basis of a constellation of teacher behaviors that were found to be present in classrooms in which student achievement was high, a module was assembled for generating very specific teacher behaviors. The main components of this program are listed below:

1. Daily review. This component is used in the introduction of the lesson, comprising a fairly short amount of time (8 minutes), and includes a focus on the concepts and skills associated with homework and on the application of several mental computation exercises.
2. Development. This component represents the greatest amount of time spent (20 minutes) on the lesson, during which the teacher attends to prerequisite skills and concepts and includes the use of lively examples, explanations, demonstrations, process explanations, illustrations, and so forth. In addition, students' comprehension is assessed using both process–product questions and controlled practice.
3. Seatwork. This component, lasting about 15 minutes, includes the opportunity for students to engage in uninterrupted and successful practice and comprises three major issues: getting all of the students involved in a sustained manner, letting the students know that their work will be checked at the end of the period, and then checking the work.
4. Homework assignment. This last component provides the students with independent practice outside of the classroom on a regular basis and includes enough work to be completed in about 15 minutes, with one to two of the problems providing review.
5. Special reviews. Two different types of reviews are included in the program: weekly and monthly. The former is conducted during the first 20 minutes of class each Monday and focuses on the skills and concepts covered during the previous week. The latter is conducted every fourth Monday and includes an opportunity to cover all of the work completed in that month.

The data supporting this program were collected over a decade, beginning in the early 1970s. On the basis of several naturalistic studies with more than 100 third- and fourth-grade teachers, several teacher behaviors were identified as having a strong relationship with student achievement (Good & Grouws, 1975). From this data base, it was determined that effective instruction could be operationalized with the following four components: (a) initiate and review instructional activities in the context of meaning; (b) minimize errors and enhance involvement for each stage of the lesson; (c) incorporate both distributed and successful practice; and (d) engage in active teaching, particularly in the developmental portion of the lesson. From these findings, a general program manual was constructed, providing a system of instruction that was to be followed each day.

In 1977, an experimental study was conducted with forty fourth-grade teachers. The results from this study supported the superiority of the program in raising the achievement scores of low-functioning students and indicated a favorable reaction by both teachers and students (Good et al., 1983). Several replications were conducted and corroborated the results from this early experimental study. A follow-up experimental study was conducted, applying the program to the teaching of verbal problem solving for sixth-grade students. The findings from this study were less clear and consistent in support of the program, though confounding was identified in the type of class structure and program implementation by the control group of teachers. Then, from 1979–1981, the program was adapted for use with a junior high school population, and an experiment was conducted in nineteen classrooms. The findings from this study indicated few differences in achievement between the experimental and control group, though issues in the implementation of the program were found, with the two groups showing great similarity on some instructional components and experimental teachers not implementing some components at times.

In general, the results from the early investigations provide clear process–product data on the effectiveness of the instructional program, but the adaptations and applications to other populations and settings are less consistently effective (Good et al., 1983). The methodology behind most of this research, however, is very well developed and programmatic, with each new investigation established on the basis of a previous study. The outcome measures were established from the content of instruction, and the observation systems were clearly delineated from prior naturalistic studies.

Direct Instruction. As described by Engelmann (1980) and Engelmann and Carnine (1982), this program is based on faultless communication and the logical development of essential features in teaching concepts, including (a) controlled rate for introducing new items; (b) juxtaposition of exemplars (positive and negative) in a well-sequenced design; (c) scripted instructional wording for the teacher; (d) active modeling and demonstration by the teacher; (e) formal use of shaping and prompting; (f) built-in procedures for fading and convertizing; (g) use of positive and negative exemplars; (h) small-group format; (i) use of signals for organizing student responses; (j) rapid instructional pace generating high rates of student responding; (k) both unison and individual responding; (l) structured error correction paradigm; (m) continuous monitoring of performance; and (n) delayed testing and practice.

The program of instruction is premised on its application within a small-group format (with three to seven students), and though not exclusively designed for special education students, it has its greatest implementation in that area. Though the program has been developed with commercial materials (e.g., Direct Instruction Strategies for Teaching and Remediation [DISTAR] [Engelmann &

Bruner, 1974] and Corrective Reading [Engelmann et al., 1978]), in practice it can be used with any curriculum.

This program has had a very long and extensive period of development, having been a major instructional model in Project Follow Through. The data from this project quite clearly support the superiority of Direct Instruction in improving the reading, math, and language skills of low-achieving students (Becker et al., 1981; Carnine, 1984; Gersten, 1985; Stebbins, St. Pierre, Proper, Anderson, & Cerva, 1977).

Summary. Although the three programs do not exhaust the range of applications of successful programs for mildly handicapped students, they do represent the best of this range. Based on very different conceptions and incorporating very different procedures, they also share several significant elements. First, they all represent active teaching, in which students are presented well-structured environments for responding. Second, they all incorporate frequent measurement and mastery monitoring, formatively evaluating students on a regular basis. Third, they have all been field tested in schools with students who are difficult to teach. Fourth, and most important, the instructional routines are well described and detailed, allowing for the precise implementation of the entire program. It is this latter aspect that provides the essential feature for replicability. While the implementation of these three programs in most schools represents an ideal, the fact remains that wide-scale implementation is limited to regional efforts.

Summary of the Review of Literature

In much of the efficacy research, placement option has been regarded as a form of treatment in itself, and the focus has, as a result, been placed largely on various administrative arrangements as the independent variable. This line of research has produced no consistent judgment regarding the superiority of either special or regular settings for educating students with mild handicaps, although there are some data suggesting that mainstream settings, including resource rooms, are associated with positive student outcomes. Interpretation of the literature also is seriously plagued by a plethora of methodological confounding, including (a) problems concerning the heterogeneity and cohort differences of the populations served; (b) the use of preexisting groups or matching of subjects on characteristics other than outcome measure; (c) the insensitivity and variability of measuring devices that often have low content validity and may not have been standardized on handicapped populations; (d) an inappropriate metric of analysis (e.g., grade or age equivalent scores) for dependent variables; and (e) a lack of specificity in describing the nature of treatment and a virtual total disregard for verifying the integrity of its delivery. Although future research may indicate that a student's age or the degree to which a student's problem is due to a repertoire or motivational deficiency interacts with the effects of setting, the past preoccupation with the setting in which instruction occurs has largely been misplaced.

In regard, then, to the question, Do students experiencing difficulty in school fare better when placed in special education settings or when allowed to remain in regular classrooms?, the appropriate response is, "Wrong question." Rather, the efficacy issue should be shifted to a focus on identifying features of instruction that lead to improved student learning. The bulk of the evidence to date suggests that distinctions among traditional remedial and special education classifications and among different placement options do not correspond to distinctions in instructional approaches that have been used. In response to the question, Is there differential programming in serving mildly handicapped students?, the answer is a resounding "No".

Implications of the Review

Current practice is fundamentally premised on aptitude-by-treatment interaction (see Arter & Jenkins, 1979, and Rudman et al., 1980, for a review of the issues involved in the integration of assessment information in the instructional program options). Classification of students, certification of teachers, and development of IEPs all reflect this perspective. The initial classification and placement of students in special education implies differential treatment based on setting as the effective variable for defining treatments. Even more specific interactions are presumed by the insistence that teachers must attain proper certification to teach certain types (classifications) of students. The assumption is that teachers with differing certifications engage in different behaviors, and, furthermore, that these behaviors are differentially effective in remediating students of various classifications. The most precise level of aptitude-by-treatment interaction occurs with the diagnostic testing of students and the consequent development of educational plans. Assessment information is assumed to be useful in the development of uniquely appropriate programs. These activities have their greatest impact on three issues in the schools: (a) generating high quality and useful information on students, (b) establishing effective programs on an empirical basis, and (c) documenting positive outcomes.

Not only are the public schools implicated but also the university and college programs that train teachers and psychologists and provide the necessary experiences for certification. Many of these programs have developed course offerings for training based on the concept of categorical disabilities. By implication, then, current training practices must be systematically examined and modified.

Given the major importance of social policy in driving the entire delivery system, it is necessary to consider the administrative aspects of special education programs, including rules, regulations, and funding. Many training programs may, in part, be a reflection of state policy and regulations. Given the legal mandate, many school systems, including elementary and secondary schools, as well as institutions of higher education, define programs in compliance with guidelines and in contrast to rational and/or empirical knowledge.

The last section of the chapter addresses the development of effective educational programs in terms of three major components that may define effective programs: the use of appropriate assessment techniques, implementation of programs with known effects, and the evaluation of outcomes. The three major levels or perspectives for viewing these areas are school-based practice, training programs, and social policy and funding. Finally, the direction of future research is presented with implications for all three components and all three perspectives.

Public School Practice

The most problematic issue characterizing current practice in special education assessment is the lack of direct connection between student test performance and instructional issues. Reynolds (1984) noted that many students are classified on the basis of an unsystematic collection of psychological traits, organic impairments, social behavior, cultural background, and other variables, with little logical or empirical connection to the educational decisions that must be made or the instruction that is to be offered.

Issues in Assessment

The observation by Reynolds is supported in the findings from a study by Thurlow and Ysseldyke (1980), in which they determined that great disparities existed between teachers and psychologists in the value they accorded to assessment information. Typically, teachers found the information far less useful for planning instruction than the psychologists thought to be the case. This lack of agreement may be a function of either (a) the utility of the information or (b) teachers' skill in using it. The former interpretation implies a problem with the content of the information, in particular as it applies to the development of instructional programs. The latter interpretation implies that the assessment information was not well understood or easily integrated into useful and direct practice in the classroom and that, with appropriate training, such information can become integrated with instruction.

Several studies have been conducted on teachers' knowledge and application of test information. Generally, it has been found that teachers seldom use formal testing information in a systematic manner; they use it more often to place students in programs but rarely to evaluate the effects of these programs, and they are not skilled in the appropriate use of this information (Lazar-Morrison, Polin, Moy, & Burry, 1980; Rudman et al., 1980; Stetz & Beck, 1979; Yeh, Herman, & Rudman, 1981). In part, this lack of knowledge may explain the findings of Ysseldyke and Thurlow (1983) regarding regular education teachers' lack of participation in the multidisciplinary team decision making. These researchers found that regular education teachers, though clearly the most important contacts in the referral process, were also actively engaged in team meetings only 27% of the time. Given their lack of skill in test interpretation, it is not surprising that they would not participate.

Teacher skill in measurement and testing involves not only the participation of teachers in the decision-making process but also the development of appropriate educational programs based on accurate and sensitive descriptions of student aptitudes. Most of these descriptions must arise out of the assessment of student performance. If teachers have few skills in this area, then it is presumptuous to assume that treatments will be specifically defined around individual students. An area of research that needs more development is the degree to which teachers can and do use test-derived data to build and adapt instructional programs.

At present, the entire scope of assessment has largely been confined to a person-centered rather than a situation-centered focus (Deno, Mirkin, & Shinn, 1978). Although assessment may be broadly defined as the collection of information (Salvia & Ysseldyke, 1985), it has typically been operationalized as the testing of students (Ysseldyke & Thurlow, 1983). In this manner, the person-centered approach views the locus of the problem as within the child and focuses the collection of information on an accurate and precise description of student characteristics. Little systematic effort has been expended in the assessment of learning environments, which implies a situation-centered approach (Engelmann et al., 1979; Messick, 1984). This latter perspective focuses assessment on the accurate and detailed description of the interactions between a learner and the environment. In this approach, both historical and current environments are assayed. Without information on the content and outcomes of previous instructional efforts, no inferences can be made regarding the capability of the student; any predictions about necessary programs and expected outcomes are even more tenuous.

One of the effects of a person-centered approach is that the information collected tends to be used in a confirmatory rather than disconfirmatory manner. For example, Ysseldyke and Thurlow (1983) reported that the probability of assessment, once students are referred, is 92%; once students are assessed, the probability of placement in special education is 73%. In essence, the focus of assessment is on confirming the existence of a problem. Interestingly, the logic of disconfirmation, though providing a bedrock for scientific methodology in the form of the null hypothesis, is scarcely even considered in the explanation of student performance. This disjunction between the manner in which research is conducted and practice is defined may well explain the current schism between what is known and what is done. Obviously, more research must be conducted that focuses on more accurate and educationally relevant descriptions of students, as well as on the development of procedures not only for conducting assessments of environments but also for using such data in making intervention decisions.

IPLEMENTATION OF EFFECTIVE PROGRAMS

In the move from assessment to the development of effec-ve practices, two problems are immediately encountered establishing (a) criteria for defining effective edu-ational programs and (b) models for delivering the pro-ams. Regardless of the assessment data and decisions, achers need to provide appropriate instructional pro-rams to individual students. In fact, it may be argued that is step is the very essence of differential programming nd that all other issues are peripheral.

As Deno and Mirkin (1977) have noted, most of the ffective teaching research is based on group design para-igms. Though the statement may be made that certain rograms appear beneficial in improving student achieve-ent in general, no particular statement may be made bout their effectiveness with individual students. Pro-ram development must be approached as a "best guess," nd then data must be collected to confirm or disconfirm he effectiveness of a given program. This approach equires far greater emphasis on formative than on sum-native evaluation.

Current practice in delivering special education pro-rams for the mildly handicapped clearly operates on a ull-out basis in which regular education is supplanted. Though the original intent of the resource room model was o include an element of consultation, the fact remains that recious little time is left for such activities. In a recent sur-vey by Evans (1980), it was determined that less than 5% of he time was spent by resource room teachers in consul-ation, while 56% of their time was spent directly instruct-ng students.

Models of consulting teachers do exist and represent a iable alternative to the pull-out model currently used. The wo most prominent are the Vermont Consulting Teacher Knight, Meyers, Paolucci-Whitcomb, Hasazi, & Nevin, 1981) and the Consulting Teacher (Idol-Maestas, 1981, 1983). Both of these programs are based on an indirect delivery of service, through which teachers work to estab-ish effective educational programs. A considerable amount of data has been collected from both programs on components and teacher competencies as well as student outcomes.

One recent application of a variation of these models was employed in a prereferral intervention system (Graden, Casey, & Bonstrom, 1985; Graden, Casey, & Christenson, 1985). Although some success was attained in this research in reducing referrals and placements, no primary student achievement data were displayed, a lack that precludes an adequate evaluation of the program. As noted in much of the efficacy research, no information is provided about the independent variables that were manipulated in keeping students out of special education. If we are to begin developing replicable models of inter-vention, it is necessary to have adequate descriptions of their components. The research on the efficacy of special education has been, and continues to be, plagued by a lack of clearly defined treatments, including precise descrip-tions of classrooms and instructional variables (Kaufman & Alberto, 1976).

EVALUATION OF PROGRAM OUTCOMES

Problems with the inadequate utilization of assessment information exist not only in the initiation of educational programs but also in the evaluation of program effects. The two major problems in this area include: (a) a serious lack of overlap between the curriculum and content of instruction and the items included in the evaluation instru-ments (Freeman et al., 1983; Jenkins & Pany, 1978; Kni-fong, 1980); and (b) a lack of systematic data utilization strategies (Skiba, Wesson, & Deno, 1982).

An example of the first issue is provided by the Freeman et al. (1983) study, in which the investigators reviewed sev-eral major curricula and several major published tests and found that the percentage of items that were systemati-cally included in both tests and curricula was low. If test data cannot be trusted to be an adequate reflection of the content of the materials used for instruction, two serious consequences are possible from their use in evaluating pro-gram effects. The most obvious implication involves the sensitivity to change: although students may improve in terms of the content of instruction, no improvement is reflected in terms of the outcome test scores. This may be due to the limited number of items appearing on a test, both in terms of the absolute number for each skill or objec-tive and the relative number appearing in both the curricu-lum and test. The findings by Marston and Deno (1982) indicate that outcomes may be differentially affected. In this study, direct measures of student performance with curriculum-based assessments reflected significant improvement in performance, though standardized tests showed no significant gains. A more subtle problem, how-ever, involves the definition of program content. If students and, by implication, teachers are evaluated by their per-formance on published standardized tests, the focus of instruction may well be constricted to include only the con-tent of the tests rather than the content of the curriculum. Hagan (1982), in a survey of teachers, found this constric-tion to be an issue, with the potential for teachers to con-centrate their teaching primarily on test items, leaving many important skills underemphasized.

The second issue in the evaluation of programs, involv-ing the inadequate utilization of data, is difficult both to determine and to remediate. For example, in much of the research on the formative evaluation of programs that employ frequent measurements of student performance, the research is inconclusive as to whether improved out-comes are a function of the use of frequent measurements, the graphic display of the data, or the utilization of the data by the teacher. Furthermore, though decision rules have been proposed for systematizing the evaluation process (Mirkin et al., 1981; White & Haring, 1980), experimen-tal verification of the use of these rules needs to be more fully established.

A recent review of this research, though, indicated that systematic formative evaluation strategies significantly can improve school achievement (Fuchs & Fuchs, 1985). These researchers reviewed twenty-one controlled studies that evaluated the effects of formative evaluation on academic achievement and included the use of behavioral techniques, frequent measurement of student performance, graphic display of progress, and the use of evaluation techniques. The main conclusion from this analysis is that students whose programs were monitored systematically and developed formatively improved almost three quarters of a standard deviation more than students whose programs were neither monitored nor systematically developed. A significant effect was also found in the use of data evaluation rules. When teachers were required to employ decision rules in the evaluation and adjustment of programs, effect sizes were greater than with the use of informal teacher judgments.

In reviewing the formative evaluation literature, Fuch and Fuchs (1985) noted that this approach to the development of individual programs is inductive, avoiding reliance on diagnostic labels, and is assessed on technically adequate measures of achievement. A more substantive advantage relates to the focus on manipulating variables that have instructional relevance for both the student and the teacher. Rather than aptitude being measured, achievement is monitored; rather than setting being the focus, teaching procedures are manipulated.

Training Programs

Issues in Assessment

The problems in assessment training can be considered from the view of teachers and psychologists. From the former perspective, the issue of assessment training relates to the development of measurement skills, while for the latter, the issue relates to the definition of a role in which the measurement skills can be used.

As noted by Yeh et al. (1981) and Lazar-Morrison et al. (1980), teachers currently lack the skills necessary either to develop a more appropriate data base or to use much of the assessment information being generated. A survey conducted by Goslin (1967) indicated that 40% of all teachers had minimal formal training (one course). The same state of affairs exists more than 15 years later. Nearly one in four teachers surveyed by Yeh et al. (1981) had not taken a course in educational measurement. Though many authors have noted the need to increase teachers' skills in developing and applying tests and testing (Ebel, 1967; Hastings, Runkel, & Damrin, 1961), little action has occurred since these calls for change (Lazar-Morrison et al., 1980). Woelner (1979) described a national picture of teacher pre-service training and certification and found few formal requirements.

Clearly, training programs must begin providing more experiences for teachers in the development and application of appropriate assessment information. This training includes concentration on the coordination of testing with other forms of assessment and the integration of this information into program development. Different educational decisions must be considered, including screening, placement, planning, evaluation, and certification (Salvia & Ysseldyke, 1985).

In contrast to this problem, in which teachers do not have the skills and need them, school psychologists often do have the skills and do not apply them. The problem in most training programs for school psychologists is the nearly exclusive reliance on intelligence and published achievement tests as the medium for the development of skills in measurement (see the Spring issue of *School Psychology Review* [Brown, Cardon, Coulter, & Meyers, 1982]) for a comprehensive appraisal of the profession). Although clearly defined programs based on the principles and practices of measurement comprise the basis for training, most effort is directed at the application of these skills in placement decisions only (Shinn, 1986). In criticizing such practice, Shinn conceptualized the process of assessment as including the determination of program outcomes, both to determine empirically the least restrictive environment and to provide a form of nondiscriminatory assessment. Yet this direction is not possible without sensitive and sensible measurement and evaluation systems capable of providing timely information. Rather, measurement skills need to be applied to the development of more classroom-relevant assessment procedures and to the evaluation of program effects both for individuals and for groups of students. Ysseldyke (1984) proposed similar changes for school psychology programs in an effort to expand the utility of their role in making a practical difference in the programming of students.

Implementation of Effective Programs

Extremely serious problems exist in the definition of many training programs for teachers and psychologists. In many states, specialized certification programs are offered to prepare teachers to work with mildly handicapped students, such as learning disabled, educable mentally retarded, and emotionally disturbed students. In Minnesota, for example, teachers must be certified in various areas in order to work with students of similar classifications. This match between certification and classification is, however, not empirically based. In fact, in a recent study by Marston (1986), learning disabled (N = 78) and educable mentally retarded (N = 49) students were randomly assigned to be taught by teachers certified to teach either learning disabled or educable mentally retarded students. If the match between certification and classification were indeed an important variable, a two-way interaction would have been predicted. That is, learning disabled students would improve differentially more when taught by a teacher trained in learning disabilities. No such interaction, however, was found. Students in both classifications improved significantly when taught by teachers of either certification. Furthermore, no differences were found in the process of instruction between the wo groups of teachers. Based on systematic observations of instruction—the Structure of Instruction Rating Scales SIRS) (Deno, King, Skiba, Sevcik, & Wesson, 1983) and CISSAR (Stanley & Greenwood, 1981)—no significant differences were found in many important classroom behaviors. In summary, the certification of teachers in specialized areas is not supported by practice in the field.

The question of certification may also be addressed by comparing the differential training of regular and special education teachers. In a recent position paper, Stainback and Stainback (1984) called for the merger of special and regular education. In response, Lieberman (1985) agreed with the position but stated that such a move was not realistic. Indeed, the irony in the current situation is that, given the lack of difference between special and regular education in the schools, in the definition of treatment and in outcomes attained, no need exists to merge them except in name and budget. They are already quite indistinguishable in practice.

Yet the training programs for special and regular education are often quite distinct from one another. Smith (1982) reported that 71% of the forty-eight states responding to a survey did not require regular classroom teachers to complete courses in special education to meet initial certification requirements; 92% did not require special education course work for recertification. Yet, in an analysis of policy that fosters integration of severely handicapped students, Brinker and Thorpe (1985) found that an integrative model was characterized by regular education foundations for special education certification and special education foundations for regular education certification. The important issue in restructuring training programs is to expose teachers to the full range of student performance, competencies, and skills in an effort to increase tolerance to individual differences and skill in developing programs in response to this diversity (Gerber & Semmel, 1984; Hersh & Walker, 1983).

Evaluation of Program Outcomes

More emphasis must be placed in training programs on the development of applied research skills to provide teachers with the necessary tools for evaluating program outcomes. The most immediately applied and direct training may be in the use of single-subject methodology (Sulzer-Azaroff & Mayer, 1977; Tawney & Gast, 1984). The focus of this evaluation paradigm is on the formative evaluation of program components to define functional relationships between instructional variables and performance outcomes (Dunst, 1979).

This methodology is particularly well suited as a response to the proposal by a National Academy of Sciences panel (Messick, 1984), in which assessment is viewed in the larger context of program development and evaluation. In their recommendations, a two-phase assessment process is described as including first, prior to any attempt at diagnosing disorders within the child, a systematic examination of the learning environment and the quality of instruction in the regular classroom. The second phase of diagnosis, involving the comprehensive assessment of within-child characteristics, is conducted only after the first phase is complete.

The panel further specified that the assessment of learning environments should include four components: (a) documentation that a school is applying procedures and practices known to be effective and supported by research; (b) observation that a student has indeed been adequately exposed to a program; (c) collection of data that indicate the student has not learned what has been taught; and, most important, (d) specification of systematic attempts to modify the content and format of instruction. This procedural schema entails a data collection system that focuses both on the precise specification of the independent variable and on the formative evaluation of outcomes (Tindal & Marston, 1985). This is also clearly the area in which the foci of research and practice are convergent, both in content and in design. Interestingly, this procedural schema has not yet been accomplished in research (Gersten, 1985), let alone in practice.

In the first component, applying procedures that have known effects, much of the process–product research cited in this chapter provides the necessary first step. Continued effort must be directed at the precise specification of curriculum materials, classroom context variables, and interactive teaching behaviors. It will include a major investment in the development of technically adequate and sensitive observation systems for assaying instructional environments. Furthermore, these systems must have high utility and a potential for immediate and reasonable application rather than a focus on basic research. This requires considerable validation research in the initial phases, followed by a program of logistics research.

The second component, involving a focus on student exposure to instructional content, must continually operate from a mastery model (Bloom, 1976). This means that time may need to be manipulated, rather than being maintained as fixed, in moving students through programs. The entire practice of grouping students within instructional groups and grades may have to change, as in the ALEM, in which students from different grades are instructed in the same material. The definition of adequate exposure must move to an empirical definition, not an a priori assumption.

The third component, the collection of data and the measurement of effects on student performance, constitutes the only and ultimate empirical basis of evaluating achievement. This necessitates that program evaluation be conducted more formally and regularly than is currently the case. The development of technically adequate measurement systems that are sensitive to changes in student performance must replace the current system of published achievement testing. A model having great application for such formative evaluation has been described by Deno, Marston, and Mirkin (1982); Deno, Mirkin, and Chiang (1982); and Deno, Mirkin, Lowry, and Kuehnle (1981).

Finally, the systematic modifications called for in the fourth component must be not only defined but also implemented with integrity. The procedures explicated by

Deno and Mirkin (1977) and Kazdin and Wilson (1978) provide a conceptual and operational basis for the implementation of such a model. This component naturally must relate back to the earlier issues in the form of a feedback loop. Obviously, the focus of this modification must be on variables highly relevant to teacher behaviors. As noted in the literature on efficacy research, setting does not appear to be a relevant variable.

Social Policy and Funding

At the very center of the controversy are the regulations supporting most current practice. At issue here is the manner in which funds are allocated and programs are administered. Considerable need exists for restructuring the entire delivery of special education programs (see the chapter by Reynolds & Lakin in this volume, and Reynolds & Wang, 1983).

Issues in Assessment

The most fundamental change may be the need to cease the current classification system, which focuses on within-child categories, and to begin funding programs based on the need for resources. As Reynolds and Lakin (see their chapter in this volume) have noted, although classification systems are meant to provide information regarding the etiology, prognosis, and prescription of treatments, the current system for classifying mildly handicapped students provides no such information relevant to these issues. Furthermore, the yoking of funding to child counts establishes a bounty system that generates an active search for students with mildly handicapping conditions and creates conditions antithetical to the establishment of proactive and successful programs (Wang & Reynolds, 1985). In this example given by Wang and Reynolds, a program with established success was removed from a school because it lowered the child count and therefore reduced funds. Though the school administration had been supportive of the instructional model, the current funding system does not support success.

The importance of state policy and its influence on practice was underscored by the recent finding by Noel and Fuller (1985) that the identification rates of handicapped students are influenced considerably by state and local educational expenditures. Another relevant finding, reported by Brinker and Thorpe (1985), is that state policy also affects the amount of integration experienced by severely handicapped students. Both of these studies clearly indicate that policy is indeed an important variable in the assessment, identification, and placement of students.

Change in policy and funding quite likely requires revamping not only the content but also the format of assessment practices. Instead of looking at within-child characteristics, assessors would focus on the content of instruction (Engelmann et al., 1979) over time (Tindal & Marston, 1985). At present, virtually no substantive attention is directed at the instructional environment, and assessment stops at the time students are placed in programs. However, if one views assessment broadly as the collection of information pertinent to the development of effective programs (Salvia & Ysseldyke, 1985), it is neither necessary nor desirable to confine it restrictively to the administration of tests prior to placement in special education.

In this form of assessment, which moves beyond the testing of students at the time of referral only, the idea of zero reject (Lilly, 1971) may truly be attained. Once a student is enrolled in a regular education program, it is impossible to remove him or her. In this proposal, regular education teachers assume the responsibility for remediating students' deficits, rather than passing off students to support specialists. Assessment is not conducted to determine placement; rather, the focus of assessment is on the development of effective programs. Students are not removed from regular education environments; rather, support services are provided by specialists in regular classrooms.

Implementation of Effective Programs

This format of assessment, in which learning environments are observed, strong instructional programs are implemented, and student performance is monitored, is strikingly similar to the manner in which research is conducted and would serve to bridge the gap between research and service. As Reynolds and Lakin (see their chapter in this volume) have suggested, it is important that schools be encouraged to investigate and to implement various practices. This process can only be accomplished if greater priority is placed on planned variation and less on compliance with limited and prescribed procedures. Reynolds and Lakin proposed a concept in which schools would be provided an experimental waiver during which time alternative procedures would be implemented and evaluated. The advantage to this approach is that an empirical basis can be established for developing the least restrictive environment for individual students.

Evaluation of Program Outcomes

To extend this concept further, schools should direct their investigations toward the cost-effectiveness of various practices in a way similar to the report by Levin, Glass, and Meister (1984). In this investigation, four different educational models were compared on two dimensions: (a) outcome on student performance and (b) cost in implementation. Using both pieces of information, the investigators established a cost-per-pupil ratio. The important application of this model is that schools need to be sensitive to both dimensions.

Finally, the most important proposal is to adopt a posture in the schools of maintaining only those programs that have been deemed effective. Although Project Follow Through was funded for several years, little impact has been made on the systematic delivery and evaluation of educational programs. The format for funding this type of search needs to be maintained, however, and insti-tionalized, including both the idea of planned variation d the systematic evaluation of outcomes. This procedure ould encourage schools to engage in constructive search and to support the evaluation of programs.

Conclusion

Little evidence exists supporting the efficacy of special lucation or the development of differential programs as a sult of the assessment-placement process. Presently, pro-rams for students with mildly handicapping conditions pically are implemented independently of assessment formation, irrespectively of less restrictive educational ptions, and entirely without regard to empirical out-mes. The major problems appear to be a lack of attention (a) developing sensitive dependent measures, (b) pre-sely describing instructional strategies, and (c) ensuring e integrity of their delivery. While limitations are appar-nt in methodology, the most serious shortcoming is in the cus of research.

As Millazzo (1970) has noted, "The issue of the efficacy f special classes is a dead one . . . we should give it a nice ineral" (p. 9). It is important in the development of future esearch that attention be directed toward variables that re functionally important in modifying student achieve-ient. This redirection of focus may be in the process and utcomes of the assessment phase, the development of ffective programs, and the evaluation of outcomes. Effort iust be directed at the development of systems for meas-ring the implementation of instruction and the conse-uent evaluation of effects. The important point is that hese two issues must be investigated as covariates, with ach variable considered in relation to, not independent of, he other variable.

Author Information

Susan Epps is Assistant Professor at the University of Oregon, Division of Counseling and Educational Psy-chology, School Psychology Program. Gerald Tindal is Assistant Professor at the University of Oregon, Division of Teacher Education, Mildly Handicapped Program.

References

Angoff, W. H. (1971). Scales, norms, and equivalent scores. In R. L. Thorndike (Ed.), *Educational measurement* (2nd ed.) (pp. 508–600). Washington, DC: American Council on Education.

Arter, J. A., & Jenkins, J. R. (1979). Differential diagnosis-prescriptive teaching: A critical appraisal. *Review of Educational Research*, **49**, 517–556.

Becker, W. C., Engelmann, S., Carnine, D. W., & Rhine, W. R. (1981). Direct Instruction Model. In W. R. Rhine (Ed.), *Making schools more effective: New directions from Follow Through* (pp. 95–154). New York: Academic Press.

Berliner, D. C. (1983). Developing conceptions of classroom environments: Some light on the T in classroom studies of ATI. *Educational Psychologist*, **18**, 1–13.

Bersoff, D. N., Kabler, M., Fiscus, E., & Ankney, R. (1972). Effectiveness of special class placement for children labeled neurologically handicapped. *Journal of School Psychology*, **10**, 157–163.

Bixler, H. H., Hildreth, G. H., Lund, K. W., & Wrightstone, J. W. (1965). *Metropolitan Achievement Tests*. New York: Harcourt, Brace & World.

Blatt, B. (1958). The physical, personality, and academic status of children who are mentally retarded attending special classes as compared with children who are mentally retarded attending regular classes. *American Journal of Mental Deficiency*, **62**, 810–818.

Bloom, B. (1976). *Human characteristics and school learning*. New York: McGraw-Hill.

Borich, G. D. (1979). Implications for developing teacher competencies from process-product research. *Journal of Teacher Education*, **30**(1), 77–86.

Brinker, R. P., & Thorpe, M. E. (1985). Some empirically derived hypotheses about the influence of state policy on degree of integration of severely handicapped students. *Remedial and Special Education*, **6**, 18–26.

Brophy, J. E. (1979). Teacher behavior and its effects. *Journal of Educational Psychology*, **71**, 733–750.

Brophy, J. (1982). How teachers influence what is taught and learned in classrooms. *Elementary School Journal*, **83**, 1–13.

Brophy, J., & Good, T. L. (1986). Teacher behavior and student achievement. In M. C. Wittrock (Ed.), *Handbook of research on teaching* (3rd ed.) (pp. 328–375). Washington, DC: American Educational Research Association.

Brown, F. G. (1970). *Principles of educational and psychological testing*. Hinsdale, IL: Dryden.

Brown, D. T., Cardon, B. W., Coulter, W. A., & Meyers, S. (Eds.). (1982). The Olympia proceedings [Special Issue]. *School Psychology Review*, **11**(2).

Budoff, M., & Gottlieb, J. (1976). Special-class EMR children mainstreamed: A study of an aptitude (learning potential) × treatment interaction. *American Journal of Mental Deficiency*, **81**, 1–11.

Burnstein, L., & Guiton, G. W. (1984). Methodological perspectives on documenting program impact. In B. K. Keogh (Ed.), *Advances in special education* (Vol. 4, pp. 21–42). Greenwich, CT: JAI Press.

Campbell, D. T. (1969). Reforms as experiments. *American Psychologist*, **24**, 409–429.

Campbell, D. T., & Stanley, J. C. (1963). *Experimental and quasi-experimental designs for research*. Chicago, IL: Rand McNally.

Carlberg, C., & Kavale, K. (1980). The efficacy of special versus regular class placement for exceptional children: A meta-analysis. *Journal of Special Education*, **14**, 295–309.

Carnine, D. (1984). Direct instruction: In search of instructional solutions for educational problems. In D. Carnine, D. Elkind, A. Hendrickson, D. Meichenbaum, R. Sieben, & F. Smith (Eds.), *Interdisciplinary voices in learning disabilities and remedial education* (pp. 1–66). Austin, TX: Pro-Ed.

Carnine, D., & Silbert, J. (1979). *Direct instruction reading*. Columbus, OH: Merrill.

Caroll, A. W. (1967). The effects of segregated and partially integrated school programs on self-concept and academic achievement of educable mentally retardates. *Exceptional Children*, **34**, 93–99.

Cartwright, G. P., Cartwright, C. A., & Ward, M. E. (1984). *Educating special learners* (2nd ed.). Belmont, CA: Wadsworth.

Cegelka, W. J., & Tyler, J. L. (1970). The efficacy of special class placement for the mentally retarded in proper perspectives. *Training School Bulletin*, **67**, 33–68.

Confrey, J., & Good, T. (1981). *Academic progress: Student and teacher perspectives* (Research proposal). East Lansing, MI: Michigan State University, Institute for Research on Teaching.

Connolly, A., Nachtman, W., & Pritchett, E. (1971). *Manual for the Key Math Diagnostic Arithmetic Test*. Circle Pines, MN: American Guidance Service.

Cook, T. D., & Campbell, D. T. (1979). *Quasi-experimentation: Design and analysis issues for field settings*. Chicago, IL: Rand McNally.

Cooper, H. M. (1982). Scientific guidelines for conducting integrative research reviews. *Review of Educational Research*, **52**, 291–302.

Corman, L., & Gottlieb, J. (1978). Mainstreaming mentally retarded children: A review of research. In N. R. Ellis (Ed.), *International review of research in mental retardation* (Vol. 9, pp. 251–275). New York: Academic Press.

Cronbach, L. J., & Snow, R. E. (1977). *Aptitudes and instructional methods: A handbook for research on interactions*. New York: Irvington.

Denham, C., & Lieberman, A. (1980). *Time to learn*. Washington, DC: National Institute of Education.

Deno, S., King, R., Skiba R., Sevcik, B., & Wesson, C. (1983). *The Structure of Instruction Rating Scale (SIRS): Development technical characteristics* (Research Rep. No. 107). Minneapolis, MN: University of Minnesota, Institute for Research on Learning Disabilities.

Deno, S., Marston, D., & Mirkin, P. (1982). Valid measurement procedures for continuous evaluation of written expression. *Exceptional Children*, **48**, 368–371.

Deno, S., & Mirkin, P. (1977). *Data based program modification: A manual*. Minneapolis, MN: University of Minnesota, Leadership Training Institute.

Deno, S., Mirkin, P., & Chiang, B. (1982). Identifying valid measures of reading. *Exceptional Children*, **49**, 36–45.

Deno, S., Mirkin, P., Lowry, L., & Kuehnle, K. (1981). *Relationships among simple measures of spelling and performance on standardized achievement tests* (Research Rep. No. 21). Minneapolis, MN: University of Minnesota, Institute for Research on Learning Disabilities.

Deno, S., Mirkin, P., & Shinn, M. (1978). Behavioral perspectives on the assessment of learning disabled children. In J. Ysseldyke (Ed.), *Synthesis of the knowledge base: Identification and assessment of learning disabled children* (Monograph No. 2). Minneapolis, MN: University of Minnesota, Institute for Research on Learning Disabilities.

Dunn, L. M., & Markwardt, F. C. (1970). *Peabody Individual Achievement Test*. Circle Pines, MN: American Guidance Service.

Dunst, C. (1979). Program Evaluation and the Education for All Handicapped Children Act. *Exceptional Children*, **12**, 24–31.

Durkin, D. (1979). Reading comprehension instruction. *Reading Research Quarterly*, **4**, 481–533.

Durkin, M. J., & Biddle, B. J. (1974). *The study of teaching*. New York: Holt, Rinehart & Winston.

Ebel, R. L. (1967). Improving the competence of teachers in educational measurement. In J. Flynn & H. Garber (Eds.), *Assessing behavior: Readings in educational and psychological measurement* (pp. 171–182). Reading, M Addison-Wesley.

Elenbogen, M. L. (1957). A comparative study of some aspects academic and social adjustment of two groups of mental retarded children in special classes and in regular class (Doctoral dissertation, Northwestern University, 1957 *Dissertation Abstracts*, **17**, 2496.

Engelmann, S. (1980). *Direct instruction*. Englewood Cliffs, N Educational Technology Publications.

Engelmann, S., & Bruner, E. C. (1974). *DISTAR Reading* Chicago, IL: Science Research Associates.

Engelmann, S., & Carnine, D. (1982). *Theory of instructio Principles and applications*. New York: Irvington.

Engelmann, S., Granzin, A., & Severson, H., (1979). Diagnosir instruction. *Journal of Special Education*, **13**, 355–363.

Engelmann, S., Johnson, G., Becker, W., Meyers, L., Carnine, D & Becker, J. (1978). *Decoding strategies: Corrective rea ing*. Chicago, IL: Science Research Associates.

Englert, C. S. (1983). Measuring special education teacher effe tiveness. *Exceptional Children*, **50**, 247–254.

Englert, C. S., & Sugai, G. (1981). *Direct Instruction Obse vation System (DIOS)*. Lexington, KY: University c Kentucky.

Epps, S., Thompson, B. J., & Lane, M. P. (1985). *Procedures fc incorporating generalization and maintenance program ming into interventions for special-education students*. De Moines, IA: Department of Public Instruction.

Epps, S., Ysseldyke, J. E., & Algozzine, B. (1983). Impact of di ferent definitions of learning disabilities on the number c students identified. *Journal of Psychoeducational Assess ment*, **1**, 341–352.

Epps, S., Ysseldyke, J. E., & Algozzine, B. (1985). An analysis c the conceptual framework underlying definitions of learnin disabilities. *Journal of School Psychology*, **23**, 133–144.

Evans, S. (1980). The consultant role of the resource teacher *Exceptional Children*, **46**, 402–403.

Eysenck, H. J. (1984). Meta-analysis: An abuse of research inte gration. *Journal of Special Education*, **18**, 41–59.

Finn, J. D., & Resnick, L. B. (1984). Issues in the instruction o mildly mentally retarded children. *Educational Researcher* **13**(3), 9–11.

Fisher, C. W., & Berliner, D. C. (1985). *Perspectives on instructional time*. White Plains, NY: Longman.

Flanagan, J. C. (1951). Units, scores, and norms. In E. F. Lindquist (Ed.), *Educational measurement* (pp. 695–763) Washington, DC: American Council on Education.

Franklin, G. S., & Sparkman, W. E. (1978). The cost effectiveness of two program delivery systems for exceptional children. *Journal of Education Finance*, **3**, 305–314.

Freeman, D. J., Kuhs, T. M., Porter, A. C., Floden, R. E., Schmidt, W. H., & Schwille, J. R. (1983). Do textbooks and tests define a national curriculum in elementary school mathematics? *Elementary School Journal*, **83**, 501–513.

Fuchs, L., & Fuchs, D. (1985, April). *Effects of systematic formative evaluation: A meta-analysis*. Paper presented at the meeting of the American Educational Research Association, Chicago, IL.

Gerber, M. M., & Semmel, M. I. (1984). Teacher as imperfect test: Reconceptualizing the referral process. *Educational Psychologist*, **19**, 137–148.

Gersten, R. (1985). Direct instruction with special education students: A review of evaluation research. *Journal of Special Education*, **19**, 41–58.

Gilmore, J. V., & Gilmore, E. C. (1968). *Gilmore Oral Reading Test*. New York: Harcourt, Brace, Jovanovich.

Glaser, R. (1977). *Adaptive education: Individual diversity and learning.* New York: Holt, Rinehart & Winston.

Glass, G. V. (1976). Primary, secondary, and meta-analysis of research. *Educational Researcher,* **5**(10), 3–8.

Glass, G. V. (1977). Integrating findings: The meta-analysis of research. *Review of Research in Education,* **5**, 351–379.

Glavin, J. P. (1973). Follow-up behavioral research in resource rooms. *Exceptional Children,* **40**, 211–213.

Glavin, J. P. (1974). Behaviorally oriented resource rooms: A follow-up. *Journal of Special Education,* **8**, 337–347.

Glavin, J. P., Quay, H. C., Annesley, R. F., & Werry, J. S. (1971). An experimental resource room for behavioral problem children. *Exceptional Children,* **38**, 131–137.

Goldstein, H., Moss, J. W., & Jordan, L. J. (1965). *The efficacy of special class training on the development of mentally retarded children* (Cooperative Research Project Report No. 619). Urbana, IL: University of Illinois, Institute for Research on Exceptional Children. (ERIC Document Reproduction Service No. ED 002 907)

Good, T. L. (1983). Classroom research: A decade of progress. *Educational Psychologist,* **18**, 127–144.

Good, T. L., & Grouws, D. A. (1975). Teacher rapport: Some stability data. *Journal of Educational Psychology,* **67**, 179–182.

Good, T. L., Grouws, D. A., & Ebmeier, H. (1983). *Active mathematics teaching.* New York: Longman.

Goslin, D. A. (1967). *Teachers and testing.* New York: The Russel Sage Foundation.

Graden, J. L., Casey, A., & Bonstrom, O. (1985). Implementing a prereferral intervention system: Part II. The data. *Exceptional Children,* **51**, 487–496.

Graden, J. L., Casey, A., & Christenson, S. L. (1985). Implementing a prereferral intervention system: Part I. The model. *Exceptional Children,* **51**, 377–384.

Greenwood, C. R., Delquadri, J. C., Stanley, S. O., Terry, B., & Hall, R. V. (1982). *Relationships among instructional contexts, student behavior, and academic achievement.* Unpublished manuscript, No. 81–081, University of Kansas, Department of Special Education and Human Development, Kansas City, KS.

Guskin, S. L. (1984). Problems and promises of meta-analysis in special education. *Journal of Special Education,* **18**, 73–80.

Guskin, S., & Spicker, H. (1968). Educational research in mental retardation. In N. O. Ellis (Ed.), *International review of mental retardation* (Vol. 3, pp. 217–278). New York: Academic Press.

Hagan, R. D. (1982). Factors influencing arithmetic performance on the Tennessee state-mandated eighth grade basic skills test. *School Science and Mathematics,* **82**, 490–505.

Hall, G. E., & Loucks, S. F. (1977). A developmental model for determining whether the treatment is actually implemented. *American Educational Research Journal,* **14**, 263–276.

Haring, N. G., & Krug, D. A. (1975). Placement in regular programs: Procedures and results. *Exceptional Children,* **41**, 413–417.

Hastings, J. T., Runkel, P. J., & Damrin, E. E. (1961). *Effects on use of tests by teachers trained in a summer institute.* Urbana, IL: University of Illinois, Bureau of Educational Research.

Haynes, M. C., & Jenkins, J. R. (1984). *Reading instruction in special education resource rooms.* Unpublished manuscript, University of Washington, Seattle.

Heller, K. A. (1982). Effects of special education placement on educable mentally retarded children. In K. A. Heller, W. H. Holtzman, & S. Messick, (Eds.), *Placing children in special education: A strategy for equity* (pp. 262–299). Washington, DC: National Academy Press.

Heller, K. A., Holtzman, W. H., & Messick, S. (1982). *Placing children in special education: A strategy for equity.* Washington, DC: National Academy Press.

Hersh, R. H., & Walker, H. M. (1983). Great expectations: Making schools effective for all students. *Policy Studies Review,* **2**, 147–188.

Idol-Maestas, L. (1981). A teacher training model: The resource/consulting teacher. *Behavioral Disorders,* **6**, 108–121.

Idol-Maestas, L. (1983). *Special educator's consultation handbook.* Rockville, MD: Aspen Systems.

Jastak, J. F., & Jastak, S. R. (1965). *The Wide Range Achievement Test,* Wilmington, DE: Guidance Associates.

Jenkins, J. R., & Mayhall, W. J. (1976). Development and evaluation of a resource teacher program. *Exceptional Children,* **43**, 21–29.

Jenkins, J. R., & Pany, D. (1978). Standardized achievement tests: How useful for special education? *Exceptional Children,* **44**, 448–453.

Johnson, D. W., Maruyama, G., Johnson, R., Nelson, D., & Skon, L. (1981). Effects of cooperative, competitive, and individualistic goal structures on achievement: A meta-analysis. *Psychological Bulletin,* **89**, 47–62.

Jones, R. L., Gottlieb, J., Guskin, S., & Yoshida, R. (1978). Evaluating mainstreaming programs: Models, caveats, considerations, and guidelines. *Exceptional Children,* **44**, 588–601.

Kaufman, M. E., & Alberto, P. A. (1976). Research on efficacy of special education for the mentally retarded. In N. R. Ellis (Ed.), *International review of research in mental retardation* (Vol. 8., pp. 225–255). New York: Academic Press.

Kaufman, M. J., Gottlieb, J., Agard, J. A., & Kukic, M. B. (1975). Mainstreaming: Toward an explication of the construct. In E. Meyen, G. Vergason, & R. Whelan (Eds.), *Alternatives for teaching exceptional children* (pp. 35–54). Denver, CO: Love.

Kazdin, A., & Wilson, T. (1978). *Evaluation of behavior therapy: Issues, evidence, and research strategies.* Lincoln, NE: University of Nebraska Press.

Knifong, J. D. (1980). Computational requirements of standardized word problem tests. *Journal of Research in Mathematics Foundation,* **11**, 3–9.

Knight, M. F., Meyers, H. W., Paolucci-Whitcomb, P., Hasazi, S. E., & Nevin, A. (1981). A four year evaluation of consulting teacher service. *Behavioral Disorders,* **6**, 92–100.

Lakin, K. C. (1983). A response to Gene V. Glass. *Policy Studies Review,* **2**, 233–240.

Lazar-Morrison, C., Polin, L., Moy, R., & Burry, J. (1980). *A review of the literature on test use* (CSE Report No. 144). Los Angeles, CA: University of California, Center for the Study of Evaluation.

Leinhardt, G., & Pallay, A. (1982). Restrictive educational settings: Exile or haven? *Review of Educational Research,* **52**, 557–578.

Leinhardt, G., & Seewald, A. M. (1981). Overlap: What's tested, what's taught. *Journal of Educational Measurement,* **18**, 85–96.

Leinhardt, G., Zigmond, N., & Cooley, W. W. (1981). Reading instruction and its effects. *American Educational Research Journal,* **18**, 343–361.

Levin, H. M., Glass, G. V., & Meister, G. R. (1984). *Cost-effectiveness of four educational interventions* (Project Report No. 84–811). Stanford, CA: Stanford University School of

Education, Institute for Research on Educational Finance and Governance.

Lilly, M. S. (1971). A training based model for special education. *Exceptional Children*, **37**, 745–749.

MacMillan, D. L., & Semmel, M. I. (1977). Evaluation of mainstreaming programs. *Focus on Exceptional Children*, **9**, 1–14.

Marshall, H. H. (1981). Open classrooms: Has the term outlived its usefulness? *Review of Educational Research*, **51**, 181–192.

Marston, D. (1986). Does categorical teacher certification benefit the mildly handicapped child? *Exceptional Children*, **53**, 423–431.

Marston, D., & Deno, S. (1982). *Implementation of direct and repeated measurement in the school setting* (Research Report No. 106). Minneapolis, MN: University of Minnesota, Institute for Research on Learning Disabilities.

Medley, D. M. (1979). The effectiveness of teachers. In P. L. Peterson & H. J. Walberg (Eds.), *Research on teaching: Concepts, findings, and implications* (pp. 11–27). Berkeley, CA: McCutchan.

Messick, S. (1984). Assessment in context: Appraising student performance in relation to instructional quality. *Educational Researcher*, **13**(3), 3–8.

Milazzo, T. C. (1970). *Special class placement or how to destroy in the name of help*. Paper presented at the 48th annual international convention of the Council for Exceptional Children, Chicago, IL. (ERIC Document Reproduction Service No. ED 039 383)

Mullen, F., & Itkin, W. (1961). The value of special classes for the mentally handicapped. *Chicago Schools Journal*, **42**, 353–363.

Myers, J. K. (1976). The efficacy of the special day school for EMR pupils. *Mental Retardation*, **14**(4), 3–11.

Noel, M. M., & Fuller, B. C. (1985). The social policy construction of special education: The impact of state characteristics on identification and integration of handicapped children. *Remedial and Special Education*, **6**, 27–35.

Nurss, J. R., & McGauvran, M. E. (1976). *Metropolitan Readiness Tests, teacher's manual, Part II: Interpretation and use of test results (Level II)*. New York: Harcourt, Brace, Jovanovich.

O'Leary, K. D., Kaufmann, K. F., Kass, R. E., & Drabman, R. S. (1970). The effects of loud and soft reprimands on the behavior of disruptive students. *Exceptional Children*, **37**, 145–155.

O'Leary, S. G., & Schneider, M. R. (1977). Special class placement for conduct problem children. *Exceptional Children*, **44**, 24–30.

Peterson, P. L. (1979). Direct instruction reconsidered. In P. L. Peterson & H. J. Walberg (Eds.), *Research on teaching: Concepts, findings, and implications* (pp. 57–69). Berkeley, CA: McCutchan.

Peterson, L., Homer, A. L., & Wonderlich, S. A. (1982). The integrity of independent variables in behavior analysis. *Journal of Applied Behavior Analysis*, **15**, 477–492.

Polloway, E. A. (1984). The integration of mildly retarded students in the schools: A historical review. *Remedial and Special Education*, **5**(4), 18–28.

Quay, H. C., Glavin, J. P., Annesley, F. R., & Werry, J. S. (1972). The modification of problem behavior and academic achievement in a resource room. *Journal of School Psychology*, **10**, 187–198.

Quay, H. C., & Peterson, D. R. (1967). *Manual for the Behavioral Problem Checklist*. Unpublished manuscript, University of Illinois.

Reschly, D. J. (1984). Beyond IQ test bias: The National Academy Panel's analysis of minority EMR overrepresentation. *Educational Researcher*, **13**(3), 15–19.

Reynolds, M. C. (1984). Classification of students with handicaps. In E. W. Gordon (Ed.), *Review of research in education* (Vol. 11, pp. 63–92). Washington, DC: American Educational Research Association.

Reynolds, M. C., & Birch, J. W. (1982). *Teaching exceptional children in all America's schools* (rev. ed.). Reston, VA: Council for Exceptional Children.

Reynolds, M. C., & Wang, M. C. (1983). Restructuring "special" school programs. *Policy Studies Review*, **2**, 189–212.

Rosenshine, B. V. (1979). Content, time, and direct instruction. In P. L. Peterson & H. J. Walberg (Eds.), *Research on teaching: Concepts, findings, and implications* (pp. 28–56). Berkeley, CA: McCutchan.

Rosenshine, B., & Furst, N. (1973). The use of direct observation to study teaching. In R. Travers (Ed.), *The second handbook of research on teaching* (pp. 122–183). Boston, MA: Rand McNally.

Rudman, H. C., Kelly, J. L., Wanous, D. S., Mehrens, W. A. Clark, C. M., & Porter, A. C. (1980). *Integrating assessment with instruction: A review (1922–1980)* (Research Series No 75). East Lansing, MI: Michigan State University, Institute for Research on Teaching.

Sabatino, D. A. (1971). An evaluation of resource rooms for children with learning disabilities. *Journal of Learning Disabilities*, **4**(2), 27–35.

Salvia, J., & Hunt, F. M. (1984). Measurement considerations in program evaluation. In B. K. Keogh (Ed.), *Advances in special education* (Vol. 4, pp. 43–68). Greenwich, CT: JAI Press.

Salvia, J., & Ysseldyke, J. E. (1985). *Assessment in special and remedial education* (3rd ed.). Boston, MA: Houghton Mifflin.

Semmel, M. I., Gottlieb, J., & Robinson, N. M. (1979). Mainstreaming: Perspectives on educating handicapped children in the public school. In D. C. Berliner (Ed.), *Review of research in education* (pp. 223–279). Washington, DC: American Educational Research Association.

Sheehan, R., & Keogh, B. K. (1981). Strategies for documenting progress of handicapped children in early education programs. *Educational Evaluation and Policy Analysis*, **3**, 59–69.

Sheehan, R., & Keogh, B. K. (1984). Approaches to evaluation in special education. In B. K. Keogh (Ed.), *Advances in special education* (Vol. 4, pp. 1–20). Greenwich, CT: JAI Press.

Shinn, M. (1986). Does anyone care what happens after the refer-test-place process? A systematic evaluation of special education. *School Psychology Review*, **15**, 49–58.

Silbert, J., Carnine, D., & Stein, M. (1981). *Direct instruction mathematics*. Columbus, OH: Merrill.

Sindelar, P. T., & Deno, S. L. (1978). The effectiveness of resource programming. *Journal of Special Education*, **12**, 17–28.

Skiba, R., Wesson, C., & Deno, S. L. (1982). *The effects of training teachers in the use of formative evaluation in reading: An experimental-control comparison* (Research Rep. No. 88). Minneapolis, MN: University of Minnesota, Institute for Research on Learning Disabilities.

Slosson, R. L. (1963). *Slosson Oral Reading Test*. East Aurora, NY: Slosson Educational Publications.

Smith, H. W., & Kennedy, W. A. (1967). Effects of three educational programs on mentally retarded children. *Perceptual and Motor Skills*, **24**, 174.

Smith, L. (1982). *A procedure for determining inservice training needs of regular classroom teachers in a mainstreaming approach to the education of the mildly handicapped.* Unpublished doctoral dissertation, University of Oregon, Eugene, OR.

Stainback, W., & Stainback S. (1984). A rationale for the merger of special and regular education. *Exceptional Children,* **51**, 102–111.

Stanley, S. O., & Greenwood, C. R. (1980). CISSAR: *Code for Instructional Structure and Student Academic Response: Observer's manual.* Kansas City, KS: University of Kansas, Bureau of Child Research, Juniper Garden Children's Project.

Stanley, S. O., & Greenwood, C. R. (1981). *Assessing opportunity to respond in classroom environments through direct observation: How much "opportunity to respond" does the minority disadvantaged student receive in school?* Unpublished manuscript, University of Kansas, Department of Special Education and Human Development, Kansas City, KS.

Stanton, J. E., & Cassidy, V. M. (1964). Effectiveness of special classes for educable mentally retarded. *Mental Retardation,* **2**(1), 8–13.

Stebbins, L. B., St. Pierre, R. G., Proper, E. C., Anderson, R. B., & Cerva, T. R. (1977). *Education as experimentation: A planned variation model* (Vol. IV). Cambridge, MA: Abt Associates.

Stetz, F., & Beck, M. (1979). *Comments from the classroom: Teachers' and students' opinions of achievement tests.* Paper presented at the meeting of the American Educational Research Association, San Francisco, CA.

Stevens, R., & Rosenshine, B. (1981). Advances in research on teaching. *Exceptional Education Quarterly,* **2**(1), 1–10.

Stokes, T. F., & Baer, D. M. (1977). An implicit technology of generalization. *Journal of Applied Behavior Analysis,* **10**, 349–367.

Sulzer-Azaroff, B., & Mayer, G. R. (1977). *Applying behavior analysis procedures with children and youth.* New York: Holt, Rinehart & Winston.

Tawney, J. W., & Gast, D. L. (1984). *Single subject research in special education.* Columbus, OH: Merrill.

Terman, L. M., & Merrill, M. A. (1960). *Stanford-Binet Intelligence Scale* (rev. ed.) Boston, MA: Houghton Mifflin.

Thurlow, M. L., Graden, J., Greener, J. W., & Ysseldyke, J. E. (1982). *Academic responding time for LD and non-LD students* (Research Rep. No. 72). Minneapolis, MN: University of Minnesota, Institute for Research on Learning Disabilities.

Thurlow, M. L., & Ysseldyke, J. E. (1980). *Instructional planning: Information collected by school psychologists vs. information considered useful by teachers* (Research Rep. No. 29). Minneapolis, MN: University of Minnesota, Institute for Research on Learning Disabilities.

Thurlow, M. L., & Ysseldyke, J. E. (1983). *Identification/classification research: An integrative summary of findings* (Research Rep. No. 142). Minneapolis, MN: University of Minnesota, Institute for Research on Learning Disabilities.

Thurlow, M. L., Ysseldyke, J. E., Graden, J., Greener, J. W., & Mecklenberg, C. (1982). *Academic responding time for LD students receiving different levels of special education services* (Research Rep. No. 78). Minneapolis, MN: University of Minnesota, Institute for Research on Learning Disabilities.

Thurston, L. L., & Thurston, T. G. (1962). *Primary Mental Abilities Test.* Chicago, IL: Science Research Associates.

Tiegs, E. W., & Clarke, W. W. (1970). *California Achievement Test.* Monterey, CA: CTB/McGraw-Hill.

Tindal, G. (1985). Investigating the effectiveness of special education: An analysis of methodology. *Journal of Learning Disabilities,* **18**, 101–112.

Tindal, G., & Marston, D. (1985). Approaches to assessment. In J. Torgeson & B. Wong (Eds.), *Psychological and educational perspectives on learning disabilities* (pp. 54–84). New York: Academic Press.

Tucker, J. A. (1980). Ethnic proportions in classes for the learning disabled: Issues in nonbiased assessment. *Journal of Special Education,* **14**, 93–105.

United States Department of Education. (1980). *Second annual report to Congress on the implementation of Public Law 94–142: The Education for All Handicapped Children Act.* Washington, DC: U.S. Office of Special Education.

Vacc, N. A. (1968). A study of emotionally disturbed children in regular and special classes. *Exceptional Children,* **35**, 197–204.

Walker, V. S. (1974). The efficacy of the resource room for educating retarded children. *Exceptional Children,* **40**, 288–289.

Wang, M. C. (1980a). Adaptive instruction: Building on diversity. *Theory Into Practice,* **19**, 122–127.

Wang, M. C. (1980b). *The degree of implementation assessment measures for the Adaptive Learning Environments Model.* Pittsburgh, PA: University of Pittsburgh, Learning Research and Development Center.

Wang, M. C. (1981). Mainstreaming exceptional children: Some instructional design and implementation considerations. *Elementary School Journal,* **81**, 195–221.

Wang, M. C., & Baker, E. T. (1985–1986). Mainstreaming programs: Design features and effects. *Journal of Special Education,* **19**, 503–525.

Wang, M. C., & Birch, J. W. (1984a). Effective special education in regular classes. *Exceptional Children,* **50**, 391–398.

Wang, M. C., & Birch, J. W. (1984b). Comparison of a full-time mainstreaming program and a resource room approach. *Exceptional Children,* **51**, 33–40.

Wang, M. C., & Gennari, P. (1983). Analysis of the design, implementation, and effects of a data-based staff development program. *Teacher Education and Special Education,* **6**, 211–226.

Wang, M. C., Gennari. P., & Waxman, H. C. (1984). The Adaptive Learning Environments Model: Design, implementation, and effects. In M. C. Wang & H. J. Walberg (Eds.), *Adapting instruction to individual differences* (pp. 191–235). Berkeley, CA: McCutchan.

Wang, M. C., Nojan, M., Strom, C. D., & Walberg, H. J. (1984). The utility of degree of implementation measures in program evaluation and implementation research. *Curriculum Inquiry,* **14**, 249–286.

Wang, M. C., Peverly, S., & Randolph, R. (1984). An investigation of the implementation and effects of a full-time mainstreaming program. *Journal of Remedial and Special Education,* **5**(6), 21–32.

Wang, M. C., & Reynolds, M. C. (1985). Avoiding the "Catch 22" in special education reform. *Exceptional Children,* **51**, 497–502.

Wang, M. C., Vaughan, E. D., & Dytman, J. A. (1985). Staff development: A key ingredient of effective mainstreaming. *Teaching Exceptional Children,* **17**, 112–121.

Wang, M. C., & Walberg, H. J. (1983). Adaptive instruction and classroom time. *American Educational Research Journal,* **20**, 601–626.

Wang, M. C., & Walberg, H. J. (in press). An investigation of classroom processes and outcomes of exemplary adaptive instruction. *International Journal of Educational Research.*

Waxman, H. C., & Walberg, H. J. (1982). The relation of teaching and learning: A review of reviews of process-product research. *Contemporary Education Review,* **1**, 103–120.

White, O. R. (1984). Selected issues in program evaluation: Arguments for the individual. In B. K. Keogh (Ed.), *Advances in special education* (Vol. 4, pp. 69–121). Greenwich, CT: JAI Press.

Woelner, E. H. (1979). *Requirements for certification for elementary schools, secondary schools and junior colleges* (44th ed.). Chicago, IL: University of Chicago Press.

Wood, S., Duncan, P., & Hansell, P. (1983). *Performance analysis and the generalization problem.* Des Moines, IA: Department of Public Instruction. (ERIC Document Reproduction Service No. ED 240 773)

Wrightstone, J. W., Justman, J., Pincus, & Lowe, R. (1956). *New York Test of Arithmetical Meanings.* New York: Harcourt, Brace, Jovanovich.

Yeh, J. P., Herman, J. L., & Rudman, L. M. (1981). *Teachers and testing: A survey of test use* (CSE Report No. 166). Los Angeles, CA: University of California, Center for the Study of Evaluation.

Ysseldyke, J. E. (1984). *School psychology: A blueprint for training and practice.* Minneapolis, MN: National School Psychology Inservice Training Network.

Ysseldyke, J. E. & Algozzine, B. (1982). *Critical issues in special and remedial education.* Boston, MA: Houghton Mifflin.

Ysseldyke, J. E., & Thurlow, M. L. (1983). *Identification/classification research: An intergrative summary of findings* (Research Rep. No. 142). Minneapolis, MN: University of Minnesota, Institute for Research on Learning Disabilities.

Ysseldyke, J. E., Thurlow, M. L., Mecklenburg, C., Graden, J., & Algozzine, B. (1984). Changes in academic engaged time as a function of assessment and special education intervention. *Special Services in the Schools,* **1**, 31–44.

SECTION 3

Noncategorical Programming for Mildly Handicapped Students

Introduction

MAYNARD C. REYNOLDS
University of Minnesota

The focus in noncategorical programs is on students who, under other arrangements, would be considered educable mentally retarded, learning disabled, and behaviorally disordered as well as students with sensory and other physical impairments who do not have multiple severe impairments. Clearly, the general topic of noncategorical programming is emerging as one of importance in special education—and as one of considerable controversy. The *Seventh Annual Report to Congress on the Implementation of Public Law 94-142: The Education for All Handicapped Children Act* (prepared and published by the U.S. Department of Education, 1985), lists 25,305 special education teachers employed in noncategorical positions. That is more than in all other single categories but three: learning disabilities (82,625 teachers); mental retardation (61,452 teachers); and emotional disturbance (26,967 teachers). Significantly, these are the three classifications of students that are most commonly joined together in noncategorical programs (see pp. 226–228 of the *Seventh Annual Report*).

Several terms are used in the chapters in this section, including *cross-categorical, multicategorical, noncategorical,* and *generic.* They all refer to programs for mildly handicapped students, but subtle differences exist among the terms. Cross-categorical tends to be used to describe programs in which children of several categories are enrolled in a single program. For example, a resource room program might serve children who have been classified in more than one of the traditional categories; it might include learning disabled and behaviorally disordered students. In this case, it is assumed that the classifications are instructionally meaningful but that programming for the students can be cross-categorical. Teachers serving in such cross-categorical programs usually have qualified themselves by completing two or more categorically oriented preparation programs. The term multicategorical is used interchangeably with cross-categorical.

The term noncategorical is used differently and refers to programs with a range of mildly handicapped children. It is not assumed that the traditional categories are useful. Reports may be made to state and federal offices showing that certain numbers of the students might be considered educable mentally retarded, learning disabled, behaviorally disordered, and so on, but, in noncategorical programs, there is a denial that such classifications are important for instructional purposes. Children with specific speech problems are usually treated separately, but, to the extent that problems are language related, they tend also to be encompassed in large part by the noncategorical rubric. In colleges and universities, a noncategorical teacher preparation program is not a simple aggregation of categorical treatment approaches but one that provides a fundamental/direct instructional perspective and training to meet the educational and social needs of children.

In the chapters that follow, attention is given mainly to noncategorical programs, although readers should be alert to occasions when specific references are made to cross-categorical or multicategorical programs. The term generic is used only occasionally, and somewhat ambiguously, in the literature. Readers will be well advised to check the meaning of the term generic in the specific context of usage.

Another distinction of importance is between situations concerned with conducting and synthesizing research and those concerned with providing education. For purposes of communication among researchers, there is reason to be tolerant of both more open and more limited approaches to definitions, depending on the nature of the research question. For example, it probably is useful for researchers to deal quite broadly with learning problems while seeking to discover the most useful ways to categorize knowledge. On the other hand, it seems quite legitimate that a network of researchers might agree to exchange scientific papers just on persons who score within a given range on general intelligence tests. It is important to be mindful of the distinction between classifications that might be agreed upon simply for scientific purposes and those which are used in the placement and instruction of children in the schools. Advocates of noncategorical programs tend to be rather conservative in that they believe that treatments associated with pupil characteristics should have demonstrated validity and utility before being applied in the schools.

Another key point to note is that categories used in special education often can be referenced either to the child or to the program. One might say that the child is blind or that he is enrolled in the braille class; one might say that the child is hungry or needs two meals per day. One of the arguments used to support noncategorical programs is that more emphasis in categorization ought to go to the program and less to the child, and that funding systems ought to be linked to the child's instructional needs rather than to the child in a category.

It should be understood, of course, that no one argues for totally abandoning all child classification activities. Most proponents of noncategorical programs acknowledge the need for distinctions that permit the sorting of essential relationships. The term noncategorical as used in special education needs to be understood in historical terms. There is a rising chorus of objection to many aspects of the present systems of categorization, but what emerges will—in its own way—be a new system of categorization. Perhaps it will be dimensional rather than typological, functional rather than etiological, based on some other distinctions, but there will be *some* system for differentiating among students and the programs used to serve them.

In planning the following chapters on noncategorical programming, it was thought that attention should go first to a general review on classification, including a consideration of the criteria that might be used to judge when a system is adequate and a synthesis and evaluation of current practices. This is provided in the chapter by James Ysseldyke, entitled "Classification of Handicapped Students."

On the conservative assumption that children ought not to be classified (or placed) in any special way within the schools except on the basis of well-confirmed evidence, the next chapter, "Avoiding or Limiting Special Education Referrals: Changes and Challenges," was planned. The decision to ask for such a chapter was also influenced by the least restrictive environment principle of PL 94-142, which suggests a preference for making the mainstream of education as powerful as possible in dealing with individual differences among students, rather than promoting opportunities for regular teachers to refer their "problem" students to special educators. Admittedly, we were also influenced by economic considerations in calling for this chapter, thinking especially about the growing frequency with which administrators and legislators are putting "caps" on special education placements and funding, and anticipating increased competition for resources among special and regular education as public school enrolments increase for the first time since the passage of PL 94-142. Ann Nevin and Jacqueline Thousand's chapter shows some of the responsible ways by which educators can put their own caps on special education referrals and placements.

The next chapter, in something of a logical sequence, looks at how special educators have been organizing noncategorical programs. In their chapter, entitled "Noncategorical Special Education Programs: Process and Outcomes," Catherine Morsink, Carol Thomas, and Judy Smith-Davis discuss how the more than 25,000 noncategorical special education teachers are employed and what the outcomes of their work are. Observers close to this scene will not be surprised to find that data are few in this area, so here we have more expressions of need than of solid research findings. Indeed, it is clear that the primary justification for noncategorical programs has been the perceived lack of justification for categorical programs.

Similarly, the fourth chapter, "Noncategorical Specia Education Personnel Preparation," is understandably long on description and short on research and evaluation. Or the other hand, what can most reasonably be expected here are careful evaluation and creative development, and this we have, in the work of Edward Blackhurst, Deborah Bott, and Donald Cross. The state of the art in some fields is defined mainly by the best thinking of learned individuals and, only later, and in limited ways, by research. There is awkwardness in the teacher preparation aspect of noncategorical programming because it needs to be planned and paced in accord with changes made in schools and in state certification practices. This chapter includes an up-to-date review of states' acceptance of noncategorical teaching as a certification specialty.

The fifth chapter in this section, entitled "Noncategorical Special Education: Models for Research and Practice," serves as the final paper in this total project of research review. More than other chapters, it is a developing statement, based on all preceding chapters but, most especially, on those dealing with learner characteristics, delivery systems and noncategorical programming. In this final chapter, Maynard Reynolds and Charlie Lakin treat problems of classification in a summary way, then discuss potential models for solving the problems, including models for political action as well as for the more technical management of classifying students and programs. Repeating themes that occur frequently in preceding papers, they turn to ways by which modern forms of special education may be joined with the adaptive education movement and the effectiveness research being conducted in regular education. In that broad framework, they believe there are challenging opportunities to renegotiate a more inclusive approach to educational research and practice. This is to say that, possibly, we can achieve an amalgam of special and regular education in research of the future, just as we witness it now in educational practice.

It should be noted that this set of chapters on noncategorical programming deals with a rapidly developing and somewhat controversial field. We have thus asked the authors to stretch themselves beyond summaries of research findings, to give their estimations of the status of practice as well as the state of the art in their respective fields. They have proposed ideas for advancing the status of both. These activities have, of course, been influenced by the backgrounds and interests of the individual authors. They do not expect to be persuasive on all matters with all readers. Most assuredly, they will appreciate responses by readers, including data on research they may have overlooked, different interpretations of the research they have reviewed, and ideas on the implications of what we know in the mid-1980s.

Classification of Handicapped Students

JAMES E. YSSELDYKE

University of Minnesota

Abstract—This chapter provides an integrative perspective of the current knowledge base on the classification of students, taking into account the lack of any major empirical test of the merits and limitations of the practice of classifying students as handicapped. Based on findings from a review of research and practice, the conclusion is drawn that current classification systems do not work well, but that there are reasonable alternatives. The chapter closes with an examination of assumptions that drive classification practices as well as suggested system changes that would eliminate some of the current barriers to the implementation of instructionally relevant alternatives.

Classification of handicapped students is an activity at the root of nearly everything that occurs in special education. Students are classified and grouped for instructional purposes. Researchers conduct their investigations on categories of exceptional students. Groups of parents and professionals organize into associations for the purpose of advocating for specific types of handicapped students. Universities educate teachers of specific types of students and organize their professional preparation programs based on disability labels. Given the prevalence of the use of classification practices, the neophyte observer could hardly help but conclude that there just must be good reasons for classifying handicapped students. Yet, it is very difficult to find strong support for classification practices in the professional literature.

I was asked to prepare an integrative review on classification of handicapped students; to review research and practice; to contrast the state of the art (what we know) with the state of practice (what we do); and to examine implications for research and practice. The preparation of this review has been a frustrating activity; it is focused more on opinions, beliefs, and practices than on research. There are many opinions on the merits and limitations of the practice of classifying students as handicapped. Yet, there is no major empirical test of the merits and limitations of doing so. The critical experiment has not been done: no one has randomly assigned normal and handicapped students to regular and special education environments and studied the short- or long-term effects on the students. There is no random assignment of students to classes, and, for obvious ethical reasons, one could not call nonhandicapped students handicapped and study the effect of doing so. Yet, we do know much about the effects of classification. It is my purpose in this paper to provide an integrative perspective of the current knowledge base on the classification of students.

Review Methods

Data sources searched for this work included those of the Educational Resources Information Center (i.e., Current Index of Journals in Education, Research in Education) and Psychological Abstracts. Two major computerized searches were conducted. In the first search, the terms *classification* (or *categorization*), *grouping* (for instructional purposes), *labeling* (of persons), and *placement* were crossed with the terms *exceptional persons, disabilities, mental retardation, learning disabilities, emotional disturbance,* and *mildly handicapped.* Studies focusing on classification as a Piagetian concept were excluded. This search produced 1,636 citations and abstracts. The second search was conducted using *aptitude-treatment-interaction* and *diagnostic teaching* as key terms. The same data bases were searched, and 1,402 citations were obtained. Each of the 3,038 abstracts identified through the two searches was read, and copies of relevant studies/papers were obtained and read.

In addition, the author used the United States Department of Education's annual reports to Congress on the implementation of PL 94-142; all editions of *The Condition of Education;* major textbooks; the Hobbs (1975) texts on *Issues in the Classification of Children;* the major text on *Placing Children in Special Education: A Strategy for Equity* (Heller, Holtzman, & Messick, 1982); major unpublished policy studies cited in the annual reports to Congress; and preliminary reports of major ongoing studies of classification practices.

In reading the literature on classification, one is struck by some interesting facts. Most of the writing on classification consists of opinion rather than research. Sometimes the opinion is data based, often it is not. The same data are used to support opposite views on classification, so that statements on this topic appear to be derived more from one's beliefs than from empirical evidence.

There are no clear-cut boundaries to the literature on classification. The act, the practice, or the topic of classification is related to or influences nearly everything that happens in special education. In preparing an integrative review, one must delimit the territory, and any such self-selection stands to be viewed as simply more opinion. Clearly, others would choose to organize their reviews in different ways. I have organized my review around the following questions:

1. Why do we classify students?
2. What relevant perspectives can be derived from the history of classification?

3. What is the state of practice?
4. What is the state of the art?
5. How does the state of practice compare to the state of the art?
6. What are the effects of classification?
7. What are the major implications for research, policy, teacher preparation, and practice?

Why Do We Classify Students?

We classify animals, plants, objects in grocery stores, and many other things in an effort to give order to our lives. School personnel classify students in an attempt to give order to the organization of schools. The classification of students, then, serves many of the same purposes served by any kind of classification. However, the classification of students also serves other purposes. Historically, students were classified so that they could be grouped for instructional purposes. It was thought, and still is thought in a number of circles, that homogeneously grouped students would profit from homogeneous instruction. Classification also has been used to serve the purposes of research, professional organizations and advocacy groups, and teacher preparation.

Research Purposes

It is argued that classification activities aid researchers. Researchers often argue that communication is facilitated when research is conducted on various types of students, and it is thought that the act of classifying subjects for research purposes facilitates the aggregation of information about specific types of students and the generalization of research findings. Yet, Taylor (1980) analyzed the extent to which researchers actually used the American Association on Mental Deficiency's classification system. He surveyed two journals, *Mental Retardation* and the *American Journal on Mental Deficiency,* for a 6-year period after issuance of the 1973 *Manual on Terminology and Classification in Mental Retardation* (Grossman, 1973). Only 28% of the articles had used the terminology and classifications recommended in the manual.

Much of the research in special education is research describing or comparing specific types of students. Yet, researchers have been repeatedly criticized for failure to describe better the populations and samples on whom they conduct their research. Smith et al. (1984) stated that:

> Many descriptions of subjects in research reports about learning disabled persons limit meaningful interpretation of the results because of their vagueness and inconsistency. Researchers are hampered in replicating or extending the research, and practitioners are uncertain about the application of the reported findings. (p. 221)

Smith et al. (1984) developed a set of standards for the description of subjects in research on learning disabled individuals.

It is confusing when researchers describe the popu lations of students on whom they conduct research simpl by using categorical labels without explicitly describin the characteristics of the subjects. Then, to make matte more confusing, some researchers proceed to conduc research on subtypes of specific types (Fisk & Rourk 1983; McKinney, 1984; Rykman & Elrod, 1983).

Professional Organizations and Advocacy Groups

It is important to note that those who classify student organize themselves politically into groups on the basis o disability labels. Thus, classification also serves the pur pose of enabling adults to organize as advocates for specifi types of students. Currently, many of the professiona organizations relevant to special education are organiz ations whose names come from the different categorie assigned to students. For example, there is the America Association on Mental Deficiency, the Council fo Students with Behavior Disorders, the Association fo Children with Learning Disabilities, and the Council fo Learning Disabilities (Ysseldyke & Algozzine, 1984). It is ironic that many of the professionals in special educatior who argue most strongly and most loudly for a noncategorical approach to service delivery and treatmen are organized into categorical associations.

Not only are there a number of professional associations for specific disabilities, but journals are devoted to specific types of exceptionalities. Thus, there is the *Journal of Learning Disabilities,* a journal called *Behavior Disorders,* and yet another entitled *Mental Retardation.*

Teacher Preparation

Most colleges and universities that educate special education teachers provide categorical training, and most states still certify teachers categorically. For example, training and certification programs exist for teachers of mentally retarded students, teachers of emotionally disturbed students, and teachers of learning disabled students. And, there are entire schools where instruction is devoted to specific categorical types of learners (e.g., there are private schools for mentally retarded students and for learning disabled students).

Teacher preparation programs in special education are certificate programs. People strive to earn a certificate permitting them to teach exceptional students. Requirements for certificates differ across states, so the organization and requirements of teacher preparation programs differ. There is usually, although not necessarily, a one-to-one correspondence between the program requirements of a college or university and the certification requirements of the state in which the college or university is located. Thus, there is considerable diversity in the preparation of special educators. Heller (1982) and Heller and Ridenour (1983) were especially critical of the mixture of educational standards and training programs.

Blackhurst, Bott, and Cross, elsewhere in this volume, ive addressed the difficult prospects of noncategorical acher preparation programs, especially in regard to forts to locate appropriate practicum and student teach-g sites.

What Relevant Perspectives Can Be Derived from the History of Classification?

arly Classification Systems

The history of classification efforts can be traced to the irly Greeks. Aristotle is usually given credit for attempt-ig the first scientific classification: his "ladder of nature." squirol (1845) proposed the first definition of mental etardation and a classification system based on the rela-ve amounts of knowledge a person had. In 1848, Samuel ridley Howe described differences between retarded eople said to be idiots, simpletons, or fools. He described ifferences between the groups. In 1910, terminology hanged when Goddard coined the term *moron* (Goddard, 919) for use in classifying retarded people. Six years iter, Alfred Binet produced a test to be used to identify tudents in need of special education (Binet, 1916). Intelli-ence testing brought an objectivity to measuring differ-nces among people. Goddard was the first to propose the se of intelligence tests, and specifically of mental ages, in he classification of retarded people. Consider the follow-ng excerpt from Goddard:

> I believe that the one- and two-year olds probably come under the group that we have always called idiots. These might again be subdivided for those who wish to draw a closer line and use the old expressions into the low grade idiot, the absolutely helpless, probably under one year of mental development; the middle idiot or those who are one-year old, those who can help themselves; and the high grade idiots, those who cannot only feed themselves, but can discriminate somewhat as to what is good to eat. Then we would, perhaps, have the imbecile group, including the ages from three to seven, again to be subdivided into the three- and four-years of age as the low grade imbecile; the five-year group would be about the middle grade imbecile; the six- and seven-year group, the high grade imbecile. All the rest would come under the highest group which has been called in a good many places the feeble-minded in the specific sense. These could again be subdivided—the eight- and nine-year-old into the low grade; the ten-year-old, the middle grade; the eleven- and twelve-year-old, the high grade. (Goddard, 1919, p. 28)

The current classification system for mental retardation is still based on degrees of intelligence as reflected in IQ scores as measured by performance on standardized measures of intelligence. Individuals are now said to evidence a level of retardation: mild, moderate, severe, or profound. Since 1959, persons also have had to demonstrate maladaptive behavior in order to be considered mentally retarded.

Classification systems in psychology and psychiatry are based on criteria agreed upon by professionals. The criteria change over time because the opinions and beliefs of professionals change over time. Clinicians who diagnose mental illness use the *Diagnostic and Statistical Manual* of the American Psychiatric Association (1980), now in its third edition. Using the third edition manual, mental disorders can be classified into one of 17 types, and these can be further differentiated. Ysseldyke and Algozzine (1984) noted that "Hippocrates' system of classifying mental disorders into mania, phrenitis, and melancholia has grown to a point where over three hundred types of problems can be identified" (p. 151).

The first system for classifying exceptional children was proposed by Horn (1924), who recommended that a classification system be used for purposes of making entitlement decisions. Horn offered a "complete classification" consisting of (a) children who are exceptional for reasons primarily mental (the most highly endowed group, the most poorly endowed group); (b) children who are exceptional for reasons primarily temperamental (incorrigible and truant children, speech defective children); and (c) children who are exceptional for reasons primarily physical (deaf children, blind children, crippled children).

Ysseldyke and Algozzine (1984) pointed out the similarity between Horn's first system of classification and the one used today. They stated:

> The "most highly endowed" are today called gifted and talented. . . . The "most poorly endowed" are today called mentally retarded. . . . The "incorrigibles and truants" of yesterday are the emotionally disturbed students of today. . . . The parallels in the categories of speech defectives, deaf, blind, and crippled should be obvious. In fact, the only difference in the list of categories recognized by the first classification system for exceptional students and the contemporary scheme is the absence of learning disabilities from the former. (p. 152)

Over time, we have added, rather than combined or deleted, categories from the classification schema. Reynolds (1984) noted that the tendency has been to expand existing categories by differentiating, for example, blind from partially sighted students and those who are deaf from those who are hard-of-hearing.

A Theoretical Framework

At least as regards relevance to practices in classifying children as handicapped, one of the most important theoretical statements on classification was the 1975 paper by Cromwell, Blashfield, and Strauss. Cromwell et al. described the practice of assigning labels to children as one in which symbols were used by senders to serve given purpose. They also pointed out that the meanings of labels change over time as the needs, intents, and responses of users of labels change. Thus, labels may be constructed or invented for the purpose of conveying certain meanings, but the meanings may change over time as a function of use.

Cromwell et al. (1975) specified the nature of the diagnostic, assessment, and prognostic process. The labels or conditions assigned to children are based on (A) historical/etiological data or on (B) current assessable characteristics. The usefulness of any diagnostic classification was said to be a function of the extent to which (C) treatments or interventions lead to (D) known outcomes or prognoses. Any time we assign a label to a student, thereby classifying him or her, the act has varying degrees of usefulness. According to Cromwell et al. (1975), classifications that are most useful and valid lead to treatments with known outcomes. Valid diagnostic paradigms are those which include both C and D data (ACD, BCD, and ABCD paradigms). In special education, we often use inappropriate and invalid diagnostic-intervention paradigms. We engage in much assessment of etiological or historical factors; we spend much time giving tests to describe pupil characteristics. This activity is valid and useful only if it leads us to design treatments or interventions with known outcomes.

Cromwell et al. (1975) specified the criteria for classification systems: classification systems must be shown to be reliable; they must provide adequate coverage; and they must be logically consistent, have clinical utility, and be acceptable to users. Cromwell et al. (1975) made a number of important recommendations for classification systems. Among their recommendations were the following:

1. Any system of classification should be dated and subject to periodic review and modification, not only because of the advancements in scientific knowledge relative to the classification data but also because public usage and surplus meanings change the meanings of labels and terms as time passes.
2. The structure of classification systems should meet the criteria of reliability, coverage, logical consistency, utility, and acceptability to users.
3. If a classification system is to be diagnostic in nature, then each diagnostic category should be understood in terms of the classes of data which contribute to its definition (historical-etiological, presently assessable characteristics) and the classes of data which determine its utility (treatment, prognosis, prevention, outcome).
4. Diagnostic classification systems should have preventive as well as treatment value.
5. Classification systems should be evaluated to determine whether the inevitable losses to the individuals are affected by the gains. The indirect gains and losses should be evaluated as well as the direct ones. (pp. 22–23)

For the most part, classification practices in special education have not been treated theoretically. There has, though, been much theorizing on why the classificatior came to exist. Rather than theorizing, special educato and psychologists who assist special educators in classify ing students spend their time trying to identify specifi tests that will differentiate specific categories of student developing measures to assess specific characteristics pre sumed to be associated with categories, trying to refin categories, and trying to make diagnostic practices mor sophisticated.

What Is the State of Practice?

As noted above, classification serves several purposes. I this section, current practice is reviewed as a function o purpose.

Classification as the Jurisdiction of States

In the United States, education is a state rather than federal responsibility. Each state has laws stating who is t be educated, and the laws are accompanied by rules, regu lations, and guidelines. The fact that laws and rules abou who is eligible for special education services are state law creates a situation in which there is considerable varianc across states in the kinds of students considered eligible fo and served in special education.

The federal government has specified that all handi capped students have the right to a free, appropriate public education. Categories of students considered handi capped and eligible for special education services are listed in Table 1, along with a count of the numbers of students who received special education services under each of the labels in the academic years from 1976–1977 through 1983–1984.

The fact that education is a state rather than a federal responsibility means that different categories or labels are used in the classification systems of different states. Chalfant (1984) studied current practice in classifying students as learning disabled. He reported that, in state guidelines, five terms are being used to describe the learning disabled population: learning disabilities, learning disabled, specific learning disabilities, perceptually impaired, and perceptual communication disorders. Epstein, Cullinan, and Sabatino (1977) studied components of state definitions of emotional disturbance. They reported that states use interchangeably the terms emotionally disturbed, behaviorally disordered, emotionally impaired, and emotionally handicapped. Two states, Massachusetts and South Dakota, do not categorize students for the purpose of eligibility determination. These states are often referred to as noncategorical states. Yet, annually, each state reports to the U.S. Department of Education the numbers of students served by category. A special education study commission in New Jersey recently recommended and held state hearings on a proposal for a categorical special education system in which the categories are based on the educational needs of each student instead of on the disability of the student (Burstein, 1985). The study commission recommended

TABLE 1
Number of Handicapped Students Ages 3 to 21 Years Served Under PL 89–313 and PL 94–142

Handicap category	1976–77	1977–78	1978–79	1979–80	1980–81	1981–82	1982–83	1983–84
Learning disabled	797,213	969,368	1,135,559	1,281,379	1,468,014	1,627,344	1,745,871	1,811,489
Speech impaired	1,302,666	1,226,957	1,216,165	1,188,967	1,170,484	1,137,919	1,134,197	1,130,569
Mentally retarded	969,547	944,909	917,880	882,173	844,180	802,264	780,831	750,534
Emotionally disturbed	283,072	288,626	301,469	331,067	348,954	341,786	353,431	362,073
Other health impaired	141,417	136,164	105,640	106,292	98,653	80,171	52,026	54,621
Multihandicapped	—	—	50,722	61,965	70,460	73,832	65,479	67,537
Hard-of-hearing	89,743	87,144	86,382	82,873	81,363	76,387	75,337	74,279
Orthopedically impaired	87,008	88,070	70,299	66,248	59,663	59,958	57,506	56,209
Visually handicapped	38,247	35,688	32,607	32,679	33,005	30,979	31,096	31,576
Deaf–blind	—	—	2,350	2,576	2,913	2,642	2,553	2,512
All conditions	3,709,913	3,776,926	3,919,073	4,036,219	4,177,689	4,233,282	4,298,327	4,341,399

Note: The information provided in this table has been compiled from the *Annual Reports to Congress on the Implementation of Public Law 94-142*, prepared by the United States Department of Education.

TABLE 2
Origins of State Definitions of Learning Disabilities

State	Federal definition	Modified federal definition	State originated definition	National joint committee definition	Noncategorical services
Alabama		×			
Alaska		×			
Arizona	×				
Arkansas	×				
California			×		
Colorado			×		
Connecticut		×			
Delaware	×				
District of Columbia	×				
Florida		×			
Georgia	×				
Hawaii	×				
Idaho	×				
Illinois		×			
Indiana	×				
Iowa			×		
Kansas			×		
Kentucky				×	
Louisiana		×			
Maine		×			
Maryland	×				
Massachusetts					×
Michigan		×			
Minnesota			×		
Mississippi		×			
Missouri	×				
Montana	×				
Nebraska	×				
Nevada			×		
New Hampshire	×				
New Jersey		×			
New Mexico			×		
New York		×			
North Carolina			×		
North Dakota	×				
Ohio	×				
Oklahoma	×				
Oregon		×			
Pennsylvania	×				
Rhode Island	×				
South Carolina	×				
South Dakota					×
Tennessee			×		
Texas	×				
Utah	×				
Vermont			×		
Virginia	×				
Washington	×				
West Virginia		×			
Wisconsin			×		
Wyoming	×				
Total	24	13	11	1	2

hat four formats be used to deliver special education services: (a) general education program with intervention, (b) general education program with related services, (c) part-time special education program, and (d) full-time special education program. Such examples illustrate the fact that different names are used to describe the same condition in different states, that some states do not classify students for eligibility purposes, and that there are new, promising, innovative ways of operating that involve classification of services rather than classification of students.

It is important to note here that the situation is more complex than the assignment of different names to similar conditions. States often use different criteria for the purpose of defining the conditions. The criteria for calling students learning disabled or mentally retarded, for example, are specified by state education agencies and may differ across states. In Chalfant's (1984) investigation, he looked not only at the differences in terminology used in different states, but also at the components of definitions. He reported that five component parts are included in state definitions of learning disabilities. These include a failure to achieve component, a psychological process component, an exclusionary component, an etiological component, and a significant discrepancy component. Chalfant reported that state definitions include either two, three, four, or all five of these components. In reviewing state guidelines, Chalfant found that twenty-four states used the federal definition of learning disabilities, twelve states had modified the federal definition in some way, one state had supplemented the federal definition with the definition of the National Joint Committee on Learning Disabilities (Hammill, Leigh, McNutt, & Larsen, 1981), and eleven states had written their own definitions. The origins of the state definitions are shown in Table 2.

Epstein et al. (1977) studied the occurrence of specific components in state definitions of behavioral disorders. The most frequently used components were (a) disorders of emotion/behavior, (b) interpersonal problems, (c) special education needed, (d) learning/achievement problems, (e) deviation from norm, and (f) severity.

One should recognize that there is considerable variability in the practice of classifying students as handicapped. But, matters get even worse. In states where conditions are called by any number of names, and where there is considerable variability in the criteria specified for labeling or classifying students and declaring them eligible for special education services, different local education agencies sometimes use state criteria and sometimes do not. The practice of classifying students cannot be understood; it can only be described. But, in describing current practice, one must recognize that (a) there are federal laws and federal definitions, (b) there are state laws and state definitions, (c) state education agencies specify criteria and procedures for classification of children, and (d) local education agencies may or may not use the criteria specified by state education agencies (Ysseldyke, 1984). In thinking about any one handicapping condition, readers must constantly remember that federal definitions are *conceptualizations* of conditions. States establish criteria for classification, and these criteria are used (or not used) in different ways to identify students and to declare them eligible for special education services.

Classification Decision Making in Schools

Much of the recent writing on current practice in the classification of exceptional children consists of opinion. People regularly write about classification, but research on classification practices is limited. Personnel at the University of Minnesota Institute for Research on Learning Disabilities conducted a series of investigations on the psychoeducational assessment and decision-making process in schools. One area of research interest focused on the ways in which school personnel used assessment information to make decisions about eligibility of students for special education services.

Multiple methodologies were used to investigate eligibility decision making. Placement teams were observed and videotaped. Computer simulation methodology was used to study the decision-making process employed by individuals. Case study methodologies were used to study bias in the decision-making process, and interviews and questionnaires were used to solicit self-reports from decision makers.

A number of generalizations were stated on the basis of many independent investigations. It was reported that "the special education team decision-making process, as currently employed in public school settings, is at best inconsistent" (Ysseldyke, Thurlow, et al., 1983, p. 77). It was found that the placement team decision-making process operated to verify problems first cited by teachers, and that placement team efforts consisted of what Sarason and Doris (1979) called a "search for pathology." It was reported that team meetings consisted largely of round-robin presentations of test data and that participants in team meetings were, for the most part, individuals who had given tests to students. Regular classroom teachers and parents participated little in team meetings (Ysseldyke, Algozzine, & Allen, 1981), and placement teams seldom met the criteria of effective functioning (Ysseldyke, Algozzine, & Mitchell, 1982).

In spite of the fact that placement team meetings consisted largely of presentation of test data and discussion of alternative placement possibilities, it was found that the classification decisions made by team members had little to do with the data presented at team meetings. Ysseldyke, Algozzine, Richey, and Graden (1982) reported very little correlation between the extent to which data supported particular decisions and the decisions that teams made. Rather, decisions were a function of "teacher squeak," the extent to which a teacher wanted a student out of his or her classroom. Beyond this, the decisions were a function of naturally occurring pupil characteristics, such as the sex, socioeconomic status, and physical appearance of the student (Ysseldyke, Algozzine, Regan, & McGue, 1981). And, it was shown that availability of services and the power that a student's parents held in the school district influenced school decisions (Christenson, Ysseldyke, & Algozzine, 1982). At the same time, it should be noted that Pfeiffer and Naglieri (1983) studied the multidisciplinary team decision-making process and argued that teams exhibited significantly less variability in placement decisions than did professionals operating alone. Pfeiffer and Naglieri argued that team decision making was superior to individual decision making.

The Minnesota researchers reported that very many nonhandicapped students are being declared handicapped. When, in a computer-simulated, decision-making investigation, decision makers were given data entirely indicative of normal or average performance, more than half of the decision makers said the normal student was eligible for special education services (Algozzine & Ysseldyke, 1981).

In a series of major investigations, the ways in which school personnel decide to classify students as learning disabled were studied. It was demonstrated that there is currently no defensible system for declaring students eligible for learning disability services. It was shown that significant numbers of normal students met state, federal, and local criteria for being classified as learning disabled. Learning disabled students could not be differentiated psychometrically from low-achieving students (Ysseldyke, Algozzine, Shinn, & McGue, 1982). When experts were asked about the definition, incidence, prevalence, or criteria for learning disability classification, there was very little agreement either conceptually or practically (Tucker, Stevens, & Ysseldyke, 1983).

The classification of learning disability does not meet the criteria for a classification system. If there is one characteristic that learning disabled students share, it is low achievement. There are no characteristics or behaviors specific to learning disability; that is, there are no characteristics that students labeled as learning disabled evidence that are not demonstrated with equal frequency by low-achieving students who are not learning disabled (Ysseldyke, Thurlow, et al., 1983).

The classification of students as learning disabled was examined further by looking at the numbers and kinds of students who would be so classified by each of seventeen commonly used sets of criteria. It was found that more than 80% of normal students could be classified as learning disabled by one or more definitions, and that over 75% of low-achieving students met the criteria for being classfied as learning disabled. At the same time, only 75% of school-identified learning disabled students met criteria for being classified as learning disabled (Ysseldyke, Algozzine, & Epps, 1983). Large numbers of students fail to acquire academic and social skills; some of those students are sorted out, classified as learning disabled, and declared eligible for special education services. Yet, there are no reliable psychometric differences between students classified as learning disabled and those simply considered to be low achieving.

School personnel still rely primarily on the use of norm-referenced psychometric measures in the classification of students. For the most part, diagnostic personnel use technically inadequate norm-referenced tests in the process of classifying students (Ysseldyke, 1979; Ysseldyke, Algozzine, Regan, & Potter, 1980b; Ysseldyke, Regan, Thurlow, & Schwartz, 1981). When diagnostic personnel are confronted with the fact that there is considerable misclassification going on, and that many of the tests currently used in making classification decisions are technically inadequate, they often argue that they rely on their clinical judgment in making classification and placement decisions. Yet, when Epps, Ysseldyke, and McGue (1984) provided teachers, psychologists, and naive judges with profiles of students' performances on norm-referenced tests and asked the judges to classify the students, hit rates were consistently 55% for the three groups.

The Minnesota researchers reported that:

> It is clear that the most important decision that gets made in the entire assessment process is the decision by a regular classroom teacher to refer a student for assessment. Once a student is referred, there is a high probability that the student will be assessed and placed in special education. (Ysseldyke, Thurlow, et al., 1983, p. 80)

This generalization was derived from a national study of referral rates. Algozzine, Christenson, and Ysseldyke (1982) found that, annually, from 3% to 5% of the school age population is referred each year for psychoeducational evaluation, that 92% of referred students are tested, and that 73% of those who are tested are declared eligible for special education services.

Reynolds has referred to the special education team decision-making process as a "capitulation conference." He made an observation that serves as an appropriate summary of the work of the Minnesota Institute:

> In general, the practice of classifying exceptional children in the schools has been carried out by professionals who have no background in the school curriculum or instruction and who base their decisions on data that are not generated in the classroom (Reynolds, 1984, p. 67)

Researchers at the Center for Educational Studies at the Research Triangle Institute (RTI) are currently engaged in an exploratory study of practices in the identification and placement of learning disabled, mentally retarded, and emotionally disturbed students. In a preliminary report published in October 1984, the researchers reported a number of initial findings. They reported that referral decisions were made using local referents, that "selection of a student for referral to special education is a function of the extent to which the student's behavior and academic progress are perceived negatively from the norm of a given school of LEA" (Hocutt, Cox, & Pelosi, 1984, p. 1). Hocutt et al. also reported that:

> The number of students referred and the severity of their problems are a function of the way in which regular education teachers are evaluated by adminis-

> trators, requirements regarding a pre-referral intervention period, and the restrictiveness of eligibility criteria/operational definitions used by an LEA to identify LD, EMR, and ED students. (p. 1)

The findings of the RTI group were congruent with those of the University of Minnesota researchers on issues of classification and decision making. The RTI group reported that:

> The proportion and education profiles of students ultimately classified as LD, EMR, or ED are a function of (1) both characteristics and number of students referred for special education; (2) the operational definitions and eligibility criteria used by an LEA; (3) individual decision making. The major factors that influence LEA identification policies and procedures (and consequently, outcomes) are federal and state laws and regulations, funding amounts and formulas, professional philosophy/training, and characteristics of the students served by a school or school district. (Hocutt et al., 1984, p. 2)

The special education assessment and decision-making process differs from state to state and from district to district within states. Classification is dependent on these assessment and decision-making practices. Thus, we see that different kinds of students are referred in different settings, that the proportion of referred students who are classified is very high, and that different kinds of students are classified in different settings. The entire referral-assessment-classification-placement process is teacher-driven.

In 1979, the Committee on Child Development and Research and Public Policy of the National Research Council established a Panel on Selection and Placement of Students in Programs for the Mentally Retarded. That panel was charged with two tasks:

> . . . (1) to determine the factors that account for disproportionate representation of minority students and males in special education programs, especially programs for mentally retarded students and (2) to identify placement criteria or practices that do not affect minority students and males disproportionately. (Heller et al., 1982, p. ix)

The panel concluded that the overall objective of assessment for purposes of placing students in special education was to improve instruction. They recommended that assessors conduct valid assessments of the learning environment as well as valid assessments of individuals. The group recommended a focus on improvement of instruction for handicapped and potentially handicapped students. The findings are similar to those reached by researchers at the Cantalician Foundation of Buffalo, New York in their study of bias in the special education assessment and decision-making process (Cantalician Foundation, Inc., 1983). These researchers, funded by the Office of Civil Rights of the United States Department of Education, studied bias in the assessment and decision-making process and concluded that the way to cut down on discriminatory assessment was to facilitate the development of effective instructional programs for mildly handicapped and minority students. They developed a narrative description of alternative instructional, referral, and assessment practices (Cantalician Foundation, Inc., 1983).

Researchers have sometimes studied school-identified populations of handicapped students with the goal of understanding current practice in classification. Garrison and Hammill (1970) studied students classified as educable mentally retarded in Philadelphia, Pennsylvania. They reported that two thirds of the students classified as mentally retarded did not meet the criteria for being so classified. Shepard and Smith (1981) studied students classified as learning disabled in Colorado (the Colorado label is perceptual-communication disorders). They reported that more than half of the students did not meet state criteria for being so classified.

Norman and Zigmond (1980) reported the results of a study of the characteristics of students labeled and served as learning disabled in school systems that were affiliated with federally funded, model demonstration centers, called Child Service Demonstration Centers (CSDCs), for students with learning disabilities. They studied the intake data from files of 1,966 students labeled and served as learning disabled in CSDCs in twenty-two states. There was a lack of consistency in the characteristics of the students served, and no specific defining variables or characteristics were identified.

Gerber (1984) critically analyzed the 1984 report to Congress on the implementation of PL 94-142 (United States Department of Education, 1984). Gerber provided data to support his contention that the report failed to alert Congress that students who are difficult to teach and manage appear to be at significant risk of erroneous classification and inequitable treatment. He based his argument on data showing considerable variability in identification and referral procedures across states and local districts and on 9 years of child-count data. Algozzine and Korinek (1985) reported the results of an analysis of the numbers of students served nationally in each condition of handicap for the years 1978 through 1982. They reported first that less than 10% of the students classified as handicapped were severely handicapped, while more than 90% of the students were labeled as either mentally retarded, emotionally disturbed, speech impaired, or learning disabled. They reported a significant increase over time in the numbers of students classified as learning disabled and a concomitant decrease in the numbers of students classified as mentally retarded.

A more detailed analysis of current practice in classifying students as handicapped was provided by Tucker (1980). He reported the results of an analysis of the enrolment of members of different ethnic groups in special education in the years 1970 through 1977. It was reported that the percentage of the total school population enrolled in special education increased from 4.1% in 1970 to 11.8% in 1977. Tucker further reported that there was a significant increase in the numbers of students classified as learning disabled and a concomitant decrease in the numbers classified as educable mentally retarded. Yet, what is interesting in the Tucker analysis is that he showed that this shift from the educable mental retardation to the learning disability classification resulted from the reclassification of large numbers of black students. Tucker's investigation illustrated very cogently the influence of social, political, and economic factors on practice in the classification of students.

Current practice in classifying students as handicapped has been shown to be arbitrary. There is so much variability in current practice that practice is often difficult to describe. It has been shown that the process of classification is dependent on the processes of referral and assessment. It has also been shown that the practice of classifying students is a teacher-driven practice and that large numbers of students are misclassified.

What Is the State of the Art?

Most of the research on classification has focused on the processes by which students are classified rather than on the effects of classification on student development and learning. Moreover, the research has not been experimental in nature. Rather, it has been either descriptive or comparative.

Descriptive Research

At least six different kinds of descriptive investigations can be identified. Researchers have (a) attempted to delineate the characteristics of specific types of students; (b) used single tests to predict the performance of single categories of students; (c) conducted investigations of the reliability of diagnoses or judgments; (d) investigated the relationship between referral and eventual classification; (e) studied placement team decision-making practices; and (f) studied alleged bias in assessment, decision making, and classification.

Characteristics of Specific Types of Students

Many investigators have conducted research on the characteristics of specific types of students (e.g., Friedman & Gillooley, 1977; Gutkin, 1979; Kaufman, Wood, & Swan, 1979; Marlowe, Coissart, Welch, & Errera, 1984). Hallahan and Kauffman (1986), Heward and Orlansky (1985), and Kirk and Gallagher (1986) included in their introductory textbooks major sections of chapters on the characteristics of specific types of categories of students.

Three major investigations in this area are prominent. Garrison and Hammill (1970) reviewed the cases of 250 children placed in Philadelphia's classes for educable mentally retarded students. Two-thirds of those students did not demonstrate characteristics typically demonstrated by mentally retarded students. They failed to meet the criteria necessary to be labeled as mentally retarded. Ysseldyke, Algozzine, Regan, and Potter (1980a) conducted a psychometric description of students enrolled in a program for severely learning disabled students. They gathered data from the school records of 124 students at a private day school for learning disabled students. The majority of students did not demonstrate the necessary criteria to be called learning disabled; rather, the overall impression was one of general poor performance. Shepard and Smith (1981) studied the files of a representative group of students labeled as having perceptual-communicative disorders in the state of Colorado. Between 59% and 74% of the pupils identified as having such disorders did not meet legal definitions or definitions in the professional literature.

Performance Predictions for Categories of Students

Investigators have also studied categories of students by attempting to predict the later performance of those students. For example, investigators have attempted to use intellectual measures to predict the academic performance of students labeled as mentally retarded. Coleman (1953) investigated the extent to which "perceptual retardation" led to reading disability, and Kass (1966) attempted to identify psycholinguistic correlates of reading disability. Simner (1984) attempted to predict readiness for school entrance on the basis of stroke direction in children's printing; Schneider and Byrne (1984) attempted to predict successful transition from self-contained special education to regular class settings.

When investigators predict, they identify correlates of later performance. Unfortunately, they have often interpreted the correlates as *causally* related to later performance rather than simply related to later performance.

The Reliability of Diagnoses or Judgments

It is inevitable that if diagnostic personnel are required to use a reasonably complex system to classify, then investigators will study the reliability with which they are able to do so. One piece of evidence showing quite clearly the lack of reliability in classification of exceptional students is the considerable variability in labels used across states, the large differences in numbers of students classified in different states, and the considerable variability among communities within states in the classification of students.

There have been many investigations of consistency in diagnosis and classification. Freeman (1971) demonstrated a lack of diagnostic consistency among clinical child psychologists. McDermott (1975, 1977) showed a lack of diagnostic consistency among school psychologists; Flor (1978) and Morrow, Powell, and Ely (1976) showed a lack of diagnostic consistency among special educators.

Spitzer and Fleiss (1974) demonstrated a lack of reliability in the diagnostic decisions of psychiatrists. Vinsonhaler et al. (1982) demonstrated a lack of reliability in the diagnostic decisions reached by reading diagnosticians.

The Relationship Between Referral and Placement

Ysseldyke and Algozzine (1984) argued that the most important decision that gets made in the entire assessment and decision-making process is the decision by a classroom teacher to refer a student for diagnosis. I noted earlier in this chapter investigations showing that 92% of referred students are tested and that 73% of tested students are declared eligible for special education services. These data were reported by Algozzine, Christenson, and Ysseldyke (1982) based on their national survey of directors of special education. Foster, Ysseldyke, Casey, and Thurlow (1984) examined the relationship between referrals and special education outcomes in a state where students are referred for psychoeducational evaluation by category of handicapping condition. Seventy-two percent of referred students were placed in some form of special education; most were placed in the category for which they were referred.

Christenson, Ysseldyke, and Algozzine (1982) examined the relationship between teachers' tolerance for specific kinds of behavior and the actions they took with specific kinds of students. A sample of 189 classroom teachers was mailed a set of case studies. Teachers received a description of a student who was demonstrating either immature behavior, perceptual-motor problems, or antisocial behavior. Teachers were asked to indicate the actions they would take with the students. Later, teachers completed the Disturbing Behavior Checklist (Algozzine, 1979) to indicate the extent to which they were bothered by specific kinds of behaviors. It was shown that teachers took the most severe actions with those students who were most like students who bother or disturb them.

Placement Team Decision-Making Practices

Many researchers have studied the process by which students are classified and have focused their investigations on the activities of placement teams. Chalfant (1984) reported that there are six kinds of teams. Some teams function to validate referrals for tests, others to develop assessment plans. Some teams integrate and interpret findings, while other teams engage in diagnostic teaching. In some instances, teams function to determine eligibility for special education services; in others they write individual educational plans. Chalfant reported that teams can and do serve more than one of these six functions, but that teams typically do not perform all of the functions.

Earlier, I reported the findings of our research on team decision making at the Minnesota Institute for Research on Learning Disabilities. We found it difficult to find team meetings that matched the specifications of the law. We found that teams functioned for the most part to verify problems first observed by teachers. We found that the team decision-making process was most often not data based, in spite of the fact that much data were reported at the meetings. We found that many team practices were unreliable and invalid.

Bias in Assessment, Decision Making, and Classification

One other area of interest for those who have studied classification has been the issue of bias in assessment, decision making, and classification. In fact, this may be the most often studied area and set of issues. This country's measurement experts have spent an enormous amount of time, effort, energy, and money trying to resolve issues relevant to bias in assessment. It is not my intent here to review the large literature on bias in assessment. The interested reader is referred to other sources (e.g., Heller et al., 1982; Jensen, 1980; Reynolds, 1984; Ysseldyke, 1977, 1979). The major issue in many recent major court cases has been alleged abuse in the assessment of students and specifically minority students. In *Larry P. v. Riles* (1972) and *PASE v. Hannon* (1980), parents of black children brought suit against school systems for alleged inappropriate use of intelligence tests in making decisions to place black students in classes for mentally retarded students. In *Lora v. Board of Education* (1978), the issue was classification of minority students as emotionally disturbed.

I referred earlier to the conclusions of the National Academy of Sciences Panel on Placement of Students in Special Education (Heller et al., 1982). That group concluded that the issue was an instructional issue and that it could best be addressed by focusing on the development of appropriate instructional interventions for all students. Cleary (1980) put the issue well when she said "the problem is the special education classes. There would be no controversy if kids blossomed when they were put into special education classes" (p. 7).

Comparative Research

The establishment and naming of categories for different handicapping conditions has led to investigations of differences between normal and average students and students assigned to different categories of mild handicaps. In addition to these investigations, researchers have focused on identifying the similarities and differences among individuals assigned to different categories of mild handicaps. Comparative research has also addressed the issue of the validity of condition-specific treatment for students assigned to various categories.

Differences Between Normal or Average and Mildly Handicapped Students

Relative to normal or average students, learning disabled students have been shown to exhibit deficient information processing (Short & Ryan, 1984; Swanson, 1982). Yet, other researchers (Samuels & Miller, 1985) have found no differences in selective attention between normal and school-identified learning disabled students.

Brooks and McCauley (1984) found information processing differences between mildly retarded students and normal or average students. And, attentional deficits have been reported for mildly retarded learners (Borkowski, Peck, & Danberg, 1983; Brooks & McCauley, 1984). Based on an extensive review of research on learning, Campione, Brown, and Ferrara (1982) reported that mildly retarded and normal learners differ on speed and efficiency of information processing, the amount of knowledge they have, the kinds of problem-solving strategies they use, and metacognition. For years, researchers have contended that mildly mentally retarded students have lower motivation than average students (Robinson & Robinson, 1976; Zigler, 1962). Now, Adelman and Taylor (1983, 1984) report motivational deficits for learning disabled students. The characteristics that previously differentiated mildly retarded and normal students now differentiate learning disabled and normal students.

I argue that the entire literature on reports of comparisons of mildly handicapped students with normal or average students is of limited theoretical and practical use. When such comparisons are made, we inevitably learn that categorical groups of students differ from normal or average students precisely on the characteristics or variables that are used to define the handicapping conditions: we learn that mentally retarded students differ on cognitive or intellectual factors, that students called emotionally disturbed differ on social/emotional factors, and that learning disabled and normal students differ on information processing or academic achievement.

I argue that the diagnostic dilemma facing the practitioner is one of differentiating low-achieving and mildly handicapped students, of sorting from all those students who are experiencing difficulties in school those to be labeled handicapped and given special education services. Johnson (1980) had 356 school psychologists read psychological reports on special education referral cases. The reports were so arranged that combinations of IQ level, emotional/social problems, and IQ-achievement discrepancies were presented. When one of the characteristics was present at greater severity than the others, predictable placement recommendations were made. When the distinctions among characteristics became fuzzy, so did the ability of decision makers to differentiate categories. In contrast to the findings of Ysseldyke and his colleagues, Johnson found that sorting factors (e.g., age, sex, socioeconomic status) did not enter into differential classification and that decision makers instead attended to salient features.

Differences Among Mildly Handicapped Students

For many years, the only kind of comparative research on categories of exceptionality was research in which the psychometric performance of categorized students was contrasted to the performance of so-called normal students. More recently, there has been a significant increase in efforts to differentiate psychometrically among categories or conditions of exceptionality (e.g., Gajar, 1979, 1980; Hallahan & Kauffman, 1976). Sherry (1982) generated descriptive data on the behavioral and psychometric characteristics of educable mentally retarded, emotionally disturbed, and learning disabled students. He had 100 subjects who were 11 and 12 years old. Sherry observed and tested twenty subjects in each of the three categories, as well as twenty students labeled as "at risk" and twenty students considered normal. Exceptional, at-risk, and normal students did not differ in behavioral characteristics. Exceptional students showed lower frequencies of non-task-oriented behavior when placed in special education resource rooms, a finding similar to that of Samuels and Miller (1985). In Sherry's investigation, the normal and at-risk students earned higher scores than any of the groups of exceptional students on the psychometric measures. There was considerable overlap in the test performance of emotionally disturbed, educable mentally retarded, and learning disabled students. Benda (1954), Bailer (1970), Lilly (1977), and Hallahan and Kauffman (1976) were all unable to differentiate among the three types of students. Consistently, investigators have been unable to differentiate reliably between the psychometric test performance of categorical groups of mildly handicapped students.

In efforts to differentiate between groups of students, research has moved from efforts to do so using single tests to actuarial prediction efforts. Researchers were unable to differentiate reliably between groups using single tests or combinations of tests; they were unable to differentiate reliably on the basis of clinical judgment. More recently, efforts have consisted of attempts to engage in systems-actuarial analysis. The most recent example of this approach is the M-MAC program (McDermott, 1984) distributed by Psychological Corporation. The program is an Apple computer program that enables users to input test scores. The program classifies the student. The program has its origins in the work of McDermott (1980), who designed a systems-actuarial method for differential identification of handicapped students. The system was written in response to observed inconsistency in diagnostic classification. The system, called *multidimensional actuarial classification,* is designed to aid in differential diagnosis. There are three stated advantages of the system. First, diagnoses are based on statistical probabilities of relationships derived through test norms rather than on clinical diagnoses derived from experiential probability, the probability of relationships based on clinicians' experiences. Second, the system does not rely on deviation in only one characteristic (i.e, intelligence), but enables consideration of multiple dimensional characteristics. In M-MAC, it is assumed that all children share common dimensions of personal qualities and differ only in the intensity and relationship among qualities. Third, it is claimed that M-MAC increases interclinician agreement in the classification of students. It is still too early to judge the extent to which the claims of the authors of this system will be realized. It is my contention that use of the system would provide reliable groups of students, and that the students would differ on the characteristics that the programmers of the system decided were important. Then we could argue at length about the extent to which the programmed differences are useful and important.

Condition-Specific Treatment

One reason for classifying students as handicapped is that doing so allegedly leads to condition-specific treatment. That is, it is assumed that students who evidence like characteristics will learn in similar ways and that identification of specific types will enable school personnel to group those types together. The assumption that different types or categories of students learn differently when taught by different methodologies is an aptitude-treatment-interaction (ATI) assumption. ATI research on categories of exceptionality has been incredibly disappointing. It has been impossible to demonstrate that students who evidence differing kinds of handicapping conditions learn differently. Indeed, this is one of the fundamental notions that drives the categorization and classification process: the notion that specific kinds of students learn differently. My reading of the professional literature in this area shows that we have demonstrated that the principles of learning apply across categories. With the exception of sensorily impaired handicapped students, the different categories of students learn in similar ways. There are not instructional strategies, techniques, or methodologies that are uniquely effective for certain categories of students.

In spite of the disappointing findings of research efforts to identify ATIs for categorical groups of handicapped students, researchers have sought to identify ATIs for certain groups within categories. Thus, for example, researchers have contrasted the performance of learning disabled students who demonstrate auditory processing disorders with the performance of learning disabled students who demonstrate visual processing disorders. In preparing this paper, I reviewed the results of hundreds of such efforts to identify ATIs. Again, the findings are disappointing.

How Does the State of Practice Compare to the State of the Art?

There is considerable disparity between the state of the art and the state of practice in the classification of students. I will not belabor that point, but simply list some clear indications of it.

1. There is currently no defensible psychometric methodology for reliably differentiating students into categories. Yet, school personnel in all but two states are required by law to use indices of pupil performance on psychometric measures to classify and place students.
2. There is no evidence to support the contention that specific categories of students learn differently. Yet, students are instructed in categorical groups on the notion that these groups of students learn differently.
3. With the exception of sensorily impaired students, categorically grouped students do not demonstrate a set of universal and specific characteristics—or, for that matter, even a single universal and specific characteristic. There is no logic to current practice.
4. The current system used by public schools to classify exceptional children does not meet the criteria of reliability, coverage, logical consistency, utility, and acceptance to users.

This is not the first effort to summarize the knowledge base, the state of the art, or the state of practice in the classification of handicapped students. When he was Secretary of Health, Education and Welfare, Elliott Richardson called for a systematic review of the classification and labeling of exceptional children. In response, Hobbs (1975) produced a two-volume text entitled *Issues in the Classification of Children*. It was generally concluded as a result of that effort that the then-current classification practices had little going for them other than administrative convenience. Hobbs recommended that such activities cease.

Reynolds (1984) prepared a careful analysis of practices in the classification of handicapped students. He concluded that:

> Clearly, the development of these largely isolated or "set aside" programs has provided a convenience for regular educators and even educational researchers who are able to theorize about individual differences without making a serious effort to implement new procedures arising from their research. (p. 88)

In 1983, Lynn pointed out that categorical special education practices are driven by funding, but that all funding is on the input side. Lynn argued that it matters not whether the programs and the categories do anyone any good. Rather, funds are awarded in proportion to the number of children found.

In 1984, a task force of school psychologists prepared a document entitled *School Psychology: A Blueprint for Training and Practice* (Ysseldyke, Reynolds, & Weinberg, 1984). In that document, it was recommended that we:

> . . . disband entirely the process of classifying mildly handicapped children in the various subcategories such as "learning disabled," "educable mentally retarded," and "behaviorally disordered" (or emotionally disturbed). Instead a child's situation would be identified as problematic only when he or she obviously was not learning or behaving in a manner that leads to personal success in schools. The major identification procedures would be curriculum-

> based and the remedies would likewise be in the curriculum realm, changing the instructional program and educational procedures to meet individual needs (p. 9).

Given the numerous negatives regarding classification activities, why do they continue? They continue because people believe they are important. We have built a massive machinery of federal funding around a categorical system: schools receive special education funds only by classifying children. We have built a teacher training enterprise around a categorical system: we train and certify teachers of mentally retarded students, teachers of deaf students, and teachers of emotionally disturbed students. We organize ourselves into professional groups on the basis of disability labels.

What are the Effects of Classification?

At the outset, it must be stated very clearly that we simply do not know for certain the effects of classifying students. There is, of course, much opinion on this topic, and a good share of the opinion has a basis in fact. People observe the good and bad things that happen to students as a result of their being classified as handicapped. And, they write about what they observe. Yet, as stated earlier, the critical experiment has not been done. We have not classified nonhandicapped students, put them in special education programs, and observed the effects. We have not done so for obvious ethical reasons. This section reviews what people have said are the alleged negative and positive effects of classification.

Alleged Negative Effects of Classification

It has been argued repeatedly and soundly that the act of classifying students has a negative effect on students, teachers, and organizations. The argument is multifaceted.

It is argued that classification creates stigma to students, that the levels that are assigned to students are stigmatizing labels. When this argument is raised, it is usually accompanied by the corollary argument that some labels are more stigmatizing than others. It is relatively easy to find this point made as an explanation for rapid, significant increases in the number of students labeled as learning disabled (Greenburg, 1984). It is argued that the label learning disabled is less stigmatizing than the labels mentally retarded or emotionally disturbed. At the same time, though, many contend that all labels are stigmatizing and label children as defective (Reynolds & Balow, 1972; Smith & Neisworth, 1975).

It is argued that the act of labeling students leads teachers to hold lowered expectations for students' performance. And, the act of labeling a student is said to affect both the labeled and the labeler (MacMillan, 1982). MacMillan (1982) stated that people often behave differently toward students after the students are labeled. Dexter (1956, 1958, 1860) argued that labeling may create a self-fulfilling prophecy as the labeled person undergoes progressively negative experiences-labeling, public degradation, institutionalization, stigmatization.

Gallagher (1976) pointed to three negatives not regularly cited by others. These were (a) categorizing can lead to a social hierarchy, (b) categorization or classification can be viewed by professionals as the end of the process and therefore not lead to change, and (c) classification is an individual treatment that can lead us to ignore the complex social and ecological issues that need reform.

Smith and Neisworth (1975) argued that one negative effect of classification, categorization, and labeling is the fact that the practice is educationally irrelevant. They argued that knowing the categories to which students are assigned provides little helpful information to teachers. They contend that teachers approach teaching a given topic in the same way, regardless of the diagnostic label assigned to a child.

Categorical practices in special education have led to the disproportionate placement of minority students. And, classification practices have led to considerable litigation. As Bersoff (1979) noted, the substantive issue in many of the recent court cases relevant to special education has been the alleged abuse in the process of assessing and classifying students.

Not only has classification led to disproportionate placement in special education, but it has often led to dead-end placement. Very few students exit special education programs to regular education programs.

One final effect of classification is referred to by Blackhurst et al. (this volume) and Blackhurst (1982). Blackhurst and his colleagues have reported that there are negative outcomes of categorical practices in special education at the professional level. In teacher training programs, there is considerable redundancy in course work, and artificial barriers among people are created when professionals organize themselves categorically into special interest groups or professional associations.

Alleged Positive Effects of Classification

It is much easier to find strong statements against the practice of classifying students than to find statements in support of such activities. People just do not often write in support of the practice of classifying students.

Gallagher (1976) identified three positive uses of labels. He said that they provide a means of classification, diagnosis, and treatment, and that labeling and classification provide a basis for research on etiology, prevention, and treatment. And, he argued that classification and labeling enable us to obtain financial support for training, research, and delivery of services.

There is little support for the first two positive aspects listed by Gallagher. Glass (1983) observed that most classification is so arbitrary that questions of treatment are irrelevant. Ysseldyke, Thurlow, et al. (1983) noted that labels are so arbitrarily assigned and subjects in research so inadequately described that we have a series of interesting research findings on unknown populations or samples of students.

It is argued that categories serve as rallying points for special interest groups (Gallagher, Forsythe, Ringelheim, & Weintraub, 1975). Indeed, I believe it is safe to conclude that we have advanced as far as we have in special education because of the efforts of parents organized categorically into advocacy groups.

Categorization and labeling are said to have positive outcomes insofar as they lead to the setting of realistic goals that children are able to accomplish (Meyers, MacMillan, & Yoshida, 1978). Yet, it is not necessary to categorize and label children in order to set realistic goals for their performance.

When all is said and done, the only clear positive effect of labeling and classification is that they are tied to legislation and lead to obtaining funds that help better the educational services that handicapped students receive.

What Are the Implications for Research, Policy, Teacher Preparation, and Practice?

In this chapter, I have delineated problems in the classification of students. There are fundamental conceptual problems in special education classification, but they are not unlike the conceptual problems faced in classification practices in psychology, psychiatry, social welfare, and society in general. The problems in this territory are enormously complex. There are no easy solutions to the problems. And, therein is a major issue for policy makers and practitioners. In spite of the complexity of the problems, there is a tremendous demand for the rapid, simple solution of those problems. There is tremendous pressure to devise "the right way" to classify students. There *is* no one right way to classify, and one right way will not be devised. Different kinds of systems are needed in different locations for the purpose of making decisions about eligibility for and delivery of special education services. However, before dealing with system change, it is important to consider a number of assumptions.

Examining Our Assumptions

Clearly, it is past time to carefully examine the assumptions that drive the practice of classifying students. Professionals disagree about whether or not specific types of students exist. Thus, they argue about whether or not there *are,* for example, mentally retarded, learning disabled, emotionally disturbed, and speech impaired students. Two issues are repeatedly confused: are there specific types of students, and are the categories useful concepts?

There can be no doubt that there are many students who experience difficulty learning in school. Many of these students *do* have cognitive deficits, some have severe perceptual problems, some have severe language problems, and others have emotional disorders. These problems can, and do, interfere with learning. But, at the same time, the concepts that drive practice have lost meaning. The terms learning disabled, mentally retarded, emotionally disturbed, behaviorally disordered, and so on have lost meaning. The conceptual definitions assigned to these terms are so general as to be nebulous. The many different operationalizations by state education agencies, and the differential compliance with state education agency criteria by local education agencies, has rendered the concepts meaningless. Yet, we address the problems in this area by trying to make the concepts more sophisticated. Task force after task force has studied ways to define the handicapping conditions. Task force reports are received and subsequently ignored by governmental agencies and professionals. When parents, professionals, advocacy groups, and others question the efficacy of categories or labels or express concerns about how eligibility decisions are made, governmental agencies institute task forces to study the problems.

Numerous committees, task forces, and study commissions have studied the conditions (categories, labels) of special education. And, there currently is as much or more conceptual confusion as there ever has been. It is time to evaluate a critical assumption: the concepts that direct current practice may make no sense.

A second assumption that begs careful examination is the assumption that all we need is a better way to operationalize the definitions that guide practice. If we cannot achieve consensus on the conceptual boundaries of our definitions of handicapping conditions, then it makes little sense to attempt achievement of consensus on classification criteria.

A third assumption that needs critical examination is the assumption that students must be classified or categorized to be eligible for special education services. We assume this to be the case, so we do it. The practice serves an administrative convenience. Yet, clearly, it needs to be carefully reexamined.

A fourth assumption that begs careful analysis is the notion that the act of classifying students helps them. There is little empirical support for this belief, yet there are few investigations that have tested directly the belief.

System Change

Reynolds (1984) identified a number of implications/directions that should be focused on here. In practice, we need to move away from test-based classification and labeling of children and to move toward classification that is "based mainly on progress in curriculum and oriented strictly to problems of instruction" (Reynolds, 1984, p. 84). Major efforts to do so are evident in the work of Wang (1980), Reynolds and Wang (1983), and Tucker (1980, 1984).

Some of the implications of the present analysis of classification practice and of research on classification are apparent, indeed obvious, in the discussion itself. And, none of the implications are new. I firmly believe that we know very well what stance we ought to take in regard to the practice of classifying exceptional children: the practice makes very little sense, and it is time to disband efforts to find new and better ways of classifying children.

In teacher preparation, we need to foster efforts to move to a generic rather than categorical basis for training those who will educate mildly and moderately handicapped students. Such a move will necessarily involve the provision of training in accommodation of individual differences to all teachers. Reynolds (1984) and Sharp (1982) have described ways of doing so.

Finally, we need a major, national research effort designed to identify the best ways to make eligibility decisions. Such an effort was specified as a recommendation in the document entitled *Barriers to Excellence: Our Children at Risk* (National Coalition of Advocates for Students, 1985). In this work, it was recommended that we:

> . . . undertake research and development efforts directed at complex funding and accountability issues. These should include waivers to selected school districts where researchers and educators are trying new approaches to child study, classification, parent involvement, instruction, and accountability. Such limited experimentation, carried out in ways which meet current accountability standards, is necessary in order to identify alternative funding and accountability mechanisms which do not encourage overclassification and misclassification of students (p. 114)

If we are to disband current practices in which norm-referenced tests are administered to students and the results of those tests used to classify or categorize the students, we need to replace those activities with some other system. What might that system look like? Reynolds and Lakin (this volume) offer a number of suggestions. They advocate the use of curriculum-based approaches similar to the Adaptive Learning Environments Model (Wang, 1980; Wang & Birch, 1984) and dimensional rather than categorical diagnoses. Clearly, there is much to support the use of curriculum-based assessment in making placement decisions (Deno, 1985; Germann & Tindal, 1985; Marston & Magnuson, 1985). One other approach, though, is the use of consultation and prereferral intervention as described by Graden, Casey, and Christenson (1985).

The prereferral intervention model is an indirect service model in which resources traditionally used to test and place large numbers of students are redirected to provide assistance to students and their teachers in the regular classroom settings where problems first arise. The goal of prereferral intervention is to implement systematically intervention strategies in the regular classroom and to evaluate the effectiveness of these strategies before a student is formally referred for testing. An objective of prereferral intervention is the delivery of interventions in the least restrictive environment and the use of data on intervention effectiveness in the making of subsequent instructional decisions. Graden et al. (1985) described the stages of the prereferral intervention process. Teachers request consultation rather than requesting testing. Consultation, observation, prereferral interventions, and conferences a[ll] precede formal referral for assessment. The major phase[s] of the prereferral intervention model include identifying, defining, and clarifying the problem; analyzing the components of the classroom ecology that effect the problem; designing and implementing interventions; and evaluating intervention effectiveness.

It is clear that current practices in the classification of students are not working well. And, there are reasonable alternatives to those practices. We need to eliminate the barriers that keep us from using and validating those alternatives.

Author Information

James E. Ysseldyke is Professor of Educational Psychology at the University of Minnesota.

References

Adelman, H., & Taylor, L. (1983). *Learning disabilities in perspective.* Chicago, IL: Scott Foresman.

Adelman, H., & Taylor, L. (1984). *Learning disabilities.* Glenview, IL: Scott Foresman.

Algozzine, B. (1979). *The disturbingness and acceptability of behaviors as a function of diagnostic label* (Research Rep No. 4). Minneapolis: University of Minnesota, Institute for Research on Learning Disabilities.

Algozzine, B., Christenson, S., & Ysseldyke, J. E. (1982). Probabilities associated with the referral to placement process. *Teacher Education and Special Education,* **5**, 19–23.

Algozzine, B., & Korinek, L. (1985). Where is special education for students with high prevalence handicaps going? *Exceptional Children,* **51**, 388–397.

Algozzine, B., & Ysseldyke, J. E. (1981). Special education services for normal students: Better safe than sorry? *Exceptional Children,* **48**, 238–243.

American Psychiatric Association. (1979). *Diagnostic and statistical manual of mental disorders* (3rd ed.). Washington, DC: Author.

Bailer, I. (1970). Emotional disturbance and mental retardation: Etiologies and conceptual relationships. In F. J. Menolascino (Ed.), *Psychiatric approaches to mental retardation.* New York: Basic Books.

Benda, C. E. (1954). Psychopathology of children. In L. Carmichael (Ed.), *Manual of child psychology.* New York: Wiley.

Bersoff, D. N. (1979). Regarding psychologists testily: Legal regulation of psychological assessment in the public schools. *Maryland Law Review,* **39**, 27–120.

Binet, A., & Simon, T. (1916). The development of intelligence in children (E. S. Kit, Trans.). Baltimore, MD: Williams & Wilkins.

Blackhurst, A. E. (1982). Noncategorical special education teacher preparation. In M. C. Reynolds (Ed.), *The future of mainstreaming: Next steps in teacher education.* Reston, VA: Council for Exceptional Children.

Borkowski, J. G., Peck, V. A., & Danberg, P. R. (1983). Attention, memory, and cognition. In J. L. Matson & J. A. Mulick (Eds.), *Handbook of mental retardation.* New York: Pergamon Press.

Brooks, P. H., & McCauley, C. (1984). Cognitive research in mental retardation. *American Journal of Mental Deficiency*, **88**, 479–486.

Brown, A. L., Bransford, J. D., Ferrara, R. A., & Campione, J. (1983). Learning, remembering, and understanding. In J. H. Flavell & E. M. Markman (Eds.), *Carmichael's manual of child psychology* (Vol. 3, pp. 77–166). New York: Wiley.

Burstein, A. (1985). *The turning point: New directions for special education*. Trenton, NJ: New Jersey Special Education Study Commission.

Campione, J. C., Brown, A. L., & Ferrara, R. A. (1982). Mental retardation and intelligence. In R. J. Sternberg (Ed.), *Handbook of human intelligence* (pp. 392–473). Cambridge, England: Cambridge University Press.

Cantalician Foundation, Inc. (1983). *Technical assistance on alternative practices related to the problem of the overrepresentation of black and minority students in special education*. Buffalo, NY: Author.

Chalfant, J. C., (1984). *Identifying learning disabled students; Guidelines for decision making*. Burlington, VT: Northeast Regional Resource Center.

Christenson, S., Ysseldyke, J. E., & Algozzine, B. (1982). Institutional and external pressures influencing referral decisions. *Psychology in the Schools*, **19**, 341–345.

Cleary, A. (1980). (Quoted in) *APA Monitor*, **11**, 7, November, 1980.

Coleman, J. C. (1953). Perceptual retardation in reading disability. *Journal of Educational Psychology*, **44**, 497–503.

The condition of education. (all editions). Washington, DC: U.S. Government Printing Office.

Cromwell, R. I., Blashfield, R. K., & Strauss, J. S. (1975). Criteria for classification systems. In N. Hobbs (Ed.), *Issues in the classification of children* (Vol. 1, pp. 4–25). San Francisco, CA: Jossey-Bass.

Deno, S. L. (1985). Curriculum-based measurement: The emerging alternative. *Exceptional Children*, **52**, 219–232.

Dexter, L. A. (1956). Towards a sociology of the mentally defective. *American Journal of Mental Deficiency*, **61**, 10–16.

Dexter, L. A. (1958). A social theory of mental deficiency. *American Journal of Mental Deficiency*, **62**, 920–928.

Dexter, L. A. (1960). Research on problems of mental subnormality. *American Journal of Mental Deficiency*, **64**, 835–838.

Epps, S., Ysseldyke, J. E., & McGue, M. (1984). Differentiating LD and non-LD students: I know one when I see one. *Learning Disability Quarterly*, **7**, 89–101.

Epstein, M., Cullinan, D., & Sabatino, D. A. (1977). State definitions of behavior disorders. *Journal of Special Education*, **11**, 417–426.

Esquirol, J. E. D. (1845). *Mental maladies*. (E. K. Hunt, Trans.). Philadelphia, PA: Lea and Blanchard. Originally published as *Maladies mentales* (1838).

Fisk, J. L., & Rourke, B. P. (1983). Neuropsychological subtyping of learning disabled children: History, methods, implications. *Journal of Learning Disabilities*, **16**, 529–531.

Flor, J. F. (1978). *Service provider agreement and special education reform*. Unpublished doctoral dissertation, Pennsylvania State University.

Foster, G. G., Ysseldyke, J. E., Casey, A., & Thurlow, M. (1984). Congruence between reason for referral and placement outcome. *Journal of Psychoeducational Assessment*, **2**, 209–218.

Freeman, M. (1971). A reliability study of psychiatric diagnosis in childhood and adolescence. *Journal of Child Psychology and Psychiatry*, **12**, 43–54.

Friedman, J. B., & Gillooley, W. B. (1977). Perceptual development in the profoundly deaf as related to early reading. *Journal of Special Education*, **11**, 347–354.

Gajar, A. H. (1979). EMR, LD, ED: Similarities and differences. *Exceptional Children*, **45**, 470–472.

Gajar, A. H. (1980). Characteristics across exceptional categories. *Journal of Special Education*, **14**, 165–173.

Gallagher, J. J. (1976). The sacred and profane use of labeling. *Mental Retardation*, **14**, 2–3.

Gallagher, J. J., Forsythe, P., Ringelheim, D., & Weintraub, F. J. (1975). Funding patterns and labeling. In N. Hobbs (Ed.), *Issues in the classification of children* (Vol. 1, pp. 432–462). San Francisco, CA: Jossey-Bass.

Garrison, M., & Hammill, D. (1970). Who are the retarded? *Exceptional Children*, **38**, 13–20.

Gerber, M. (1984). The Department of Education's Sixth Annual Report to Congress on P.L. 94–142: Is Congress getting the full story? *Exceptional Children*, **51**, 209–224.

Germann, G., & Tindal, G. (1985). An application of curriculum-based assessment: The use of direct and repeated measurement. *Exceptional Children*, **52**, 244–265.

Glass, G. (1983). The effectiveness of special education. *Policy Studies Review*, **2**, 65–78.

Goddard, H. H. (1919). *Psychology of the normal and subnormal*. New York: Dodd, Mead.

Graden, J. L., Casey, A., & Christenson, S. L. (1985). Implementing a prereferral intervention system: Part I. The model. *Exceptional Children*, **51**, 377–388.

Greenburg, D. (1984). The 1984 Annual Report to Congress: Are we better off? *Exceptional Children*, **51**, 203–208.

Grossman, H. (Ed.). (1973). *Manual of terminology and classification in mental retardation*. Washington, DC: American Association on Mental Deficiency.

Gutkin, T. (1979). Bannatyne patterns of Caucasian and Mexican-American learning disabled children. *Psychology in the Schools*, **16**, 178–182.

Hallahan, D. P., & Kauffman, J. M. (1976). Learning disabilities versus emotional disturbance versus retardation. In D. P. Hallahan & J. M. Kauffman (Eds.), *Introduction to learning disabilities: A psychobehavioral approach*. Englewood Cliffs, NJ: Prentice-Hall.

Hallahan, D. J., & Kauffman, J. M. (1986). *Exceptional Children*. Englewood Cliffs, NJ: Prentice-Hall.

Hammill, D., Leigh, J., McNutt, G., & Larson, S. C. (1981). A new definition of learning disabilities. *Learning Disability Quarterly*, **4**, 336–343.

Heller, H. W., (1982). Professional standards for preparing special educators: Status and prospects. *Exceptional Education Quarterly*, **2**, 77–86.

Heller, K. A., Holtzman W., & Messick, S. (1982). *Placing children in special education: A strategy for equity*. Washington, DC: National Academy Press.

Heller, H. W., & Ridenour, N. (1983). Professional standards: Foundation for the future. *Exceptional Children*, **49**, 294–298.

Heward, W. L., & Orlansky, M. D. (1985). *Exceptional children*. Columbus, OH: Charles Merrill.

Hobbs, N. (1975). *Issues in the classification of children* (Vols. 1 and 2). San Francisco, CA: Jossey-Bass.

Hocutt, A. M., Cox, J. L., & Pelosi, J. (1984). An exploration of issues regarding the identification and placement of LD, MR, and ED students. In *A policy-oriented study of special education's service delivery system, Phase 1: Preliminary study* (RTI Report No. RTI/2706-06/OIES). Durham,

NC: Research Triangle Institute, Center for Educational Studies.

Horn, J. L. (1924) *The education of exceptional children: A consideration of public school problems and policies in the field of differentiated education.* New York: The Century Company.

Howe, S. G. (1848). Report of commission to inquire into the conditions of idiots of the Commonwealth of Massachusetts. Boston, MA: Senate Document No. 51, 1–37. Also in M. Rosen, G. R. Clark, & M. S. Kivitz (Eds.), *The history of mental retardation* (Vol. 1, pp. 33–60). Baltimore, MD: University Park Press.

Jensen, A. R. (1980). *Bias in mental testing.* New York: Free Press.

Johnson, V. M. (1980). Analysis of factors influencing special educational placement decisions. *Journal of School Psychology,* **18**, 191–202.

Kass, C. E. (1966). Psycholinguistic disabilities of children with reading problems. *Exceptional Children,* **32**, 533–539.

Kaufman, A. S., Wood, M. M., & Swan, W. W. (1979). Dimensions of problem behaviors of emotionally disturbed children as seen by their parents and teachers. *Psychology in the Schools,* **16**, 207–216.

Kirk, S. A., & Gallagher, J. J. (1986). *Educating exceptional children.* Boston, MA: Houghton Mifflin.

Larry P. v. Riles, Civil action N. L. -71-2270, 343 F. Supp. 1306 (N. D. Calif. 1972).

Lilly, M. S. (1977). A merger of categories: Are we finally ready? *Journal of Learning Disabilities,* **10**, 115–121.

Lora v. Board of Education, New York City, 75 Civ. 917 (E.D. New York 1979).

Lynn, L. E. (1983). The emerging system for educating handicapped children. *Policy Studies Review,* **2**, 21–58.

MacMillan, D. (1982). *Mental retardation in school and society* (2nd ed.). Boston, MA: Little, Brown.

Marlowe, M., Coissart, A., Welch, K., & Errera, J. (1984). Hair mineral content as a predictor of learning disabilities. *Journal of Learning Disabilities,* **17**, 418–421.

Marston, D., & Magnuson, D. (1985). Implementing curriculum-based assessment in special and regular education settings. *Exceptional Children,* **52**, 266–276.

McDermott, P. A. (1975). Characteristics of diagnostic decision-making behaviors among groups of pre- and post-practicum trainee and experienced school psychologists. (Doctoral dissertation, Temple University). *Dissertation Abstracts International,* **36**, 3520-A.

McDermott, P. A. (1977). Measures of diagnostic data usage as discriminants among training and experience levels in school psychology. *Psychology in the Schools,* **14**, 323–331.

McDermott, P. A. (1980). A systems-actuarial method for the differential diagnosis of handicapped children. *Journal of Special Education,* **14**, 7–20.

McDermott, P. (1984). *McDermott multidimensional actuarial classification.* San Antonio, TX: Psychological Corporation.

McKinney, J. D. (1984). The search for subtypes of specific learning disabilities. *Journal of Learning Disabilities,* **17**, 43–50.

Meyers, C., MacMillan, D., & Yoshida, R. (1978). Validity of psychologists' identification of EMR students in the perspective of the California decertification experience. *Journal of School Psychology,* **16**, 3–15.

Morrow, H. W., Powell, G. D., & Ely, D. D. (1976). Placement of placebo: Does additional information change special education placement decisions? *Journal of School Psychology,* **14**, 186–191.

National Coalition of Advocates for Students. (1985, January) *Barriers to excellence: Our children at risk.* Boston, MA Author.

Norman, C. A., & Zigmond, N. (1980). Characteristics of children labeled and served as learning disabled in school systems affiliated with child service demonstration centers. *Journal of Learning Disabilities,* **13**, 542–547.

PASE v. Hannon, 74C 3586 (N. D. Ill. 1980).

Pfeiffer, S. I., & Naglieri, J. A. (1983). An investigation of multidisciplinary team decision making. *Journal of Learning Disabilities,* **16**, 588–590.

Reynolds, M. C. (1984). Classification of students with handicaps. In E. W. Gordon (Ed.), *Review of research in education* (Vol. II. pp. 63–92). Washington, DC: American Educational Research Association.

Reynolds, M. C., & Balow, B. (1972). Categories and variables in special education. *Exceptional Children,* **38**, 357–366.

Reynolds, M. C., & Wang, M. C. (1983). Restructuring "special" school programs: A position paper. *Policy Studies Review,* **2**, 189–212.

Robinson, N., & Robinson, H. (1976). *The mentally retarded child.* New York: McGraw-Hill.

Rykman, D. B., & Elrod, G. F. (1983). Once is not enough. *Journal of Learning Disabilities,* **16**, 87–89.

Samuels, S. J., & Miller, N. L. (1985). Failure to find attentional differences between learning disabled and normal children on classroom and laboratory tasks. *Exceptional Children,* **51**, 358–376.

Sarason, S., & Doris, J. (1979). *Educational handicap, public policy, and social history.* New York: Free Press.

Schneider, B., & Byrne, B. M. (1984). Predictors of successful transition from self-contained special education to regular class settings. *Psychology in the Schools,* **21**, 375–380.

Sharp, B. (1982). *Dean's Grant projects: Challenge and change in teacher education.* Washington, DC: American Association of Colleges for Teacher Education.

Shepard, L., & Smith, M. L. (1981). *Evaluation of the identification of perceptual-communicative disorders in Colorado* (Final Rep.). Boulder: University of Colorado, Laboratory of Educational Research.

Sherry, L. (1982). *Behavioral and psychometric characteristics of educable mental retarded, emotionally handicapped, learning disabled, at risk, and normal students.* Unpublished manuscript, University of North Carolina, Department of Learning/Instruction, Special Education Program, Charlotte.

Short, E. J., & Ryan, E. B. (1984). Metacognitive differences between skilled and less-skilled readers: Remediating deficits through story grammar and attribution training. *Journal of Educational Psychology,* **76**, 225–235.

Simner, M. L. (1984). Predicting school readiness from stroke directions in children's printing. *Journal of Learning Disabilities,* **17**, 397–399.

Smith, D. D., Deshler, D., Hallahan, D., Lovit, T., Robinson, S., Voress, J., & Ysseldyke, J. (1984). Minimum standards for the description of subjects used in learning disabilities research reports. *Learning Disability Quarterly,* **7**, 221–225.

Smith, R. M., & Neisworth, J. T. (1975). *The exceptional child: A functional approach.* New York: McGraw-Hill.

Spitzer, R. L., & Fleiss, J. J. (1974). A re-analysis of the reliability of psychiatric diagnosis. *British Journal of Psychiatry,* **125**, 341–347.

Swanson, H. L. (1982). Controversy: Strategy or capacity deficit. *Topics in Learning and Learning Disabilities,* **2**(2), entire issue.

aylor, R. L. (1980). Use of the AAMD classification system: A review of recent research. *American Journal of Mental Deficiency*, **85**, 116–119.

ucker, J. (1980). *Non-test-based assessment*. Minneapolis, MN: National School Psychology Inservice Training Network.

ucker, J. (1984). *School psychology in the classroom*. Minneapolis, MN: National School Psychology Inservice Training Network.

'ucker, J., Stevens, L., & Ysseldyke, J. E. (1983). Learning disabilities: The experts speak out. *Journal of Learning Disabilities*, **16**, 6–14.

Inited States Department of Education. (1984). *Sixth annual report to Congress on the implementation of Public Law 94–142: The Education for All Handicapped Children Act*. Washington, DC: Author.

'insonhaler, J. F., Weinshank, A. B., Wagner, C. C., Poplin, R. M. (1982). *Diagnosing children with educational problems: Characteristics of reading and learning disabilities specialists and classroom teachers* (Research Series No. 117). East Lansing, MI: Michigan State University Institute for Research on Teaching.

Wang, M. C. (1980). Adaptive instruction: Building on diversity. *Theory Into Practice*, **19**, 122–127.

Wang, M. C., & Birch, J. W. (1984). Effective special education in regular classes. *Exceptional Children*, **50**, 391–398.

Ysseldyke, J. E. (1977). Implementation of the nondiscriminatory assessment provisions of Public Law 94–142. In *Developing criteria for the evaluation of the protection in evaluation procedures provisions* (pp. 143–194). Washington, DC: Department of Health, Education and Welfare, United States Office of Education.

Ysseldyke, J. E. (1979). Issues in psychoeducational assessment. In G. D. Phye & D. J. Reschly (Eds.), *School psychology: Perspectives and issues*. New York: Academic Press.

Ysseldyke, J. E. (1984, June). *Current U.S. practice in making psychoeducational decisions*. Paper presented at the Congress of the Research Institute Voor het Onderwijs in Het Noorden, Groningen, The Netherlands.

Ysseldyke, J. E., & Algozzine, B. (1984). *Introduction to special education*. Boston, MA: Houghton Mifflin.

Ysseldyke, J. E., Algozzine, B., & Allen, D. (1981). Regular education teacher participation in special education team decision making. *Elementary School Journal*, **82**, 160–165.

Ysseldyke, J. E., Algozzine, B., & Epps, S. (1983). A logical and empirical analysis of current practice in classifying students as handicapped. *Exceptional Children*, **50**, 160–166.

Ysseldyke, J. E., Algozzine, B., & Mitchell, J. (1982). Special education team decision making: An analysis of current practice. *Personnel and Guidance Journal*, **60**, 308–313.

Ysseldyke, J. E., Algozzine, B., Regan, R., & Potter, M. (1980a). *A descriptive study of students enrolled in a program for the severely learning disabled* (Research Rep. No. 45). Minneapolis: University of Minnesota, Institute for Research on Learning Disabilities.

Ysseldyke, J. E., Algozzine, B., Regan, R., & Potter, M. (1980b). Technical adequacy of tests used by professionals in simulated decision making. *Psychology in the Schools*, **17**, 202–209.

Ysseldyke, J. E., Algozzine, B., Richey, L., & Graden, J. (1982). Declaring students eligible for learning disability services: Why bother with the data? *Learning Disability Quarterly*, **5**, 37–44.

Ysseldyke, J. E., Algozzine, B., Shinn, M., & McGue, M. (1982). Similarities and differences between low achievers and students classified learning disabled. *Journal of Special Education*, **16**, 73–85.

Ysseldyke, J. D., Regan, R. R., Thurlow, M. L., & Schwartz, S. Z. (1981). Current assessment practices: The cattle dip approach. *Diagnostique*, **6**, 16–27.

Ysseldyke, J. E., Reynolds, M. C., & Weinberg, R. A. (1984). *School psychology: A blueprint for training and practice*. Minneapolis, MN: National School Psychology Inservice Training Network.

Ysseldyke, J. E., Thurlow, M. L., Graden, J. L., Wesson, C., Algozzine, B., & Deno, S. L. (1983). Generalizations from five years of research on assessment and decision making. *Exceptional Education Quarterly*, **4**(1), 75–94.

Zigler, E. (1962). Rigidity in the feebleminded. In E. P. Trapp & R. Himmelstein (Eds.), *Readings on the exceptional child*. New York: Appleton-Century-Crofts.

Avoiding or Limiting Special Education Referrals: Changes and Challenges

ANN NEVIN and JACQUELINE THOUSAND

University of Vermont

Abstract—The major theme of this chapter is that as mainstream education broadens its tolerance for individual differences, few—if any—students need to be referred for services delivered outside the system. Reports from "state-of-the-art" research and practice are described and integrated with position statements. The paper focuses on underlying methods that strengthen the mainstream: adaptations of curricula and classroom management systems; teacher development and administrative management strategies; and early interventions and parental support. Recommendations for policy, training, and research are discussed.

The purpose of this chapter is to review the research and practices related to systems for avoiding or limiting referral of students for special education services. It should be noted that referral of a specific student remains the right and responsibility of parents and professionals who seek the most appropriate educational program for adapting the educational environment to meet that student's special needs. Systems for limiting or avoiding referrals are not intended to abridge that right or to abrogate that responsibility. Furthermore, it is important to emphasize that we are not focusing on simply reducing the number of students perceived to need special services, nor are we suggesting that there are fewer students who will need specialized instruction. In fact, we are interested in discovering systems to increase the resourcefulness of educators in creating more effective programs to assure the academic and social progress of all students. There is, therefore, an underlying theme of prevention, rather than intervention, that prevails in the broader text. This chapter intends to question why students are ever referred out of the general education system where general educators provide effective instruction for all students.

The specific context for this review can be illustrated by the results of a study conducted by the National Academy of Sciences in 1982 (Heller, Holtzman, & Messick) which recommended more scrutiny and reorganization of the general education system in order to correct the overreferral and overplacement of students in special education programs. The movement to "cap," or limit, service delivery for certain handicapping conditions, such as learning disability, also indicates the context for considering strategies to strengthen the mainstream educational system.

Our hypothesis is that, as mainstream education broadens its tolerance of individual differences, fewer students will be referred for services delivered *outside* of the system. In short, referrals can be avoided as general educators improve their instructional delivery system. General educators who develop broader tolerance in educating students with wide ranges of individual differences can be seen as both the impetus for and the result of strengthening the mainstream. New directions for the role and function of special educators within the general education system can thus be considered.

The boundary issues for this topic, those issues not typically considered to have a special education focus, include teacher development and systems development research and practices. These boundary issues were reflected in the profiles constructed for a search of the computerized data base for 1974 through 1984 reports and research articles entered in the Educational Resources Information Center (ERIC) and a search of the projects currently funded by Special Education Programs, U.S. Office of Education. Four areas were searched: (a) prereferral strategies involving teacher development, (b) prereferral strategies focusing on administration, (c) strengthening the mainstream, and (d) effects of early intervention.

Review of the State of the Art: Research and Practice

The major purpose of this section is to discuss and integrate current research, practices, and position statements related to systems that avoid or limit referral of students for position education services. The state of the art and the state of practice are presented concurrently.

Strengthening the Mainstream: Curricular and Ecological Adaptations

In this section, the research and practice related to methods that directly strengthen the mainstream education system are discussed. The section begins with a presentation of research relating to the principles of effective schools. Research relating to effective instructional techniques and to other general education interventions are then addressed. Specific implications of knowledge of applied behavior analysis are discussed, as are specific techniques such as peer tutoring and adaptation of curricula.

Principles of Effective Schools Research

There is a growing body of research on "effective schools" that indicates public schools can design achievement-oriented environments for *all* students. This research shows that, when general educators change the curriculum or the classroom instructional system, such changes *can* have a positive impact on all students, including those with handicaps. Edmond's (1979) criteria for an effective school is that "the children of the poor achieve minimal mastery of basic school skills that describe minimally successful pupil performance for the children of the middle class . . . an effective school is instructionally successful for all children" (p. 13). Based on an extensive review of the effective schools literature, Hersh (1981) defined effective as student academic achievement as measured by standardized achievement tests. Edmonds (1979), Brookover and Lezotte (1979), and Hersh (1981) identified, in comprehensive reviews, characteristics associated with effective schools. These characteristics include (a) administrative leadership for instructional behaviors, coupled with public rewards and incentives, that lead to student achievement; (b) expectations from administrators and teachers for student achievement (including clearly specified academic and social goals and a tightly coupled curriculum); (c) emphasis on teaching activities that result in high academic learning time; (d) frequent monitoring of homework and student progress; and (e) orderly, safe environments.

The variables researched in the effective schools literature suggest that administrators can manipulate the school environment toward student achievement. Not only are these clusters of classroom/school characteristics individually associated with pupil achievement, but efforts to incorporate them into a unified instructional design have also shown positive results for pupils identified as mildly handicapped. A system-wide demonstration of the effect of teachers acquiring those skills has been provided by Wang and associates at the University of Pittsburgh (e.g., Wang & Gennari, 1983; Wang, Vaughan, & Dytman, 1985). Wang and Gennari (1983) reported, for example, components of effective adaptive learning environments that result in successful instruction of students, including students with handicaps, in the mainstream.

Mastery Learning, Individualized Learning, and Cooperative Learning Systems

Similarly, the effective instruction literature suggests specific variables that teachers can manipulate that result in higher achievement. Several general education instructional techniques that are successful in increasing achievement have been identified by current educational researchers: mastery learning (Block, 1974); individualized learning (Bloom, 1980; Froh & Muraki, 1980) and cooperative learning (Johnson & Johnson, 1975; Johnson, Maruyama, Johnson, Nelson, & Skon, 1981; Slavin, 1984). These techniques have been shown to be effective with students who have handicaps. Hiscox and William (1979) reported the use of mastery learning techniques in Chapter 1 programs serving disadvantaged youth. Nevin, Johnson, and Johnson (1982); Nevin, Skieber, and Polewski (1984); and Wilcox, Sbardellati, and Nevin (in press) described the effective use of cooperative learning or group contingencies to improve the academic and social behaviors of mainstreamed students with handicaps.

Other General Education Interventions

Other general education innovations that have been effective in educating students with handicaps include resource room programs (Lott, 1975; Rainer & McCool, 1974; Schultz, 1978; Welsh & Ligon, 1980); peer tutoring programs (Laycock & Schwartzberg, 1976; Semmel, 1980); lowering of class size (Noli, 1980); increasing academic learning time (Aufderheide, 1981); and mainstreaming of bilingual students (Shore, 1981). These interventions offer a growing data base showing the effectiveness of teacher-controlled variables in school-based programs for students with handicaps as well as for nonhandicapped students.

Applied Behavior Analysis

Another strategy for strengthening mainstream education is to ensure teachers are skilled in using applied behavior analysis techniques. Hall, Lund, and Jackson (1968); Hall and Copeland (1972); and Haring, Lovitt, Eaton, and Hansen (1978) represent researchers and public school practitioners in both general and special education who agree on the knowledge of applied behavior analysis as a body of principles and techniques specifically designed to change important human behaviors within practical educational settings. A consequence of teachers being skilled in using applied behavior analysis is an increased ability to include in regular classes handicapped students who had formerly been excluded. Teachers with applied behavior analysis skills can test the effects of a particular program and treat each implementation as a new experiment, thus creating data-based teaching systems (Deno & Merkin, 1977). Instructional events are categorized as antecedents and consequences and evaluated on the basis of the observed accelerating and decelerating effects on the target behavior of the learners.

Peer Tutoring

Peer and cross-age tutoring programs are examples of adaptations of classroom ecology that have gained a research and practice data base as an effective method of teaching students with special education needs. When combined with principles and procedures of applied behavior analysis, frequent monitoring and supervision, peer tutoring programs have been found to be effective. They have been used to teach arithmetic to elementary school children (Harris & Sherman, 1973; Johnson &

Bailey, 1974); reading to senior high school students (Ritter & Idol-Maestas, 1982); spelling, arithmetic, and word recognition to elementary school children (Hawkes & Paolucci-Whitcomb, 1980; Jenkins, Mayhall, Peschka, & Jenkins, 1974); and social initiations to withdrawn children (Lancioni, 1982). Role reversal is also an important instructional option in which the student identified as handicapped can serve in the role of tutor (Osguthorpe, Eiserman, Shisler, Top, & Scruggs, 1984). General educators who implement tutorial programs for handicapped students in regular classrooms require reinforcement and assistance from administrators and specialists in preparing materials and tutors and in evaluating and redesigning programs (Semmel, 1980).

Curricular Adaptations

The ability of teachers to adapt curricula is another example of an effective teacher behavior that facilitates the mainstreaming of students with identified handicaps. Larrivee and Vacca (1982) reported that general education teachers who received comprehensive training in a variety of psychoeducational techniques and curricular approaches were able to increase academic growth for mainstreamed students while simultaneously accomplishing similar gains for all of their students. Haughton (1976) reported on Project PREM (Preparing Regular Educators for Mainstreaming), a competency-based pre-service and in-service training program based on a diagnostic-prescriptive model and pilot tested with 107 teachers. Teachers in the training program showed gains in skills and knowledge related to individualizing instruction, which led to their increased flexibility in adapting curricula for students with handicaps.

Cantrell and Cantrell (1976) showed that, by offering support to regular class teachers, the need for special education can be reduced. Cantrell (1979) created an instrument to measure the classroom's ability to adapt to students with special needs. The indices included rating on teacher contact, teacher movement, teacher attitudes in relation to student needs (such as math and reading scores, absences, support services, etc.). The implication of the Cantrells' work is that, as a student's needs increase, the needs for the classroom to adapt also increase. They have shown promising methods for assessing needs and for offering early interventions that reduce the rates of problematic classroom situations.

The literature on approaches to general improvement of regular classes as a way of preventing special education referrals (by assuming better educational progress by most pupils) is obviously broader than has been encompassed here. For further discussion of this topic, see other chapters in this volume (e.g. those by Reynolds & Lakin and Walberg & Wang). In addition, a good general summary of relevant research is provided in the book recently edited by Wang and Walberg (1985); a practical summary of efforts to improve teacher education for the same purpose has been provided by Sharp (1982).

Prereferral Interventions: Teacher Development and Administrative Strategies

This section reviews research and practice relating to approaches that reduce the likelihood of educators referring students for special education. These approaches are categorized according to teacher development strategies, such as in-service training, and to administration strategies, such as case management systems.

Traditional Referral Process

Ysseldyke et al. (1983) have summarized their 5 years of research on the assessment and decision-making process for service delivery for students with learning disabilities. In studies of current referral practices, they found that teachers were referring students in increasing numbers, sometimes because of administrative, teacher, or system variables rather than because of the students' actual ability–performance discrepancies. They also found that, once referred, students were tested *almost automatically*, and that, once tested, a large majority are directly placed in the category for which they were referred (Algozzine, Christenson, & Ysseldyke, 1982).

Two major interventions that have been identified as effective in interrupting this domino effect and decreasing special education referrals are teacher development through in-service training and case management strategies. Administrative strategies typically involve both rearranging management responsibilities for general and special education personnel and retraining educators.

Changing Educators' Beliefs and Practices

In order to avoid or limit special education referrals, beliefs held by both general and special education personnel need to be changed. For example, before special educators will encourage integration, they must believe that general education systems *can* appropriately serve students with handicaps (Thousand, 1985). Similarly, general educators must believe they can positively affect the education of students with handicaps (Harasymiw & Horne, 1975; Larrivee & Cook, 1979; Stephens & Braun, 1980; Stewart, 1983) and that they will receive necessary administrative and educational support for integrating students with handicaps (Larrivee & Cook, 1979; Perry, 1980; Shotel, Iano, & McGilligan, 1972; Stephens & Braun, 1980).

A promising model for describing how beliefs affect attitudes and intentions, and subsequent actual performances, has been researched by Ajzen and Fishbein (1973, 1977, 1980). Changing beliefs, then, becomes a viable and appropriate focus for training—one that is the responsibility and function of teacher trainers at universities and colleges, and of local school administrators, who directly affect the belief systems of educators at the pre-service and in-service levels.

Fishbein and Ajzen (1975) have argued that people hold many beliefs about the consequences of a particular behavior and that they also hold beliefs about what influential others want them to do in relation to their performance of a particular behavior. Both sets of beliefs determine a person's attitudes, perceptions of social norms, and intentions to perform the behavior of interest. Therefore, to change an educator's behavior, attention must be paid both to the beliefs of influential others and to the beliefs held by the educator.

In accordance with Fishbein and Ajzen's theory, then, systems likely to result in decreased special education referrals will be those that address changes in the beliefs not only of the regular educators who are initiating the referrals but also of special educators and administrators. Thousand (1985) assessed the effectiveness of the so-called Fishbein Model in predicting special educators' structuring of student integration opportunities from measures of teachers' intentions, social norms, attitudes, and beliefs about what significant others thought they should do. It was found that measures of teachers' actual provision of integration opportunities was predicted by their intention to structure integration opportunities and by a specific set of beliefs about the consequences of integration. It was strongly recommended that the identified beliefs be incorporated into teacher in-service training programs.

Evaluation of In-Service and Management Strategies

Very few researchers have directly evaluated the effects of in-service training or management change efforts. Those who have include Turnbough (1979), Tobias (1982), Gennari (1982), Marble (1980), Fleming and Fleming (1983), Knight (1981), and Luth (1981). These data-based reports clearly suggest that implementation of specific in-service training or administrative changes can result in a decrease in the number of students referred for special education services as teachers are supported in serving students in the regular education system.

Turnbough (1979) implemented a criterion-referenced referral and placement system for fifteen rural, Georgian school districts. The number of inappropriately placed students in the districts were reduced from 18% to 4.4% as a result of the project. Similarly, Tobias (1982) reported the effectiveness of a referral, evaluation, and placement training program pilot tested in three New York City school districts that resulted in a reduction of disproportionate numbers of ethnic and racially different students in special education programs.

Although there is a plethora of reports describing in-service training materials and methods, only two provided direct measurement of their effectiveness. Gennari (1982) described a data-based staff development program providing teachers with basic skills experiences intended for adapting to students' individual learning needs. This system provides a "self-monitoring tool," which assists school personnel in becoming independent in establishing and maintaining adaptive learning environments. Degree o program implementation, school district staff develop ment plans, and monthly training logs were evaluated ove a one-year period to access the patterns of changes i degree of program implementation for 138 teacher (Wang & Gennari, 1983). Results reveal improvement i programs for students with handicaps.

Cole (1978) described the effectiveness of a pre-servic course on the attitudes, knowledge, and skills of teachers Course evaluations indicate increases in basic knowledg and skills in making judgments about student achievemen and related effectiveness of instruction.

Marble (1980) provided a data-based analysis of th effects of training material. The impact analysis of a informational document, entitled "The Slow Learner i the Secondary Schools," indicates improvement in atti tudes of regular classroom teachers after participation although the most common provision for special educatio was referral to the learning assistance center, thus indica ting that referral actions did not change.

Case Management Systems

A combination management and in-service training system is exemplified by the staff support team, or the case management team, approach. Stokes (1981) reported the effects of building-based teams, while Fleming and Fleming (1983) provided preliminary data on the usefulness of a multidisciplinary team in handling referrals efficiently.

Necessary conditions for implementing a prereferral intervention system have been delineated by Graden, Casey, and Christenson (1985). The system relies on the indirect consultative or training-based model such as was suggested by Lilly (1971). The goal of the prereferral model is to prevent inappropriate student placements in special education and, simultaneously, to decrease future student referrals by increasing the competencies of regular classroom teachers. A teacher experiencing an instructional or social interaction problem with a student is offered support from an assigned consultant, who taps existing school resources (such as a special education teacher, a psychologist, or another classroom teacher who previously has had a similar problem). Case management teams or child study teams are formed at the building level to monitor programs. Data supporting the use of this model have been reported by Chalfant (1979) and Graden, Casey, and Bonstrom (1985). Of the six pilot sites studied by Graden, Casey, and Bonstrom, four reported a decreased trend after prereferral intervention in the numbers of students tested and placed in special education programs and an upward trend in the use of consultative services. As stated by Graden, Casey, and Christenson (1985), the case management model attempts to address two major criticisms of traditional testing and placement practices. First, the test results often are not instructionally relevant or helpful to teachers. Second, when students are declared ineligible, referring teachers are left without useful suggestions and students do not receive alternative interventions.

In the Chalfant (1979) case management model, teacher assistance teams were formed at the building level to provide "day-to-day peer problem-solving groups for teachers" (p. 85). In one report of effectiveness of the model (as measured by teacher reports as well as by changes in the students referred to the teams), of the 200 children referred to the twenty-three teacher assistance teams, 133 successfully avoided being referred to special education. The teams successfully resolved the problems of 133 students (including three mainstreamed handicapped students); fifty-four students were referred for further special education services and were found to be eligible for specific special education placements. In only thirteen cases were students' problems not resolved. These results indicate that a team problem-solving method is a viable option for traditional special education referral and placement (Chalfant, Pysh, & Moultrie, 1979).

Consulting Teacher Systems

A consultation/training role as a comprehensive service delivery model for special education was first proposed by Lilly (1971). The consultation/training model provided a framework for prevention through sharing knowledge and skills.

Knight (1981) reported on the effectiveness of a consulting teacher training model with high school teachers promoting cooperative team teaching between general and special educators to serve handicapped students within the regular classroom. Specific findings were that workshops were the least effective intervention, whereas courses with team teaching or consultation assistance were most effective in creating change in teacher behaviors. Teachers receiving courses with team teaching or consultation assistance were more likely to implement procedures in their classrooms that resulted in appropriate instruction for handicapped students. Such instructional interventions included cooperative learning groups, specific skills training of students in learning strategies, and the implementation of a math curriculum incorporating a continuous progress monitoring system. Luth (1981) reported an effective staff development model that supplemented workshops with technical assistance and specific feedback concerning effectiveness of consultants.

Empirical evidence supporting a consultation training-based intervention system has been provided by Idol-Maestas, Nevin, and Paolucci-Whitcomb (1985, 1986); Knight, Meyers, Paolucci-Whitcomb, Hasazi, and Nevin (1981); Lew, Mesch, and Lates (1982); and Miller and Sabatino (1978). Specifically, Miller and Sabatino (1978) showed no difference in academic gains between students receiving consultation plus regular classroom intervention and resource room intervention alone. Teacher behaviors, however, were judged as slightly superior in the consultation model. Knight et el. (1981) showed statistically significant increases in progress of students with handicaps receiving services in districts where consulting teachers had worked with classroom teachers for more than 6 years. Results also suggest that the increased skills of regular educators receiving consultation were responsible, at least in part, for the improvement in students. Teachers in schools with a consulting teacher assumed more direct roles and engaged in more direct activities with handicapped learners' referral, assessment, curriculum development, implementation of teaching/learning activities, and evaluation when compared to their counterparts. Additional empirical validation of the effectiveness of the consulting teacher pre-intervention model in relation to academic progress of handicapped students is offered by Idol-Maestas, Lloyd, and Lilly (1981); Lew et al. (1982); and Nelson and Stevens (1981).

The school psychology literature hints at similar results indicating the success of the training role of consultants. Indeed, even more complex is the suggestion that the mental set or expectation of the consultant can directly influence the behaviors (i.e., referral to outside resources vs. direct planning implementations of interventions) of teachers who requested assistance. Tombari and Bergan (1978) reported the results of a study designed to identify how consultants' cues affected how teachers described students' problems. More specifically, "medical model" cues (as distinguished from "behavioral model") resulted in teachers being pessimistic about their ability to solve the stated problem.

In summary, research to date supports the implementation of intervention strategies for avoiding special education placement by directly supporting and training regular school personnel in the implementation of effective interventions with learners experiencing handicaps. Alternative special education assessment, decision making, and service delivery also are being explored and reported in the literature.

Expanding What Is Possible

The purpose of this section is to review the research and practice relating to early intervention, parental support, and transition models for reducing rates of referral to special education.

Early Intervention

A comprehensive review of research investigating the efficacy of various types of early intervention programs with handicapped, at-risk, and disadvantaged preschoolers currently is in progress at the Early Intervention Research Institute (EIRI) at the Utah State University Affiliated Exceptional Child Center. Among the research efforts of the EIRI has been the application of meta-analysis techniques to analyze early intervention efficacy studies. Results from an analysis of 162 studies are now available in interim reports (Bush & White, 1983; White, 1984; White & Casto, 1984; White, Mastropieri, & Casto, 1984). It should be noted that, until this effort, no early intervention efficacy review has cited more than sixty studies. In addition, few reviews have employed such well-designed and well-documented procedures for locating studies and analyzing methodological integrity.

Preliminary results reported by White and Casto (1984) confirm what has been claimed since the 1960s, when early intervention model demonstration efforts were initiated: Early intervention has substantial, immediate, positive benefits for handicapped as well as at-risk and disadvantaged children. As for the long-range, enduring impact of early intervention, few data are available (White, 1984).

For the subset of efficacy studies involving handicapped children judged by White and colleagues to be methodologically sound and of good quality (White, 1984), none report follow-up data later than one year after the termination of intervention. Only two studies with a focus on handicapped children have gathered data later than 2 years after intervention terminated. One of the two follow-up studies is a retrospective study (Moore, Fredericks, & Baldwin, 1981), which found severely handicapped 9-, 10-, and 11-year-olds with 2 or more years of early intervention outperforming handicapped peers with one year or no preschool. The other study is a follow-up study of a sample of students ages 5–8 years from thirty-two Handicapped Children's Early Education Programs (HCEEPs). This second study was conducted by the Batelle Institute (Stock et al., 1976) for the Bureau for the Education of the Handicapped and found 90% of the HCEEP graduate sample placed in special education rather than regular education programs, despite teachers' ratings of HCEEP graduates as more advanced in cognitive and social skill areas relative to similarly handicapped peers with no HCEEP experience.

Given the dearth of longitudinal data regarding the performance of handicapped children who have participated in early intervention programs (Bush & White, 1983; Casto, White, & Taylor, 1983; Ramey, Bryant, & Suarez, 1984; White, 1984; White, Mastropieri, & Casto, 1984), White and colleagues concluded that "the question of whether early intervention for handicapped children results in long-term benefits is essentially unanswered and unaddressed" (White, 1984, p. 25).

For disadvantaged (low-income) children, more data are available. However, readers are cautioned about extrapolating findings from disadvantaged to handicapped children. For disadvantaged preschoolers, the most common outcome measures have been IQ and academic achievement. In general, a "wash out" effect is observed. The greater the time since termination of the intervention program, the less benefit observed. At one month after intervention, there is a drop of about one third of a standard deviation for outcomes measures. As noted by White (1984), 3 years following intervention, the average differences between control children and children having received early education intervention is essentially zero. The same general findings were observed when only high quality studies were examined. With quality studies, however, a small residual effect remained 3 years following intervention.

Two important research efforts involving disadvantaged children take exception to the trend found in the meta-analysis for effects to washout in successive years of schooling. In 1976, the Longitudinal Studies Consortium, chaired by Lazar, was established to pool data from the twelve major early intervention projects of the 1960s and to conduct a collaborative follow-up of the original subjects. In the 10-year follow-up conducted by the Consortium (Lazar & Darlington, 1982), washout effects following preschool were still found for intelligence and achievement measures. However, more salient and important findings were that early intervention significantly reduced the number of children assigned to special classes and reduced the number of children retained in a grade. Lazar and Darlington concluded that measurable educational benefits can be experienced by disadvantaged children following their exit from diverse but well-designed and carefully implemented early intervention programs.

The second research effort that shows no washout effect is directed at longitudinal follow-up of Perry Preschool Project graduates (Weikart, Bond, & McNeir, 1978; Weikart, Epstein, Schweinhart, & Bond, 1978). The Perry Preschool Project 15-year-old follow-up study (Schweinhart & Weikart, 1981) and the soon-to-be-published 19-year-old follow-up study (J. Clements, personal communication, February 9, 1984, reported in White, 1984) show substantial and important differences favoring the 123 children who attended the Perry Preschool early intervention program over their randomly assigned control group peers on academic motivation, homework completion, evaluation of schooling, scholastic achievement, high school graduation rates, employment, delinquent behavior, and criminal records. Most important to the focus of this chapter are the findings regarding special education placements. For Perry Preschool graduates, placements in programs of special education were almost cut in half. Whereas 39% of control children were placed in programs of special education, only 19% of experimental group learners received special education services for one year or more by the end of high school.

Independent variables. An analysis of sixty-four review articles published from 1966 to 1982 on the efficacy of early intervention revealed ten intervention and subject variables most frequently cited by the reviewers as potential mediating variables (Bush & White, 1983). Degree of parental involvement; degree of structure in intervention; training/competence/attitude of intervenor; nature of intervention (e.g., philosophical orientation or type of curriculum); length/intensity of intervention; and use of operant conditioning principles were the most frequently cited intervention variables. Subject variables included age at which intervention begins; socioeconomic status; degree of environmental stimulation/deprivation in home setting; parent–child relationship; and family integrity.

A subsequent meta-analysis (White, 1984) was conducted with five of the ten frequently cited variables—degree of structure in intervention; training of intervenor; age at which intervention begins; intensity/duration of intervention; degree of parental involvement—to determine whether values frequently claimed for these variables were empirically supported. Based primarily on intervention studies with disadvantaged rather than handicapped children, it was found that more highly structured programs with detailed outcome objectives supported by task analyses and procedures and criteria for advancing pupils to new objectives and materials were more effective than programs without these components. Available research examining the training backgrounds of intervenors is scarce. The research that does exist suggests that both professionals and paraprofessionals can be effective and that highly trained intervenors are slightly more effective than those with less training. The research leaves substantially unresolved all issues concerning intensity and duration and age at which to begin intervention, although, for disadvantaged and at-risk children, some evidence favors more intense programs of longer duration. Despite the widespread belief that parental involvement is central to program effectiveness (Bricker, Bailey, & Bruder, 1984; Bronfenbrenner, 1974; Dunst & Rheingrover, 1981), the meta-analysis performed at Utah State University (White, 1984) found no particular advantage for programs with parental components, leaving the parental involvement question as yet unanswered. All in all, conditions under which early intervention is most effective have yet to be empirically explored and identified (Reynolds, Egan, & Lerner, 1983).

Future examinations of program variables need to address questions such as the following: (a) "Is one form/model of intervention more effective than another in selected areas under specified conditions?" (Swan, 1981, p. 2); (b) "What type of child with which handicapping conditions is most positively affected by a particular intervention strategy?"; and (c) "Which strategies can be manipulated to give the most positive results?" (Reynolds et al., 1983, p. 54). Other examinations need to address questions specifically related to post-early intervention determinants of school success—questions such as, "What post-preschool settings and features of those settings are most beneficial in maintaining or increasing the preschool benefits?" (Moore et al., 1981). In efforts to answer these questions, very likely, previously unexplored independent program, student, and family variables will be examined, and new and innovative intervention approaches such as Zeitlin's (1981) program, which focuses upon helping handicapped preschoolers and parents to become more adaptive and cope better with stress, should emerge.

Dependent variables. Strain (1984) effectively argued that one of the most pervasive and dysfunctional assumptions in early intervention efficacy research is that a time-limited educational intervention will result in relatively permanent behavior change. Strain is one of a growing number of researchers (Beckman & Burke, 1984; Bronfenbrenner, 1974; Dunst & Rheingrover, 1981; Dunst, Vance, & Gallagher, 1983; Ramey & Baker-Ward, 1982; Sameroff & Chandler, 1975; Yarrow, 1979) who have observed that the critical nature of early experience is not as clear as it once appeared and that a more transactional (Sameroff & Chandler, 1975); ecological (Bronfenbrenner, 1974); lifespan (Schweinhart & Weikart, 1981); systems-level (Dunst & Rheingrover, 1981) perspective concerning early intervention is warranted. From a transactional point of view, the child, changed by his or her experiences in the environment, continues to interact with the environment, changes it, and is changed by it. Early intervention experiences, then, are only part of an ever-expanding child life; development is modified continuously by a myriad of variables as the child grows. In fact, it has been proposed that the critical mechanism *maintaining* child change over time is not the program per se, but the parents and the attitudinal and behavioral changes they acquire during and sustain following the time-limited early intervention (Bricker et al., 1984).

A transactional perspective concerning early education efficacy research necessitates the consideration of a wide variety of outcome variables and the time period over which they are measured. Outcome measures also must be more closely tied than they have been in previous research to the goals of intervention (Strain, 1984; White & Casto, 1984). If enhancement of child intelligence is the sole goal of early intervention efforts, then traditional cognitive measures (e.g., IQ and achievement tests) may be sufficient measures of program efficacy. However, if we hold that exclusive use of IQ tests is neglectful of information on other behaviors that have an impact on a child's ability to cope with environmental demands (Zigler & Trickett, 1978), the need for identifying and measuring other areas of potential program impact on a handicapped child, his or her family, and fellow nonhandicapped peers and community members becomes obvious (Dunst et al., 1983; White, 1984).

Bricker and Dow (1980) reported evidence that children who acquire competencies in pre-academic, communication, and self-help areas as a result of early education programs seem to make transitions to and function in less restrictive class placements. The public school system, then, is a consumer of early intervention programs in that program graduates do eventually move into the school system, and the school system is one place where social validation of treatment effects should occur. Some infrequently measured but important public school dimensions suggested for examination are learner avoidance of or extent of need for special education services (Karnes, Schwedel, Lewis, Ratts, & Esry, 1981; Schweinhart & Weikart, 1981; Zeitlin, 1981); performance on specific tasks, amount of time spent in integrated settings, motivation and social adjustment (Bricker et al., 1984); and acquisition of skills critical for survival in regular kindergarten or first grade (Vincent et al., 1980).

Other outcome variables suggested for more in-depth evaluation include the social competence, mental health, communication skills, and daily living skills of the child (White, 1984); the emotional and physical well-being of different family members, reduction in the burdens and demands of rearing a handicapped child, and the style and quality of parent–child interactions (Dunst et al., 1983). If such variables are included in future early intervention programs as program goals and outcome measures, it may no longer be necessary to judge as intervention failures those learners with multiple handicaps or severe brain damage who do not make developmental progress with intervention, but whose families, peers, or community members experience personal and social benefits (Bricker & Dow, 1980; Dunst et al., 1983).

Finally, if a transactional, lifespan perspective is taken in early intervention efficacy research, additional efforts must be made to extend longitudinal data collection through the high school years into adulthood (as Schweinhart & Weikart, 1981, have done). For more severely disabled persons, progress toward independent functioning in integrated community, home, and work situations as well as in school settings is the overriding educational priority, rendering traditional academic measures of school success relatively meaningless. So, then, for at least some students, longitudinal educational follow-up measures need to be expanded to include assessments of early education graduate accomplishments in areas of independent living, school and community integration, vocational opportunity, and personal well being.

Parental Support

The rationale for parental support includes several distinctions. The transactional perspective discussed above suggests that parental support is *central* to the longitudinal success of handicapped, disadvantaged, and at-risk children. If Bricker and colleagues (1984) are correct in their contention that it is the parent who ensures maintenance of learner success into the public school years, then it is critical to help parents identify the support they want and need starting at the time they first learn of their child's handicap and continuing through their child's adulthood. The passage of PL 94-142 marked the beginning of a shift in the way in which parents of children with handicaps were viewed by the professionals serving their children (Turnbull & Turnbull, 1982). Historically, both general and special educators have held a number of beliefs and attitudes about families of children with handicapping conditions. The most predominant beliefs have been: (a) parents are not willing or able to work with their handicapped children, (b) parents have unrealistic expectations for their handicapped children, (c) parents do not know how to teach their handicapped children, (d) parents need professionals to help them, and (e) parents contribute to the problems of their handicapped children (Vincent, Laten, Salisbury, Brown, & Baumgart, 1981). These negative assumptions or beliefs have been particularly destructive—not only because they are mostly erroneous, but also because they have tended to foster an adversarial parent–teacher relationship in which both parties have perceived their efforts to be at cross-purposes (Donnellan & Mirenda, 1984). Such a relationship has, in turn, interfered with parents' freedom to decide the degree to which they have assumed the role and responsibility of an educational decision maker, a freedom which PL 94-142 is designed to produce (Turnbull, 1983). The shift in home–school relations facilitated by PL 94-142 has been from the predominantly negative relationship just described (Darling & Darling, 1982; McAfee & Vergason, 1979; Rubin & Quinn-Curran, 1983) to the present situation, in which the emphasis is on developing parent–professional partnerships (Fuqua, Hegland, & Karas, 1985; Weigerink, Hocutt, Posante-Lora, & Bristol, 1980).

Bronfenbrenner (1974) suggested that parental support efforts *at the very least* should enable parents to encourage and support their children's public school educational activities at home and at school. Some evidence suggesting that a parental support focus in early intervention can influence subsequent school outcomes for learners with handicaps was provided by Zeitlin (1981). His study describes public placement of thirty-six handicapped children involved in an early intervention program that focused on assisting 3- to 5-year-olds and their parent to cope with stress, become more adaptive, and acquire other related skills. The children were a heterogeneous population with the labels neurologically impaired, communicatively handicapped, autistic, retarded, or emotionally disturbed. Of the thirty-six children, twenty-three were placed in regular classes, seventeen with resource room support. The remaining thirteen were placed in special education classes. These results provide some support for the contention that parents' adaptability is essential in maintaining their children's progress in regular education programs, in spite of the generally negative findings in meta-analyses conducted by White and colleagues, as cited earlier.

Transition/Generalization Models

Recently, strategies for ensuring more successful transition of at-risk and handicapped early education pupils into regular school programs have been identified and developed (Vincent et al., 1980). The strategies involve the systematic determination and incorporation into early education curriculum of "survival skills," those developmental and pre-academic areas that kindergarten and first-grade teachers expect all entering students to demonstrate in their classrooms on the first day of public school. As defined by Vincent et al., survival skills include such behaviors as attending to task, raising hand for attention, sitting in seat, and turn taking.

Successful transition also requires the identification and incorporation into early intervention teaching practices those instructional strategies and overall classroom structures actually employed in the next, public school, regular education environments. There are two primary reasons for this particular need. Given the literature documenting that behavior learned and displayed under one set of conditions does not necessarily generalize to other, more natural, and, possibly, more ambiguous settings (Stokes & Baer, 1977), it is critical that the early childhood special educator teach survival skills in an environment that gradually approximates the structure of the regular kindergarten or first-grade classroom into which early education graduates hopefully will move. For transfer and generalization to be effective, strategies for identifying survival skills must also include an examination and analysis of activities and opportunity to work in child-guided rather than teacher-guided activities (Vincent et al., 1980).

A second reason for incorporating less restrictive teaching practices into early intervention programs is the need to gradually increase the handicapped learner's ability to acquire, as well as generalize, new skills within regular classroom environments while decreasing the need for more restrictive special education practices in promoting continued skill acquisition (Vincent et al., 1980). The establishment of a continuum of instructional strategies that vary according to their degree of restrictiveness would provide early intervention programs with the needed sequence for gradually approximating the structure of the regular kindergarten and first-grade classroom.

Summary and Evaluation of the Gap Between Research and Practice

The state of the art (research) and the state of practice with respect to special education referral and placement have been presented concurrently. Models that rely on a transactional and interactional perspective provide the most promise in effectively strengthening the mainstream to limit and avoid the need for special education services. To date, research that incorporates theory into practice has reported a few outcomes in relation to avoidance of special education referral and placement.

The research findings that are well substantiated include:

1. There are programs that can be introduced in mainstream school operations that successfully increase tolerance for individual differences and reduce the rates of referral to special education.
2. Administrative and support systems can be implemented that result in increased reliance on the general rather than the special education system to provide intensive alternative education in the mainstream.
3. In-service training can result in increased skills of regular educators in providing direct intervention in the mainstream for students with handicaps.
4. Principles of effective instruction and effective schools have demonstrated utility in reducing referral rates of students to special education.
5. Consultation as a service delivery model has been demonstrated to benefit students with handicaps.
6. Although the evidence is somewhat equivocal on the effects of parental involvement in school programs, there is some supporting evidence for the effectiveness of models that emphasize involvement of parents in the development of programs for students as a strategy for avoiding special education placement of young learners entering the public school system.
7. The operation of well-structured preschool programs for at-risk students reduces substantially the number of children enrolled in such programs who are later referred to and enrolled in special education programs.

Recommendations

This section is devoted to recommendations intended to close the gap between research and practice. The ultimate goal of these recommendations is to assure that every student who has special needs will be provided with an appropriate program, regardless of the nature, etiology, or prognosis related to his or her special needs. In short, the *need* for labeling, categorizing, and subsequent placement and program monitoring of students (i.e., the apparent functions of the current special education delivery system) will decrease as these functions are accomplished by the strengthened mainstream system. Concomitantly, new directions for special education functions can be considered.

Our recommendations are presented under three broad general headings: research, training, and policy.

Research

Areas of needed research include: (a) further exploration of early education and other programs that may yield preventative effects, that is, reduce the rate at which handicaps are identified among children; (b) the extent to which parental involvement actually impacts on educational programs; the strategies that most directly affect parental involvement; and how, specifically, parental involvement relates to effective service delivery; (c) long-term outcomes of prereferral efforts as effective strategies in enhancing education in the mainstream; and (d) studies involving application of ideas developing within the so-called effectiveness research that offer promise of strengthening mainstream education as a resource for all children.

Training

A critical dimension in closing the gap between the state of the art and the state of practice in further efforts to integrate general and special education is the training of personnel in new practices. Models and techniques for providing such training need to be developed.

Recently, the Fishbein Model has emerged as a theoretical and empirically supported research base for conceptualizing changes in educators' beliefs and related changes in their behavior. This model might be helpful in predicting and developing training programs expressly aimed at changing student referrals to and placement in special education programs. Finally, tests of the effectiveness of these new training models need to measure actual changes in educators' expressed attitudes or intentions as well as their behaviors.

POLICY

As documented by Weatherly and Lipsky (1977), policies are implemented at the service delivery level only when they match the capacity of the implementers—in essence, educators as implementers (practitioners) actually operationalize the policy. Therefore, it is important to look to practitioners as well as to political figures as one thinks about policies. However, here we concentrate briefly on only a few policy implications of the review that has been provided. There appears to be growing flexibility in options for special education services; there is more readiness for change than was evident a decade ago when PL 94-142 became law. The economics of the present situation are caused by such flexibility. In many places, there is concern about "capping" the number of exceptional children served in special environments. This creates additional pressure for a faster development of abilities to serve exceptional children in regular classes and schools. The principle of least restrictive environment requires the same kind of change.

One quite radical proposal for change was offered by Stainback and Stainback (1984). They suggested that the special education system should be merged totally with general education into a unified system structured to meet the needs of all students. The basic arguments for a single, unified system reflect an awareness of the disadvantages and inefficiency of operating dual systems and an acknowledgement that instructional needs of students fail to warrant separate systems. It seems likely, however, that somewhat less radical forms of integration will be observed in at least the near future.

It is clear that, with appropriate training and support, the general education system can be strengthened to meet the individual needs of students with handicaps. Policies that foster developments in this direction are much needed and can be supported by research findings expressed as state of the art.

A number of model projects have demonstrated success in unifying regular and special education—even for quite severely handicapped students: for example, the School and Community Integration Project (SCIP) (Fox, Schutz, Thousand, & Williams, 1984) and the Homecoming Project (Thousand, Reid, & Godek, 1984). In both of these projects, severely handicapped learners formerly placed in regionalized, segregated, special education classes were successfully returned to their local neighborhood schools. "Homecoming teams" (comprised of the local regular class teacher receiving the student, the student's parents, the local special educators and administrators, and the special education consultant) were identified as responsible for the planning and implementation of social and academic programs. Successful integration occurred when local schools assumed "ownership" of the student. That is, local school staff believed that the student should be educated in their school, that they were competent to educate that student locally, and that they received the support from administrators, special educators, and parents. Moreover, achievement as measured by the proportion of Individualized Educational Program objectives achieved annually by severely handicapped students placed in integrated settings was correlated significantly with degree of interaction with nonhandicapped students (Brinker & Thorpe, 1984). Basically, these projects show that local school districts can create effective criteria and reinforcement for greater tolerance of individual differences. The administrators in participating districts no longer reinforce teachers for referring students out of regular education but, instead, solicit the mutual collaboration of parents and specialists in creating viable systems for "sticking with" students who have severe difficulties in learning.

Conclusion

The reduction of referrals of students for special education is a complex problem. The history of special education shows a continuing separatist refrain, with a host of philosophical, legal, political, and financial themes. It is not and will not be easy to reverse this tradition. On the other hand, the arguments and necessity for change seem compelling. Lessons still may be learned from Dunn (1968), who pointed out that much special education for mildly retarded students was *not* justifiable. The literature (i.e., research base) still does not say that separate placement leads to great advantages for students with special education needs, nor does it suggest that integration without interventions within the general education system will work any better. What is required is creative reformation of schools in general. Such reformation will involve new relationships between special and general education, with much emphasis on training and role change of school personnel (Lilly, 1971; Reynolds, 1965); on use of special education resources as developmental capital (Deno, 1972); and with a great deal of responsible experimental education (Burrello, Tracy, & Schultz, 1973). We are encouraged by the zeitgeist that leads us—even forces us—to work toward the re-unification of general and special education. A substantial and growing research base is available to undergird that process.

Author Information

Ann Nevin is Professor and Jacqueline Thousand is Assistant Professor, both at the College of Education and Social Services, University of Vermont.

References

Ajzen, I., & Fishbein, M. (1973). Attitudinal and normative variables as predictors of specific behaviors. *Journal of Personality and Social Psychology*, **27**, 41–57.

Ajzen, I., & Fishbein, M. (1977). Attitude-behavior relations: A theoretical analysis and review of empirical research. *Psychological Bulletin*, **84**, 888–918.

Ajzen, I., & Fishbein, M. (1980). *Understanding attitudes and predicting social behavior*. Englewood Cliffs, NJ: Prentice-Hall.

Algozzine, B., Christenson, S., & Ysseldyke, J. (1982). Probabilities associated with the referral to placement process. *Teacher Education and Special Education,* **5**(3), 19–23.

Aufderheide, S. (1981). Individualized teaching strategies and learning time: Implications for mainstreaming. *Physical Educator,* **38**(1), 20–25.

Beckman, P. J., & Burke, P. J. (1984). Early-childhood special education: State of the art. *Topics in Early Childhood Special Education,* **4**(9), 19–32.

Block, J. (1974). *Schools, society, and mastery learning.* New York: Holt, Rinehart & Winston.

Bloom, B. (1980). The new direction in education: Alterable variables. *Phi Delta Kappan,* **61**, 382–385.

Bricker, D., Bailey, E., & Bruder, M. B. (1984). The efficacy of early intervention and the handicapped infant: A wise or wasted resource. *Advances in Developmental and Behavioral Pediatrics,* **5**, 373–423.

Bricker, D. D., & Dow, M. G. (1980). Early intervention with the young severely handicapped child. *Journal of the Association for the Severely Handicapped,* **5**(2), 130–142.

Brinker, R. P., & Thorpe, M. E. (1984). Integration of severely handicapped students and the proportion of IEP objectives achieved. *Exceptional Children,* **51**, 168–175.

Bronfenbrenner, U. (1974). Developmental research, public policy, and the ecology of childhood. *Child Development,* **45**, 1–5.

Brookover, W., & Lezotte, L. (1979). *Changes in school characterization coincident with changes in school achievement.* (Occasional Paper No. 17). East Lansing: Michigan State University, Institute for Research on Teaching.

Burrello, L., Tracy, M., & Schultz, E. (1973). Special education as experimental educators. *Exceptional Children,* **40**, 39–44.

Bush, D. W., & White, K. R. (1983, April). *The efficacy of early intervention: What can be learned from previous reviews of the literature?* Paper presented at the annual meeting of the Rocky Mountain Psychological Association, Snowbird, Utah.

Cantrell, M. L. (1979, April). *Measures of student diversity and individualized instruction in the classroom.* Paper presented at the Annual International Convention of the Council for Exceptional Children, Dallas, TX.

Cantrell, R. P., & Cantrell, M. L. (1976). Preventive mainstreaming: Impact of a supportive service program on children. *Exceptional Children,* **43**, 381–385.

Casto, G., White, K., & Taylor, C. (1983). *Final report 1982–83 work scope.* Logan: Utah State University, Early Intervention Research Institute.

Chalfant, J. (1979). *Evaluation report of a teacher assistance model: In-service training for teachers and administrators* (USOE Grant No. G007801745). Tucson: University of Arizona.

Chalfant, J., Pysh, M., & Moultrie, R. (1979). Teacher assistance teams: A model for within building problem solving. *Learning Disability Quarterly,* **2**, 85–96.

Cole, H. P. (1978, May). *Growth of attitudes, knowledge, and skill required by P.L. 94–142 among preservice teachers.* Paper presented at the University of Missouri, St. Louis First Behavioral Studies Conference.

Darling, R. B., & Darling, J. (1982). *Children who are different.* St. Louis, MO: C. V. Mosby.

Deno, E. (1972). *Instructional alternatives for exceptional children.* Reston, VA: Council for Exceptional Children.

Deno, S., & Mirkin, P. (1977). *Data-based program modification: A manual.* Reston, VA: Council for Exceptional Children.

Donnellan, A. M., & Mirenda, P. M. (1984). Issues related to professional involvement with families of individuals with autism and other severe handicaps. *The Association for Severely Handicapped Journal,* **9**(2), 16–22.

Dunn, L. (1968). Special education for the mildly retarded—is it justifiable? *Exceptional Children,* **35**, 5–22.

Dunst, C. J., & Rheingrover, R. J. (1981). An analysis of the efficacy of early intervention with organically handicapped children. *Evaluation and Program Planning,* **4**, 287–323.

Dunst, C. J., Vance, S. D., & Gallagher, J. L. (1983, April). *Differential efficacy of early intervention with handicapped infants.* Paper presented at the Council for Exceptional Children National Conference, Detroit, MI.

Edmonds, R. (1979). Some schools work and more can. *Social Policy,* **9**(5), 28–32.

Fishbein M., & Ajzen, I. (1975). *Belief, attitude, intention, and behavior: An introduction to theory and research.* Reading, MA: Addison-Wesley.

Fleming, D., & Fleming, E. (1983). Consultation with multidisciplinary teams: A program of development and improvement of team functioning. *Journal of School Psychology,* **21**, 367–376.

Fox, W., Schutz, R., Thousand, J., & Williams, W. (1984, December). *Establishing parent and professional partnerships.* Paper presented at the National Parent/Professional Conference, Washington, DC.

Froh, R., & Muraki, E. (1980, October). *Modification and discontinuance of mastery learning strategies.* Paper presented at Midwestern Educational Research Association, Toledo, OH.

Fuqua, R. W., Hegland, S. M., & Karas, S. C. (1985). Processes influencing linkages between preschool handicap classrooms and homes. *Exceptional Children,* **51**, 307–314.

Gennari, P. (1982, March). *The data-based staff development program: Design, implementation, and effects.* Paper presented at the annual meeting of the American Educational Research Association, New York.

Graden, J., Casey, A., & Bonstrom, O. (1985). Implementing a prereferral intervention system: II. The data. *Exceptional Children,* **51**, 487–496.

Graden, J., Casey, A., & Christenson, S. (1985). Implementing a prereferral intervention system: I. The model. *Exceptional Children,* **51**, 377–384.

Hall, R. V., & Copeland, R. (1972). The responsive teacher model: A first step in shaping school personnel as behavior modification specialists. In F. Clark, D. Evans, & L. Hamerlynck (Eds.), *Implementing behavior programs for schools* (pp. 125–131). Champaign, IL: Research Press.

Hall, R. V., Lund, D., & Jackson, D. (1968). Effects of teacher attention on study behavior. *Journal of Applied Behavior Analysis,* **1**, 1–12.

Harasymiw, S. J., & Horne, M. D. (1975). Integration of handicapped children: Its effects on teacher attitudes. *Education,* **96**, 153–158.

Haring, N., Lovitt, J., Eaton, M., & Hansen, C. (1978). *The fourth R: Research in the classroom.* Columbus, OH: Merrill.

Harris, V., & Sherman, J. (1973). Effects of peer tutoring and consequences on the math performance of elementary classroom students. *Journal of Applied Behavior Analysis,* **6**, 587–597.

Haughton, D. D. (1976). *Project PREM: Final Report for Year 1 (Preparing Regular Educators for Mainstreaming).* Washington, DC: U.S. Department of Health, Education, and

Welfare/Office of Education, Bureau of Education for the Handicapped.

Hawkes, K., & Paolucci-Whitcomb, P. (1980). Helping teachers use peer tutoring: A consultation model. *The Pointer,* **24**(3), 47–55.

Heller, K., Holtzman, W., & Messick, S. (Eds.). (1982). *Placing children in special education: A strategy for equity.* Washington, DC: National Academy Press.

Hersh, R. (1981). *What makes some schools and teachers more effective?* [Position Paper]. Eugene: University of Oregon, College of Education.

Hiscox, S., & Williams, B. (1979, April). *When you don't plan to be there long: Evaluating Title I mastery learning programs.* Paper presented at the annual meeting of the American Educational Research Association, San Francisco, CA.

Idol-Maestas, L., Lloyd, S., & Lilly, M. S. (1981). Implementation of a noncategorical approach to direct service and teacher education. *Exceptional Children,* **48**, 213–219.

Idol-Maestas, L., Nevin, A., & Paolucci-Whitcomb, P. (1985). *Facilitators' manual for collaborative consultation: Principles and techniques.* Reston, VA: Council for Exceptional Children, Project RETOOL.

Idol-Maestas, L., Nevin, A., & Paolucci-Whitcomb, P. (1986). *Collaborative consultation.* Rockville, MD: Aspen.

Jenkins, J., Mayhall, W., Peschka, C., & Jenkins, L. (1974). Comparing small group and tutorial instruction in resource rooms. *Exceptional Children.* **40**, 245–250.

Johnson, M., & Bailey, J. (1974). Cross-age tutoring: First graders as arithmetic tutors for kindergarten children. *Journal of Applied Behavior Analysis,* **7**, 223–231.

Johnson, D., & Johnson, R. (1975). *Learning together and alone.* Englewood Cliffs, NJ: Prentice-Hall.

Johnson, D. W., Maruyama, G., Johnson, R., Nelson, D., & Skon, L. (1981). The effects of cooperative, competitive, and individualistic goal structures on achievement: A meta-analysis. *Psychological Bulletin,* **89**, 47–62.

Karnes, M. B., Schwedel, A. M., Lewis, G. F., Ratts, D. A., & Esry, D. R. (1981). Impact of early programming for the handicapped: A follow-up study into the elementary school. *Journal of the Division of Early Childhood,* **4**, 62-79.

Knight, M. (1981). Impact: Interactive model for professional action and change for teachers. *Journal of Staff Development,* **2**(2), 103–113.

Knight, M., Meyers, H., Paolucci-Whitcomb, P., Hasazi, S., & Nevin, A. (1981). A four year evaluation of consulting teacher services. *Behavioral Disorders,* **6**, 92–100.

Lancioni, G. (1982). Normal children as tutors to teach social responses to withdrawn mentally retarded schoolmates: Training, maintenance, and generalization. *Journal of Applied Behavior Analysis,* **15**, 17–40.

Larrivee, B., & Cook, L. (1979). Mainstreaming: A study of the variable affecting teacher attitude. *Journal of Special Education,* **8**, 1–11.

Larrivee, B., & Vacca, J. (1982). *Training teachers to apply teaching behaviors which provide for the successful integration of the mildly handicapped. Identifying effective teaching behaviors for mainstreaming.* Research Report submitted to Office of Special Education and Rehabilitative Services, Washington, DC.

Laycock, V., & Schwartzberg, I. (1976). *Mainstreaming through peer assisted learning.* (ERIC Document Reproduction No. ED 143 150).

Lazar, I., & Darlington, R. (1982). Lasting effects of early education: A report from the consortium for longitudinal studies. *Monographs of the Society for Research in Child Development,* **47**(2–3, Serial No. 195).

Lew, M., Mesch, D., & Lates, B. J. (1982). The Simmons College generic consulting teacher program: A program description and data-based application. *Teacher Education and Special Education,* **5**(2), 11–16.

Lilly, M. S. (1971). A training-based model for special education. *Exceptional Children.* **37**, 745–749.

Lott, L. (1975). *Strategies and techniques for mainstreaming: A resource room handbook.* (Available from Supervisory for Special Education Programs [Monroe County Intermediate School District, 1101 S. Raisinville Road, Monroe, MI 48161].)

Luth, F. (1981). Support systems for mainstreaming: A means of effective staff development. *Journal of Staff Development,* **2**(2), 114–122.

Marble, W. (1980). *An evaluation of the professional development sequence on "The slow learner in the secondary school."* Report submitted to Burnaby (British Columbia) School District.

McAfee, J. K., & Vergason, G. A. (1979). Parent involvement in the process of special education: Establishing the new partnership. *Focus on Exceptional Children,* **11**(2).

Miller, T., & Sabatino, D. (1978). An evaluation of the teacher consultant model as an approach to mainstreaming. *Exceptional Children,* **45**, 86–91.

Moore, M. G., Fredericks, H. D., & Baldwin, V. L. (1981). The long-range effects of early childhood education on a trainable mentally retarded population. *Journal of the Division for Early Childhood,* **4**, 93–109.

Nelson, M., & Stevens, K. (1981). An accountable consultation model for mainstreaming behaviorally disordered children. *Behavioral Disorders,* **6**, 82–91.

Nevin, A., Johnson, R., & Johnson, D. (1982). Effects of group and individual contingencies on academic performance and social relations of special needs students. *Journal of Social Psychology,* **116**, 41–59.

Nevin, A., Skieber, E., & Polewski, C. (1984). A regular classroom teacher implements cooperative learning. *The Pointer,* **28**, 19–21.

Noli, P. (1980, April). *Implications of class size research.* Paper presented at the annual meeting of the American Association of School Administrators, Anaheim, CA.

Osguthorpe, R. T., Eiserman, W., Shisler, L., Top, B. L., & Scruggs, T. E. (1984). *Handicapped children as tutors.* [1983–84 Final Report]. Provo, UT: Brigham Young University, David O. McKay Institute of Education.

Parker, C. (1975). *Psychological consultation: Helping teachers meet special needs.* Reston, VA: Council for Exceptional Children.

Perry, H. L. (1980). The effect of special education supportive services on teacher attitudes toward regular class integration of mildly handicapped children (Doctoral dissertation, George Washington University, 1979). *Dissertation Abstracts International,* **40**(9A), 5003–5004.

Rainer, A., & McCool, J. (1974). *Resource room approach to mainstreaming: Learning Center. Integrated alternative to special education.* Washington, DC: U.S. Department of Health, Education and Welfare/Office of Education, Bureau of Elementary and Secondary Education.

Ramey, C., & Baker-Ward, L. (1982). Psychosocial retardation and the early experience paradigm. In D. Bricker (Ed.), *Intervention with at-risk and handicapped infants.* Baltimore, MD: University Park Press.

amey, C., Bryant, D., & Suarez, T. (1984). Preschool compensatory education and the modifiability of intelligence: A critical review. In D. Detterman (Ed.), *Current topics in human intelligence*. Norwood, NJ: Ablex.

eynolds, L., Egan, R., & Lerner, J. (1983). Efficacy of early intervention of preacademic deficits: A review of the literature. *Topics in Early Childhood Special Education,* 3(3), 47–56.

eynolds, M. C. (1965). The capacities of children. *Exceptional Children,* **3**, 337–342.

itter, S., & Idol-Maestas, L. (1982). *A peer tutor program in reading for senior high school students.* Unpublished manuscript, University of Illinois, Department of Special Education, Urbana-Champaign.

ubin, S., & Quinn-Curran, N. (1983). Lost, then found: Parents' journey through the community service maze. In M. Seligman (Ed.), *The family with a handicapped child: Understanding and treatment* (pp. 63–94). New York: Grune & Stratton.

ameroff, A. J., & Chandler, M. J. (1975). Reproductive risk and the continuum of caretaking causality. In F. D. Horowitz (Ed.), *Review of child development research* (Vol. 4, pp. 187–244). Chicago, IL: University of Chicago Press.

chultz, J. (1978, March). *Assessment of learning centers as a teaching/learning strategy in mainstreamed classes.* Paper presented at the annual meeting of the American Educational Research Association, Ontario, Canada.

chweinhart, L. J., & Weikart, D. P. (1981). Effects of the Perry Preschool Program on youths through age 15. *Journal of the Division for Early Childhood,* **4**, 29–39.

Semmel, M. (1980). Tutoring mainstreamed handicapped pupils in regular classrooms. *Education Unlimited,* **2**(4), 54–56.

Sharp, B. (1982). *Dean's Grant Projects: Challenge and change in teacher education.* Washington, DC: American Association of Colleges for Teacher Education.

Shore, R. (1981). *Fort Hamilton and Grover Cleveland High School project ELITES: Education for Life Through Extended Services* [ESEA Title VII Final Report]. Submitted to Office of Bilingual Education and Minority Languages Affairs (Ed.), Washington, DC.

Shotel, J. R., Iano, R. P., McGilligan, J. R. (1972). Teacher attitudes associated with the integration of handicapped children. *Exceptional Children,* **38**, 677–683.

Slavin, R. (1984). Review of cooperative learning research. *Review of Educational Research,* **50**, 315–342.

Stainback, W., & Stainback, S. (1984). A rationale for the merger of special and regular education. *Exceptional Children,* **51**, 102–111.

Stephens, T. M., & Braun, B. L. (1980). Measures of regular classroom teachers' attitudes toward handicapped children. *Exceptional Children,* **48**, 292–294.

Stewart, F. K. (1983). Teacher attitudes and expectations regarding mainstreaming of handicapped children. *Teacher Education and Special Education,* **6**(1), 39–50.

Stock, J., Wnek, L., Newborg, E., Schenck, J., Gabel, J., Spurgeon, M., & Ray, H. (1976). *Evaluation of handicapped children's early education program (HCEEP)* [Final report to Bureau of Education for the Handicapped, U.S. Office of Education]. Columbus, OH: Batelle.

Stokes, S. (1981). Staff support teams: A vehicle for individualized staff development. *Journal of Staff Development,* **2**(2), 93–102.

Stokes, T., & Baer, D. (1977). An implicit technology of generalization. *Journal of Applied Behavior Analysis,* **10**, 349–367.

Strain, P. S. (1984). Efficacy research with young handicapped children: A critique of the status quo. *Journal of the Division of Early Childhood,* **9**, 4–10.

Swan, W. W. (1981). Efficacy studies in early childhood special education: An overview. *Journal of the Division of Early Childhood,* **4**, 1–4.

Tarrier, R. (1978). *Mainstreamed handicapped students in occupational education: Exemplary administrative practices.* Report submitted to City University of New York and New York State Education Department of Occupational Education Supervision.

Thousand, J. (1985). *Social integration and parent involvement: Special education teacher attitudes and behaviors.* Unpublished doctoral dissertation, University of Vermont, Burlington.

Thousand, J., Reid, R., & Godek, J. (1984, November). *Homecoming: A consulting model for educating learners with severe handicaps in their local schools.* Paper presented at the 11th Annual International Conference of the Association for the Severely Handicapped, Chicago, IL.

Tobias, R. (1982). *Project referral, evaluation and placement training, 1980–1981, Title VI-D* [Final Evaluation Report and System Design Requirements for the Child Assistance Program for the Division of Special Education, New York City Board of Education]. Submitted to Management Analysis Center, Inc., Washington, DC.

Tombari, M., & Bergan, T. (1978). Consultant uses and teacher verbalizations, judgments, and expectancies concerning children's adjustment problems. *Journal of School Psychology,* **16**, 212–219.

Turnbough, T. (1979). *Implementing criterion-referenced referral and placement of special education students in fifteen school districts through development and application of an administrative system* [Individual Practicum Report]. Fort Lauderdale, FL: Nova University.

Turnbull, A. P. (1983). Parent-professional interactions. In M. Snell (Ed.), *Systematic instruction of the moderately and severely handicapped* (2nd ed.) (pp. 18–43). Columbus, OH: Merrill.

Turnbull, A. P., & Turnbull, H. R., III. (1982). Parent involvement in the education of handicapped children: A critique. *Mental Retardation,* **20**, 115–122.

Vincent, L. J., Laten, S., Salisbury, C., Brown, P., & Baumgart, D. (1981). Family involvement in the educational process of severely handicapped students: State of the art and directions for the future. In B. Wilcox & B. York (Eds.), *Quality education services for the severely handicapped: The federal investment* (pp. 164–179). Washington, DC: U.S. Department of Education, Office of Special Education.

Vincent, L., Salisbury, C., Walter, G., Brown, P., Gruenewald, L., & Powers, M. (1980). Program evaluation and curriculum development in early childhood/special education: Criteria of the next environment. In W. Sailor, B. Wilcox, & L. Brown (Eds.), *Methods of instruction for severely handicapped students.* Baltimore, MD: Paul Brookes.

Walberg, H. (1984). Improving the productivity of America's schools. *Educational Leadership,* **4**(8), 19–30.

Wang, M. C., & Gennari, P. (1983). Analysis of the design, implementation, and effects of a data-based staff development program. *Teacher Education and Special Education,* **6**, 211–216.

Wang, M. C., Vaughan, E. D., & Dytman, J. A. (1985). Staff development: A key ingredient of successful mainstreaming. *Teaching Exceptional Children,* **17**(2), 112–121.

Wang, M. C., & Walberg, H. J. (1985). *Adapting instruction to individual differences.* Berkeley, CA: McCutchan.

Weatherly, R., & Lipsky, M. (1977). Street level bureaucrats and institutional innovation. *Harvard Educational Review,* **47,** 171–197.

Weigerink, R., Hocutt, A., Posante-Lora, R., & Bristol, M. (1980). Parent involvement in early education programs for handicapped children. In J. J. Gallagher (Ed.), *New directions for exceptional children: Ecology of exceptional children* (pp. 67–85). San Francisco, CA: Jossey-Bass.

Weikart, D. P., Bond, J. T., & McNeir, J. T. (1978). *The Ypsilanti Perry Preschool Project: Preschool years and longitudinal results* (Monographs of the High/Scope Educational Research Foundation No. 3). Ypsilanti, MI: High/Scope Press.

Weikart, D. P., Epstein, A. S., Schweinhart, L., & Bond, J. T. (1978). *The Ypsilanti Preschool Curriculum Demonstration Project* (Monographs of the High/Scope Educational Research Foundation No. 4). Ypsilanti, MI: High/Scope Press.

Welsh, D., & Ligon, G. (1980). *Project RISE: Reading achievement in ALSO Junior High School Education (1978–1979) Interim Evaluation Report.* Report submitted to U.S. Department of Health, Education, and Welfare, Washington, DC.

White, K. R. (1984). *An integrative review of early intervention.* Logan: Utah State University. Early Intervention Research Institute.

White, K. R., & Casto, G. (1984). An integrative review of earl intervention efficacy studies with at-risk children: Impli cations for the handicapped. Logan: Utah State University Early Intervention Research Institute.

White, K. R., Mastropieri, M., & Casto, G. (1984). An analysis o special education early childhood projects approved by th joint dissemination review panel. *Journal of the Division fo Early Childhood,* **9,** 11–26.

Wilcox, J., Sbardellati, E., & Nevin, A. (in press). Integratin a severely handicapped girl in a first grade classroon with cooperative learning groups. *Teaching Exceptiona Children.*

Yarrow, L. J. (1979). Historical perspectives and future develop ment in infant development. In J. Osofsky (Ed.), *Handbook of infant development* (pp. 897–917). New York: Wiley.

Ysseldyke, J., Thurlow, M., Graden, S., Wesson, C., Algozzine B., & Deno, S. (1983). Generalization from five years o research on assessment and decision-making: The University of Minnesota Institute. *Exceptional Children Quarterly,* **4** 75–93.

Zeitlin, S. (1981). Learning through coping: An effective preschool program. *Journal of the Division for Early Education,* **4,** 53–61.

Zigler, E., & Trickett, P. (1978). IQ, social competence, and evaluation of early childhood intervention programs. *American Psychologist,* **33,** 789–798.

Noncategorical Special Education Programs: Process and Outcomes

CATHERINE VOELKER MORSINK
University of Florida
CAROL CHASE THOMAS
University of North Carolina at Wilmington
and JUDY SMITH-DAVIS
University of Nevada at Reno

Abstract—The rationale for noncategorical programs, including the similarity of student characteristics and the effectiveness of methods across categories, is presented. Because the evidence is inconclusive, however, cautions against oversimplification are stated. Four elements of effective methodology across settings and categories are abstracted, and existing practices are described in noncategorical early childhood, secondary, resource room, and transition programs. The discrepancies between best and actual practice are summarized as major issues, and the implications for research, practice, and policy are outlined.

Rationale for Noncategorical Programs

Like other chapters in this volume, this discussion focuses on special/supplemental education programs for students who are variously labeled as learning disabled, educable mentally retarded, or emotionally disturbed/behaviorally disordered and for those who have minor deviations in sensory or physical functioning. Categorical approaches to the delivery of services to such students are theoretically based on the assumptions that all students with similar labels have similar characteristics and abilities/disabilities and that, consequently, these students can be expected to respond similarly to the same types of educational programs. Conversely, noncategorical approaches are based on the rationale that these types of students cannot be separated precisely and accurately into categories and that such separations are not useful in prescribing educational practices with differential probabilities of success. These arguments for noncategorical programs, as well as the cautions against the over- or premature use of such programs, are discussed briefly below.

Similarity of Characteristics

Theoretically, students classified as learning disabled, educable mentally retarded, and emotionally disturbed have measurably different learning and behavioral characteristics. An educable mentally retarded student has a lower IQ (generally in the range of 50–75), with an academic achievement rate, and, often, a social development rate, substantially below that of his or her peers. A learning disabled student has an average or above-average IQ, test performance showing unusual scatter, and academic achievement deficits in specific areas, as compared with overall assessed aptitude (IQ). An emotionally disturbed student has conduct/personality problems that may or may not be accompanied by academic deficits.

In reality, however, there are numerous similarities among the three groups along the dimensions of underachievement, personal adjustment, and adaptive behavior. For this reason, attempts to separate the three categories by common measures of characteristics have been less than successful. Hallahan and Kauffman's (1977) work, for example, raised questions about the similarity of etiologies and of interventions, with the concluding inference that diagnosis is difficult and irrelevant.

Research over the past two decades has been permeated with evidence that psychometric categorization of students is limited both in reliability and in practical applicability. For example, Santostefano (1964) found that measures of cognitive scanning and flexibility, previously shown to differentiate diagnostic categories in adults, did not discriminate groups of children classified as brain injured, orphaned, and normal when IQ was controlled. Kaufman (1981), using the Wechsler Intelligence Scale for Children-Revised (WISC-R) (Wechsler, 1974), found that students labeled as learning disabled, educable mentally retarded, emotionally disturbed, reading disabled, and normal had similar verbal/performance discrepancies on this test. Norman and Zigmond (1980) found that children labeled as learning disabled and served by Child Service Demonstration Centers varied widely in the severity of the discrepancy between academic achievement and measured potential for achievement and that some of these children, labeled as learning disabled, had IQ scores of 69 or below. A number of researchers have found that children variously classified as learning disabled, educable mentally retarded, or emotionally disturbed share common academic difficulties, particularly in the area of reading

(Cegelka & Cegelka, 1970; Garrison & Hammill, 1971; Kirk, 1964; Stennett, 1969; Stone & Rowley, 1964; Weinstein, 1969; Zax, Cowen, Rappaport, Beach, & Laird, 1968). Similarly, Bryan and Bryan (1981) showed that learning disabled students often have difficulties in social perceptions as well as in academic skills.

The ambiguity in categorical classification is intensified by the fact that definitions of the three categories are neither consistent among states nor stable over time. For example, twenty-five states revised their definitions of learning disability between 1973 and 1975; these definitions were often contradictory (Mercer, Forgnone, & Wolking, 1976). In a follow-up review, Mercer, Hughes, and Mercer (1985) found that only 44% of the states now use the 1977 *Federal Register* ("Procedures for Evaluation," 1977) definition without modifications, while 28% use it with slight variation. Twenty-four percent of the states use different definitions, and 4% have no definition for learning disability. In the area of emotional disturbance, Epstein, Cullinan, and Sabatino (1977) revealed that there were eleven components in the various states' definitions, many of which were contradictory and ambiguous. For the category of educable mental retardation, a change in the American Association on Mental Deficiency (AAMD) definition in 1973 (Grossman, 1973) presented a further complicating factor in that a large number of students (previously labeled as educable mentally retarded) no longer met the new criteria for classification as retarded.

Discrepancies in state eligibility have resulted in large disparities among states in the percentages of students classified as educable mentally retarded (from 0.49% in Alaska to 4.14% in Alabama); learning disabled (from 0.83% in New York to 5.20% in Maryland); and emotionally disturbed (from 0.04% in Mississippi to 3.09% in Utah) (Applied Urbanetics Policy Research, 1980). The classification issue is complicated further by the current increases in poverty, family instability, substance abuse, and illegitimate births (Preston, 1984) and by a concomitant increase in the number of school-age children with low academic achievement, poor task completion, and social maladjustment (Colbert, Newman, Ney, & Young, 1982; Gickling, 1985). Attempts to sort these children into categories on the basis of existing definitions have been disappointing.

Effectiveness of Methods Across Categories

The lack of evidence that specific teaching methods are differentially effective for students labeled as learning disabled, educable mentally retarded, and emotionally disturbed is a second reason for supporting noncategorical programs for mildly handicapped students. An extensive review of textbooks in these three categories not only failed to indicate that specific teaching strategies and materials were effective for one category as opposed to others, but it also suggested that, in many cases, methods were effective for some students within a diagnostic category but ineffective for others within the same category.

Lack of Support for Categorical Methods

The recommendations of specialists in the fields of learning disability, educable mental retardation, and emotional disturbance were analyzed through a review of twenty-seven chapters of major texts written between 197[illegible] and 1984 (Morsink, 1984). (These works included Algozzine, Schmid, and Mercer, 1981; Berdine and Blackhurst 1981; Birch, 1974; Blake, 1974; Blankenship and Lilly 1981; Bruininks, Warfield, and Stealey, 1982; Cartwright Cartwright, and Ward, 1981; Hallahan and Kauffman 1982; Lerner, 1980; Little, 1982; Lovitt, 1978; McDowell Adamson, and Wood, 1982; Mercer, 1983; Morsink, 1981 Nelson, 1981; Payne and Thomas, 1978; Reeve and Kauffman, 1978; Reid and Hresko, 1981; Reynolds and Birch 1977; and Whelan, 1982.) From this analysis, Morsink concluded that professionals were recommending methods that matched children's behaviors rather than their categories. That is, the professionals were saying that mildly handicapped students in any category may have academic deficits, and if they do, they should be taught basic skills that learning disabled, educable mentally retarded, or emotionally disturbed students may have behavioral problems, and, if they do, their behavior should be modified, and that children in any of these categories may need more concrete materials, more practice, more specific feedback on their performance in order to learn, and so on. The consensus seemed to be that, for mildly handicapped (as opposed to moderately or severely retarded, disabled, or disturbed) students, methods could not be prescribed by category, and that effectiveness could only be determined by initially matching teaching strategies to learner strengths and weaknesses and then using continuous measurement systems. These suggestions for adapting instructional programs to meet the needs of mildly handicapped students can logically be grouped into three educationally relevant clusters: physical environment modifications, instructional strategies, and classroom management suggestions. These and other related clusters are discussed in more detail in other sources (e.g., Morsink, 1984; Smith & Neisworth, 1975).

Evidence of Success Across Categories

Independent summaries of the research on effective methods of teaching educable mentally retarded (Algozzine, 1984), emotionally disturbed (Valcante, 1984), and learning disabled (Morsink, Branscum, & Boone, 1984) students suggest that the same methods have been used successfully with students in all three categories. Moreover, in many of these studies, the investigators have concluded that the procedure used was effective for some students but not for others within the sample studied. Research on these methods is summarized briefly in Table 1.

In a review statement, Algozzine, Algozzine, Morsink, and Dykes (1984) conclude that, because of confounding variables, it is difficult to identify a particular method as

TABLE 1
Studies of Effectiveness of Selected Teaching Methods for Three Categories of Mildly Handicapping Conditions

Teaching method	Studies of effectiveness		
	Learning disability	Emotional disturbance	Educable mental retardation
DISTAR/ Direct instruction	Bateman, 1979 Lloyd, Cullinan, Heins, & Epstein, 1980 Maier, 1980	Epstein & Cullinan, 1982	Isaacs & Stennet, 1980
Continuous measurement/ precision teaching	Lovitt, 1975 Lloyd, Hallahan, Kosiewicz, & Kneedler, 1982	Hewett, Taylor & Artuso, 1969 Bellafiore & Salend, 1983 Booth & Fairbank, 1983	Tawney, 1977 Knowlton, 1978
Structure	Lewis & Kass, 1982 Foster & Torgesen, 1983	Hewett, Taylor, & Artuso, 1969	Spitz, 1973 Broome & Wambold, 1977
Controlled practice	Lovitt & Hansen, 1976 Haines & Torgesen, 1978 Bos, 1982 Lewis & Kass, 1982 Conners, 1983	Grassi, 1971 Polsgrove, Reith, Friend, & Cohen, 1980	Fisher & Zeaman, 1973 Glidden, Bilsky, & Pawelski, 1977 Nelson & Cummings, 1981
Applying, generalizing information	Lovitt, 1975 Deshler, Alley, Warner, & Schumaker, 1981 Rose & Gottlieb, 1981 Pany, Jenkins, & Schreck, 1982	Lebsock & Salzberg, 1981	Lobb & Childs, 1973 Nelson & Cummings, 1981 Borkowski & Varnhagen, 1984
Behavior modification	Lovitt, 1975 Nagle & Thwaite, 1979 Swanson, 1981	Kuypers, Becker, & O'Leary, 1968 Alexander & Apfel, 1976 Bellafiore & Salend, 1983 Booth & Fairbank, 1983	Tawney, 1977 Raber & Weisz, 1981 LaGreca, Stone, & Bell, 1983
Reinforcement or specific correction of academic responses	Thorpe, Chaing, & Drach, 1981 Kosiewicz, Hallahan, Lloyd, & Graves, 1982 Rose, McEntire, & Dowdy, 1982 Jenkins, Larson, & Fleisher, 1983	Noffsinger, 1971 Clements & Tracy, 1977	Cawley, 1968 Evans, 1970 Nelson & Cummings, 1981
Interpersonal skills instruction	Bryan & Bryan, 1978 Tollefson, Tracy, Johnsen, Buenning, Farmer, & Barke, 1982	Morgan, Young, & Goldstein, 1983	Raber & Weisz, 1981 LaGreca, Stone, & Bell, 1983

differentially effective for students with a particular diagnostic label but not for students with other mild handicaps. Consequently, it is not yet possible either to describe a set of characteristics or to prescribe a set of methods that applies always and only to students by diagnostic category.

Furthermore, researchers trying to determine whether methods are differentially effective by category have found it difficult to draw inferences from samples that lack common characteristics. Some studies have been conducted with samples of learning disabled, educable mentally retarded, or emotionally disturbed students who have met state criteria. In other cases, students in the samples have met state criteria, but categorical definitions have varied so much across states and over time that no inferences about aptitude-by-treatment interactions could be drawn. In still other cases, researchers have failed to describe their samples carefully. The problem of heterogeneity in the populations being studied extends to all three existing categories: learning disability (see Mercer, 1985); emotional disturbance (see Lakin, 1982); and educable mental retardation (see Zigler, Balla, & Hodapp, 1984). Zigler et al. (1984) summarized the problem in this way: "Studies done by different investigators in different places may vary in these dimensions [i.e., characteristics], so interpretation and generalization are fruitless" (p. 215). These findings support the earlier observations of Hobbs (1975, 1978), who systematically reviewed classification practices and related research and concluded that the knowledge base for definitions and programs designed around them was inadequate.

Cautions Against Oversimplification

Although there is an abundance of evidence to suggest that students presently classified as mildly handicapped have so much in common and seem to profit from such similar interventions that they can be treated noncategorically, there are still some disturbing questions about the finality of this conclusion. Many of these questions are related to the concern that categorical approaches may be inadequately or inappropriately discredited and that there is a need for further study.

Lack of Conclusive Evidence

Long-term studies of exceptional learners within the three diagnostic categories of concern provide some evidence for the existence of real difference among the categories. Gajar (1979), in an extensive review of the characteristics of students labeled as educable mentally retarded, learning disabled, and emotionally disturbed, found that certain measures could distinguish the three types of students accurately about 82% of the time. These measures were IQ, reading level, test score scatter, and conduct/personality problems. In the Gajar study, it appeared more difficult to identify the emotionally disturbed students accurately than the students in the other two subgroups.

There is also evidence that differences in characteristics by category become more obvious as the severity of a student's handicap increases. For example, for students whose mental retardation is attributable to organic (as opposed to environmental) causes, there are measurable differences in the structures of their intelligence on Piagetian tasks that go beyond simple differences in IQ scores (Zigler et al., 1984). Mildly to moderately retarded students also may have deficiencies in social skills (Kehle & Barclay, 1979) or in memory problems that involve difficulty with semantic organization (August 1980). In early studies of learning disabilities, 75% of the students studied were found to have neurological impairments (Myklebust & Boshes, 1969). More recently, Swanson (1982) showed that the difficulties of learning disabled students go beyond lack of skill mastery and short attention span to problems in comprehending conceptual rules. Similarly, an emotionally disturbed student may have complex behavioral disorders or personality problems that require extensive behavior modification or psychotherapeutic treatment.

As is shown later, existing noncategorical (or multicategorical) placements frequently include students in all three categories whose handicaps are moderate to severe as well as mild. This range of individual differences is so large (both in depth and in breadth) that it becomes impossible for the teacher to provide appropriate instruction (Hocutt, Cox, & Pelosi, 1984). Nevertheless, the training of teachers in noncategorical classrooms is frequently limited to a single methods class emphasizing the teaching of academic skills (Huntze & Simpson, 1983; McDowell et al., 1982).

Need for Further Study

Clearly, there is a need for further research before this issue can be resolved. Further efforts must be made by researchers to describe accurately the academic and behavioral characteristics of the populations they study, to reduce the heterogeneity of their samples, and to specify, when possible, the subcategories within the larger category (Lakin, 1982; Torgesen & Dice, 1980; Zigler et al., 1984). Perhaps, in lieu of the search for alternative methods, research should explore the three groups' needs for alternative curricula (e.g., the need of educable mentally retarded students for a functional curriculum emphasizing real-life experiences in career/vocational education and the need of emotionally disturbed students for more extensive education in social skills development [Forgnone, McBride, Cronis, & Smith, in press]). Further study of the level of program intensity (as opposed to categorical placement) required for various learning disabled students might also be fruitful (Mercer, 1986). Mercer suggested that intensity might include more one-to-one instruction and a greater degree of teacher reinforcement. It may also provide a longer period of time for mastery (Bryant, Payne, & Gettinger, 1982).

In addition to investigations of alternative curricula and program intensity, further investigation of some of the causes of disability seems warranted. According to Rice (1983), for example, new research is needed on the role and limitations of the link between language and cognition, from which more viable remedial programs for specific students could evolve. Until these issues can be explored, a conclusive recommendation to teach mildly handicapped students either categorically or noncategorically should be regarded as premature.

State of the Art

Common Elements of Effective Methodology Across Categories

From a review of the literature and from a synthesis of classroom observation reports, it appears that a logical way to discuss methods of serving students classified as learning disabled, educable mentally retarded, and emotionally disturbed is to describe the common elements of effective instruction for these students. These elements can be found in reports on studies of normal learners (Walberg, 1984), nonclassified students with low socioeconomic backgrounds (Stevens & Rosenshine, 1981), and students who have unlabeled reading disabilities (Gettinger, 1982); and in research syntheses on mildly handicapped students both in regular classes (Larrivee, 1982; Wang & Birch, 1984a, 1984b) and in special classes (Jenkins & Mayhall, 1976; Sindelar & Deno, 1978).

Larrivee (1982) reviewed general education teacher effectiveness literature (Medley, 1977), constructed instruments for classroom observation from the factors that described effective teachers, and used these instruients in classroom observations. In a pilot study, she observed twelve teachers and concluded that behaviors similar to those reported in the general education teacher effectiveness literature also characterized the teachers who were effective with mildly handicapped students. In an observational study of 38 classrooms for learning disabled, educable mentally retarded, and emotionally disturbed students, Algozzine, Algozzine, Morsink, and Dykes (1984) confirmed the presence of a number of these behaviors and concluded that they were similar for teachers of the three groups of students; in other words, the teacher behaviors did not differ by category of exceptionality.

Earlier summaries of research on the effectiveness of the resource room (Jenkins & Mayhall, 1976), and on the extension of the engineered classroom to students classified as educable mentally retarded, learning disabled, and emotionally disturbed and grouped together for instruction, indicate that the programs incorporating similar elements were successful across categories. It is the effectiveness of generic methods across categories, rather than the prescription of methods by category, that is supported by the literature.

Researchers have concluded that effective teachers of mildly handicapped students are those who almost never use criticism; they have and communicate high expectations, present task-oriented instruction, reinforce on-task behavior, and use high rates of contingent praise (Gable, Hendrickson, Shores, & Young, 1983; Larrivee, 1982). They also are able to adapt their instruction by using alternative strategies, allowing for individual learning rates, and providing a variety of learning options that accommodate student differences (Wang, Gennari, & Waxman, 1985). It is hypothesized, then, that effective teachers of learning disabled, educable mentally retarded, and emotionally disturbed students provide (a) teacher-directed instruction; (b) extensive opportunities for active academic responding, with feedback; (c) contingent reinforcement for appropriate behavior; and (d) instruction adapted to individual students' needs. These methods appear effective across categories, although the reader should note that results for one level of handicap (i.e., mild) do not necessarily apply to other levels (i.e., moderate or severe). Separation of these four elements of effective methodology—teacher-directed instruction, active academic responding, contingent reinforcement, and adaptive instruction—is arbitrary, for the purpose of describing them more clearly. In practice, the programs described under these four elements often included aspects of several or all four elements, and an inference that only one of the four accounts for the overall effectiveness of a given program would go beyond the data. We hypothesize that all four of the elements facilitate the learning of mildly handicapped students across categories. (It could, perhaps, be argued also that these elements facilitate learning for all students but that they are more critical for, or need to be used more extensively with, mildly handicapped students.) Definitions of and supporting research for these methods are summarized briefly below.

Teacher-Directed Instruction

For the purpose of this discussion, teacher-directed instruction is defined as instruction that is planned and presented by the teacher. It is academically focused, systematic, and presented in sequential order of difficulty, beginning with a student's present level of achievement. It is characterized by teacher modeling and low-order question asking and is most commonly presented in a group setting (Gettinger, 1982), although it also may be delivered in a tutorial mode (Jenkins & Mayhall, 1976). Teacher-directed instruction is contrasted with instruction that consists of brief teacher responses to the questions of learners working independently.

Direct instruction, a specific example of teacher-directed instruction, has been found effective across the three categories (Bateman, 1979; Cotton & Savard, 1982; Englemann & Carnine, 1982; Epstein & Cullinan, 1982; Isaacs & Stennett, 1980; Lloyd, Cullinan, Heins, & Epstein, 1980; Maggs, 1980; Stephens, 1980). The key elements of direct instruction also have been successful in special education programs across the three categories in teaching for transfer (Gettinger, 1982); high-level answers (Maier, 1980); generalization (Lloyd, Saltzman, & Kauffman, 1981); and problem solving (Goldstein & Goldstein, 1980). Direct instruction is highly controlled and often features a script for the teacher. The term teacher-directed instruction is used in the present review because it is more inclusive, and because it is supported by the general teacher effectiveness research (Medley, 1977).

Active Academic Responding

Teacher-directed instruction typically features a large amount of learner practice, and the effects of controlled practice cannot be separated from the effects of teacher presentation. For the purpose of this discussion, however, controlled practice—the learner's response—is separated from teacher-directed instruction, the teacher's presentation. The factor that is isolated here has been identified as time-on-task, academic learning time, or more recently, active academic responding. The concept of active academic responding, however, goes beyond the concept of time-on-task, which may include periods when a student only appears to be working or is making a passive response, such as looking or listening. Active academic responding is defined as a measurable response on the part of a learner—written, manipulative, verbal, or gestural—that follows a teacher's question or request for performance. It may include independent work sheet or workbook completion, provided that this activity is closely and continuously supervised.

Academic learning time has been shown consistently to correlate with student achievement (Walberg, 1984). It also has been shown that mildly handicapped students require more learning time, more trials to criterion, and more practice than normal learners (Fisher & Zeaman, 1973; Heron & Skinner, 1981). Moreover, it has been shown that handicapped students' opportunities for verbal interactions with their teachers increase as group size decreases (Bryan & Wheeler, 1976; Kaufman, Agard, & Semmel, 1986), and that learning disabled, educable mentally retarded, and emotionally disturbed students are more attentive and interested when placed in smaller classes (Kaufman et al., 1986; Sherry, 1979). Conversely, handicapped students placed in larger classes may increase their levels of passive responding (Richey, Miller, & Lessman, 1981).

Either one-to-one instruction with a teacher or peer or verbally interactive small-group instruction can increase students' opportunities for active responding (Gettinger, 1982; Kaufman et al., 1986). The important element seems to be the provision of controlled practice, with positive teacher (or peer tutor) feedback (Cox & Wilson, 1981; Gable, Hendrickson, Shores, & Young, 1983; Larrivee, 1982; Wang & Birch, 1984b) rather than smaller class size per se.

Contingent Reinforcement

For the purpose of this discussion, contingent reinforcement is related to behavior management, while teacher feedback focuses on academic performance. While academic feedback is specific and may be used either to confirm or correct a student's accuracy, contingent reinforcement is positive rather than corrective; it may be either general or specific. Contingent reinforcement is social—usually delivered as verbal or nonverbal praise—though it may extend to tangible reinforcement, such as that which is given through a token economy or some other form of tangible reward system. The objective, of course, is that the student will ultimately be able to engage in self-management when the teacher's reinforcement has faded (Rosenbaum & Drabman, 1979).

Support for contingent reinforcement goes back to the body of literature related to keeping students on task by minimizing disruptions (Florida State Department of Education, 1983). More than a decade ago, Shores, Cegelka, and Nelson (1973) summarized special education research across categories, showing that any teacher attention to a behavior may increase the frequency of that behavior, even when the teacher's attention is a reprimand. Contingent reinforcement includes clear statements of rules; planned ignoring of inappropriate behavior; and positive reinforcement of alternative (acceptable) behavior demonstrated by another student.

Adaptive Instruction

The cluster of methods known as adaptive instruction includes those through which a teacher, rather than working in an inflexible way with an entire group, individualizes instruction to accommodate student differences. The application of adaptive instruction to mildly handicapped students in the mainstream has been studied extensively by researchers at the University of Pittsburgh's Learning Research and Development Center (Wang et al., 198[illegible]; Wang & Vaughan, 1985).

Adaptations include, for example, those which matc[illegible] individual students' needs for repeated practice (Fisher [illegible] Zeaman, 1973; Heron & Skinner, 1981; Lewis & Kas[illegible] 1982; Nelson & Cummings, 1981); lower reading levels [illegible] simplified language (Cawley, 1968; Hessler & Kitche[illegible] 1980; Magee & Newcomer, 1978; Noel, 1980; Ogletree [illegible] Uylaki, 1976); and specific learning strategies that enab[illegible] students to monitor their understanding of print materia[illegible] (Bellafiore & Salend, 1983; Conners, 1983; Lloyd, Halla[illegible]han, Kosiewicz, & Kneedler, 1982; Schumaker, Deshle[illegible] Alley, & Warner, 1983; Wong & Jones, 1982).

Adaptive instruction includes the use of alternativ[illegible] materials, media, classroom structures, and reinforcemen[illegible] schedules, as well as those obvious modality emphases use[illegible] for students with mild visual or auditory disabilities. I[illegible] does not extend to the prescription of methods by category since there is a growing body of research that suggests differential effects for various methods according to individual differences within categories (Ganchow, Wheeler, & Kretschmer, 1982; Reisburg, 1982).

Commonality of Practices Across Settings

There is evidence that the four elements discussed abov[illegible] are descriptive of effective practices across various settings. These settings include resource rooms and such othe[illegible] settings as self-contained and mainstream classrooms.

Resource Rooms

Jenkins and Mayhall (1976) summarized previous conflicting results from studies of resource rooms and concluded that the conflicts were the result of studying programs with inconsistent variables. To correct this problem, they abstracted from previous research the features that had been identified as effective. Then, in a series of summative experiments, they tested the whole model. They identified three factors that could cluster as directed instruction: one-to-one tutoring, either by a teacher or by a supervised cross-age tutor; direct service (rather than consultation); and daily instruction. They also described the importance of active academic responding with teacher feedback in their identification of active tutorial practice with daily measurement and feedback. The importance of adaptive instruction can be inferred from Jenkins and Mayhall's insistence that one-to-one instruction produced the greatest student learning. Later studies of effectiveness, described in the section on effectiveness of methods across categories, support the need for these components, with the exception of one-to-one instruction. It should be noted, however, that most one-to-one instruction in current resource rooms is not teacher-directed instruction; it is independent study monitored by the teacher.

After identifying the components, Jenkins and Mayhall evaluated overall program effectiveness in a series of three experiments. In all cases, it was found that both the special and the regular class students who received resource room programming with these identified components outperformed the students in the control groups. The investiators concluded that these components are descriptors of ffective resource rooms.

The importance of contingent reinforcement was shown y O'Connor, Stuck, and Wyne (1979). They identified lementary students who were one or more years behind in nath and reading and who had low percentages of on-task erformance. The students were chosen for intensive esource room programming. Ten children each partici-ated in groups for a 3–8-week intervention phase, while a omparison group of the same number stayed in a regular lassroom. Following intervention, it was found that the esource room students had greater on-task achievement nd scored significantly higher in reading and math. The mprovement both in on-task behavior and in academics emained for 4 months after the students returned to the egular classroom full time. Two experiments were con-lucted: one for second and third graders in an affluent chool, and a second for sixth-grade black students in an conomically depressed school. In both cases, the exper-mental group was placed in a resource room part time; the program adhered to strict behavioral procedures, including positive reinforcement with a token economy and individual timers, individualized academics, charting of performance, and time out. All these procedures are included in the description of contingent reinforcement. It appears that the treatment—rather than the resource room placement per se—accounted for the program's effectiveness.

Richey et al. (1981) conducted two interesting experiments on learning disabled students' attention, independence, and task orientation. In the first study, they compared eighteen disabled students' behaviors in regular and special classes. In the regular class, achievement was positively correlated with passive responding; in the resource room, achievement was correlated with attending. The study also shows that students were more distractible in the regular class, that passive responding in the regular class increased over time, and that passive responding decreased over time in the resource room. In the second study, the researchers attempted to determine which teacher interactions most affected the learning disabled students' approaches to the classroom. They found that ten learning disabled students received mixed messages about expectations. Although teachers gave them more positive and less negative reinforcement than they gave to the learning disabled students' peers, the teachers also ignored almost one third of the learning disabled students' interaction attempts. This practice may lead learning disabled students to believe that their behaviors are satisfactory when they are not. Like the earlier studies, this one seems to show that it was not the placement but the type of treatment provided (active academic responding with teacher feedback) that characterized the resource room's effectiveness.

Self-Contained and Regular Classrooms

Cox and Wilson (1981) found that the self-contained special class program was more effective than either the resource room or the regular class with specialist consultation in increasing the reading achievement of learning disabled students. A carefully planned instructional program, with more teacher-directed instruction, was the element that distinguished the self-contained setting from the other two kinds of classes.

The regular classroom can also be an effective learning environment for mildly handicapped students, so long as it includes selected program features that provide for diverse student populations, particularly those students who require greater-than-usual instructional support (Wang & Baker, 1985–1986; Waxman, Wang, Anderson, & Walberg, 1985). The Adaptive Learning Environments Model developed by Wang and her associates (Wang & Birch, 1984a, 1984b; Wang et al., 1985) is an example of a program designed with such features, including a curriculum that combines direct prescriptive instruction in academic skills with methods for facilitating student inquiry, self-management, and social cooperation; ongoing analysis of learner needs and skills; and interactive, individually prescribed instruction to meet individual needs.

The applicability of elements of effectiveness such as those noted above across settings suggests that the critical factor is not the setting but, rather, the way in which instruction is delivered and managed. In their study of the efficacy of resource rooms, Sindelar and Deno (1978) concluded that the important question was, *How* does the program work?, rather than simply, Does it work? More recently, the recommendations of a National Academy of Sciences (NAS) panel regarding special classes for mentally retarded students (Messick, 1984) support this conclusion.

Similarly, the conclusions of Walberg (1984), based on a synthesis of approximately 3,000 research studies, lend support to the effectiveness of common elements across general education settings. Walberg identified nine factors grouped under the headings of aptitude, instruction, and environment, that appear to be casual influences on student learning. Within the category of instruction, methods emphasizing reinforcement, acceleration, readiness training, and cues/feedback seem to have the greatest impact on learning (effects of approximately 1 standard deviation). Several other methods appear to have relatively strong effects (0.3–0.8 standard deviation). These include cooperative learning, personalized/adaptive instruction, tutoring, and diagnostic-prescriptive teaching. Walberg also pointed out that instructional time has an overall correlation of 0.38 with learning outcomes, but that simple increases in time produce diminishing rates of return in learning. Walberg suggested that "the more powerful factors appear to benefit all students in all conditions; but some students appear to benefit somewhat more than others under some conditions" (p. 22). And, in his discussion of the benefits of instruction based on individual needs, Walberg concluded:

> These related methods may attain their success by helping students to concentrate on the specific goals they individually need to achieve, or by freeing them

from the pervasive seatwork and recitation in groups that may suit only the middle third of the students. (p. 23)

The State of Practice

At the present time, there are a number of noncategorical or multicategorical programs operating in all but two states. They are found most often at the preschool and secondary levels, where mildly handicapped students who are academically "at risk" and those who are in need of career/vocational training have the most in common. At the elementary school level, the resource room is the prevalent delivery system for noncategorical programs, particularly in rural areas, while transition programs are used at both elementary and secondary levels to assist decertified students in bridging the gap between special education placement and the general education program. These four types of programs are illustrated below. This discussion is followed by a description of certification patterns and a summary of actual practices in these various settings, as determined by classroom observations.

Some authors distinguish among noncategorical, cross-categorical, and multicategorical programs. In noncategorical programs, mildly handicapped students are not labeled or are given a generic label such as mildly handicapped. In cross-categorical and multicategorical programs, mildly handicapped students labeled as learning disabled, educable mentally retarded, and emotionally disturbed (and, perhaps, also classified as having mild visual, hearing, or physical disabilities) are combined in a single program. For the purpose of this discussion, these distinctions are noted when made in the research reviewed but are not viewed as having practical relevance except for teacher certification.

Early Childhood Programs for At-Risk Children

Preschool/early childhood is the period when noncategorical programs for mildly handicapped children are the most defensible. There are fewer normative data on an individual child's cognitive, behavioral, and social skills at the preschool level. During this time, the same developmental lags may characterize children who have mild learning disabilities and those who are educable mentally retarded; it is also difficult to distinguish children who are mildly emotionally disturbed from those with learning disabilities or mild retardation on the basis of their social/behavioral deficits. Many parents and educators are reluctant to label children before they have even begun attending school for fear that the label may create negative self-fulfilling prophecies (Lerner, 1985; Mercer, 1983).

Rationale and Program Types

The value of early intervention for children considered to be at risk due to environmental factors or mildly handicapping conditions has been demonstrated for a number of years, as illustrated in the landmark research of Skeels and Dye (1939); Kirk (1958); Bereiter and Englemann (1966) and Skeels (1966). However, major emphasis on early intervention can still be considered a fairly recent phenomenon since most of the efforts have been initiated during the past two decades. Support for such efforts has increased through the years with the establishment of the Handicapped Children's Early Education Program (HCEEP) in 1968 to fund model preschools; the requirement of at least a 10% enrolment of handicapped children in Head Start programs in 1972; the availability of Preschool Incentive Grants under PL 94-142 (1975); and the allocation of monies for more severely handicapped persons under the Developmental Disabilities Act (1978). The support available from these sources has enabled states to attempt to rectify the problem reported by Gallagher (1979) that two thirds of the handicapped preschoolers who needed services were not receiving them. As White, Mastropieri, and Castro (1984) reported, eighteen states now require early intervention programs, and several other states have legislation pending.

Bailey and Wolery (1984) attributed this increased attention to early intervention to a progressive change in the way society views children, an emphasis on individual needs as exemplified by civil rights movements on behalf of all minority groups, a focus upon environmental influences on child growth and development processes, and societal and governmental interest in education. Although much progress has been made, much remains to be done to increase funding, train personnel, and increase public awareness (Kershman, 1985).

Noncategorical early intervention programs for mildly handicapped students have utilized a number of intervention strategies. These include psychoeducational interventions, direct instruction models, language development programs, and programs emphasizing parental support. Some of the programs have featured a combination of strategies. Head Start, Follow Through, and the HCEEP have been the major vehicles for the delivery of programs to mildly handicapped at-risk children.

Summary of Effectiveness

Although the effectiveness of early intervention programs is now widely endorsed, the research results on organically handicapped and at-risk children are equivocal at best. In their review of forty-nine studies that used pre-experimental, quasi-experimental, or true experimental designs to determine the effectiveness of interventions with organically impaired infants, Dunst and Rheingrover (1981) found numerous threats to internal validity in the majority of the studies. They stated that, although they were not concluding that early intervention does not work, they could not affirm the effectiveness of such programs based on the studies reviewed because the experimental designs rendered the results uninterpretable. In a similar review of twenty-seven studies of early intervention with biologically impaired infants and young children,

Simeonsson, Cooper, and Scheiner (1982) also noted problems with scientific research criteria but stated that, in spite of the limitations, they felt that the research did provide some qualified support for the effectiveness of such efforts.

Psychoeducational interventions with environmentally deprived or at-risk children who later might be labeled as educable mentally retarded, learning disabled, or mildly emotionally disturbed have also shown mixed results. The early research on Head Start programs created quite a bit of controversy when the findings revealed that the summer programs did not produce cognitive or affective gains that were maintained through the primary grades and that the full-year programs produced only limited effects on cognitive skills and no measurable impact on affective development that could still be noted up through Grade 3 (cf. Cicirelli, Evans, & Schiller, 1970; Smith & Bissell, 1970).

Later research on the Follow Through programs designed to continue the educational efforts begun in Head Start appeared to provide support for direct instruction teaching models (see summary in Becker & Carnine, 1981), but these studies also were subjected to a number of reanalyses and reinterpretations (e.g., House, Glass, McLean, & Walker, 1978). The actual impact of the Head Start experience on handicapped children cannot be readily ascertained because the data typically are embedded in the total program results (Turnbull & Blacher-Dixon, 1981).

Other longitudinal studies of low-income children have demonstrated promising outcomes. Lazar and Darlington (1982) reported on a follow-up of children who had been in eight, well-run, preschool programs similar to Head Start and found that significantly fewer children in the preschool programs were later placed in special education classrooms or retained in a grade. Schweinhart and Weikart (1981) found similar long-term results in their study of 123 children from 3 to 19 years of age who were involved in the Perry Preschool Project (Schweinhart & Weikart, 1981). When compared to a control group, the children who had received preschool programming showed superior academic achievement, fewer special education placements, and fewer grade retentions.

Demonstration projects funded by the HCEEP have resulted in the development of a number of curriculum and assessment materials. In addition, some of the projects have yielded evidence of long-term gains. For example, Weiss (1981) described the Inclass Reactive Language (INREAL) intervention program for 3–5-year-old language handicapped and bilingual children. The major goal of the project was to improve the language and related learning skills of the children. Data gathered 3 years after the INREAL program had concluded show that the use of these procedures resulted in the need for substantially fewer remedial reading, speech pathology, and learning disability placements.

A number of the HCEEP projects have been reviewed for effectiveness and recommended for wide distribution and replication by the Joint Dissemination Review Panel (JDRP), a group comprised of equal numbers of members from the United States Department of Education and the National Institute of Education. Two recent analyses of twenty-one of the HCEEP projects endorsed by the JDRP indicate a number of methodological problems in these studies similar to those noted in other early intervention program research. Odom and Fewell (1983) stated that the projects had a number of experimental design flaws, but they felt that most of the flaws were understandable or unavoidable. White et al. (1984) replicated and extended the work of Odom and Fewell in order to analyze critically the efficacy of the projects. Their study revealed that all of the projects suffered from major threats to internal validity, such as maturation, selection bias, regression toward the mean, and practice in test taking. Also, they noted that the majority of the studies used only pretest-posttest designs, and few of them used control or alternative treatment groups. They concluded that the HCEEP projects included in these analyses were consistent with current thinking about early intervention in that they emphasized, for example, the importance of involving parents, using structured teaching strategies, and starting the programs with handicapped children as soom as is feasible; but, because of the methodological problems, the data could not be seen as conclusive documentation to support these positions.

Establishing a research base for the efficacy of noncategorical early childhood programs is very difficult considering the limited research, the inclusion of children with a variety of handicapping conditions and severity levels in most projects, and the methodological weaknesses evident in almost all of the studies. Threats to internal validity must be controlled, and designs other than pretest-posttest procedures should be used in future research (White et al., 1984). In addition, indices of progress, such as the Proportional Change Index developed by Wolery (1983), need to be further refined and tested in order to allow comparisons of program efficiency for children of various ages and handicapping conditions. In response to pressure from the public and legislators for cost-effectiveness and program-efficiency data, Strain (1984) advocated consideration of the nature of educational interventions and attention to the problems inherent in administering tests that are normed on nonhandicapped populations and that are given by unfamiliar examiners; he proposed that efforts be focused instead upon replicating the best practices in the field. Bailey and Wolery (1984) also cautioned against stressing statistical significance at the expense of clinically significant changes that are indicative of important functional achievements in a young child's life.

Noncategorical Secondary Programs

Noncategorical practices have been implemented frequently at the secondary level. The rationale for noncategorical secondary programs is similar to the general rationale for noncategorical programs—that mildly handicapped students are similar and difficult to categorize. At the secondary level, noncategorical programs may be more the norm than the exception because there are fewer students identified as mildly handicapped, and grouping them by category would not be cost-effective, particularly in small districts. Also, at the secondary level, most mildly handicapped students have similar instructional needs, primarily for remediation of basic academics and for development of social and vocational skills.

In the present review, no studies were located in which researchers systematically compared secondary noncategorical with categorical programs. A large number of descriptions of secondary practices were located, however. These are outlined in greater detail in *The Secondary Practices Portfolio* (Smith-Davis, Johnson, Fairchild, Johnson, & Prothro, 1984), which is available through Dissemin/Action and which provided the information for the review of programs that follows. Secondary practices that deal with special education noncategorical or multicategorical programs and have some data to support their effectiveness are summarized below. Those which describe alternative education for unlabeled students are not included. The main features of these programs that seem to contribute to their effectiveness are highlighted. The programs are classfied into two types: those which emphasize basic education, and those which focus on career/vocational training.

Basic Education

Noncategorical and multicategorical approaches to teaching basic skills to mildly handicapped secondary students vary widely. Modified programs, course work, or graduation requirements are included in the approaches utilized to meet individual needs.

Secondary programs that feature adapted course work within the regular program exist in Philadelphia, Pennsylvania; Pueblo, Colorado; Greenville, South Carolina; Syracuse, New York; Portland, Oregon; and St. Louis, Missouri. Typical adaptations include modifications in instructional materials, use of objectives, evaluation of competencies, and graduation requirements. Many of these programs include counseling for students, as well as skill development, and some operate on a school team approach that provides support for individualized instruction. The St. Louis program is unique in that it focuses on strategies to provide students with a working knowledge of the legal system, to strengthen decision-making skills, and to reinforce basic skills.

In secondary programs at Jonesboro, Arkansas and High Point, North Carolina, mildly handicapped students are taught learning strategies rather than basic skills per se. These learning strategies are broken down into steps that can be generalized across subject areas and applied to problem solving in various areas of academic content.

Career/Vocational Programs

A number of noncategorical or multicategorical programs are available in secondary career/vocational education. Nationwide, programs in the area of career/vocational education illustrate vast differences in interpretation of ways in which to meet the postschool needs of handicapped secondary school students. Program approaches include emphasis on prerequisite behaviors, strengthening of positive attitudes and decision-making skills, presentation of academic/basic skills in a vocational context, and exploration of career/vocational choices in simulated or real-life situations. All of the programs noted below, as described by Smith-Davis, Johnson, et al. (1984), include career/vocational education to some degree, and all include some data on effectiveness.

Several of the programs pair academic work with life skills or vocational material. The Boston Mountains Educational Cooperative Career Awareness Program (CAP) has developed a curriculum that pairs specific academic skills with selected occupations to show students that school subjects are not only important but also relevent. Similarly, the Packets to Assist Literacy (PALS) program in Chipley, Florida, has created materials to increase reading comprehension in four areas: employability skills, health, money management, and food preparation. Preparation for life after school and gainful employment are also the main objectives of a self-contained special program in Winston-Salem, North Carolina; the program combines vocational and basic skills classes.

The Career and Personal Decision Making Skills Program for young adolescents in Boston, Massachusetts is illustrative of a program that emphasizes the improvement of self-discipline and decision-making skills. The curriculum includes education in current social issues as well as in job awareness and prevocational skills. Decision-making activities are stressed throughout the curriculum.

Some programs focus specifically on the exploration of and preparation for vocational options following high school. In an Albuquerque, New Mexico program, students explore a variety of vocational options in a career exploration class. Project DISCOVERY in Red Oak, Iowa, provides a systematic approach to career/vocational exploration by using kits featuring computer hardware and software components. In the Experience-Based Career Education program in Fond du Lac, Wisconsin, handicapped junior and senior high school students spend 4 days a week at any of 250 community experience sites of their choosing to investigate, first hand, a particular career.

Resource Room Programs

The use of resource rooms as a service delivery option for mildly handicapped students became popular in the early to mid-1970s. Prior to that time, mildly handicapped students had been served noncategorically in programs of a similar nature, which were classified as remedial reading. Initially, the resource rooms were primarily elementary; as elementary students became older without being "cured," resource rooms were established at the middle and high school levels. Early in their development, resource rooms served students grouped by skill deficits for small-group instruction. Many of the programs emphasized social/behavioral skills development. Currently, most resource rooms follow a regular class schedule and provide instruction to large, flexible groups. Individualization is facilitated through the use of student folders containing worksheets geared to Individualized Educational Program (IEP) objectives. Noncategorical or multicategorical resource room programs are especially prevalent in rural areas, where they are more cost-effective than categorical placements. In the following section, descriptive data on resource rooms are provided, and issues related to the resource room's effectiveness are presented.

Descriptions of Programs

According to D'Alonzo, D'Alonzo, and Mauser (1979), there are five types of resource rooms: categorical, cross-categorical, noncategorical, specific skills, and itinerant. These investigators provided a checklist of facilities and services, with the recommendation that approximately twenty students per class be served. Adamson (1983) summarized noncategorical resource room services for secondary school students. He indicated that most students are served approximately half the day and that, when they return to the regular environment, they are faced with the same conditions that created their referral.

More detailed descriptions of current resource room patterns were provided by Friend and McNutt (1984). These authors pointed out that forty-nine of the fifty states and the District of Columbia have resource rooms classified as noncategorical or multicategorical. Their descriptive data on characteristics of resource room programs as reported by state departments of education are presented in Table 2.

Issues in the Evaluation of Resource Rooms

In the present review, only two studies were located in which noncategorical resource rooms were compared with categorical resource rooms. The first (Sparks & Richardson, 1981) focused on the efficacy of placements for learning disabled students only and offered tentative results. In the second study (Dulle & Childs, 1985), the investigators compared categorical with noncategorical placement (both resource room and self-contained) for 229 students classified as learning disabled, educable mentally retarded, and emotionally disturbed, only half of whom remained in the programs through posttesting. The investigators indicated that their results suggest that the categorical and multicategorical approaches were equally effective, but they acknowledged several methodological problems. They also stated that parents and professionals raised numerous objections to the multicategorical programs. It appears that parents of students classified as learning disabled are particularly resistant to noncategorical programs.

One of the problems in drawing conclusions from research on the effectiveness of resource rooms is that many early programs operated without any systematic collection of data on effectiveness. Chaffin (1974) located and reviewed thirty early programs that emphasized some type of part-time placement while retaining students in a mainstream classroom. Of the thirty programs, twenty were operating in public schools; ten had no evaluation information, while others had case studies/questionnaires; and four had minimal-level, data-based evaluations showing the programs to be effective. Among these programs was one in the Fountain Valley School District of California, in which 81% of the students reached learning goals in reading, while 89% did so in math; and the Pickney Project, a university-school collaborative project at the University of Kansas, in which students all demonstrated overall gains on the Peabody Individual Achievement Test (PIAT) (Dunn, 1970) of about 0.5 and general information gains of 0.9. These two early programs did feature continuous evaluation of student progress.

One of the major concerns in the evaluation of the noncategorical resource room is effectiveness is whether or not students maintain the gains they make in resource room programs. Ito (1980) conducted a follow-up study of the reading gains of students placed part-time in a resource room to see if they had maintained gains after one year in the regular classroom. He found that students did increase their reading rates in the resource room but that these gains were not maintained after one year. These findings are similar to those of Galvin, Quay, Annesley, and Werry (1971) regarding behaviorally disordered students who had been placed in resource rooms and failed to maintain gains after they returned to the regular classroom.

Neubauer (1979) attempted to determine to what extent and under what conditions improved performance in a pull-out setting can assist a student's reintegration into the mainstream environment. Neubauer pointed out that resource room curricula focus on basic skills instruction and that a reintegrated student frequently has difficulties with science and social studies because of specialized vocabulary and study skills. Neubauer urged that resource room curricula should emphasize two kinds of generalization: from specific to applied skills, and from one setting to another. Kuhlman (1981) successfully used a prop—a good luck charm—that a student carried from the resource room to the regular class as a reminder that the student should apply learned skills when in the mainstream. Adamson (1983) described how secondary students can generalize skills when generalization is taught directly and when follow-up consultation is provided.

It appears, then, that, despite the existence of numerous descriptions of resource rooms, there is little or mixed evidence of their effectiveness. It should be emphasized here that the issue is not the effectiveness of the resource room versus other service delivery models. The issue is the effectiveness of categorical versus noncategorical resource rooms. On this question, there is almost no data-based evidence.

TABLE 2
Characteristics of Resource Room Programs as Reported by State Departments of Education

States	Year begun	Type of teacher certification	Type of resource room used	Time students spend in resource room	Percent of all handicapped served in resource room (estimated)
Alabama	1970[a]	E	CI	NR	UN
Alaska	UN	E	M	N	UN
Arizona	NR	E	CM	O	71%
Arkansas	1975[a]	E	CNI	H	54%
California	1977	S	MI	H	42%
Colorado	1973	E	CMI	N	67%
Connecticut	1967	E	M	N	92%
Delaware	UN	E	M	H	UN
Dist. of Columbia	1967[a]	E	CMNI	H	90%
Florida	1974	E	CMI	T	70%
Georgia	1970s[a]	E	M	H	UN
Hawaii	1975[a]	E	M	T	24%
Idaho	1967	G	MI	N	75%
Illinois	1964	E	CMI	H	70%
Indiana	1978	E	M	H	UN
Iowa	1963	E	CMI	T	40%
Kansas	1960s[a]	E	CMI	H	94%
Kentucky	1972[a]	E	CMI	H	36%
Louisiana	1976	EG	MI	T	47%
Maine	1973	E	M	H	82%
Maryland	1968	G	M	T	67%
Massachusetts	1974	S	N	T	96%
Michigan	NR	E	CMI	N	25%
Minnesota	1975[a]	E	CMI	H	73%
Mississippi	UN	E	MI	T	83%
Missouri	1974	ES	CMI	N	86%
Montana	1977[a]	G	MI	N	71%
Nebraska	1973[a]	E	MI	T	54%
Nevada	UN	E	CM	N	84%
New Hampshire	UN	EG	CMNI	H	46%
New Jersey	1969[a]	G	CMN	T	17%
New Mexico	1972[a]	EG	CMI	T	51%
New York	1968	G	CMI	H	20%
North Carolina	1970[a]	E	CMI	T	98%
North Dakota	UN	E	CM	H	NR
Ohio	1973[a]	E	C	N	UN
Oklahoma	UN	E	CMI	H	UN
Oregon	1973[a]	EG	MI	N	66%
Pennsylvania	1969[a]	E	CM	H	17%
Rhode Island	1978[a]	S	CMI	N	70%
South Carolina	1973	E	CMI	H	49%
South Dakota	UN	G	N	T	20%
Tennessee	1973	EG	CM	T	54%
Texas	1970	EG	CMI	T	96%
Utah	1970	ES	CMI	T	85%
Vermont	1971[a]	G	M	T	70%
Virginia	1970	E	CMI	N	86%
Washington	UN	N	M	N	UN
West Virginia	1968	E	CMI	T	UN
Wisconsin	UN	E	CMI	H	23%
Wyoming	UN	E	CMI	N	UN

Codes

General:	NR	= No Response.
	UN	= Unknown, respondent indicated information not available.
Year begun:	a	= Approximation of year begun.
Type of certification:	E	= Certificate in area(s) of exceptionality to be served.
	S	= Special resource teacher certificate.
	G	= Generic special education teacher certificate.
	N	= No specific requirements.
Type of resource room:	C	= Categorical.
	M	= Multicategorical.
	N	= Noncategorical.
	I	= Itinerant.
Time in resource room:	H	= Up to, but not more than, half the school day.
	T	= Other time specified or recommended.
	N	= Time not specified.
	O	= Other.

Note: From "Resource Room Programs: Where Are We Now?" by M. Friera and G. McNutt, 1984, *Exceptional Children*, **51**, 152–153, Copyright 1984 by the Council For Exceptional Children. Registered by permission.

Transition Programs Between Regular and Special Education

Like resource programs, noncategorical transition programs span the elementary through high school levels. Designed to provide support services for students returning to the mainstream from special education categorical programs, they have been used for more than a decade, particularly in Texas and California, but recently they have attracted renewed attention. (Schneider & Bryne, 1984; Slade, 1984).

The reintegration of handicapped students from special classes into the mainstream of education has stimulated much interest at legal, philosophical, social, and educational levels. There are a number of difficulties involved in the transition between special and regular class placement for noncategorical mildly handicapped students. Yoshida, MacMillan, and Meyers (1976) pointed out the social and legal issues that caused California to revise its criteria for classification as educable mentally handicapped in an effort to prevent the overidentification of minority students. MacMillan, Meyers, and Yoshida (1978) also described the perceptions of classroom teachers regarding decertified educable mentally handicapped students and regular class cohorts. They showed that the students in transition programs were perceived as having lower ability and social acceptance, although the enrolment of decertified students did not appear to have an impact on the regular class instruction.

Program Descriptions

Many programs utilize a consulting teacher approach to facilitate a smooth transition between regular and special class settings (Haight, 1984). Although this individual is most commonly called a consultant or a diagnostic-prescriptive teacher, other titles also have been assigned. This individual generally is involved in in-service with or individualized training of the regular classroom teacher, is available as a consultant regarding student behavioral, instructional, or other problems as necessary, and may also provide diagnostic and coordination services. Generally, this specialist is assigned to more than one school. Many school districts utilize a resource room teacher as the main transition facilitator. Working within their individual schools, these teachers offer crisis intervention, curriculum advice, and counseling for regular teachers and transition students. Other schools provide modified settings or special intermediary programs as a means of making a successful transition. Additionally, programs preparing a regular student body for the increased influx of handicapped peers into the educational environment are receiving more attention. Materials designed to foster both understanding of handicapped students and acceptance of others' differences are becoming more readily available.

Factors That Affect Reintegration

A review of available literature on reintegration has isolated numerous factors to be considered in successful transition programs. Fundamental to most approaches is the assignment of a specific individual to act as an intermediary in the process. This individual, regardless of title, works with the student and the receiving teacher to facilitate a smooth transition for both (Radford-Hill, 1984). Additionally, some models are now available to structure the integration process (Hundert, 1982). General areas they consider include administrative issues, selection of likely transition students, preparation of students, preparation of receiving personnel, preparation of materials, and follow-up of reintegration. South Dakota, in particular, has developed these guidelines in the form of a needs assessment for the successful reintegration of handicapped students. Specific details have also been provided by Slade (1984) and Schneider and Byrne (1984).

Description of National Certification Patterns

A final element of the description of existing noncategorical and multicategorical programs is a summary of certification patterns in more than half of the United States and its territories. This pattern is particularly prevelant in remote rural areas.

Certification of special education personnel is conducted across the United States in one or more of the following patterns: categorical, noncategorical, and /or multicategorical. In categorical certification, personnel are certified and trained to teach in a specific area of handicap. In a noncategorical model, they are typically certified according to the level of severity of the handicaps of the pupils they teach. Multicategorical models utilize personnel certified to teach in more than one handicap area.

Even when noncategorical or multicategorical approaches are taken, many jurisdictions include categorical certification for personnel in areas pertaining to sensory handicaps, severe handicaps, and other low-prevalence handicaps. Moreover, certain specialists (e.g., speech pathologists) are generally certified apart from special education.

Current information on certification practices has been gained from a study of fifty-seven jurisdictions (the fifty states, the District of Columbia, the Bureau of Indian Affairs, and five territories) (Noel, Smith-Davis, & Burke, in press). Details on noncategorical and multicategorical certification appear in the Appendix to this chapter. Further information on the topic of state certification practices can be found in this volume's chapter by Blackhurst, Bott, and Cross.

Summary of Existing Practices

Noncategorical and multicategorical programs are operating at preschool, elementary, and secondary levels throughout the nation. They are particularly prevalent in rural or sparsely populated areas such as South Dakota, in which the small numbers of students in each category make generic programs more cost effective. At the preschool level, noncategorical programs are recommended as a way of serving children who are at risk but not readily distinguishable by category, or those for whom a premature label might create a self-fulfilling prophecy. At the secondary level, multicategorical programs are used most often to serve students who have been previously labeled differentially but who have programmatic needs (e.g., for remediation of basic academics or for career/vocational education) in common.

Resource rooms and transition programs are now being used more frequently than self-contained classrooms to serve mildly handicapped students noncategorically. Twenty-seven jurisdictions have teacher certification that is primarily categorical, while in thirty others, certification is primarily noncategorical or multicategorical; some type of noncategorical programs operate, however, in all but two states. There is some evidence of the effectiveness of noncategorical and multicategorical programs, but there are no comparative results suggesting that either categorical or noncategorical programs have a greater impact on students' achievement or adjustment.

Major Issues in Noncategorical Programs

Although the rationale for noncategorical and multicategorical programs is well established and there are a number of such programs in place, there are still some concerns about their existence. These concerns center on two issues: these programs do not function in the real world as they have been designed in theory to function; and changes in these special education programs over the time seem to be creating greater discrepancies between best and actual practice in noncategorical programs. Each of these issues is discussed briefly below. The discussion includes information gained through two recent national surveys (Noel et al., in press; Smith-Davis, Burke, & Noel, 1984) of personnel at state departments of education—perhaps the individuals in the best position to observe the actual operation of noncategorical programs.

Reality Not Equivalent To Theory

In theory, noncategorical and multicategorical programs are designed to serve mildly handicapped students who are similar in age and in learning needs. Since the early 1980s, however, there has been a growing trend to move handicapped students into less and less restrictive environments. In practice, this means that more mildly to moderately handicapped children are being moved into regular education programs and into resource room/regular classroom instruction in multicategorical groups. Multicategorical grouping, while increasingly prevalent among mildly to moderately handicapped children, is not, however, reserved for this population. Multicategorical resource room instruction also is provided in some districts for groups that combine deaf–blind, multihandicapped, and other severely handicapped students. Further, in some cases in which small numbers of handicapped children are present, more severely involved children may be placed for instruction with mildly to moderately handicapped students. The overall evidence suggests that multicategorical placement does not always follow decisions based on educational quality but often reflects districts' responses to shrinking fiscal and personnel resources as well as administrative convenience; another problem is that multicategorical resource room placement creates more students per teacher (Noel et al., in press; Smith-Davis, Burke, & Noel, 1984).

In the surveys conducted in all the states, the District of Columbia, and several territories in 1982 and 1984, respondents in more than half of the jurisdictions reported concerns about the multicategorical grouping of handicapped children for instruction, and, in several jurisdictions, task groups were taking a second look at the multicategorical resource room model. These concerns were not directed toward the wisdom of the multicategorical resource room model itself but, rather, toward its abuse in practice. Parents of handicapped children also have been reported to share these concerns. Indeed, when proposals to initiate multicategorical programming were introduced in several jurisdictions, they were defeated by parental opposition (Noel et al., in press; Smith-Davis, Burke, & Noel, 1984).

In the face of the trend to move more and more students into resource room or regular class placements, three jurisdictions are turning in the opposite direction by electing to reduce resource room placements in favor of more self-contained instructional settings. In each case, the efficacy of the resource room in genuinely bringing about positive educational changes in handicapped students has been seriously questioned, not only by educational authorities but also by regular education teachers to whose classes these students return each day, and by parents (Noel et al., in press).

In one such jurisdiction, the major problem reported is the qualifications of resource room teachers; it is believed that these personnel cannot be expected to deal with the diversity of needs and learning styles and the number of children represented in multicategorical resource rooms. In another jurisdiction, which has been dealing for some time with the issue, the State Board of Education has announced that current arrangements (termed *holding tanks*) will no longer exist by 1987 because any teacher will have to be certified in each area that he or she serves (i.e., personnel teaching multicategorical groups will have to become certified in all of the handicap areas they serve). A third jurisdiction conducted a 5-year analysis of the multicategorical resource room as a service delivery mode, and the results show that students who were initially placed in resource rooms less than 50% of the school day eventually spent more, rather than less, of their time in such placements. Increased time in the resource room was shown to be related to progression through the grades and to be dependent on reading ability and on the entire general problem of low-achieving students. The results of this analysis lead to the conclusion that the prevailing reason for students to remain in resource rooms is nonsuccess in regular classroom programming—a difficulty shared by handicapped and low-achieving students alike (Noel et al., in press).

Program approval also has become a touchy issue. In

wo states, there was an initial interest in establishing a few oncategorical or multicategorical programs on an expermental basis, particularly in sparsely populated areas. Guidelines were established, and these units had to be pproved as exceptions. So many of these units have been stablished, however, that advocacy groups have initiated legal actions against them, claiming that benign approval exists for all. Indeed, most states have well-developed guidelines (e.g., for students' educational levels, social development, physical development, and management needs) that are not being implemented. Additionally, here are concerns about abuses of noncategorical models hat fail to serve the students who fall between classifications (e.g., those who have IQs of 70–84 or reading levels of Grades 2–3) and, conversely, about those which open their programs to all underachieving students. In particular, there is concern about the 119% increase in students classfied as learning disabled over the past 7 years; many of these students are served in noncategorical placements (Foster, 1984).

Among other concerns revealed by respondents surveyed in 1982 and 1984 (Noel et al., in press; Smith-Davis, Burke, & Noel, 1984) are the following.

- There is considerable questioning as to whether college and university training programs can adequately train multicategorical personnel in 4 years, about the depth of training provided in higher education programs, and about the manner in which districts program for mildly to moderately handicapped students.
- Generalists are not found to be universally well prepared to serve a diversity of students, and exorbitant demands often are placed on them in terms of caseloads and preparation for the various students they will see in a day or a week. This concern about the diversity of responsibilities and number of skills required of teachers in multicategorical situations is multiplied when caseloads and inappropriate groupings of students present personnel with demands that even the best and most experienced teachers cannot meet. In some locations, districts may request variances to enlarge the categories of handicap or age levels that can be served in a multicategorical resource room or an interrelated class. It is in such cases as these that the diversity of students' handicaps and learning needs can become excessively demanding. The Hocutt et al. (1984) study cited earlier provides new evidence that noncategorical programs for students with similar levels of severity and specific deficits work but those which combine large numbers of students with multicategorical disabilities do not. The latter practice may have, unfortunately, occurred as a cost-effectiveness measure and a superficial response to demands for compliance with the letter of the law.
- Many professionals question the wisdom of serving emotionally disturbed students in multicategorical settings. This is a concern not only about the impact such students have on the behavior of others but also about their unique instructional needs and varying intellectual capacities—all of which may indicate the need for educational placement apart from multicategorical groups that include retarded and learning disabled students.
- In many cases in which the demand for personnel exceeds supply, the most widespread response of jurisdictions is to issue temporary certification to personnel who do not demonstrate the training, background, experience, or other qualifications necessary for the positions to which they are assigned. Thus, uncertainties about the preparation of multicategorical teachers can be coupled with the necessity of assigning marginally qualified people to the multicategorical group. Further, in some jurisdictions, a teacher certified in any one area of handicap may be permitted to teach in any other category—a practice guaranteed to cluster students with teachers whose skills are less than adequate for the range and dimensions of the multicategorical setting.
- Since 1982, secondary education for handicapped students has received increasing attention as a result of federal emphasis on transitional programming that prepares these students for adult life. Currently, most jurisdictions are making greater efforts to achieve the interagency cooperation that is necessary to extend vocational opportunities to handicapped students, and there are accelerated efforts to create programs in which secondary handicapped students can earn Carnegie units and standard high school diplomas. Nonetheless, secondary education continues to be viewed as an alarmingly weak link in the special education continuum (Noel et al., in press). A major problem is the lack of qualified personnel to provide instruction at the secondary level.
- In many states, particularly those west of the Mississippi River, even multicategorical grouping is not the solution for small districts in sparsely populated areas, where it is not uncommon to find a one-room school with one teacher responsible for up to eight grades. Such multigrade instruction may also include, from time to time, one or more mildly to moderately handicapped students. In these circumstances, superintendents report the need not for greater categorization of students and specialization of teachers but, rather, for what are termed "competent generalists"—general education teachers with skills in curricular sequencing across grades, direct instruction and incremental learning, individualized instruction, responding to varying individual learning styles, cross-age grouping of children for instruction, planning and managing multiple activities, and using problem-solving approaches to working with children. A multigrade rural or remote school is essentially a situation in which all children must receive individual instruc-

tion geared to their learning styles, grade levels, and other variables (Noel et al., in press; Scott, 1984).

Program Changes Over Time

Between the early 1970s and the present time, a number of changes have occurred in the special education programs that serve mildly handicapped students. One such change is in the prevalance of directed teaching. Extensive observations of 521 regular, self-contained, and resource room classes participating in the Programmed Re-entry into Mainstream Education (PRIME) project (Kaufman, Semmel, & Agard, 1973) in Texas during 1971–1972 (Kaufman et al., 1986) reveal that there were, at that time, many similarities between the regular and special classes, including the amount of time the teacher was the central focus, directing lessons for whole or small groups. In contrast, 607 observations in forty-four special classrooms, including thirty-eight classrooms for educable mentally handicapped, learning disabled, and emotionally disturbed students in Florida during 1983–1984 reveal that most of the "instruction consisted of teacher supervision, with students engaged in completing work sheets independently while teachers circulated to provide assistance" (Algozzine et al., 1984).

There is a difference not only in the amount of time the teacher spends directing instruction but also in the type of instruction provided. In actual practice, the curricula provided for most elementary (McBride & Forgnone, 1985) and secondary (Noel et al., in press) multicategorical programs are focused almost entirely on the development of academic skills to meet state competency standards. Multicategorical resource rooms at the secondary level are reported to be oriented to basic skills remediation and tutorial assistance, with an emphasis on the process rather than the product and with little career/vocational education or postschool planning.

Other contrasts are also becoming apparent. Early resource room programs featured temporary experimental placements, with continuous measurement of student progress and systematic team review after 3–6 months (Chaffin, 1974), an ideal procedure, which is less possible now because of legal requirements and paperwork demands. A small number of students were given intensive, direct services by a specialist, as opposed to a large number being given indirect services (e.g., teacher consultation). The latter practice has been shown to provide services for a larger number of students but to reduce the number of "cures" among more seriously involved students (Wixson, 1980).

Early in the implementation of the resource room model, Brown, Kiraly, and McKinnon (1979) raised questions about its effectiveness, particularly in terms of the role and function of the resource room teacher. They raised questions about small-group as opposed to individualized instruction and about whether the resource room teacher should provide in-service and consultation to the classroom teacher. The heavy load of paperwork, scheduling, and communication with other teachers were cited as problems. Other constraints included the need for providing services to a large number of students (eighteen per day) for periods of only about 30 minutes each. At this time, it is not uncommon for resource room teachers to serve thirty or more students per day. Many of these students have widely disparate needs (Hocutt et al., 1984).

Implications for Research, Practice, and Policy

Although there is a strong rationale and a sound theoretical base for noncategorical/multicategorical programs, there are a number of weaknesses in the actual implementation of these programs. These weaknesses suggest that there is a need for further study before a decision on the efficacy of noncategorical programs can be made.

Earlier in this paper, four elements of effective instruction for mildly handicapped students were identified. They were teacher-directed instruction, active academic responding, contingent reinforcement, and adaptive instruction. If these elements are descriptors of effective programs, then current practice in noncategorical/multicategorical programs (particularly in resource rooms) is discrepant from best practice. Further study of each of each of the four descriptors is recommended.

- Although individual or small-group (with similar needs), teacher-directed instruction is desirable, many noncategorical classes are too large for direct tutoring or consist of students with too many kinds of handicaps to be grouped effectively for instruction (Hocutt et al., 1984); much instruction consists of independent work sheet completion, with the teacher circulating to provide periodic assistance (Algozzine et al., 1984). Moreover, there is a need for further study of teacher-directed instruction, because researchers have recently raised questions about the comprehensiveness, focus, and linguistic clarity of teachers' classroom discourses and their impact in student learning (Nelson, 1984; Silliman, 1984).
- Although high rates of active academic responding with teacher feedback are desirable, the average student spends less than 45 minutes per day in active responding time (Thurlow, Ysseldyke, Graden, Greener, & Mecklenberg, 1982). This average extends across teacher-perceived levels of behavioral (Graden, Thurlow, Ysseldyke, & Algozzine, 1982) and academic (Greener, Thurlow, Graden, & Ysseldyke, 1982) competence and appears similar across groups regardless of label or level; in a specific academic subject, such as second-grade reading, actual responding time per day may be as little as 10 minutes (Graden et al., 1982). Moreover, opportunities for student–teacher interactions have been shown to decrease as class size increases (Bryan & Wheeler, 1976). There is a need for further study of the effects of active academic responding on student learning, including the

impact of class size on students' opportunity to respond.

— Although high rates of contingent reinforcement are desirable, special education teachers of mildly handicapped students give low rates of contingent praise, with teachers of learning disabled and emotionally disturbed students using a preponderance of disapprovals (Gable, Hendrickson, Young, Shores, & Stowitschek, 1983). In general, it seems that teachers give slightly more academic encouragement to mildly handicapped students than to their nonhandicapped peers, but they give the mildly handicapped students low rates of contingent reinforcement for appropriate social behavior (Gable, Hendrickson, Shores & Young, 1983). Also, students respond to teacher criticism by ignoring the teacher (Gable, Hendrickson, Shores, & Young, 1983; Gable, Hendrickson, Young, Shores, & Stowitschek, 1983). Thurlow et al. (1982) found that teachers of learning disabled students spent little time giving either approval or disapproval, though rates were higher for disapproval. Algozzine et al. (1984) found that the teachers of learning disabled, educable mentally retarded, and emotionally disturbed students in their study used general praise or neutral feedback and that these teachers' students were largely on-task but not intensely or enthusiastically involved in learning. There is a need for further study of the effects of various types of teacher response on the learning and behavior of handicapped children. Both approval and disapproval should be studied as contingent responses (for a discussion of differential effects of praise, see Morsink, Soar, Soar, & Thomas, 1986).

— Even though instruction adapted to the special learning needs of mildly handicapped students is desirable, most instruction provided in resource rooms for mildly handicapped students is focused on low-level academic skills (McBride & Forgnone, 1985; Noel et al., in press); it is characterized by little differentiation in format (i.e. little use of media, learning centers, games, activities) and consists primarily of textbook reading and/or work sheet completion with delayed or infrequent teacher feedback (Algozzine et al., 1984). There is a need for further study of the effects of adaptive instruction on the learning of handicapped children. New strategies by Wang and her colleagues (Wang & Birch, 1984a, 1984b; Wang et al., 1985) seem particularly promising.

A further complication arises from the fact that many teachers currently placed in categorical and in non- or multicategorical classes are only temporarily certified or are unqualified for their positions. It is suggested that careful study of this situation might reveal the consequences of the injudicious use of unqualified personnel. At this time, however, comparisons of categorical versus noncategorical programs, with control for the levels of personnel preparation, have not been conducted. Research on this issue is recommended.

In summary, it appears that the current situation is similar to the state of the art in resource room implementation, as reported by Jenkins and Mayhall in 1976 and summarized by Sindelar and Deno in 1978: Such diversity exists among programs entitled noncategorical or multicategorical that reliable comparisons cannot be made between these and the similarly diverse programs entitled categorical. As suggested by these investigators, issues regarding research and practice should focus on identification of the instructional and teacher training variables that enhance student learning and adjustment rather than on the simple comparison of programs with different titles.

Although the present research synthesis does not provide clear directions for policy change, it appears that even a cautious scholar might abstract the following.

— Every program for mildly handicapped students should be staffed with a well-prepared teacher who is capable of providing clear, direct instruction with active academic responding, managing simultaneous activities, providing contingent reinforcement, and adapting instruction to individual needs as determined by ongoing measurement of student achievement. Continuing the practice of emergency certification may intensify the learning problems of handicapped students, and it further complicates the task of researchers.

— All efficacy studies accepted for future professional publication should include clear descriptions of both learner characteristics and the specific intervention strategies implemented. It has been counterproductive to attempt to infer the efficacy of categorical or noncategorical programs when the diversity within subjects and treatments has exceeded the differences between or among them.

— The issues of administrative convenience and cost-effectiveness should not take precedence over the larger issue of benefit to students. It is only temporarily less expensive to group students who cannot be managed, to place too many students in a program, or to select an environment that is theoretically less restrictive but actually not more facilitative. The long-range consequences of such policies are serious: Dedicated teachers leave the profession; mildly handicapped students develop fewer academic, social, and career/vocational skills and may become more liabilities than potential contributors to society; and conscientious researchers are unable to isolate significant variables that could be used to advance the state of the art.

The conclusion that mildly handicapped students should be served noncategorically or categorical in self-contained, resource, or mainstream classrooms is premature, based on the existing evidence. The conclusion that policy changes should follow rather than precede careful study is long overdue.

Acknowledgment

The authors wish to thank Junean Krajewsk for her assistance in summarizing work on secondary noncategorical programs.

Author Information

Catherine Voelker Morsink is Professor/Chair of Special Education at the University of Florida. Carol Chase Thomas is Assistant Professor of Special Education at the University of North Carolina at Wilmington. Judy Smith-Davis is Consultant in Special Education at the University of Nevada at Reno.

References

Adamson, P. (1983). Linking two worlds: Serving resource students at the secondary level. *Teaching Exceptional Children*, **15**, 70–75.

Alexander, R., & Apfel, C. H. (1976). Altering schedules of reinforcement for improved classroom behavior. *Exceptional Children*, **43**, 97–99.

Algozzine, K. (1984). *Specialized competencies for EMH teachers: A review of the literature.* Gainesville: University of Florida, Department of Special Education.

Algozzine, R., Algozzine, K., Morsink, C., & Dykes, M. K. (1984). *Summary of the 1983–84 ESE classroom observations, using COKER.* Gainesville: University of Florida, Department of Special Education.

Algozzine, R., Schmid, R., & Mercer, C. (1981). *Childhood behavior disorders.* Gaithersburg, MD: Aspen.

Applied Urbanetics Policy Research. (1980). State profiles prepared for the Office of Special Education (Contract No. 300–78–0467). Washington, DC: Author.

August, G. (1980). Input organization as a mediating factor in memory: Comparison of EMR and nonretarded individuals. *Journal of Experimental Child Psychology*, **30**, 125–143.

Bailey, D. B., & Wolery, M. (1984). *Teaching infants and preschoolers with handicaps.* Columbus, OH: Merrill.

Bateman, B. (1979). Teaching reading to learning disabled and other hard-to-teach children. In B. L. Resnick & P. A. Weaver (Eds.), *Theory and practice of early reading* (Vol. 1, pp. 227–260). Hillsdale, NJ: Erlbaum.

Becker, W., & Carnine, D. (1980). Direct instruction: An effective approach to educational intervention with disadvantaged and low performers. In B. B. Lahey & A. E. Kazdin (Eds.), *Advances in clinical child psychology* (Vol. 3, pp. 429–474). New York: Plenum.

Bellafiore, L., & Salend, S. (1983). Modifying inappropriate behavior through a peer confrontation system. *Behavioral Disorders*, **8**, 274–279.

Berdine, W., & Blackhurst, A. E. (1981). Mental retardation. In A. E. Blackhurst & W. Berdine (Eds.), *An introduction to special education* (pp. 310–353). Boston, MA: Little, Brown.

Bereiter, C., & Englemann, S. (1966). *Teaching disadvantaged children in the preschool.* Englewood Cliffs, NJ: Prentice-Hall.

Birch, J. (1974). *Mainstreaming educable mentally retarded children in regular classes.* Reston, VA: Council for Exceptional Children.

Blake, K. (1974). *Teaching the retarded.* Englewood Cliffs, N Prentice-Hall.

Blankenship, C., & Lilly, M. S. (1981). *Mainstreaming studen with learning and behavior problems: Techniques for t classroom teacher.* New York: Holt, Rinehart & Winston.

Booth, S. R., & Fairbank, D. W. (1983). Videotape feedback as behavior management technique. *Behavioral Disorders,* 55–59.

Borkowski, J. G., & Varnhagen, C. K. (1984). Transfer of lear ing strategies; Contrast of self-instructional and tradition training formats with EMR children. *American Journal Mental Deficiency*, **88**, 369–379.

Bos, C. S. (1982). Getting past decoding: Assisted and repeat reading as remedial methods for LD students. *Topics Learning and Learning Disabilities*, **1**(4), 51–57.

Broome, K., & Wambold, C. L. (1977). Teaching basic mat facts to EMR children through individual and small grou instruction, pupil teaming, contingency contracting, an learning center activities. *Education and Training of th Mentally Retarded*, **12**, 120–124.

Brown, L., Kiraly, J., & McKinnon, A. (1979). Resource room Some aspects for special educators to ponder. *Journal Learning Disabilities*, **12**, 480–482.

Bruininks, R., Warfield, G., & Stealey, D. (1982). The mentall retarded. In E. Meyen (Ed.), *Exceptional children an youth* (pp. 196–261). Denver, CO: Love.

Bryan, T., & Bryan, J. (1978). Social interactions of LD childre *Learning Disability Quarterly*, **1**, 33–38.

Bryan, T., & Bryan, J. (1981). Some personal and social experi ences of learning disabled children. In B. K. Keogh (Ed.) *Advances in special education* (Vol. 3, pp. 147–186). Green wich, CT: JAI Press.

Bryan, T., & Wheeler, R. (1976). Teachers' behaviors in classe for severely retarded, trainable, LD and normal children *Mental Retardation*, **14**(4), 41–45.

Bryant, N. D., Payne, H., & Gettinger, M. (1982). Applying the mastery learning model to sight word instruction fo disabled readers. *Journal of Experimental Education* **50**(3), 116–121.

Cartwright, P., Cartwright, C., & Ward, M. (Eds.). (1981) Emotional disturbance, mental retardation, and learning disabilities. In *Educating special learners* (pp. 157–253) Belmont, CA: Wadsworth.

Cawley, J. F. (1968). Word recognition performance of mentally handicapped and average children: Implications for classroom diagnosis. *Mental Retardation*, **6**(3), 28–31.

Cegelka, P., & Cegelka, W. (1970). A review of research: Reading and the educable mentally handicapped. *Exceptional Children*, **37**, 187–200.

Chaffin, J. (1974). Will the real "mainstreaming" program please stand up! (or . . . should Dunn have done it?). *Focus on Exceptional Children*, **6**(October), 1–18.

Cicirelli, V., Evans, J., & Schiller, J. (1970). The impact of Head Start: A reply to the report analysis. *Harvard Educational Review*, **40**, 105–129.

Clements, J. E., & Tracy, D. B. (1977). Effects of touch and verbal reinforcement on the classroom behavior of emotionally disturbed boys. *Exceptional Children*, **43**, 453–454.

Colbert, P., Newman, B., Ney, P., & Young, J. (1982). Learning disabilities as a symptom of depression in children. *Journal of Learning Disabilities*, **15**, 333–336.

Conners, F. (1983). Improving school instruction for LD children: The Teachers College Institute. *Exceptional Education Quarterly*, **4**(1), 23–44.

ɔtton, K., & Savard, W. (1982). *Topic summary report: Direct instruction.* San Francisco, CA: Northwest Regional Education Laboratory.

ɔx, L., & Wilson, A. (1981). A comparison of academic gains in reading among mildly LD students in three program structures. *Reading Improvement,* **18,** 132–137.

'Alonzo, B., D'Alonzo, R., & Mauser, A. (1979). Developing resource rooms for the handicapped. *Teaching Exceptional Children,* **11,** 91–96.

eshler, D., Alley, G., Warner, M., & Schumaker, J. (1981). Instructional practices for promoting skill acquisitions and generalization in severely LD adolescents. *Learning Disability Quarterly,* **4,** 415–421.

ulle, P., & Childs, P. (1985, April). *Categorical vs. cross-categorical programming.* Paper presented at the International Conference of the Council for Exceptional Children, Anaheim, CA.

unn, L. (1970). *Peabody Individual Achievement Test.* Circle Pines, MN: American Guidance Service.

unst, C. J., & Rheingrover, R. M. (1981). An analysis of the efficacy of infant intervention programs with organically handicapped children. *Evaluation and Program Planning,* **4,** 287–323.

nglemann, S., & Carnine, D. (1982). *Theory of instruction: Principles and applications.* New York: Irvington.

pstein, M., & Cullinan, D. (1982). Using social comparison procedures in educating behaviorally disordered pupils. *Behavioral Disorders,* **7,** 219–224.

pstein, M., Cullinan, D., & Sabatino, P. (1977). State definitions of behavior disorders. *Journal of Special Education,* **11,** 417–426.

vans, R. A. (1970). Use of associative clustering in the study of reading disability: Effects of presentation mode. *American Journal of Mental Deficiency,* **74,** 765–770.

isher, M. A., & Zeaman, D. (1973). An attention-retention theory of retardate discrimination learning. In N. R. Ellis (Ed.), *The international review of research in mental retardation* (Vol. 6, pp. 171–257). New York: Academic Press.

lorida State Department of Education, Office of Teacher Education, Certification and Inservice Staff Development. (1983). *Domains of the Florida Performance Measurement System.* Tallahassee: Author.

Forgnone, C., McBride, J., Cronis, T., & Smith, G. (in press). Mental retardation is not a mildly handicapping condition: Implications for a special curriculum. *Journal of Research and Development in Education.*

Foster, K., & Torgesen, J. (1983). The effects of directed study on the spelling performance of two subgroups of learning disabled students. *Learning Disabilities Quarterly,* **6,** 252–257.

Foster, S. (1984, April 25). Rise in LD pupils fuels concern in state districts. *Education Week,* pp. 1, 18.

Friend, M., & McNutt, G. (1984). Resource room programs: Where are we now? *Exceptional Children,* **51,** 150–155.

Gable, R., Hendrickson, J., Shores, R., & Young, C. (1983). Teacher-handicapped child classroom interactions. *Teacher Education and Special Education,* **6,** 88–95.

Gable, R., Hendrickson, J., Young, C., Shores, R., & Stowitschek, J. (1983). A comparison of teacher approval statements across categories of exceptionality. *Journal of Special Education Technology,* **6,** 15–22.

Gajar, A. (1979). Educable mentally retarded, learning disabled, emotionally disturbed: Similarities and differences. *Exceptional Children,* **45,** 470–472.

Gallagher, J. (1979). Rights of the next generation of children. *Exceptional Children,* **46,** 98–105.

Galvin, J., Quay, H., Annesley, F., & Werry, J. (1971). An experimental resource room for problem children. *Exceptional Children,* **38,** 131–137.

Ganchow, L., Wheeler, D., & Kretschmer, R. (1982). Contextual effects on reading of individual words by reading disabled adolescents with SLD. *Learning Disability Quarterly,* **5,** 145–151.

Garrison, M., & Hammil, D. (1971). Who are the retarded? *Exceptional Children,* **38,** 13–20.

Gettinger, M. (1982). Improving classroom behaviors and achievement of learning disabled children using direct instruction. *School Psychology Review,* **11,** 329–336.

Gickling, E. (1985). The forgotten learner. *Nevada Public Affairs Review,* **1,** 19–22.

Glidden, L. M., Bilsky, L. H., & Pawelski, C. (1977). Sentence mediation and stimulus blocking in free recall. *American Journal of Mental Deficiency,* **82,** 84–90.

Goldstein, H., & Goldstein, M. (1980). *Reasoning ability of mildly retarded learners. What research and experience say to the teacher of exceptional children* (NIE Contract #400–76–0119). Reston, VA: Council for Exceptional Children.

Graden, J., Thurlow, M., & Ysseldyke, J. (1982). Instructional ecology and academic responding time for students at three levels of teacher-perceived behavioral competence. (Research Rep. No. 73). Minneapolis: University of Minnesota, Institute for Research on Learning Disabilities.

Graden, J., Thurlow, M., Ysseldyke, J., & Algozzine, B. (1982). *Instructional ecology and academic responding time for students in different reading groups* (Research Rep. No. 79). Minneapolis: University of Minnesota, Institute for Research on Learning Disabilities.

Grassi, J. (1971). Effects of massed and spaced practice on learning in brain-damaged, behavior-disorders, and normal children. *Journal of Learning Disabilities,* **4**(5), 8–12.

Greener, J., Thurlow, M., Graden, J., & Ysseldyke, J. (1982). *The educational environment and students' responding times as a function of students' teacher-perceived academic competence* (Research Rep. No. 86). Minneapolis: University of Minnesota, Institute for Research on Learning Disabilities.

Grossman, H. (Ed.). (1973). *Manual on terminology and classification in mental retardation.* Washington, DC: American Association on Mental Deficiency.

Haight, S. C. (1984). Special education teacher consultant: Idealism versus realism. *Exceptional Children,* **50,** 507–515.

Haines, D., & Torgesen, J. (1978). The effect of incentives on research and short-term memory in children with reading problems. *Learning Disability Quarterly,* **2,** 28–55.

Hallahan, D., & Kauffman, J. (1977). Labels, categories, behaviors: ED, LD, and EMR reconsidered. *Journal of Special Education,* **11,** 139–149.

Hallahan, D., & Kauffman, J. (1982). Learning disabilities; emotional disturbance; mental retardation. In D. Hallahan & J. Kauffman (Eds.), *Exceptional Children* (2nd ed.) (pp. 37–180). Englewood Cliffs, NJ: Prentice-Hall.

Heron, T., & Skinner, M. (1981). Criteria for defining regular classroom as the least restrictive environment for learning disabled students. *Learning Disability Quarterly,* **4,** 115–121.

Hessler, G. L., & Kitchen, D. W. (1980). Language characteristics of a purposive sample of early elementary LD students. *Learning Disability Quarterly,* **3,** 36–41.

Hewett, F. M., Taylor, F. D., & Artuso, A. A. (1969). The Santa Monica Project: Evaluation of an engineered classroom design with emotionally disturbed children. *Exceptional Children,* **35**, 523–529.

Hobbs, N. (Ed.). (1975). *Issues in the classification of children.* San Francisco, CA: Jossey-Bass.

Hobbs, N. (1978). Classification options: A conversation with N. Hobbs on exceptional child education. *Exceptional Children,* **44**, 494–497.

Hocutt, A. M., Cox, J. L., & Pelosi, J. (1984). *A policy-oriented study of special education's service delivery system. Vol. I. An exploration of issues regarding the identification and placement of LD, MR, and ED students* (RTI Rep. No. RTI/2706–06/OIFR). Research Triangle Park, NC: Research Triangle Institute, Center for Educational Studies.

House, E. R., Glass, G. V., McLean, L. D., Walker, D. F. (1978). No simple answer. Critique of the Follow Through evaluation. *Harvard Educational Review,* **48**, 128–160.

Hundert, J. (1982). Some considerations of planning the integration of handicapped children into the mainstream. *Journal of Learning Disabilities,* **15**, 73–80.

Huntze, S., & Simpson, R. (1983). In J. Grosenick, S. Huntze, & C. Smith (Eds.), *National needs analysis/leadership training project: Noncategorical issues in programming for behaviorally disordered children and youth* (USDOE Grant #G0081–01817, pp. 30–55). Columbia: University of Missouri, Department of Special Education.

Isaacs, L., & Stennett, R. (1980). The DISTAR Reading Program in junior opportunity classes: Phase IV—Positive results after three full years of instruction. *Special Education in Canada,* **54**, 18–20.

Ito, R. (1980). Long-term effects of resource room programs on LD children's reading. *Journal of Learning Disabilities,* **13**(6), 322–326.

Jenkins, J., Larson, K., & Fleisher, L. (1983). Effects of error correction on world recognition and reading comprehension. *Learning Disability Quarterly,* **6**, 139–145.

Jenkins, J., & Mayhall, W. (1976). Development and evaluation of a resource teacher program. *Exceptional Children,* **43**, 21–29.

Kaufman, A. S. (1981). The WISC–R and learning disabilities: State of the art. *Journal of Learning Disabilities,* **14**, 520–526.

Kaufman, M., Agard, J., & Semmel, M. (1986). *Mainstreaming: Learners and their environments.* Cambridge, MA: Brookline Books.

Kaufman, M., Semmel, M., & Agard, J. (1973). *Project PRIME: Interim report 1971–1972—Purposes and procedures.* Washington, DC: U.S. Office of Education, Bureau of Education for the Handicapped.

Kehle, T., & Barclay, J. (1979). Social characteristics of mentally handicapped students. *Journal of Research and Development in Education,* **12**, 46–56.

Kershman, S. M (1985). Early childhood education. In W. H. Berdine & A. E. Blackhurst (Eds.), *An introduction to special education* (2nd ed.) (pp. 89–144). Boston, MA: Little, Brown.

Kirk, S. A. (1958). *Early education of the mentally retarded.* Urbana: University of Illinois Press.

Kirk, S. A. (1964). Research in education. In H. Stevens & R. Heber (Eds.), *Mental retardation: A review of research* (pp. 57–99). Chicago, IL: University of Chicago Press.

Knowlton, E. (1978). *A fading technique for teaching sight vocabulary.* Lexington: University of Kentucky, Department of Special Education.

Kosiewicz, M., Hallahan, D., Lloyd, J., & Graves, A. (198[illegible]). Effects of self-instruction and self-correction procedures [illegible] handwriting performance. *Learning Disability Quarterly,* [illegible] 71–78.

Kuhlman, C. (1981). *A procedure to facilitate generalization [illegible] academic performance* (Microfilm No. 81–06830). A[illegible] Arbor, MI: University Microfilms International.

Kuypers, D. S., Becker, W. C., & O'Leary, K. D. (1968). How [illegible] make a token system fail. *Exceptional Children,* **3[illegible]** 101–109.

LaGreca, A. M., Stone, W. L., & Bell, C. R. (1983). Facilitati[illegible] the vocational-interpersonal skills of mentally retarded ind[illegible]viduals. *American Journal of Mental Deficiency,* **8[illegible]** 270–278.

Lakin, K. C. (1982). Research-based knowledge and profession[illegible] practices in special education for emotionally disturb[illegible] students. In C. R. Smith & B. J. Wilcots (Eds.), *Iow[illegible] Monograph: Current issues in behavior disorders.*

Larrivee, B. (1982). Identifying effective teaching behaviors f[illegible] mainstreaming. *Teacher Education and Special Educatio[illegible]* **5**, 2–6.

Lazar, I., & Darlington, R. (1982). Lasting effects of early ed[illegible]cation: A report from the consortium for longitudinal studie[illegible] *Monographs of the Society for Research in Child Develo[illegible]ment,* **47** (Serial No. 195).

Lebsock, M. S., & Salzberg, C. L. (1981). The use of role play an[illegible] reinforcement procedures in the development of generalize[illegible] interpersonal behavior with emotionally disturbed-behavi[illegible] disordered adolescents in a special education classroo[illegible] *Behavioral Disorders,* **6**, 150–163.

Lerner, J. W. (1980). *Learning disabilities: Theories, diagnosi[illegible] and teaching strategies* (3rd ed.). Boston, MA: Hought[illegible] Mifflin.

Lerner, J. W. (1985). *Learning disabilities: Theories, diagnosis, and teaching strategies* (4th ed.). Boston, MA: Hought[illegible] Mifflin.

Lewis, R., & Kass, C. (1982). Labelling and recall in learnin[illegible] disabled students. *Journal of Learning Disabilities,* **15** 238–241.

Little, L. (1982). The learning disabled. In E. Meyen (Ed.) *Exceptional children and youth* (pp. 304–345). Denver, CO: Love.

Lloyd, J., Cullinan, D., Heins, E., & Epstein, M. (1980). Direc[illegible] instruction: Effects on oral and written language comprehension. *Learning Disability Quarterly,* **3**, 70–76.

Lloyd, J., Hallahan, D., Kosiewicz, M., & Kneedler, R. (1982). Reactive effects of self-assessment and self-recording o[illegible] attention to task and academic productivity. *Learning Disability Quarterly,* **5**, 216–227.

Lloyd, J., Saltzman, N., & Kauffman, J. (1981). Predictable generalization in academic learning as a result of preskills and strategy training. *Learning Disability Quarterly,* **4**, 203–216.

Lobb, H., & Childs, R. (1973). Verbal control and intradimensional transfer of discrimination learning in mentally retarded vs. intellectually average subjects. *American Journal of Mental Deficiency,* **78**, 182–192.

Lovitt, T. (1975). Applied behavior analysis and LD: Part II. Research. *Journal of Learning Disabilities,* **8**(8), 504–518.

Lovitt, T. (1978). The learning disabled. In N. Haring (Ed.), *Behavior of exceptional children* (2nd ed.) (pp. 155–192). Columbus, OH: Merrill.

Lovitt, T., & Hansen, C. (1976). The use of contingent skipping and drilling to improve oral reading and comprehension. *Journal of Learning Disabilities,* **9**, 20–26.

MacMillan, D., Meyers, C., & Yoshida, R. (1978). Regular class teachers' perceptions of transition program for EMR students and their impact on the students. *Psychology in the Schools,* **15,** 19–103.

Magee, P., & Newcomer, P. (1978). The relationship between oral language skills and academic achievement of LD children. *Learning Disability Quarterly,* **1,** 63–67.

Maggs, R. (1980). Direct Instruction: Why it works. *American Journal of Special Education Technology,* **12,** 7–12.

Maier, A. (1980). The effect of focusing on the cognitive processes of learning disabled children. *Journal of Learning Disabilities,* **13,** 143–147.

McBride, J., & Forgnone, C. (1985). Emphasis of instruction on provided LD, EH and EMR students in categorical and cross-categorical resource programs. *Journal of Research and Development in Education,* **18,** 50–55.

McDowell, R., Adamson, G., & Wood, F. (1982). *Teaching emotionally disturbed children.* Boston, MA: Little, Brown.

Medley, D. (1977). *Teacher competence and teacher effectiveness: A review of process-product research.* Washington, DC: American Association of Colleges for Teacher Education. (ERIC Document Reproduction Service No. ED 143 629)

Mercer, C. D. (1983). *Students with learning disabilities* (2nd ed.). Columbus, OH: Merrill.

Mercer, C. D. (1986). Learning disabilities. In N. G. Haring & L. McCormick (Eds.), *Exceptional children and youth* (4th ed.) (pp. 119–159). Columbus, OH: Merrill.

Mercer, C., Forgnone, C., & Wolking, W. (1976). Definitions of learning disabilities used in the United States. *Journal of Learning Disabilities,* **9,** 376–386.

Mercer, C., Hughes, C., & Mercer, A. (1985). Definitions of learning disabilities used by state education departments. *Learning Disability Quarterly,* **8,** 45–55.

Messick, S. (1984). Assessment in context: Appraising student performance in relation to instructional quality. *Educational Researcher,* **13** (3), 3–8.

Morgan, D., Young, K. R., & Goldstein, S. (1983). Teaching behaviorally disordered students to increase teacher attention and praise in mainstreamed classrooms. *Behavioral Disorders,* **8,** 265–273.

Morsink, C. (1981). Learning disabilities. In A. E. Blackhurst & W. Berdine (Eds.), *Introduction to special education* (pp. 354–390). Boston, MA: Little, Brown.

Morsink, C. (1984). *Teaching special needs students in regular classrooms.* Boston, MA: Little, Brown.

Morsink, C., Branscum, G., & Boone, R. (1984). *Specialized competencies for SLD teachers: A review of related literature.* Gainesville: University of Florida, Department of Special Education.

Morsink, C., Soar, R., & Thomas, R. (1986). Research on teaching: Opening the door to special classrooms. *Exceptional Children,* **53,** 32–40.

Myklebust, H., & Boshes, B. (1969). *Minimal brain damage in children* (Final report, U.S. Public Health Service Contract 108–65–142, U.S. Department of Health, Education, and Welfare). Evanston, IL: Northwestern University Publication.

Nagle, R., & Thwaite, B. (1979). Modeling effects on impulsivity with LD children. *Journal of Learning Disabilities,* **12,** 331–336.

Nelson, C. M. (1981). Behavior disorders. In A. E. Blackhurst & W. Berdine (Eds.), *An introduction to special education* (pp. 391–430). Boston, MA: Little, Brown.

Nelson, N. (1984). Beyond information processing: The language of teachers and textbooks. In G. Wallach & K. G. Butler (Eds.), *Language learning disabilities in school age children* (pp. 154–178). Baltimore, MD: Williams & Wilkins.

Nelson, R. B., & Cummings, J. A. (1981). Basic concept attainment of educable mentally handicapped children: Implications for teaching concepts. *Education and Training of the Mentally Retarded,* **16,** 303–306.

Neubauer, L. (1979). A fine-grain analysis for maximizing the effect of resource room instruction (Microfilm No. 79–01082). Ann Arbor, MI: University Microfilms International.

Noel, M. (1980). Referential communication abilities of LD children. *Learning Disability Quarterly,* **3,** 70–75.

Noel, M., Smith-Davis, J., & Burke, P. J. (in press). *Personnel to educate the handicapped: 1984 status report.* College Park: University of Maryland, Institute for the Study of Exceptional Children and Youth.

Noffsinger, T. (1971). The effects of reward and level of aspiration on students with deviant behaviors. *Exceptional Children,* **37,** 355–364.

Norman, C. A., & Zigmond, N. (1980). Characteristics of children labeled and served as learning disabled in school systems affiliated with Child Service Demonstration Centers. *Journal of Learning Disabilities,* **13,** 542–547.

O'Connor, P., Stuck, G., & Wyne, M. (1979). Effects of a short term intervention resource room program on task orientation and achievement. *Journal of Special Education,* **13,** 322–326.

Odom, S. L., & Fewell, R. R. (1983). Program evaluation in early childhood special education: A meta-evaluation. *Educational Evaluation and Policy Analysis,* **5,** 445–460.

Ogletree, E. J., & Uylaki, W. (1976). A motoric approach to teaching multiplication to the mentally retarded child. *Education and Training of the Mentally Retarded,* **11,** 129–134.

Pany, D., Jenkins, J., & Schreck, J. (1982). Vocabulary instruction: Effects on work knowledge and reading comprehension. *Learning Disability Quarterly,* **5,** 202–215.

Payne, J., & Thomas, C. (1978). The mentally retarded. In N. Haring (Ed.), *Behavior of exceptional children* (2nd ed.) (pp. 97–122). Columbus, OH: Merrill.

Polsgrove, L., Reith, H. J., Friend, M., & Cohen, R. (1980). An analysis of the effects of various instructional procedures on the oral reading performance of high school special education students. *Monograph in Behavior Disorders,* pp. 125–133.

Preston, S. (1984). Children and the elderly in the U.S. *Scientific American,* **251,** 44–49.

Procedures for evaluation of specific learning disabilities. (1977). *Federal Register,* **42**(250), 65082–65085.

Raber, S. M., & Weisz, J. R. (1981). Teacher feedback to mentally retarded and nonretarded children. *American Journal of Mental Deficiency,* **86**(2), 148–156.

Radford-Hill, S. (1984, March). *Perspectives on advocacy and school psychology* (Preliminary report of the NASP/NCAS Task Force on School Advocacy and School Psychology). Kent, OH: National Association of School Psychologists.

Reeve, R., & Kauffman, J. (1978). The behavior disordered. In N. Haring (Ed.), *Behavior of exceptional children* (2nd ed.) (pp. 123–154). Columbus, OH: Merrill.

Reid, D. K., & Hresko, W. (1981). *A cognitive approach to LD.* New York: McGraw-Hill.

Reisburg, L. (1982). Individual differences in LD students' use of contextual cuing. *Learning Disability Quarterly,* **5,** 91–99.

Reynolds, M. C., & Birch, J. W. (1977). Learning disabilities and behavior disorders: Mental retardation. In M. C. Reynolds & J. W. Birch (Eds.), *Teaching exceptional children in all America's schools* (pp. 261–342). Reston, VA: Council for Exceptional Children.

Rice, M. (1983). Contemporary accounts of the cognitive/language relationship: Implications for speech-language clinicians. *Journal of Speech and Hearing Disorders,* **48**, 347–359.

Richey, D., Miller, M. & Lessman, J. (1981). Resource and regular classroom behavior of learning disabled students. *Journal of Learning Disabilities,* **14**, 163–166.

Rose, T., & Gottlieb, J. (1981). Transfer of training: An overlooked component of mainstreaming programs. *Exceptional Children,* **48**, 175–176.

Rose, T., McEntire, E., & Dowdy, C. (1982). Effects of two error-correction procedures on oral reading. *Learning Disability Quarterly,* **5**, 100–104.

Rosenbaum, M., & Drabman, R. (1979). Self-control training in the classroom: A review and critique. *Journal of Applied Behavior Analysis,* **12**, 467–485.

Santostefano, S. (1964). Cognitive controls and exceptional states in children. *Journal of Clinical Psychology,* **20**, 213–218.

Schneider, B. H., & Byrne, B. M. (1984). Predictors of successful transition from self-contained special education to regular class settings. *Psychology in the Schools,* **21**, 375–380.

Schumaker, J., Deshler, D., Alley, G., & Warner, M. (1983). Toward the development of an intervention model for LD adolescents: The University of Kansas Institute. *Exceptional Education Quarterly,* **4**(1), 45–74.

Schweinhart, L. J., & Weikart, D. P. (1981). Effects of the Perry Preschool Program on youths through age 15. *Journal of the Division for Early Childhood,* **4**, 29–39.

Scott, R. J. (1984). *Teaching and learning in remote schools: A dilemma beyond rural education.* Rosslyn, VA: National Information Center for Handicapped Children and Youth.

Sherry, S. (1979). *Behavioral characteristics of educable mentally retarded, emotionally handicapped, and learning disabled students.* Unpublished doctoral dissertation, University of Florida, Gainesville.

Shores, R., Cegelka, P., & Nelson, C. M. (1973). Competency based special education teacher training. *Exceptional Children,* **40**, 192–197.

Silliman, E. (1984). Interactional competencies in the instructional context: The role of teaching discourse in learning. In G. Wallach & K. G. Butler (Eds.), *Language learning disabilities in school age children* (pp. 288–318). Baltimore, MD: Williams & Wilkins.

Simeonsson, R. J., Cooper, D. H., & Scheiner, A. P. (1982). A review and analysis of the effectiveness of early intervention programs. *Pediatrics,* **69**, 635–641.

Sindelar, P., & Deno, S. (1978). The effectiveness of resource programming. *Journal of Special Education,* **12**, 17–28.

Skeels, H. (1966). Adult status of children with contrasting early life experiences: A follow-up study. *Monographs of the Society for Research in Child Development,* **31** (Serial No. 105).

Skeels, H., & Dye, H. (1939). A study of the effects of differential stimulation on mentally retarded children. *Proceedings and Addresses of the American Association on Mental Deficiency,* **44**, 114–139.

Slade, D. (1984). Helping LD students make transitions: Six suggestions. *Academic Therapy,* **19**, 543–547.

Smith, M. S., & Bissell, J. S. (1970). Report analysis: The impact of Head Start. *Harvard Educational Review,* **40**, 51–104.

Smith, R., & Neisworth, J. (1975). *The exceptional child: A functional approach.* New York: McGraw-Hill.

Smith-Davis, J., Burke, P. J., & Noel, M. (1984). *Personnel to educate the handicapped in America: Supply and demand from a programmatic viewpoint.* College Park: University of Maryland, Institute for the Study of Exceptional Children and Youth.

Smith-Davis, J., Johnson, K., Fairchild, R., Johnson, S., & Prothro, H. (1984). *The secondary practices portfolio.* Reno, NE: Dissemin/Action, Inc.

Sparks, R., & Richardson, S. (1981). Multicategorical/cross-categorical classrooms for LD students. *Journal of Learning Disabilities,* **14**, 60–61.

Spitz, H. H. (1973). Consolidation facts into the schematized learning and memory system of educable retardates. In N. R. Ellis (Ed.), *International review of research in mental retardation* (Vol. 6, pp. 149–170). New York: Academic Press.

Stennett, R. (1969). Emotional handicap in the elementary years: Phase or disease? *American Journal of Orthopsychiatry,* **36**, 444–449.

Stephens, E. (1980). Direct instruction research with moderately and severely retarded in Australia: A review. *American Journal of Special Education Technology,* **12**, 41–46.

Stevens, R., & Rosenshine, B. (1981). Advances in research on teaching. *Exceptional Education Quarterly,* **2**(1), 1–9.

Stone, F., & Rowley, V. (1964). Educational disability in emotionally disturbed children. *Exceptional Children,* **30**, 423–426.

Strain, P. S. (1984). Efficacy research with young handicapped children: A critique of the status quo. *Journal of the Division for Early Childhood,* **9**, 4–10.

Swanson, L. (1981). Modification of comprehension deficits in LD children. *Learning Disability Quarterly,* **4**, 189–201.

Swanson, L. (1982). Conceptual process as a function of age and enforced attention in learning-disabled children: Evidence for deficient rule learning. *Contemporary Educational Psychology,* **7**, 152–160.

Tawney, J. W. (1977). *Practice what you preach: A project to develop a contingency managed "methods" course, and to measure the effects of this course by in-field evaluation* (Final Report). Lexington: University of Kentucky, Department of Special Education.

Thorpe, H., Chaing, B., & Drach, C. (1981). Individual and group feedback systems for improving oral reading accuracy in LD and regular children. *Journal of Learning Disabilities,* **14**, 332–334.

Thurlow, M., Ysseldyke, J., Graden, J., Greener, J., & Mecklenberg, C. (1982). *Academic responding time for LD students receiving different levels of special education services* (Research Rep. No. 78). Minneapolis: University of Minnesota, Institute for Research on Learning Disabilities.

Tollefson, N., Tracy, D., Johnsen, E., Buenning, M., Farmer, A., & Barke, C. (1982). Attribution patterns of LD adolescents. *Learning Disability Quarterly,* **5**, 14–20.

Torgesen, J., & Dice, C. (1980). Characteristics of research on learning disabilities. *Journal of Learning Disabilities,* **13**, 531–535.

Turnbull, A. P., & Blacher-Dixon, J. (1981). Preschool mainstreaming: An empirical and conceptual review. In P. S. Strain & M. M. Kerr (Eds.), *Mainstreaming of children in schools: Research and programmatic issues* (pp. 71–100). New York: Academic Press.

Valcante, G. (1984). *Specialized competencies for teachers of mildly emotionally handicapped students: A review of literature*. Unpublished manuscript, University of Florida, Department of Special Education, Gainesville.

Walberg, H. J. (1984). Improving the productivity of America's schools. *Educational Leadership*, **41**, 19–30.

Wang, M. C., & Baker, E. T. (1985–1986). Mainstreaming programs: Design features and effects. *Journal of Special Education*, **19**, 503–525.

Wang, M. C., & Birch, J. W. (1984a). Comparison of a full-time mainstreaming program and a resource room approach. *Exceptional Children*, **51**, 33–40.

Wang, M. C., & Birch, J. W. (1984b). Effective special education in regular classes. *Exceptional Children*, **50**, 391–398.

Wang, M. C., Gennari, P., & Waxman, H. C. (1985). The Adaptive Learning Environments Model: Design, implementation, and effects. In M. C. Wang & H. J. Walberg (Eds.), *Adapting instruction to individual differences* (pp. 191–235). Berkeley, CA: McCutchan.

Wang, M. C., & Vaughan, E. (1985). *Handbook for the implementation of adaptive instruction programs. Module 1: Theory and practice*. Pittsburgh, PA: University of Pittsburgh, Learning Research and Development Center.

Waxman, H. C., Wang, M. C., Anderson, K. A., & Walberg, H. J. (1985). Adaptive education and student outcomes: A quantitative synthesis. *Journal of Educational Research*, **78**, 228–236.

Wechsler, D. (1974). *Wechsler Intelligence Scale for Children—Revised*. New York: Psychological Corporation.

Weinstein, L. (1969). Project Re-Ed schools for emotionally disturbed children: Effectiveness as viewed by referring agencies, parents, and teachers. *Exceptional Children*, **35**, 703–711.

Weiss, R. S. (1981). INREAL intervention for language handicapped and bilingual children. *Journal of the Division for Early Childhood*, **4**, 40–51.

Whelan, R. (1982). The emotionally disturbed. In E. Meyen (Ed.), *Exceptional children and youth* (pp. 346–381). Denver, CO: Love.

White, K. R., Mastropieri, M., & Casto, G. (1984). An analysis of special education early childhood projects approved by the Joint Dissemination Review Panel. *Journal of the Division for Early Childhood*, **9**, 11–26.

Wixson, S. (1980). Two resource room models for serving learning and behavior disordered pupils. *Behavioral Disorders*, **5**, 116–125.

Wolery, M. (1983). Proportional Change Index: An alternative for comparing child change data. *Exceptional Children*, **50**, 167–170.

Wong, B., & Jones, W. (1982). Increasing metacomprehension in normally achieving students through self-questioning training. *Learning Disability Quarterly*, **5**, 228–240.

Yoshida, R., MacMillan, P., & Meyers, C. (1976). The decertification of minority group EMR students in California: Student achievement and adjustment. In R. E. Jones (Ed.), *Mainstreaming and the minority child* (pp. 215–232). Reston, VA: Council for Exceptional Children.

Zax, M., Cowen, E., Rappaport, J., Beach, D., & Laird, J. (1968). Follow-up of children identified early as emotionally disturbed. *Journal of Consulting and Clinical Psychology*, **32**, 369–374.

Zigler, E., Balla, D., & Hodapp, R. (1984). On the definition and classification of mental retardation. *American Journal of mental Deficiency*, **89**, 215–230.

Appendix: Jurisdictions With Completely or Primarily Noncategorical or Multicategorical Teacher Certification, 1985

Alaska. Certification in regular education, with endorsements in special education and specialization in: learning disabilities, mental retardation, physical handicaps, resource room, severe handicaps, visual handicaps, emotional disturbance, hearing handicaps. The state-noted specialization does not restrict the areas in which the certificate holder can work; it simply specifies the area of specialization in which the holder is trained. Although the certificate looks like categorical certification, it is in fact a comprehensive certificate.

American Samoa. All teachers are certified in regular education, and in-service training prepares them for special education. American Samoa has severe problems in recruiting personnel, and this certification pattern helps to offset these difficulties.

Arkansas. Generic noncategorical certification has become even more generic with a special education certificate that now covers mild to severe handicaps. Categorical certification covers speech, hearing, vision, severe handicaps, and severe emotional disturbance.

Connecticut. A single certificate covers multiple categories, and categorical certificates cover specialty areas.

District of Columbia. Certification is primarily noncategorical, with categorical certification in low-prevalence areas.

Guam. Certification is noncategorical (mild handicaps, moderate handicaps, severe handicaps).

Hawaii. Personnel are certified in special education, with specification of the area of emphasis: generic (mental retardation and learning disabilities), hearing impairment, visual impairment, and other low-prevalence handicaps. The overall special education certification allows personnel with a specific area of emphasis to teach in other specialty areas of special education, but this is not done unless manpower supplies in given areas are inadequate.

Idaho. Certification is in general special education, with categorical endorsements. The endorsements do not restrict the areas in which a person can work but specify the area of specialization in which a person is trained.

Kentucky. Multicategorical certification (educable mental retardation, learning disabilities, behavior disorders, and physical handicaps) is used for personnel in mild to moderate handicaps. Categorical certificates are issued in severe handicaps and other low-prevalence handicaps.

Louisiana. Certification has been categorical, but seven new certification areas became effective in 1985: mildly and moderately handicapped, severely handicapped, hearing impaired, visually impaired, speech/language impaired, noncategorical preschool, gifted and talented.

Maryland. Noncategorical generic certification is based on age level (infant–primary, elementary–middle school, secondary–adult). Categorical endorsements are issued in vision, speech, and severe handicaps.

Massachusetts. New certification policies that became effective in 1982 cover: teachers of young children, aged 3–7; severe special needs, K to 12; moderate special needs, K to 12; special needs/audition; vision; speech, language, and hearing; generic consulting teacher—all levels.

Montana. Certificates are awarded in general elementary or secondary education, with a noncategorical special education endorsement, and areas of emphasis in severely handicapped, developmental disabilities, and learning disabilities. The areas of emphasis indicate the training of the certificate holder.

Nebraska. Noncategorical certification is by age level (elementary, junior high school, and high school), with specific endorsements for low-prevalence handicaps and for categories in mild handicaps at the master's level. The educable/trainable mentally retarded endorsement has been replaced with a mild/moderate endorsement covering several handicaps.

New Jersey. There is generic multicategorical certification, with categorical certificates in auditory impairment and in visual impairment.

New Mexico. Certification is in regular education, with categorical endorsements in special education and one generalist endorsement. The state operates special education programs according to four levels of severity of handicap, with the A level comprising more mildly handicapped students and the D level comprising the most severe educational handicaps.

New York. Noncategorical certification covers mental retardation, emotional disturbance, behavioral impairment, and learning disability. Categorical certification covers deafness, blindness, and speech impairment.

North Carolina. Certification is cross-categorical (mildly handicapped), with categorical specialty certification in low-prevalence areas, specific learning disabilities, speech and language, gifted and talented. Both categorical and noncategorical certification are available for resource teachers and consulting teachers. There are plans to change the current early childhood special education certification to a categorical basis and to add certification for adaptive physical education.

Northern Mariana Islands. Certification is generic; a single certificate covers all areas of special education. The Northern Marianas also experience serious recruitment problems.

Pennsylvania. Noncategorical certification covers mental retardation, emotional disturbance, physical handicaps, behavioral impairments, and learning disabilities. Categorical certification covers deafness, blindness, and speech impairment.

Puerto Rico. Certification is generic; a single certificate covers all areas of special education. Puerto Rico is, however, in the process of changing over to specialized endorsements in four categories: mild handicaps, severe handicaps, communication disorders, and visual handicaps.

Rhode Island. Certification is noncategorical for mild/moderate, and moderate/severe educational handicaps. Categorical certification covers physical handicaps, visual impairment, hearing impairment, deaf–blind, and speech/language impairment.

South Dakota. Certification is noncategorical, except for categorical speech/hearing.

Tennessee. The number of endorsements for teachers has been reduced. In special education, five earlier endorsements have been collapsed into one endorsement in special education. Now there are four areas of endorsement for education of handicapped students: deafness; speech; vision; and special education (which is noncategorical special education, subsuming largely learning disabilities, mental retardation, and behavior disorders).

Texas. Texas has done away with the endorsement in learning disabilities/emotional disturbance/mental retardation. Certification now covers: elementary generic, K to 12; secondary generic, K to 12 (e.g., for persons who specialize in a subject area and also are certifiable in special education); a separate speech certificate; and a separate certificate in auditory handicaps. In addition to these four certificate areas, there are three other endorsement areas: visually handicapped; severely disturbed/autistic; and severely handicapped. These certification areas are at the undergraduate level; new certification policies for graduate level personnel await state board approval.

Utah. Generic multicategorical certification covers resource room teachers (mildly and moderately handicapped). Categorical certification covers speech impairment and personnel to teach deaf-blind students. There is separate certification for severe handicaps.

Vermont. Certification is noncategorical (mildly handicapped, moderately handicapped, and severely handicapped).

Virgin Islands. Certification is generic; a single certificate covers all categories, but there are special requirements for speech/language personnel, occupational therapists, and physical therapists.

Washington. Certification is in regular education, with noncategorical endorsements in mild/moderate handicaps, severe handicaps, and preschool.

Wyoming. Certification is noncategorical, with categorical specialist endorsements in some areas.

Noncategorical Special Education Personnel Preparation[1]

A. EDWARD BLACKHURST, DEBORAH A. BOTT and DONALD P. CROSS

University of Kentucky

Abstract—Noncategorical special education personnel preparation is the process of preparing personnel to work with students who have mild learning, behavioral, or physical disabilities. It is viewed as an alternative to personnel preparation practices delivered according to traditional categories of disability. This chapter describes the rationale for noncategorical personnel preparation practices. Trends in noncategorical teacher certification standards and resulting teacher preparation programs are explored. Implications of noncategorical personnel preparation for the education of regular teachers and related personnel are examined. Recommendations for public policy, legislation, service delivery, and research are also presented.

Historically, special education teachers have been educated and certified according to the diagnostic category of the students to be taught (e.g., learning disabled, educable mentally retarded). In recent years, however, the trend has been to revise teacher education and certification programs along noncategorical lines. Typically, noncategorical teacher preparation programs combine the areas of mild behavioral disorders, educable mental retardation, and mild learning disability, although other categories are included in some states. In addition to the term *noncategorical,* such programs are frequently referred to as *generic, cross-categorical,* or *multicategorical.*

Some people differentiate among the terms. For example, some consider noncategorical certification to refer to certification to teach students who have a specific level of handicap (e.g., mild handicap, severe handicap), while cross-categorical or multicategorical certification refers to certification to teach in more than one disability area. Occasionally, the noncategorical approach has been applied to severely and multiply handicapped learners. For example, Hart (1972) described a teacher preparation practicum in which severely handicapped students were grouped according to the skill area in which they were experiencing learning problems (i.e., self-care, socialization, motor development) rather than type of disability.

For the purpose of this chapter, the term noncategorical programs will be used to refer to programs that prepare personnel to work primarily with students who have mild learning, behavioral, or physical disabilities. The term will be used synonymously with generic, cross-categorical, or multicategorical programs.

[1] Portions of this paper are reprinted from an earlier review by the senior author (Blackhurst, 1981).

The purposes of this chapter are to describe the rationale for noncategorical personnel preparation practices in special education, to review the trends in noncategorical teacher certification practices, to examine noncategorical personnel preparation practices, and to explore the implications that the delivery of noncategorical special education services have for the preparation of regular education personnel. The chapter closes with a list of implications that noncategorical personnel preparation practices have for public policy, legislation, service delivery, and needed research.

Although our original intent was to survey the research related to the above topics, it became apparent that there is a paucity of research in these areas. Most decisions and practices related to noncategorical personnel preparation appear to have been based primarily upon theory and expert opinion rather than upon data from research studies. This chapter reviews the research findings that have been reported; however, it is not restricted to the research literature. A number of the seminal positions that have influenced noncategorical personnel preparation are also reviewed in order to provide a context for existing practices.

Rationale for Noncategorical Approaches

Noncategorical approaches to special education teacher preparation was the initial topic discussed at the first annual conference of the Teacher Education Division of the Council for Exceptional Children (CEC) in 1978. In keynoting that conference, Reynolds (1979) criticized categorical approaches to the practices of labeling and categorizing exceptional children and the effect that such practices have had on teacher education. He stated:

> Unfortunately, the ways we have been classifying and grouping children in special education and tracking teachers for training in special education . . . have not been fully rational. Despite all our concerns with providing the best education possible for children and training enough teachers to serve them, we have never thought through the question of what is a rational scheme for classifying and grouping children, nor the other side of the coin, what is the best way to organize and conduct teacher-education programs to support such a scheme. . . . Let's face it: These categories are neither natural nor rational. (p. 5)

Reynolds went on to propose a solution to the problem. He suggested a continuation of specialized (categorical) training programs for teachers of students with visual impairments, hearing disorders, communication disorders, and severe and profound handicaps, but he argued for noncategorical approaches for students diagnosed as educable mentally retarded, emotionally disturbed, orthopedically handicapped, or learning disabled.

It should be noted that not all people are in favor of noncategorical approaches to educating mildly handicapped students and the concomitant noncategorical teacher education. For example, Lieberman (quoted in an interview with James, c. 1984) strongly opposed noncategorical approaches on a number of grounds. He claimed that teachers need to have an in-depth understanding of a child's problems and their etiology to be effective teachers. He also claimed that children from different diagnostic categories will not mix appropriately when placed in the same resource room or special class. In addition, he stated that noncategorical approaches encourage the practice of inappropriate placement of children who are having difficulties in school but are not diagnosed as having a disability. Finally, he proposed that the movement to "delabel" children will not be effective because people will continue to use categorical labels to describe the children.

Some parents of mildly handicapped students, especially parents of learning disabled students, are opposed to the concept of noncategorical services. Parents make up a large portion of the membership of the Association for Children With Learning Disabilities (ACLD). A 1983 position statement for ACLD dealt with the topic of cross-categorical resource rooms and specifically mentioned teacher preparation (ACLD, 1983). The authors of the ACLD statement felt that noncategorical training programs were not adequate preparation for teaching learning disabled students, especially those students with severe learning disabilities. Many parents were concerned that noncategorical programs evolved as a way for states to reduce the funding and services available to mildly handicapped students (Vallecorsa, 1983).

Those in favor of the use of diagnostic labels also argue that administrators need to be able to categorize children in order to qualify for state financial support. Labels can also help focus public attention and legislation on a particular problem. One could argue further that, if one set of labels were eliminated, it would soon be replaced by another and that labels are useful in discussing children with similar characteristics (Blackhurst, 1985).

It is not known how widely these divergent opinions are held; however, there is some evidence that professionals tend to support Reynolds' position rather than the one advocated by Lieberman. Landmark research related to the futures of special education was conducted in 1973 by CEC for a project on professional standards (Reynolds, 1973). A Delphi (Weaver, 1971) study of 1,041 professionals indicated support for the approach advocated by Reynolds. On a 7-point scale of "desirability" of the development of noncategorical approaches to teacher education for children with mild intellectual and emotional problems, respondents generated a mean rating of 4.46 and a median of 4.95, with a 2.17 standard deviation.

Of course, the above Delphi survey data were collected a number of years ago. It is not known how professionals would react if asked the same questions today. As discussed later in this chapter, however, the trends appear to be moving in favor of the position advocated by Reynolds.

Proponents of noncategorical teacher education generally argue against labeling children and delivering educational services according to diagnostic category. In the early 1970s, a project on classification of exceptional children was conducted by Hobbs (1975). His conclusions included the following points: (a) labels are applied imprecisely; (b) labeled children are stigmatized; (c) labels yield too little information for planning; (d) the classification of children with multiple problems in terms of a dominant set of attributes leads to the neglect of other conditions; (e) classification tends to be deviance oriented; (f) classification systems are insensitive to the rapid changes that take place in children; and (g) classification of a child can result in the disregard of important etiological factors. Additional information concerning the effects of labeling was summarized by Ysseldyke and Algozzine (1982).

Smith and Neisworth (1975, pp. 8–9) further elaborated on the arguments against categorization:

1. Categories are educationally irrelevant. Simply knowing the diagnostic category into which a student has been placed provides little helpful information for teachers. For example, teachers would probably approach the task of teaching reading to students labeled as learning disabled in the same way they would to those labeled as educable mentally retarded or emotionally disturbed.
2. Categorical groupings overlap. Because children may exhibit a wide range of behaviors affecting their educational performance, they do not fit neatly into single categories. Indeed, it is not uncommon to hear of different diagnosticians applying different diagnostic labels to the same children.
3. Categories label children as defective. Labeling practices imply that the cause of an educational or developmental problem rests solely with the child. The result of such labeling is that stereotypes are developed and that negative expectations emerge in people who work with labeled children.
4. Special education instructional materials are not category specific. With only a few exceptions, such as captioned films for deaf students or braille readers for blind students, instructional materials can be used with a variety of students, regardless of their categorical labels.
5. Preparation of teachers along traditional categorical lines results in redundancy of course work and barriers within the profession. Overlaps in course content are particularly evident in categorical courses dealing with methods of teaching. Although communication may be facilitated within groups of professionals who profess interest in a particular

area of special education, categorical specialization serves as a barrier to communication between groups.

6. Patterns of funding for special education have perpetuated the categorical approach. For all of its positive features, the 1975 Education for All Handicapped Children Act (PL 94-142), and its 1983 amendments (PL 89-199), reinforce categorical emphases through its requirements to identify and classify students in order to qualify for reimbursement. State funding for special education programs at the local level and funding for university teacher preparation programs also perpetuate categorical practices.

There is some evidence that teaching competencies for the different categories of mildly handicapped students are similar. Blackhurst, McLoughlin, and Price (1977) identified the competencies they believed to be important for noncategorical special education teachers. These were based upon an analysis of the similarities among four categorical teacher certification programs at the University of Kentucky: educable mentally retarded, emotionally disturbed, learning disabilities, and orthopedically handicapped.

Prior to establishing a noncategorical undergraduate preparation program at the University of Charleston, comparisons were made among the program objectives for teachers of behaviorally disordered, mentally retarded, and learning disabled students, as defined by the West Virginia Department of Education (Newhouse, 1981). The analysis revealed a great deal of repetition, especially in knowledge of the curricular process, assessment and diagnosis, legal responsibilities, and interdisciplinary teams.

More recently, Carri (1985) surveyed 180 public school resource teachers. From this pool, he randomly selected twenty teachers of children with learning disabilities, twenty teachers of children with behavioral disorders, and twenty teachers of mentally retarded children. A questionnaire was administered to evaluate the skills and competencies these teachers reported as necessary for teaching their respective students. No differences were found between the competencies reported by teachers of mentally retarded children and those reported by teachers of learning disabled children. Teachers of children with behavioral disorders did report some differences, however. Differences were reported in the areas of assessing and evaluating pupil behavior, curriculum design and use, professional information, administrative duties, and communicating and interacting with teachers and peers. The Carri report contains insufficient information to be able to interpret the exact nature of the differences in each of these areas. In general, however, it appears that the teachers were more similar than different in their interpretation of the importance of various competencies.

To this point, the discussion has relied primarily on the opinions of professionals. However, as Idol-Maestas, Lloyd, and Lilly (1981) pointed out, "no better demonstration of the wisdom of noncategorical service delivery can be made than to bring about dramatic gains in children carrying different labels, using equivalent instructional techniques" (p. 214). These authorities presented data on the academic performance of children with a variety of diagnostic labels who improved as a result of receiving noncategorical direct instructional services from resource/consulting teachers.

Noncategorical services for special education students may be delivered in regular classrooms as well as in pull-out programs and self-contained special education classrooms. Wang and Birch (1984) reported on the effectiveness of a full-time mainstreaming program, the Adaptive Learning Environments Model (ALEM), in which children labeled as learning disabled, gifted, socially and emotionally disturbed, and visually impaired received all educational services within the regular classroom. Data indicated that the ALEM was an effective approach to delivering special services based on individual need rather than category of handicap. Wang (1981) reported that special educators working within an ALEM classroom or school are best organized in a noncategorical manner.

It has also been argued by Stephens, Blackhurst, and Magliocca (1982) that, as more teachers with noncategorical certification become available, educational services for exceptional children in the schools should improve. Such teachers should be better prepared to teach children who exhibit a variety of educational characteristics, with a corresponding salutary effect on child performance.

Noncategorical teaching certification can result in more efficient administration of special education programs. School officials should have greater flexibility in the use of their special education staff members, and noncategorical teachers should be better prepared for a changing job market (Stephens & Joseph, 1982). For example, although funding may still come from state and federal sources for categorical programs, special education students should be able to be mixed and grouped in different ways because the organization and operation of the special education programs would not be dependent upon the availability of teachers who are also certified in specific categorical areas. Thus, the resource room for educable mentally retarded students and the one for learning disabled students need not exist as such; students placed in a resource room could be grouped on the basis of educationally relevant characteristics (e.g., academic skill strengths or deficits) instead of on the basis of diagnostic labels.

The final argument in favor of noncategorical approaches relates to the potential for the reduction of stereotyping of special education students who have been labeled. Categorical teacher preparation programs have a tendency to perpetuate the use of diagnostic labels and the concomitant reinforcement of negative stereotypes. As Gillung and Rucker (1977) discovered, regular educators and some special educators had lowered expectations for children who were labeled than for children with identical behaviors who were not labeled. Such lowered expectations could result in less than optimal instructional programs, with the result of lowered achievement on the part of the labeled students.

The elimination of categorical certification areas such as educable mentally retarded, emotionally disturbed, and learning disabled, coupled with the development of noncategorical personnel preparation programs and the revision of service delivery systems, should help to reduce the negative stereotypes that have evolved over the years. Of course, as noted earlier, it could be argued that, if one set of labels were replaced by another, the new labels would gradually assume the stereotypes associated with the old. This may well happen, however, the proposed change in orientation can also be viewed as a catalyst for developing revised expectations that focus upon the positive aspects of exceptional students and the special education services delivered to them.

For reasons such as those described in this section, noncategorical approaches to special education teacher preparation appear to be more logical than categorical approaches. However, it should be emphasized that the perceived failure of categorical approaches does not validate noncategorical ones. Although there is considerable logical appeal for noncategorical approaches, there is a need for additional empirical evidence to comfortably support one type of approach over another.

It should also be reemphasized that noncategorical approaches seem to be most appropriate for those students who have mild disabilities. This caveat is supported by the research of Smith-Davis, Burke, and Noel (1984). In their 1982 national survey, they interviewed a number of concerned professionals who questioned the wisdom of attempting to include preparation for teaching children with severe and low-prevalence handicaps in generic certification programs. It was the opinion of their respondents that to do so represented unsound teacher education practice.

Trends in Noncategorical Certification Practices

As noted in the previous section, in the early 1970s, CEC surveyed over 1,000 professional educators as part of a project to develop professional standards for special education personnel (Reynolds, 1973). Using the Delphi research technique, respondents were asked to estimate the likelihood and desirability of various occurrences in special education in the future. Results of this study predicted that, by 1983, the trend would be to reduce special education teacher certification in the areas of educable mental retardation, learning disability, and emotional disturbance in favor of more general certification in special education. In addition, with the exception of regular education teachers, respondents reported that the collapsing of these categories was desirable. Respondents also indicated that separate categories in the fields of speech, hearing, and vision would probably be maintained. Subsequently, CEC published *Guidelines for Personnel in the Education of Exceptional Children* (1976). The results of the Delphi survey were reflected in this document in the form of Guideline 3.3, which stated: "Certification in special education should provide for those personnel who develop generic competencies to perform effectively with variously handicapped persons as well as those who develop highly specialized competencies to work with some exceptional people" (p. 45).

History and Current Status

The first reported study of the status of noncategorical special education certification was conducted by Gilmore and Argyros (1977), who examined certification guidelines and found that the majority of states granted certification according to disability category. They concluded that eleven states offered some form of "generic certificate" in 1977. Two years later, Barresi and Bunte (1979) replicated this study and reported that fourteen states had some form of generic certification; however, there was some question about the criterion for determining whether a state offered categorical certification (Blackhurst, 1981).

In 1979, Belch surveyed the certification officers of the fifty states plus the District of Columbia. He was interested in finding out how many of those jurisdictions offered noncategorical teacher certification, how many were moving in that direction, and how many states had categorical certificates and no plans to change. Belch found that twelve jurisdictions (24%) offered noncategorical certificates, with another seven moving in that direction.

Smith-Davis et al. (1984) conducted a survey in 1982 and found that half of the certification jurisdictions (the fifty states, District of Columbia, Guam, and Puerto Rico) had noncategorical, cross-categorical, or multicategorical certification standards. They found that most states with noncategorical certification requirements also had categorical certificates for teachers of children with sensory handicaps, severe handicaps, and other low-prevalence handicaps. Separate certificates were also provided for speech, occupational, and physical therapists.

Chapey, Pyszkowski, and Trimarco (1985) replicated Belch's study to determine whether changes in noncategorical certification practices had occurred by the mid-1980s. Two errors were detected in the Chapey et al. findings, however. Kentucky was listed as a categorical state, when, in fact, it was one of the earliest states to adopt noncategorical certification standards. Similarly, Pennsylvania was listed as a categorical state, even though it has a noncategorical certificate for teachers of mentally and/or physically handicapped students (G. P. Cartwright, personal communication, January 3, 1986).

The authors of the present review conducted their own mail and telephone survey of certification officers of the fifty-one jurisdictions originally surveyed by Belch. Ten discrepancies were found with the Chapey et al. study (Arizona, District of Columbia, Kentucky, Mississippi, Missouri, North Carolina, Oklahoma, Pennsylvania, Rhode Island, and South Carolina). The findings of the authors' survey are reported in the 1986 column of Table 1. Data reported in the 1979 column of Table 1 reflect the findings of Belch (1979).

TABLE 1
Trends in Noncategorical Certification Practices (No = Categorical; Yes = Noncategorical)

Jurisdiction	1979	1986	Jurisdiction	1979	1986	Jurisdiction	1979	1986
AL	No	No	KY	Yes	Yes	ND	No	No
AK	No*	Yes	LA	No*	No	OH	No	No
AZ	No	No	ME	No*	No	OK	No	No
AR	No	Yes	MD	No	Yes	OR	Yes	Yes
CA	No	Yes	MA	Yes	Yes	PA	Yes	Yes
CO	No	No	MI	No	No	RI	No*	Yes
CT	Yes	Yes	MN	No	No	SC	No*	No
DE	No	Yes	MS	No*	Yes	SD	No	Yes
DC	Yes	Yes	MO	No*	No	TN	Yes	Yes
FL	No	Yes	MT	No	Yes	TX	Yes	Yes
GA	No	No	NE	No*	No	UT	No	No
HI	No	Yes	NV	No	Yes	VT	Yes	Yes
ID	Yes	Yes	NH	Yes	Yes	VA	No	No
IL	No	No	NJ	No	Yes	WA	No*	Yes
IN	No	No	NM	No*	Yes	WV	No	No
IA	No	No	NY	Yes	Yes	WI	No	No
KS	No	No	NC	No*	Yes	WY	No*	Yes

* Moving toward noncategorical certification
Note: Data in 1979 Column are from "Toward Noncategorical Teacher Certification in Special Education—Myth or Reality?" by P. J. Belch, 1979, *Exceptional Children,* **46,** 130. Copyright 1979 by Council for Exceptional Children. Adapted by permission.

The data presented in Table 1 indicate that twelve of the fifty-one jurisdictions (24%) offered noncategorical certification in 1979, while twenty-nine (57%) had noncategorical certificates in 1985. According to Chapey et al. (1985), respondents from an additional nine jurisdictions in 1985 also indicated that it would be their preference to have noncategorical certification. Interestingly, of the seventeen jurisdictions that added noncategorical certificates between 1979 and 1986, only seven (41%) indicated that they were moving in that direction in 1979. Although slightly less than one-half of the jurisdictions are still categorical, it is clear that there has been a definite trend toward noncategorical certification. Whether this trend continues remains to be seen.

One should be cautious in interpreting the data in Table 1. It should not be concluded that because one state is listed as noncategorical it has certification standards similar to another state with noncategorical certification. There is considerable variance in the states' definitions of noncategorical certification standards. In addition, many of the jurisdictions listed as having noncategorical certificates continue to maintain categorical certification options.

Establishing Certification Standards

State certification standards dictate the form and substance of noncategorical teacher preparation programs (Stephens & Joseph, 1982). Blackhurst (1981) described a number of issues that are typically encountered when state standards are being developed for noncategorical special education teaching certificates. In dealing with establishment of standards, certification committees usually try to determine which previously defined categorical areas should be included, whether certification should be based upon severity of disability, and the ways in which age levels should be addressed. There may be discussion of categories and whether, in fact, categorical differences *do* exist. For example, should students with physical disabilities be included in noncategorical certification? Some may argue that the only instructional modifications needed for teaching students with such disabilities relate to the adaptation of the physical environment and the provision of adapted instructional materials and equipment. Others may argue that considerably more is involved in teaching children who may have more severe disabilities such as cerebral palsy.

Another issue that deserves attention relates to the roles and functions performed by teachers who will hold noncategorical certificates. Will these teachers serve as special class teachers, resource teachers, consulting teachers, team teachers in mainstreamed settings, or in some combination of these roles? In the roles they will hold, what functions must be performed and what competencies should be required? Unless consensus can be reached in answering these questions, it is virtually impossible to agree upon curriculum standards.

The relationship of the special education certificate to the general education certificate also must be decided. Some states have a separate certificate in special education. Others offer special education as an endorsement of an elementary or secondary certificate, and still others require dual certification in special and general education. Some will argue that a single certificate is all that is needed; others will argue that special education teachers need to be familiar with what goes on in the elementary or secondary classes if they are to be effective resource teachers. Advocates of the latter position will support certification in either elementary or secondary education to provide teacher trainees with practicum experience in the regular classroom.

The problem of levels is also raised in discussion of certification standards. Should the certificate cover all grade levels, K through 12, or should it be divided into appropriate levels, such as preschool, primary, or secondary? Some will argue for the broad curriculum in order to provide more flexibility for teachers and for administrators who may be employing them. Others will argue that the various levels require different competencies and that all of these competencies cannot be developed through a single certification program.

All of the aforementioned issues represent broad conceptual or philosophical issues that must be resolved prior to the specification of the actual competency or curriculum requirements by committees involved with the development or revision of certification standards.

State Certification Reciprocity

If existing conditions are any indication, it appears likely that certification requirements of the different states will continue to vary greatly. This variance will, undoubtedly, complicate problems in reciprocity of teacher certification. That is, what might be acceptable for noncategorical certification in some states might not be acceptable for a similarly named certificate in others. Certifying agencies in states with noncategorical certification also are currently encountering difficulties in making determinations about what certificates to issue to those teachers with categorical certification who move to their states.

The problem of reciprocity of teacher certification is being addressed. According to Mackey (1980), the Interstate Agreement on Qualification of Educational Personnel, an interstate compact originally developed in 1964, was developed to facilitate reciprocal certification in all areas of education. In late 1979, agreements were signed to extend the compact for 5 years. Nearly 70% of the states are signatories of that agreement.

According to Mackey, the problem of incompatible special education certification among the various states has created difficulty in implementing the compact for special education teachers. However, members who signed the agreement were well aware of the problem and have been working toward its resolution in conjunction with the National Association of State Directors of Teacher Education and Certification.

Because of variability in certification requirements and the problem of interstate reciprocity, it will be interesting to see whether national standards for special education certification or licensure will emerge. Many people are opposed to such a procedure, although a number of other professionals support it. Heller (1982) wrote a very provocative article in support of national certification standards.

Noncategorical Personnel Preparation Practices

This section of the review presents information related to the development of college and university programs to prepare special education personnel for noncategorical teaching assignments. The status of noncategorical preparation programs is described. A discussion of topics related to design of the curriculum, program implementation, staffing, and evaluation follows.

Status of Noncategorical Personnel Preparation

Under the sponsorship of the Teacher Education Division of CEC, a national survey of special education personnel preparation programs was conducted by Geiger and reported in 1983. The purpose of the survey was to produce a directory of institutions of higher education (IHEs) that prepare special educators. Although not specifically designed to identify noncategorical preparation programs, the respondents were asked to indicate the special education categories in which training was offered at various degree levels.

The authors of the present review analyzed the data in the Geiger directory to determine the number of IHEs reporting noncategorical offerings. The directory contains a total of 698 IHEs that were identified as providing some form of special education presonnel preparation program. Of this number, 174 did not respond to the questionnaire. Although the nonrespondents were included in the directory, it was not possible to determine the types of programs that were offered at those institutions.

Of the remaining 524 that reported information about their programs, 239 indicated that they offered some form of noncategorical training. There is an interesting correspondence between the percentage of IHEs offering noncategorical personnel preparation programs (45.6%) and the percentage of jurisdictions that had noncategorical certification programs or were moving in that direction (47%) in 1979 (see Table 1). Since IHEs must adhere to the certification practices of their respective jurisdictions, similar percentages would be expected. These data appear to confirm such expectations. (The Teacher Education Division of CEC was in the process of replicating the Geiger survey in mid-1986.)

There was a wide variety of different terms used by the IHEs to describe their noncategorical programs (e.g., noncategorical, generic, cross-categorical, learning and behavior disorders). As with the different noncategorical certification practices of the states, one should not assume that the noncategorical personnel preparation programs of different IHEs are similar in content or approach.

Designing a Noncategorical Curriculum

When noncategorical certification standards or guidelines are established by state certification agencies, college and university faculties must develop curricula that are esponsive to those guidelines. Most colleges and universi- ies moving in this direction are faced with the problem of onverting existing categorical teacher preparation pro- rams to noncategorical ones. As Blackhurst (1979) noted, pecial education departments must deal with at least the ollowing issues:

> What are the basic assumptions underlying the development of the program? What functions must graduates of the programs be able to perform? What competencies are associated with each function? What objectives should be included and how should these be evaluated? What content should be included? How should the program be structured in terms of courses and practica? What formative and summative evaluation questions should be addressed? What resources are available to support the program? How will the program be managed? (p. 40)

Christopolos and Valletutti (1972) mentioned several of the issues described above when they identified urgent problems inherent in noncategorical preparation of teachers. They raised several additional points, such as the needs to establish a feasible rate for implementation of the program, to meet state certification requirements, and to persuade school officials to employ generalists. Influencing the hiring practices of schools would appear to be beyond the scope of teacher preparation programs, but hiring practices obviously influence program graduates and, eventually, the types of services delivered to handicapped children.

Other design issues for noncategorical training programs include clarifying the type of student served by such school programs and providing the breadth and depth of knowledge that would allow graduates to adequately serve the target population (Vallecorsa, 1983). This knowledge would include the ability to use formative and summative evaluation data, allowing an educator to critically examine the quality of the noncategorical school program. Vallecorsa also stated that teachers in training must understand the nature and intent of the cross-categorical training they receive.

Blackhurst et al. (1977) identified some sixty issues that were addressed during one university's efforts to convert from a categorical to a noncategorical curriculum. They also presented a model that can be used to guide noncategorical curriculum development efforts. Additional details of how to implement that model were provided in another work by Blackhurst (1977).

Implementing Noncategorical Curricula

The literature contains several descriptions of noncategorical special education personnel preparation programs (Blackhurst, 1981; Heward et al., 1981; Pierce, 1981; Stephens & Joseph, 1982). Reports of the success of most of these are limited primarily to anecdotal evidence and reactions of either the faculty who operate them or the students who are enrolled in them. Validation data are largely lacking about the effectiveness of such programs, although Knight, Christie, Egner, Paolucci, and Bates (1976) did provide data related to rate of task completion of students in one such program.

Unless a new program is being initiated, most noncategorical programs are the result of a revision of categorical curricula. Once a curriculum revision has been completed, however, additional problems may be encountered. For example, provisions must be made for students who entered a categorical program either to complete that program or to convert to the new program. The implication is that dual programs may need to be maintained until currently enrolled "categorical" students are graduated.

Because federal and state funds for special education programs are issued primarily on a categorical basis, most local school districts operate their special education programs along categorical lines, with special classes and resource rooms being provided for learning disabled students, educable mentally retarded students, and so forth. Consequently, it is difficult to locate practicum sites that capture the essence of noncategorical programming. Inappropriately structured programs or programs bound to diagnostic categories do not provide good models for students to emulate in their student teaching and other practicum experiences.

Faculty at some institutions are faced with a dilemma when their philosophy of personnel preparation favors a noncategorical approach while state certification is awarded on a categorical basis. This need not be a deterrent to those who hold such beliefs, however. It has been shown that categorical university curricula can be successfully modified to approximate a noncategorical approach to categorical certification requirements (Blackhurst, Cross, Nelson, & Tawney, 1973; Heward et al., 1981; Nelson, Berdine, & Boyer, 1978).

Staffing

Conversion to noncategorical certification programs also creates problems with respect to the staffing of teacher preparation programs. In most cases, faculty members must assume new roles and/or teaching responsibilities for which they may not have been specifically prepared. Stephens and Joseph (1982) observed that, frequently, the emphasis in a noncategorical program is on how the practitioners, rather than the teacher trainers, should change. Faculty members may need to undertake in-service programs to upgrade their teaching skills.

Because many doctoral programs still train their students on a categorical basis, special education departments with revised programs may encounter difficulty in finding appropriately prepared faculty members. Basic to the staffing problem is the issue of what qualifications faculty members should have in order to be employed in noncategorical teacher preparation programs. It is unclear whether the faculty should be comprised of a number of specialists who will work together to train generic personnel.

Evaluation

There are few reports of the effectiveness of noncategorical personnel preparation efforts in the literature. Formative studies of a noncategorical program in a state offering categorical certification were reported by Blackhurst et al. (1973) and Nelson et al. (1978). Data presented in these reports, however, were based primarily on reports of student satisfaction and anecdotal evidence from faculty.

Smith-Davis, Morsink, and Wheatley (1984) have provided a useful resource for college faculty who are interested in improving the quality of their special education teacher preparation programs. Their document can be used as a workbook to establish baseline descriptions of personnel preparation programs, including those that are structured on a noncategorical basis. The baseline information can then be used as the basis for evaluating progress in implementing the program.

Guidelines for actually conducting evaluations of personnel preparation programs have been described in the useful work of Brinkerhoff, Brethower, Hluchyj, and Nowakowski (1983a; 1983b). These investigators have provided guidelines for conducting evaluations of special education personnel preparation programs and a workbook to facilitate the development of such evaluations. An example of how to evaluate an effort to make a transition from a categorical to a noncategorical personnel preparation program is included in that work (Blackhurst, 1983).

Although there are a few data-based reports in the literature, it is evident that evaluative studies of noncategorical personnel preparation programs are lacking. A need clearly exists to validate the practices that are being implemented primarily on the basis of theory and personal opinion. The report of Idol-Maestas et al. (1981), which was cited earlier, represents a step in the right direction. These authorities examined the progress of students who were recipients of instruction from personnel trained in a noncategorical program. Learner-referenced evaluation studies such as this one produce data upon which sound implementation decisions can be made.

Training for Regular Education Teachers

With the 1975 passage of PL 94-142, school personnel were mandated to educate handicapped students in the "least restrictive environment." This provision of the law has resulted in increased efforts to integrate mildly handicapped students into the regular classroom for portions of their educational program—a practice commonly referred to as *mainstreaming*. Thus, regular teachers are now frequently called upon to assume part of the responsibility of teaching handicapped students who are capable of profiting from regular class instruction. Many of these teachers now find themselves responsible for planning and implementing instructional lessons for students who have the ability to master the subject matter but who may exhibit mild learning or behavior problems. Others must accommodate the needs of students who have sensory impairments or physical disabilities that require modifications in the classroom environment, instructional materials, and teaching methods to facilitate learning.

The idea of mainstreaming has logical appeal. All children are entitled to a free and appropriate education in our democratic system. It makes sense to educate all children who can profit from regular class instruction together. Not only is it good for the mainstreamed students, but a strong case can be made for the notion that mainstreaming is good for other students as well. Mainstreaming should help to improve attitudes toward people with handicaps, which should stimulate a greater tolerance for individual differences in our society.

Unfortunately, however, there are many potential problems between the conceptualization of mainstreaming and its implementation. The National Education Association (NEA) addressed some of the relevant issues and concerns of teachers in their "NEA Resolution 77–33" (Ryor, 1977). Among these is a concern about teacher preparation for mainstreaming. Many regular classroom teachers did not believe they had the competencies necessary for mainstreaming to be effective. Such concerns prompted several studies on identification of mainstreaming competencies to give direction to the development of pre-service and in-service teacher education programs.

Mainstreaming Competency Identification Studies

One of the first competency identification efforts in the area of mainstreaming was a survey of fourteen colleges and universities that were conducting programs to prepare regular classroom teachers to mainstream mildly handicapped students (Goldhammer, Rader, & Reuschlein, 1977). This research yielded a list of some 464 competencies clustered into thirteen areas: nature of mainstreaming, nature of the handicap, attitudes, resources, teaching techniques, learning environment, learning styles, classroom management, curriculum, communication, assessing student needs, evaluating student progress, and administration.

At about the same time that Goldhammer and his associates were conducting their survey, Redden and Blackhurst (1978) reported research directed at identifying competencies of elementary teachers who were mainstreaming handicapped students. Using a research procedure known as the critical incident technique (Flanagan, 1962), 828 specific incidents in which teachers had been either effective or ineffective in their mainstreaming efforts were collected from 184 elementary teachers. After eliminating redundancies, some 271 different tasks were identified that seemed to be important. These tasks were clustered into thirty-one competency statements, which were subsequently grouped into six areas of teacher functioning: developing orientation strategies for mainstream entry, assessing needs and goal setting, planning teaching strategies and use of resources, implementing teaching strategies and utilization of resources, facilitating learn-ng, and evaluating learning. The complete list of tasks is available in Redden's (1976) work.

The next large-scale effort at identifying mainstreaming competencies was conducted by Reynolds, Birch, Grohs, Howsam, and Morsink in 1980. This work was the topic of a national study conducted in conjunction with the Dean's Grants projects (discussed later in this chapter). Reynolds and his colleagues described ten clusters of competencies as the domains of professional competence that appear to be important for all teachers who are involved in individualized instruction. These ten domains are curriculum, teaching basic skills, pupil and class management, professional consultation and communications, teacher–parent relationships, student–student relationships, exceptional conditions, referral, individualized teaching, and professional values. A useful document, titled *A Common Body of Practice for Teachers: The Challenge of PL 94-142 to Teacher Education,* was published by the American Association of Colleges for Teacher Education as a result of this work. A series of knowledge-base reviews and resource units were also developed, based upon the ten clusters of competence (Lakin & Reynolds, 1982).

At first glance, the results of these three major studies of mainstreaming competencies are overwhelming. One study identified nearly 500 competencies, another identified some 270 tasks, while the third generated ten competency domains that encompass a very broad spectrum of teaching skills. In analyzing these three major studies of mainstreaming competencies, however, Blackhurst (1982) concluded that the great majority of the competencies that were identified are competencies that all good teachers should possess, regardless of whether or not they are teaching mainstreamed students.

The investigations cited above do appear to have identified some competencies, however, that are associated directly with mainstreaming. These relate to knowledge about legal mandates, characteristics of exceptional children, participation in school-wide planning for mainstreaming, procedures for preparing special students for entry into the regular class, preparation of regular students for entry of special students into the class, integration of handicapped students into the regular classroom, curriculum and teaching accommodations that can be made for children with physical and sensory impairments, and ways to work with specialists of various types and with parents of mainstreamed students.

Stephens, Blackhurst, and Magliocca (1982) provided an extended treatment of the topic of teacher competencies for mainstreaming. They elaborated on the three studies previously noted and discussed those competencies that have been identified as being unique to mainstreaming efforts. In addition, they described how teachers can pursue a professional development program to improve their teaching competencies. A checklist was also provided that teachers can use to perform a self-analysis of the areas in which they need additional training.

When identifying competencies, however, it is important to attend to the caveat of Shores, Cegelka, and Nelson (1973). These authorities cautioned against the uncritical acceptance of competency statements based simply upon face validity. They called for studies to generate data that would determine whether possession of a particular competency has an effect on child performance.

Teacher Certification Requirements

Caution should be exercised in validating professional practice against federal legislation. However, it could be postulated that, because federal law requires that special education students receive a portion of their education in regular classrooms when appropriate, and because there appear to be competencies specifically related to mainstreaming, one might expect that course content related to mainstreaming would be a requirement in teacher preparation programs. There appears to be a trend toward such a requirement; however, implementation is slow.

In a survey conducted in 1976, Byford (1979) assessed the availability of undergraduate, graduate, and in-service skill courses for regular educators in diagnostic, remediation, and behavior management techniques for mildly handicapped students. Colleges and universities in the United States Office of Education's Region III area were asked to list courses available before 1970 and since 1970. The survey revealed some response to mainstreaming, with the majority of relevant courses available at the undergraduate level. Byford concluded that there was still not a widespread attempt to train regular educators to deal with mildly handicapped students in the mainstream.

In 1980, Patton and Braithwaite (1980–1981) conducted a survey of certification requirements for elementary and secondary teachers. They found that only ten states required a course on special education as part of their preservice teacher preparation programs. Four years later, Ganschow, Weber, and Davis (1984) replicated this study and found that seventeen states required one special education course, two had a two-course requirement, seven had specific guidelines related to special education training, and eight made a general reference to competencies about handicapping conditions in their teacher certification guidelines. Two other states were in the process of considering requirements for one course. Thus, in 1984, twenty-one states required at least one course or were in the process of requiring one course on exceptionalities for their regular education teachers-in-training.

There is some discrepancy in the literature, however. Chapey et al. (1985) reported that two fewer states (fifteen) required at least one special education course for regular education majors than did Ganschow et al. (1984), who reported that seventeen states had such requirements. It is unknown whether certification standards changed or whether errors occurred in reporting or analysis.

According to Ganschow et al., an additional fifteen states referred to competencies about handicaps in their guidelines for certification, confirming the research of Smith and Schindler (1980). However, Ganschow et al. (1984) expressed concern about this finding. They claimed that "SEAs which set general . . . guidelines cannot rigorously enforce the compliance of educational institutions to provide their students with relevant experiences" (p. 75). If there is validity to this claim, when the fifteen states are coupled with the fourteen states that have no requirements or guidelines, then 58% (29) of the states do not mandate content related to teaching handicapped students for their elementary or secondary teachers. Although it has been more than a decade since PL 94-142 was passed, it appears that significant inadequacies exist in preparing elementary and secondary teachers to educate handicapped children in their classrooms.

Training for Related Personnel

No data were located concerning the extent to which personnel with related responsibilities for the education of students with mild disabilities receive appropriate pre-service or in-service education. It would seem to be important to include such content in the curricula for the preparation of school psychologists, guidance counselors, social workers, principals, school superintendents, general instructional supervisors, and others involved in the delivery of educational services to this group of students. Training for educational leaders is particularly important; it has been the authors' experience that the extent to which educational practices are implemented in schools is directly related to the knowledge and degree of commitment of administrators responsible for the day-to-day operation of the schools.

Similarly, the training of school psychologists appears to be extremely critical for successful noncategorical programming. In all likelihood, school psychologists who diagnose and label students on a categorical basis contribute barriers to successful implementation of noncategorical programs. The National Association of School Psychologists adopted a resolution in early 1985 calling for noncategorical service delivery systems (J. L. Graden, personal communication, April 24, 1985). If future training programs for school psychologists reflect the intent of this resolution, the aforementioned barriers should be reduced.

Need for In-Service Training

Although revisions in pre-service curricula can ensure that future personnel receive appropriate training, a major remaining problem is the provision of meaningful in-service training programs to persons already delivering educational services in the schools. Technology may hold some promise for providing in-service training. For example, Cartwright and Cartwright (1973) used computer-assisted instruction to provide course work dealing with the identification of students in regular classrooms who were in need of special education services. Blackhurst (1978) provided a variety of examples of ways in which different technologies can be used in the delivery of special education in-service training.

Of course, traditional methods of providing in-service training can also be employed (e.g., Bishop, 1976). Because there has been concern about the effectiveness of short-term, in-service training without follow-up (e.g. Stephens & Hartman, 1978), some have attempted innovative approaches to in-service training. For example Coulter (1985) used a technique, called shadowing, for providing in-service training on curriculum-based assessment to pupil-appraisal personnel. Shadowing provided immediate feedback to professionals who were practicing new skills in their work environments.

The Adaptive Learning Environments Model (ALEM), mentioned earlier, also has implications for pre-service and in-service education related to noncategorical programming for children. As of 1985, four universities (California State University at Los Angeles, Long Island University, the University of Kentucky, and the University of Minnesota) were conducting demonstration projects coordinated by the Learning Research and Development Center at the University of Pittsburgh. The demonstration projects involved implementation of the ALEM within the framework of a college–school collaborative model for personnel preparation (Wang, 1983). The aim of the project is to coordinate the work of colleges of education and school improvement efforts in elementary and secondary schools. This college–school collaborative model involves systematic in-service and pre-service preparation and can be applied to a variety of innovative practices.

Dean's Grant Projects

Between 1975 and 1982, more than 260 "Dean's Grants" were funded by the Federal Bureau of Education for the Handicapped (Sharp, 1982). The primary purpose of these grants was to stimulate and support changes in the preparation of elementary and secondary teachers and related personnel to better prepare them to serve handicapped children mainstreamed into regular education programs. The projects bore their unusual name because deans of the participating schools, colleges, and departments of education were required to be the directors of the projects. By closely involving the deans, it was thought that the likelihood of effecting administrative and curricular change would be maximized.

A work edited by Sharp (1982) summarized the activities of the Dean's Grants and their accomplishments. Among the conclusions cited by contributing authors in Sharp's monograph were the following:

1. Approximately three-fourths of the teacher preparation programs had revised their teacher preparation curricula to include content related to teaching handicapped children.
2. Less than half of the programs included practica with handicapped students for elementary or secondary teacher education students.
3. Approximately 87% of participating institutions reported that regular education faculties were knowledgeable about provisions of PL 94-142.
4. There was a paucity of follow-up data to evaluate the effectiveness of program graduates.

It appears that the Dean's Grants projects had a significant impact on personnel preparation practices. New courses on exceptional children were established in many universities. Units and instructional modules related to teaching learners with disabilities were also incorporated into existing courses. Since funding for the Dean's Grants projects has been terminated, it would be interesting to conduct an investigation to determine whether changes implemented during the funding period remain and the extent to which related activities are currently being conducted.

Future Considerations

This review of noncategorical personnel preparation practices has raised far more questions than it has answered. From an analysis of the literature on the topic, there appear to be a number of implications for future consideration and action. Some of these are presented in this section. It should be emphasized, however, that these implications represent the opinions of the reviewers and are not based upon an empirical foundation, which, as has been pointed out earlier, is essentially nonexistent. The implications for policy, legislation, service delivery, and research that are described in this section are based upon the assumption that noncategorical personnel preparation practices are desirable. Although there is considerable sentiment to support this contention, there is not unanimity on the topic.

Policy Implications

Perhaps the major policy implication raised by the issue of noncategorical personnel preparation relates to teacher certification practices. Because of varying philosophies, the special education teacher certification standards of the various states create major problems in reciprocal certification. A teacher holding noncategorical certification in one state may not meet the noncategorical certification standards of another. This situation creates real nightmares for certification officers and confusion and frustration among professionals whose personal situations require that they move to new geographical areas.

Because the American tradition places primary responsibility for educational policy at the local and state levels, it is likely that philosophical differences will continue to perpetuate differing certification standards. If so, the problem of reciprocal certification will remain. A solution to the problem may rest with the development of a national policy on noncategorical teacher certification, which could take the form of national licensure for special education teachers.

It should be noted that national licensure for teachers is anathema to many people; however, several professions (e.g., medicine) have had various forms of national licensure or certification for years. In fact, the American Speech–Language–Hearing Association (ASLHA) has a national certification model that enables the individual states to maintain their autonomy in setting licensure standards for persons providing private speech, language, or hearing services, yet provides them with a way to resolve the problem of issuing licenses to people who apply from other jurisdictions.

In the ASLHA model, persons may elect to apply for the Certificate of Clinical Competence (CCC), which is awarded based upon a variety of educational and performance criteria, a national accrediting examination, and a supervised clinical fellowship year of employment following completion of a master's degree. People holding the CCC typically meet criteria for a license to engage in private practice in different states.

Some states (e.g., Ohio) have incorporated the ASLHA standards into their teacher certification requirements. Most states, however, permit the practice of speech therapy in schools without the ASLHA certificate. Those states maintain separate certification requirements for professionals who provide services to students with speech or communication disorders. In some states, people holding an ASLHA certificate of clinical competence will automatically be awarded certification to work in the schools, while other states may require additional courses to earn such certification.

If a model similar to that of the ASLHA were to be adopted, a professional organization, such as CEC, could develop standards to be used as the basis for a national special education certificate or license. Careful consultation with the various certification jurisdictions during the planning period would ensure that holders of the national certificate would be acceptable candidates for teacher certification in those jurisdictions. Application for the license would be on an elective basis. Those who planned to stay within a particular state might be content to apply for state certification, while those who anticipated frequent relocations might find the national license more appealing.

A combination of state and national certification and licensure would maintain the autonomy of the various states, as has been the tradition. At the same time, a national system could resolve the major problem of reciprocal certification. Other merits of a national licensure system for special education teachers have been described by Heller (1982), while other authorities have argued against such practices (Blatt, 1981). There is definite disagreement on the topic. As Birch and Reynolds (1982) pointed out, however, one of the marks of a profession is to have nationally recognized standards and procedures for ensuring that its members adhere to those standards. These authorities claimed that special education has the status of a "semi-profession" because it does not meet these criteria (among others).

Perhaps movement toward national certification and licensure would help promote full recognition of special education as a profession, as well as help resolve the problem of noncategorical certification reciprocity. Such a movement would need to be approached cautiously, however. Although national licensure might result in greater consistency in qualifications of professionals, care would need to be taken to ensure the validity of any national standards or guidelines.

The Teacher Education Division (1986) of CEC was collaborating with the National Council for the Accreditation of Teacher Education in 1985 and 1986 to develop guidelines for the accreditation of special education personnel preparation programs. The guidelines being developed by those agencies encompass a wide range of personnel preparation programs, however, and are not restricted to noncategorical programs.

Legislative Implications

Early in this review, it was pointed out that maintenance of diagnostic categories is useful for drawing attention to the problems and needs of groups of people with similar characteristics. Nowhere is this rationale more evident than in federal and state legislation. Funds and services are made available for special education purposes largely on the basis of categorical definitions.

It is unlikely that there soon will be a change in the categorical orientation of special education legislation. Many educational and rehabilitative programs are funded and operated on a categorical basis, school census data are maintained by category, and parents and others advocate for specific categorical groups. These are very strong forces that militate against change in current categorical practices. However, if there is merit to noncategorical approaches, there is a need to begin to recognize them in legislation and accompanying regulations. If noncategorical legislation is found to be politically infeasible, the issue could be approached by acknowledging that categorical definitions may be necessary in order to provide the basis for appropriating funds and for administrative decision making. Once funding has been obtained, however, educational services could be delivered in a noncategorical fashion, based upon the educational needs of the children to be served.

The major implication here is the need to develop educational programs for legislators, policymakers, parents, and other advocates. Such educational programs should focus upon the issues related to noncategorical programming and its potential benefits. Policy makers who understand the implications and intent of noncategorical programming should be more likely to support efforts to move the field in that direction.

Service Delivery Implications

Perhaps the greatest benefit of having teachers who hold noncategorical certification is the potential for improving the delivery of educational services to children with mild disabilities. As pointed out at the beginning of this review, the delivery of educational services based upon diagnostic category is not the optimal procedure. The most rational approach to educating children is to base instruction upon their *educationally relevant* characteristics.

Effective special education teachers are those who have been trained to identify the educational strengths and weaknesses of children, plan programs of instruction in response to those strengths and weaknesses, implement the programs, evaluate the effectiveness of their efforts, and modify instruction based upon effectiveness data. Noncategorical personnel preparation programs focus on the preparation of teachers who have such skills, regardless of diagnostic category.

Although data are again lacking, it has been the authors' observation, having worked in Kentucky, a state in which noncategorical teacher certification has been in effect since 1978, that the availability of teachers trained to work with children based upon their educational needs instead of their diagnostic category has an impact on the delivery of educational services. Although financing for school programs continues to be operated along categorical lines in the state, some school districts are taking advantage of the skills of noncategorically certified teachers through the development of different instructional delivery systems. For example, greater use is being made of resource room programs that can respond to a variety of different children.

Noncategorical teacher preparation relates to the predicted de-emphasis on special class placement in favor of serving mildly handicapped students in regular classrooms. A teacher who is prepared to view learning problems in terms of a child's profile of academic strengths and weaknesses rather than diagnostic labels will be in a better position to collaborate with colleagues in serving special needs students in regular classrooms. Labels are particularly irrelevant in the mainstream, as no placement decisions are required.

Pugach and Lilly (1984) observed that teacher education programs frequently reflect the current status of educational practice rather than lead the field toward meaningful change. They stressed the need for teacher preparation programs to adjust to the predicted changes in the nature of special services for mildly handicapped learners. Some of the implications for personnel preparation discussed by Pugach and Lilly relate directly to the noncategorical viewpoint, especially the need to prepare all teachers to deal with a wide range of abilities and to expect that students will need diverse methods of instruction.

The implication is that instructional delivery systems can be more flexible and relevant to children's needs when teachers have been appropriately prepared in programs having a noncategorical orientation. It should be emphasized, however, that the delivery systems must be planned intelligently. Caution must be taken to guard against the attitude that all mildly handicapped children can be placed together for instruction simply because a teacher with noncategorical certification is available. Such is not necessarily the case. Placement and grouping decisions must be made on the basis of the characteristics displayed by individual children. Schubert and Glick (1981) studied successful mainstreaming programs and cited several criteria that reflected successful practices. They claimed that students to be mainstreamed should be (a) capable of doing at least some work at or above grade level; (b) able to remain on task in the regular classroom without as much assistance as might be available to them in the resource room; (c) able to fit into the routine of the regular class; (d) capable of functioning socially in the regular class; and (e) capable of working in the regular classroom without a great deal of extra assistance, special materials, or adaptive equipment that must be provided by the regular class teacher.

Research Implications

As noted several times in this chapter, very little research on the topic of noncategorical teacher preparation has been reported in the literature. This section presents a number of research topics and questions that should be addressed as a part of any future research agenda. The topics are organized around issues related to elements of the curriculum design model that was mentioned previously (Blackhurst, 1977; Blackhurst et al., 1977). Consequently, data generated from an examination of the topics would have direct, practical implications for personnel preparation practices.

It should be emphasized that the items in this research agenda are not intended to be exhaustive. Rather, they are illustrative of some of the major topics that should be addressed by researchers. They also reflect the biases of the authors, who favor competency-based approaches to teacher education.

PHILOSOPHICAL ISSUES

Those who attempt to implement noncategorical approaches to teacher education should have a well-articulated philosophy that can serve as the conceptual underpinning for program implementation. The faculty should specify the values and beliefs that relate to the preparation of special education teachers for noncategorical teaching positions. Although philosophical differences may vary from training program to training program, there are some basic questions that need to be answered that would have implications for the development of the philosophies of all faculty.

— Are there differences in the educationally relevant characteristics among children who have been assigned to different diagnostic categories? If so, what are they? What are the similarities among the groups?
— As severity of disability increases, do differences among children in different diagnostic categories become more apparent?
— What is the most effective method of delivering instruction to teacher education students (e.g., field-based, competency-based, modularized)?
— What role should field experiences and practica play in a personnel preparation program? What is the optimal blend of field experiences and practica? How can students receive adequate practicum experiences to ensure that they will be prepared for the variety of settings they may find themselves in after graduation?
— How can personnel be prepared to be flexible enough to adapt to new or different special education service delivery models that may emerge in the schools?
— Are there differences in effectiveness of various noncategorical service delivery models (e.g., consulting teacher, resource room, team teaching)? If so, what implications do these differences have for personnel preparation programs?
— If philosophical differences among professionals involved in noncategorical teacher education programs cannot be resolved, how can programs be developed to accommodate the differences?

ISSUES RELATED TO ROLES OF GRADUATES

There is a need to develop firm definitions of the various roles that noncategorical teachers must perform in public schools. The identification of these roles and the functions associated with them have direct implications for the design of curricula.

— Are the roles that teachers must assume different for students who have been assigned to different diagnostic categories?
— How do the roles of noncategorical teachers change according to the types of settings in which children are educated?
— How do the ages and grade placements of children affect teachers' roles?

ISSUES RELATED TO COMPETENCIES

After teachers' roles and their associated functions have been defined, it is necessary to identify the competencies associated with each. It is insufficient to simply identify competencies through speculation. Competencies must be validated if training programs are to be effective.

— What competencies are required of noncategorical teachers?
— Are different competencies needed depending upon the diagnostic category of the child being taught?
— What effect do placements and ages of children have on the competencies required of their teachers?

ISSUES RELATED TO INSTRUCTIONAL OBJECTIVES

In designing any teacher preparation curriculum, it is important to have precisely stated objectives to guide the instructional program.

— What objectives are associated with each of the noncategorical teacher competencies?
— Under what conditions should the objectives be demonstrated?

— How should the objectives be evaluated? What should be accepted as evidence that the objectives have been mastered?

Issues Related to Content of Curriculum

Decisions concerning content focus on questions about what will be taught in the noncategorical curriculum. Determination must be made about existing instructional methods and materials that are appropriate plus those that must be developed and/or adapted for use in a program.

— What criteria should be used for selecting content for noncategorical programs?
— Since many texts are "categorical," should students be required to study those that are relevant? Should categorical content be presented separately, and then integrated; or should content be integrated as the students progress through a program?
— What are the effects of using categorical terminology? What are the alternatives?
— How can content related to areas such as technology, career education, assessment, and other topics be best integrated into a curriculum?

Issues Related to Program Structure

The structure of a program relates to the system for delivering course work, practica, and related experiences to students. Numerous questions related to the most effective ways to structure these experiences can be asked.

— What courses should be designed for the delivery of instruction? How should these be sequenced?
— What should be the length of the program?
— How should practica be integrated with courses?
— How effective are different approaches to instruction (e.g., computer-assisted instruction, adjunct auto-instruction, micro-teaching)?

Issues Related to Program Implementation

Implementation of a curriculum should follow logically from the previous activites. Other than those issues that relate to the implementation of any personnel preparation program, there are several that are of particular concern to those designing noncategorical programs.

— How can faculty who were previously in categorical areas be reeducated and reoriented to noncategorical programs?
— Should classes be team taught by categorical experts or should faculty be expected to prepare for new teaching roles?
— What type of faculty in-service is necessary for effective program implementation?
— How can meaningful noncategorical practicum experiences be developed for students if schools are operating programs on a categorical basis? If only categorical practicum sites are available, should students be required to have experiences in several of these?
— How can an effective transition be made for those currently enrolled in categorical programs?
— What criteria should be established for selection and retention of students?
— How can student competencies be monitored and by whom?

Issues Related to Program Evaluation

Program evaluation is critical when embarking upon noncategorical personnel preparation programs. Such evaluation is required to determine program effectiveness and to serve as the basis for program revision. Both formative and summative evaluation efforts are needed to address such questions as those noted below.

— Are students developing competencies that are required for noncategorical teaching?
— What difficulties do students encounter in the programs and after graduation?
— Do graduates have difficulty getting jobs after graduation? Once employed, do they have any difficulty in adapting to the demands of their employers?
— How effective are program graduates? What are the perceptions of their supervisors?
— Do handicapped students learn as a result of the efforts of teachers trained in noncategorical programs?
— Do handicapped students learn more from teachers who have been trained in categorical preparation programs or from those who have been trained in noncategorical ones?

Undoubtedly, one could raise a host of other research issues and questions about noncategorical teacher education programs. Of the questions noted above, however, the last two are the most important. These cut to the core of the issue, yet are perhaps the most difficult to study because of the potential amount of uncontrollable variance that is inherent in conducting learner-referenced research on teacher effectiveness.

Conclusions

It appears that the prediction of movement toward noncategorical special education teacher preparation programs made by members of the profession in the early 1970s is gradually being fulfilled, albeit slower than predicted and slower than some might like. As of early 1986, slightly more than half of the states (57%) had adopted noncategorical certification standards. Since colleges and universities must provide programs consistent with certification standards, it is assumed that institutions of higher education in states requiring noncategorical certification are changing to noncategorical curricula. This speculation seems to be supported by our analysis of Geiger's (1983) national directory of special education personnel preparation programs.

There appears to be some movement in providing additional training to regular teachers in ways to work with handicapped students. Such movement is reflected in certification standards and guidelines requiring such training and in university curricula that include special education content in the elementary and secondary education programs. Some authorities believe that many of the current efforts are insufficient.

Although there are several problems associated with the development of noncategorical certification and teacher preparation practices, these problems appear to be outweighed by the potential benefits. Some of the benefits, such as improved personnel preparation curricula, are immediately apparent. Other benefits, such as reduction of stereotypes, will probably not be realized for several years. The availability of teachers with noncategorical certification also has the potential for serving as a catalyst to modify the ways in which educational services are delivered to special education students in public schools.

As noted throughout this chapter, there is a paucity of empirical data upon which to base decisions about noncategorical certification standards and teacher preparation curricula. Considerable attention has been devoted to the identification of the issues that are involved in moving toward a noncategorical approach. The challenge now is to conduct studies that will generate the data needed to make informed decisions about the resolution of those issues.

Author Information

A. Edward Blackhurst is Professor, Deborah A. Bott is Assistant Professor, and Donald P. Cross is Associate Professor, all at the University of Kentucky, Department of Special Education.

References

Association for Children With Learning Disabilities [ACLD]. (1983, April). ACLD position statement: Cross-categorical resource programs. *ACLD Newsbriefs*, **149**, 5–6.

Barresi, J., & Bunte, J. (1979). *Special education certification practices: A summary of a national survey*. Paper prepared for the Policy Options Project. Reston, VA: Council for Exceptional Children.

Belch, P. J. (1979). Toward noncategorical teacher certification in special education—myth or reality? *Exceptional Children*, **46**, 129–131.

Birch, J. W., & Reynolds, M. C. (1982). Special education as a profession. *Exceptional Education Quarterly*, **2**(4), 1–13.

Bishop, L. J. (1976). *Staff development and instructional improvement*. Boston, MA: Allyn & Bacon.

Blackhurst, A. E. (1977). Competency-based special education personnel preparation. In R. D. Kneedler & S. G. Tarver (Eds.), *Changing perspectives in special education* (pp. 156–182). Columbus, OH: Merrill.

Blackhurst , A. E. (1978). Using telecommunication systems for delivering inservice training. *Viewpoints in Teaching and Learning*, **54**(4), 27–40.

Blackhurst, A. E. (1979). Curriculum planning as an element of quality control in special education personnel preparation. *Teacher Education and Special Education*, **2**, 39–41.

Blackhurst, A. E. (1981). Noncategorical teacher preparation: Problems and promises. *Exceptional Children*, **48**, 197–205.

Blackhurst, A. E. (1982). Competencies for teaching mainstreamed students. *Theory into Practice*, **21**, 139–143.

Blackhurst, A. E. (1983). A department evaluates curriculum change. In R. W. Brinkerhoff, D. M. Brethower, T. Hluchyj, & J. R. Nowakowski (Eds.), *Program evaluation: A practitioner's guide for trainers and educators—Sourcebook/casebook* (pp. 303–324). Boston, MA: Kluwer-Nijhoff.

Blackhurst, A. E. (1985). Issues in special education. In W. H. Berdine & A. E. Blackhurst (Eds.), *An introduction to special education* (2nd ed.) (pp. 45–85). Boston, MA: Little, Brown.

Blackhurst, A. E., Cross, D. P., Nelson, C. M., & Tawney, J. W. (1973). Approximating non-categorical teacher education. *Exceptional Children*, **39**, 284–288.

Blackhurst, A. E., McLoughlin, J. A., & Price, L. M. (1977). Issues in the development of programs to prepare teachers of children with learning and behavior disorders. *Behavioral Disorders*, **2**, 157–168.

Blatt, B. (1981). We get the teachers we deserve. *Journal of Learning Disabilities*, **14**, 475–480, 493.

Brinkerhoff, R. W., Brethower, D. M., Hluchyj, T., & Nowakowski, J. R. (1983a). *Program evaluation: A practitioner's guide for trainers and educators—Design manual*. Boston, MA: Kluwer-Nijhoff.

Brinkerhoff, R. W., Brethower, D. M., Hluchyj, T., & Nowakowski, J. R. (1983b). *Program evaluation: A practitioner's guide for trainers and educators—Sourcebook/casebook*. Boston, MA: Kluwer-Nijhoff.

Byford, E. M. (1979). Mainstreaming: The effect on regular teacher training programs. *Journal of Teacher Education*, **30**(6), 23–24.

Carri, L. (1985). Inservice teachers' assessed needs in behavioral disorders, mental retardation, and learning disabilities: Are they similar? *Exceptional Children*, **51**, 411–416.

Cartwright, G. P., & Cartwright, C. A. (1973). Early identification of handicapped children: A CAI course. *Journal of Teacher Education*, **24**, 128–134.

Chapey, G. D., Pyszkowski, I. S., & Trimarco, T. A. (1985). National trends for certification and training of special education teachers. *Teacher Education and Special Education*, **8**, 203–208.

Christopolos, F., & Valletutti, P. (1972). A noncategorical and field-competency model for teacher preparation in special education. *Journal of Special Education*, **6**, 115–120.

Coulter, W. A. (1985). Implementing curriculum-based assessment: Considerations for pupil appraisal professionals. *Exceptional Children*, **52**, 277–281.

Council for Exceptional Children. (1976). *Guidelines for personnel in the education of exceptional children*. Reston, VA: Author.

Flanagan, J. (1962). *Measuring human performance*. Pittsburgh, PA: American Institutes for Research.

Ganschow, L., Weber, D. B., & Davis, M. (1984). Preservice teacher preparation for mainstreaming. *Exceptional Children*, **51**, 74–76.

Geiger, W. L. (1983). *1983 National directory of special education teacher preparation programs.* Washington, DC: National Information Center for Handicapped Children and Youth.

Gillung, T. B., & Rucker, C. H. (1977). Labels and teacher expectations. *Exceptional Children,* **43**, 464–465.

Gilmore, J. T., & Argyros, N. S. (1977). *Special education certification: A state of the art survey.* Albany, NY: The State Education Department, Office for the Education of Children With Handicapping Conditions.

Goldhammer, K., Rader, B. T., & Reuschlein, P. (1977). *Mainstreaming: Teacher competencies.* East Lansing, MI: Michigan State University, College of Education.

Graden, J. L. Personal communication, April 24, 1985.

Hart, V. (1972). *A team teaching practicum for teacher preparation in multiple handicaps.* Nashville, TN: George Peabody College for Teachers. (ERIC Document Reproduction Service No. ED 101 502)

Heller, H. W. (1982). Professional standards for preparing special educators: Status and prospects. *Exceptional Education Quarterly,* **2**(4), 77–86.

Heward, W. L., Cooper, J. O., Heron, T. E., Hill, D. S., McCormick, S., Porter, J. T., Stephens, T. M., & Sutherland, H. A. (1981). Noncategorical teacher training in a state with categorical certification requirements. *Exceptional Children,* **48**, 206–212.

Hobbs, N. (1975). *The futures of children.* San Francisco, CA: Jossey-Bass.

Idol-Maestas, L., Lloyd, S., & Lilly, M. S. (1981). A noncategorical approach to direct service and teacher education. *Exceptional Children,* **48**, 213–220.

James, L. (1984). Lieberman comments on licensing trend. *Newsletter of the Minnesota Association for Children with Learning Disabilities* (pp. 6–7).

Knight, M. F., Christie, L., Egner, A. N., Paolucci, P., & Bates, B. J. (1976). Rate of task completion for evaluating and monitoring a field-based graduate training program. In L. E. Fraley & E. A. Vargas (Eds.), *Behavior research and technology in higher education* (pp. 99–114). Gainesville, FL: University of Florida, Department of Psychology.

Lakin, K. C., & Reynolds, M. C. (1982). Public Law 94-142 as an organizing principle for teacher education curricula. In B. L. Sharp (Ed.), *Dean's grant projects: Challenge and change in teacher education.* Washington, DC: American Association of Colleges for Teacher Education.

Mackey, C. C., Jr. (1980). Interstate certification and special education. *Teacher Education and Special Education,* **3**(2), 20–26.

Nelson, C. M., Berdine, W. H., & Boyer, J. R. (1978). The evolution of a non-categorical competency-based special education methods course. *Journal of Special Education Technology,* **2**(2), 37–46.

Newhouse, J. (1981). A cross-disciplinary special education preparation program: An undergraduate experimental model. *Journal of Teacher Education,* **32**(4), 38–41.

Patton, J. M., & Braithwaite, R. L. (1980–1981). PL 94-142 and the changing status of teacher certification/recertification. *Yearbook of Special Education* (6th ed.) (pp. 157–160). Chicago, IL: Marquis Academic Media.

Pierce, M. M. (1981). The responsive teacher program in Vermont. *Journal of Special Education Technology,* **4**(1), 57–62.

Pugach, M., & Lilly, S. M. (1984, February). *Reconceptualizing support services for classroom teachers: Implications for teacher education.* Paper presented at the 36th Annual Meeting of the American Association of Colleges for Teacher Education, San Antonio, TX. (ERIC Document Reproduction Service No. ED 240 079)

Redden, M. R. (1976). *An investigation of mainstreaming competencies of regular elementary teachers.* Unpublished doctoral dissertation, University of Kentucky, Lexington.

Redden, M. R., & Blackhurst, A. E. (1978). Mainstreaming competency specifications for elementary teachers. *Exceptional Children,* **44**, 615–617.

Reynolds, M. C. (1973). *Delphi survey: A report of rounds I and II.* Reston, VA: Council for Exceptional Children.

Reynolds, M. C. (1979). Categorical vs. noncategorical teacher training. *Teacher Education and Special Education,* **2**, 5–8.

Reynolds, M. C., Birch, J. W., Grohs, D., Howsam, R., & Morsink, C. V. (1980). *A common body of practice for teachers: The challenge of PL 94-142 to teacher education.* Washington, DC: American Association of Colleges for Teacher Education.

Ryor, J. (1977). Integrating the handicapped. *Today's Education,* **66**(3), 24–26.

Schubert, M. A., & Glick, H. M. (1981). Least restrictive environment programs: Why are some so successful? *Education Unlimited,* **3**(2), 11–13.

Sharp, B. L. (Ed.). (1982). *Dean's grant projects: Challenge and change in teacher education.* Washington, DC: American Association of Colleges for Teacher Education.

Shores, R. E., Cegelka, P. T., & Nelson, C. M. (1973). Competency based special education teacher training. *Exceptional Children,* **40**, 192–197.

Smith, J. E., Jr., & Schindler, W. J. (1980). Certification requirements of general educators concerning exceptional pupils. *Exceptional Children,* **46**, 430–432.

Smith, R. M., & Neisworth, J. T. (1975). *The exceptional child: A functional approach.* New York: McGraw-Hill.

Smith-Davis, J., Burke, P. J., & Noel, M. (1984). *Personnel to educate the handicapped in America: Supply and demand from a programmatic viewpoint.* College Park, MD: University of Maryland, Institute for the Study of Exceptional Children and Youth.

Smith-Davis, J., Morsink, C., & Wheatley, F. W. (1984). *Quality in personnel preparation for education of the handicapped: The baseline book.* Vienna, VA: Dissemin/Action.

Stephens, T. M., Blackhurst, A. E., & Magliocca, L. A. (1982). *Teaching mainstreamed students.* New York: Wiley.

Stephens, T. M., & Hartman, A. C. (1978). Inservice education: Its murky past and uncertain future. *Viewpoints in Teaching and Learning,* **54**(4), 1–3.

Stephens, T. M., & Joseph, E. A. (1982). Decategorizing teacher preparation in special education. *Education and Treatment of Children,* **5**(4), 395–404.

Teacher Education Division [TED]. (1986, January 22). *The validation of quality practices in personnel preparation for special education* (Special Document for TED members). Reston, VA: Council for Exceptional Children, TED.

Vallecorsa, A. L. (1983). Cross-categorical resource programs: An emerging trend in special education. *Education,* **104**, 131–136.

Wang, M. C. (1981). Mainstreaming exceptional children: Some instructional design and implementation considerations. *Elementary School Journal,* **81**, 195–221.

Wang, M. C. (1983). *A college–school collaborative model for personnel preparation.* Pittsburgh, PA: University of Pittsburgh, Learning Research and Development Center.

Wang, M. C., & Birch, J. W. (1984). Comparison of a full-time mainstreaming program and a resource room program. *Exceptional Children,* **51**, 33–40.

Weaver, W. T. (1971). The DELPHI forecasting method. *Phi Delta Kappan,* **52**, 267–271.

Ysseldyke, J. E., & Algozzine, B. (1982). *Critical issues in special and remedial education.* Boston, MA: Houghton Mifflin.

Noncategorical Special Education: Models for Research and Practice

MAYNARD C. REYNOLDS and K. CHARLIE LAKIN

University of Minnesota

Abstract—This chapter concerns noncategorical programming for mildly handicapped children. It provides a critical summary of problems in contemporary approaches to child classifications and program organization in special education, as well as a review of alternative procedures. Several strategies for attempting to reform the classificatory and delivery systems are offered, with most attention focused on what is termed a "waiver for performance" approach. It is suggested that recent research on the effectiveness of instruction and schools provides a new and promising basis for improving programs for mildly handicapped students both in regular and in special education.

To consider the topic of noncategorical special education it is necessary to address general issues about the differential diagnosis of children. In special education, that has always been a very difficult problem—in both conceptual and practical terms. Differential diagnosis of children is a very important activity, for the way children are classified dictates much of special education program organization, funding, and teacher preparation; it determines which students are legally entitled to receive special education and related assistance, and it may influence the kinds of assistance they will receive and where they will receive it.

Earlier reviews (Heller, Holtzman, & Messick, 1982; Hobbs, 1975, 1980) and other papers in this volume offer evidence that the present methods of classifying children for special education are inadequate, making it difficult to compile research findings, leading to illogical statistical variances among the states in the prevalence of disabilities, and, far too often, to "special" treatments that are in no way specifically related to diagnostic classification. It does not appear that the special education system is evolving toward more specific and valid categories. To the contrary, there may be a rising turn against the whole process of categorization. The number of schools using mixed category, noncategorical, or cross-categorical programs is rising. In a one-year period, from the 1981–1982 to the 1982–1983 school years, the number of noncategorical teachers employed in special education programs in the United States rose from 16,177 to 25,305 (U.S. Department of Education, 1985).

In this chapter, we examine ideas relating to noncategorical approaches to special education, especially for mildly handicapped students.[1] In this venture, it is necessary to examine all of education for two reasons: first, because special education for mildly handicapped students exists primarily as a function of what is left undone at any given time by regular education, that is, mildly handicapped students are, in the vast majority of cases, drawn from the ranks of those students who are not succeeding in regular education; and second, because through implementation of the "least restrictive environment" principle of PL 94-142, most mildly handicapped students receive significant portions of their schooling in regular education classes. We have also chosen to examine a broad range of ideas about differentiations in school programs and change processes, including some of the political aspects. Diagnostic practices are based, in part, on tradition and political/economic forces, as well as on professional considerations. Changes are almost always controversial and, thus, political. Also considered are various issues concerning the nature of diagnostic classification and the alternative models that may be useful in attempts to bring order to a rather untidy scene. To set the context for the broad and complex review that follows, we begin with a brief historical statement.

A Brief History and a Statement of Challenge

The history of education for handicapped students can be written in at least two different ways. The first, and, probably, the most common approach, at least among researchers, is akin to finding and reporting the source of a great river and then tracking it to its broad outflow to the sea. In the field of education for children who are blind, for example, historians often cite the work of Louis Braille, inventor of the braille reading system, as a small beginning step that generated through time a broad set of educational activities in behalf of blind persons (Davidson, 1971). Such an approach to history emphasizes technical and professional developments or research and pays little attention to what was happening in general to blind persons or to the economic, social, political, and educational contexts within which developments were occurring. The descriptions pro-

[1] For the purposes of this chapter, *mildly handicapped* denotes students who frequently are classified as educable mentally retarded, learning disabled, and emotionally disturbed but not psychotic or autistic, as well as those who have physical and sensory impairments but who do not have additional severely disabling conditions. The term also encompasses students with language development problems (in their first or primary language) of less than a severe degree; many such students are classified in the schools as having language or speech problems. We believe that there is more agreement among professionals, advocates, and others about the classification of children who are severely/profoundly handicapped.

vided usually begin with a discovery, an invention, and/or research and then follow with a steady, almost linear, story of progress.

A second, and quite different, approach focuses on larger features, trends, and issues in the school and life situations of handicapped persons. Such an approach shows, for example, that hundreds of thousands of academic "laggards," a term used early in the twentieth century but also as late as 1959 (by Davies, p. 173) to characterize students who, in time, became known as educable mentally retarded or learning disabled, were excluded from the schools in the United States in early decades of the twentieth century, and that efforts to provide an education for these pupils were an important, even essential, facet of the development of contemporary special education. In this second approach, special education is seen as part of general education, whose history tells of exclusionary policies that have been (and continue to be) overturned only gradually and by very strong and persistent efforts.

In the early decades of the twentieth century, when the passage of child labor laws excluded children from industrial work, such children, and the many other children kept out of schools for failure to succeed, idled in the streets of the large cities—dangerously, some thought. This was the framework for the passage of compulsory school attendance laws in many states. Yet, schools were ill prepared to adapt to the needs of many children who came from the streets. There were several possible responses to this situation. First, schools could have accommodated the widening range of pupil characteristics through changes in organizational and instructional systems. Second, schools could have remained relatively rigid, and students who did not fit in well could have been siphoned off to special tracks, classes, or schools, or be excused, expelled, or otherwise deprived of education on the grounds that they could not benefit from regular schools. As the second response prevailed, special education for mildly handicapped students developed as a function of the limited capacity of regular schools to accommodate individual differences. In this role, special education was part of a sophisticated form of exclusion.

It is not a mere coincidence that Alfred Binet's work on intelligence testing, started at about the turn of the twentieth century in France and quickly adapted for use in the United States, was oriented to predicting which students were likely not to perform well in regular school programs (see Binet & Simon, 1914). The strategy was that students with poor prognoses would be set aside in special programs, not because of evidence that they would achieve better when taught in the special places but only because they were expected to do relatively less well than their peers in regular places. As Cronbach put it, "when ability tests became available they were used by the schools—to put it bluntly—to decide which pupils should be allowed to drop by the wayside or to vegetate in an undemanding slow classroom" (1967, p. 24).

It is noteworthy that it was the availability of the ability (IQ) test that permitted the definitions of handicapping conditions to be extended to include mental retardation early in the present century and, later, to include the category of learning disabilities. Without the intelligence test, it would hardly have been possible for the American Association on Mental Deficiency (AAMD) in 1910, when it was called the American Association for the Study of the Feebleminded, to expand the traditional system for classifying persons as retarded, which previously included only the categories "idiot" and "imbecile," to include the category "moron" (Goddard, 1910). Only by use of intelligence tests was a moron readily separable from his or her more capable peers. The society listened when Goddard (1914), after testing the entire population of a school district, concluded not just that 2% had scored in what was considered the "defective range," but that 2% were "so mentally defective as to preclude any possibility of their ever being made normal and able to take care of themselves as adults" (p. 2). From there it was a small step to segregate such students, and, as Davies noted in his 1959 revision of his classic 1930 review of the history of programs for persons with mental retardation in the United States, "the special classes, at first frankly an expedient to rid the schools of an overwhelming burden, are now recognized to have a rightful place in the educational system" (p. 173). In the more recent case of learning disabilities, it has been common practice to use IQ tests to estimate educability and then to note those children whose actual achievements fall far below what has been predicted for them; extreme cases of discrepancy have been labeled as learning disabled. The institutionalization of programs based on IQ tests and kindred procedures could not, of course, change, or make any more valid, the premises on which they were founded.

The point to note in these introductory comments is that the history of special education for mildly handicapped students is not told very well or completely in a review of research; in truth, the history includes large exclusionary aspects. So-called handicapped students have seldom been carefully classified and/or selected for programs on the basis of evidence demonstrating value for them. Much more often they have been simply "de-selected" from programs in which it has been difficult or inconvenient to serve them. Research has sometimes contributed to such de-selection processes, for example, by emphasizing simple predictive technologies rather than stressing instructional interventions and program evaluation. The contemporary educational system contains evidence of continued exclusion, showing that early beliefs about handicaps (e.g., as God's curse), genetic origins of handicaps (as the result of depravity), and the distinct and different psychological make-up of handicapped children probably have not been fully eliminated (Gardner, 1984).

In the past decade, however, the general trend in the schools of the nation has been to become more inclusive, to gradually assimilate a larger and more diverse proportion of the nation's young people into the regular schools (U.S. Department of Education, 1985). This trend is reflected in efforts to accommodate within regular classes and schools greater numbers of handicapped, minority, migrant, bilingual, and other children "at the margin." Called the *mainstreaming movement,* it is based on the principle of the least restrictive environment as expressed persuasively in court decisions *Pennsylvania Association for Retarded Children [PARC] v. Pennsylvania,* 1972) and in law (PL 94-142, 1975), and it raised with much urgency the question of how the renegotiation of relations between regular and special education should proceed. Is it necessary to retain many of the traditional categories and classification processes or can the emerging programs be less categorical, even noncategorical, while yet giving important attention to individual differences among pupils and to instruction that is adaptive to individual needs?

The basis of new efforts to include marginal students in the regular schools can be traced importantly to the *Brown v. Board of Education* decision of 1954. This decision established that separate educational facilities for different racial groups are inherently unequal and that operating schools in such separate ways is unconstitutional, specifically in violation of the equal protection aspects of the Fourteenth Amendment to the Constitution. The decision provided what Gilhool, (1976) termed the "modern source" for the "zero reject and integration imperatives" (p. 12). A link from the decision to policies on the integration of handicapped students in regular school programs was anticipated by John W. Davis, counsel for a defendant in *Brown v. Board of Education.* Davis argued as follows before the Supreme Court:

> May it please the court, I think if the appellant's construction of the Fourteenth Amendment should prevail here, there is no doubt in my mind that it would catch the Indian within its grasp just as much as the Negro. If it should prevail, I am unable to see why a State would have any further right to segregate its pupils on the ground of sex or on the ground of age or on the ground of mental capacity. (Quoted in Gilhool, 1976, p. 12)

Much has occurred to affect special education since 1954, most of which does not need to be recounted here. In principle, the United States now has a pervasive set of inclusive school systems that are dedicated to maximum integration of all students. Yet, the facts of the present situation reflect the long history of education, with special programs still quite separate in organization and still reflecting the legacy of exclusion and the tendency to classify children into quite narrow categories.

Writing in a somewhat different context, Robins and Helzer (1986) have this to say about a proper classification system: If a class or category

> has the same pattern of symptoms across cases and over time and is associated with known precursors, leads to the predictable degrees of impairment if untreated, and responds to specific treatments, the chances that it is a valid diagnosis are greatly increased. (p. 427)

Special education classification systems are not very impressive or valid when judged in this framework. The patterns of organization for special programs and systems of student classification vary remarkably from one state to another (Comptroller General, 1981). When systems of classification are ostensibly the same (i.e., use the same categories), the state-by-state variations in prevalence contravene any plausible distribution of phenotypes (Algozzine & Korinek, 1985; Glass, 1983; U.S. Department of Education, 1985). Evidence supporting specific links between diagnostic classification and instruction in special education is lacking (Heller et al., 1982; New York City Commission on Special Education, 1985), yet, massive amounts of time and money are spent on these procedures (Ysseldyke & Algozzine, 1983; Ysseldyke & Thurlow, 1983). All manner of arguments, in and out of the courts, challenge contemporary child study procedures and placements and the programs based on them *PARC v. Pennsylvania,* 1972; Stainback & Stainback, 1984; Wang & Reynolds, 1985). Legislators worry about the burgeoning size and costs of special programs for mildly handicapped students, especially for students assigned to the learning disability category, a category that seems to have few definable limits.

In his review, Hobbs warned that "nothing less than the future of children is at stake" (1975, p. 1) in the ways children are classified and placed in school programs. He did not see the use of traditional special education classifications as the innocuous but necessary bureaucratic requirement for funding purposes that some contend it to be; rather, he saw it as an impediment in the efforts to help children in need. He later summed up the traditional approaches of schools to the classification and placement of children as "a major barrier to the efficient and effective delivery of services to them and their families" (1980, p. 274).

Hobbs (1975) proposed that child study processes be directed to decisions about the services needed by children, with a de-emphasis on the children's "deficiencies" and more emphasis on the instructional interventions and related services likely to be helpful to them. Categorical funding systems, he proposed, should be linked to the services provided rather than to placement of children in categories. For example, in Hobbs's view, reimbursement might involve paying a set number of dollars per hour of tutoring in braille, for psychological testing, or for one-on-one tutoring in reading, or even for two square meals a day if that were what a child needed. Thus, specific services rather than a labeled child would trigger the flow of dollars. A school district's use of reimbursable services could be contained by prescribing levels of cost sharing—perhaps adjusted according to the wealth of a district—among local, state, and federal governments.

A study conducted by a National Academy of Sciences (NAS) panel (Heller et al., 1982) was prompted by a request from the Office of Civil Rights, U.S. Department of Education, to investigate the disproportional rates of placement of minority children and males in special education programs. Although the panel found the rate of placement of black children in classes for educable mentally retarded pupils to be about three times higher than for white children (Heller et al., 1982), it quickly identified the problem as much broader than that of disproportional placements. The NAS panel took a conservative position on child classification, stipulating that "it is the responsibility of the placement team that labels and places a child in a special program to demonstrate that any differential label used is related to a distinctive prescription for educational practices . . . that lead to improved outcomes" (p. 94). Weighing current practice against such a standard, it concluded the "we can find little empirical justification for categorical labeling that discriminates mildly mentally retarded children from other children with academic difficulties" (p. 87). The NAS panel went on to stress the need for important changes that would improve prereferral, referral, and placement systems for total school systems, not just for special education.

A serious response to the issues raised by Hobbs and the NAS panel would require the transformation of the child study and placement systems throughout the nation, probably toward something less categorical, in a traditional sense, than present practices. But, this is not to say that the change process would be simple. Because professional and advocacy organizations have important roles in setting policies regarding the classification of children and in organizing school programs, they would play equally important roles in considering changes. Indeed, the survival of traditional classification systems probably lies as much in the organizations' demarcations of professional boundaries as in the consistent application of procedures in differential diagnosis.

The acceptance of a category of pupils, for example, as being learning disabled has created collateral enterprises of teaching, teacher supervision, child assessment, teacher training, advocacy, product development, research and scholarly writing, and professional organization. Such enterprises are (or, at least, are often perceived to be) dependent upon the retention of that particular category of pupils. This parallelism of classificatory systems and professional and advocacy activities greatly complicates the problems of restructuring the field, particularly among groups that feel, often correctly, that they have reached their present status only through hard-fought efforts. Advocates often believe that the children for whom they have advocated and won increased special education services actually form a discrete subpopulation. But, the potential resistance of professional and advocacy organizations not withstanding, there can be little question that the way this society has approached the education of mildly handicapped students needs careful reconsideration. Indeed, there is an urgent need for such reconsideration for reasons going well beyond the problems intrinsic to traditional special education programs.

There are forces operating to promote change, of course. The maintenance of discrete categorical programs is costly in many ways, especially in rural areas (Sage & Fensom, 1985). Also to be considered are a rising number of professional voices expressing intellectual and moral frustration about the current required systems of classification, which continue to be operated even against evidence of nonvalidity (Algozzine & Korinek, 1985; Glass, 1983; Kavale & Mattson, 1983; Lilly, 1986; Reynolds, 1984; Wood & Lakin, 1982; Ysseldyke & Thurlow, 1983).

The Natural Limits of Contemporary Special Education

Additional urgency for reexamining contemporary special education delivery systems, specifically including a search for new models of categorizing children, derives from a clearly predictable future increase in the number and proportion of school-age children who are at risk of being placed in special education programs. A number of socioeconomic factors, described in greater detail below, will contribute to this growth. These factors suggest that millions of children with academic and social problems will be added to the roles of public schools in the near future.

Population Growth

Total school populations will grow substantially during the rest of this century. In analyzing the future demands to be placed on special education programs in the United States, it is important to begin by noting the growing size of the general school-age population. Since the passage of PL 94-142 in 1975, states and localities have been greatly aided in their abilities to fund expanded special education programs by a substantial decrease in the size of the nation's population of school-age children and youth. In 1975, there were approximately 51 million children and youth of school age in the United States; a decade later there were 44 million. This demographic shift created a particularly favorable environment for meeting the increased costs, space requirements, and staffing of special education in the decade after the passage of PL 94-142. These conditions, however, are now changing. It is estimated by the Bureau of the Census that, by 1995, there will be over 48 million children of school age (5–17 years old) in the United States. By the year 2000, the total number of school-age children (an estimated 50 million) will have returned almost to the 1975 level (U.S. Bureau of the Census, 1982, 1983).

The figures cited above would, in themselves, suggest substantial pressure on districts to find the resources necessary to serve a growing special education population while, for the first time since the passage of PL 91-142, also serving a growing regular education population. Raising the resources to provide a larger version of the contemporary education system will pose enough of a problem for districts given the current social and economic climates (e.g., general resistance to increasing the taxes that support schools, particularly among the 63% of all households that do not contain children; growing costs and pressure to provide services for the rapidly growing population of older citizens; a large federal budget deficit); however, the nature of the problem to be faced by schools in the near future will be considerably more complex.

The 50 million school-age children in the year 2000 will be significantly different from the school-age children of 1975. Rising rates on socioeconomic variables that operate as predictors of children being identified as mildly handicapped and low in academic achievement suggest that a higher proportion of children will be considered handicapped in the year 2000. Some of the evidence for this conclusion is briefly summarized below.

Identification as Handicapped and Minority Children

Minority children are currently much more likely to be identified as mildly handicapped and minority enrolments in U.S. schools will continue to grow at a substantially higher rate than those of white pupils. For example, according to the Office of Civil Rights of the U.S. Department of Education (1982), while 4.7% of white school children were identified as mildly handicapped (learning disabled, mildly retarded, or emotionally disturbed) in 1980, 7.2% of black children were so identified. Because the population of minority children and youth is growing far more rapidly that that of white children, these statistics have implications for the future size of special education populations. In 1970, 15.2% of U.S. children below 18 years of age were non-white; in 1980, 17.4%. By 1990, it is projected that 19.3% of U.S children below the age of 18 will be minority children, by 2000, over 21% (U.S. Bureau of the Census, 1981, 1983). In 1980, the fertility rate (live births per 1,000 women between 15 and 44 years old) for white women was 65. For non-white women it was 89 (National Centre for Health Statistics, 1981). By far the fastest growing demographic segment of the United States population is Hispanic (growing by over 50% between 1970 and 1980). This subpopulation has a high proportion of children participating in bilingual, migrant, special, or Chapter 1 education programs.

It is important to note that relatively high proportions of minority children in today's schools have remedial academic needs that exist irrespective of whether they are identified as handicapped. As an example of these needs, in the 1981 National Survey of Children, 39% of black children versus 16% of white children were identified by their teachers as "needing remedial reading" instruction (Child Trends, 1985). That these needs can be attributed to complex social and economic conditions does not diminish them, nor does it diminish the responsibility that educational institutions have and will continue to have for responding effectively to them.

In sum, if one assumes stability in the current disproportional assignment of minorities to special education as mildly handicapped in the future, special education programs will need to continue to grow more rapidly than the currently expanding regular education programs. If one assumes little or no growth in special education, it is clear that new alternative programs or improved effectiveness among existing programs will be necessary to meet the growing needs.

Children in Poverty

Children from poor families are currently much more likely to be identified as needing remedial instruction or as being mildly handicapped, and the number of children living in poverty conditions is increasing. In the 1981 National Survey of Children (Child Trends, 1985), teachers indicated that 35.1% of the sampled school children in families with an income of less than $10,000 needed remedial reading and that 16.7% were "slow learners" or "learning disabled." In contrast, teachers of sampled children in the median family income range of $20,000–$35,000 identified 12.3% of pupils as needing remedial reading, and 7.4% as being slow learners or learning disabled (Child Trends, 1985). Because of the substantial growth in the proportion of our nation's children living in poverty (in 1980, the poverty level was an annual income of $9,287 for a family of four), the association between growing up in poverty and the perceived need for remedial and/or special educational services appears to imply a greater future demand for special education and similar educational services. In 1970, 14.9% of children below 18 years of age were living below the poverty level; by 1981, that percentage had increased to 19.5% (U.S. Bureau of the Census, 1982). In 1980, ninety women per 1,000 women in the 18–44 age range living in families with incomes under $10,000 gave birth to children. This rate was dramatically higher than the fifty-six women (in the same age range) per 1,000 families with incomes over $20,000 who gave birth to children. Relatedly, 9.2% of women 18–44 years of age who had not finished high school gave birth to children in 1980 as compared with 6.1% of women having graduated from college (U.S. Bureau of the Census, 1982). There have been some recent fluctuations in the total percentage of the total U.S. population living in poverty, but the data suggest that the number of children living in poverty, already high, has continued to increase.

Other Factors

Other factors that have a less well-documented, but probable, effect on the likelihood of increased special education or remedial service placements include (a) increasing proportions of children under 18 years of age living with one or fewer natural parents—from 15% in 1970 to 25% in 1982; (b) increasing proportions of children whose mothers are employed—from 32% in 1970 to 50% in 1982; and (c) increasing survival of babies of low birth weight (below 3 lb 4 oz)—from 28% living one year beyond birth in 1960 to 52% in 1980—and the associated incidence of severe congenital abnormality and/or development delay of low birth weight children when compared to normal children (12% vs. 2%; Zill, 1985).

Because the variables described above are highly interrelated (e.g., minority children tend to be poor children), it is difficult to project accurately what would be the future special education enrolment in the absence of modified standards of pupil identification and placement. Suffice it to say that, should current practices be projected into the future, they would create a demand for special education services that could be considerably larger than at present in terms of total pupils, proportion of pupils receiving special education, total costs, and proportion of total school budgets allocated to special education and related services. These costs must be carefully weighed against the society's willingness to expand its commitment to such children, particularly in light of competing interests such as those of the growing regular education populations, aging populations, and the sizable majority of households without children. Particularly, given the lack of efficacy data to support the value of many present programs, social support should not be naively anticipated. Indeed, in the absence of sufficient reason to count on support for expanding special education for mildly handicapped students (in some places already evident in limitations, or "caps" on children identified as learning disabled), perhaps the questions policy makers and educators ought to be thinking about now are (a) How can existing resources be used most efficiently to fulfill the intended purposes of special education for mildly handicapped students?; or (b) How will decisions be made about who will and who will not be helped should a state of educational triage be forced by inadequate funding for special education and other categorical programs? We propose to examine ideas and research relating to the first question in anticipation of avoiding the second.

Effective Schooling for Mildly Handicapped Students

A major movement for the general improvement of educational programs is underway that seems to hold possibilities for considerable benefit to mildly handicapped students. According to Cross (1984), during the 1980s there have been (by the end of 1984) about thirty national reports and nearly 300 state task force reports on improving the general quality of education. This is a special period in American education (not unique, but special). Reform is in the air, there is a sense that we must somehow improve what we are doing.

Much of the educational reform being proposed appears to focus on making instruction more demanding and more uniform for all students. Public officials are calling for higher standards. This focus is not improper; many current curricula have been watered down and many students have not been challenged. But such a focus is not sufficient. There is danger that the call for higher standards will cause a concentration of effort and resources on and a commitment to only gifted students. In a seminal report, international in scope, Coleman and Husen (1985) recorded a belief that, if intensification of education takes place mainly through "increasing demands on students, without changes that affect either motivation or environmental constraints that inhibit achievement, it also brings with it increased failures" (p. 67). It is critical that standards be based on the expectation that schools will provide valuable, equitable, and integrated educational opportunities to pupils of all backgrounds and aptitudes.

Knowledge-Based School Reform

Despite serious questions about what some reformers would have the schools become and to what children they would direct scarce resources, we find some aspects of the current school reform movement(s) to be encouraging; among these are the enthusiasm and concern generated. But concerns for education can be transient and cyclical (we have had enthusiastic efforts at school reform in every decade since the end of the Second World War). Two things bode well for the current reforms, however. First, they are examining the foundation of what schools should be expected to accomplish in this society; and, second, they are coming on the heels of a decade of active inquiry about what factors are associated with relatively more or less effective educational programs.

In the past, educators have shown optimism for almost any innovation and have adopted methods and materials based solely on the testimony of perceived experts. However, it is now possible to undertake educational improvement efforts on a promising base of research. Before proceeding to a discussion of that research, we touch briefly on the important topic of outcomes. What should be the outcomes of education? What outcomes are of such importance as to justify special forms of education when ordinary procedures are not successful?

The Right to Education: The Cultural Imperatives

In *Brown v. Board of Education* (1954), the Supreme Court's unanimous decision outlined clearly why the right to education must exist in this society and what the focus of schooling should be in response to that right. Education, the Justices agreed,

> is required in the performance of our most basic responsibilities. Today it is the principal instrument in . . . preparing [the child] for later . . . training, and in helping [the child to] adjust normally to his environment. In these days, it is doubtful that any child may reasonably be expected to succeed in life if he is denied the opportunity of an education. (*Brown v. Board of Education*, 1954, p. 484)

The first essential purpose of schooling is to respond to the individual's learning needs in performing "the most basic responsibilities of [his/her] society" (*Brown v. Board of Education,* 1954, p. 484). These basic responsibilities can be referred to as the "cultural imperatives," the essential skills of contemporary social living. These are the domains in which educators are expected to be extremely persistent in their teaching efforts.

The term cultural imperatives was used by the late George Stoddard (1961) in contrast to what he termed the "cultural electives." In modern America, we might say that language development is a cultural imperative—at least as important to survival in a complex culture as calcium is for bones. We would not say that learning to play the piano is a cultural imperative, but it is a cultural elective. The imperatives are important for everybody and are to be treated insistently and persistently by educators; the electives, on the other hand, are for individual selection. This leads to the questions: Are there cultural imperatives in our society, and what are they?

Several perspectives are helpful in answering the questions about cultural imperatives, and one of them comes directly from the field of special education. What aspects of learning by children in our society seem so important that we take extraordinary steps to provide special help when learning is proceeding badly? That question can be answered with fair precision using data from special education. More than 10 billion dollars a year is spent in support of special education in the United States for children showing difficulties in these areas:

- — basic literacy and communication skills (reading, speaking, listening, arithmetic, etc.)
- — social behavior (cooperative, nondestructive, law-abiding behavior, good citizenship, etc.)
- — self-help (toileting, feeding, dressing, etc.)
- — economic efficiency (economic usefulness at home, self-support, employability, etc.)
- — health (physical stamina, good nutrition, safety, mobility, etc.)

A second perspective is provided by examining statements by major policy commissions and boards, those responsible for setting policies for the schools. In a review of such statements in the United States, Birch and Johnstone (1975) found that "themes involving home, health, personal development, citizenship, human relations and self-support" (pp. 29–30) were dominant.

The similarity of the lists of imperatives generated by policy makers and derived from special education is striking. Almost identical results are observed from a third perspective, curricula created for severely handicapped students (Brown, Nietupski, & Hamre-Nietupski, 1976). In this case, the curriculum makers necessarily orient themselves to the most basic or ultimate requirements for survival in a complex culture. Persons least likely to thrive in our society are those who are illiterate, ineffective in communications, unable to cooperate in and contribute to group life, unable to provide for their own physical needs, and noncontributive in an economic sense. It is to promote learning in these domains that we operate the most basic parts of the public school system and supplement that system with a special system when necessary.

Summarizing across these several perspectives, it can be proposed that the cultural imperatives in the late twentieth century in the United States include (a) life maintenance skills, such as self-help skills (dressing, toileting), health (hygiene, nutrition), safety, and consumerism; (b) basic literacy skills, such as reading, arithmetic, and language; (c) social skills, as demonstrated in acceptable group behavior and cooperation; and (d) orientation toward self-development (motivation to learn, desire to be independent, skills involved in self-management and economic usefulness). We believe that schools are responsible for focusing efforts in these areas of cultural imperatives for all students. In considering classification (categorical) systems to be used in the schools, it will be necessary, we believe, to attend to students who show difficulties in these areas. It probably will not be necessary to use special classification systems for students who have difficulties learning to play the piccolo or to use a cross-cut saw, but attention will need to go to those who fail to learn to read, to toilet themselves, or to behave acceptably in group life. If, as proposed later, attention were to shift to direct curriculum-based measures as a preferred approach to diagnosis and classification of students, these would be the general variables of prime importance—the cultural imperatives.

Because academic skills are such basic tools in our culture, and because they tend not to develop incidentally from experience outside of school, educators have a particular responsibility to teach them effectively. Much is known about the conditions under which their development occurs; this knowledge base has grown out of research on those instructional practices and environmental and curricular features of classrooms and schools which are associated with variations in academic attainment by students in different settings. This research, and related work in development and dissemination, are at only embryonic stages but already have shown power to affect the rates of children's learning. Given the absence of evidence that academic attainments of mildly handicapped students are a function of a different set of factors than the attainments of nonhandicapped students, parsimony would require attention to this research's potential to serve as a general foundation for improving the teaching and learning of mildly handicapped students. So far, this knowledge and literature have not been widely included in discussions about special education programs, although they are beginning to be (see Algozzine & Maheady, 1986). (See also the report of the broad evaluation of mixed category programs as conducted in Pennsylvania [Sage & Fensom, 1985]. In that study, it was concluded that most mixed category programs were working well and, that when they were not, it was most likely the result of "other factors" that would operate negatively in any program.)

In following sections, we summarize the effectiveness literature, examine its implications for restructuring the education of mildly handicapped students as part of renegotiated arrangements between regular and special education, and present ideas for future research—especially those related to models for revising categorical approaches to special education.

Predictors of Educational Effects

The effectiveness literature has been widely accepted as a practical basis for improving education, possibly for the following reasons. First, there is widespread acceptance of the idea that pupil achievement in basic academic skills is *the* important dependent variable in educational research. The effectiveness research has focused on academic skills. Second, this research tends to focus on independent variables that are alterable in the school or classroom. The value of independent variables that are associated with pupil achievement but that can be manipulated by educators is greater than those over which educators have relatively little control (e.g., IQ, family background, class size). Third, both independent and dependent variables in this research tend to be highly satisfying to the common sense of researchers, educators, and the general public.

A number of models for structuring the effectiveness literature for use by teachers have become very popular. For example, Hunter's (1980) model transforms much of this body of research into guiding principles of teaching, which can be scanned quickly by teachers to facilitate principled approaches to planning, conducting, and evaluating instruction. The model serves to bring a scattered knowledge base into a convenient, quite coherent, and usable form. It adds little to the knowledge base, but it makes the base teachable and usable.

Before summarizing the findings of the effectiveness research, it is important to note that these studies, individually and collectively, have limitations. For example, usually the individual research projects were conducted in short periods of time and, thus, do not yield clear evidence of long-term effects. Some of the research compares only the extremes of effective and ineffective schools or schools that are very different in the aptitudes of their students. Much of this research overlooks individual pupil variability on the dependent measures. It could, therefore, be argued that relevance of this literature to mildly handicapped students has not been demonstrated. On the other hand, and at least equally important, neither has the irrelevance of this literature to mildly handicapped students been demonstrated.

The effectiveness research, it must be recognized, is associative, not causal. Do well-ordered classrooms produce higher achievement or do the requirements of higher achievement cause well-ordered classrooms?

Finally, it should be recognized that the literature itself does not define precise action; the action must be inferred. For example, virtually all reviews conclude that the amount of time students spend directly engaged in educational tasks is positively associated with higher achievement, but the value of suggestions like Tomlinson's (1981) that schools use parent volunteers and aids to increase academic engagement can only be inferred. Nevertheless, we are greatly encouraged by the rich literature on successful efforts to increase in classrooms those conditions which are generally predictive of increased pupil attainment.

In preparing this summary, we benefited greatly from the prior research synthesis efforts of Berbow (1980); Berliner (1982); Block (1984); Brookover, Beady, Flood, Schweitzer, and Wisenbaker (1979); Brophy and Evertson (1976); Denham and Lieberman (1980); Rosenshine (1976); and Wang and Walberg (1985). If in any way this review differs from other summaries, it is in not attempting to merge individual predictors of pupil attainment into general clusters (e.g., positive classroom climate). This more generic cataloguing of studies was avoided primarily because of a sense that the research can often be most useful in efforts to increase the attainments of students (including handicapped individuals) when the variables are treated as individual, manipulable conditions that can be directly targeted for intervention.

Two specific limitations of this review should also be noted. First, it omits attention to the recurring finding that administrative variables are significant to pupil attainments. The importance of school leaders in establishing effective schools is well established, but, presumably, their efforts are manifested through conditions such as those summarized below. Second, the reader is provided with only one or two references to each variable. Referral to the reviews noted above is recommended as an introduction to the massive body of research making up the teacher/school effectiveness literature.

In keeping with the general perspective outlined above, effects have been organized here under four target areas for intervention: environmental (school, classroom characteristics); instructional (nature and extent of teaching, monitoring, and reinforcement); curricular (types, quality, and appropriateness of instructional objectives and materials); and individual (aptitude and motivation of learner). Each of these four categories of research is summarized below.

Environmental Characteristics Predicting Educational Effects

A number of environmental factors have been found consistently to be evident in successful educational environments (schools and classrooms in which students are demonstrating relatively high academic attainment).

Discipline and order. Successful educational environments operate with a basic set of generally understood, agreed upon, and enforced rules. Students know where they should be and what they must do, are expected to act on that knowledge, and are aware of the consequences of doing/not doing so (Edmonds, 1979; Rutter, Maugham, Mortimore, Ouston, & Smith, 1979).

Lack of disruptiveness. Successful educational environments tend to have lower levels of unruly and disruptive behavior than unsuccessful environments (Rollins, McCandless, Thompson, & Brassell, 1974; Weber, 1971).

Teacher directedness. Successful educational environments tend to be those in which the teacher is clearly in control of instructional activities and student behavior. What goes on in the classroom derives from the teacher's social and academic authority (Wynne, 1980).

Productivity. Successful educational environments tend to be those in which there are clear expectations, support, and monitoring of student behavior and in which positive student outcomes are stressed (Brookover et al., 1979; Rutter et al., 1979).

Teaching orientation. Successful educational environments tend to be those in which teachers spend relatively more class time in teaching and less class time in managerial, disciplinary, or other nonacademic activities (Rutter et al., 1979).

Student–teacher rapport. Successful educational environments tend to have teachers who are perceived to be empathetic and personally concerned with individual students' academic and nonacademic successes and difficulties (Rutter et al., 1979).

Instructional Characteristics Predicting Educational Effects

A number of instructional factors have been found to be associated with student achievement. They include the following.

Time available for instruction. Instruction tends to be more effective in schools in which students have relatively high amounts of time available for instruction because they miss fewer days of school (Wiley, 1976; Wiley & Harnischfeger, 1974); because instructional time is increased through monitored homework (Worsham, 1981); or because the school day/year is longer.

Academically productive time. Instruction tends to be more effective in classrooms in which academically productive time is maximized, that is, in which more time is allocated to academic tasks and relatively lower amounts are allocated to discretionary/nonproductive activities (Stallings, 1980).

Time on task. Instruction tends to be more effective in classrooms in which students spend more time actively engaged in academic tasks (Bloom, 1986; Rutter et al., 1979).

Academic Learning Time (ALT). Instruction tends to be more effective in classrooms in which more time is spent on tasks that students can perform at a high rate of success (Rosenshine & Berliner, 1978).

Ratio of students to instructors. Instruction tends to be more effective in classrooms in which greater opportunity for attention to individual instruction is provided. This can be increased by having smaller classes or by bringing additional help into the classroom (Phi Delta Kappa, 1980).

Systematic reinforcement of achievement. Instruction tends to be more effective in classrooms in which pupil achievement is systematically and publicly reinforced on an individual and group basis (Brookover et al., 1979; Wynne, 1980).

Feedback on pupil performance. Instruction tends to be more effective in classrooms in which frequent, *objective* feedback is provided to pupils on their performance and immediate, focused reviewed instruction is provided when needed (Good & Grouws, 1979; Rutter et al., 1979).

Orientation to learning. Achievement tends to be greater in classes in which students are carefully and systematically oriented to the learning task, that is, informed of the objectives and expectations of the assignment and its relation to previously learned skills and concepts (Block & Burns, 1976).

Efforts to improve instruction. Instruction tends to be more effective in schools in which staff development activities specifically related to instructional methods and classroom management are provided; activities that are school wide and focus on continuous, long-term staff development are most effective (Edmonds, 1979; Leithwood & Montgomery, 1982; Venezky & Winfield, 1979).

Increased instructional time through peer or cross-age tutoring. The use of peers in cross-age tutoring programs has been shown to produce improved academic skills among tutees but to have no consistent academic effects on tutors (Cohen, Kulik, & Kulik, 1982).

Cooperative goal structuring. Instruction tends to be more effective in classrooms in which heterogeneous cooperative groups are used as part of the instructional program (Johnson, Maruyama, Johnson, Nelson, & Skon, 1981).

Curricular Characteristics Predicting Educational Effects

A number of general curricular characteristics have been found to be associated with high student achievement. In addition, some specific characteristics of curricula within particular subject-matter domains have been shown to be related to achievement within those domains (e.g., phonics approaches to reading tend to be more effective than sight–word approaches). The following points have been observed quite consistently about the general structure and organization of curricula.

Curricula linking instruction to current academic status. A student achieves more when instruction is based on objective assessment of his or her current academic status and when there is continuity in curriculum placement as the student moves through the grade levels (Walberg, 1984).

Curricula providing frequent checkpoints of progress. Students achieve more through curricula that provide frequent checks on learning for the purposes of feedback, providing additional instruction, and planning for next steps through a sequence of skills (Evertson, 1982; Wynne, 1980).

Curricula that focus on mastery of critical basic skills. Curricula tend to be effective that focus on basic academic skills and that assure the mastery of prerequisite skills before introducing new skills/concepts (Block & Burns, 1976; Levin, 1981).

Curricula that provide direct instruction. The amount of time students spend receiving teacher-directed instruction in specific skills is positively related to their achievement (Becker, 1977).

Continuity of curricula and instructional staff. Schools in which higher continuity is maintained in the content and sequencing of curricula and in the teachers who instruct students within the curricula tend to be more effective (Wang & Walberg, 1985).

Individually paced curricula. Self-paced curricula (curricula of sequenced skills that students move through at their own rates of mastery) tend to produce overall higher rates of achievement, particularly for high- and low-achieving students (Walberg, 1984; Weber, 1971).

Modifiable Individual Characteristics Predicting Educational Effects

As noted, the literature on effective schools identifies numerous variables in the environment, curricula, or instructional system that can be altered to predictably affect pupils' academic attainments. These are presented as system factors. In addition, a number of manipulable individual characteristics also have been found to be associated with educational effects. These treatable characteristics differ from the relatively stable characteristics associated with student achievement (e.g., socioeconomic status) in that efforts by the schools can be reasonably hypothesized to affect these variables. Among these variables are characteristics that can be grouped under the categories of ability, motivation, attention, and attribution.

Ability

1. *Cognitive entry skills.* A strong predictor of a student's mastery of any particular skill is his or her prior mastery of its prerequisite skills. Indeed, cognitive entry skills are a better predictor of task achievement than IQ (Bloom, 1980; Coleman et al., 1966).

Motivation

1. *Educational orientation.* Students who have higher expectations for educational achievement tend to have higher achievement (Felixbrod & O'Leary, 1974).
2. *Reinforcement of attainment.* Students who perceive academic attainment to have relatively high relevance to their goals or aspirations tend to achieve more than other students (Gawronski & Mathis, 1965; Speedie, Hobson, Feldhusen, & Thurston, 1971).

Attention

1. *Student attendance.* Students who attend school more days and classes more hours achieve more academically (Wiley, 1976; Wiley & Harnischfeger, 1974).
2. *Attention to task.* Students who spend greater amounts of time attending to academic tasks that are appropriate to their existing skill levels are more successful in mastering those tasks (Rutter et al., 1979).
3. *Organizational skills.* Students who have been trained in organizational and study skills increase their academic achievement (Palincsar & Brown, 1984).
4. *Impulsivity.* Students who tend to respond relatively impulsively tend to do less well academically than students who are more reflective; relatively impulsive students who have been taught strategies for reflective responding tend to improve their academic performance (Messer, 1976).

Attribution

1. *Locus of control.* Students who perceive themselves to have relatively high control over their lives and *specifically take primary responsibility for their own learning* tend to achieve more in school (Stallings & Kaskowitz, 1974; Wang, 1983).

Relating Effective Schooling to Special Education

We believe that the preceding research findings are important in examining the state of practice in special education for mildly handicapped students today and in looking toward its future. It is clear that special education in its current forms (special classes, resource rooms, individual diagnoses and treatments) cannot be expanded to include all children and youth who need supplemental help in today's schools and will be even less able to subsume the growing numbers of students who may require supplemental instruction in the future.

It should also be observed that special education for mildly handicapped students in its present form often runs counter to principles of effective instruction and, thus, should not be extended even if such extension is economically and politically feasible. For example, many children enrolled in special education pull-out programs have fewer minutes of academically engaged time each day because of the time spent moving from class to class and getting down to work once they arrive in the various settings (see Doss & Holley, 1982). Undoubtedly, students in pull-out programs also experience many discontinuities in programs because different materials are used in the various settings or because the different teachers have not been able to communicate fully about coordinating the programs. Many special education students may be spending considerable time in academically nonproductive process training (e.g., Arter & Jenkins, 1979; Hammill & Larsen, 1974; Kavale, 1981). Special education classes may well have higher rates of disruption, less homework, and lower expectations for students, and/or instill in students lower expectations of themselves than in regular classes. What is relatively clear is that special education programs do not, per se, tend to produce greater academic achievement among their participants than do regular class alternatives (see Madden & Slavin, 1983).

To say that results of special programs are sometimes disappointing is not to say that alternative programs, such as mainstreaming, have better results. Indeed, there is some evidence that mainstreaming may have negative effects, as in the case of attitudes toward mentally retarded pupils (Gottlieb, Corman, & Curci, 1984; see also the entire volume relating to attitudes, edited by Jones, 1984). To hypothesize why special education tends to have effects that are, on the average, smaller and less consistent than might be expected given the increased per pupil resources allocated to it, one might well turn to the preceding predictors of academic achievement. It seems reasonable to assume that special education programs have not produced higher pupil achievement because they have not evinced greater congruence with the environmental, instructional, or curricular characteristics noted above than have the settings against which they have been compared. Conversely, it would be expected that programs that reflect the preceding factors would have better results with their students, irrespective of the classification of students or the certification status of their teachers.

An analysis of factors affecting the relative effectiveness of programs is not, of course, unambiguous in interpretation. The research findings could be used to argue that special education self-contained classrooms and resource rooms ought to be strengthened through careful attention to the effectiveness literature. Indeed, one would expect such arguments, except for what seem to be the more parsimonious ways to use this literature, in the first instance, to develop effective regular education programs in accord with the principle of the least restrictive environment. A similar application of the effectiveness literature in all special education programs is, of course, also appropriate and important.

For the future, a strategy that has obvious promise, but, so far, has been little tried, is, first, to create more effective classrooms (to make satisfactory achievement more predictable for all students) and, second, to work intensively with students who show the least progress by concentrating on the same characteristics (but as attributes of individuals) that are associated with better progress. For example, if a child has difficulty in attending to academic tasks, the problem is addressed first in the class as a whole and, second, by use of a behavior modification program or other procedures specifically targeted on increasing the on-task behavior of the individual child. The point of emphasis is that program modification related to effectiveness *can be applied both to the academic situation (environmental, instructional, curricular factors) and/or to particular children needing special help.* Increased efforts to improve the academic situations of regular classrooms could obviate the need for specialized classification and interventions for many students; individualized interventions focused on personal characteristics that enhance an individual's ability to benefit from instruction could remove the need for pull-out programs for many more. This double press for improvement, that is, on both the effectiveness of instruction in general and on characteristics of individuals who are in difficulty, could well be one of the main approaches in research and practical development for special educators in the near future. Such an approach is proposed here not as *the* solution, but as one major domain for research and as an approach to practical problems of teaching mildly handicapped pupils.

The proposal to organize efforts around the effectiveness literature is something like asking a modern Alfred Binet to start his work once more, again focusing on the prediction of academic performance, but with two limitations this time—first, that only variables permitting manipulation by teachers be used and, second, that research showing effects be the basis for selecting variables. Regular schools and special education programs constituted on such a basis would be vastly different from the present programs built mostly around concepts and attitudes associated with Binet's early work. In the next section, we outline approaches to improving the quality of research on education as well as its relevance to the schooling of mildly handicapped pupils.

Increasing the Effectiveness of Research on Mildly Handicapped Students

It is unfortunate that, in the development of special education practices, research-based justification was not required prior to the creation of categories and category-related treatments for mildly handicapped students. The failure to establish the requirement can be understood in historical terms, but it is urgently important to repair that deficiency now. In the preceding section, it was suggested that schools should de-emphasize the traditional approach to child study and focus instead on characteristics of school environments and pupils known to affect learning. An impressive array of research findings on school and instructional effectiveness was cited for use in this process; nevertheless, more and better ideas are still needed. In this section, attention is given to other starting points and strategies in designing research of the future. To begin, some quite elementary research concepts, which unfortunately are frequently overlooked, are summarized.

Definition of Classes

So far, classificatory ideas have been treated in this review in less than precise ways. To sharpen the discussion, a distinction must be made first between a class, or category (terms used interchangeably in this chapter), and a taxon. All taxons are classes, but not all classes are taxons (Meehl & Goldberg, 1982). Most classes or categories used in education are determined by setting a cutting point on variables used to describe children (Reynolds, 1984). For example, children may be classified as retarded if their IQs are below 70; students are defined as learning disabled if they show discrepancies beyond some defined magnitude between their achievements and the expectations held for them. The classes or categories resulting from such processes are not defined causally or theoretically in any significant way; and they do not identify taxons or true types of children. They are more like the class of students admitted to a particular college or course.

Many discussions of the categories of special education proceed on the assumption that the categories are true types or taxons. Occasionally, it is made to seem illegal, if not sinful, that a child is misclassified as retarded or emotionally disturbed, the assumption being that there really is a "taxon out there"—in some Platonic sense—and that the child is the victim of a poor diagnosis. To claim misdiagnosis, one would need to be able to define clearly what is a correct diagnosis, and therein lies the problem. Textbooks, too, frequently discuss causes of learning disabilities or behavior problems as if those classes were taxons, failing to recognize that, to a considerable extent, the classes are administrative conveniences with boundaries created out of political and economic considerations as much as by professional considerations. In the case of mental retardation, for example, the definition was moved a whole standard deviation on the IQ scale on the basis of a decision by a small committee in the 1973 version of the AAMD classification manual (Grossman, 1973).

A further clarification is needed to distinguish between definitions that are curriculum based and those that involve dispositional elements (Meehl, 1972). Iron is magnetizable, as some other metals are not; thus iron may be said to have the disposition of being magnetizable. In human terms, it is possible, in some cases, to order a series of dispositions or conditionals that eventuate in a particular problem. For example, consider a child who has phenylketonuria (PKU). Specifically, consider the case of an untreated PKU child who shows poor academic achievement in school (1st order), arising from limited general intelligence (2nd order), that stems from an inappropriate diet (3rd order) for a child who is a PKU genotype (4th order), which, in turn, is based on the genetic carrier status of the parents (5th order). In contrast, if the problem is defined simply at the level of poor achievement, the diagnosis could be described as curriculum based. At times, however, definitions, and, thus, classificatory decisions, are complicated by invoking certain of the conditionals or predispositional states as parts of the definition.

In the field of learning disabilities the most commonly employed definition, and the one used by the U.S. Department of Education, requires that a significant discrepancy be shown between ability (or "capacity") and achievement in a basic area, such as reading, plus evidence of "disorder in one or more of the basic psychological processes involved in understanding or in using language" (U.S. Office of Education, 1977, p. 42478). It is the reference to the underlying or basic psychological processes (meaning attention, perception, memory, etc.) that moves the definition beyond the curriculum level to the presumed predispositions (Reynolds, 1984). The learning disabilities dilemma in special education is similar to the problem encountered by the American Psychiatric Association, which, in the second version of the *Diagnostic and Statistical Manual of Mental Disorders* (DSM II) (American Psychiatric Association, 1968), defined psychoneuroses in a way that presumed the validity of the psychoanalytical view of causation. Getting out of that trap in the preparation of the third (1980) edition of the manual was a major professional *and political* challenge for the organization (Robins & Helzer, 1986). Such a challenge now faces special education.

In schools, it is very common to move from a curriculum level to a psychological level of disposition in considering educational problems. School psychologists are the chief gatekeepers for special education; they are the persons called upon to classify children as retarded, learning disabled, or emotionally disturbed. They operate mainly on the level of presumed psychological predispositions. From there, the analysis can become more complicated by moving to an organic level, which is primarily the domain of physicians. Cruickshank (1972, p. 383) illustrated that perspective and tendency when he said that learning disabilities (1st order) are "essentially and almost always the result of perceptual problems [2nd order and psychological] based on the neurological system" (3rd order and medical).

Definitions that cut across several orders of disposition are enormously complex and usually difficult to justify on the basis of clear research evidence. That is one of the reasons, quite clearly, why there has been such great difficulty in defining what is meant by learning disability, mental retardation, and emotional disturbance. The situation is made all the more complex because, often, there are no good measurement techniques to get at the variables included in the definitions.

The problems of classification for educational purposes become especially difficult when one considers several categories simultaneously and how the various categorical programs can be coordinated—for example, considering special education, Chapter 1 (for economically disadvantaged students), migrant education, and English-as-a-second-language programs. Each of these fields has its own boundaries. Federally supported migrant education programs, for example, apply only to children of families engaged in agricultural or fishing industries. By the time one considers all of the defining terms in migrant education and then tries to achieve interactions with special education, the resulting classes of children are by no means taxonic. Solutions to these problems of categorizing (or not categorizing) pupils must be addressed first through realization that the classes we deal with are not taxonic; they are administrative conveniences, greatly influenced by contextual (economic, political, etc.) factors as well as by variables relating to instructional needs. Solutions will require careful reflection on the purposes served by classification, our next topic.

Purposes of Classification

The choice of a system of classification ought to be based, above all, on the purposes to be served. As Robbins (1966) put it some years ago, the use of a classification system "implies that the category chosen is good for something" (p. 5). Being clear about purposes is especially difficult for special educators because, historically, they have turned to nonteaching professions, usually psychology or medicine, for their classificatory systems and procedures. Unfortunately, these professions often have adopted systems that offer only poor diagnostic reliability and poor applicability to educational systems. Thus, teachers often complain that many of the diagnoses performed by psychologists and physicians seem irrelevant to instructional purposes.

A general purpose of classification is to assure clear communications among researchers so that a knowledge base can be accumulated. In reporting a particular research finding, it is essential that each researcher be very clear and consistent in describing the subjects used as well as other features of the study; otherwise, later researchers will not know how to replicate the study (i.e., use similar subjects and conduct a similar study) or how to synthesize the findings with those of other researchers, and practitioners will encounter great difficulty in judging when research findings may be relevant to given practical situations. The field of special education has fallen short of minimal standards in the area of clear communication about research and domains of applicability.

One obvious place to seek progress is in the research journals. Editors should insist that research reports include clear descriptions of the subjects used and essential information on other topics. Basic information on subjects, such as age, sex, school placement, socioeconomic status, and selection criteria should be provided routinely. Giving identifying details on criteria for selection of research subjects is especially important. There is no evidence of anything near this level of precision in reporting research on mildly handicapped children. At present, the common way of identifying subjects for research on emotionally disturbed children, for example, is simply to study children who have been placed in classes for emotionally disturbed students (Wood & Lakin, 1982). MacMillan, Meyers, and Morrison (1980) discussed similar problems in research on mentally retarded children as have Keogh and MacMillan (1983) with research on learning disabled children. Indeed, textbooks that ostensibly teach professionals how to teach the child-type emotionally disturbed are based on studies of children ranging from kindergartners who are identified as being restless on their mats at nap time to hospitalized adolescents who exhibit serious disruptive and assaultive behavior. To merge the findings on the child-type emotionally disturbed from studies with such a range of subjects is meaningless in the extreme. Wood and Laken (1982) characterized the procedures for classification recorded in research reports on emotionally disturbed students as so inadequate that it would be impossible to replicate the studies. They stated that "we are deceived if we think we know about whom it is that most authors of research reports are writing" (p. 44).

Professional and research societies can help in this domain by establishing standards of subject description to facilitate the exchange of research information. It would help if relatively simple and open definitions were used for research communications, understanding that such definitions implied no necessary applicability in schools or to other settings. For example, editors of research journals addressing limited cognitive development might agree to report studies only on populations in which all members fall more than one standard deviation below the general population mean on accepted measures of general intellectual ability. To repeat, it would be necessary to state clearly that such a policy served only to set out a general domain within which research reports would be exchanged and not to define a population for special education placement or other classificatory purpose until the reliability and validity (association with differentially beneficial treatment) of the class or various subclasses were validated through research.

The Role of Classification Activity in Contemporary Education

In practical work with handicapped children, it is common to speak of three purposes of classification: (a) to specify etiology; (b) to make a prognosis; and (c) to select (and sometimes finance) a treatment (Zubin, 1967). Each purpose is discussed briefly below.

Etiology

Much of the thinking about the classification of handicapped children in the schools has been in an etiological vein; it is the so-called "medical model" at work. It assumes that there must be some biological errors involved to produce these handicapped children. However, for educational purposes, etiology usually has little or no relevance. In a study of child patients at a psychiatric facility, for example, Sinclair, Forness, and Alexson (no date) found that "use of psychiatric diagnosis in conjunction with psychoeducational test data does not appreciably translate into specific educational placements any better than the use of psychoeducational test data alone" (p. 14). In most cases, it matters very little whether a student's learning difficulties stem from brain injury or from another cause. Occasionally, etiology can influence decisions about an instructional program (e.g., if the cause of a child's low vision is a progressive illness, then the child's instructional program can be expanded to include braille, which he or she will need in the future). The facts of etiology may be relevant to the prevention of problems, but they relate to instruction only if they dictate differences in how particular children should be taught. It is of interest to note that, even in medicine and other clinical professions, there have been moves away from the so-called medical model. Robins and Helzer (1986) put it this way: "classification should arise out of observation of phenomenology and course of illness rather than out of improved etiological theories" (p. 410).

Prognosis

Attempts at predicting the long-term course of a child's disability or educational progress also have limited usefulness (Reynolds, 1984; Zubin, 1967). Teachers are employed to influence learning, not just to predict it. Teachers should be concerned with whether one approach or method of instruction will work better than another with a particular child. Thus, teachers should always be making multiple short-term prognostications for each student and then choosing the more promising instructional approach. This kind of prognostication is logically and practically different from general predictions about what to expect of a given child, and still more different from a prognosis concerning disease processes.

Allocation to (or Design of) an Instructional Program

Assignment to an instructional situation is the legitimate purpose of classification in the schools. The educator's orientation is not to the recovery from defects or prevention of pathology but to the enhancing of children's knowledge and skills. This view puts an emphasis on teaching and learning, always positively framed and in a cultural context. There is still much talk among educators about *dysfunctions, deficits, impairments,* and *disabilities,* as if these were the starting points in education and recovery from or remediation of them were the goal—but it is human development, with the competencies and breadth it gives to life, that is the goal. A teacher prevents reading disabilities, of course, by teaching reading or its prerequisites with greater resourcefulness and better effects to more children; and problems in algebra are prevented by teaching basic arithmetic more effectively. But it is the allocation of students to specific programs and to developmental rather than deficit-oriented programs of instruction, assuming there are alternatives, that is the purpose of classification in the schools (Reynolds & Birch, 1982).

Educators have not been alone, in recent years, in advancing the need for a developmental perspective. For example, Skinner (1981) stated explicitly that "if a classification is to be clinically useful, then the information it provides must enhance decision making with respect to what treatment intervention is most appropriate for a particular patient or group of similar patients" (p. 77). Kendall concluded that "in the last resort *all* diagnostic concepts stand or fall by the strength of the prognostic and therapeutic implications they embody" (1975, p. 40). Levy (1963) explicated the diagnostic processes relating to alternative treatments similarly, in these words: Diagnosis has "as its ultimate goal the provision of a basis for the anticipation of behavior . . . under various contingencies" (p. 157).

Clearly, the classification of students as handicapped will vary across professions because each offers or calls for different forms of treatment. For the educator, a student is blind when he or she must be taught to read without the use of sight (e.g., through the use of braille or optacon methods). For educators, a deaf student is one for whom the development of language and communications skills cannot be based on functional audition: instruction of deaf students must proceed through other functioning modalities. However, when other categories of handicapping conditions are considered, the situation becomes less clear. Although many other students are classified for special education purposes, it is not always obvious that the category indicates the need for a specific kind of specialized assistance, and it is for failures precisely in this domain that the field of special education has been faulted by the NAS review panel (Heller et al., 1982).

This discussion of the purposes of classification can be summed up as follows: first, it would be very helpful if scientific researchers and publishers would clarify the classification domains in which they prepare and disseminate research reports. These domains probably should be given relatively open definitions so that a wide variety of research can be reported without too much worry at the outset about boundary problems. However, it is critical that publishers of scientific reports insist on a full description of subjects used so that readers interested in replication or synthesis will be well informed. Second, it is suggested that, for educators, the appropriate purpose of classification is the allocation of students to instructional programs with the highest promise; it is assumed here that alternative programs are available or can be created. Indeed, it is the business of special education to help create alternative programs, and how children are allocated to the various programs is the issue considered here.

A Look to the Future

In this section, we consider a variety of professional and research issues and their political contexts. We do so out of the belief that educational practice for mildly handicapped children within the traditional diagnostic framework is not justified on the basis of existing evidence. Even communications about this domain are in disrepair. Differences in values and perceptions abound and are draining significant amounts of the intellectual and financial resources allocated to improving education for children and youth with mild handicaps. The problem is to find ways of breaking out of this very difficult situation that will encourage research and innovation of the most responsible kinds—which we assume to mean, in the main, that they are data-based.

The present situation in child classification for purposes of providing special education programs clearly is in need of attention. Although we know that special education per se has not been a predictor of educational attainments (Carlberg & Kavale, 1980; Madden & Slavin, 1983), we have begun to learn about some of the factors that are. In this section, we consider strategies to shift policy in directions that take fuller advantage of the present knowledge and that may involve increased sharing of responsibility among regular and special educators for programs in service for children with learning problems (Will, 1986).

Approaches to Change

A number of strategies for the amelioration of the present situation in special education for mildly handicapped students can be devised. For the purposes of this discussion, we set out three options that represent qualitatively different policy approaches and that also can be seen as fitting along a continuum of governmental intrusion into the status quo. We refer to these three strategies as the "reactive strategy," the "waivers for performance approach," and the "Food and Drug Administration (FDA) approach."

The Reactive Strategy

One possibility in facing the current challenges to the validity of special education for mildly handicapped students is simply to make reactive changes as economic, political, and other forces operate. Because the key factors in policy decisions at the present time appear to be economic (e.g., to curtail the growth in special education costs) and political (e.g., to respond to charges of racial bias in special education classification), the policy solutions deriving from the reactive approach tend to be narrowly focused, largely administrative, and considerably removed from the "level of the lesson." Examples of solutions in this context are merely to place enrolment caps on programs for learning disabled students or to use terms that are perceived to be less disparaging (at least temporarily) to classify minority students. When people complain that disproportionate numbers of minority children are being diagnosed as retarded, for example, the gatekeepers simply increase the proportion diagnosed as learning disabled (Tucker, 1980). However, such solutions seldom address the fundamental problems and, therefore, usually fail to improve the quality of practices. What is more, such solutions are particularly prone to upset the delicate balances in systems; for example, some legislators and administrators may call for a cap on the rapidly growing percentage of students labeled as learning disabled, while others call for a reduction in the number of minority students classified by the more pejorative labels. These policies are incompatible, they propose no instructional improvements, and they work out to be particularly disadvantageous for poor and minority children.

Reactive solutions may relieve temporary pressures, but, in fact, they reflect, and, in time, can only exacerbate, the kinds of problems noted. We foresee a strong possibility that caps on children labeled as learning disabled, already evident in some places, will be applied in many places in the next few years. Should this happen, presumably increased pressures would be felt to relabel large numbers of students as educable mentally retarded (the number of educable mentally retarded students decreased sharply between 1976 and 1983 as preference shifted to the use of the learning disabilities label) (U.S. Department of Education, 1985). Also, more students might be expected to be labeled as speech impaired or something else, and the labeling of children would be based even more on political and economic considerations and less on objective assessments of individuals. Teachers would be frustrated because many children with substantial needs would be left without extra assistance.

Not all reactive approaches are negative in outcome, nor can they all be considered as merely "muddling along." But such approaches leave unresolved a number of questions—among them the following:

1. PL 94-142 was passed to assure an appropriate education to handicapped students. How can the schools maintain or justify long-term public support for special education programs that have been shown to operate with few reliable technical or professional distinctions and few specific and predictable treatment effects for mildly handicapped children?
2. PL 94-142 stresses maximum inclusion of handicapped students in regular school programs. How can educators continue to advocate integration while lacking strong efforts to develop and maintain regular education programs that are powerful enough to accommodate mildly handicapped students and while working under the constraints of financial disincentives for integrated programming (Wang & Reynolds, 1985)?
3. PL 94-142 calls for appropriate diagnosis/assessment of students. How can educators justify continuing to demand that school psychologists and other gatekeepers perform functions in the classification of students that they increasingly recognize as technically, intellectually, and morally unjustifiable,

thus creating problems for children and causing the demoralization of the professional staff (National Association of School Psychologists, 1985)?

But the issues are not limited to questions of the formal defensibility of the response to PL 94-142. There are more subtle issues about the effectiveness of that response. For example, in a period of stress on cost-effectiveness, how long can support be maintained for supplemental programs that withhold service and program adaptations from students at incipient stages of difficulty that would prevent further deterioration of performance? Procedures are quite well known for improving instruction in basic academic skills at the early education and primary school levels (procedures that reduce rates of special education placements at a later time) (Lazar, Darlington, Murray, Royce, & Snipper, 1982). Most present classification and funding systems do not support these promising early interventions. In the area of personnel preparation, how can colleges and universities justify the costs of preparing teachers separately for the several categorical licenses when there is little or no evidence to indicate that the treatments they are taught to provide have any differential association with the categories of mild handicaps?

In short, the reactive strategy makes little proactive use of available research and scholarly analysis. Reactive responses are unlikely to do more than temporarily deflect existing problems. They tend to reduce pressures, but they leave solutions to other actors and to a later time. Reactive responses contribute to extreme variations in the quality of education received by mildly handicapped students by providing equal sanction and economic support to virtually any kind of program offered in the name of special education. They relegate persons and agencies in positions that imply educational leadership to a role of bursar.

The Waivers for Performance Approach

A modestly proactive strategy would be one in which governmental agencies that now regulate special education, including its required classification procedures, would grant flexibility through "waivers"[2] of regulatory requirements to selected states and communities that wish to experiment with (and carefully monitor) alternative procedures of organizing and delivering educational programs for mildly handicapped students. For example, several communities might submit plans for use of noncategorical, curriculum-based classification systems in which a student's current rate of progress (or lack thereof) in the school's curriculum would determine whether he or she received special assistance at any given time. A school district might agree to run parallel categorical identification systems (traditional and curriculum based) for an experimental period (e.g., 3–5 years), or to compare performance in the experimental system with that in a traditional program in a neighboring district to test the accountability features of the new system. Through study of the parallel systems, checks could be made to see whether the experimental system would identify all or most of the children now identified as learning disabled, emotionally disturbed, and educable mentally retarded; whether it could be equally accountable for services to them; whether it could target services on existing needs cost-effectively; whether it would lead to equal or improved academic, social, and psychological benefits to students traditionally identified as handicapped; and/or whether it could provide benefits to nonhandicapped students. It would be necessary, under the waiver for performance strategy, for the sponsoring agency to offer assurance that funding that is now provided under the various categories would not be reduced for participating districts during the experimental period. In return, districts would assure these agencies that they would not increase their special education budgets under the waiver and that all legal requirements (e.g., due process rights, preparation of Individualized Educational Programs) would be satisfied.

The waiver approach assumes that a number of responsible but different approaches to special education classification and delivery are feasible and that it would be beneficial to promote experimental trials of a number of such different ideas. The recent report on mixed category programs in Pennsylvania (Sage & Fensom, 1985) gives examples of some of the kinds of approaches to be expected. The waiver approach would require the careful consideration of proposals by state boards of education and federal officials before the granting of waivers of various policies, rules, and regulations; and that consideration would ensure deliberations on policy matters while the experimental programs operate in the schools and also give policy leaders the opportunity to decide on the kinds of outcomes data to require. Such discussions and the shift toward research on outcomes data in shaping policy would be gains for all concerned.

It would be a further gain for the waiver strategy, but more difficult politically, if experimental programs were permitted to extend to areas beyond contemporary special education. It was noted in the NAS study (Heller et al., 1982) that the distinctions between special education programs and those for disadvantaged students (such as students served in Chapter 1 programs) have little or no credibility. Ysseldyke and Thurlow (1983) have made similar observations based on their research. Most Chapter 1 programs provide tutoring for pupils whose progress in reading and/or arithmetic is slow. That is also the case in

[2]For some people, the idea of waivers may seem negative in tone. Perhaps it would be preferable to stress the enlargement of experimental programs with the waiver aspect being only incidental to the more positively framed new or experimental approaches. The term as used here is meant to reflect essentially the same federal–state relationship created in the Medicaid waiver for home and community-based services authorized in the Omnibus Budget Reconciliation Act in 1981. In giving the Secretary of Health and Human Services the authority to waive existing Medicaid long-term care standards for states wishing to establish alternative community services for people who would otherwise be institutionalized, Congress intended to facilitate placement in the least restrictive placement by not making federal Medicaid funding contingent on treatment in a Medicaid-certified institution.

many learning disability programs, which means that the distinction between Chapter 1 pupils and learning disabled pupils is marginal. It might be assumed that, under a waiver for performance strategy, programs combining the pupil assessment, teaching, and program evaluation resources of special education and Chapter 1 programs would be popular. Hopefully, experimental efforts would encompass other categorical programs as well, such as migrant education, bilingual education, English-as-a-second-language instruction, and Indian education.

If a number of school districts and states were entered into waivers for performance experiments, they could be brought together occasionally, along with external participants (e.g., university faculty, public officials, advocates, parents), to share their experiences and data. A special research community would thus be created to help summarize and disseminate results of the studies and to stimulate discussion of related policy issues.

The waiver for performance approach would put research into a central position in the identification of promising alternative practices, administrative arrangements, and means of resource allocation that respond to critical problems in categorical education programs. This strategy would offer possibilities for data-based policy and regulatory changes. Although such a strategy would encourage alternatives to current practice, it need not in any way threaten the rights of handicapped children to a free and appropriate education. Indeed, it would not involve broad changes in statutes or of regulations, only selected and time-limited waivers of regulations along with guarantees that no funding disincentives would be created for school districts trying approved new approaches.

We believe that it would be both necessary and wise for governmental agencies to be quite clear and demanding about the standards they would use in considering and granting waivers of the kinds discussed above. In many states and communities, experience is being gained under the Medicaid waivers that also apply to some handicapped children. The Medicaid waiver program has grown very rapidly and successfully, in part, we believe, because the standards for operating under the waivers were thoughtfully developed and widely disseminated. Examples of the guidelines that could be developed for special education programs conducted under a waiver strategy appear in Figure 1. We especially note the importance of observing the *rights* that handicapped children have under PL 94-142; for example, to due process, to the development of individualized plans for education, and to fair and impartial assessments. These and other rights must be protected, we believe, under any experimental trials of noncategorical programs. By establishing specific standards by which waiver applications would be assessed prior to approval, federal and state education agencies could be reasonably assured that alternative programs would pose no serious academic or social hazard for participating students. At the same time, these agencies could promote careful examination of the value of promising alternatives while still providing mildly handicapped students with the basic rights and protections afforded by PL 94-142.

FIGURE 1. Rights without labels—proposed guidelines for evaluating the appropriateness of granting a waiver of existing categorical program regulations for an experimental period.

I. General Quality of Academic Program

A. *Productivity*. Does the alternative program incorporate recognition of those factors that have been shown to be associated with academic attainment? For example, does an alternative program provide students with access to orderly and productive environments, equal or greater academic teaching time, systematic and objective feedback on performance, and well-sequenced curricula?

B. *Responsiveness*. Does the alternative have procedures and means to identify and respond to individual academic problems?

C. *Appropriateness*. Does the alternative focus equal or greater attention on areas of basic skills?

D. *Timeliness*. Does the alternative identify learning problems among the school population and allocate teaching resources to their remediation at least as quickly as or earlier than in traditional categorical programs?

E. *Generalizability*. Does the alternative attend to needs for school learning to be generalized to life beyond the schools?

II. Integration

A. *Least Restrictive Alternative*. Does the alternative assure use of the least restrictive (most integrated) setting feasible for education of the involved students?

B. *Presentation*. Does the alternative tend to present mildly handicapped students as being as normal and as competent as much as is feasible given their disabilities and/or academic deficiencies?

C. *Stigmatization*. Does the alternative provide less (or no more) stigmatization by labeling for mildly handicapped students?

III. Teaching Staff

A. *Qualifications*. Do mildly handicapped students in the alternative program receive education from teachers who are as well qualified as teachers in traditional categorical programs?

IV. Individualized Educational Programs

A. *Individual Assessment*. Does the alternative program involve the assembling of types and amounts of educationally relevant information on mildly handicapped students to permit the development of an appropriate individualized program and the monitoring of its effectiveness?

B. *Program Plans.* Does the alternative program involve the development of specific individualized goals and objectives for students?

C. *Parent Involvement.* Does the alternative program provide a means for parental involvement in planning, reinforcing, and monitoring students' educational achievements?

V. Program Outcomes

A. *Assessment Team.* Does the alternative program have an assessment plan for examining effectiveness that includes a qualified assessment team and advisory board (including regular and special educators, school administrators, parents, advocates, and qualified evaluators)?

B. *Measurement of Effects.* Does the alternative program have a planned methodology for assessing its relative effects on the educational progress of students in major curricular domains (e.g., control groups, contrast groups, rates of progress in two school districts' standardized testing programs in a one-group time series design)?

C. *Cost–Benefit.* Does the alternative program assessment plan contain a hypothesized cost–benefit (e.g., to offer equal service for less cost or improved service for equal costs) and have a reasonable strategy for comparing costs with traditional programs?

VI. Assurances

A. *Parental Choice.* Does the alternative program provide parents with the choice of selecting a traditional categorical program for their child?

B. *Eligibility.* Does the alternative program establish clear limits on the range of students who will be eligible for the program (e.g., academic abilities/readiness, behavioral standards), conditions for demission, and assurances of unbiased treatment of characteristics not specified in the eligibility standards?

C. *Due Process.* Does the alternative program contain due process mechanisms by which complaints about placement and program quality can be redressed?

The FDA Approach

If the reactive strategy were put at one end of a continuum of governmental intervention into the highly problematic status quo in special education, an aggressively proactive strategy, what we have labeled the FDA (Federal Drug Administration) approach, could be seen at the other. Whereas, at present, the role of the federal government is loosely defined, and largely limited to the disbursement of funds, in the FDA approach, the federal Department of Education would have a clearly defined obligation and commitment to use its vested authority (and budget) to promote demonstrably effective approaches to educating mildly handicapped students and to support research dedicated to that same purpose. Such a role would be analogous to that of the FDA.

Briefly stated, with respect to pharmacological products, the purpose of the FDA is to ensure that drugs made available to the public are safe and effective for their intended use and that they are properly labeled. The FDA develops standards for the initial development and testing of drugs, regulates claims made by producers of pharmaceuticals once drugs are approved, investigates reports of harmful effects of drugs and requires corrective action where warranted, and gathers information on the extent of use and effects of pharmaceutical agents. The Health Affairs branch of the FDA operates a clearinghouse of medical, scientific, and legal/policy information for health care professionals. In short, the FDA has a mandate to take the potential benefits and dangers of pharmaceutical agents very seriously and to operate in a comprehensive way in the interests of the consumers of drugs.

A strong case can be made for the potential benefits of an FDA-type model in special education, in which diagnostic and treatment practices that are ineffective, unsafe, or improperly labeled are too often exhibited. For example, it is quite clear that perceptual, perceptual-motor, optometric, psycholinguistic, multisensory, and many other treatments of learning disabilities would be found to be ineffective if the Department of Education were to apply scrutiny to their application. Many other treatments (e.g., many psychoeducational approaches to behavioral disorders) would be found to be improperly labeled in that they claim benefits that have never been demonstrated. But far from regulating the use or claims for such treatments, the Department of Education and most state counterparts reimburse their use as readily as an hour of remedial reading. It is noteworthy that the Department of Education recently published a small document entitled *What Works* (1986). With further development of that document, along with the development of complementary documents that could be entitled *What Doesn't Work* and *What Needs Substantiation,* the agency would be in a position to sanction educational practices and to assist more localized levels of government in developing and monitoring effective practices.

If the Department of Education were to take a more proactive interest in the quality of education received by mildly handicapped students, it need not limit itself only to sorting out present practices according to their validity but could involve itself in setting standards for the assessment of new curricula and training materials and for monitoring the appropriateness of claims made for approved products. An agency having such functions might be expected to have a major positive impact on the practices of professionals and the discriminating use of services by consumers.

An FDA-type role would not necessarily need to be regulatory to improve the effectiveness of special education; it could be merely informative. But it is patently wrong to argue that the federal government, which now disperses over one billion dollars annually for special education, has neither the right nor the responsibility to concern itself with how the money is used. An FDA approach would substantially modify the traditional federal government role in education by significantly increasing its intrusion into the programs of state and local governments. Note, however, that the safety and effectiveness of the pharmaceuticals monitored by the FDA have been seen as worth the intervention into the historical relation between patients and physicians.

Of course, there are limitations to an FDA approach. Unlike pills of uniform chemical composition, any treatment in special education can be claimed to be different when it is delivered by different teachers. Endless recitations of specific examples of the successes of generally ineffective practices could be used to thwart efforts to clean house in special education. The fact that educational practices traditionally have been controlled locally would not bode well for increased federal monitoring. On the other hand, it seems reasonable that, in return for the millions of dollars that federal agencies pass on to states and local schools for special education, there might be some forceful leadership at the federal level to ensure that practices are not harmful or mislabeled.

Choosing an Approach

Having presented a range of policy strategies for improving the practice of special education for mildly handicapped students, we turn to an elaboration of what we see as the most prudent directions for research and practice of the future. Aspects of the reactive strategy are appealing. Not only does the status quo always have its comforts; actually, if one comprehensively studies the literature on noncategorical programs, it is obvious that many creative alternatives to traditional special education have been developed by state and local districts that are basically muddling along, meeting the exigencies of educating mildly handicapped students as effectively as they can. Clearly, such efforts should continue; however, at the same time, it can hardly be said that toleration of such localized efforts represents adequate state or federal policy.

There is also considerable reason to argue that federal and state government should become more "FDA like," that is, more involved in differentiating between useful and unuseful practice and more active in promoting the former and discouraging the latter. Such a proactive role could be an important and helpful step in ending the "anything goes" era of special education. One very great problem is the difficulty of assembling a convincing body of evidence to support either traditional special education programs or the noncategorical alternatives to it. Indeed, noncategorical education for mildly handicapped students derives much more of its support from its place as a logical alternative to traditional practices and from the least restrictive environment principle, than from a sizable literature showing its effectiveness in its own right.

In large measure, it is this reality that makes the waiver for performance option so appealing. Its requirement of controlled experimentation on some of the important programmatic issues raised in this and other papers in this volume could be extremely important to future practices in educating mildly handicapped students. Some of the particular issues and alternatives are discussed below.

Using Appropriate Models of Child Classification

Clearly, a number of alternative methods of child classification in educational settings are available, and they need to be evaluated. Here we consider some possible options to try under controlled conditions, possibly under a waiver for performance strategy.

Curriculum-based assessment and program planning approaches evaluate student progress and prescribe academic exercises based on individual students' progress through standard curricular sequences. Such approaches are not concerned with group and grade-level comparisons but, instead, are used to monitor where a student is in a curriculum, whether he or she is progressing satisfactorily through it, and whether program modifications are needed. In terms of the levels of disposition analysis proposed earlier, curriculum-based approaches are at the first level, or at the level of the lesson; and that is the safe and appropriate level for classification where approaches at various levels of disposition removed from the level of the lesson are unproven or doubtful.

An example of the curriculum-based approach is presently provided in an experimental program in Montevideo, a small town in Minnesota. The Montevideo schools have defined their curriculum very precisely in the basic skills areas, particularly in regard to reading and arithmetic. The curriculum is segmented and sequenced; competency tests are used for each segment; pupils proceed from unit to more advanced unit in the curriculum only when they have mastered each skill or achieved necessary prerequisite knowledge. Programs are highly individualized in the sense that each child is taught at an individually appropriate level. Teachers use small-group and large-group instructional methods, as well as individual teaching. Direct instruction by teachers is common. Data showing when each child enters and exists from each unit of instruction are stored in a microcomputer. School days are numbered continuously for each new class of first graders, so that first grade covers days 1–180, second grade covers roughly days 181–360, and so on. Data on children are cumulated over the school years. Using the day numbers as markers, the teacher can call up records on the school progress of any pupil at any time. Those pupils whose progress is below the 20th percentile, for example, can be flagged easily for special attention. It is by the use of such a "progress in curriculum" criterion that the classification system becomes curriculum based. It contrasts with the system currently used almost everywhere in the United States—the identification of children as handicapped in some category as the entry to the system. A curriculum-based approach seeks data on whether children are progressing in the curriculum as the first step; the classification as handicapped usually seems irrelevant.

Actually, a parallel identification and classification system of the traditional kind is operated in Montevideo, but data assembled in Spring 1984 show that use of a simple 20th-percentile dividing line in curriculum progress would have identified all students who might otherwise have been labeled as educable mentally retarded, learning disabled, or emotionally disturbed (Peterson, Heistad, Peterson, & Reynolds, 1985; see also Tucker, 1985). All so-called handicapped children were identified in a totally unobtrusive way simply by calling for a computer printout on students whose rates of progress in arithmetic, reading, or both was below the 20th percentile (using local norms). No loss in accountability to students identified in the traditional special education categories was occurring in Montevideo, and none would have occurred by use of the new system. After being identified, of course, the diagnosis of a child proceeds into studies of cognitive abilities, family supports, and other matters that may be important and helpful in planning instruction; but the basic identification process at Montevideo is curriculum based; it is clear and relevant to instruction. The children identified are those for whom the regular school program is not working, defined in terms of pupils' rates of progress through the curriculum. The program sends up a signal showing that instruction requires modification because it is not working for some students. Attention in this system goes immediately to program modification rather than to characteristics of the child that may lead only to categorization.

The curriculum-based approach focuses mainly at the level of the lesson, on detailed specification of what a child already knows and does not know in the domains of the curriculum. It is precise about the cognitive entry characteristics necessary to the acquisition of new skills in an instructional domain (Bloom, 1980). The review by Tobias (1976) of studies in which achievements in the curriculum areas were examined as aptitudes that interact importantly with instructional procedures in the same teaching areas stands starkly alone within the aptitude-treatment-interaction (ATI) research for its emphasis on achievement variables as aptitudes, yet, it is, perhaps, the most relevant ATI research conducted to date for instructional purposes. More attention of this kind by researchers seems fully warranted.

The curriculum-based approach assumes that educators ought to be conservative about considering the supposedly underlying levels of disposition unless and until the knowledge base for such consideration is very clear. It suggests, for example, that educators and psychologists who claim that learning difficulties are embedded in underlying cognitive processing deficits or neurological problems ought to be held to a very high level of confirmation about those claims before being admitted to practice in the schools. The skepticism should be even greater if the claim is made that, by teaching for underlying processes, one achieves significant (indirect) transfer to reading skills or other curriculum areas. Findings in that context are mostly negative (Arter & Jenkins, 1979).

Curriculum-Based Approaches Within Broad-Based Instructional Systems

The preceding example of the Montevideo schools actually is not simple and is not limited to using curriculum-based approaches to child classification. The Montevideo schools have a broad, school-wide system (it encompasses all aspects of both regular and special education) of individualizing instruction for all pupils. Almost all special education students spend all of their school day in regular classrooms. Special teachers go into these rooms as co-professionals with regular teachers, but they concentrate on students who are having difficulties and need intensive, highly structured, and direct instruction by a teacher.

The total system is known as the Adaptive Learning Environments Model (ALEM), developed at the University of Pittsburgh (Wang, 1980; Wang, Gennari, & Waxman, 1985). At its core is a management system for individualizing instruction and assigning considerable self-responsibility to pupils for managing their own progress through the curriculum. It has a detailed monitoring system to reflect the degree of implementation of the model, a teacher-training system, and a parent involvement program. Systems have been worked out for coordinating the work of regular and special education teachers in developing comprehensive curricula to teach students with widely ranging levels of ability and academic status. The system focuses on teaching basic skills. The schools in Montevideo confirm an observation made by Farrow and Rogers (1983) in their field study of how local districts successfully address the least restrictive environment principle. They concluded that "LEAs [Local Education Agencies] having the most success in achieving LRE have pursued broad-based strategies that both draw on a wide range of services and infuse the entire school district with LRE principles" (pp. x–xi).

Dimensional Rather Than Categorical Diagnosis

In curriculum-based systems, child study focuses on dimensions of variability rather than on categories. For example, if studies are made of reading ability or of psychological attributes, the results are expressed directly by scores, assuming a continuum, rather than in categories, such as mentally retarded. In their review of the 1980 edition of the *Diagnostic and Statistical Manual of Mental Disorders* of the American Psychiatric Association (1980), Eysenck, Wakefied, and Friedman (1983), in a brief section looking to the future, wrote that "categorical diagnosis must be replaced with dimensional assessment" (p. 185). They went on to point out that categorical diagnosis may be appropriate when there is a "specific causal species of pathogen," "major gene defects," or "specific dietary deficiencies;" but most problems encountered in school are not of such kinds and "the alternative to categorical diagnosis is dimensional assessment" (p. 185). Why use categories, they asked, when "the single score on the intelligence dimension provides much clearer information" (p. 186)? A similar case for dimensional rather than categorical approaches has been advanced more recently by Robins and Helzer (1986).

Reynolds and Balow (1972) made similar suggestions some years earlier, suggesting weather phenomena as an analogy. If temperature, humidity, and atmospheric pressure can be measured quite reliably and validly, why not use the measures directly and fully to characterize the weather on a particular day rather than simply describing it as "hot and muggy"? In studying children, some important dimensions, such as intelligence and achievement, can be described with good validity on the basis of careful testing or observations. Why not leave it at that, with all the precision possible? Such an approach assumes, of course, that means of identification, such as progress in curriculum, will be used instead of the traditional categories to identify children whose situations need improvement and to motivate the necessary social action to support special education programs.

A move toward dimensional diagnosis offers opportunities for a rapprochement between the fields of special education and adaptive education within the educational research community as well as in practical programs of the schools. It is noteworthy that a special interest group on research in special education has been created quite recently within the American Educational Research Association. Noteworthy also is the explicit attention to handicapped children in some of the recent adaptive education literature; see Johnson and Johnson (1981), Leinhardt, Bickel, and Palley (1982), Slavin, Madden, and Leavey (1982), Torgeson (1982), and Wang and Walberg (1985).

A Composite Approach

The preceding approaches can be combined, and, in fact, doing so appears to be an advantageous way to proceed in the integration of instructional and child study processes. Consider the following hypothetical scenario.

First, children are identified on the basis of progress in curriculum variables. It might be declared policy, for example, that all children whose rates of progress through the basic skills curricula (addressing the cultural imperatives) fall below the 20th percentile (based on local norms) will be identified for special study and for cooperative, detailed planning with parents. This procedure does not suggest anything in the way of a typology; it suggests, instead, that there is a wide range in the responsiveness of children to the instruction offered in the schools and that there ought to be a definite (reliable, universally applied) system for dealing with students and situations when progress is lacking or very slow.

Second, a careful study of the instructional and broader life situation of the child in question is made. The NAS panel (Heller et al., 1982) suggested that an analysis should be made first of the classroom and the child's broader life situation; and treatment should also begin there. In structuring the study of the child and his or her situation, we turn to what is known about effective schooling. To repeat briefly, the diagnosis would look at the following school-related areas.

- Environmental Characteristics. Discipline and order, disruptiveness, teacher directedness, productivity, teaching orientation, and student–teacher rapport.
- Instructional Characteristics. Academic learning time; ratio of students to instructors; systematic reinforcement of achievement; feedback on pupil performance; orientation to learning; efforts to improve instruction; peer and cross-age tutoring; homework (checked); and cooperative goal structuring.
- Curricular Characteristics. Curricula linked to current academic status of individuals, frequent checkpoints of curricula and instructional staff, and individually-paced curricula.

The best evidence we have indicates that the preceding features are associated with desired rates of learning. Various systems for the management of instruction are being advanced to facilitate the application of all or most of the principles involved, and much of it is being dealt with under the rubric of adaptive education. Accordingly, these are the best-known starting points in diagnosis when a child is not learning.

But then we return to study of the child. Let us assume that the school is doing all that is possible as part of its regular operations to run effectively and that specialists are deployed to consult with regular teachers to develop immediately the necessary modifications in the program for pupils showing problems. Furthermore, we assume that the schools are applying broad systems procedures to provide instruction in accordance with all that is known about effective schools. Even with all such efforts, however, it is likely that some students will not show adequate progress and, inevitably, that 20% of the students will fall below the 20th percentile on local norms for progress in reading, arithmetic, and other subjects.[3] These children are the ones proposed for special study in the hypothetical scenario.

The third step, then, is to proceed to study the selected children in collaboration with the parents. Psychologists and other professionals assist in the studies, not by classifying the children in traditional ways, but by helping in the search for improved approaches to instruction. Psychologists, and others who participate in the study, scan all that they know and then help to assemble indicators of how the individual child might be better managed and taught both in school and at home. Measurements are treated mainly as variables, except when there is evidence supporting a

[3]We make no special point about the 20th percentile, except that there is some evidence that this boundary point tends to pick up all or nearly all of the so-called mildly handicapped students. Other break points may serve well in particular situations.

typology or pointing toward particular treatments or instructional approaches. What is known from ATI studies, sub-type cluster studies, behavioral analyses, or any other procedures is applied here. In total, the purpose of the diagnostic process is to create more promising environmental arrangements and instructional processes for each child. We are not proposing throwing away IQs, data on cognitive processes, findings of neurological studies, or anything else that might have validity and be helpful, but that the entire process of diagnosis be *disciplined* and *focused* on the one topic of designing a school program that is promising as a means of increasing the child's mastery of important skills and knowledge.

We propose that the literature on effective schooling is highly useful in this process. If a child shows an achievement problem in basic areas, interventions can be directly focused on that problem. If a problem is noted in the child's attentiveness, the solution may be to employ a specialist in behavior analysis and modification to organize a specific program to improve on-task behavior or attention. If the child has missed some of the essential cognitive skills necessary to proceed to a next stage in instruction, a temporary tutoring arrangement may be useful in remediating the specific problem. Thus, the effectiveness literature could be used to the maximum extent possible, as a way of structuring child study, just as it is also used to study the child's instructional environment.

Disability-Centered Research

In the search for models that have promise as a basis for research and practice in special education, stress has been placed on effectiveness research, on studies of comprehensive systems of sequenced curricula, and on instructional practices and environmental organization that maintain mildly handicapped students in regular classrooms. This is not to suggest the discouragement of disability-centered research. The aim is only to discourage the equating of an hypothesis with a discovery, a testimonial with demonstration of product effectiveness, or the presumption that, because people are somehow shown to be quantitatively different in some dimension, they are qualitatively or categorically different and, thus, should be treated differently. These notions are unacceptable and harmful and should be totally discredited except when confirmed solidly by research findings.

It is possible (even necessary) that instructionally meaningful categories of students can be identified, of course. The effectiveness of group instruction always depends upon the characteristics of group members, and it is both wise and necessary to be proactive, at times, in forming groups or classes. It is the matter of particulars about how classes are formed and treated that needs to be checked for validity. We think that information on the current status of students in the curriculum domain is most likely to be useful, but there is good reason to continue the search for other approaches as well.

Further work in the area of profile clusters or subtypes within categories of exceptionality seems potentially fruitful. This approach examines data on multiple dimensions concerning mildly handicapped students. In effect, one looks at pupils in a complex hyperspace to see if regions of density emerge to suggest various typologies (McKinney, 1984; Morris, Blashfield, & Satz, 1981). This search for subtypes has appeal, but it has its doubtful aspects as well. It can be doubted that the approach has ever resulted in discovering classes that are taxonic. However, it may well lend itself to the development of hypotheses about treatment of subtypes that can be tested.

A modified version of the subtype approach is one that uses groups that have been established on some external basis and then checks to see if some profile similarities might exist within the subtypes. For example, suppose that a Fernald method (Fernald, 1943) of teaching reading were used with a large group of poor readers. The question might then be asked, Do the students who show a good response to the Fernald approach have common characteristics? From there, obviously, one could go on to similar studies of other teaching methods, systems, and materials to test for unique relationships between characteristics of students and responses to treatments. This procedure is somewhat similar to that used in the development of the Strong Vocational Interest Inventory (Strong, 1947) and the Minnesota Multiphasic Personality Inventory (Hathaway & McKinley, 1942) in that external classifications (people successful in various occupations in the case of the Strong) were used as a starter and then searches were made to discover associated patterns of responses on test items and scales. The results have been impressive and massive, showing how profiles of test scores can be used as an approach to diagnosis and classification.

The subtype approach, when it starts with treatment variations, is a version of ATI methodology in that it gives attention simultaneously to aptitudes and treatments and seeks to understand, as the ultimate goal, how to allocate students optimally among the several kinds of instruction. Similarly, this approach illustrates the "matching" strategies advanced by Hunt and Sullivan (1974), among others. In sum, we do not see the state of knowledge in special education as contrary to classification, but it does provide much evidence on which to challenge traditional diagnostic approaches to classification for the purposes of providing differentiated education.

Certain cautions must be considered if we are to expect useful results in disability-centered research. First, as noted earlier, we must be as clear as possible in describing the subjects of research (Keogh et al., 1982). Second, we must begin to control research for the factors that are already known to predict the rates of learning. It simply is not adequate to discover, for example, that a certain subpopulation of learning disabled students achieved more with Program A than with Program B if the academic learning time was greater in Program A than in Program B. In short, we must expect researchers to use controls for those conditions already known to affect outcomes. As surely as air pressure affects the volume of gases, classroom climates and instructional practices affect pupil progress, and to make any claims about applying the methods of science, special education researchers must take into account the factors known to affect outcomes in such settings.

Conclusion

There is much to accomplish in both the science and art of educating handicapped students. It may be that the art is not good because the science has been so poor. But we are not without knowledge to guide our future. One, perhaps unfortunate, social function that special education for mildly handicapped students has fulfilled is the reduction within regular classrooms of students who are relatively hard to teach. As noted by one of the patriarchs of special education, J. E. Wallace Wallin:

> Great relief was [and still is] afforded the normal pupils and the regular grade teachers by the removal of the flotsam and jetsam, the hold backs and drags, who retarded the progress of the class and often created difficult problems of discipline. (1924, p. 171)

Educators need not be satisfied with such unredemptive purposes. Much has been learned about which of the specialized treatments endemic to special education classes hold little promise; and they can be stopped. Researchers are beginning to learn about the environmental, instructional, and curricular conditions that predict pupil achievement, and much is known about how to attain these conditions. This knowledge can be used to construct educational systems, evaluate those systems, and control research for those conditions that affect pupil achievement, always checking at the margins to be sure that education for handicapped students has profited from the growing foundation of general principles for education.

Author Information

Maynard C. Reynolds is Professor of Educational Psychology, and K. Charlie Lakin is Senior Scientist, Department of Educational Psychology, both at the University of Minnesota.

References

Alexson, J., & Sinclair, E. (undated). *DSM III and school placement: A comparison between inpatients and outpatients.* Los Angeles, CA: University of California at Los Angeles, Mental Retardation and Child Psychiatry Program.

Algozzine, B., & Korinek, L. (1985). Where is special education for students with high prevalence handicaps going? *Exceptional Children,* **51**, 388–394.

Algozzine, R., & Maheady, L. (Eds.). (1986). In search of excellence: Instruction that works in special education classrooms [Special Issue]. *Exceptional Children,* **52**(6).

American Psychiatric Association. (1968). *Diagnostic and statistical manual of mental disorders* (2nd ed.). Washington, DC: Author.

American Psychiatric Association. (1980). *Diagnostic and statistical manual of mental disorders* (3rd ed.). Washington, DC: Author.

Arter, J. A., & Jenkins, J. R. (1979). Differential diagnosis—prescriptive teaching: A critical appraisal. *Review of Educational Research,* **49**, 517–555.

Becker, W. (1977). Teaching reading and language to the disadvantaged: What have we learned from field research? *Harvard Educational Review,* **47**, 518–543.

Berbow, C. (1980). *Review of instructionally effective schooling literature* (Urban Diversity Series, No. 70). New York: Columbia University, Teachers College.

Berliner, D. (Ed.). (1982). *Research on teaching: Implications for practice.* Washington, DC: National Institute of Education.

Binet, A., & Simon, T. (1914). *Mentally defective children.* London, England: E. Arnold.

Birch, J. W., & Johnstone, B. K. (1975). *Designing schools and schooling for the handicapped.* Springfield, IL: Charles C. Thomas.

Block, E. (1984). *Effective schooling: A summary of research.* Washington, DC: Educational Research Service.

Block, J. H., & Burns, R. B. (1976). Mastery learning. In L. S. Schulman (Ed.), *Review of research in education* (Vol. 4, pp. 3–49), Itasca, IL: Peacock.

Bloom, B. S. (1976). *Human characteristics and school learning.* New York: McGraw-Hill.

Bloom, B. S. (1980). The new direction in educational research: Alterable variables. *Phi Delta Kappan,* **61**, 382–385.

Brookover, W. B., Beady, C. H., Flood, P. K., Schweitzer, J., & Wisenbaker, J. (1979). *School systems and school achievement: Schools can make a difference.* New York: Praeger.

Brophy, J. E., & Evertson, C. M. (1976). *Learning from teaching: A developmental perspective.* Boston, MA: Allyn & Bacon.

Brown v. Board of Education, 347 U.S. 483 (1954).

Brown, L., Nietupski, J., & Hamre-Nietupski, S. (1976). The criterion of ultimate functioning. In M. A. Thomas (Ed.), *Hey, don't forget about me* (pp. 2–15). Reston, VA: Council for Exceptional Children.

Carlberg, C., & Kavale, K. (1980). The efficacy of special versus regular class placement for exceptional children: A meta-analysis. *Journal of Special Education,* **14**, 295–309.

Child Trends. (1985). *The school aged handicapped* (NCES 85–400). Washington, DC: U.S. Government Printing Office.

Cohen, P. A., Kulik, J. A., & Kulik, C. C. (1982). Educational outcomes of tutoring: A meta-analysis of findings. *American Education Research Journal,* **19**, 237–248.

Coleman, J. S., Campbell, E. Q., Hobson, C. J., McPartland, J., Mood, A. M., Weinfold, F. D., & York, R. L. (1966). *Equality of educational opportunity.* Washington, DC: U.S. Government Printing Office.

Coleman, J. C., & Husen, T. (1985). *Becoming adult in a changing society.* Paris, France: Centre for Educational Research and Development, Organization for Economic Cooperation and Development.

Comptroller General. (1981). *Disparities still exist in who gets special education.* Washington, DC: General Accounting Office.

Cronbach, L. J. (1967). How can instruction be adapted to individual differences? In R. M. Gagne (Ed.), *Learning and individual differences* (pp. 23–39). Columbus, OH: Merrill.

Cross, K. P. (1984). The rising tide of school reform reports. *Phi Delta Kappan,* **65**, 167–172.

Cruickshank, W. M. (1972). Some issues facing the field of learning disability. *Journal of Learning Disabilities,* **5**, 380–383.

Davidson, M. (1971). *Louis Braille, the boy who invented books for the blind.* New York: Hastings House.

Davies, S. P. (1930). *Social control of the mentally deficient.* New York: Columbia University Press.

Davies, S. P. (1959). *The mentally retarded in society.* New York: Columbia University Press.

Denham, C., & Lieberman, A. (Eds.). (1980). *Time to learn.* Washington, DC: National Institute of Education.

Deno, S. L. (1985). Curriculum-based measurement: The emerging alternative. *Exceptional Children,* **52**, 219–232.

Doss, D., & Holley, F. (1982). *A cause for national pause: Title I school wide projects.* Austin, TX: Austin Independent School District, Office of Research and Evaluation.

Edmonds, R. R. (1979). Effective schools for the urban poor. *Educational Leadership,* **37**, 15–27.

Education for All Handicapped Children Act. (1977). Federal Register, August 23, 1977, pp. 42474–42514, CFR Title 45, Sections 121a. 1–121a, 754.

Evertson, C. M. (1982). Differences in instructional activities in higher and lower achieving junior high school English and mathematics classrooms. *Elementary School Journal,* **82**, 329–351.

Eysenck, H. J., Wakefield, J. A., & Friedman, A. F. (1983). Diagnosis and clinical assessment: The DSM III. *Annual Review of Psychology,* **34**, 167–193.

Farrow, F., & Rogers, C. (1983). *Policies which address out-of-district placements and assure education in the least restrictive environment.* Washington, DC: The Centre for the Study of Social Policy.

Felixbrod, J. J., & O'Leary, K. D. (1974). Self-determination of academic standards by children: Toward freedom from external control. *Journal of Educational Psychology,* **66**, 845–850.

Fernald, A. M. (1943). *Remedial techniques in basic school subjects.* New York: McGraw-Hill.

Gardner, E. M. (1984, May). The education crisis: Washington shares the blame. *Backgrounder,* p. 351.

Gawronski, D. A., & Mathis, C. (1965). Differences between over-achieving, normal-achieving, and under-achieving high school students. *Psychology in the Schools,* **2**, 152–155.

Gilhool, T. K. (1976). Changing public policies: Roots and forces. In M. C. Reynolds (Ed.), *Mainstreaming: Origins and implications* (pp. 8–13). Reston, VA: Council for Exceptional Children.

Glass, G. V. (1983). Effectiveness of special education. *Policy Studies Review,* **2**, 65–78.

Goddard, H. H. (1910). Feeblemindedness: A question of definition. *Journal of Psycho-Aesthenics,* **33**, 220.

Goddard, H. H. (1914). *School training of defective children.* New York: World.

Good, T., & Grouws, D. (1979). The Missouri mathematics effectiveness project. *Journal of Educational Psychology,* **71**, 355–362.

Gottlieb, J., Corman, L., & Curci, R. (1984). Attitudes toward mentally retarded children. In R. L. Jones (Ed.), *Attitudes and attitude change in special education* (pp. 143–156). Reston, VA: Council for Exceptional Children.

Grossman, H. J. (Ed.). (1973). *Manual on terminology and classification in mental retardation.* Washington, DC: American Association on Mental Deficiency.

Hammill, D. D., & Larsen, S. C. (1974). The effectiveness of psycholinguistic training. *Exceptional Children,* **41**, 5–14.

Hathaway, S. R., & McKinley, J. C. (1942). *Minnesota Multiphasic Inventory.* Minneapolis, MN: University of Minnesota Press.

Heller, K. A., Holtzman, W. H., & Messick, S. (Eds.). (1982). *Placing children in special education: A strategy for equity.* Washington, DC: National Academy Press.

Hobbs, N. (1975). *The futures of children.* San Francisco, CA: Jossey-Bass.

Hobbs, N. (1980). An ecologically oriented service-based system for the classification of handicapped children. In E. Salzinger, J. Antrobus, & J. Glick (Eds.), *The ecosystem of the "risk" child* (pp. 271–290). New York: Academic Press.

Hunt, D. E., & Sullivan, E. V. (1974). *Between psychology and education.* New York: Holt, Rinehart & Winston.

Hunter, M. (1980). *Mastery teaching.* El Segundo, CA: TIP Publications.

Johnson, D. W., Maruyama, G., Johnson, R., Nelson, D., & Skon, L. (1980). The effects of cooperative, competitive and individualistic goal structures on achievement. *Psychological Bulletin,* **89**, 47–62

Johnson, R., & Johnson, D. (1981). Building friendship between handicapped and nonhandicapped students: Effects of cooperative and individualistic instruction. *American Educational Research Journal,* **18**, 415–423.

Jones, R. L. (Ed.). (1984). *Attitudes and attitude change in special education.* Reston, VA: Council for Exceptional Children.

Kavale, K. (1981). Functions of the Illinois Test of Psycholinguistic Abilities (ITPA): Are they trainable? *Exceptional Children,* **47**, 496–510.

Kavale, K. A., & Mattson, P. D. (1983). One jumped off the balance beam: Meta-analysis of perceptual motor training. *Journal of Learning Disabilities,* **16**, 165–173.

Kendell, R. E. (1975). *The role of diagnosis in psychiatry.* Oxford, England: Blackwell.

Keogh, B. K., & MacMillan, D. L. (1983). The logic of sample selection: Who represents what? *Exceptional Education Quarterly,* **4**(3), 84–96.

Keogh, B. K., Major-Kingsley, S., Omori-Gordon, H. P., & Reid, H. (1982). *A system of marker variables for the field of learning disabilities.* New York: Syracuse University.

Lazar, I., Darlington, R., Murray, J., Royce, J., & Snipper, A. (1982). *Lasting effects of early education: A report from the Consortium for Longitudinal Studies* [Monograph of the Society for Research in Child Development]. **47**, 1–151.

Leinhardt, G., Bickel, W., & Pallay, A. (1982). Unlabeled but still entitled: Toward more effective remediation. *Teachers College Record,* **84**(2), 391–422.

Leithwood, K. A., & Montgomery, D. J. (1982). The role of the elementary school principal in program improvement. *Review of Educational Research,* **52**, 309–337.

Levin, T. (1981). *Effective instruction.* Alexandra, VA: Association for Supervision and Curriculum Development.

Levy, L. M. (1963). *Psychological interpretation.* New York: Holt, Rinehart & Winston.

Lilly, M. S. (1986, March). The relationship between general and special education. *Counterpoint,* p. 10.

MacMillan, D. L., Meyers, C. E., & Morrison, G. M. (1980). System-identification of mildly mentally retarded children: Implications for interpreting and conducting research. *American Journal of Mental Deficiency,* **85**, 108–115.

Madden, N. A., & Slavin, R. E. (1983). Mainstreaming students with mild handicaps: Academic and social outcomes. *Review of Educational Research,* **53**, 519–569.

McKinney, J. D. (1984). The research for subtypes of specific learning disability. *Annual Review of Learning Disabilities,* **2**, 19–26.

Meehl, P. E. (1972). Specific genetic etiology, psychodynamics and therapeutic nihilism. *International Journal of Mental Health,* **1**, 10–27.

Meehl, P. E., & Goldberg, R. R. (1982). Taxometric methods. In P. L. Kendall & J. N. Butcher (Eds.), *Handbook of research methods in clinical psychology.* New York: Wiley.

Messer, S. (1976). Reflection—impulsivity: A review. *Psychological Bulletin,* **83**, 1026–1053.

Morris, R., Blashfield, R., & Satz, P. (1981). Neuropsychology and cluster analysis: Potentials and problems. *Journal of Clinical Neuropsychology,* **3**, 79–99.

National Centre for Health Statistics. (1981). *Final natality statistics, monthly vital statistics report.* Washington, DC: Author.

National Coalition of Advocates for Students and National Association of School Psychologists. (1985). *Advocacy for education for all children: A position statement.* Boston, MA: Author.

New York City Commission on Special Education. (1985). *Special education: a call for quality.* New York: The City of New York, Office of the Mayor.

Office of Civil Rights, U.S. Department of Education. (1982). *Elementary and Secondary School Rights Survey.* Washington, DC: Author.

Palincsar, A. S., & Brown, A. (1984). Reciprocal teaching of comprehension fostering and comprehension monitoring activities. *Cognition and Instruction,* **1**, 117–175.

Pennsylvania Association for Retarded Children v. Pennsylvania, 343 F. Supp. 279 (E.D. Pa. 1972).

Peterson, J., Heistad, D., Peterson, D., & Reynolds, M. C. (1985). Montevideo Individualized Prescriptive Instructional Management System. *Exceptional Children,* **52**, 239–243.

Phi Delta Kappa. (1980). *Why do some urban schools succeed?* Bloomington, IN: Author.

Reynolds, M. C. (1984). Classification of students with handicaps. In E. W. Gordon (Ed.), *Review of research in education* (Vol. 11, pp. 63–92). Washington, DC: American Educational Research Association.

Reynolds, M. C., & Balow, B. (1972). Categories and variables in special education. *Exceptional Children,* **38**, 357–366.

Reynolds, M. C., & Birch, J. W. (1982). *Teaching exceptional children in all America's schools* (2nd ed.). Reston, VA: Council for Exceptional Children.

Robbins, L. L. (1966). An historical review of classification of behavior disorders and one current perspective. In L. D. Eron (Ed.), *The classification of behavior disorders.* Chicago, IL: Aldine.

Robins, L. N., & Helzer, J. E. (1986). The current state of psychiatric diagnosis. *Annual Review of Psychology,* **37**, 409–432.

Rollins, H., McCandless, B., Thompson, M., & Brassell, W. (1974). Project success environment: An extended application of contingency management in inner-city schools. *Journal of Educational Psychology,* **66**, 167–178.

Rosenshine, B. (1976). Academic engaged time, content covered, and direct instruction. *Journal of Education,* **160**(3), 38–66.

Rosenshine, B. V., & Berliner, D. C. (1978). Academic engaged time. *British Journal of Teacher Education,* **4**, 3–16.

Rutter, M., Maugham, B., Mortimore, P., Ouston, J., & Smith, A. (1979). *Fifteen thousand hours: Secondary schools and their effects on children.* Cambridge, MA: Harvard University Press.

Sage, D. D., & Fensom, H. C. (1985). *A study of mixed category special education programs in the Commonwealth of Pennsylvania.* Harrisburg, PA: State Department of Public Instruction.

Sinclair, E., Forness, S., & Alexson, J. (no date). *Psychiatric diagnoses: A study of its relationship to school needs.* Unpublished manuscript, University of California, Mental Retardation and Child Psychiatry Program, Los Angeles, CA.

Skinner, H. A. (1981). Toward the integration of classification theory and methods. *Journal of Abnormal Psychology,* **90**, 68–87.

Slavin, R. E., Madden, N. A., & Leavey, M. (1982, March). *Combining cooperative learning and individualized instruction: Effects on the social acceptance, achievement and behavior of mainstreamed students.* Paper presented at the annual meeting of the American Educational Research Association, New York.

Speedie, S., Hobson, S., Feldhusen, J., & Thurston, J. (1971). Evaluation of a battery of noncognitive variables as long-range predictors of academic achievement. In *Proceedings of the 79th Annual Convention of the American Psychological Association.*

Stainback, W., & Stainback, S. (1984). A rationale for the merger of special and regular education. *Exceptional Children,* **5**, 102–111.

Stallings, J. A. (1980). Allocated academic learning time revisited. *Educational Researcher,* **9**(1), 11–16.

Stallings, J. A., & Kaskowitz, D. (1974). *Follow Through classroom observation evaluation, 1972–1973.* Menlo Park, CA: Stanford Research Institute.

Stoddard, G. (1986). *The dual progress plan.* New York: Harper & Brothers.

Strong, E. K., Jr. (1943). *Vocational interests of men and women.* Palo Alto, CA: Stanford University Press.

Tobias, S. (1976). Achievement treatment interactions. *Review of Educational Research,* **46**, 61–74.

Tomlinson, T. M. (1981, May). *Student ability, student background and student achievement: Another look at life in effective schools.* Paper presented at the Educational Testing Service Conference on Effective Schools, New York.

Torgeson, J. K. (1982). The learning disabled child as an inactive learner: Educational implications. *Topics in Learning and Learning Disabilities,* **2**(1), 45–52.

Tucker, J. A. (1980). Ethnic proportions in classes for the learning disabled. *Journal of Special Education,* **14**, 93–105.

Tucker, J. A. (Ed.). (1985). Curriculum-based assessment [Special Issue]. *Exceptional Children,* **52**(3).

U.S. Bureau of the Census. (1981). Estimates of the population of the United States by age, sex, and race: 1970 to 1981. *Current Population Reports* (Series P25, No. 917). Washington, DC: Author.

U.S. Bureau of the Census. (1982). *Statistical Abstracts of the United States, 1982–1983.* Washington, DC: U.S. Government Printing Office.

U.S. Bureau of the Census. (1983). Projections of the populations of the United States: 1982 to 2050. *Current Population Reports* (Series P25 No. 922). Washington, DC: Author.

U.S. Department of Education. (1985). *Seventh annual report to Congress on the implementation of Public Law 94–142: The Education for All Handicapped Children Act.* Washington, DC: Author.

U.S. Department of Education. (1986). *What works.* Washington, DC: Author.

Venezky, R., & Winfield, L. (1979). *Schools that succeed beyond expectations in reading.* Newark: University of Delaware, College of Education. (ERIC Document Reproduction Service No. ED 177 484)

Walberg, H. (1984). Improving the productivity of America's schools. *Educational Leadership*, **41**, 19–30.

Wallin, J. E. W. (1924). Classification of mentally deficient and retarded children for instruction. *Journal of Psycho-Aesthenics*, **29**, 166–182.

Wang, M. C. (1980). Adaptive instruction: Building on diversity. *Theory Into Practice*, **19**(2), 122–127.

Wang, M. C. (1983). Development and consequences of students' sense of personal control. In J. M. Levine & M. C. Wang (Eds.), *Teacher and student perceptions: Implications for learning* (pp. 213–248). Hillsdale, NJ: Erlbaum.

Wang, M. C., Gennari, P., & Waxman, H. C. (1985). The Adaptive Learning Environments Model: Design, implementation, and effects. In M. C. Wang & H. J. Walberg (Eds.), *Adapting instruction to individual differences* (pp. 191–235). Berkeley, CA: McCutchan.

Wang, M. C., & Reynolds, M. C. (1985). Avoiding the "Catch 22" in special education reform. *Exceptional Children*, **51**, 497–502.

Wang, M. C., & Walberg, H. J. (Eds.). (1985). *Adapting instruction to individual differences*. Berkeley, CA: McCutchan.

Weber, G. (1971). *Inner-city children can be taught to read: Four successful schools*. Washington, DC: Council for Basic Education.

Wiley, D. (1976). Another hour, another day. Quantity of schooling, a potent path for policy. In W. Sewell, R. Hauser, & D. Featherman (Eds.), *Schooling and achievement in American society*. New York: Academic Press.

Wiley, D. E., & Harnischfeger, A. (1974). Explosion of a myth: Quantity of schooling and exposure to instruction, major educational vehicles. *Educational Researcher*, **3**(1), 7–12.

Will, M. L. (1986). Educating children with learning problems: A shared responsibility. *Exceptional Children*, **52**, 411–415.

Wood, F. H., & Lakin, K. C. (1982). Defining emotionally disturbed/behaviorally disordered populations for research purposes. In F. H. Wood & K. C. Lakin (Eds.), *Disturbing, disordered or disturbed? Perspectives on the definition of problem behavior in educational settings* (pp. 29–48). Reston, VA: Council for Exceptional Children.

Worsham, M. E. (1981). *Student accountability for written work in junior high school classes*. Austin: University of Texas, Research and Development Center for Teacher Education.

Wynne, E. A. (1980). *Looking at schools: Good, bad and indifferent*. Lexington, MA: D.C. Health.

Ysseldyke, J. E., & Algozzine, B. (1983). LD or not LD: That's not the question. *Journal of Learning Disabilities*, **16**, 29–31.

Ysseldyke, J. E., & Thurlow, M. L. (1983). *Identification/classification research: An integrative summary of findings* (Research Rep. No. 142). Minneapolis: University of Minnesota, Department of Educational Psychology.

Zill, N. (1985, June 25). *How is the number of children with severe handicaps likely to change over time?* Testimony prepared for the Subcommittee on Select Education of the Committee on Education and Labor, U.S. House of Representatives.

Zubin, J. (1967). Classification of the behavior disorders. In P. R. Farnsworth, O. McNemar, & Q. McNemar (Eds.), *Annual review of psychology* (Vol. 18, pp. 373–406). Palo Alto, CA: Annual Reviews.

Author Index

Subject Index